UNDERSTANDING
PSYCHOLOGY

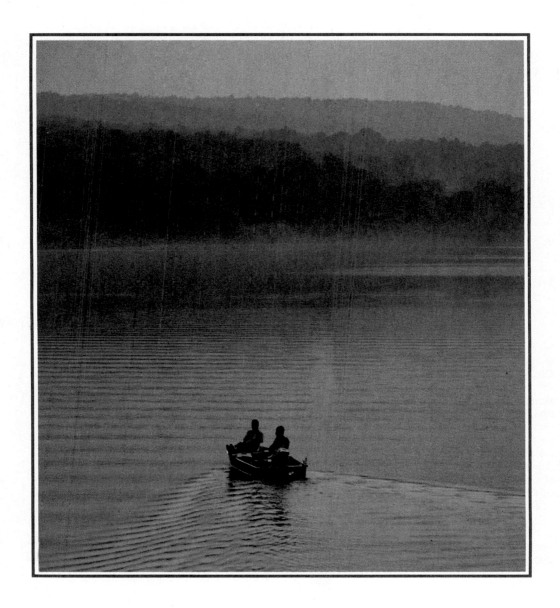

GLENCOE

Macmillan/McGraw-Hill

Lake Forest, Illinois; Columbus, Ohio; Mission Hills, California; Peoria, Illinois

PROGRAM CONSULTANT

Anne V. Gormly
Professor of Psychology
Trenton State College
Trenton, NJ

TEACHER REVIEWERS

Margaret Ann Carter
Ann Arbor Public Schools
Ann Arbor, MI

Walter G. Dabrowski
Pemberton High School
Pemberton, NJ

Robert N. Gilbert
Palatine High School
Palatine, IL

UNIVERSITY REVIEWER

Robert Stahl
Arizona State University

Send all inquiries to:
GLENCOE DIVISION
Macmillan/McGraw-Hill
936 Eastwind Drive
Westerville, OH 43081

ISBN 0-02-800180-x (Student Text)
ISBN 0-02-800181-8 (Teacher's Edition)
ISBN 0-02-800182-6 (Teacher's Resource Binder)

Printed in the United States of America

2 3 4 5 6 7 8 9 10 A-HAW   00 99 98 97 96 95 94 93 92

CONTENTS

UNIT 1

LEARNING AND COGNITIVE PROCESSES

UNIT 2

THE WORKINGS OF MIND AND BODY

UNIT 3

THE LIFE SPAN

UNIT 4

PERSONALITY AND INDIVIDUALITY

UNIT 5

ADJUSTMENT AND BREAKDOWN

UNIT 6

HUMAN RELATIONS

Chapter 17. Human Interaction   425

UNDERSTANDING PSYCHOLOGY

CHAPTER 1

Introducing Psychology

Key Terms:

applied science
basic science
hypothesis
introspection
psychiatry
psychology

What is it that fascinates psychologists about ordinary behavior? What exactly do they study? One way to answer this question is to look at a slice of life through a psychologist's eyes.

Ruth, a college student, decides to have lunch at the school cafeteria. She walks to the cafeteria, gets in line, chooses tuna salad and orange juice, and pays at the counter. She then looks around for someone to sit with. She doesn't see any close friends, so she goes to a table by herself, sits down, and begins to eat.

A few minutes later, Gary, a young man in Ruth's English class, comes over to join her. When Ruth looks up at him, she no longer feels like eating. She thinks Gary is very good looking, but he never speaks to Ruth unless he's missed a class and wants to borrow her notes. She greets him coolly, but Gary sits down anyway and begins to tell a long, rambling story about *A Visit from the Little Green People*, the horror movie on TV he stayed up to watch last night. Meanwhile, Ruth remembers that Gary missed this morning's English class and catches him eyeing her notebook.

Ruth fantasizes dumping her lunch on Gary's neatly groomed hair, but instead she gets up to leave. Gary attempts a casual smile and asks to borrow her notes. Now Ruth is more than annoyed. Although her English notebook is in plain sight, she tells him curtly that she is sorry but she has left her notes in the library—to which, as a matter of fact, she must return right away. As she leaves the cafeteria, she glances back and sees Gary still sitting at the table. He looks depressed. Suddenly, she feels a bit depressed herself.

This is a simple story, but from a psychologist's point of view, the behavior was complex. First of all, Ruth decided to have lunch because of her *physiological* (physical) *state*—she was hungry. She may also have

Objectives:

After studying this chapter, you should be able to

- describe the range of topics that are covered in an introductory course in psychology.
- cite the questions psychologists ask and describe how research is performed.
- explain the three most important trends within psychology.
- summarize the specialized fields of psychology.

Figure 1.1 Studying psychology can help you gain a perspective on your own behavior.

Figure 1.2
Where we might see two people
sitting and talking, a psychologist
might see a sequence of complex
behaviors.

been motivated by *cognitive* (factual) elements—she knew she must eat now because she had classes scheduled for the next few hours. When she entered the cafeteria, she *perceived* sensory stimuli different from those outside, but she paid little attention to the new sights, sounds, and smells, except to note that the food smelled good and the line was mercifully short. She went through the line and paid for her food—*learned behavior* not too different from that of a hungry rat that runs a maze for a food reward.

Ruth looked for a *social group* to join, but found none to which she belonged. She sat alone until Gary joined her. He felt free to do so because in most schools there is an informal rule, or *norm*, that students who have a class together may approach each other socially. (This rule usually does not apply to members of a looser group, such as commuters who ride the same bus.) Ruth *remembered* how Gary had behaved toward her in the past and realized that he was about to follow the same note-borrowing routine. This triggered the *emotional* reaction of anger. However, she did not dump her food on his head as a two-year-old might have done, but acted in a way that was more appropriate to her stage of *development*. We can assume that her response was characteristic of her *personality:* she told the young man that she didn't have the notes (even though he had seen them) and left.

In the example above, if such situations occurred often, and if they were always followed by depression, either student's behavior could indicate psychological *disturbance*. If Gary always relied on others for help and manipulated people to get his way, his behavior might be a sign of disorder. So might Ruth's, since she interprets simple requests as demands but finds herself unable either to meet or refuse the request in a direct way. However, in this context, neither student's behavior seems *abnormal*.

Viewed in this way, an apparently simple event raises many questions about why people behave and feel as they do. How is their behavior influenced by their physiological states? What motivates them to choose one action instead of another? Nearly all of the topics covered in this book are reflected in a psychologist's perception of this brief story.

WHY STUDY PSYCHOLOGY?

Students are usually attracted to the study of psychology because they hope to gain a better understanding of people. You may be studying psychology for more specific and personal reasons. As you read this book, you will discover new ways of looking at yourself and of interpreting the behavior of other people. The daily events you might ordinarily take for granted may now become fuel for thought. Two things you will gain by learning about psychology are insight into behavior and new practical information on how to deal with situations in everyday life.

Insight

Psychology can provide useful insight into your own and other people's behavior. For example, suppose a student is convinced that he is hopelessly shy and doomed forever to feel uncomfortable in groups. Then he learns through social psychology that different kinds of groups tend to have different effects on their members. He thinks about this for a while and notes that, although he is miserable at parties, he feels fine at meetings of the school newspaper staff and in the group he works with in the biology laboratory (in technical terms, he is much more uncomfortable in unstructured social groups than in structured, task-oriented groups). Realizing that he is uncomfortable only in some groups brings relief. He is not paralyzingly shy; he just does not like unstructured groups. He is not alone in his feelings.

There is something to learn about each of us in *Understanding Psychology*. You, too, may find that because of something you read in one chapter or another, you see yourself in a new way.

Of course, you must be careful in applying your new insight. Few people are more obnoxious than the student who has had one psychology course and proceeds to terrorize family, friends, and strangers with an analysis of every action. Many puppies and kittens have become the unlucky targets of a psychology student's newly learned training methods.

"A little learning is a dangerous thing," according to an old cliché, but the more psychology you study, the more respect you will gain for the complexity and diversity of human behavior. An introductory psychology course is just one investment in a lifelong process of education about yourself and others.

Practical Information

Some of the chapters in this book include material that has a practical application in everyday life. You will learn concrete and detailed ways to carry out a number of useful procedures psychologists have developed.

For example, Chapter 2 describes the systematic way of dispensing rewards and punishments that psychologists call *shaping* (Figure 1.3). You will definitely find this useful if you ever have to train a puppy, and you may find yourself wondering how you are shaping the behavior of people around you. Perhaps you have two friends who are always happy to join you for coffee or a movie but who never bring any money along. You have loaned them money many times and, just as many times, they have failed to pay you back. You know they can afford to pay their share, and you have told them so repeatedly. They are good friends, however, so you end up paying their way again and again. In doing so, you are rewarding or reinforcing an undesirable behavior pattern. Is that what you really want to do?

Chapter 3 includes a description of several *mnemonic devices*, or memory aids, that will help you retain information by rote. The poem beginning "Thirty days has September," which helps many people remember the number of days in each month, is an example. With mnemonic devices, you usually associate each item on a list with something easier to remember, such as a mental picture, rhyme, or phrase. Although this may require time and effort, memory experts have shown that it is worth the trouble. The techniques described may help you memorize almost any list of words or numbers—the names of the presidents of the United States and their dates in office (for a history course), the authors and titles of books (for an English course), telephone numbers, shopping lists, and so on.

In reading the chapter on child development, you may recall similar experiences you had in your own childhood. The chapter on disturbance

Figure 1.3
Kissing is a response that is subject to shaping. Here the response is emitted tentatively and would probably be repeated only after a considerable time if it produced no result. The kiss is reinforced, however, and immediately the response increases in frequency and in vigor.

and breakdown may help you understand difficult periods in your own life and in the lives of those around you. Chapter 16 will tell you about the different kinds of therapy available to people who are experiencing severe or chronic difficulties. Of course, you should not jump to conclusions on the basis of this introduction to psychology. It takes a trained professional to diagnose and treat developmental and psychological problems (as Chapter 16 explains).

OVERVIEW OF PSYCHOLOGY

Defining Psychology

Psychology is the study of human behavior and mental processes. It covers everything that people think, feel, and do. Psychologists differ in how much importance they place on specific types of behavior. For example, some psychologists believe that you should study only behavior that you can see, observe, or measure directly. Ruth's behavior of selecting and paying for her food, choosing a table, and refusing to lend her notes to Gary are all examples of behaviors that are observable. Some psychologists believe that our fantasies, thoughts, and feelings are also important kinds of human behavior, even though these behaviors are not directly observable. Ruth may infer or guess that Gary is sad by the expression on his face, but she cannot directly observe his emotional reaction.

While psychologists may differ on which kinds of human behavior are important, they do agree that the study of behavior must be systematic. The use of a systematic method of asking and answering questions about why people think, act, and feel as they do reduces the chances of coming to false conclusions about behavior. Consider the old story of the blind men and the elephant. A long time ago three very wise but blind men were out on a journey when they came across a sleeping elephant. Because they could not see the elephant, they did not know what was blocking their way so they set about to discover what they could about the obstacle. As it happened, each man put his hands on a different section of the elephant, examining it in great detail and with much thought. The first man, having felt the elephant's trunk, described a creature that was long, wormlike, and quite flexible. "No, no! You must be mistaken," said the second man who was seated on the back of the elephant, "This creature is wide, very round, and does not move very much." The man who was holding one of the elephant's tusks added his description of a small, hard, pointed creature. Each of these men was correct in his description of what he felt, but, in order to understand the elephant fully, they needed to combine their accumulated knowledge. The study of human behavior is similar. Many different approaches are necessary to understand the complex richness of human behavior.

We each like to think we understand people. We spend time observing others (and ourselves) and form conclusions about people in general from

Many different approaches are necessary to understand the complex richness of human behavior.

our daily interactions. Sometimes the conclusions we draw, however, are not accurate because we are not systematic in our "study" of people. Check the accuracy of some of your conclusions by responding true or false to the statements in Figure 1.4. Then compare your answers with the correct ones found at the end of this chapter (page 18).

The Scientific Basis of Psychology

Psychologists rely on the *scientific method*. This means that they reach their conclusions by identifying a specific problem or question, formulating a hypothesis, collecting data through observation and experiment, and analyzing the data.

By asking specific, well defined questions, psychologists can gain insight into the behavior pattern they are studying. Asking a precise question about a limited aspect of behavior is basic to psychological research. Forming a *hypothesis* to explain the behavior is also a basic method of research. A **hypothesis** is an "educated guess"—the researcher has some evidence for suspecting a specific answer. In a hypothesis, researchers state what they expect to find, expressed in such a way that it can be proved or disproved. A psychologist might, for example, make the following hypothesis: People who have similar opinions on important issues in their lives are more likely to be attracted to each other than people who have very different opinions. The psychologist would then test the hypothesis in a way that would enable him or her to collect data. A survey might be conducted, for example, or questionnaires sent out. Finally, the psychologist would analyze the data (see the Appendix, page 487). The

Figure 1.4
Test your intuitions about human behavior by answering true or false to the statements below. Turn to page 16 for the answers.

1. The behavior of most lower animals—insects, reptiles and amphibians, most rodents, and birds—is instinctive and unaffected by learning.
2. For the first week of life, a baby sees nothing but a gray blur regardless of what he or she "looks at."
3. A child learns to talk more quickly if the adults around the child habitually repeat the word he or she is trying to say, using proper pronunciation.
4. The best way to get a chronically noisy schoolchild to settle down and pay attention is to punish him or her.
5. Slow learners remember more of what they learn than fast learners.
6. Highly intelligent people— "geniuses"—tend to be physically frail and socially isolated.
7. On the average, you cannot predict from a person's grades at school and college whether he or she will do well in a career.
8. Most national and ethnic stereotypes are completely false.
9. In small amounts, alcohol is a stimulant.
10. LSD causes chromosome damage.
11. The largest drug problem in the United States, in terms of the number of people affected, is marijuana.
12. Psychiatry is a subdivision of psychology.
13. Most mentally retarded people are also mentally ill.
14. A third or more of the people suffering from severe mental disorder are potentially dangerous.
15. Electroshock therapy is an outmoded technique rarely used in today's mental hospitals.
16. The more severe the disorder, the more intensive the therapy required to cure it; for example, schizophrenics usually respond best to psychoanalysis.
17. Quite a few psychological characteristics of men and women appear to be inborn; in all cultures, for example, women are more emotional and sexually less aggressive than men.
18. No reputable psychologist "believes in" such irrational phenomena as ESP, hypnosis, or the bizarre mental and physical achievements of Eastern yogis.

hypothesis might prove to be wrong—that is, the researcher may find that there are no differences between the two groups.

There are many hypotheses, but real answers to general questions are arrived at only by general agreement on the part of the experts after years of research on many different aspects of a problem.

The Goals of Psychology

As psychologists go about their systematic and scientific study of people, they have several goals. Overall, psychologists seek to do four things— describe, explain, predict, and control behavior.

The first task for any scientist or psychologist is to gather information about the behavior being studied and to present what is known. For example, we described Ruth's behavior in the cafeteria. A psychologist, however, would not be content with simply stating the facts; he or she would also be interested in explaining why people behave as they do. Such an explanation often goes beyond what can be observed to include ideas about why people react in certain ways.

Psychologists present their ideas in the form of hypotheses, which can be grouped together into theories. A theory represents past hunches or trial explanations about the facts observed. Psychological theories are tentative; they are always on trial because they are subject to change as more information about people and their behaviors is gathered. Theories do, however, allow us to fulfill the first two goals of psychology—to describe and explain observed behavior.

The third goal of psychology is to be able to predict, as a result of accumulated knowledge, what people will think, feel, or do in certain situations. By studying descriptive accounts linking certain behaviors together, psychologists can predict certain events.

Finally, psychologists seek to go beyond description, explanation, and prediction to influence or control behavior in helpful ways. Although many psychologists are involved in doing basic research to find out more about human behavior, other psychologists are more interested in discovering ways to use what is already known about people to benefit others. Some psychologists are interested in both **basic science,** or research, and **applied science,** or practical applications of the principles discovered in basic science research.

Psychologists who are studying the ability of infants to perceive visual patterns are doing basic research. They would not be concerned with the implication their findings might have on the design of a crib. Psychologists studying rapid eye movement in sleep research are also involved in basic science. If they discover that one individual has a sleep disturbance, they will try to understand and explain the situation, but they will not try to correct it. That is a job for applied scientists, such as clinical psychologists. An example of a psychologist involved in applying psychological principles rather than discovering them is a consultant to a toy manufacturer.

Why is this distinction important? The reason is that the transfer of findings from basic to applied science can be tricky. The following example illustrates this.

Psychologists seek to go beyond description, explanation, and prediction to influence or control behavior in helpful ways.

Figure 1.5
This engraving depicts a forest scene, doesn't it? If you answer yes, it may be because you looked only at the "framed area." If we had said, "Look at the muddy road," you would have seen that the forest is simply a reflection in a puddle. The same thing happens in psychology. Attending to one theoretical view prevents a researcher from seeing others.

Psychologists doing basic research have found that babies raised in institutions such as orphanages are seriously retarded in their physical, intellectual, and emotional development. Wayne Dennis (1960), among others, traces this to the fact that these babies have nothing to look at but a blank, white ceiling and white crib cushions, and are handled only when they need to be fed or changed. However, we have to be very careful not to apply this finding too broadly. Because children who lack stimulation tend to develop poorly, we can't conclude that by providing children with maximum stimulation—playing with them continually, having music piped into their rooms, surrounding them with fancy toys—we can guarantee that they will grow up emotionally sound and intellectually superior. On the contrary, it appears that most babies do best with a medium level of stimulation (White, 1969). In basic science, we are provided with specific findings: what happened in one study conducted at one time and in one place. To generalize these specific findings into a list of general rules (as the blind wise men did) would be misleading.

Understanding Psychology focuses on psychology as a basic research science. The research findings provide the foundations on which practical applications are built. However, we give you some idea of the range of applications in psychology by including many subsections (in yellow) called "Using Psychology."

A BRIEF HISTORY OF PSYCHOLOGY

Even though psychology is one of the newer sciences, the study of human behavior began with the ancient Greek philosophers. In the fifth and sixth centuries B.C., they began to study human behavior and decided that people's lives were dominated not so much by the gods as by their own minds: people were rational.

These early philosophers attempted to interpret the world they observed around them in terms of human perceptions—objects were hot or cold, wet or dry, hard or soft, and these qualities influenced people's experience of them. Although the Greek philosophers did not rely on systematic study, they did set the stage for the development of the science of psychology through their reliance on observation as a means of knowing about people.

Much later, seventeenth century philosophers introduced the idea of *dualism*, the concept that the world is divided into two elements (in this case, mind and matter). The mind accounted for our thoughts and feelings. Matter referred to our physical being, our bodies. Mind and matter were believed to be completely independent of each other. Furthermore, since the mind was believed to be part of God's domain, it was not subject to the same kind of investigation as the more material aspects of life. The mind was studied by theologians, while matter was studied by other scholars in universities.

The French philosopher René Descartes helped mold current psychological study when he wrote that there was a link between mind and body. He reasoned that the mind controlled the body's movements, sensations, and perceptions. His approach to understanding human behavior was based on the assumption that the mind and body influence each other to create a person's experiences. Exactly how this interaction takes place is still being studied today.

Toward the end of the seventeenth century, the British philosopher John Locke contributed yet another important concept to the foundation for modern psychology. Locke believed in the concept of *empiricism*, that all knowledge is obtained through observation and experience. He said that infants come into this world with blank minds, with no experiences. The term he used to describe the mind of the human infant was *tabula rasa* (Latin for blank tablet). Whatever experiences a person has in life are written into this blank tablet. Knowledge, then, is the result of a buildup of experiences. Locke's ideas have influenced education as well as psychology.

Psychology as a Discipline

The establishment of psychology as a separate, formal field of study began in 1879 in Leipzig, Germany, when Wilhelm Wundt started his Laboratory of Psychology. In fact, Wundt is referred to as the founder of psychology as a science. Although he was trained in physiology—the study of how the body works—his real interest was in the study of the human mind. In his laboratory, he modeled his research on the mind after that in other natural sciences he had studied. He developed a method of self-observation called **introspection** to collect information about the mind. In carefully controlled situations, trained subjects reported their thoughts, and Wundt tried to map out the basic structure of thought processes. Wundt's experiments were very important historically, not so much because he ad-

MORE about...

Psychology as the Study of Physiological Processes. In addition to the ways psychology has been studied in the past, some psychologists today also focus on the physiological bases of behavior. Psychologists who subscribe to the physiological perspective contend that behavior can be best understood by looking at its biological or physical causes. *Physiological psychologists* (also called *biopsychologists*) believe that most or all psychological events are the result of a underlying biological or chemical processes. Many physiological psychologists do research on the functioning of the nervous system, study how brain cells communicate with each other, and explore the relationship between hormones and behavior.

Physiological psychologists often conduct research on animals in order to understand basic physiological processes. These results can then be applied to the study of more complicated behavior of human beings. Recent successes in treating problems such as depression and schizophrenia with drugs lend support to the physiological position that to understand human behavior we must understand its underlying physiological processes.

vanced our understanding of the mind, but because his work attracted many students who carried on the tradition of psychological research.

A close rival for the honor of founder of psychology is the American psychologist William James. James, the first American psychologist, was more involved in writing than research. (His brother, Henry James, was a great American writer.) In his text *Principles of Psychology* (1890), James speculated that thinking, feeling, learning, remembering—all of the activities of the mind—serve one major function, to help us survive as a species. Rather than focusing on the structure of the mind as Wundt did, James focused on the functions of the conscious mind. Although James did not produce any significant experimental findings, his writings and theories are still influential. In Chapter 6, you will learn more about James' ideas on motivation and emotion.

Psychology as the Study of Unconscious Processes

While the first psychologists were interested in understanding the conscious mind, Sigmund Freud, a physician who practiced in Vienna until 1938, was more interested in the unconscious mind. He believed that our conscious experiences are only the tip of the iceberg, that beneath the surface are primitive biological urges that are in conflict with the requirements of society and morality. According to Freud, these unconscious motivations and conflicts are responsible for much human behavior. He thought that they were responsible for many medically unexplainable physical symptoms that troubled his patients.

Freud used a new method for indirectly studying unconscious processes. In this technique, known as *free association*, a patient said everything that came to mind—no matter how absurd or irrelevant it seemed—without attempting to produce logical or meaningful statements. The person was instructed not to edit or censor the thoughts. Freud's role, that of *psychoanalyst*, was to be objective; he merely sat and listened, then interpreted the associations (Figure 1.6). Free association, Freud believed, revealed the operation of unconscious processes. Freud also believed that dreams are expressions of the most primitive unconscious urges. To learn more about these urges, he developed *dream analysis*—basically an extension of free association—in which the patient applied the same technique to his or her dreams (Freud, 1940).

While working out his ideas, Freud took careful, extensive notes on all his patients and treatment sessions. He used these records, or case studies, to develop and illustrate a comprehensive theory of personality—that is, of the total, functioning person (Hall and Lindzey, 1978). Freud's theory of personality will be discussed in Chapter 11.

In many areas of psychology today, Freud's view of unconscious motivation remains a powerful and controversial influence. Modern psychologists may support, alter, or attempt to disprove it, but most have a strong opinion about it. The technique of free association is still used by psychoanalysts, and the method of intensive case study is still a major tool for investigating behavior.

Figure 1.6
Sigmund Freud in his Vienna office, 1938.

Psychology as the Study of Individual Differences

Sir Francis Galton, a nineteenth-century English mathematician and scientist, wanted to understand how heredity (inherited traits) influences a person's abilities, character, and behavior (Figure 1.7). Galton (1869) traced the ancestry of various eminent people and found that greatness runs in families. (This was appropriate, since Galton himself was considered a genius and his family included at least one towering intellectual figure, a cousin named Charles Darwin.) He therefore concluded that genius or eminence is a hereditary trait. This conclusion was like the blind men's ideas about the elephant. Galton did not consider the possibility that the tendency of genius to run in eminent families might be a result of the exceptional environments and socioeconomic advantages that also tend to run in such families.

Figure 1.7
Sir Francis Galton, who invented procedures for testing abilities and characteristics that are still used in modern personality and intelligence tests.

The data Galton used were based on his study of biographies. However, not content to limit his inquiry to indirect accounts, he went on to invent procedures for directly testing the abilities and characteristics of a wide range of people. These tests were the primitive ancestors of the modern personality tests and intelligence tests that virtually everyone who reads this book has taken at some time. Galton also devised statistical techniques that are still in use today.

Although Galton began his work shortly before psychology emerged as an independent discipline, his theories and techniques quickly became central aspects of the new science. In 1883 he published a book, *Inquiries into Human Faculty and Its Development*, that is regarded as having defined the beginnings of individual psychology. Galton's writings raised the issue of whether behavior is determined by heredity or environment—a subject that has become the focus of controversy, especially in recent years. Gal-

Psychology in China. Psychology in modern China lags far behind the United States, but the roots of psychological testing can be traced to the ancient Chinese. Several thousand years ago, the Chinese developed and used written tests to evaluate abilities in areas such as law and poetry.

In more recent times, Chinese psychologists seeking training often came to the United States. After World War II, the People's Republic of China was established and communist rule predominated. Because of China's communist orientation, psychology came under the influence of Soviet ideology. Pavlovian psychology became the standard, and Chinese psychologists were required to learn Russian.

Chinese psychologists attempted to establish their own identity in the 1960s but suffered a setback during the repressive Cultural Revolution, when psychology was removed from university curricula. Many psychologists were sent to labor farms, and some even committed suicide. There are now more than 2,000 psychologists in China. These psychologists are encouraged to study practical issues, especially in education.

ton's influence can also be seen in the current widespread use of psychological tests.

Psychology as the Study of Observable Behavior

The pioneering work of Russian physiologist Ivan Pavlov, who won the Nobel prize in 1904, charted another new course for psychological investigation. In a now-famous experiment, Pavlov rang a tuning fork each time he gave a dog some meat powder. The dog would naturally salivate the moment it saw the meat powder. After Pavlov repeated the procedure several times, the dog would salivate when it heard the tuning fork, even if no food appeared. It had been conditioned to associate the sound with the food.

The concept of the conditioned reflex—a response (salivation) elicited by a stimulus (the tuning fork) other than the one that first produced it (food)—was used by psychologists as a new tool, as a means of exploring the development of behavior. Using this tool, they could begin to account for behavior as the product of prior experience. This enabled them to explain how certain acts and certain differences among individuals were the result of learning.

Psychologists who stressed investigating observable behavior became known as *behaviorists*. Their position, as formulated by American psychologist John B. Watson (1924), was that psychology should concern itself *only* with the observable facts of behavior. Watson further maintained that all behavior, even apparently instinctive behavior, is the result of conditioning and occurs because the appropriate stimulus is present in the environment.

Although it was Watson who defined and solidified the behaviorist position, it is B. F. Skinner, the contemporary American psychologist, who refined and popularized it. Skinner attempted to show how, in principle, his laboratory techniques might be applied to society as a whole. In his classic novel *Walden Two* (1949), he portrayed his idea of Utopia—a small town in which conditioning, through rewarding those who display behavior that is considered desirable, rules every conceivable facet of life.

Skinner has exerted great influence on both the general public and the science of psychology. His face is familiar to television audiences, and his book *Beyond Freedom and Dignity* (1971) became a bestseller (Figure 1.8). A number of Walden Two communities have been formed in various parts of the country, and many people toilet-train their children, lose weight, quit smoking, and overcome phobias by using Skinner-inspired methods.

Skinner has been widely criticized, for many people are convinced that he seeks to limit personal freedom with his "manipulative" conditioning techniques. He has also been heartily applauded as a social visionary. In any event, his theories and methods have been highly influential in psychology. Behaviorist-inspired techniques compete with more traditional psychotherapy for use in the treatment of various psychological disorders. The techniques of *reinforcement*, or controlled reward and punishment, have become increasingly popular in education, and Skinner's teaching machine was the forerunner of modern computerized programmed instruction. Moreover, a vast number of today's psychologists use Skinner's research methods to obtain precise findings in their laboratory experiments.

Humanistic psychology developed as a reaction to the behavioral movement. Humanistic psychologists, notably Abraham Maslow, Carl Rogers, and Rollo May, describe human nature as active and creative rather than passively reacting to external stimuli. Unlike behaviorists, humanists feel that the human mind is able to influence and change the world in which it functions.

PSYCHOLOGY AS A PROFESSION

What Is a Psychologist?

Perhaps the best way to answer this question is to ask who is not a psychologist. Although your parents may tell you they know a lot about human behavior and may have been studying your behavior all your life, they are not psychologists because of it. Psychologists are people who have been trained to observe and analyze behavior patterns, to develop theories on behavior, and to apply what they know to influence behavior. Just as there are many different branches of medicine, there are many different fields of psychology. The principle ones are described below.

People often confuse the terms "psychologist" and "psychiatrist." These are different professions. **Psychiatry** is a specialty of medicine. After a psychiatry student completes medical school, he or she continues training in psychiatric medicine and learns to treat people with disturbed behavior. Psychiatrists work mainly in hospitals and have their own private practices; unlike psychologists, they can prescribe drugs to treat their patients. Sometimes, a psychiatrist works with a psychologist in testing, evaluating, and treating patients. Unlike psychologists, most psychiatrists are not involved in much research; they focus their efforts primarily on helping their patients deal with emotional difficulties.

Specialty Fields in Psychology

Psychology today covers an enormous range of specialty fields. Psychologists are employed in advertising, education, and criminology. Some psychologists are studying death, art, and robots. Psychological themes and terminology have become part of everyday life, and of novels, films, and television programs.

In the process of expanding its scope, psychology has been divided into a number of subfields. Clinical and *counseling psychology* are the most popular. Specialists in this field are usually referred to as *psychotherapists*. Clinical psychologists help people deal with their personal problems. They

Figure 1.8
Behaviorist B. F. Skinner has influenced large numbers of people with his techniques of conditioning behavior by rewards and punishments.

? FACT OR FICTION

Forensic psychologists apply psychology to legal issues.

Fact. *Forensic psychology* is a relatively new but growing area of psychology. It attempts to apply psychological principles to the legal system. A forensic psychologist might provide testimony as an expert witness in a trial, be employed to counsel inmates at a correctional facility, or have a job working with police authorities assisting them in solving criminal cases.

Answers to Figure 1.4
All of the statements in Figure 1.4 are false. As you read the different chapters in this book, you will learn more about the correct answers to these statements and the research that psychologists have conducted to prove these theories false.

Figure 1.9
(Opposite) Psychologists at work. (a) One to one therapy. (b) An automated instructional system designed by educational psychologists. (c) Administering a standard intelligence test. (d) A therapist working with a mentally disturbed child. (e) Space vehicles designed with the help of psychologists. (f) Doing research on sleep and dreaming. (g) Videotaping a family interaction for later use in family therapy. (h) Brain research: an experiment in chemical stimulation of the brain.

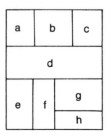

work mainly in private offices, mental hospitals, prisons, and clinics. Some specialize in giving and interpreting personality tests designed to determine whether a person needs treatment and, if so, what kind. Counseling psychologists usually work in schools or industrial firms, advising and assisting people. Your school may have a special type of counseling psychologist, known as a school psychologist, who is trained to help young people with their problems.

A large number of specialists study *personality psychology, social psychology*, and *developmental psychology*. These psychologists are usually involved in basic rather than applied science. Personality psychologists study personality development and traits and devise personality tests. Social psychologists study groups and the way they influence individual behavior. Some are particularly interested in public opinion and devote much of their time to conducting polls and surveys. Most developmental psychologists focus on children from birth to about age fifteen. In recent years, however, some have been leaning toward the "life-cycle" or "cradle-to-grave" approach—that is, studying development as something that continues from birth to old age.

Educational psychology deals with topics related to teaching children and young adults, such as intelligence, memory, problem solving, and motivation. Specialists in this field are concerned with evaluating teaching methods, devising tests, and developing new instructional devices for films and television.

Community psychology is a relatively new area of community mental health. A psychologist who specializes in this area may work in a mental health or social welfare agency operated by the state or local government or by a private organization. A community psychologist may help design, run, or evaluate a mental health clinic in a remote area.

Industrial psychology is another area of specialization. Industrial psychologists have developed methods to boost production, improve working conditions, place applicants in jobs for which they are best suited, train people, and reduce accidents.

Finally, about a fourth of all psychologists are engaged in *experimental psychology*. These psychologists do everything from testing how electrical stimulation of a certain area of a rat's brain affects its behavior, through studying how disturbed people think, to observing how different socioeconomic groups vote in elections. They are basic scientists rather than applied scientists.

What psychologists think about, what experiments they have done, and what this knowledge means form the subject of this book. Psychology is dedicated to answering some of the most interesting questions of everyday life: What happens during sleep? How can bad habits be broken? Is there a way to measure intelligence? Why do crowds sometimes turn into mobs? Do dreams mean anything? How does punishment affect a child? Can memory be improved? What causes psychological breakdowns? In trying to answer such questions, psychology ties together all that has been discovered about human behavior and feelings in order to look at the total human being. The picture is far from complete, but much of what is known will be found in the chapters that follow.

SUMMARY

Use the following outline as a tool for reviewing this chapter. Copy the outline onto your own paper, leaving spaces between headings to make notes about key concepts.

 I. Why Study Psychology?

    A. Insight

    B. Practical Information

 II. Overview of Psychology

    A. Defining Psychology

    B. The Scientific Basis of Psychology

    C. The Goals of Psychology

 III. A Brief History of Psychology

    A. Psychology as a Discipline

    B. Psychology as the Study of Unconscious Processes

    C. Psychology as the Study of Individual Differences

    D. Psychology as the Study of Observable Behavior

 IV. Psychology as a Profession

    A. What Is a Psychologist?

    B. Specialty Fields in Psychology

CONCEPTS AND VOCABULARY

1. What are some advantages of learning about psychology?

2. What is the first step in psychological research?

3. What are four goals of psychology?

4. What is the concept of dualism? When was it first introduced?

5. Who established the idea of *empiricism* and *tabula rasa*? What is the meaning of each of these terms?

6. Who established the first psychology laboratory and is considered the founder of psychology as a science?

7. What method of study did Wundt develop to collect information about the mind?

8. According to William James, what was the single function of all the activities of the mind?

9. What type of motivations did Freud study? What methods did he use in his studies?

10. Is Freud's view of unconscious motivation still influential?

11. What did Sir Francis Galton want to understand? What area of psychology did he begin?

12. What is the name given to psychologists who investigate observable behavior? Can you name three of these psychologists? Who influenced the formation of communities based on learning, or conditioning, principles? What is the name given to these communities?

13. What is the most popular subfield of psychology? What type of psychologist usually works in schools? What type might work in a factory?

CRITICAL THINKING

1. **Synthesize.** Write your own definition of psychology. Is your definition different from one you would have written before reading the chapter? Put the definition in a safe place and take it out and read it at the end of the course to see if you still agree with it.

2. **Apply.** How is psychology involved in your life? Make a list of all the ways in which psychology affects your life. (Hint: Traffic signs and classroom interiors are often designed by psycholo-

gists.) Keep in mind the different specialties of psychology you read about in the chapter.

3. **Evaluate.** Psychology is generally thought of as a helpful science and is expected to produce happier people, accident-free and more productive workers, and greater understanding of interpersonal relationships. However, well-meaning people throughout history have also applied what they considered to be sound "psychological" techniques that have actually tormented or totally destroyed their intended beneficiaries. Can you see any possibilities today where psychological knowledge could be used against the best interests of an individual or society?

APPLYING KNOWLEDGE

1. Make a list of various professions or occupations. List the ways a psychologist might contribute to better functioning within the occupation or profession. What kind of psychologist do you think would be most helpful in performing each job?

2. Much of psychology is, in effect, an attempt to express the nature of human behavior. Make a list of characteristics or behavioral tendencies that you think apply to all people. Compare your list with those of other students in the class.

3. The history of psychology includes the names of many individuals who are not well known to the public. How many of the psychologists mentioned in this chapter were you already familiar with? Could you have identified their contributions to the field of psychology? Choose five people you know and ask them for a brief definition of psychology. Take notes on their answers. Next, ask them to name any important people in the field of psychology, either past or present. Are you surprised by the results of your ques-

tioning? If the people you questioned did not know any important psychologists, explain why you think this was the case. Report the results of your questioning to the class.

ANALYZING VIEWPOINTS

1. Psychology is usually thought of as a science. Psychologists rely on the scientific method, testing hypotheses by collecting information, analyzing data, and conducting additional experiments. But is psychology a science in the same way that biology or chemistry is a science? Can you study human behavior in the same way as you can biological phenomena? Are there any characteristics or "laws," comparable to established laws in physics, that are universally true for all humans? Write an essay that argues both sides of the issue, using what you learned in this chapter as well as your own thoughts and ideas. Begin your essay with a basic definition of science. Locate a definition of science in one of your textbooks or in the library.

BEYOND THE CLASSROOM.

1. Go to the library and ask the librarian where you can find information on careers. Tell the librarian you are doing a project for school on careers in the field of psychology. Read what you can find about the different careers that exist within the field of psychology. If you know a psychologist, arrange an interview with that person. How did he or she choose the field of psychology? What education was needed? What are the most rewarding aspects of the job? Are there negative parts of the job? Which type of psychologist would you choose to be? Why? Report what you learn about careers in psychology to your class.

UNIT 1

Learning and Cognitive Processes

CHAPTER 2

Learning: Principles and Applications

Key Terms:

aversive control
avoidance conditioning
behavior modification
classical conditioning
conditioned reinforcer
conditioned response (CR)
conditioned stimulus (CS)
discrimination
escape conditioning
extinction
feedback
fixed-interval schedule
fixed-ratio schedule
generalization
learning
negative reinforcement
neutral stimulus
operant conditioning
primary reinforcers
punishers
reinforcement
response chains
shaping
signals
token economy
transfer
unconditioned response (UCR)
unconditioned stimulus (UCS)
variable-interval schedule
variable-ratio schedule

Learning is basic to our understanding of human behavior. It is involved in nearly all aspects of life. As young infants, we learn to hold ourselves upright, to walk, and to use our hands. Later, we learn to run, to play baseball, and to use a can opener. We learn to read, to write, to memorize information to help us pass an exam. We learn how to get people to give us what we want by asking, bargaining, being nice, or pouting. We even learn to be afraid of the dentist or of taking exams, and then we learn to overcome these fears. We also learn how to learn. **Learning** can be defined as a relatively permanent change in behavior that results from experience.

Not all of the behaviors that we learn are acquired in the same way. Furthermore, the same behavior can be learned in different ways. For example, we may learn to fear the dentist because we associate the dentist with the experience of pain. We may have acquired a fear of the dentist because every time we express our fears, our parents or friends give us special attention and comfort. We may never have gone to the dentist, but we may have learned to fear him or her by watching someone else's reaction to a dentist. These examples represent the three basic types of learning that have been studied by psychologists: *classical conditioning, operant conditioning,* and *modeling.*

CLASSICAL CONDITIONING

Like many great discoveries, Ivan Pavlov's discovery of the principle of classical conditioning was accidental. Around the turn of the century, this Russian scientist had been studying the process of digestion. Pavlov wanted to understand how a dog's stomach prepares to digest food when something is placed in the dog's mouth. Then he noticed that the mere sight

Objectives:

After studying this chapter, you should be able to

- describe the principles and techniques of classical conditioning.
- outline the principles, techniques, and applications of operant conditioning.
- cite the factors involved in the process of learning.
- apply the principles of learning to human behavior.

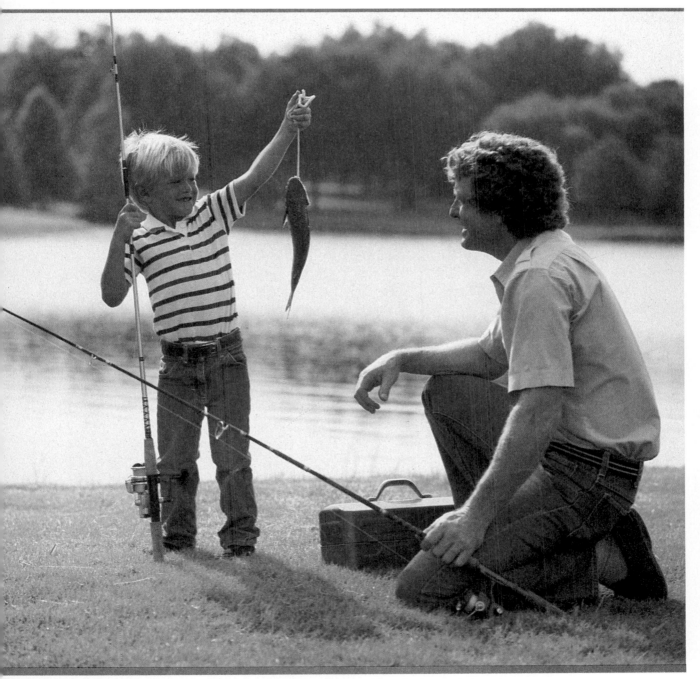

Figure 2.1 Skill at a sport is learned behavior, as is almost everything else human beings do.

or smell of food was enough to start a dog salivating. Pavlov became fascinated with these "psychic secretions" that occurred before food was actually presented, and decided to investigate how they worked.

Pavlov's Experiment

Pavlov (1927) began his experiments by ringing a tuning fork and then immediately placing some meat powder on the dog's tongue. He chose the tuning fork because it was a **neutral stimulus**—that is, one that had nothing to do with the response (salivation). After only a few times, the dog started salivating as soon as it heard the sound, even if food were not placed in its mouth (Figure 2.2). Pavlov went on to demonstrate that any neutral stimulus will cause an unrelated response if it is presented regularly just before the stimulus (here, food) that normally induces that response (salivation).

Pavlov distinguished among the different elements of his experiment as follows. He used the term "unconditioned" to refer to natural stimuli and to automatic, involuntary responses. Such responses include blushing, shivering, being startled, or salivating. In the experiment, food was the **unconditioned stimulus (UCS):** a stimulus that leads to a certain response without previous training. (A dog doesn't have to be taught to salivate when it smells meat.) Food normally causes salivation. This is an **unconditioned response (UCR):** a response that occurs naturally and automatically when the unconditioned stimulus is presented.

Under normal conditions, the sound of a tuning fork would not cause salivation. The dog had to be taught, or *conditioned*, to associate this sound with food. An ordinarily neutral stimulus that, after training, leads to a response such as salivation is termed a **conditioned stimulus (CS).** The salivation it causes is a **conditioned response (CR).** A conditioned response is learned. A wide variety of stimuli may serve as conditioned stimuli for salivation: the sight of food or an experimenter entering the room, the sound of a tone, a flash of light. Controlling an animal's or a person's

Figure 2.2
The apparatus Pavlov used to study conditioned salivation in dogs. The harness held the dog steady, while the tube leading from the dog's mouth deposited saliva on an arm connected to the recorder on the left. Drops of saliva moved the pen, making a permanent record of the salivation response to such stimuli as food and sights or sounds associated with food.

responses in this way so that an old response becomes attached to a new stimulus is called **classical conditioning.** A number of different "reflex" responses that ordinarily occur automatically can be conditioned to occur whenever the correct conditioned stimulus occurs. These include responses produced by the glands, such as salivation or weeping, and responses of our internal muscles, such as those of the stomach. In general, these responses are controlled by the autonomic nervous system and are very much involved in our emotions, as we will see in Chapter 4, "Body and Behavior."

General Principles of Classical Conditioning

Acquisition of a classically conditioned response generally occurs gradually. With each pairing of the artificial, conditioned stimulus with the natural, unconditioned stimulus, the learned response is strengthened. In Pavlov's experiment, the more frequently the tuning fork was paired with the food, the more often the tone elicited salivation (the conditioned response). The timing of the association between the conditioned stimulus (the tone) and the unconditioned stimulus (food) also influences learning. Pavlov tried several different conditioning procedures in which he varied the time between the conditioned stimulus and the unconditioned stimulus. Sometimes he presented the tone before the food was presented. Other times, he presented the tone at the same time as the food. Generally, he found that classical conditioning was more reliable and effective when the conditioned stimulus was presented just before the unconditioned stimulus. He found that presenting the CS about half a second before the UCS gave the best results.

In the same set of experiments, Pavlov also explored the phenomena of *generalization* and *discrimination*. **Generalization** occurs when an animal responds to a second stimulus similar to the original conditioned stimulus. When Pavlov conditioned a dog to salivate at the sight of a circle (the CS), he found that the dog would salivate when it saw an oval as well. The dog had generalized its response to include a similar stimulus. Pavlov was later able to do the opposite, to teach the dog to respond only to the circle by always pairing meat powder with the circle but never pairing it with the oval. He thus taught the dog a **discrimination:** the ability to respond differently to different stimuli.

Generalization and discrimination are complementary processes and are part of our everyday life. For example, assume a person has come to associate the sound of a dentist's drill (CS) with a nervous reaction (CR). After several exposures to a dentist's drill, the person may find that he or she has generalized this uncomfortable feeling to the sound of other, nondental drills. Later, the person may learn to discriminate between the sound of a dentist's drill and other drills.

A classically conditioned response, like any other behavior, is subject to change. Pavlov discovered that if he stopped presenting food after the sound of the tuning fork, the sound gradually lost its effect on the dog. After he repeatedly struck the tuning fork without giving food, the dog no longer associated the sound with the arrival of food—the sound of the

The Case of Little Albert

John B. Watson and Rosalie Rayner (1920) showed how conditioning could be used on a human infant. They experimented with a well-adjusted eleven-month-old child named Albert. They presented Albert with many objects, including a rat, a rabbit, blocks, a fur coat, and a hairy Santa Claus mask. Albert showed no fear of any of these objects—they were all neutral stimuli for the fear response.

Watson and Rayner decided that they would attempt to condition Albert to fear rats. They began by placing a furry white rat in front of him. Albert would reach out to touch it and, each time he did, one of Watson's assistants would sound a metal bar with a hammer behind Albert's head. The first time the metal bar was struck, Albert fell forward and buried his head in a pillow. The next time he reached for the rat and the bar was struck, Albert began to whimper. The noise, the unconditioned stimulus, brought about a natural, unconditioned response, fear. After only a few such pairings, the rat became a *conditioned stimulus* that elicited a *conditioned response*, fear.

After Watson and Rayner conditioned Albert to fear rats, they presented him with a rabbit. Albert now reacted fearfully to the rabbit. The researchers found that the degree of fear Albert felt toward other neutral stimuli depended upon how much they resembled the furry white rat. His conditioned fear response had generalized to include the rabbit. Other furry white objects, such as the fur coat and Santa Claus mask, also caused Albert to cry and try to escape whenever Watson and Rayner presented them, although the response was not so great as when the rabbit was presented.

One of the most frequent criticisms of Watson and Rayner's experimental demonstration of a conditioned fear in Little Albert was that they were successful in teaching a previously healthy, well-adjusted child to be fearful. Apparently, the researchers knew at least one month ahead of time that Albert would be leaving the study and yet they made no attempt to extinguish his conditioned fears (Harris, 1979). Ethical researchers today would not repeat the Little Albert study, because of the potential psychological harm to the young child.

One of Watson's students, Mary Cover Jones (1924, 1974), developed an extinction procedure to reduce people's existing fears. Peter was a boy who was extremely fearful of rabbits. Jones helped Peter eliminate his fear by extinction and by pairing the feared object (the rabbit) with pleasant experiences such as eating ice cream or receiving special adult attention.

tuning fork was no longer able to elicit the salivation response. Pavlov called this effect **extinction** because the conditioned response had gradually died out.

Even though a classically conditioned response may be extinguished, this does not mean that the person has completely unlearned the conditioned response. After a period of time in which the conditioned stimulus is not presented, the previously extinguished conditioned response may reappear when the conditioned stimulus is presented again. This *spontaneous recovery* does not bring the conditioned response back to its full strength before extinction, however. For example, the amount of salivation

Pavlov's dog produced during spontaneous recovery was much less than the amount produced during the conditioning period. Furthermore, presenting the tone several times without food resulted in gradual loss of the salivation response.

A good example of extinction and spontaneous recovery is the following. Every time you are in the shower and the water pressure drops, the water suddenly turns very hot. You learn to associate the normally neutral stimulus of a drop in water pressure with your automatic startle reaction to the hot water surge. Even after you finally repair your plumbing so that hot water no longer follows a drop in water pressure, it may take several showers before you no longer react to a water pressure change. You eventually extinguish the startle reaction. Then you go away for a period of time. When you return, you again react with a startle whenever the water pressure changes. You have had a spontaneous recovery of your conditioned startle reaction. Then, after several showers without any hot water assaults, you no longer have a reaction.

Classical Conditioning and Human Behavior

Classical conditioning was discovered in learning experiments with animals, but, as we have seen, the principles of classical conditioning apply to human learning as well.

Using the principle of classical conditioning, a practical solution to the problem of bedwetting was discovered by O. Hobart Mowrer and his wife Mollie (1938). One reason bedwetting occurs is that children do not wake up during the night when they have a full bladder. Instead, they wet the bed while they are sleeping. The Mowrers developed a device known as the *bell and pad*. It consists of two metallic sheets perforated with small holes and attached by wires to a battery-run alarm. The thin, metal sheets are placed under the child's bed sheets. When the sleeping child moistens the sheet with the first drops of urine, the circuit closes, causing the alarm to go off and wake the child. The child can then use the bathroom. The alarm is the unconditioned stimulus which produces the unconditioned response of waking up. The sensation of a full bladder is the conditioned stimulus which, before conditioning, did not produce wakefulness. After several pairings of the alarm (UCS) and the full bladder (CS), the child is able to awaken to the sensation of a full bladder without the help of the alarm. This technique has proved to be a very effective way of treating bedwetting problems.

To identify the elements in this conditioning example and compare them to Pavlov's experiment, see Figure 2.3.

Taste Aversions. Suppose you go out on a date to a fancy restaurant. You may decide to try an expensive appetizer you've never had, such as snails. Then suppose that, after dinner, you go on to a concert and become violently ill. You will probably develop a taste aversion—you will never be able to look at another snail without becoming at least a little nauseated.

TWO EXAMPLES OF CLASSICAL CONDITIONING

Figure 2.3
The classical conditioning procedure involves three phases—before, during, and after training. The learner responds to the neutral stimulus (the CS) with a conditioned response.

	Stimulus	Response
Pavlov's Experiment		
BEFORE CONDITIONING	Tone (neutral stimulus) →	Does not produce response of salivation
	Food (UCS) →	Salivation (UCR)
DURING CONDITIONING	Tone (CS) and Food (UCS) →	Salivation (UCR)
AFTER CONDITIONING	Tone (CS) →	Salivation (CR)
Mowrer's Experiment		
BEFORE CONDITIONING	Full bladder (neutral stimulus) →	Does not produce response of wakening
	Alarm (UCS) →	Awakening (UCR)
DURING CONDITIONING	Full bladder (CS) and Alarm (USC) →	Awakening (UCR)
AFTER CONDITIONING	Full bladder (CS) →	Awakening (CR)

Your nausea reaction to snails is an example of classical conditioning. What makes this type of conditioning particularly interesting to learning theorists is that, when people or other animals become ill, they seem to decide, "It must have been something I ate," even if they haven't eaten for several hours. In the above situation, it is unlikely that the concert hall in which you were sick will become the conditioned stimulus. Nor will other stimuli from the restaurant—the wallpaper pattern or the type of china used. What's more, psychologists can even predict which part of your meal will be the conditioned stimulus: you will probably blame a new food, one that you haven't had before. Thus, if you get sick after a meal of salad, steak, and snails, you will probably learn to hate snails, even if they are really not at fault.

John Garcia and R. A. Koelling (1966) first demonstrated this phenomenon with rats. The animals were placed in a cage with a tube containing flavored water. Whenever a rat took a drink, lights would flash and clicks would sound. Then the rats were divided into two groups. Some rats were given an electric shock after they drank. All these rats showed traditional classical conditioning: the lights and the sounds became conditioned stimuli, and they tried to avoid them in order to avoid a shock. Other rats were not shocked, but were injected with a drug that made them sick after they drank and the lights and sounds occurred. These rats developed an aversion not to the lights or the sounds but only to the taste of the flavored water.

This special relationship between food and illness was used in a study (Gustavson *et al.*, 1974) that made coyotes hate the taste of lamb by giving them a drug to make them sick when they ate sheep. This is an important application because sheep farmers in the western United States would like to eliminate the coyotes that threaten their flocks, while naturalists are opposed to killing the coyotes. The experimenters realized that coyotes could be trained to eat other kinds of meat, and thus learn to coexist peacefully with sheep.

Figure 2.4
A rat pressing a bar in a Skinner box. The Skinner box is an artificial environment in which lights, sounds, rewards, and punishments can be delivered and controlled and in which some of the animal's behaviors, such as bar pressing, can be recorded by automatic switches.

OPERANT CONDITIONING

Suppose a dog is wandering around the neighborhood, sniffing trees, checking garbage cans, looking for a squirrel to chase. A kind person sees the dog and tosses a bone out of the kitchen door to it. The next day, the dog is likely to stop at the same door on its rounds, if not go to it directly. The kind person produces another bone, and another the next day. The dog becomes a regular visitor.

Suppose a child is unhappy because his younger sister seems to be capturing their mother's attention. He begins to pout and act aggressively toward his sister. Right away his mother stops attending to the younger sister to reprimand him. Even though the mother's attention is negative, the boy seems to like it; a short time later, he is back again harassing his sister and earning another reprimand from his mother.

Both stories are examples of **operant conditioning**—that is, learning from the consequences of behavior. The term "operant" is used because the subject (the wandering dog and the boy in our examples) *operates* on or causes some change in the environment, producing a result that influences whether it will operate in the same way in the future. Depending on the effect of the operant behaviors, the learner will repeat or eliminate these behaviors—to get rewards or avoid punishment.

Operant conditioning differs from classical conditioning in two important ways. First, in order for operant conditioning to occur, the learner must behave in a way that produces some consequences. The control of the learning is in the hands of the learner. If the learner takes no action, no operant conditioning can occur.

A second difference between operant and classical conditioning concerns the kinds of behavior that are acquired. In classical conditioning, the most effective learning occurs with automatic, reflexive behavior. Operant conditioning is not limited to reflexive responses, but may involve the acquisition of a wide range of voluntary behaviors.

Reinforcement

B. F. Skinner (1974) is the psychologist most closely associated with operant conditioning. He and his colleagues believe that most behavior is influenced by one's history of rewards and punishments. Suppose you want to teach a dog to shake hands. One way would be to give the animal a pat on the head or a biscuit every time it lifts its paw up to you. The biscuit or pat is called a positive reinforcer. In this example, the dog will get the message and shake hands again to get another reward. **Reinforcement** can be defined as a stimulus or event that affects the likelihood that a behavior will be repeated. The nature of the reinforcement depends on the effect it has on the learner. Examples of reinforcers that people respond to are social approval, money, and extra privileges.

Your dog will stop shaking hands when you forget to reward it for the trick and withdraw reinforcement. Extinction will occur, but it will take time. In fact, for a while after you stop rewarding it, the dog will probably become impatient, bark, and paw even more insistently than it did before.

Figure 2.5
Practice is an important part of learning to play a musical instrument. Beginners spend many hours practicing scales and simple tunes. Once they master the basics, they can move on to more complicated arrangements.

Schedules of Reinforcement

One important factor in operant conditioning is the type and frequency of reinforcement. You might suppose that behavior would best be acquired by reinforcing every response. This is called a *continuous schedule* of reinforcement. However, the best results are not obtained from a continuous schedule. When positive reinforcement occurs only intermittently or on a partial schedule, the responses are generally more stable and more persistent.

Consider, for example, two vending machines in the cafeteria. You have found that the first machine always delivers the candy bar you have selected. You have never lost any money in it, and you have always received a positive reinforcement (your candy bar). The second machine is unreliable. Sometimes you get your candy bar after you put your money in. At other times you get nothing: no candy bar, no money returned. Now, suppose one day you find that the first, reliable machine does not give you your candy bar. From which machine would you continue to try to get a reinforcement (candy bar)? You would probably not choose the first, more reliable machine, because you would assume that you would not get a candy bar from it no matter how long you tried. You would probably continue to try the second vending machine, because you know that sometimes it works and sometimes it doesn't. You would not consider it unusual when it failed to work, and you would expect that, after a few tries, it would give you your selection.

This example shows how intermittent reinforcement causes responses to be generally more stable and persistent than a continuous schedule of reinforcement.

Although intermittent reinforcement may be arranged in a number of ways, four basic methods, or schedules, have been studied in the laboratory. Schedules of reinforcement may be based either on the *number* of correct responses that the organism makes between reinforcements (*ratio* schedules) or on the *amount of time* that elapses before reinforcement is made available (*interval* schedules). In either case, reinforcement may appear on a regular, or fixed, schedule or on an irregular, or variable, schedule. The four basic schedules result from the combination of these four possibilities. People respond differently to each type.

In a **fixed-ratio schedule,** reinforcement depends on a specified quantity of responses, such as rewarding every fourth response. The student who receives a good grade after completing a specified amount of work and the typist who is paid by the number of pages completed are on fixed-ratio schedules. People tend to work hard on fixed-ratio schedules, pausing briefly after each reward. However, if the amount of work or number of responses to be completed before the next reward is great, the student or pieceworker is likely to show low morale and few responses at the beginning of each new cycle because there is a long way to go before the next reinforcement.

A **variable-ratio schedule** requires that an average number of responses be made for each reinforcement. Instead of the fixed number of responses being set, as in the fixed-ratio schedule, the number of responses needed for a reinforcement changes from one time to the next. Slot machines are a good example of a variable-ratio schedule. They are set to pay off after a varying number of attempts. Gamblers often overlook this feature of slot machines and continue to deposit coins at a steady high rate, believing (mistakenly) that the more they do so, the sooner they will hit the jackpot. Casino operators encourage this response by giving out free tokens to newcomers. Yet the casino operators also control the variable ratio for the jackpot. Generally, people on variable-ratio schedules of reinforcement tend to work or respond at a steady high rate.

On a **fixed-interval schedule,** reinforcement is available after a predetermined time. Reinforcement can occur after a certain number of minutes, hours, or days, but the time interval is always the same. People who are reinforced under a fixed-interval schedule are likely to decrease responding right after a reinforcement, but as the end of the interval draws near again, their rate of response may increase rapidly. Workers who are paid every Thursday may be more motivated to come to work on Thursday morning (payday) than on Friday (the day after payday). Absenteeism is generally much lower on payday.

On a **variable-interval schedule,** the time at which a reinforcer will be available varies throughout the conditioning procedure. An example of a variable-interval reinforcement would be a call from a prospective employer that you knew would come at some point, but you did not know when. You would probably jump up to answer the phone for hours so that no one in the family would answer it first, even though you did not know whether an individual call was going to be the reinforcer (the call from the employer). No matter how long you continued your answering behavior, you could not increase the likelihood of hearing his or her voice. You would continue your answering behavior because you knew that it would pay off eventually. Similarly a pigeon (such as the one in Figure

Figure 2.6
This pigeon is showing signs of emotional upset common in extinction of an operantly conditioned response. The bird was trained to obtain food from the square hole by pecking at the key in the round hole. When the experimenter switched off the circuit that made the arrangement work, the bird pecked the key for a while and then, finding no food, began to jump around and flap its wings.

2.6) that is on a variable-interval schedule tends to peck at the key much more regularly than an animal on a fixed-interval schedule, because the amount of time it will take to be reinforced is unknown.

In summary, ratio schedules are based on events, while interval schedules are based on time. In general, responses are learned better and are more resistant to extinction when reinforced on a variable rather than on a fixed schedule. However, to be effective, the reinforcement (including punishment) must be consistent for the same type of behavior even though it does not have to follow every time. Most reinforcers in human relationships are on a variable schedule because of the complexity of behavior and because we cannot predict how people will interact.

Signals

In operant conditioning, stimuli that are associated with receiving rewards or punishment become **signals** for particular behaviors. For example, we learn to cross a street only when the traffic light is green and to answer the phone only when it rings. These signals simply indicate that if you cross the street or answer the phone, a reinforcer is likely to follow in the form of safe arrival on the other side of the street or of a voice on the phone.

Just as organisms generalize among and discriminate between conditioned stimuli in classical conditioning, they also generalize among and discriminate between stimuli that serve as signals in operant conditioning. For example, the child who has been rewarded for saying "doggie" every time he or she sees the family's basset hound may generalize and say "doggie" when he or she sees a sheep, a cow, or a horse. These animals are similar enough to the hound for them to become signals that "doggie" will produce a reward. Discrimination results when "doggie" fails to produce a reward in these other cases. The child learns to confine the use of the word to dogs and to respond differently when seeing sheep, cattle, or horses.

Because signals are guides to future rewards and punishments, they often become rewards or punishers in themselves. In such cases, the signal is called a **conditioned reinforcer** because without the conditioning process, it would be like a neutral stimulus having no positive or negative value to a person. With conditioning, almost any stimulus can acquire almost any value.

One experimenter (Wolfe, 1936) demonstrated this with chimpanzees. Poker chips have no value for chimps—they aren't edible and they aren't very much fun to play with. This experimenter, however, used operant conditioning to teach chimps to value poker chips as much as humans value money. He provided the animals with a "Chimp-O-Mat" that dispensed peanuts or bananas, which are **primary reinforcers,** or natural rewards. (Chimps like these foods.) To obtain food, the chimps had to pull down on a heavily weighted bar to obtain poker chips, then insert the chips in a slot in the machine (Figure 2.7). In time, the poker chips became conditioned reinforcers. Their value was evident from the fact that the

Figure 2.7
Using the Chimp-O-Mat to "buy" peanuts and bananas with poker chips obtained by pulling down on a heavily weighted bar. Through operant conditioning, this chimp had learned to value something that was neither edible nor fun to play with.

chimpanzees would work for them, save them, and sometimes try to steal them from one another.

There is no need to look only to animals for examples of this phenomenon. Smiles have little value for newborn babies, and words of approval have no meaning. In time, however, babies learn that these expressions and sounds mean that an adult is about to pick them up, cuddle them, perhaps feed them (primary reinforcers). The smiles and sounds of approval signal a reward. In time, children begin to value smiles, praise, and other forms of social approval in and of themselves.

Aversive Control

People often use the word "reinforcement" to refer only to the pleasant consequences of behavior. Psychologists, however, use it to refer to anything that increases the frequency of a behavior. Unpleasant or aversive consequences (as opposed to pleasant ones) influence much of our everyday behavior. **Aversive control** refers to this type of conditioning, or learning. There are two ways in which unpleasant events, or aversive stimuli, can affect our behavior: as negative reinforcers or as punishers.

Negative reinforcement.   In **negative reinforcement,** a painful or unpleasant stimulus is removed or is not applied at all if a certain kind of
behavior occurs. The removal of unpleasant consequences increases the
frequency of a behavior (Figure 2.8). There are two types of negative
reinforcement learning that psychologists have studied in detail: *escape
conditioning* and *avoidance conditioning*. In **escape conditioning,** the behavior a person engages in causes an unpleasant event to stop. Consider
the case of a child who hates liver and is served it for dinner—a thoroughly
repulsive experience. She whines about the food and gags while eating it.
At this point, her mother removes the liver. The gagging and whining
behavior has been thus negatively reinforced, and the child is likely to
gag and whine in the future when given an unpleasant meal. This kind
of learning is called escape conditioning because the behavior has enabled
the child to escape the liver meal.

In **avoidance conditioning,** the person's behavior has the effect of preventing an unpleasant situation from happening. In our example, if the
girl's past whining and gagging behavior had stopped the mother from
even serving the liver, we would identify the situation as avoidance conditioning; the child would have avoided the unpleasant consequences in
advance.

Punishment.   The most obvious form of aversion control is not negative
reinforcement, but punishment. If you want to stop a dog from pawing
at you when it wants attention, you should link your attention to it with
a punishment such as a smack on the rump with a newspaper. Such
actions are called **punishers.**

As with reinforcers, the events or actions that serve as punishers depend
on their effect on the learner. In the opening example on operant conditioning, the mother's reprimands that were meant to be punishers were
actually reinforcers because of the effect they had on the boy, who wanted

Figure 2.8
A rat makes the correct choice in a
trial on the Lashley jump stand.
Learning is rapid in this apparatus
because an incorrect choice
produces aversive consequences:
The rat bumps its nose on the
closed door (horizontally striped in
this case) and falls into the net
below.

Figure 2.9
An analysis of the relationship between the behavior of a child and the behavior of his parents. (from left to right and from top to bottom) The child is about to engage in a positively reinforcing activity (playing in the mud), but his parents are emitting a behavior (forbidding him to play in the mud). He punishes their forbidding behavior with an aversive stimulus (a violent tantrum). Their forbidding behavior decreases in strength and they give in. The parents' giving-in behavior is now negatively reinforced by the removal of the aversive tantrum. The child's tantrum is positively reinforced by playing in the mud. The results of this conditioning process are that tantrums are now more likely, forbidding is less likely, and giving in is more likely. The new behavior may generalize to a new yet similar situation.

attention. Perhaps sending him to his room every time he harassed his sister would have been an appropriate punisher; this unpleasant stimulus would have prevented him from repeating the behavior.

In punishment, an unpleasant consequence occurs and decreases the frequency of the behavior that produced it. Negative reinforcement and punishment operate in opposite ways: in negative reinforcement, escape or avoidance behavior is *repeated*, and in punishment, behavior that is punished is *not repeated*.

Psychologists have found several disadvantages in using aversive stimuli to change behavior. For one thing, aversive stimuli can produce unwanted side effects such as rage, aggression, and fear. Then, instead of having to change only one problem behavior, there may be two or more. For example, children whose parents rely on spanking to control disobedience may also have to deal with the problem of their children's increased aggressiveness toward other children.

A second problem with aversive stimuli is that people learn to avoid the person delivering the aversive consequences. In the cases of parents or teachers who punish often, children learn to stay away from them. One consequence of this is that parents and teachers have less opportunity to correct the children's inappropriate behavior. Also, punishment is likely to suppress rather than eliminate behaviors.

FACTORS THAT AFFECT LEARNING

Studies of more complex forms of learning have revealed that several factors can help or hinder the process. Among them are feedback, transfer, and practice.

Feedback

Finding out the results of an action or performance is called **feedback.** Without feedback, you might repeat the same mistakes so many times that you develop a skill incorrectly—you would never learn what you were doing wrong. Even if you were performing correctly, you would not be receiving reinforcement for continuing. If, for example, you always wore earplugs while you practiced the piano, you would never know just how bad your version of "Chopsticks" sounded.

Transfer

Often a skill that you have already learned can help you to learn a new skill. If you have learned to play the saxophone, it will be much easier for you to learn to play the clarinet. You can **transfer** skills you already have such as reading notes and converting them into responses of your lips, tongue, and fingers to the clarinet. When previously learned responses help you learn a new task, it is called *positive* transfer.

When a previously learned task hinders learning, *negative* transfer has occurred. An American may find driving in England to be more difficult than it is for an Englishman who is learning to drive. In England the steering wheel is on the opposite side of the car, and people drive on the opposite side of the road. The learned skill of driving American style makes it difficult to perform the necessary new mental and motor tasks. An American's responses are often the exact opposite of what is needed.

Practice

Practice, the repetition of a task, helps to bind responses together. It is the key element that makes for smooth and fluent movement from response to response.

Because practice takes time, psychologists have been interested in determining how to use that time most efficiently. They have found that whatever type of skill a person is learning, it is usually better to space out practice rather than do it all at once.

It is possible to practice by imagining oneself performing a skill. Athletes imagine themselves making golf swings over and over again or mentally shooting free throws in basketball to improve their performance. Psychologists call such effort *mental practice*. Although it is not as effective as the real thing, it is better than nothing at all.

LEARNING STRATEGIES

It would be difficult to solve problems if people had to relearn the solution process each time a problem occurred. Fortunately, when you learn to solve one problem, some of the problem-solving experiences may transfer to other, similar problems. Once you learn certain strategies for solving problems and learning tasks, you will usually have an easier time on your next attempts. (Such problem-solving strategies are also discussed in Chapter 3.) Strategies are affected by their consequences just as less complex reasons are. If a strategy works, the person or animal is likely to use it again. Many learned principles for dealing with life are valuable; others may actually be handicaps.

Learning to Learn

Harry Harlow (1949) has shown that animals can learn to learn—they can learn to use strategies for solving similar problems and tasks. He gave a monkey the problem of finding a raisin under one of two wooden lids, one red and one green (Figure 2.10). The raisin was always hidden under the green lid. Because the experimenter kept changing the position of the lids, the monkey took a while to realize that color was important, not location.

When the monkey had learned to always pick the green lid, the experimenter changed the problem. Now the monkey had to choose between triangular and circular lids. The raisin was always placed under the circular lid, and the experimenter again changed the location of the lids on each trial. As before, it took several tries for the monkey to learn that the shape of the lid, not its location, indicated where the raisin would be. After doing a number of problems like these, the monkey began to learn that the difference between the two lids always contained the key to the problem. Eventually the monkey could solve any similar two-choice problem with, at most, one error.

The learning of strategies and principles is extremely important in human behavior. In school you practice such skills as reading books, writing essays, and taking tests. In many cases the particular things you have learned will be less important in the long run than what you have learned about learning generally. Learning to extract information from a book, for example, will be helpful whether the book is about physics, grammar, or cooking. Just as Harlow's monkey acquired a general method for quickly solving particular problems, you are acquiring a general strategy for learning particular pieces of information.

Helplessness and Laziness

Psychologists have shown that general learning strategies can affect a person's relationship to the environment. For example, if a person has numerous experiences in which his actions have no effect on his world, he may learn a general strategy of helplessness or laziness.

Martin Seligman did a number of experiments to show how learned helplessness developed in animals. He strapped dogs into a harness from which they could not escape, and then gave them a series of shocks at irregular intervals. After days of shock treatment, the dogs were unharnessed. Now they could escape the shocks or avoid them entirely simply by jumping over a hurdle into a safe compartment. More than half the dogs failed to learn to jump. When several dogs that had not been shocked were also tested, almost all of them quickly learned to jump to safety. Apparently, many of the dogs in the first group had learned to stand and endure the shocks, resigned to the fact that any effort to escape would be useless.

Later experiments showed that people reacted in the same way. In the first stage of one study (Hiroto, 1974), some college students were able to turn off an unpleasant loud noise, while others had no control over it. Later, all were placed in a situation in which they merely had to move a lever to stop a similar noise. Only the ones who had control over the noise in the first place learned to turn it off. The others did not even try.

It is not hard to see how these results can apply to everyday situations. In order to be able to try hard and to be full of energy, people must learn that their actions *do* make a difference. If rewards come without effort, a person never learns to work (learned laziness). If pain comes no matter how hard one tries, a person gives up (learned helplessness).

Seligman believes that learned helplessness is one major cause of depression. He has revised his theory (Abramson, Seligman, and Teasdale, 1978; Miller and Seligman, 1982) so that it is now somewhat more detailed than his earlier theory, which was based primarily on animal studies. He reasons that, when people are unable to control events in their lives, they generally respond in one of the following ways. They may be less motivated to act and thus stop trying. They may have trouble learning to bring about new outcomes or may stop thinking. They may experience a lowered sense of self-esteem and think negatively about themselves. They may also feel depressed.

Seligman identified three important elements of helplessness: *stability*, *globality*, and *internality*. Stability refers to the person's belief that the state of helplessness results from a permanent characteristic. For example, a student who fails a math test can decide that the problem is either temporary ("I did poorly on this math test because I was sick") or *stable* ("I never have done well on math tests and never will"). Similarly, the person can decide that the problem is either specific ("I'm no good at

Figure 2.10
Harry Harlow presented monkeys with pairs of lids like those shown here and required them to learn strategies for determining which lid in each pair covered a morsel of food. After being presented with a few hundred such problems, the monkeys learned to use the same strategy for dealing with each new pair.

Shaping Complicated Behaviors in Animals. Psychologists have used shaping to condition very complicated behavior patterns in animals. Pigeons have been taught to play Ping-Pong and play songs on a small piano. During World War I, the British trained sea gulls to detect enemy submarines in the English Channel. To train them, the British sent their own submarines out in the Channel while dropping food on the surface. Soon the sea gulls would follow submarines from the air without the presence of food, and the sighting of sea gulls over the Channel became a signal of the possible presence of German subs.

During World War II, B. F. Skinner was involved in a project that trained pigeons to guide missiles to enemy targets. The pigeons were gradually reinforced for pecking at images of enemy targets projected on a screen. Although these "top gun" pigeons were quite accurate, they were never actually used in real combat.

More recently, the U.S. Navy has trained dolphins to detect enemy divers and locate undersea mines. Also, sea lions have been taught to recover antisubmarine rockets so that the Navy can evaluate the rockets' performance.

math tests") or *global* ("I'm just dumb"). Both stability and globality focus on the student—on *internal* reasons for failure. The student could have decided that the problem was external ("This was a bad math test") instead of internal. People who attributed an undesirable outcome to their own inadequacies will probably experience depression along with guilt and self-blame. Those who attribute their problems to their own inadequacies and see these personal shortcomings as enduring traits that apply to all situations are likely to suffer from severe depression.

The revision of Seligman's theory is important because it is a good example of several new trends in behaviorism. As learning theorists begin to study people rather than animals, they are finding that some of the old behavior models are too simple because they focus simply on what people *do*. What people *think* is also important.

LEARNING COMPLICATED SKILLS

When you acquire a skill such as knitting, photography, shooting a basketball, or talking persuasively, you learn more than just a single new stimulus-response relationship. You learn a large number of them, and you learn how to put them together into a large, smooth-flowing unit. Psychologists have devoted considerable attention to how new responses are acquired and to how they are put together in complex skills.

Shaping is a process in which reinforcement is used to sculpt new responses out of old (Figure 2.11). An experimenter can use this method to teach a rat to do something it has never done before and would never do if left to itself. He can shape it, for example, to raise a miniature flag. The rat is physically capable of standing on its hind legs and using its mouth to pull a miniature-flag–raising cord, but at present it does not do so. The rat probably will not perform this unusual action by accident, so the experimenter begins by rewarding the rat for any action similar to the wanted responses, using reinforcement to produce successive, or closer and closer, approximations of the desired behavior.

Imagine the rat roaming around on a table with the flag apparatus in the middle. The rat inspects everything and finally sniffs at the flagpole. The experimenter immediately reinforces this response by giving the rat a food pellet. Now the rat frequently sniffs the flagpole, hoping to get another pellet, but the experimenter waits until the rat lifts a paw before he gives it another reward. This process continues, with the experimenter reinforcing close responses and then waiting for even closer ones. Eventually, he has the rat on its hind legs nibbling at the cord. Suddenly the rat seizes the cord in its teeth and yanks it. Immediately the rat is rewarded, and it begins pulling rapidly on the cord. A new response has been shaped.

Shaping has been used to teach language skills to impaired children.

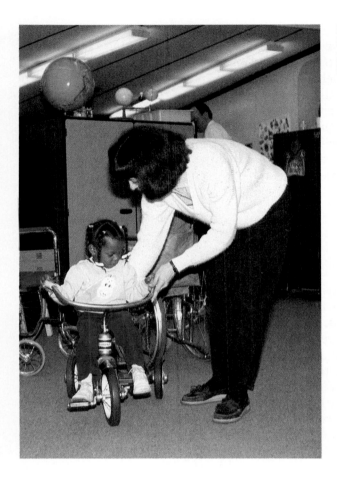

Figure 2.11
Psychologists shape behavior by using reinforcement to sculpture new responses out of old ones. This instructor is shaping behavior as she teaches this disabled preschooler to ride a tricycle.

Psychologists at first reward the children for simple sounds, such as "bah." Later the children are only rewarded for complete words, such as "beans," and later for complete sentences, such as "Beans, please." Many such children have successfully learned to use some language by this method (Lovaas *et al.*, 1967).

Combining Responses: Chaining

In order to learn a skill, a person must be able to put various new responses together. Responses that follow one another in a sequence are put together in **response chains.** Each response produces the signal for the next one. For example, to hammer a nail into a board, you would have to put together the following chain of responses: pick up the hammer, pick up the nail, position the nail, swing the hammer, hit the nail, swing the hammer, hit the nail, and so on until the nail is completely sunk in. Each hit of the nail is a signal that you are striking it correctly, and the nail's being flush with the board's surface is a signal that no further responses are required.

In learning, chains of responses are organized into larger *response patterns*. For example, the complex skill of swimming has three major chains that are combined to make up the whole swimming pattern: an arm-stroking chain, a breathing chain, and a leg-kicking chain (Figure 2.12). After much practice, you no longer have to think about the different steps involved. The behavior takes on a rhythm of its own: the chains of responses flow naturally as soon as you dive into the water.

It is often necessary to learn simple responses before mastering the complex pattern. If you cannot hit a nail with a hammer, you certainly cannot build a house. Therefore, before a person can learn to perform a particular skill, he or she must learn all the subordinate skills that make the larger skill possible.

MODELING

Up to this point it would seem that there are two types of learning: emotional responding, conditioned by the close association of neutral and unconditioned stimuli; and operant responses, learned either by reward or punishment. However, the informal observations you have been making all your life concerning learning probably suggest to you that there is more to learning than this—that, in fact, we most often learn by imitating others. This is especially true of social responses—when we learn how to behave in a new situation by watching how others behave. When you go to a concert for the first time, you may be very hesitant about where to go, when to enter (especially if you are late), when to clap, how to get a better seat after the first intermission, and so on. So you observe others, follow them, and soon you are an "old hand."

Figure 2.12
In learning a skill, responses that follow one another in sequence are put together in chains, and the chains are then organized into response patterns. The complex skill of swimming has three major parts: arm stroke, breathing, and leg kicking.

We would expect imitation to be responsible for more basic forms of behavior as well, when the proper response is essential to life. Trial-and-error learning is not useful if the punishment for failure to emit the response is to be eaten by a predator. Thus, correct avoidance behavior often must be learned by imitating.

The general term for this kind of learning is *modeling*. It includes three different types of effects. In the simplest case the behavior of others simply increases the chances that we will do the same thing. We clap when others do, look up at a building if everyone else is looking there, and copy the styles and verbal expressions of our peers. No learning occurs in this case, in the sense of acquiring new responses. We simply perform old responses that we otherwise might be using.

The second type of modeling is usually called *observational learning*, or simply, imitation. In this sort of learning an observer watches a model perform a behavior and is later able to reproduce it closely, though the observer was unable to do this before observing the model. An example is watching someone use an unfamiliar tool, either live or on film, and afterward being able to handle the tool yourself.

A third type of modeling involves disinhibition. When an observer watches someone else engage in a threatening activity without being punished, the observer may find it easier to engage in that behavior later. For example, someone with a snake phobia may watch another person handling snakes. Such observation may help to alleviate the phobia. This procedure is used in clinical work, as we will see in the chapter on therapies.

What happens when an observer learns by watching? Early theorists believed that we have some sort of "instinct" for imitation, and, indeed, it is probable that some animals do imitate automatically, especially when they are very young and have good models constantly around them: their parents. Operant-conditioning theorists such as Skinner have suggested that imitation itself is a kind of response, one that is often reinforced because it works so well. That is, the behavior of others come to function as a discriminative stimulus for a sort of matching behavior, which is then reinforced because it works on the environment or because other persons tend to reinforce such matching (as when a mother praises her child for correctly imitating her words).

USING PSYCHOLOGY

Behavior Modification

The term "behavior modification" often appears in magazine articles describing research on changing people's behavior through drugs, "mind control," or even brain surgery. In fact, it is none of these things. **Behavior modification** refers to the systematic application of learning principles to change people's actions and feelings.

MORE about...

Spatial Learning. Both classical and operant conditioning revolve around time. In Pavlov's demonstration of classical conditioning, the sound of a tuning fork came before food. In operant conditioning, a dog given a biscuit after lifting its paw learns to "shake hands."

In addition to these two types of conditioning, psychologists have studied a third form, spatial learning, which involves learning the location of things in the environment. Psychologists who study spatial learning claim that humans explore their environment and form internal cognitive maps. These maps help us to master new environments. Do you remember how confusing school was on your first day? You quickly formed a cognitive map, and this spatial learning explains why by now you could probably find your way around blindfolded.

Psychologists have found that spatial learning occurs not only in humans, but also in animals. They believe that cognitive maps account for the facts that chimps quickly learn to detect food hidden in an area, rats learn their way around a maze, and honeybees find their way back to the hive.

? FACT OR FICTION

Most psychologists believe that alcoholics can "learn" to be social drinkers.

Fiction. Although attempts have been made to use behavior modification on alcoholics to teach them to be social drinkers, these attempts have generally been unsuccessful. Most psychologists believe that alcoholics simply cannot learn to drink in moderation. Thus, attempts at behavior modification usually involve abstaining completely from alcohol as a first and necessary step on the road to recovery.

When you give your little brother a quarter to leave you alone, that is very much like behavior modification. What distinguishes behavior modification from common-sense approaches is the fact that it involves a careful series of well-defined steps to change behavior. The success of each step is carefully evaluated to find the best solution for a given situation.

The behavior modifier usually begins by defining a problem very carefully in concrete terms. For example, a mother might complain that her son is messy. If she used behavior modification to reform the child, she would first have to define "messy" in objective terms: he does not make his bed in the morning, he drops his coat on the couch when he comes inside, and so on. She would not worry about where his bad habits come from. Rather she would work out a system of rewards and punishments aimed at getting Johnnie to make his bed, hang up his coat, and so on.

Both operant- and classical-conditioning principles have been used in behavior modification. Classical-conditioning principles are particularly useful in helping people to overcome fears, and we shall discuss them when we consider the problem of treating abnormal behavior (Chapter 16). In addition, as you will see in the following examples, operant-conditioning principles have also been applied to everyday problems.

Computer-Assisted Instruction

The famous Greek teacher Socrates taught his students by a conversational method very similar to what *computer-assisted instruction (CAI)* is using today. CAI is a refinement of the concept of programmed instruction which was introduced by S. L. Pressey (1926) and refined by B. F. Skinner in the 1950s.

The essential concept of programmed instruction is based on operant conditioning. The material to be learned is broken down into simpler units called "frames"; each time the student demonstrates that she or he has learned the information in a frame, the student is given positive reinforcement in the form of new information, choices, or point rewards similar to those used in video games. Each question, or "prompt," builds on information already mastered. The computer knows (as does the student) exactly what the learner understands on the basis of the student's answers to questions. These questions can be multiple choice, true or false, fill-in-the-blanks, or conversational in format.

Figure 2.13
A modern technique in teaching is computer-
assisted instruction (CAI). Computers ask the
student a question, get a response, and tell the
student if the answer is right or wrong.

There are several advantages to this system of instruction over conventional classroom methods. The learner has
immediate feedback about whether he or she understands
the material. The learner reviews only material he or she
does not understand. There is constant incentive to learn
because of many positive reinforcements. This method also
avoids aversive aspects of classroom learning, including a
sense of failure for wrong answers in class or on tests. The
student can progress at an individual rate, depending on
how well rather than how fast he or she learns.

In most variations of CAI, the student can "talk" with
the computer by typing in various comments or writing
on the screen with a special pen. In the *branching* system
of information delivery, the student can choose between
paths of instruction after she or he makes a response. The
paths can be remedial or supplementary. If the student
responds incorrectly, she or he is taken back to the original
question that led to the path she or he was on. There is
also a simpler, *linear*, system in which such choices are not
included.

After completing a course taught by CAI, the student is either given a letter grade automatically (according to how much of the course was completed) or takes a test to see how much information was retained.

Almost every study comparing this method of instruction with conventional classroom methods has shown it to be superior in student retention of the material. The only problem sometimes experienced with CAI is that students may not finish the courses when there is no set timetable of instruction. Other disadvantages are expense and lack of human interaction.

Several principles of learning psychology are at work in CAI. The student is learning complex material through a response chain. She or he is reinforced constantly on a fixed schedule. Knowledge is being shaped in a systematic and predictable way. The student is able to have a dialogue with the instructor on every point, which is impossible for a class of students in a conventional setting.

Token Economies

Psychologists tried an experiment with a group of extremely disenchanted boys in Washington, D.C. In fact, the boys had been labeled "uneducable" and placed in the National Training School. The experimenters used what is known as a **token economy** to motivate the boys. The youngsters received points for good grades on tests. They could "cash" these points in for such rewards as snacks, lounge privileges, or items in a mail-order catalog. In other words, they created a system that worked like the Chimp-O-Mat, discussed earlier. Within a few months, a majority of the students showed a significant increase in IQ scores (an average gain of twelve and a half points). The boys continued to improve in the months that followed, showing that they were, indeed, educable (Cohen and Filipczak, 1971).

In another experiment teachers used a token economy to teach preschoolers in a Head Start program to write, and compared their scores on writing tests with those achieved by children who did not participate in a token economy. The youngsters who received tokens, which they could exchange for food, movies, and other rewards, improved dramatically. Equally important, they seemed to be developing a very positive attitude toward school. The youngsters who did not receive tokens made very little progress (Miller and Schneider, 1970).

Thus, in token economies, people are systematically paid

to act appropriately. In the real world, behaviorists argue, the rewards are just as real; they are simply less systematic. In overcrowded mental hospitals, for example, the only way some patients can get attention is by "acting crazy." Most staff members simply don't have time to bother with people who are not causing trouble. Since attention from the staff is reinforcing for these patients, in effect people are rewarded for undesirable behavior. By systematically rewarding only desirable behavior, token economies have been set up in prisons, mental hospitals, halfway houses, and classrooms. (See also Chapter 16.)

Self-Control

In token economies, a researcher sets up an elaborate system of reinforcers to get people to act the way he or she wants. One of the most important new trends in behavior modification is a growing emphasis on asking people to set up personal systems of rewards and punishments to shape their own thoughts and actions.

In the past, behaviorists limited their studies to observable behavior (Chapter 1), and made little attempt to observe or change the way people thought. Then, as more learning researchers began to study humans (instead of focusing exclusively on animals), it became obvious that what people *do* is only part of the story. As we described above, for example, Martin Seligman recently expanded his theory of learned helplessness to try to explain why some people develop long-lasting depressions while others seem to get over them. Part of the difference, Seligman argues, is based on what people *think*—that is, how they interpret their failures.

As in any application of behavior modification, the first step in self-control is to define the problem. A person who smokes too much would be encouraged to actually count how many cigarettes he smoked every hour of the day and note what kinds of situations led him to smoke. (After a meal? When talking to friends? Driving to work?) Similarly, a person who had a very poor opinion of herself would have to define the problem more concretely. She might begin by counting the number of self-deprecating remarks she made and thoughts she had. Researchers have found that just keeping track of behavior in this way often leads a person to start changing it.

The next step may be to set up a single behavioral contract. One soda lover who had trouble studying decided that she would only allow herself a Pepsi after she studied for half an hour. Her cola addiction remained strong, but her study time increased dramatically under this system. A behavioral contract simply involves choosing a reinforcer (buying a new shirt, watching a favorite TV program) and making it contingent on some unpleasant but necessary act (getting to work on time, washing the kitchen floor). These contracts are most likely to succeed if you also use successive approximations—starting with an easy task and gradually making it more difficult. For example, you might begin by studying ten minutes before rewarding yourself, and gradually increase it to an hour.

Behavior modifiers are now developing and testing many other techniques to help people learn to control themselves.

Improving Your Study Habits

One psychologist designed a program to help students improve their study habits and tried it on a group of volunteers. The students were told to set a time when they would go to a small room in the library they had not used before, taking only the materials they wanted to study. They were then to work for as long as they remained interested—and *only* for as long as they were interested. As soon as they found themselves fidgeting, daydreaming, becoming drowsy or bored, they were to make the decision to stop studying. There was only one condition. They had to read one more page, or solve one more simple problem, before they left. Even if this made them want to study longer, they were instructed to hold to their decision to leave the library, go for a cup of coffee, call a friend, or do whatever they wanted to do.

The next day they were asked to repeat the same procedure, adding a second page to the amount they read between the time they decided to leave and the time they actually left the library. The third day they added a third page, and so on. Students who followed this procedure found that in time they were able to study for longer periods than before, that they were studying more effectively, and that they didn't mind studying so much.

Why did this procedure work? Many students force themselves to study. One common technique is to go to the library to avoid distractions. The result may be hours spent staring at a book without really learning anything. Repeated failures to get anything accomplished and sheer

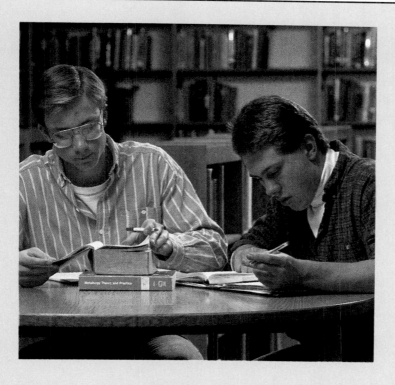

Figure 2.14
The library need not become a conditioned aversive stimulus if you learn how to build positive reinforcement into your studying routine.

discomfort turn studying into a dreaded chore. The library becomes a conditioned aversive stimulus—you hate it because you've spent so many uncomfortable hours there. The procedure was designed to change these feelings.

Requiring students to leave as soon as they felt distracted helped to reduce the negative, punishing emotions associated with studying. The students stopped when these feelings began. Studying in a new place removed the conditioned aversive stimulus. Thus, aversive responses were not conditioned to the subject matter or the room, as they are when students force themselves to work.

Second, the procedure made use of successive approximations. The students began by reading just one page after they became bored, and only gradually increased the assignment. This also reduced the aversive response to studying. The task no longer seemed so difficult.

Finally, when they left their work, the students received two kinds of positive reinforcement. They had the satisfaction of knowing they had followed the procedure and had completed an assignment (namely, one more page), and they were free to do something they enjoyed. Thus they rewarded or reinforced themselves for however much studying they did (Fox, 1966). You might try this procedure.

Use the following outline as a tool for reviewing this chapter. Copy the outline onto your own paper, leaving spaces between headings to make notes about key concepts.

    I. Classical Conditioning

        A. Pavlov's Experiment

        B. General Principles of Classical Conditioning

        C. Classical Conditioning and Human Behavior

   II. Operant Conditioning

        A. Reinforcement

        B. Schedules of Reinforcement

        C. Signals

        D. Aversive Control

  III. Factors that Affect Learning

        A. Feedback

        B. Transfer

        C. Practice

  IV. Learning Strategies

        A. Learning to Learn

        B. Helplessness and Laziness

   V. Learning Complicated Skills

        A. Combining Responses: Chaining

  VI. Modeling

1. What type of learning is involved when an old response becomes attached to a new stimulus? What terms did Pavlov use for each of the following elements in his experiments with dogs: food, the dog's salivation response at the sight of food, the sound of the tuning fork, the animal's salivation response to the sound of the tuning fork? What term did he use to explain the effect of repeatedly striking the tuning forks without providing food?

2. Who is the psychologist closely associated with operant conditioning? Which type of learning—operant conditioning or classical conditioning—emphasizes that the stimulus elicits the response?

3. What are positive consequences called? Negative consequences? Can you name two ways to have a behavior repeated and two ways to prevent a behavior from being repeated?

4. What are the four types of intermittent schedules of reinforcement?

5. What are some examples of primary reinforcers? What type of reinforcer is money?

6. Aversive stimuli can be used in two ways. What are they? How are they different? People can avoid unpleasant events or escape from them. Can you explain the difference?

7. How did Martin Seligman develop learned helplessness in animals? A person who has learned helplessness is more likely to be depressed. If a person feels helpless and depressed after taking an exam, what two things is this person likely to be thinking about?

8. What is the process in which a person is reinforced for closer and closer approximations of the desired behavior? What is the name of the sequence in which one response produces the signal for the next response?

9. What are the three types of modeling?

1. **Analyze.** Which of the schedules of reinforcement do your instructors generally use in conducting their classes? How would your classes be different if they used the other schedules? Give examples for your answers and justify your reasoning.

2. **Apply.** Businesses often make use of conditioning techniques in their commercials. They associate the name of their product with pleasant tunes or exciting scenes, so that the name alone will elicit conditioned relaxation or excitement. Think of specific ads that use these techniques. Describe several selling methods that use operant conditioning.

3. **Analyze.** In the experiment on learned helplessness, the animals that were unable to change their situation for long periods of time seemed unable or unwilling to change when the possibility was opened to them. What implications do such experiments have for humans? Can you think of situations in your life that have had the effect of learned helplessness?

APPLYING KNOWLEDGE

1. Select some particular area of study that you find difficult or unpleasant. Whenever you sit down to study this subject, play one of your favorite tapes or CDs as you study. Do this for two weeks and then analyze your reactions. Have your feelings toward the music become associated with the subject of study? Do you find it easier to learn and remember? Explain your findings in light of what you know about conditioning techniques.

2. Conduct an operant-conditioning experiment of your own to modify the behavior of a member of your family or a friend. Tell him or her as much or as little as you choose, but carefully record everything that you do tell this person. Use positive reinforcement only, and record all

results. Using the procedures given in the chapter, write a paper describing your experiment in behavior modification.

ANALYZING VIEWPOINTS

1. Much has been written about the deficiencies in American education today. Some commentators cite the decline in test scores as evidence that the students of today do not measure up to their peers of a generation ago. Many reasons are given, including the amount of time spent watching television rather than reading or studying. Others argue that television has had little or no impact on the quality of education in America. Write an essay supporting both viewpoints. Be sure to include what you have learned from the chapter about how people learn. Read recent magazine and newspaper articles for more information on the causes of the decline in the American educational system.

BEYOND THE CLASSROOM

1. Go to a public place where you can watch parents and children interacting with each other. Shopping malls, fast food restaurants, and supermarkets are ideal settings to observe parents attempting to control children *and* children attempting to control parents. Watch a parent-child interaction long enough to identify an aversive stimulus the parent or child may be using to control behavior. What particular behavior of the child is the parent attempting to change? What particular behavior of the parent is the child attempting to change? Are they successful? Can you identify the disadvantages to both parent and child of using aversive stimuli in the situation you have observed? What changes would you recommend?

CHAPTER 3

Memory and Thought

Key Terms:

central processing
chunking
concept
confabulation
creativity
directed thinking
eidetic memory
feature extraction
image
input
insight
long-term memory
memory
mnemonic devices
nondirected thinking
output
proactive interference
recall
recognition
recombination
repression
retrieval
retroactive interference
rule
selective attention
sensory storage
set
short-term memory
symbol

Is anything more complex than the human mind?

Consider all the material stored in your memory: your social security number, the capital of South Dakota, "The Star Spangled Banner," your first love's phone number, the major generals of the Civil War, the starting lineup for the Boston Red Sox, your best friend in first grade, and so on. What kind of incredible filing system allows you to instantly recover a Beatles song or your favorite recipe? How does all that information fit in your head?

Going beyond memory, how do we think? How do we solve problems? How do we create ideas? No mysteries are more fundamental, and researchers are just beginning to investigate human thought. Psychologists refer to all cognitive and mental activities—from memorizing lists of numbers to writing poems and inventing new technologies—as *information processing*. This involves three steps: input, central processing, and output. **Input** is the information people receive from their senses. **Central processing** is the storing (in memory) and sorting (by thought) of this information in the brain. **Output** refers to the ideas and actions that result from processing.

TAKING INFORMATION IN

Information is any event that reduces uncertainty. For example, when a traffic light changes from red to green, it provides you with information—it reduces your uncertainty about whether you should step on the gas. Information is transmitted through the senses in many forms—voices, musical sounds, sweet tastes, pungent odors, colorful images, rough textures, pain-

Objectives:

After studying this chapter, you should be able to

- describe the concept of information processing.
- identify the different types of memory systems.
- explain the different theories that account for memory.
- describe the psychological perspective on thought, the units of thought, and the basic types of thought.
- define problem solving and outline the development of problem-solving strategies.

Figure 3.1 No mysteries are more fundamental than how we think, remember, solve problems, and create ideas.

ful stings. At any given moment a confusing array of sights, sounds, smells, and other sensations compete for your attention. If you accepted all these inputs, you would be completely overwhelmed. Two processes help people to narrow sensory inputs to a manageable number: selective attention and feature extraction.

Selective Attention

The ability to pick and choose among the various available inputs is called **selective attention.** For example, if you are at a large party where the music is turned up and everyone is talking, you can focus on a friend's voice and ignore all other sounds. In a way, selective attention is like tuning in a specific television channel.

Unlike a television dial, however, selective attention does not completely block out the other programs or stimuli. You may be listening attentively to what a friend is saying, but at the same time you are unconsciously monitoring information that is coming in over other channels. If your name is mentioned in a conversation going on three feet away, you will notice it and tune into that input. If someone strolls by dressed in a

Figure 3.2
The "filter model" of how we listen to the input to only one ear at a time during shadowing. (After Broadbent, 1958.)

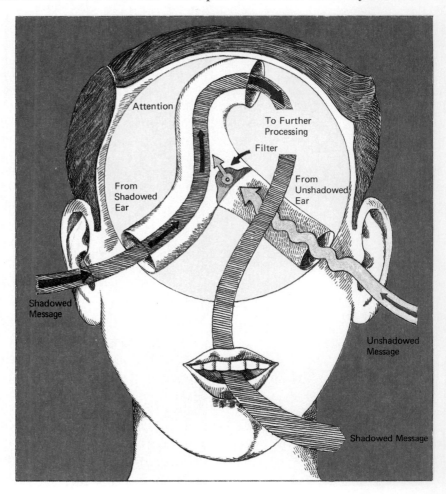

bathing suit, snorkel, and fins, you will notice him. The "cocktail-party phenomenon," as selective attention is sometimes called, allows you to concentrate on one thing without tuning out everything else that is happening.

In laboratory experiments, researchers have shown how selective attention affects the brain (Hernández-Peón, 1961). For example, if people are asked to pay attention to an auditory stimulus, the brain waves that record their response to sound will get larger. While this is happening, the brain waves that record their response to what they see will get smaller because they are not paying close attention to visual stimuli. If the same people are asked to pay attention to visual stimuli, the reverse occurs: visual brain waves increase while auditory brain waves decrease. A similar experiment has shown that a certain kind of brain wave diminishes but does not disappear when people are given a problem to solve or are drawn into conversation. Such experiments seem to indicate that the brain somehow evaluates the importance of the information that comes in over different channels. Top-priority information is allowed to reach the highest brain centers, whereas unimportant information is suppressed (Figure 3.2).

What makes one input more important than another? Information leading to the satisfaction of such needs as hunger and thirst has top priority. (A person who is very hungry, for example, will pay more attention to his dinner than to the dinner-table chitchat.) We also give priority to inputs that are strange and novel, such as an individual who comes to a party dressed for snorkeling. A third director of attention is interest: the more interested you are in something, the more likely you are to notice it. For example, most people "tune in" when they hear their name mentioned; we're all interested in what other people have to say about us. Likewise, if you become interested in chess, you will suddenly begin to notice newspaper articles about chess, chess sets in store windows, and references to chess moves in everyday speech (for example, "stalemate"). These inputs are not new. They were there last year and the year before, but you simply weren't interested enough to notice them.

Feature Extraction

Selective attention is only the first step in narrowing down input. The second step is to decide which aspects of the selected channel you will focus on. This process, called **feature extraction,** involves locating the outstanding characteristics of incoming information (Figure 3.3). If you want to identify the make of a car, you look for certain features—the shape of the fenders, the proportion of height to length, and so on. For the most part, you ignore such features as color, upholstery, and tires, which tell you little about the make of the car. Similarly, when you read, you focus on the important words, skimming over such words as "the," "and," or "for example."

Being able to extract the significant features of an input helps a person to identify it and compare it to other inputs. For example, you are able to distinguish faces from one another and, at the same time, see resemblances. You may notice that all the members of a family have similar

Figure 3.3
Can you spot the hidden faces in this picture? To find them, it is necessary for you to extract those features that define a human face from a large amount of irrelevant and misleading information.

noses, yet you are able to recognize each person on the basis of other features.

Obviously, feature extraction depends to some extent on experience—on knowing what to look for. This is especially true where fine distinctions must be made. It takes considerable expertise to distinguish an original Rembrandt from a skillful forgery. Most of us cannot distinguish between two accomplished pianists playing the same concerto, but an expert who knows what to listen for can.

Like selective attention, feature extraction is an evaluative process. If you are reading a novel for pleasure, you may look for the "juicy" parts. If you're reading a historical biography to prepare for an exam, you'll probably still look for the juicy parts. When you don't find any, you go ahead and concentrate on the other facts.

STORING INFORMATION

In order to be used, the inputs that reach the brain must be registered, held onto, perhaps "filed" for future reference. We call the storage of inputs **memory.** Psychologists distinguish among three kinds of memory, each of which has a different purpose and time span. **Sensory storage** holds information for only an instant; **short-term memory** keeps it in mind for about twenty seconds; **long-term memory** stores it indefinitely.

Sensory Storage

The senses—sight, hearing, and so on—seem to be able to hold an input for a fraction of a second before it disappears. For example, when you watch a movie, you do not notice the gaps between frames. The actions seem smooth because each frame is held in sensory storage until the next frame arrives.

Sperling (1960) demonstrated this phenomenon in an ingenious experiment. He used a tachistoscope (a device that presents a picture for a very brief time) to present a group of letters to people for a twentieth of a second. Previous studies had shown that if you present a stimulus like this

$$
\begin{array}{ccc}
T & D & R \\
S & R & N \\
F & Z & K \\
\end{array}
$$

people will usually be able to tell you four or five of the letters. Sperling believed that people took a mental photograph of the letters, and were able to read back only a few before the picture faded. He told the people in his experiment that after he flashed the letters on the tachistoscope screen, he would present a tone. Upon hearing a high tone, the subjects were to tell him the top row, a medium tone the middle row, and a low tone the bottom row. Once people learned this system, they were indeed able to remember any row of letters. Thus, he proved that the subject retains a brief image of the whole picture so that he or she can still read off the items in the correct row *after* the picture has left the screen.

The information held momentarily by the senses has not yet been narrowed down or analyzed. It is like a short-lived but highly detailed photograph or tape recording. However, by the time information gets to the next stage—short-term memory—it has been analyzed, identified, and simplified so that it can be conveniently stored and handled for a longer time.

Short-Term Memory

The things you have in your conscious mind at any one moment are being held in short-term memory. Short-term memory does not necessarily involve paying close attention. You have probably had the experience of listening to someone only partially and then having that person accuse you of not paying attention. You deny it, and, in order to prove your innocence, you repeat to him, word for word, the last words he said. You can do this because you are holding the words in short-term memory. Usually, however, the sense of what he was saying does not register on you until you repeat the words out loud. Repeating the words makes you pay attention to them. This is what psychologists mean by rehearsal.

Rehearsal. To keep information in short-term memory for more than a few seconds, you have to repeat it to yourself, in your mind or out loud. When you look up a telephone number, for example, you can remember the seven digits long enough to dial them *if* you repeat them several times. If you are distracted or make a mistake in dialing, the chances are you will have to look the number up again. It has been lost from short-term memory.

Psychologists have measured short-term memory by seeing how long a subject can retain a piece of information without rehearsal. The experimenter shows the subject a card with three letters on it, such as CPQ. However, at the same time the experimenter makes the subject think about something else in order to prevent her from rehearsing the letters. For example, she might ask the subject to start counting backward by threes from 798 as soon as she flashes the card. If the subject performs this task for only a short time, she will usually remember the letters. But if she is kept from rehearsing for more than eighteen seconds, the information is forgotten. Thus, short-term memory seems to last for less than twenty seconds without rehearsal.

Short-term memory can hold only about seven unrelated items.

Chunking. Short-term memory is limited not only in its duration, but in its capacity as well. It can hold only about seven unrelated items, If, for example, someone quickly reels off a series of digits to you, you will be able to keep only about seven or eight of them in your immediate memory. Beyond that number, confusion among them will set in. The same would be true if the unrelated items were a random set of words. We may not notice this limit to our capacity because we usually do not have to store so many unrelated items in our immediate memory. Either the items are

Figure 3.4
Glance quickly at the left figure in this pair, then look away. How many dots did you see? Now do the same with the right figure. You were probably more sure and more accurate in your answer for the right figure because the organization of the dots into a small number of chunks makes it easier to process the information.

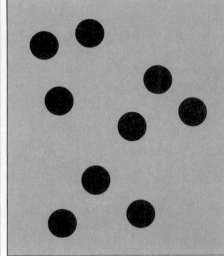

related (as when we listen to someone speak) or they are rehearsed and placed in long-term memory.

The most interesting aspect of this limit, discovered by George Miller (1956), is that it involves about seven items of any kind. Each item may consist of a collection of many other items, but if they are all packaged into one "chunk" then there is still only one item. Thus we can remember about seven unrelated sets of initials, such as COMSAT, DDT, SST, or the initials of our favorite radio stations, even though we could not remember all the letters separately. This occurs because we have connected, or "chunked," them together previously, so that DDT is one item, not three.

One of the tricks of memorizing a lot of information quickly is to chunk together the items as fast as they come in. If we connect items in groups, we have fewer to remember. For example, we remember new phone numbers in two or three chunks (555–6794 or 555–67–94) rather than as a string of seven digits (5–5–5–6–7–9–4). As Figure 3.4 illustrates, we use chunking to remember visual as well as verbal inputs.

Even with chunking, short-term memory is only a temporary device. It contains information labeled "of possible interest." If the information is worth holding onto, it must be transferred to long-term memory.

Long-Term Memory

Long-term memory is where we store information for future use. It can be thought of as a kind of filing cabinet or storage bin for names, dates, words, and faces. When we say someone has a good memory, we usually mean he or she can recall a great deal of this type of information. But long-term memory also contains representations of countless experiences and sensations. You may not have thought about your childhood home for years, but you can probably still visualize it.

Long-term memory involves all the processes we have been describing. Suppose a person goes to see a play. As the actors say their lines, the sounds flow through sensory storage. Selective attention screens out other sounds, and feature extraction turns sounds into words. These words accumulate in short-term memory and form meaningful phrases and sentences.

The viewer attends to the action and changing scenery in much the same way. Together, they form chunks in her memory. An hour or two later, she will have forgotten all but the most striking lines, but she has stored the *meaning* of the lines and actions in long-term memory. The next day, she may be able to give a scene-by-scene description of the play. Throughout this process, the least important information is dropped and only the essentials are retained (Figure 3.5). A month or two later, the woman may remember only a brief outline of the plot and perhaps a few particularly impressive moments. In time she may not remember anything about the play. Other, more recently stored items block access to earlier memories or may even replace them. But if she sees the play again, she will probably recognize the lines of the play and anticipate the actions. Although it has become less accessible, it is still stored in long-term memory.

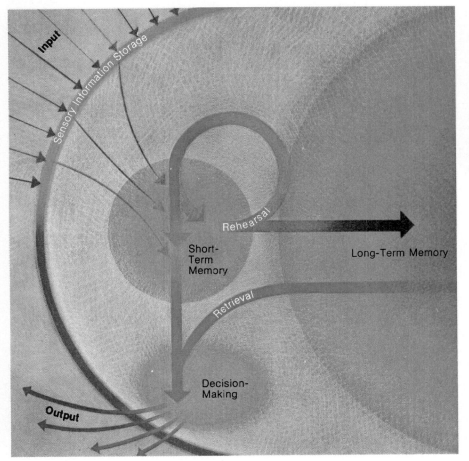

Figure 3.5
The flow of information processing. Input to the senses is stored temporarily, and some of it is passed on into short-term memory. Information may be kept in short-term memory by rehearsal or it may be passed on to long-term memory. Material stored in both short- and long-term memory is used in making decisions. The decision process results in outputs such as talking, writing, or moving.

Memory and the Brain

What happens in the brain when something is stored in long-term memory? This question is highly controversial. Although psychologists agree that some physiological changes must occur in the brain, they do not know what these changes are.

Some researchers believe that memory is due to changes in the form of protein molecules in the brain. In one experiment, a number of mice were trained to run through a maze, avoiding alleys where they would receive an electric shock. Then the mice were injected with a chemical known to disrupt protein production in the brain. Afterward, the mice could no longer remember the safe way out of the maze (Flexner, 1967). Recently, researchers (Flood, Bennett, and Orme, 1975) have been able to control the amount of "amnesia" in mice by injecting varying amounts of the chemical for certain time periods after the training task. The more of the protein-blocking chemical the mice receive, the more forgetful they become. One theory is that senility in the aged may be related to the end of protein production in the brain.

Another theory focuses on chemical-electrical changes in the brain. It may be that memory develops when the characteristics of the synapses change chemically. (As explained in Chapter 5, synapses are the gaps between nerve cells.) When something is learned, some pathways in the brain are facilitated and others inhibited. To date, it is impossible to say which of these theories is closer to the truth.

To complicate matters further, there is some controversy about just where memories are located in the brain. Karl Lashley (1929) argued that no one cell, or group of cells, can be removed to destroy a memory. Indeed, he found that he had to destroy most of the upper part of a rat's brain to erase the memory of a problem it had learned to solve. As a result, many psychologists believe that the same memories may be stored in several parts of the brain, so that destroying one area simply removes one copy. More recently, Richard Thompson (1976) and others have questioned Lashley's view. They believe that more sophisticated physiological techniques may be able to identify specific learning pathways.

All these ideas remain highly speculative. Many psychologists believe, however, that a better understanding of the processes underlying memory will be reached in the near future.

RETRIEVING INFORMATION

Stored information is useless unless it can be retrieved from memory. Once you've forgotten to send a card for your mother's birthday, it's not very consoling to prove that you have the date filed away in your brain. We've all experienced the acute embarrassment of being unable to remember a close friend's name. There are few things in life more frustrating than having a word "on the tip of your tongue," but just not being able to remember it.

The problem of memory is to store many thousands of items in such a way that you can find the one you need when you need it. The solution to **retrieval** is organization. Since human memory is extraordinarily efficient, it must be extremely well organized. Psychologists do not yet know how it is organized, but they are studying the processes involved in retrieval for clues.

Recognition

Human memory is organized in such a way as to make recognition quite easy—people can say with great accuracy whether or not something is familiar to them. If someone asked you the name of your first-grade teacher, for example, you might not remember it. But chances are that you would recognize the name if you heard it. Similarly, a multiple-choice test may bring out knowledge that a student might not be able to show on an essay test. The ability to recognize suggests that much more information is stored in memory than one might think.

The process of **recognition** provides insight into how information is stored in memory. We can recognize the sound of a particular musical instrument (say, the piano) no matter what tune is being played on it. We can also recognize a tune no matter what instrument is playing it. This pattern of recognition indicates that a single item of information may be "indexed" under the several "headings" so that it can be reached in a number of ways. Thus, "the attractive teller at the Five Cents Savings Bank" might be indexed under "Five Cents Savings Bank," "service people," "potential friends," "blondes," and possibly under several other headings as well. The more categories an item is filed in, the more easily it can be retrieved.

USING PSYCHOLOGY

Eyewitness Testimony

One situation in which recognition is extremely important (sometimes a matter of life or death) is in the courtroom. It is very convincing to a judge or jury when an eyewitness points to someone in the room and says, "That's the one who did it."

A psychologist who is deeply involved in the issue of eyewitness testimony is Elizabeth Loftus. She has shown (1974) that even after it had been proved that the eyesight of a witness was too poor for her to have seen a robber's face from where she stood at the scene of a robbery, the jury was still swayed by her testimony.

Lawyers can cite many cases of people falsely accused by eyewitnesses whose testimonies later proved to be inaccurate. In one such case, fourteen eyewitnesses agreed that the defendant had robbed a California supermarket

PSYCHOLOGY UPDATE

Selective Memory Problems. Memory problems can sometimes take a surprising twist. One example is the peculiar condition known as *prospagnosia*, in which the patient is unable to recognize familiar faces—even his or her own mirror image. People who have this condition can still perceive other aspects of faces, however, such as whether a person's expression is happy or sad.

Prospagnosia usually results from a stroke or head injury, and it illustrates how remarkably narrow or selective memory problems can sometimes be.

As another example of a selective problem, consider the case of a 34-year-old man who suffered a stroke. Afterwards, he regained his previous abilities—except that he found it nearly impossible to name common fruits and vegetables. He could, however, pick out the objects if the names were read to him. Selective problems such as these suggest that memories are organized into categories. Somehow, an individual category may become disconnected from the memory system as a whole.

and shot a policeman. However, later evidence proved that he was nowhere near the scene of the crime.

Elizabeth Loftus (1974) has done a fascinating series of experiments showing that when people are asked to recall the details of auto accidents, they, too, are likely to distort the facts. After groups of college students saw a filmed accident, she asked some of them, "About how fast were the cars going when they hit each other?" The average estimate was 34 miles per hour. When she substituted the word "smashed" for "hit" in the above question, another group of students remembered the cars as going significantly faster—41 miles per hour.

Figure 3.6
Three sketches of the "Son of Sam" killer show that eyewitnesses have different memories of his appearance.

Sam: the latest sketches
Cops' update alters description

The first drawing of Son of Sam made on July 29, 1976 after the Bronx killing of Donna Lauria, 18.

On Nov. 27 the .44-caliber killer struck for the third time. Victim Donna DeMasi, 17, saw him like this.

In the same Nov. 27 shooting, Joanne Lomino, 19—paralyzed for life—supplied the details for this sketch.

Loftus (1979, 1980) has also found that a person's memory of an event can be distorted in the process of remembering it. Shocking events, such as those involving violence, can disrupt our ability to form a strong memory. Without a strong, clear memory of the event, the eyewitness is more likely to incorporate misinformation into the recall. For example, if a police officer asks a witness to describe the gun used in a robbery, the witness may recall a gun even though the robber never revealed a weapon.

Defense attorneys are well aware of the effects that leading questions can have on people's memories. Expert testimony by psychologists on the nature of human memory and on the factors that influence the accuracy of an identification may be needed to convince jurors to be more critical in their appraisal of eyewitness testimony. Even after being cautioned by experts on human memory, however, jurors still tend to believe that the eye is a camera and that recall is like a videotape.

Recall

More remarkable than the ability to recognize information is the ability to recall it. **Recall** is the active reconstruction of information. Just think about the amount of recall involved in a simple conversation. Each person uses hundreds of words involving all kinds of information, even though each word and bit of information must be retrieved separately from the storehouse of memory.

Recall involves more than searching for and finding pieces of information, however. It involves a person's knowledge, attitudes, and expectations. This was demonstrated in the following experiment. The researcher showed a group of young children a bottle of colored water, tilted as shown in Figure 3.7. The children were then asked to draw what they had seen from memory. Most of their drawings did not look at all like the original arrangement. However, six months later, when the same children were asked to draw the bottle they had seen, many did much better (Figure 3.8). Apparently they now had a better idea of what the tilted bottle *should* look like (Inhelder, 1969).

Because of this process of reconstruction, memories may change over time. They may be simplified, enriched, or distorted, depending on the individual's experiences and attitudes. This is why we sometimes make mistakes in memory. One type of mistake is called **confabulation:** a person "remembers" information that was never stored in memory. Confabulation generally occurs when an individual remembers parts of a situation and fills in the gaps by making up the rest. This is precisely what eyewitnesses to a crime often do—they fill in the holes in their memory with reasonable guesses, without even being aware that they are doing it.

Some people do not need to reconstruct information, because they have an **eidetic memory,** usually referred to as a "photographic memory." People with eidetic memories can remember with amazing accuracy all the details of a photograph, or pages of a text, or an experience on the basis of short-term exposure. There is some controversy about just how common

Memories may be simplified, enriched, or distorted over time.

Figure 3.7
Children between the ages of five and seven were shown a bottle half filled with colored water and suspended at an angle, such as is shown in this drawing. After each child had seen this arrangement he was asked to draw it from memory. Some of the results of this experiment are shown in Figure 3.8a, b.

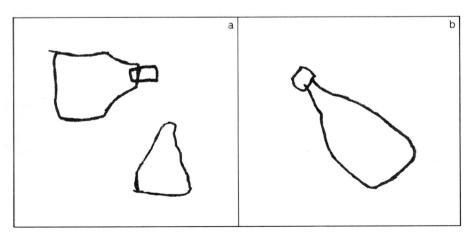
a   b

Figure 3.8
Drawings produced by children who had been shown an arrangement like that depicted in Figure 3.7. (a) The five- to seven-year-old children were not too successful in reproducing this arrangement from memory. (b) A drawing done by one of these children six months later. Even though the child had had half a year to forget what he had seen, his reproduction of the arrangement actually improved because he had developed a better idea of what bottles look like and of how water behaves.

photographic memory is. Several researchers have suggested that it is more common in children than in adults.

The Mind of a Mnemonist.   One of the best documented cases of a man with an astounding memory is presented in A. R. Luria's delightful book *The Mind of a Mnemonist* (1968). In the 1920s, a newspaper reporter came to Luria's laboratory to participate in a memory experiment. The Russian psychologist was amazed to learn that S. (as he called the reporter) could easily repeat lists of thirty, fifty, or seventy numbers after he heard them once. He could repeat them backward and forward with equal ease. And when Luria asked him for some of the same lists more than fifteen years later, S. still remembered them.

Perhaps as a result of Dr. Luria's tests, S. began another career as a professional mnemonist: he would repeat complicated lists supplied by people in the audience. How did he do it? Every word or number would conjure up rich visual images which S. easily remembered. For example, in one performance the audience provided him with the following nonsensical formula:

$$N \cdot \sqrt{d^2 \, x \, \frac{85}{vx}} \quad \cdot \quad \sqrt[3]{\frac{276^2 \cdot 86x}{n^2v \cdot 264} \, n^2b} \; = \qquad sv \, \frac{1{,}624}{32^2} \cdot r^2 \, s.$$

S. was able to repeat this perfectly after studying it for a few minutes. He later told Dr. Luria a story he made up to help remember the formula:

"Neiman *(N)* came out and jabbed at the ground with his cane (.). He looked up at a tall tree which resembled the square root sign ($\sqrt{}$), and thought to himself: 'No wonder the tree has withered and begun to expose its roots. After all, it was here when I built these two houses' *(d²)*" (49). And so on.

But being a professional mnemonist is not all roses. One of S.'s biggest problems was learning to forget. His brain was cluttered with old lists of words, numbers, and letters. Even when he tried to relax, his mind would be flooded with vivid images from the past. S. also had trouble reading: every word brought a sea of images, and he had trouble focusing on the underlying meaning of a passage. Partly because of these problems, Dr. Luria wrote, "S. struck one as a disorganized and rather dull-witted person" (65).

Forgetting

Everyone experiences a loss of memory from time to time. You're sure you've seen that person before but can't quite place her. You have the word on the tip of your tongue, but. . . . When information that once entered long-term memory cannot be retrieved, it is said to be forgotten. Forgetting may involve decay, interference, or repression.

Some inputs may fade away, or decay, over time. Items quickly decay in sensory storage and short-term memory, as indicated above. It is not

Remembering High School Classmates

Few of us will ever forget our high school days, with all their glory and pain. But how many of us will remember the names and faces of our high school classmates ten, twenty, thirty, and even forty years after graduation? According to a recent study, apparently more of us than you might think.

To find out just how long our long-term memory is, researchers showed nearly 400 high school graduates, ranging in age from seventeen to seventy-four, pictures from their high school yearbooks. Here are some of the surprising results:

- 35 years after graduation, people could identify the faces of 9 out of 10 of their classmates. The size of the high school made no difference in their response.
- 15 years after graduation, subjects could recall 90 percent of their classmates' names.
- Name recall began to fade to between 70 and 80 percent by the time people reached their late thirties.
- Women generally had better memories for names and faces than men.

Researchers explain these amazing results by looking to the way we collect this information in the first place. Our storehouse of names and faces is built over our four-year high school career, and continual repetition helps cement this knowledge in our memories for decades.

So if you're afraid you're going to forget all the classmates you will leave behind, take heart. They'll probably be part of your memory for a very long time.

For more details, see Harry P. Bahrick, Phyllis O. Bahrick, and Roy P. Wittinger, "Those Unforgettable High School Days," *Psychology Today,* December, 1974.

certain, however, whether long-term memories can ever decay. We know that a blow to the head or electrical stimulation of certain parts of the brain can cause loss of memory. The memories lost are the most recent ones, however; older memories seem to remain (see box). The fact that apparently forgotten information can be recovered through meditation, hypnosis, or brain stimulation suggests that at least some memories never decay. Rather, interference or repression causes people to lose track of them.

Interference refers to a memory being blocked or erased by previous or subsequent memories. This blocking is of two kinds: proactive and retroactive. In **proactive interference** an earlier memory does the blocking. In **retroactive interference** a later memory does the blocking. Suppose you move to a new home. You now have to remember a new address and phone number. At first you may have trouble remembering them because the memory of your old address and phone number gets in the way (proactive interference). Later, you know the new information, but have trouble remembering the old data (retroactive interference).

It may be that interference actually does erase some memories permanently. In other cases the old data have not been lost. The information is in your memory somewhere, if only you could find it. According to Sigmund Freud, sometimes blocking is no accident. A person may subconsciously block memories of an embarrassing or frightening experience. This kind of forgetting is called **repression.** The material still exists in the person's memory, but it has been made inaccessible because it is so disturbing. (We discuss repression further in Chapter 11.)

USING PSYCHOLOGY

Mood and Memory

In 1968, Sirhan Sirhan assassinated Robert Kennedy in a Los Angeles hotel. Sirhan was in a highly agitated state when he killed Kennedy. When questioned about it immediately afterward, he had no recollection of the event. A hypnotist was called in. The hypnotist re-created the events of the murder. As Sirhan listened, he became agitated and recalled more and more details of the murder. Sometimes while he was in a trance he described events aloud; at other times he recorded his memories by writing them down automatically, without being aware of what he was writing (Bower, 1981). In his non-hypnotized state, Sirhan was never conscious of these memories and even denied that he had committed the murder.

Sirhan Sirhan's case is a dramatic example of *state-dependent memory*. The theory of this type of memory is based on the assumption that events learned in a certain emotional state can be remembered better when one is put back into the same state.

To learn more about the influence of mood on memory, psychologist Gordon Bower conducted a series of laboratory experiments. In one study, he hypnotized a group of subjects and made them feel happy. While they were in that happy state, he gave them a list of words to learn. At another session, he hypnotized them again, but put them in a sad mood and gave them a different list of words to learn. Later, the subjects were hypnotized again and were asked to recall one of the lists they had been given previously. Bower found that the subjects who tried to recall a list in the same mood as that in which they learned it could remember more of the words than subjects who tried to recall the list they had learned while in the other mood.

Bower also had subjects keep daily records of the emotional events in their lives. Later, he hypnotized them and asked them to recall the incidents they had recorded. Bower found that subjects who were placed in a sad mood recalled more unpleasant events in their daily lives than subjects who were hypnotized to be in a happy mood. Also, subjects recalled more unpleasant events from their childhood when they were in a sad mood than they recalled happy events when in a happy mood.

One explanation for this mood-dependent recall offered by Bower is that mood serves as a cue for retrieving information. When a memory is stored, it is associated with a specific emotion as well as with specific actions or people. The emotional state later functions as a marker in our memory of the specific event. When we are in the same mood, we are more likely to be able to find the memory thus marked.

There are some practical implications of Bower's research. First, if you want to maximize your recall of material, one way to do so is to recall the material in a circumstance or emotional context similar to the one in which the material was learned. For example, if you match a mood of tension while studying for an exam with a tense mood while taking an exam, you can expect to do better in recalling the studied material. Often, students are relaxed while studying for an exam, but anxious while taking it—a bad match for recall, according to Bower.

SQ3R. "SQ3R" is an effective study method that can be applied to textbooks. It involves five steps. Step one is to *Survey*. When beginning a chapter, read through the section headings quickly to see what is going to be covered. Next comes *Question*. Change each section heading into a question. This helps you keep in mind what is to be learned. For example, the title of the adjacent section in this book is "Improving Memory." You might, therefore, pose the question, "How can memory be improved?" Step three is to *Read* the chapter. As you do, try to answer the questions you posed. In step four, *Recite*, either write brief notes covering the highlights of the reading or recite the main points out loud. Finally, *Review* the main points by asking the questions again and then writing or reciting the answers. By the time you finish doing all four steps, you should have learned much about the text, partly because, by using the SQ3R method, you have actively thought about the material.

Improving Memory

Techniques for improving memory are based on efficient organization of the things you learn and on chunking information into easily handled packages. Meaningfulness, association, lack of interference, and degree of original learning all influence your ability to retrieve data from memory.

The more meaningful something is, the easier it will be to remember. For example, you would be more likely to remember the six letters DFIRNE if they were arranged to form the word FRIEND. Similarly, you remember things more vividly if you associate them with things already stored in memory or with a strong emotional experience. As pointed out earlier, the more categories a memory is indexed under, the more accessible it is. If an input is analyzed and indexed under many categories, each association can serve as a trigger for the memory. If you associate the new information with strong sounds, smells, tastes, textures, and so on, any of these stimuli could trigger the memory. The more senses you use when trying to memorize something, the more likely it is that you will be able to retrieve it. This is a key to improving your memory.

For similar reasons, a good way to protect a memory from interference is to *overlearn* it—to keep on rehearsing it even after you think you know it well. Another way to prevent interference while learning new material is to avoid studying similar material together. Instead of studying history right after political science, study biology in between. Still another method is to space out your learning. Trying to absorb large amounts of information at one sitting results in a great deal of interference. It is far more effective to study a little at a time.

Figure 3.9
Here is a mnemonic device for remembering that Picasso (which sounds like "pickax") was a Cubist. Often, the sillier the mental picture, the better it is for retrieving the information you have trouble remembering.

Mnemonic Devices.   **Mnemonic devices** are techniques for using associations to memorize information. The ancient Greeks memorized speeches by mentally walking around their homes or neighborhoods and "placing" each line of a speech in a different spot. Once they made the associations, they could recall the speech by mentally retracing their steps and "picking up" each line. A more familiar mnemonic device is the rhyme we use to recall the number of days in each month ("Thirty days has September"). Another is the phrase "Every Good Boy Does Fine," in which the first letters of the words are the same as the names of the musical notes on the lines of a staff (E, G, B, D, and F); the notes between the lines spell FACE.

Another useful mnemonic device is to form mental pictures containing the information you want to remember—the sillier the better. Suppose you have trouble remembering the authors and titles of books, or which artists belong to which schools of painting. To plant the fact in your mind that John Updike wrote *Rabbit, Run*, you might picture a RABBIT RUNning UP a DIKE. To remember that Picasso was a Cubist, picture someone attacking a giant CUBE with a PICKAX (which sounds like Picasso) (Lorayne and Lucas, 1974: 166–169) (Figure 3.9).

Mnemonic devices are not magical. Indeed, they involve extra work—making up words, stories, and so on. But the very effort of trying to do this may help you to remember things.

CENTRAL PROCESSING OF INFORMATION

If storage and retrieval were the only processes we used to handle information, human beings would be little more than glorified cameras and projectors. But, in fact, we are capable of doing things with information that make the most complex computers seem simple by comparison. These processes—thinking and problem solving—are most impressive when they show originality or creativity.

Thinking

Thinking may be viewed as changing and reorganizing the information stored in memory in order to create new information. By thinking, humans are able to put together any combination of words from memory and create sentences never devised before—such as this one.

Units of Thought. The processes of thought depend on several devices or units of thought: images, symbols, concepts, and rules.

The most primitive unit of thought is an **image,** a mental representation of a specific event or object. The representation is not usually an exact copy; rather, it contains only the highlights of the original. For example, if an adult tries to visualize a grandmother who died when he was seven, he would probably remember only a few details—perhaps the color of her hair or a piece of jewelry that she wore.

A more abstract unit of thought is a **symbol,** a sound or design that represents an object or quality. The most common symbols in thinking are words: every word is a symbol that stands for something other than itself. An image represents a specific sight or sound, but a symbol may have a number of meanings. The fact that symbols differ from the things they represent enables us to think about things that are not present, to range over the past and future, to imagine things and situations that never were or will be. Numbers, letters, and punctuation marks are all familiar symbols of ideas that have no concrete existence.

When a symbol is used as a label for a class of objects or events with certain common attributes, or for the attributes themselves, it is called a

Figure 3.10
This problem was devised by psychologist Edward De Bono, who believes that conventional directed thinking is insufficient for solving new and unusual problems. His approach to problem-solving requires use of nondirected thinking in order to generate new ways of looking at the problem situation. The answer to this problem is provided in Figure 3.15.

An old money-lender offered to cancel a merchant's debt and keep him from going to prison if the merchant would give the money-lender his lovely daughter. Horrified yet desperate, the merchant and his daughter agreed to let Providence decide. The money-lender said he would put a black pebble and a white pebble in a bag and the girl would draw one. The white pebble would cancel the debt and leave her free. The black one would make her the money-lender's, although the debt would be canceled. If she refused to pick, her father would go to prison. From the pebble-strewn path they were standing on, the money-lender picked two pebbles and quickly put them in the bag, but the girl saw he had picked up two black ones. What would you have done if you were the girl?

concept. "Animals," "music," "liquid," and "beautiful people" are examples of concepts based on the common attributes of the objects and experiences belonging to each category. Thus the concept "animal" separates a group of organisms from such things as automobiles, carrots, and Roquefort cheese. Concepts enable us to chunk large amounts of information. We do not have to treat every new piece of information as unique since we already know something about the class of objects or experiences to which the new item belongs.

The fourth and most complex unit of thought is a **rule,** a statement of a relation between concepts. The following are examples of rules: a person cannot be in two places at the same time; mass remains constant despite changes in appearance.

Images, symbols, concepts, and rules are the building blocks of mental activity. They provide an economical and efficient way for people to represent reality, to manipulate and reorganize it, and to devise new ways of acting. A person can think about pursuing several different careers, weigh their pros and cons, and decide which to pursue without having to try them all.

Kinds of Thinking. People think in two distinct ways. The first, called **directed thinking,** is a systematic and logical attempt to reach a specific goal, such as the solution of a problem. This kind of thinking depends heavily on symbols, concepts, and rules. The other type, called **nondirected thinking,** consists of a free flow of thoughts through the mind, with no particular goal or plan, and depends more on images (Figure 3.10).

Nondirected thinking is usually rich with imagery and feelings. Day-dreams, fantasies, and reveries are typical examples. People often engage in nondirected thought when they are relaxing or trying to escape from boredom or worry. This kind of thinking may provide unexpected insights into one's goals and beliefs. Scientists and artists say that some of their best ideas emerge from drifting thoughts that occur when they have set aside a problem for the moment.

In contrast, directed thinking is deliberate and purposeful. It is through directed thinking that we solve problems, formulate and follow rules, and set, work toward, and achieve goals.

Problem Solving

One of the main functions of directed thinking is to solve problems—to bridge the gap, mentally, between a present situation and a desired goal. The gap may be between hunger and food, a column of figures and a total, lack of money and bills to pay, or cancer and a cure. In all these examples, getting from the problem to the solution requires some directed thinking.

Strategies.   Problem solving depends on the use of strategies, or specific methods for approaching problems. One strategy is to break down a complex problem into a number of smaller, more easily solved problems. For example, it is the end of the semester and your life is falling apart. You don't even have time to tie your shoelaces. You solve the problem by breaking it down into small pieces: studying for a science exam; finishing that overdue paper; canceling your dinner date; scheduling regular study breaks to maintain what's left of your sanity; and so on.

For some problems, you may work backward from the goal you have set. Mystery writers often use this method: They decide how to end the story ("who did it") and then devise a plot leading to this conclusion.

Another problem may require you to examine various ways of reaching a desired goal. Suppose a woman needs to be in Chicago by 11:00 A.M. on July 7 for a business conference. She checks train departures and arrivals, airline schedules, and car-rental companies. The only train to Chicago that morning arrives at 5:00 A.M. (too early), and the first plane arrives at 11:30 A.M. (too late). So she decides to rent a car and drive.

To determine which strategy to use in a particular situation, most of us analyze the problem to see if it resembles a situation we have experienced in the past. A strategy that worked in the past is likely to work again. The more unusual the problem, the more difficult it is to devise a strategy for dealing with it.

Set.   There are times when certain useful strategies become cemented into the problem-solving process. When a particular strategy becomes a habit, it is called a **set**—you are "set" to treat problems in a certain way. For example, a chess player may always attempt to control the four center

Figure 3.11

Given the materials pictured here, how would you go about mounting the candle vertically on a wooden wall in such a way that it can be lit? This problem was formulated by Carl Duncker to test how well people are able to overcome functional fixedness. The solution is presented in Figure 3.15.

squares of the chessboard. Whenever her opponent attacks, she responds by looking for ways to regain control of those four squares. She has a "set" for this strategy. If this set helps her to win, fine. Sometimes, however, a set interferes with problem solving, and then it is called *rigidity*. You probably know the old riddle, "What is black, white, and read all over? A newspaper." When you say the riddle, the word "read" sounds like "red," which is why some people cannot guess the answer. "Read" is heard as part of the black and white set—it is interpreted as being a color. If you asked, "What is read by people every day and is black and white?" the correct answer would be obvious. And boring.

One form of set that can interfere with problem solving is functional fixedness—the inability to imagine new functions for familiar objects. In experiments on functional fixedness, people are asked to solve a problem that requires them to use a familiar object in an unfamiliar way (Duncker, 1945). Because they are set to use the object in the usual way, people tend to pay attention only to the features of the object that relate to its everyday use (see Figure 3.11). They respond in a rigid way.

Another type of rigidity occurs when a person makes a wrong assumption about a problem. In Figure 3.12, for example, the problem is to connect the dots with four straight lines without lifting your pencil. Most people have trouble solving this puzzle because they falsely assume that they must stay within the area of the dots.

People trying to solve the kind of problem shown in Figure 3.13 experience a third kind of rigidity. Most people look for direct methods of solving problems and do not see solutions that require several intermediate steps.

Rigidity can be overcome if the person realizes that his or her strategy is not working and looks for other ways to approach the problem. The more familiar the situation, the more difficult this will be. Rigidity is less likely to occur with unusual problems.

Creativity

Creativity is the ability to use information in such a way that the result is somehow new, original, and meaningful. All problem solving requires

Figure 3.12

Connect these dots with four straight lines without lifting your pencil. The solution appears in Figure 3.15.

Figure 3.13
How would you go about solving this problem: Eight soldiers need to cross a river, but the only way to cross is in a small boat in which two children are playing. The boat can carry at most two children or one soldier. How do the soldiers get across? You'll find the answer in Figure 3.15.

some creativity. Certain ways of solving problems, however, are simply more brilliant or beautiful or efficient than others. Psychologists do not know exactly why some people are able to think more creatively than others, although they have identified some of the characteristics of creative thinking—including flexibility and the ability to recombine elements to achieve insight.

Flexibility. Flexibility is, quite simply, the ability to overcome rigidity. Psychologists have devised a number of ingenious tests to measure flexibility. One test is shown in Figure 3.14. The individual is asked to name a word that the three words in each row have in common. To do this, a person must be able to think of many different aspects of each of these words. Another test of flexibility is to ask people how many uses they can imagine for a single object, such as a brick or a paper clip. The more uses a person can devise, the more flexible he or she is said to be. Whether such tests actually measure creativity is debatable. Nevertheless, it is obvious that inflexible, rigid thinking leads to unoriginal solutions, or no solutions at all.

Recombination. When the elements of a problem are familiar but the required solution is not, it may be achieved by **recombination,** a new mental rearrangement of the elements. In football and basketball, for example, there are no new moves—only recombinations of old ones. Such recombination seems to be a vital part of creativity. Many creative people say that no truly great poem, no original invention, has ever been produced by someone who has not spent years studying his or her subject. The creative person is able to take the information that he or she and others have compiled and put it together in a totally new way. The brilliant philosopher and mathematician Sir Isaac Newton, who discovered the laws of motion, once said, "If I have seen further, it is by standing on the shoulders

Figure 3.14
A test devised to measure flexibility in thinking. The task is to name a single word that all three words on a line have in common. For example, the answer to the first item is "foot." (The other answers are given in Figure 3.15.)

1.	stool	powder	ball
2.	blue	cake	cottage
3.	man	wheel	high
4.	motion	poke	down
5.	line	birthday	surprise
6.	wood	liquor	luck
7.	house	village	golf
8.	card	knee	rope
9.	news	doll	tiger
10.	painting	bowl	nail
11.	weight	wave	house
12.	made	cuff	left
13.	key	wall	precious
14.	bull	tired	hot
15.	knife	up	hi
16.	handle	hole	police
17.	plan	show	walker
18.	hop	side	pet
19.	bell	tender	iron
20.	spelling	line	busy

of giants." In other words, he was able to recombine the discoveries of the great scientists who had preceded him to uncover new and more far-reaching truths.

Another result of brilliant recombination is Samuel Taylor Coleridge's unusual poem "Kubla Khan." Scholars have shown that almost every word and phrase came directly from Coleridge's past readings and personal experiences. Coleridge recombined these elements during a period of non-

hen the girl put her hand into the bag to draw out the fateful pebble, she fumbled and dropped it, where it was immediately lost among the others. "Oh," she said, "well, you can tell which one I picked by looking at the one that's left." The girl's lateral thinking saved her father and herself.

1.	foot	11.	light
2.	cheese	12.	hand
3.	chair	13.	stone
4.	slow	14.	dog
5.	party	15.	jack
6.	hard	16.	man
7.	green	17.	floor
8.	trick	18.	car
9.	paper	19.	bar
10.	finger	20.	bee

Figure 3.15
Solutions to the problems presented in the chapter. Note that in each case the solution requires breaking certain habits of thought. (a) In the De Bono money-lender problem, it is difficult to imagine that control of the situation can be taken out of the hands of the powerful money-lender. (b) Solving the Duncker candle problem requires one to look at the matchbox and candle box as more than containers to be discarded. The presence of the useless piece of string usually serves to confuse problem solvers. (c) As the text points out, the solution to this problem is blocked if the person avoids going beyond the boundaries of the dots. (d) The answers to the test of flexibility require that the individual ig- nore common associations and look for unusual ones. (e) The first steps in solution of the river problem. Once the solver discovers the first step in the problem's solution, he or she may become further bogged down if he doesn't realize the lengthy cyclical nature of the process required.

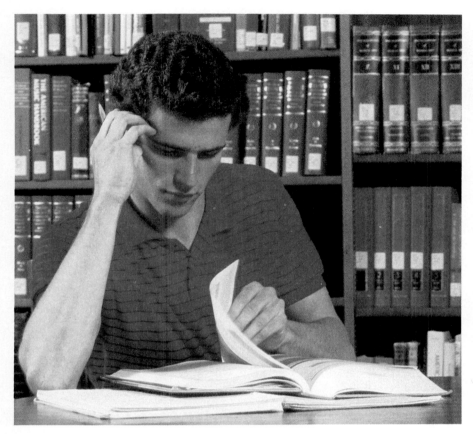

Figure 3.16
Most of us have experienced insight or the "aha" experience at some time. Can you recall the most recent time you experienced frustration, abandoned the task for a while, and suddenly the solution seemed to come out of nowhere?

directed thinking—drug-induced sleep. He awoke with the entire poem in his mind, but was only able to commit part of it to paper before he was interrupted by a knock at his door. When Coleridge went back to his poem, it had vanished from his mind.

Insight. The sudden emergence of a solution by recombination of elements is called **insight**. Insight usually occurs when problems have proved resistant to all problem-solving efforts and strategies. The scientist or artist reaches a point of high frustration and temporarily abandons the task. But the recombination process seems to continue on an unconscious level. When the person is absorbed in some other activity, the answer seems to appear out of nowhere. This sudden insight has appropriately been called the "aha" experience.

Certain animals appear to experience this same cycle of frustration, temporary diversion (during which time the problem "incubates"), and then sudden insight. For example, Wolfgang Köhler (1925) placed a chimpanzee in a cage where a cluster of bananas was hung out of its reach. Also in the cage were a number of wooden boxes. At first the chimpanzee tried various unsuccessful ways of getting at the fruit. Finally it sat down, apparently giving up, and simply stared straight ahead for a while. Then suddenly it jumped up, piled three boxes on top of one another, climbed to the top of the pile, and grabbed the bananas.

SUMMARY

Use the following outline as a tool for reviewing this chapter. Copy the outline onto your own paper, leaving spaces between headings to make notes about key concepts.

I. Taking Information In

   A. Selective Attention

   B. Feature Extraction

II. Storing Information

   A. Sensory Storage

   B. Short-Term Storage

   C. Long-Term Storage

   D. Memory and the Brain

III. Retrieving Information

   A. Recognition

   B. Recall

   C. Forgetting

   D. Improving Memory

IV. Central Processing of Information

   A. Thinking

   B. Problem Solving

   C. Creativity

CONCEPTS AND VOCABULARY

1. Information processing involves three steps. List and define them.

2. What are the first two processes that help people narrow sensory inputs?

3. What factors make one input more important than another?

4. Name the three types of memory. How long is information retained in each type?

5. List two strategies for expanding the limits of short-term memory.

6. What are the two theories that explain the activities in the brain when something is stored in long-term memory?

7. What are the two types of interference that block memory? Can you develop a mnemonic device to remember their definitions?

8. Describe six methods to improve your memory.

9. List the four units of thought in order of increasing complexity.

10. What are the two kinds of thinking?

11. When a problem-solving strategy becomes a habit, what is it called? Give one example of how this can interfere with problem solving.

12. What are three characteristics of creative thinking?

CRITICAL THINKING

1. **Analyze.** In the middle of an ordinary activity, like reading a book, stop for a moment and listen for sounds you normally block out. Jot down the sounds you hear and try to identify them. Why don't you usually hear them? Under what circumstances would you notice them?

2. **Analyze.** Relax and engage in nondirected thinking—let your thoughts wander. Things may come into your mind that you thought you had forgotten or that you didn't know you knew. Or reflect on a recent dream you had— where might the various images have come from?

3. **Evaluate.** Suppose you wanted to put together a jigsaw puzzle. What are the problem-solving strategies you might use? Which one do you think would work the best?

4. **Synthesize.** Try to remember what you were doing on your last birthday. As you probe your memory, verbalize the mental steps you are

going through. What does this exercise tell you about your thought processes?

APPLYING KNOWLEDGE

1. Mentally determine where the light switches in your home are located and keep track of them in your head. Do you have to use visual images to count the switches? To keep track of the number? If not, could you do it with images if you wanted to?

2. Try this simple learning task on your friends. Give them a list of numbers to memorize: 6, 9, 8, 11, 10, 13, 12, 15, 14, 17, 16, and so on. Tell some of them simply to memorize the material. Tell others that there is an organizational principle behind the number sequence, and to memorize the number with the aid of the principle (which they must discover). In the sequence above, the principle is "plus 3, minus 1." Is one group better at remembering the list than the other? Based on what you know from the chapter, why do you think this is so?

3. Try the following game to demonstrate the reconstructive aspects of recall. (You will need at least seven or eight people—the more the better.) Before you gather the group together, write or copy a very short (not more than three or four paragraphs) story containing a fair amount of descriptive detail. Memorize, as best you can, the story, and whisper it to one member of the group, making sure the others are out of earshot. Then instruct your listener to whisper the story to another player, and so on until all the players have heard it. When the last person has been told the story, have him or her repeat it aloud to the entire group. Then read the original story from your written copy. Chances are good that the two versions are quite a bit different.

Discuss among yourselves how, when, and why the story changed.

ANALYZING VIEWPOINTS

1. This text discusses the validity of eyewitness testimony in court cases. When an eyewitness identifies an individual as the person who committed the crime, the evidence can be very convincing to the jury. However, there are many cases of people who are falsely accused by eyewitnesses. In fact, innocent people have served time in jail for crimes they did not commit because of inaccurate eyewitness testimony. Should eyewitness testimony be used in the courtroom? Why or why not? Write a paper that argues both sides of the issue. Use what you know about the nature of human memory and studies of eyewitness testimony. You may also want to look for magazine and newspaper articles that report on specific crimes where eyewitness testimony was used.

BEYOND THE CLASSROOM

1. Think of a significant news event that has happened in the past ten years, such as the explosion of the *Challenger* space shuttle, or the tearing down of the Berlin Wall. Ask people of different ages (e.g., a teenager, a parent or teacher, a grandparent) what they remember about the event. After they have described their memories, ask them how they went about trying to recall the event. What do their answers tell you about long-term memory? What do their answers tell you about how people retrieve information from memory? Did you find any differences in the memories of teenagers, adults, or the elderly? How can these differences be explained? Report to the class on your findings.

UNIT 2

The Workings of Mind and Body

CHAPTER 4

Body and Behavior

You are your brain. Your pleasant personality, your wry sense of humor, and your favorite color are all coded in the thirteen billion nerve cells of your brain. Ordinarily, we pay no attention to our biological nature. But your reliance on the physical properties of the nervous system would become painfully obvious if you were involved in a car accident that damaged your brain: your personality, your memories, and even your sense of humor might be affected.

The Greek physician Hippocrates was the first to notice that head injuries often disturbed thought and behavior. In the twenty-five centuries since his observations, many attempts have been made to explain how this mass of soggy gray tissue could create the theory of relativity, the Sistine Chapel ceiling, and the energy crisis. But the mind remains a mystery to itself.

Some of the most exciting developments in psychology are going on in the brain sciences, and this chapter will help you to understand the newspaper and magazine articles reporting new discoveries that you will probably be reading for the next twenty-five years. In addition to describing the organization of the nervous system, we will discuss studies of lower animals and the possible role of genes in complex human behavior.

THE NERVOUS SYSTEM

In some ways, the nervous system is like the telephone system in a city. Messages are constantly traveling back and forth. As in a telephone system, the messages are basically electrical. They travel along prelaid cables,

Objectives:

After studying this chapter, you should be able to

- name the parts and functions of the nervous system.
- identify the structure and functions of the human brain.
- discuss the different ways psychologists study the brain.
- describe the endocrine system.
- summarize research on the effects of heredity and environment.

Figure 4.1 The control of our bodies rests with our brains. It is the brain and the nervous system that enable us to sit, stand, skate, run—and to think and plan.

Once a neuron begins to "fire," it can be stopped if the original stimulation is weak.

Fiction. Transmission between neurons or nerve cells occurs when the cells are stimulated past a minimum point and emit a signal. The neuron is said to "fire." The firing of neurons occurs in line with the all-or-none principle, which states that when a neuron fires it does so at full strength. If a neuron is not stimulated past the minimum level, it does not fire at all.

linked with one another by relays and switchboards. In the body, the cables are **nerve fibers.** The relays are **synapses,** the gaps that occur between individual nerve cells. The switchboards are special cells that are found along the lines of communication (called *interneurons*) and the networks of nerve cells found in the brain and spinal cord. One major difference is that a telephone system simply conveys messages, while the nervous system actively helps to run the body.

The brain monitors what is happening inside and outside the body by receiving messages from **receptors**—cells whose function is to gather information. The brain sifts through these messages, combines them, and sends out orders to the **effectors**—cells that work the muscles and internal glands and organs. For example, receptors in your eye may send a message to the brain such as "Round object. Size increasing. Distance decreasing rapidly." Your brain instantly connects this image with information from memory to identify this object as a baseball. Almost simultaneously your brain orders the effectors in your arms to position themselves so you don't get beaned in right field.

How the Nervous System Works

Messages to and from the brain travel along the nerves, which are strings of long, thin cells called **neurons** (see Figure 4.2). Chemical-electrical signals travel down the neurons much as flame travels along a firecracker fuse. The main difference is that the neuron can "burn" over and over

Figure 4.2
A few of the billions of neurons in the human body, shown tens of thousands of times bigger than they really are. Neurons connect with each other at the synapses, where chemical substances cross the gap from one nerve cell to another. In that way, messages can travel through the body.

again, hundreds of times a minute.

Each neuron is long and thin, with branching or brushlike extensions (Figure 4.2). One end receives the message and the other, which can be as much as three feet long, transmits the electro-chemical impulse to the next neuron. The next neuron picks up chemicals called **neurotransmitters** from across the synapse (gap). The neurotransmitters can excite the next neuron or stop it from transmitting (inhibition). The neurotransmitters are like the valves in a water system that allow flow in only one direction.

The intensity of activity in each neuron depends on how many other neurons are acting on it. Each individual neuron is either ON or OFF, depending on whether the majority of neurons acting on it are exciting it or inhibiting it. The actual destination of nerve impulses produced by an excited neuron, as they travel from one neuron to another, is limited by what tract in the nervous system they are on. Ascending tracts carry sensory impulses to the brain; descending tracts carry motor impulses from the brain.

Some of the actions that your body takes in response to impulses from the nerves are voluntary acts, such as lifting your hand to turn a page (which actually involves many impulses to many muscles). Others are involuntary acts, such as changes in the heartbeat, in the blood pressure, or in the size of the pupils. The term **somatic nervous system** refers to the part of the nervous system that controls voluntary activities. The term **autonomic nervous system** refers to the part of the nervous system that controls involuntary activities—those that ordinarily occur "automatically," such as heartbeat, stomach activity, and so on.

The autonomic nervous system itself has two parts: *sympathetic* and *parasympathetic*. The **sympathetic nervous system** prepares the body for dealing with emergencies or strenuous activity. It speeds up the heart to hasten the supply of oxygen and nutrients to body tissues. It constricts some arteries and relaxes others so that blood flows to the muscles, where it is most needed in emergencies and strenuous activity. It increases the blood pressure and suspends some activities, such as digestion. In contrast, the **parasympathetic nervous system** works to conserve energy and to enhance the body's ability to recover from strenuous activity. It reduces the heart rate and blood pressure and helps bring the body back to normal.

All of this takes place automatically. Receptors are constantly receiving messages (hunger, the need to swallow or cough) that alert the autonomic nervous system, via the *thalamus* in the brain, to carry out routine activities. Imagine how difficult it would be if you had no autonomic nervous system and had to think about it every time your body needed to digest a sandwich or perspire.

Structurally, the nervous system is divided into two parts (Figure 4.3): the brain and **spinal cord** (the **central nervous system (CNS)**); and smaller branches of nerves that reach the other parts of the body (the **peripheral nervous system (PNS)**). More than three-fourths of the body's neurons are in the brain, which weighs about 3 pounds. The nerves of the peripheral system that branch out from the spinal column are about as thick as a pencil. Those in the extremities, such as the fingertips, are invisibly small. All parts of the nervous system are protected in some way: the brain by

Figure 4.3
The central nervous system (CNS) and the peripheral nervous system (PNS) in the human body.

Central Nervous System

Peripheral Nervous System

Figure 4.4
A cross section of the human brain, showing the subcortex, or "old brain," and the cerebral cortex, or "new brain."

the skull and several layers of sheathing; the spinal cord by the vertebrae; and the peripheral nerves by layers of sheathing. The bony protection of the spinal cord is vital. An injury to the spinal cord could prevent the transmittal of messages from the brain to the muscles, and could result in paralysis.

The spinal cord extends into the brain through a widening called the *brainstem.* Generally, this part of the brain and the other physically "lower" sections of the brain control "lower" functions (such as sleeping, chewing, and salivation) that we share with all other animals. The correct name for this part of the brain is the **subcortex.** It is often referred to as the "old brain" because it is thought to have evolved millions of years ago in our prehuman ancestors. At the back and bottom of the old brain is the **cerebellum.** This structure looks somewhat like a miniature version of the brain as a whole. One of its main functions is to control posture and balance.

The "higher" thinking processes are housed in the "new brain." The outer layer of the new brain consists of the **cerebral cortex.** The inner layer is the **cerebrum.** The cerebral cortex and cerebrum surround the subcortex as a halved peach surrounds the pit (Figure 4.4). The cerebral cortex gives you the ability to learn and store complex and abstract information, and to project your thinking into the future. It is your cerebral cortex that allows you to see, read, and understand this sentence. The

Figure 4.5
The structures of the subcortex. (This illustration shows the brain as it would appear if it were sliced exactly in half from front to back.)

cortex, or bark, of the cerebrum is the site of most conscious thinking processes, yet it is less than a half-inch thick.

Precisely which areas of the cerebral cortex control which activities is not completely known, but information is being gathered and brain maps are being made. To help them describe the location of certain activities, scientists refer to sites on different **lobes,** or regions, of the brain (Figure 4.6). The information that is available is based on observations of people and laboratory animals with brain or nerve damage. Scientists have also gathered information by stimulating parts of the brain during surgery (this is painless), and by conducting tests that measure the activity in different areas of the brain.

Some areas of the cortex receive information from the skin senses and from muscles. The amount of brain tissue connected to any given body part is based on the sensitivity of that area, not on its size (Figure 4.7). For example, the highly developed sense of touch in the hand involves a much larger brain area than that of the relatively insensitive calves. The part of the cortex that receives information is called the **somatosensory cortex.** The **motor cortex** sends information to control body movement. The motor cortex is also divided according to need: the more sophisticated the movements have to be (such as those used in speaking), the bigger the brain area involved. The *association areas* mediate between the other two and do the actual synthesizing of information.

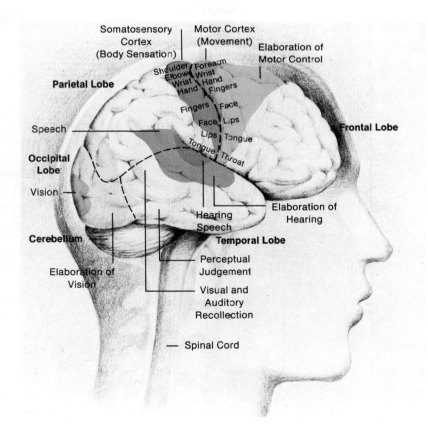

Figure 4.6
An external view of the brain from the side. Most of the areas exposed here are parts of the "new" brain. The functions of the cerebral cortex are not fully understood; areas whose behavioral importance is known are indicated.

Figure 4.7
Two views of the same half of the brain, sliced in half between the parietal and frontal lobes (along the groove that separates the somatosensory cortex from the motor cortex). The areas of greatest sensitivity (left) and motor control (right) are listed. The funny little men depict how the body would look if areas of greatest sensitivity and motor control were proportionate in the body to their size in the brain.

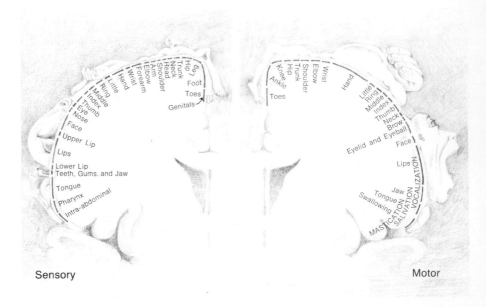

Sensory   Motor

The brain processes a vast number of incoming and outgoing messages every second, but not all of them reach the cerebral cortex. Some parts of the lower brain (such as the **reticular activating system** and the **thalamus**) filter out all but the most important messages. Exactly how the parts of the brain process so much information is being studied. It seems that patterns of stimuli and appropriate responses are stored in the memory so that when a pattern of incoming impulses is screened by the lower parts of the brain, they are compared to other, previous patterns. This is an ongoing process.

The brain's ability to process many experiences at once make it so superior to the most sophisticated computer that scientists can never hope to match its capabilities. They are still trying to determine the different functions and interactions of the parts of the brain. Some studies suggest that the **frontal lobes** control creativity and personality: they enable people to be witty, sensitive, or easygoing. Evidence for this theory is provided by the case of Phineas Gage. A quarryman, he was injured in an explosion in the mid-1800s. The force of the blast drove an iron stake through Gage's head, damaging the frontal lobes (Figure 4.8). Remarkably, Gage survived and was back at work in a few months. The accident did not impair his bodily functions or his memory or skills. However, Gage's personality changed dramatically. This once trustworthy and dependable man became childish, fitful, impatient, and capricious. Later studies of large numbers of people with similar brain damage suggest that planning future action, emotional control, and the ability to pay attention depend on the frontal lobes.

Figure 4.8
This drawing was adapted from one of the sketches made by the doctor who attended Phineas Gage. It shows the path taken by the iron stake that was propelled through Gage's skull.

The Hemispheres of the Brain

The cortex is divided into two hemispheres that are roughly mirror images of each other. (Each of the four lobes is present in both hemispheres.) The two hemispheres are connected by a band of nerves called the **corpus callosum,** which carries messages back and forth between the two. Each hemisphere is connected to half of the body in a crisscrossed fashion. The motor cortex of the left hemisphere of the brain controls most of the right side of the body; the right hemisphere motor cortex controls most of the left side of the body. Thus a stroke that causes damage to the right hemisphere will result in numbness or paralysis on the left side of the body. Researchers have also found a number of more subtle differences between the sides of the brain: in right-handed people, the left hemisphere controls language, while the right hemisphere is involved in spatial tasks.

Many psychologists became interested in differences between the cerebral hemispheres when "split brain" operations were tried on epileptics like Harriet Lees. For most of her life Ms. Lees's seizures were mild and could be controlled with drugs. However, at age twenty-five they began to get worse, and by thirty Lees was having as many as a dozen violent seizures a day. An epileptic seizure involves massive electrical activity that begins in one hemisphere and spreads to the other. To enable this woman to live a normal life, doctors decided to sever the corpus callosum so that seizures could not spread.

The operation was a success—Lees has not had a seizure since. But psychologists were even more interested in the potential side effects of this dramatic operation. Despite the fact that patients who had this operation now had "two separate brains," they seemed remarkably normal. Researchers went on to develop a number of ingenious techniques to try to detect subtle effects of the operation. To understand the procedures, you need to know a little about brain anatomy. For example, the left half of each eye is connected to the right hemisphere and the right half of each eye is wired to the left hemisphere. To get a message to only one hemisphere at a time, the researchers asked each split-brain patient to stare at a dot while they briefly flashed a word or a picture on one side of the dot. If the word "nut" was flashed to the right of the dot, it went to the left hemisphere. The patient could usually read it quite easily under these circumstances, because the left hemisphere controls language for most right-handed people.

But when the same word was flashed to the right hemisphere (left side of each eye), the patient was not able to repeat it. For an ordinary person, the word "nut" would quickly go from one side of the brain to the other via the corpus callosum. Since this patient's corpus callosum had been cut, however, the message could not get from the nonverbal right hemisphere to the verbal left. Even more amazing was the fact that the patient really did recognize the word: with her left hand (which is also connected to the right hemisphere), she could pick out a nut from a group of objects hidden behind a screen. But even after she correctly picked out the nut and held it in her hand, still she could not remember the word!

In another experiment, a picture of a nude woman was flashed to the right hemisphere (left side of each eye) of another split-brain patient (Figure 4.9). This woman laughed but said she saw nothing. Only her left hemisphere could speak and it did not see the nude; but the right hemisphere, which did see the nude, produced the laugh. When the woman was asked why she laughed, she acted confused and couldn't explain it.

Planning the future, controlling emotions, and paying attention seem to depend on the frontal lobes of the brain.

Figure 4.9
The presentation of a visual stimulus to a single hemisphere of a person who has undergone split-brain surgery. The patient reacts with amusement to the picture of the nude woman flashed on the left side of the screen but is unable to say why.

Right-handed children are genetically predisposed to develop verbal left hemispheres, but the actual specialization develops over the years. If a child suffers damage to the left hemisphere, the right hemisphere will take over the function of speech. The child may learn more slowly than other children, but he or she will learn to speak. However, almost all adults who suffer damage to the left hemisphere have extreme difficulty speaking—if they can speak at all. The effects of right-hemisphere damage are less clear, but they probably include problems with spatial abilities.

Though this specialization of labor is particularly relevant for people with brain damage, it also involves normal people. One group of studies, for example, has looked at the brain waves (or EEG—see below) of right-handed people as they perform verbal and spatial tasks. The EEG shows greater activity in the right hemisphere for spatial tasks like memorizing geometrical designs, remembering faces, or imagining an elephant in a swing. But when the same people were asked to perform verbal tasks—writing a letter in their heads, thinking of words that begin with "t," and listening to boring passages from the *Congressional Record*—their EEG showed relatively greater activity in the left hemisphere (Hassett, 1978). Even more interesting, and far easier to observe, is the fact that normal people tend to move their eyes in a certain way depending on which hemisphere they are using (see box).

Which Way Do the Eyes Move?

Did you know that the direction your eyes move when you think about a question may indicate which side of the brain you are using for the answer?

Ask a friend the following four questions, and secretly watch whether she first looks to the right or the left as she considers each:

1. Make up a sentence using the words "code" and "mathematics."
2. Picture the last automobile accident you saw. In which direction were the cars going?
3. What does the proverb "Easy come, easy go" mean?
4. Picture and describe the last time you cried.

Questions 1 and 3 are verbal, nonemotional questions; a right-handed person should use the left hemisphere to answer and, as a result, tend to look to the right. Questions 2 and 4 are spatial-emotional questions that require the right hemisphere and should, on the average, yield more eye movements to the left than the right.

For more details, see G. E. Schwartz, R. Davidson, and F. Maer, "Right Hemisphere Lateralization for Emotion in the Human Brain: Interactions with Cognition," *Science*, 190 (1975): 286–288.

These clear differences between the hemispheres apply primarily to right-handed people. Some left-handers have the opposite pattern of cerebral dominance—language is found in the right hemisphere. More commonly, lefties have less dramatic differences between the halves of the brain.

One by-product of all the research on cerebral dominance has been to increase interest in the phenomenon of handedness. About nine out of ten people prefer to use their right hand, and this seems to be a distinctly human characteristic with a long history. Even the people pictured in Egyptian tomb paintings usually use their right hand (Figure 4.10). Jeannine Herron (1976) has argued that left-handers are a discriminated-against minority. Teachers often try to get young children to use their right hands. The French word for left is *gauche*, which in English means clumsy or socially inept, as in "left-handed compliment." There is no scientific basis, Herron argues, for believing that right-handed is better.

About nine out of ten people are right-handed.

HOW PSYCHOLOGISTS STUDY THE BRAIN

Mapping the brain's mountains, canyons, and inner recesses has supplied scientists with fascinating information about the role of the brain in behavior. Psychologists who do this kind of research are called physiological

Figure 4.10
An Egyptian tomb painting showing people at work, using their right hands.

psychologists. Among the methods they use to explore the brain are recording, stimulation, and lesioning.

Recording

By inserting wires called **electrodes** into the brain, it is possible to detect the minute electrical changes that occur when neurons fire (Figure 4.11). The wires are connected to electronic equipment that amplifies the tiny voltages produced by the firing neurons. Even single neurons can be monitored. For example, two researchers placed tiny electrodes in the sections of cats' and monkeys' brains that receive visual information. They found that different neurons fired, depending on whether a line, an edge, or an angle was placed before the animal's eyes (Hubel and Wiesel, 1962).

The electrical activity of whole areas of the brain can be recorded with an **electroencephalograph (EEG).** Wires from the EEG machine are taped to the scalp so that millions upon millions of neurons can be monitored at the same time (Figure 4.12). Psychologists have observed that the overall electrical activity of the brain rises and falls rhythmically and that the

Figure 4.11
This rat has an electrode implanted in an area of its "old" brain. Each time the animal presses the lever, a tiny pulse is delivered to its brain. The extremely high rates of lever-pressing performed by animals with such implants indicate that a "pleasure center" is probably being stimulated by the electricity.

pattern of the rhythm depends on whether a person is awake, drowsy, or asleep (as illustrated in Chapter 7). These rhythms, or brain waves, occur because the neurons in the brain tend to increase or decrease their amount of activity in unison.

EEGs can be used to monitor the brain disorder that causes epilepsy. When an epileptic seizure occurs, abnormal electrical activity begins in a small piece of damaged brain tissue. It then spreads to neighboring areas of the brain. By monitoring brain waves on an EEG, doctors can determine what kind of surgical procedure (if any) would reduce violent seizures. Another test has been developed that measures brain activity by revealing the amount of glucose consumed by neurons in the brain. This technique, called a *positron emission tomography* (*PET*) scan, can be used to locate tumors and seizure activity.

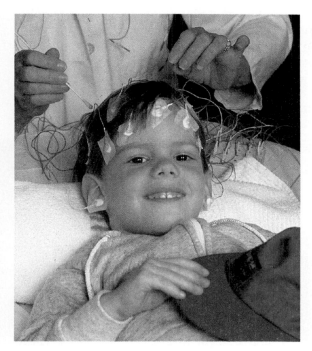

Figure 4.12
Measuring brain waves using an electroencephalograph (EEG) machine.

Stimulation

Electrodes may be used to set off the firing of neurons as well as to record it. Brain surgeon Wilder Penfield stimulated the brains of his patients during surgery to determine what functions the various parts of the brain perform. In this way he could localize the malfunctioning part for which surgery was required, for example, for epilepsy. When Penfield applied a tiny electric current to points on the temporal lobe of the brain, he could trigger whole memory sequences. During surgery, one woman heard a familiar song so clearly that she thought a record was being played in the operating room (Penfield and Rasmussen, 1950).

Using the stimulation technique, other researchers have shown that there are "pleasure" and "punishment" centers in the brain. One research team implanted electrodes in certain areas of the "old brain" of a rat, then placed the rat in a box equipped with a lever that the rat could press. Each time the rat pressed the lever, a mild electrical current was delivered to its brain. When the electrode was placed in the rat's "pleasure" center, it would push the lever several thousand times per hour (Olds and Olds, 1965) (see Figure 4.11).

Scientists have used chemicals as well as electricity to stimulate the brain. In this method, a small tube is implanted in an animal's brain so that the end touches the area to be stimulated (Figure 4.13). Chemicals can then be delivered through the tube to the area of the brain being studied. Such experiments have shown that different chemicals in the hypothalamus can affect hunger and thirst in an animal.

Stimulation techniques have aroused great medical interest. They have been used with terminal cancer patients to relieve them of intolerable pain without using drugs. A current delivered through electrodes implanted in certain areas of the brain seems to provide a sudden temporary relief (Delgado, 1969). Furthermore, some psychiatrists have experimented with similar methods to control violent emotional behavior in otherwise uncontrollable patients.

Figure 4.13
The technique for stimulating the inside of a rat's brain with chemicals. (a) The rat is prepared for brain surgery. (b) A small funnel at the top of a tiny tube is permanently implanted in the rat's skull. The other end of the tube is deep inside the brain. (c) A small amount of some chemical that affects the nervous system is passed into the tube in a solution of water.

a

b

c

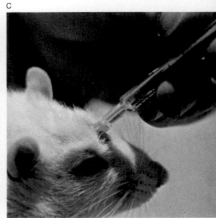

The Courts and Psychosurgery

In 1973, a Michigan court made an important decision which limited psychosurgery.

L.S., a criminal who had been charged with first-degree murder and rape, had been confined to a Michigan mental hospital for eighteen years when he agreed to have brain surgery to try to make him less violent. Legal services lawyer Gabe Kaimowitz brought suit to prevent the operation.

Both L.S. and his parents had given written consent for the operation. But it became clear in court that neither completely understood the implications of the procedure. Furthermore, L.S. suspected that he might be released earlier if he went along with the operation.

The court ruled that the operation should not be done even though L.S. had said he wanted it. Involuntarily confined patients, the court said, simply cannot give legally adequate consent to experimental high-risk procedures like psychosurgery. Thus, the legal status of certain types of psychosurgery is now in doubt.

For more details, see Carol Wade Offir, "The Movement to Pull Out the Electrodes," *Psychology Today,* 7 (May 1974): 69–70.

Lesions

Scientists sometimes create lesions by cutting or destroying part of an animal's brain. If the animal behaves differently after the operation, they assume that the destroyed brain area is involved with that type of behavior. For example, in one classic lesion study, two researchers removed a certain area of the subcortex (or "old brain") from rhesus monkeys. Normally, these animals are aggressive and vicious. After the operation they became less fearful and at the same time less violent (Kluver and Bucy, 1937). The implication was that this area of the brain controlled aggression. Subsequent researchers have learned that the relations revealed by this type of research are far more subtle and complex than people first believed.

USING PSYCHOLOGY

Psychosurgery

We have already discussed the use of lesions in treating violent epileptic seizures (by severing the corpus callosum). Experiments with animals suggested to some researchers that it might be possible to treat certain behavioral problems with similar operations. Brain surgery aimed at changing people's thoughts and actions is called **psychosurgery.**

PSYCHOLOGY UPDATE

Brain Damage: The Role of Glutamate. Strokes or head injuries often cause brain damage. Within several minutes, brain cells begin to die. Since this process happens so quickly, it had been thought that little could be done to prevent permanent brain damage. However, recent research by neuroscientists suggests otherwise. They contend that although brain cells that are directly on the site of the injury die quickly, adjacent cells are damaged and die by a chemical process that occurs hours after the initial event. This chemical process revolves around glutamate—an excitatory chemical in the brain. Usually, only small amounts of glutamate are released and stimulate adjacent neurons. However, a stroke or head injury disrupts the brain's chemical balance and results in large amounts of glutamate being released. A chain reaction of overstimulation begins in cells near the initial injury. These overstimulated cells are damaged and ultimately die. This may be why a brain-injured person's condition continues to worsen for hours after the initial injury. Scientists are currently looking for ways to reduce this flow of glutamate in order to reduce brain damage.

The first great wave of psychosurgery was from about 1935 to 1955. A number of studies had showed that monkeys were less upset by frustration after portions of the frontal lobe of their brains were destroyed. A similar operation, called a prefrontal lobotomy, was tried on about 50,000 mental patients in the United States and Great Britain. These operations often seemed to help people who had serious mental problems. But they also had some undesirable side effects.

After the frontal lobes were destroyed, many patients lost the ability to deal with new information or pursue goals. For example, a woman who was a very innovative cook before her operation had trouble with new recipes afterward. Even more distressing was the fact that when she went out food shopping, she would sometimes get distracted and would forget why she had left the house (Valenstein, 1973: 298). But it is hard to draw a firm conclusion about the overall effects of frontal lobotomies. After reviewing all the available evidence, Elliot Valenstein wrote: "There is certainly no grounds for either the position that all psychosurgery necessarily reduces people to a 'vegetable status' or that it has a high probability of producing miraculous cures. The truth, even if somewhat wishy-washy, lies in between these extreme positions. There is little doubt, however, that many abuses existed" (Valenstein, 1973: 315). But the matter became academic in the mid-1950s because new drugs were introduced that became the treatment of choice in mental hospitals.

Within the last fifteen years, however, new operations have been introduced, and people have become interested in psychosurgery once again. Instead of destroying large portions of the frontal lobes, these operations used sophisticated techniques to destroy very small areas of tissue deep inside the brain. These operations quickly became controversial, particularly when they were used to change people who had a history of violent behavior. (Michael Crichton's best-selling novel *The Terminal Man* gave a fictional account of one such operation that went wrong.) In recent years, psychosurgeons have operated on about 400 people per year in the United States.

Public attention brought psychosurgery into the courts and the political arena. In 1974, Congress appointed the eleven-member National Commission for the Protection of Human Subjects of Biomedical and Behavioral Research to study several controversial areas. In October 1976, they released their report on psychosurgery. At this time, public and scientific opinion was generally opposed to psychosurgery. The commission's conclusions were, in the words of one reporter

(Culliton, 1976), "surprisingly favorable." They did not approve the older technique of frontal lobotomy, but they did say that some of the newer operations seemed to work. For example, an operation called a cingulotomy (destruction of a major subcortical structure) seems to be very helpful for some people who suffer from pain and severe depression.

The complexity of these operations on the brain and the philosophical issues raised by the idea of changing the way people act by changing their brains guarantees that psychosurgery will remain controversial for some time to come.

THE ENDOCRINE SYSTEM

The nervous system is one of two communication systems for sending information to and from the brain. The second is the endocrine system. The **endocrine system** sends chemical messages called **hormones.** The hormones are produced in the endocrine glands and are distributed by the blood and other body fluids. (The names and locations of these glands are shown in Figure 4.14.) The hormone messages are like letters in a postal system. They can circulate throughout the bloodstream, but they can be delivered only to a specific address: the particular organ of the body that they influence. The endocrine glands are also called ductless glands because they release hormones directly into the bloodstream. In contrast, the *duct glands,* or *exocrine glands,* release their contents through small holes, or ducts, onto the surface of the body. Examples of duct glands are sweat glands and tear glands.

Under the direction of the **hypothalamus** in the brain, the **pituitary gland** acts as the "master gland." The pituitary gland secretes a large number of hormones, many of which control the output of hormones by other endocrine glands. The hypothalamus monitors the amount of hormones in the blood and sends out messages to correct imbalances.

What do these hormone messages tell the body to do? They carry messages to organs involved in regulating and storing nutrients so that, despite changes in conditions outside the body, cell metabolism can continue on an even course. They also control growth and reproduction, including ovulation and lactation (milk production) in women.

The **thyroid gland** produces the hormone thyroxin. Thyroxin stimulates certain chemical reactions that are important for all tissues of the body. Too little thyroxin makes people feel lazy and lethargic; too much makes them overactive. The adrenal glands become active when a person is angry or frightened. They release adrenalin into the bloodstream. The adrenalin causes the heartbeat and breathing to increase. These and other changes help a person feel the extra energy he or she needs to handle a difficult situation.

Through the combined action of the nervous and endocrine systems,

Figure 4.14
The endocrine glands.

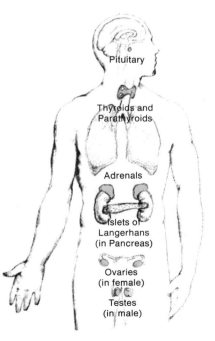

the brain monitors and controls most human behavior. In the next chapter we will see how the endocrine system influences behavior we normally attribute to psychological causes—emotion and motivation.

THE RELATIONSHIP BETWEEN HUMANS AND ANIMALS

Much of the research described in this chapter has been done primarily with lower animals. Researchers often study animals because they cannot perform a risky operation on a human being without a better reason than scientific inquiry. The research that has been done on humans has either occurred as a part of some necessary medical operation or has involved observing people who have suffered an injury by accident.

It is now commonly accepted that the study of animals can help in the study of human beings, even though direct experiments on humans would be even more useful if they could be done. Animal studies are especially valuable in medicine and physiology. Drugs, vaccines, and new forms of surgery are regularly tested on animal subjects. The reason such research is considered useful is that human beings are believed to have evolved from more primitive animal origins, and their bodies are therefore similar to the bodies of other animals.

The Evolution of Behavior

What many people often do not realize is that evolution applies not only to anatomy and physiology but also to behavior. Charles Darwin, the biologist who in 1859 published his theory of evolution, believed that all animal

Figure 4.15
There are many similarities between human behavior and animal behavior. At this penguin gathering, for example, there are penguins in pairs and by themselves. Some are aloof, some are enjoying the sunshine, and some are simply observing the scene.

species are related to one another. Consequently, the structure of their bodies and their behavior patterns can be distinguished and compared just as one may compare a child's nose or his temper to that of his father. The bones in a bird's wing are different but comparable to the bones in a human arm; the way birds flock together can be compared to the way humans gather in groups (Figure 4.15). And just as the parts of a chimpanzee's brain can be compared to a human's, so can a chimpanzee's ability to solve problems be compared to human thinking ability.

Darwin's theory does not mean that humans do not possess unique qualities, but it does make it possible to think of humans as members of a particularly complex, interesting species instead of as totally different from other animals.

Ethology

One of the major outgrowths of Darwin's theory of evolution is **ethology,** the study of the natural behavior patterns of all species of animals from a biological point of view. They attempt to understand how these patterns have evolved and changed, and how they are expressed in humans. Ethologists call these natural patterns **species-specific behaviors,** behaviors that are characteristic of a particular animal species. By observing animals in their natural environment, ethologists hope to discover the links between a species' surroundings and its behaviors.

Ethologists have found that the behavior and experience of more primitive animals (such as insects or fish) are less flexible, or more stereotyped, than the behavior of higher animals, such as apes or humans. Stereotyped behaviors consist of patterns of responses that cannot change readily in response to changes in the environment. They work well only if the environment stays as it was when the behavior pattern evolved.

For example, when a horse is confronted with danger and requires a quiet escape, it is impossible for it to tiptoe away. Its escape behavior consists of only three patterns: walking, trotting, and galloping. Each pattern is a distinct series of movements that vary little from one horse to another, and all normal horses display these patterns. These are called **fixed action patterns** because they are inflexible—an animal can react to certain situations only in these ways.

Fixed action patterns are one kind of **instinct**—a behavior pattern that is inborn rather than learned. People often misuse the word "instinct" to refer to behaviors that become automatic after long practice. A professional baseball player may be described as "instinctively" making the right play, for example. But ethologists use the term "instinct" to refer only to those abilities that seem to be inherited.

Ethologists have found that animals are born with special sensitivities to certain cues in the environment (as well as with special ways of behaving). These cues are called sign stimuli. For example, Niko Tinbergen showed that the male stickleback, a small fish, will attack a model of another stickleback if it has a red belly. Even if the model is distorted, as in Figure 4.16, the male will still attack. Yet if it sees a very lifelike model of a stickleback without a red belly, the male will leave it alone. In this case, the

Figure 4.16
The bright red belly of the male stickleback is a sign stimulus for attack from other sticklebacks. They will attack red-bellied models like the ones below before they will respond to a realistic model of a stickleback that does not have a red belly.

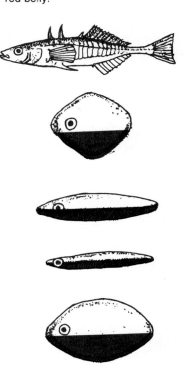

MORE about...

Using Ethology to Study Human Behavior. Human ethology is the study of human behavior as it naturally occurs. Ethologists make comparisons between human and animal behaviors as part of their investigations.

One study investigated whether people crossing the street looked both ways before they crossed. When males and females crossed together, males looked both ways more often than females. Human ethologists see a similarity between this finding and the behavior of monkey and baboon troops living in the wild, whose adult males serve as lookouts. A human ethologist might say that humans have exchanged "cheetahs for Chevrolets" as the focus of their lookout behaviors.

Basketball fans know that Michael Jordan sticks out his tongue when he is attempting a difficult shot. Similarly, it has been found that expert billiard players stick out their tongues more often when making hard shots than when attempting relatively easy shots. According to ethologists, a tongue display acts as a nonverbal signal that interaction is not desired. For humans, the tongue displays seem to indicate that the person does not want to be interrupted because of the need to concentrate in a difficult situation.

sign stimulus that triggers attack is the color red. In other species other sign stimuli can trigger certain behaviors.

Do sign stimuli occur in humans? Although instincts are less common and less powerful in human behavior, there is evidence that some stereotyped behaviors exist. For example, Konrad Lorenz found that a "parental instinct" seems to be aroused by the appearance of the human baby. When he compared human infants to other young animals, he noticed that they all seem to display a similar set of sign stimuli which appear to stir up parental feelings. Short faces, prominent foreheads, round eyes, and plump cheeks all seem to arouse the parental response.

Sociobiology

Closely related to ethology is another new discipline that studies the hereditary basis of social behavior in animals and humans to determine whether these behaviors are inherited from remote ancestors. This science, known as **sociobiology,** draws on the findings of biology, anthropology, and psychology. It has attracted a great deal of attention, and an even greater amount of controversy. In 1975, Harvard zoologist Edward O. Wilson published *Sociobiology: A New Synthesis,* in which he defined the new discipline as "the systematic study of the biological basis of all social behavior" (1975a: 595). Wilson surveyed the social behavior of all known primates and suggested that certain traits humans share with almost all other primates—prolonged maternal care of offspring, for instance, and male dominance over females—may have been passed along to us in our genes.

Sociobiologists regard their discipline as the last phase of the revolution begun by Charles Darwin. It tries to fill a major gap in Darwin's theory of natural selection: nature's goal is individual survival and reproduction, yet several traits of humans and other animals seem to work directly against this goal. Soldier ants will fight to the death, thus contributing to saving their group from invaders. A bird will often call out a warning to other birds that a predator is nearby, though the warning call itself alerts the enemy to that particular bird's whereabouts and risks the bird's life. Dolphins have been known to band together and support a stricken companion on the surface of the water where it can breathe (Wilson, 1975b). And, of course, among humans, parents die rescuing their children from fires, and soldiers throw themselves suicidally on grenades to save their buddies.

Sociobiologists fit all these acts of self-sacrifice into nature's economy. They explain that altruism itself favors genetic gain: the individual risks itself, but the result of this behavior is that other individuals who share its genes may survive (Figure 4.17). The soldier ant, which is sterile, protects its queen, which then lives to produce more of the soldier ant's kind. The bird who calls a warning in effect also protects its kind, and this increases the chance that its genes will survive, as does the behavior of the mother who saves her baby. The battlefield hero dies confident that the nation will keep his family safe to reproduce—and thus to perpetuate his own genes. The noted British biologist J. B. S. Haldane once joked that he would give his life for his two brothers, each of whom shares about half his genes, or for eight cousins (cited in *Time,* August 1, 1977, 56).

Figure 4.17
Sociobiologists explain firefighters risking their lives to save others as yet another aspect of natural selection: the individual risks itself, but the species survives.

Sociobiology seeks to explain other social behaviors, even aggression, in terms of genetic advantage. The bully who kicks sand in the ninety-seven-pound weakling's face is actually sending a message to the weakling's girl friend: "I have good genes. You ought to mate with me."

The idea that genes determine human social behavior has been so controversial that Wilson has been picketed and even had water thrown in his face at the otherwise sedate 1978 meeting of the American Association for the Advancement of Science. Some critics, notably Richard Lewontin, Stephen Gould, and other members of the Harvard-based Sociobiology Study Group, have expressed fear that sociobiology can be used to support the political, economic, and legal status quo. According to the logic of sociobiology, these must have been determined by our genes (reported in Wade, 1976).

Other critics point out that there is no hard evidence that specific genes exist for altruism, aggression, or other social behaviors, but only theories and guesswork (Washburn, 1978). They also point out that animals may behave very selfishly indeed. Among the lions of the Serengeti plain in East Africa, lionesses have been observed driving their own cubs away from food if the catch was small; many of these cubs have died of starvation. Of

Figure 4.18 A baboon troop in the wild. Although many people believe that primate males dominate females, relations between the sexes are actually quite complicated.

1,400 herring gull chicks studied during one period, 23 percent were killed by attacks from adults of their own species as they strayed from the nest (Marler, 1976).

Along the same lines, anthropologists have repeatedly contested the popular belief that human males are innately aggressive and dominant over females. The supporters of this argument often cite studies of baboons that document male aggression and dominance over females. Opponents point out that the baboons observed in these studies were in a game park, an abnormal environment that exposed them to a heavy concentration of predators (especially human ones) and to a high level of tension. Among baboon troops that live undisturbed in the forest, however, it is female baboons who determine the troop's movements. Males exhibit very little aggression and little dominance (Pilbeam, 1972).

If baboon behavior can vary so widely in different environments, it is even more likely that human behavior will do so. Genes may very well be an important component of human social behavior, but they cannot entirely determine it. If the children of two great athletes are never permitted to exercise, their genes will never make them athletes. Indeed, the flexibility of human social behavior, the extreme differences in various cultures and in different contexts, is almost uniquely human (Pilbeam, 1972). Only human beings construct cultures, passing on large and growing accumulations of learning from generation to generation and thereby to a certain extent overcoming the slow process of genetic evolution. Only human beings exhibit a wide variety of culturally determined behaviors, such as wearing black to funerals in some countries and white in others.

The question of the extent to which heredity does determine human social behavior is far from settled. But Wilson and some other sociobiologists believe that humankind is flexible and must be so, and that genetic inclinations need not always be obeyed and sometimes should not be. Evolution takes place so slowly that we may still be inheriting behavior patterns that were adaptive in prehistoric times but that are no longer useful in our radically different world. In the Stone Age it may well have been important to raise as many healthy children as possible; on today's crowded planet it is not. When humans lived in hunter-gatherer societies, it might have been necessary to wage war against all foreigners in order to survive; now war could mean the end of humankind (Wilson, 1975b). The major contribution of sociobiology has been to remind us that genes do count, but that human beings have the capacity to learn a wide range of behaviors and to unlearn those that cease to be adaptive.

HEREDITY AND ENVIRONMENT

People often argue about whether human behavior is instinctive (due to heredity) or learned (due to environment). Do people learn to be good athletes, or are they born that way? Do people learn to do well in school, or are they born good at it? Do people learn to be homosexual, or are they born that way? The reason for the intensity of the argument may be that many people assume that something learned can probably be changed, whereas something inborn will be difficult or impossible to change. This is wrong. Whenever psychologists investigate a particular case, they find that the issue is not that simple. Inherited factors and environmental conditions always act together in complicated ways. Asking whether heredity or environment is responsible for something turns out to be like asking "What makes a cake rise, baking powder or heat?" Obviously, an interaction of the two is responsible.

Inherited factors and environment always act together in complicated ways.

The argument over the nature-nurture question has been going on for centuries. Sir Francis Galton, a cousin of Charles Darwin, was one of the first to preach the importance of nature in the modern era. In 1869 he published *Hereditary Genius*, a book in which he analyzed the families of over 1,000 eminent politicians, religious leaders, artists, and scholars. He found that success ran in the families and concluded that heredity was the cause.

But most psychologists have emphasized the importance of the environment. The tone was set by John Watson, the father of behaviorism, who wrote in 1930: "Give me a dozen healthy infants, well-formed, and my own specified world to bring them up in and I'll guarantee to take any one at random and train him to become any type of specialist I might select—doctor, lawyer, artist, merchant-chief, and, yes, even beggarman and thief, regardless of his talents, penchants, tendencies, abilities, vocations, and race of his ancestors" (Watson, 1930: 104).

Watson's view now seems a bit extreme. Recent studies that directly looked for evidence of genetic influence on human traits have focused on three general areas: cognitive abilities (like IQ), mental illness, and personality. The argument over IQ (see Chapter 12) has been particularly loud and long, but each of the other areas is also controversial.

One way to find out whether a trait is inherited is to study twins. Identical twins develop from a single fertilized egg (thus, they are called monozygotic) and share the same genes. Fraternal twins develop from two fertilized eggs (thus, dizygotic), and their genes are no more similar than those of brothers or sisters.

Figure 4.19
Because identical twins share the same genes as well as the same environment, studying them is one way to find out whether a trait is inherited or learned.

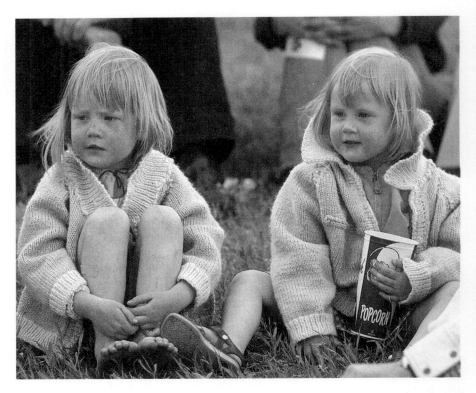

Obviously, twins growing up in the same house share the same general environment. But identical twins who grow up together also share the same genes. So, if identical twins prove to be more alike on a specific trait than fraternal twins do, it probably means that genes are important for that trait.

For example, many twin studies have been done on the inheritance of mental disease. Schizophrenia is the most common form of serious mental illness and affects about 1 percent of the world population (see Chapter 15). Studies have shown that if one twin becomes schizophrenic, the other twin is three to six times more likely to become schizophrenic if he is an identical twin rather than a fraternal twin (Rosenthal, 1970). Thus, schizophrenia is at least partly genetic. However, it is also clear that in many cases, one identical twin develops schizophrenia and the other does not. Thus, environmental factors are also important.

There are several other ways of studying the nature-nurture problem in humans. In a few cases, identical twins have been separated at birth by adoption agencies or whatever. These twins show the effects of the same genes in different environments. Although such cases are relatively rare, they are extremely important from a scientific point of view. It is also possible to see whether adopted children more closely resemble their biological parents (thus suggesting the importance of genes) or their adoptive parents (emphasizing the influence of environment). Although many such studies are going on, the nature-nurture question will probably continue to be controversial, at least until people gain a more sophisticated understanding of how heredity and environment interact to produce behavior.

Psychologists at the University of Minnesota have been studying identical twins who were separated at birth and reared in different environments (Holden, 1980). One of the researchers, Thomas Bouchard, reports that despite very different social, cultural, and economic backgrounds, the twins shared many common behaviors. For example, in one set of twins (both named Jim), both had done well in math and poorly in spelling while in school, both worked as deputy sheriffs, vacationed in Florida, gave identical names to their children and pets, bit their fingernails, had identical smoking and drinking patterns, and liked mechanical drawing and carpentry. These similarities and others suggest that heredity may contribute to behaviors that we normally associate with experience.

Many researchers now believe that many of the differences among people can be explained by considering heredity as well as experience. Contrary to popular belief, the influence of genes on behavior does not mean that nothing can be done to change the behavior. Although it is true that it is difficult and undesirable to change the genetic code that may direct behavior, it is possible to alter the environment in which the genes operate. The genetic disorder phenylketonuria (PKU) is a case in point. PKU is a single gene defect which, if undetected and untreated, results in severe mental retardation. A simple blood test at birth (Figure 4.20) can reveal the presence of PKU, which afflicts about 1 in 20,000 whites (it is rare among blacks). Afflicted infants can be placed on a special diet until the brain develops and is no longer in danger. Thus, although PKU is inherited, its effects can be changed by controlling the environment.

Figure 4.20
The test for PKU, a simple prick on the heel, is now given automatically to all newborns, since early detection can prevent the ravages of this congenital disease.

SUMMARY

Use the following outline as a tool for reviewing this chapter. Copy the outline onto your own paper, leaving spaces between headings to make notes about key concepts.

I. The Nervous System

   A. How the Nervous System Works

   B. The Hemispheres of the Brain

II. How Psychologists Study the Brain

   A. Recording

   B. Stimulation

   C. Lesions

III. The Endocrine System

IV. The Relationship Between Humans and Animals

   A. The Evolution of Behavior

   B. Ethology

   C. Sociobiology

V. Heredity and Environment

CONCEPTS AND VOCABULARY

1. Explain how messages travel to and from the brain through the nervous system. What are the neurotransmitters?

2. What are the two types of nervous systems? Which system does the spinal cord belong to?

3. What activities does the somatic nervous system control?

4. What are the two parts of the autonomic nervous system? Which part uses up the energy in the body?

5. What is the part of the cortex that receives information?

6. What functions does the subcortex control?

7. What two parts of the lower brain work to filter out all but the most important messages before they reach the cerebral cortex? How do parts of the brain process such a large amount of information?

8. What is one of the main functions of the cerebellum?

9. What are the four lobes of the cerebral cortex? What is the main function of each?

10. The cortex of the brain is divided into the left and the right hemispheres. Which side of the body does each hemisphere control? What kinds of tasks does each hemisphere control in right-handed people? What is the function of the corpus callosum?

11. What are the three methods used to study the brain?

12. What is the name of the chemical system of communication between the body and the brain? How are the messages of this system transmitted? Which gland is the center of control for this system? What other gland helps in regulating general bodily activity?

13. What is the study of the natural behavior patterns of animals from a biological point of view?

14. How do ethologists use the term *instinct?*

15. What is the name of the science that studies the hereditary basis of social behavior? What is the major contribution of this science?

16. One way to find out whether a trait is inherited is to compare the behavior of identical and fraternal twins. Explain how this works.

CRITICAL THINKING

1. **Synthesize.** Suppose a person suffers a stroke which causes damage to the frontal lobes. What aspects of the person's behavior would you expect to see change? What if the damage oc-

curred in the occipital lobe instead? What problems would you expect the person to experience?

2. **Evaluate.** What aspects of your personality, your way of acting, and your appearance are most obviously the result of heredity? Which seem to be more related to your environmental upbringing? What factors make it difficult to decide whether hereditary or environmental factors are of greatest influence?

APPLYING KNOWLEDGE

1. Ask several of your friends (individually) to perform some mental task, such as multiplying 31 by 24 in their heads, or counting the number of letters in a simple phrase (such as "early to bed"). Observe which way their eyes shift as they begin to think about the problem. If their eyes shift to the right, which hemisphere is being used to do the counting? Which hemisphere is doing the counting if their eyes shift to the left?

2. Observe species-specific behaviors in cats, dogs, or any other animals you see regularly. If you have an animal that you can observe carefully, try to identify fixed action patterns that are common to the animal's species. Do they exist in any form in yourself?

ANALYZING VIEWPOINTS

1. Within the field of psychology, there is a debate about the role that heredity plays in determining behavior as compared to the role of the environment. Some psychologists argue that behavior is genetically predetermined. For example, they believe that great athletes are born with the talent and drive to succeed. On the other hand, some psychologists believe that behavior is determined more by environmental factors. These psychologists argue that someone born with average athletic abilities could be developed into a great athlete with the proper exercise and coaching. Write an essay supporting each side of the issue. Use what you learned in the chapter about the contributions of heredity and environment to human behavior. You may also want to read magazine articles or biographies of athletes to gather more information.

2. Much of what we know about the brain and its functioning has come from studies performed on animals. In recent years, however, animal rights groups have begun to protest the use of animals in experiments, citing the inhumane treatment of animals used in laboratory experiments. List the pros and cons of using animals for psychological research. Read recent magazine and newspaper articles for more information on the topic.

BEYOND THE CLASSROOM

1. Choose the family of a friend or neighbor that you know well. Ask the family for permission to study and report on the family members before you begin this project. Spend several hours visiting with the family. Carefully observe the personalities and behaviors of the parents and different siblings. Try to identify the dominant traits and characteristics of each family member. What is each family member's personality? Do family members have similar personalities, or is one person easygoing and another nervous and tense? Are there vast differences in personality between the oldest and the youngest child? What does each family member do better than most people? Is there a special ability, such as musical talent, that all family members share? Which of the traits and characteristics you identified are due to heredity? Which do you think are due to environmental factors? What evidence did you find of the interaction of heredity and the environment in determining personality and behavior? Report to the class on your findings.

CHAPTER 5

Sensation and Perception

Key Terms:

absolute threshold
auditory nerve
binocular fusion
color blindness
cones
constancy
decibel
difference threshold
extrasensory perception (ESP)
Gestalt
illusions
kinesthesis
lens
motion parallax
olfactory nerve
optic nerve
parapsychology
pitch
psychophysics
pupil
referred pain
retina
retinal disparity
rods
signal-detection theory
stereopsis
subliminal advertising
vestibular system
Weber's law

In the next few seconds, something peculiar will start hap pening to the material youa rereading. Iti soft ennotre alized howcom plext heproces sofrea ding is. Afe w sim plerear range mentscan ha veyoucomp lete lycon fused!

As you can see, your success in gathering information from your environment, interpreting this information, and acting on it depends considerably on its being organized in ways you expect.

Your knowledge of the external world—and of your internal state as well—comes entirely from chemical and electrical processes occurring in the nervous system, particularly in the brain. Physical change in the external or internal environment triggers chemical, electrical, and mechanical activity in sense receptors. After complex processing in the nervous system, a pattern of activity is produced in certain areas of the brain. You experience this electrical activity as a sensation—awareness of colors, forms, sounds, smells, tastes, and so on. Usually you experience some meaningful whole—you see Groucho Marx, hear Paul McCartney's voice, smell an old, dirty sock—rather than a collection of sensations. The organization of sensory information into meaningful wholes is knows as perception.

This process can be seen in the act of eating. When someone puts two hamburgers in front of you, receptors in your eyes send a message to the brain: the all-beef patties are stacked together in the sesame seed bun, along with some lettuce. Receptors in your nose may tell you there's ketchup and cheese inside, while other receptors in your mouth send messages about pickles and some mysterious sauce. As you grasp this gourmet delight in your hands, receptors in your fingers tell you that the roll is soft and warm. And the brain combines all these inputs into one unified perception: it's a Big Mac.

Objectives:

After studying this chapter, you should be able to

- describe the field of study known as psychophysics.
- define the concepts of threshold, Weber's Law, and signal detection.
- describe the nature and functioning of the sense organs.
- outline the principles involved in perception.

Figure 5.1 We "take in" information through our senses. Through sight, sound, touch, and smell we perceive the world around us.

Avoiding Motion Sickness.
One sensation you may be familiar with is "motion sickness." This condition occurs when a person's body is in motion and the inner ear becomes overstimulated or confused. Here are some things you can do to avoid motion sickness:

When you are flying try to position yourself where there is the least movement. Airline passengers sitting next to the wings have the smoothest ride. Recline your seat if possible. Avoid large meals, but try to take frequent small amounts of fluids and simple foods.

If you are riding in a car, avoid reading. You are less likely to get sick if you watch the ground or the horizon. The visual input helps you maintain equilibrium. One reason that small children are especially prone to motionsickness is that they cannot see out of the car and so they lose visual contact with their environment.

In this chapter we will look at each of these steps more closely, focusing on how each organ converts physical changes into chemical-electrical signals to the brain and how perceptions are built from this information. In the last section we will discuss the possibility of gaining information without the known senses—through the process of extrasensory perception.

SENSATION

The world is filled with physical changes–an alarm clock sounds; the flip of a switch fills a room with light; you stumble against a door; steam from a hot tub billows out into the bathroom, changing the temperature and clouding the mirror. All these changes result in sensations–of loudness, brightness, pain in the elbow you bump, heat, tastes, smells, and so on. Any aspect of or change in the environment to which an organism responds is called a stimulus. An alarm, an electric light, and an aching muscle are all stimuli for human beings.

A stimulus can be measured in some physical way—by its size, its duration, its intensity, its wavelength, and so on. A sensory experience can also be measured (at least, indirectly). But a sensory experience and a stimulus are not the same. For example, the same English muffin (stimulus) might taste (sensory experience) one way if you had just eaten and quite a different way if you hadn't eaten anything for a week. On the other hand, the same sensory experience (flashing lights, for example) might be produced by different stimuli (a blow to the head or a fireworks display).

Psychologists are interested in the relationship between physical stimuli and sensory experiences. In vision, for example, the sensation of color corresponds to the wavelength of the light, whereas brightness corresponds to the intensity of this stimulus.

What is the relationship between color and wavelength? How does changing a light's intensity affect one's sensation of its brightness? The psychological study of such questions is called **psychophysics.** The goal of psychophysics is to develop a quantified relationship between stimuli from the world (such as frequency and intensity) and the sensory experiences (such as pitch and loudness) produced by them.

Threshold

In order to establish laws about how people sense the external world, psychologists first try to determine how much of a stimulus is necessary for a person to sense it at all. How much energy is required for someone to hear a sound or to see a light? How much of a scent must be in the room before one can smell it? How much pressure must be applied to the skin before a person will feel it?

To answer such questions, a psychologist might set up the following experiment. First, a person (the subject) is placed in a dark room and is instructed to look at the wall. He is asked to say "I see it" when he is able to detect a light. The psychologist then uses an extremely precise machine that can project a low-intensity beam of light against the wall. The experimenter turns on the machine to its lowest light projection. The subject says nothing. The experimenter increases the light until finally the subject responds, "I see it." Then the experimenter begins another test in the opposite direction. He starts with a clearly visible light and decreases its intensity until the light seems to disappear. Many trials are completed and averaged. The **absolute threshold**—the smallest amount of energy that will produce a sensation—is defined as the amount of energy that a subject can see about half the time.

Interestingly enough, thresholds determined in this way are not as absolute as psychologists first believed. The point at which the person says "I see it" may vary with the instructions he is given ("Say you see it only if you're absolutely certain" versus "If there's any doubt, say you see it") or even the order in which the stimuli are presented.

Under ideal conditions, the senses have very low absolute thresholds. That is, sensations will be experienced with very small amounts of stimulation. For example, the eardrum registers a sound if it moves as little as 1 percent of the diameter of a hydrogen molecule. If the ear were any more sensitive, you might hear the sound of air molecules bumping into each other (Geldard, 1972). Similarly, the eye is about as sensitive as it could possibly be.

If the ear were any more sensitive, you might hear the sound of air molecules bumping into each other.

USING PSYCHOLOGY

Subliminal Advertising

On September 12, 1957, an advertising executive held a press conference to announce a revolutionary breakthrough in marketing techniques: **subliminal advertising.** The word "subliminal" comes from the Latin: *sub* ("below") and *limen* ("threshold"). The words "Eat Popcorn" and "Coca-Cola" had been flashed on a movie screen in a New Jersey theater on alternate nights for six weeks, according to the executive. Although the flashes were so brief (1/3,000 of a second, once every five seconds) that none of the moviegoers even seemed to notice them, popcorn sales rose 18.1 percent and Coca-Cola sales went up 57.7 percent.

The public response to this announcement was long, loud, and hysterical. In a TV interview, Aldous Huxley predicted that it would be possible to manipulate people politically with this technique "by about 1964" (quoted in Brown, 1963: 184). Congressmen called for FCC regulations, while several state legislatures passed laws banning subliminal ads.

Meanwhile, more test results began to appear. When the man who made the original claims staged another test for the FCC a few months later, the results were equivocal. Later, WTWO-TV in Bangor, Maine, flashed the words "If you have seen this message, write WTWO" on the screen for 1/60 of a second every day for a week. Nobody wrote. A Seattle radio station experimented with auditory subliminal ads. During regular programming, a very low whisper in the background repeated "TV's a bore" and "Isn't TV dull?" (These experimenters had planned to add the message "TV causes eye cancer," but decided they'd better not risk it.) There is no reason to believe that these ads had any effect.

British television got into the act by flashing the message "Pirie breaks world record" during a ballet program. At the end of the show, an announcer asked the 4.5 million viewers to write to the station if they had noticed anything unusual. Four hundred thirty replies were received; 20 of them repeated the message verbatim and another 134 were close to being right.

The idea for subliminal ads was a natural outgrowth of a long series of controversial studies on *subliminal perception*—the ability to notice stimuli that affect only the unconscious mind. Most of these earlier studies involved presenting verbal or visual material at intensities that were considered too low for people to perceive. However, a more critical look at the studies revealed several flaws in the way they were designed and carried out. For example, the original New Jersey study was done by nonpsychologists working for the Subliminal Projection Company. No attempt was made to assess or control factors other than the subliminal message that might have influenced the purchase of Coke or popcorn. The temperature in the theater or the length of the movie might have contributed to the increase in sales. Unfortunately, the study was not presented in enough detail to be evaluated by scientists.

Even if it is possible for people to perceive information at very low levels of intensity, there is not much evidence that these weak, often limited, messages would be more powerful than conscious messages in influencing people. The idea may be appealing to some advertising executives looking for a way to increase sales. There is a growing consensus among psychologists who have done controlled studies, however, that subliminal advertising does not work.

Sensory Differences and Ratios

Another type of threshold is the **difference threshold** or just noticeable difference. This refers to the smallest change in a stimulus that will produce a change in sensation. So to return to our example of the person tested in a dark room, a psychologist would test for the difference threshold by gradually increasing the intensity of a visible light beam until the person says, "Yes, this is brighter than the light I just saw." With this technique, it is possible to identify the smallest increase in light intensity that will be noticeable to the human eye.

Psychologists also have found that a particular sensory experience depends more on *changes* in the stimulus than on the absolute size or amount of the stimulus. For example, if you put a three-pound package of food into an empty backpack, the sensation of weight will be greatly increased. But if you add the same amount to a hundred-pound backpack, the sensation will hardly increase at all. This is because the sensation produced by the added weight reflects a proportional change—and three pounds does not provide much change in a one-hundred-pound load.

In psychophysics, this idea is known as **Weber's law:** the larger or stronger a stimulus, the larger the change required for an observer to notice that anything has happened to it (to experience a just noticeable difference) (Weber, 1834).

The amount of stimulus change necessary to produce some increase in sensory experience is different for different cases, but it is almost always proportional. Suppose, for example, that you have a glass of unsweetened lemonade. In order to make it sweet, you add two spoonfuls of sugar. Now to make the lemonade taste "twice as sweet," you must add six spoonfuls—three times the original amount of sugar. Then you discover that in order to make the lemonade "four times as sweet," you must add a total of eighteen spoonfuls (Figure 5.2). Each time the sweetness doubles, the amount of sugar triples (see Stevens, 1962).

Figure 5.2
A change in sensory experience is proportional to the amount of physical change. In this case, each time the amount of sugar triples, the sweetness of the lemonade doubles.

PSYCHOLOGY UPDATE

Seeing in the Dark. Certain workers, such as radar operators, sometimes need to keep their eyes adapted to darkness, even when they take a rest break in a well-lit room. They can do this by wearing goggles that admit only red light. The red goggles work because, as described in the text, the eye has two kinds of receptor cells, called rods and cones. It is the cones that allow us to see colors. Since the red light admitted by the goggles stimulates only the cones, the adaptation level of the rods is not affected. It is, in fact, as if the rods were still in darkness.

When the worker returns to a dim room and removes the goggles, the rods will be highly sensitive and night vision will be good. Though the cones are now light-adapted, they will not interfere with vision unless the perception of color becomes especially important.

Phantom Limb Pain

Every night Andy woke covered in a cold, soaking sweat. The pain that filled his left hand was more than he could bear. It felt like a razor-sharp scalpel was being jabbed deeper and deeper into the palm of his hand. No one had prepared him for this pain—not even the doctors who had amputated his left hand two years before.

The *phantom limb pain* we've just described is one of the most bizarre phenomenons in medicine. It may take the form of tingling feelings, warmth, coldness, heaviness, or intense pain in a limb that is no longer there.

About one-third of all amputees report phantom limb pain, which in most cases continues for about a year. But as doctors and some unfortunate amputees know, pain may last for decades.

Evidence suggests that phantom limb pain has no single cause. Irritation of the stump, abnormal sympathetic nervous system activity, and emotional disturbance may all play a role. But no one is sure exactly how these factors contribute to the pain or how to rid an amputee of the agony he feels in a limb that is no longer there.

For more details, see Ronald Melzack, *The Puzzle of Pain;* New York: Basic Books, 1973.

By experimenting in this way with variations in sounds, temperatures, pressures, colors, tastes, and smells, psychologists are learning more about how each sense responds to stimulation. Some senses produce huge increases in sensation in response to small increases in energy. For example, the pain of an electric shock can be increased more than eight times by doubling the voltage. On the other hand, the intensity of a light must be increased many times to double its brightness.

Sensory Adaptation

Psychologists have focused on people's responses to changes in stimuli because they have found that the senses are tuned to change: they are most responsive to increases and decreases, to new events rather than to ongoing, unchanging stimulation. This is because our senses have a general ability to adapt, or adjust themselves, to a constant level of stimulation. They get used to a new level and respond only to changes away from it.

A good example of this process of adaptation is the increase in visual sensitivity that you experience after a short time in a darkened movie theater. At first you see only blackness, but after a while your eyes adapt to the new level, and you can see seats, faces, and so on. Adaptation occurs for the other senses as well. Receptors in your skin adapt to the cold water when you go for a swim; disagreeable odors in a lab seem to disappear after a while; street noises cease to bother you after you've lived in a city for a time. Without sensory adaptation, you would feel the constant pressure of the clothes on your body, and other stimuli would seem to be bombarding all your senses at the same time.

Motivation and Signal-Detection Theory

Sensory experience does not depend on stimulus alone, however. A person's ability to detect a stimulus also depends on motivation. The individual does not simply receive a signal passively. Rather, the individual's perceptual system makes a decision as to its presence, though the decision-making process is usually entirely unconscious.

Thus the nervous new radar operator may see blips on his screen when there are none while the overrelaxed veteran may not notice the unexpected. To use a more complex example, if you've been thinking a lot about your old boy friend, you may think you see him walking down the street when it's really somebody else. On the other hand, you probably wouldn't expect to meet your piano teacher at a football game, and you might not notice him if he showed up there. Thus, feelings, expectations, and motivation influence whether or not you experience a sensation.

Signal-detection theory studies the mathematical relations between motivation, sensitivity, and sensation (Green and Swets, 1966). Detection thresholds involve recognizing some stimulus against a background of noise. A radar operator must be able to detect an airplane on a radar screen even when the plane's blip is faint and difficult to distinguish from blips

Figure 5.3
Air controllers must be able to detect an airplane on the radar screen even when the plane's blip is faint and difficult to distinguish from blips caused by natural phenomena such as flocks of birds or bad weather.

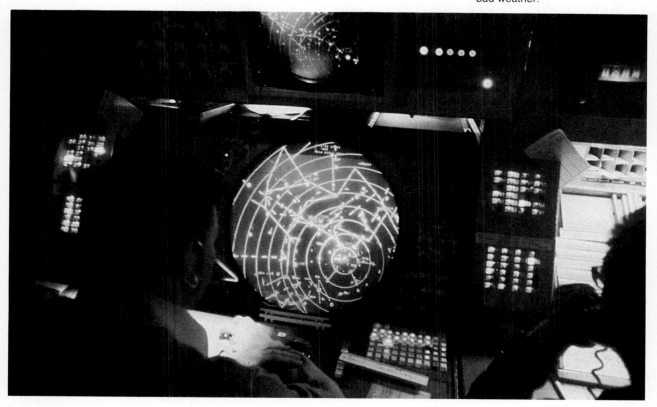

caused by flocks of birds or bad weather, which can produce images that are like visual "noise" (Figure 5.3). Consider radar operators watching a screen in wartime during a storm. How do they decide whether a blip on the screen is an enemy plane or a patch of noise? If they were to call out massive armed forces for every blip, they would create chaos. But if one bomber was mistakenly identified as noise, the results could be disastrous. The radar operator's judgment will be influenced by many factors, and different operators appear to have different sensitivities to blips. Moreover, a specific individual's apparent sensitivity seems to fluctuate, depending on the situation. For example, being watched by a superior will probably affect the operator's performance, as will fatigue or other distractions.

In studying the difficulties faced by radar operators, psychologists have reformulated the concept of absolute threshold to take into account the many factors that affect detection of minimal stimuli. As a result, the signal-detection theory abandons the idea that there is a single true absolute threshold for a stimulus. Instead it adopts the notion that the stimulus, here called a signal, must be detected in the face of noise, which can interfere with detection of the signal. Thus signal detection is similar to standing in a noisy bus terminal, listening for the announcement of your bus departure time over the loudspeaker. Although the volume of the loudspeaker remains constant, you will have more or less difficulty in detecting your "signal," depending on the amount of noise in the bus terminal.

THE SENSES

Although people are thought to have five senses, there are actually more. In addition to vision, hearing, taste, smell, and touch, there are several skin senses and two "internal" senses: *vestibular* and *kinesthetic*.

Each type of sensory receptor takes some sort of external stimulus—light, chemical molecules, sound waves, pressure—and converts it into a chemical-electrical message that can be understood by the brain. So far we know most about these processes in vision and hearing. The other senses have received less attention and are more mysterious in their functioning.

Figure 5.4
The process of vision. (a) A cross-section of the human eye, showing the passage of light. Note that the retina receives an inverted image of the external world, although people are never aware of this inversion. The place where the optic nerve leaves the eye is called the blind spot because it is the only spot on the retina where no sensation takes place. (b) The cell structure of the retina. Note that the light-sensitive cells (the rods and cones) are those furthest from the light, not the closest as one might expect. Light arriving at the retina must pass through various other cells before striking the rods and cones, which convert it into nervous impulses. The impulses then pass through these other cells to be coded and organized before traveling over the optic nerve to the brain.

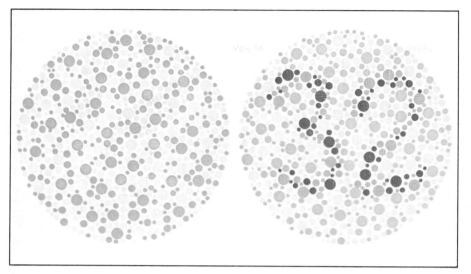

Figure 5.5
A test for color blindness. You should be able to see numerals in the dot patterns that make up these two figures. If you cannot distinguish the numerals in the circle on the left, you may be yellow-blue color-blind. If you cannot see those on the right, you may be red-green color-blind. Color-blind people use brightness differences to distinguish objects that most other people distinguish by color. In this test the dots are carefully equated for brightness, so the only way to see the numerals is to see the color differences. Due to the limitations of color printing, the illustration here may not pick up all cases of color blindness. (The Dvorine Pseudo-Isochromatic Plates.)

Vision

Vision is the most studied of all the senses, reflecting the high importance we place on our sense of sight. Vision provides a great deal of information about one's environment and the objects in it—the sizes, shapes, and locations of things, and their textures, colors, and distances.

How does vision occur? Light enters the eye through the **pupil** (see Figure 5.4a) and reaches the **lens,** a flexible structure that focuses light on the **retina**. The retina contains two types of light-sensitive receptor cells: **rods** and **cones** (see Figure 5.4b). These cells are responsible for changing light energy into chemical and electrical impulses, which then travel over the **optic nerve** to the brain.

Cones require more light than rods before they begin to respond; they work best in daylight. Rods are sensitive to much lower levels of light than cones and are particularly useful in night vision. There are many more rods (75 to 150 million) than there are cones (6 to 7 million), but only cones are sensitive to color. Rods and cones can be compared to black-and-white and color film. Color film takes more light and thus works best in daylight; sensitive black-and-white film works not only in bright light but in shadows, dim light, and other poor lighting conditions.

Color Blindness.   When some or all of a person's cones do not function properly, he or she is said to be **color-blind.** There are several kinds of color blindness; most color-blind people do see *some* colors (Figure 5.5). For example, some people have trouble distinguishing between red and green. Other people are able to see red and green but cannot distinguish between yellow and blue. A very few people are totally color-blind. They depend on their rods, so to them the world looks something like black-and-white television programs—nothing but blacks and whites and shades of gray.

Color blindness affects about 8 percent of American men and less than 1 percent of American women. It is believed to result from a hereditary defect in the cones. This defect is carried in the genes of women whose vision is usually normal. These women pass the color-blindness genes on to their sons, who are born color-blind (see Wald, 1964).

Figure 5.6
To experience stereoscopic depth perception, take a tall, thin piece of cardboard and place it perpendicular to the page on the line that marks the separation of the two pictures. Then, with the edge of the cardboard resting between your eyes (as shown in the drawing), look at the left photo with your left eye and the right photo with your right eye and try to let the two images come together as one. (It helps to concentrate on the white dot.) If you are successful in fusing the images, the scene will suddenly jump out in depth. This process of binocular fusion contributes continuously to your ability to perceive depth.

Binocular Fusion and Stereopsis. Because we have two eyes, located about 2.5 inches apart, the visual system receives two images. But instead of seeing double, we see a single image, probably a composite of the views of two eyes. The combination of the two images into one is called **binocular fusion.**

Not only does the visual system receive two images, but there is a difference between the images on the retinas. This difference is called **retinal disparity.** You can easily observe retinal disparity by bringing an object such as an eraser close to your eyes. Without moving it, look at the eraser first with one eye, then with the other. You will see a difference in the two images because of the different viewpoint each eye has. When you open both eyes you will no longer see the difference, but will instead see the object as solid and three-dimensional, if you have good binocular vision. **Stereopsis** refers to the phenomenon of seeing depth as a result of retinal disparity (Figure 5.6).

Figure 5.7
The hearing process. Sound vibrations in the air strike the eardrum and set in motion a chain of three bones—the malleus (hammer), the incus (anvil), and the stapes (stirrup). The stapes strikes another drum on the cochlea—a long, coiled, fluid-filled tube with a skin-like membrane running down the middle of it. The vibrations on this membrane stimulate hair-like cells that in turn stimulate the adjacent sensory nerve cells. The snail-like cochlea in this picture is also shown in cross section, with wavy pink lines representing the electrical impulses that will travel to the brain.

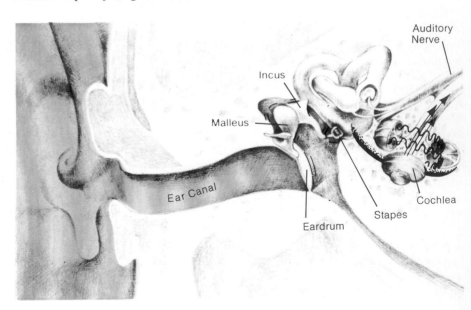

Hearing

Hearing depends on vibrations of the air, called sound waves. Sound waves from the air pass through various bones and fluids (shown in Figure 5.7) until they reach the inner ear, which contains tiny hairlike cells that move back and forth (much like a field of wheat waving in the wind). These hair cells change sound vibrations into chemical-electrical signals that travel through the **auditory nerve** to the brain.

The sensation of loudness depends on the strength of the vibrations in the air. This strength, or energy, is measured in **decibels.** The sounds we hear range upward from zero decibels, the softest sound the human ear can detect, to about 140 decibels, which is roughly as loud as a jet plane taking off. Any sound over 110 decibels can damage hearing, and any sound that is painful when you first hear it *will* damage your hearing if you hear it often enough. Figure 5.8 lists the decibel levels of some common sounds.

Pitch depends on sound frequency, or the rate of the vibration of the medium through which the sound is transmitted. Frequencies range from low to high: low frequencies produce deep bass sounds; high frequencies produce shrill squeaks. If you hear a sound composed of a combination of different frequencies, you can hear the separate pitches even though they occur simultaneously. For example, if you strike two keys of a piano at the same time, your ear can detect two distinct pitches.

Sounds are located through the interaction of the two ears. When a noise occurs on your right, for example, the sound comes to both ears, but it reaches your right ear a fraction of a second before it reaches the left. It is also slightly louder in the right ear. These differences often tell you which direction it is coming from.

Smell and Taste

Smell and taste are known as the chemical senses because their receptors are sensitive to chemical molecules rather than to light energy or sound waves. For you to smell something, the smell receptors in your nose must come into contact with the appropriate molecules. These molecules enter your nose in vapors, which reach a special membrane in the nasal passages on which the smell receptors are located. These receptors send messages about smells over the **olfactory nerve** to the brain.

For you to taste something, appropriate chemicals must stimulate receptors in the taste buds on your tongue. Taste information is relayed to the brain along with data about the texture and temperature of the substance you have put in your mouth.

Some scientists have proposed that all smells are made up of six qualities: flowery, fruity, spicy, resinous, putrid, and burned (Henning, 1916). Other scientists have come up with a similar scheme for taste, which they say is composed of four primary qualities, shown in Figure 5.9: sour, salty, bitter, and sweet (Beebe-Center, 1949).

Much of what is referred to as taste is actually produced by the sense of smell, however. You have undoubtedly noticed that when your nose is blocked by a cold, foods usually taste bland.

Figure 5.8
The decibel ratings for various common sounds. Sound actually becomes painful at about 130 decibels. Decibels represent ratios: A 20-decibel difference between two sounds indicates that one sound is ten times more intense than the other. Thus a vacuum cleaner puts ten times as much pressure on your eardrums as conversation does.

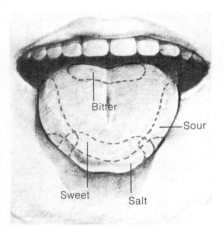

Figure 5.9
A map of the human tongue, indicating the areas that seem more sensitive to one kind of stimulation than to others. Interestingly, it is possible to be taste-blind as well as color-blind: A chemical called phenylthiocarbamide (PTC) tastes extremely bitter to some people and is quite tasteless to others.

Sex and Smell

Many animals communicate by means of odors, as any dog owner whose pet has gone into heat knows. Is it possible that people too communicate by scents? No one knows for sure, but there have been some fascinating studies suggesting that this may be the case.

Martha McClintock tested the "old wives' tale" that women's menstrual cycles synchronize when they live together. She found that the menstrual cycles of college roommates and friends did indeed become more similar as the school year progressed. She believed that pheromones—scented chemical messengers—were the cause.

Richard Michael has shown that female rhesus monkeys secrete certain substances that seem to make them more sexually attractive. In 1974, he reported that human females secrete the same chemical. But so far, no one has been able to prove that the odor increases human sexual desire.

For more details, see James Hassett, "Sex and Smell," *Psychology Today,* 11 (March 1978), pp. 40–45.

Sensations of warmth, cold, and pressure also affect taste. Try to imagine eating cold chicken soup or drinking a hot Pepsi, and you will realize how important temperature is to the sense of taste. Now imagine the textural differences between a spoonful of pudding and a crunchy chocolate bar, and you will see how the texture of food also influences taste.

The chemical senses seem to play a relatively unimportant role in human life when compared to their functions in lower animals. Insects, for example, often depend on smell to communicate with one another, especially in mating. In humans, smell and taste have become more a matter of esthetics than of survival (see box).

The Skin Senses

Receptors in the skin are responsible for providing the brain with at least four kinds of information about the environment: pressure, warmth, cold, and pain.

Sensitivity to pressure varies from place to place in the skin. Some spots, such as your fingertips, are densely populated with receptors and are, therefore, highly sensitive. Other spots, such as the middle of your back, contain relatively few receptors. Pressure sensations can serve as protection. For example, feeling the light pressure of an insect landing on your arm warns you of the danger of being stung.

Some skin receptors are particularly sensitive to hot or cold stimuli. In order to create a hot or cold sensation, a stimulus must have a temperature greater or less than the temperature of the skin. If you plunge your arm into a sink of warm water on a hot day, you will experience little or no sensation of its heat. If you put your arm in the same water on a cold day, however, the water will feel quite warm.

Many kinds of stimuli—scratches, punctures, severe pressure, heat, and cold—can produce pain. Their common property is real or potential injury to bodily tissues. Pain makes it possible for you to prevent damage to your body—it is an emergency system that demands immediate action.

Because pain acts as a warning system for your body, it does not easily adapt to stimulation—you rarely get "used to" pain. Pain tells you to avoid a stimulation that is harmful to you. Without this mechanism, you might "adapt" to a fire when you stand next to it. After a few minutes you would literally begin to cook, and your tissues would die.

Balance

The body's sense of balance is regulated by the **vestibular system** inside the inner ear. Its prominent feature is the three semicircular canals, as shown in Figure 5.10. When your head starts turning, the movement causes the liquid in the canals to move, bending the endings of receptor hair cells. The cells connect with the vestibular nerve, which joins the auditory nerve with the brain.

The stimuli for vestibular responses include movements such as spinning, falling, and tilting the body or head. Overstimulation of the vestibular sense by such movements can result in dizziness and "motion sickness," as you probably have experienced by going on amusement-park rides or by spinning around on a swivel stool. Although you are seldom directly aware of your sense of balance, without it you would be unable to stand or walk without falling or stumbling.

Body Sensations

Kinesthesis is the sense of movement and body position. It cooperates with the vestibular and visual senses to maintain posture and balance. The sensation of kinesthesis comes from receptors in and near the muscles, tendons, and joints. When any movement occurs, these receptors immediately send messages to the brain.

Without kinesthetic sensations, your movements would be jerky and uncoordinated. You would not know what your hand was doing if it were behind your back, and you could not walk without looking at your feet. Furthermore, complex physical activities, such as surgery, piano playing, and acrobatics, would be impossible.

Another type of bodily sensation comes from receptors that monitor internal body conditions. These receptors are sensitive to pressure, temperature, pain, and chemicals inside the body. For example, a full stomach stretching these internal receptors informs the brain that the stomach has ingested too much.

Little is known about pain from the interior of the body except that it seems to be deep, dull, and much more unpleasant than the sharply localized pain from the skin. In some cases, internal pain receptors may send inaccurate messages. They may indicate, for example, that a pain is located in the shoulder when in reality the source of irritation is in the lower stomach. Such sensation of pain in an area away from the actual source is called **referred pain.**

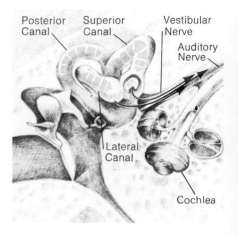

Figure 5.10
The vestibular system. The organs of balance consist of three semicircular canals at right angles to one another, filled with a freely moving fluid. Continuous motion in a straight line produces no response in this system, but starting, stopping, turning, speeding up, or slowing down makes the fluid in at least one of the canals move, stimulating the hair cells attached to the canal walls. These hair cells convert the movement into electrical impulses that are sent to the brain via the auditory nerve.

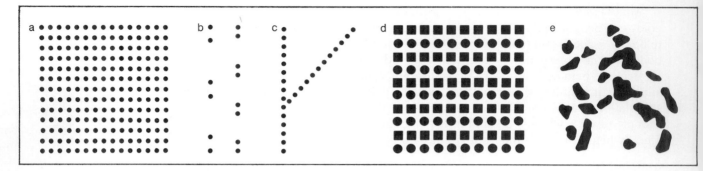

Figure 5.11
Principles of perceptual organization. Human beings see patterns and groupings in their environments rather than disorganized arrays of bits and pieces. For example, it is impossible to look at the array of dots in (a) without seeing shifting patterns of squares and lines. In (b), elements that are close to one another seem to belong together. However, as (c) shows, continuity can be more important: Although the bottom dot in the inclined series is closer to the vertical series, it is not seen as belonging to the vertical row. It is seen as a continuation of the inclined row and therefore as part of it. (d) Similar elements seem to belong to one another and therefore one sees the array as a set of horizontal rows rather than vertical columns, as one might if all the elements were the same. In (e) a principle known as closure is demonstrated. The breaks are ignored; what is seen is a "whole."

PERCEPTION

People do not usually experience a mass of colors, noises, warmths, and pressures. Rather we see cars and buildings, hear voices and music, and feel pencils, desks, and close friends. We do not merely have sensory experiences; we perceive objects. The brain receives information from the senses and organizes and interprets it into meaningful experiences—unconsciously. This process is called perception.

Principles of Perceptual Organization

Through the process of perception, the brain is always trying to build "wholes" out of the confusion of stimuli that bombards the senses. The "whole" experience that comes from organizing bits and pieces of information into meaningful objects and patterns is called a **Gestalt.** Here, the whole is greater than the sum of the parts. ("Gestalt" is a German word meaning pattern or configuration.)

Gestalt psychologists have tried to identify the principles the brain uses in constructing perceptions (Koffka, 1963). Some of the principles they have discovered are demonstrated in Figure 5.11. For example, they have found that people tend to see dots in patterns and groups. Thus when you look at Figure 5.11a, you see shifting patterns of lines and rectangles, not just an array of dots. Two principles that people use in organizing such patterns are proximity and similarity. If the elements of the pattern are close to one another or are similar in appearance, they tend to be perceived as belonging to one another. These principles are demonstrated in Figures 5.11b, c, and d.

The Gestalt principles of organization help to explain how people group their sensations and fill in gaps in order to make sense of the world. In music, for instance, you tend to group notes on the basis of their closeness to one another in time—you hear melodies, not single notes. Similarity and continuity are also important. They allow you to follow the sound of a particular voice or instrument even when many other sounds are occurring. For example, you can follow the sound of a bass guitar through a song.

Figure-Ground Perception

One form of perceptual organization is the division of experience into figure and ground. Look at Figure 5.12. What do you see? Sometimes the figure looks like a white vase against a black background. At other times it appears to be two black faces against a white background.

Figure-ground perception is the ability to discriminate properly between figure and ground. When you look at a three-dimensional object against the sky, you have no trouble distinguishing between the object and its background. It is when something is two-dimensional, as in Figure 5.12, that you may have trouble telling the figure from the ground. Nevertheless, such figure-ground perceptions give clues as to the nature of perception. The fact that a single pattern can be perceived in more than one way demonstrates that we are not passive receivers of stimuli.

Figure and ground are important in hearing as well as in vision. When you follow one person's voice at a noisy meeting, that voice is a figure and all other sounds become ground. Similarly, when you listen to a piece of music, a familiar theme may "leap out" at you: the melody becomes the figure, and the rest of the music merely background.

Perceptual Inference

Often we have perceptions that are not based entirely on current sensory information. When you hear barking as you approach your house, you assume it is your dog—not a cat or a rhinoceros or even another dog. When you take a seat in a dark theater, you assume it is solid and will hold your weight even though you cannot see what supports the seat. When you are driving in a car and see in the distance that the road climbs up a steep hill, then disappears over the top, you assume the road will continue over and down the hill, not come to an abrupt halt (Figure 5.13).

This phenomenon of filling in the gaps in what our senses tell us is known as perceptual inference (Gregory, 1970). Perceptual inference is

Figure 5.12
What did you see the first time you looked at this famous illustration? Whatever you saw, you saw because of your past experiences and current expectations. People invariably organize their experience into figure and ground. Whatever appears as figure receives the attention, is likely to be remembered, and has a distinctness of form that is lacking in the vague, formless ground. But, as this figure shows, what is meaningless ground one minute may become the all-important figure the next.

Figure 5.13
Perceptual inference: Even though you cannot see it, you assume that the road will continue beyond the slight rise—not stop abruptly at the limits of your vision from the car.

largely automatic and unconscious. We need only a few cues to inform us that a noise is our dog barking or that a seat is solid. Why? Because we have encountered these stimuli and objects in the past and know what to expect from them in the present. Perceptual inference thus sometimes depends on experience. On the other hand, we are probably born with some of our ability to make perceptual inferences. For example, experimenters have shown that infants just barely able to crawl will avoid falling over what appears to be a steep cliff—thus proving that they perceive depth (Gibson and Walk, 1960). (See Figure 5.14.)

Learning to Perceive

In large part, perceiving is something that people *learn* to do. For example, infants under one month will smile at a nodding object the size of a human face, whether or not it has eyes, a nose, or other human features. At about

Figure 5.14
The visual cliff apparatus. A human infant of crawling age (about six months) will usually refuse to cross the glass surface over the "deep" side even if his mother is on the other side and is urging the child to join her. The infant is perfectly willing to cross the "shallow" side to reach his mother, however. Even though the child can feel the hard solid glass surface beneath him, he refuses to venture out over an edge that appears to be a sudden drop.

Figure 5.15
A cut-away view of the apparatus used to show that active involvement is necessary for perceptual learning. Both kittens are receiving roughly the same visual input as they move in relation to the vertical stripes painted on the walls of the cylinder, but one kitten is producing the changes in what it sees by its own muscular movements. The other kitten sees similar changes because of the way it is harnessed to the first kitten, but what it sees has nothing to do with its own movements. This second kitten was found not to have developed the ability to see depth in this situation, while the active kitten developed depth perception normally.

twenty weeks, however, a blank oval will not make most babies smile, but a drawing of a face or a mask will. The baby has learned to distinguish something that looks like a person from other objects. Babies twenty-eight weeks and older are more likely to smile at a female than a male face. By thirty weeks most smile more readily when they see a familiar face than when they see someone they do not know. But it takes seven or eight months for babies to learn to recognize different people (Ahrens, 1954).

Experiments show that people and animals must be actively involved in their environments to develop perception. An experiment with newborn kittens demonstrates this. A number of kittens were raised in the dark until they were ten weeks old. Then they were divided into two groups: actives and passives.

For three hours a day an active kitten and a passive kitten were linked together, as shown in Figure 5.15. The kittens were harnessed in such a way that every action of the active kitten moved the passive kitten an equal distance, forward, backward, up, down, and from side to side. The visual stimulation for the two kittens was approximately the same, but the active animal produced its *own* changes in stimulation (by walking, for example). The other kitten was merely a passive receiver of stimulation. When the kittens were tested later, the passive one was not able to discriminate depth—to judge how close or far away various objects were. But the active kitten developed this ability normally. Not until the passive kitten had been allowed to live normally for two days—to move around in a visual environment of its own—did it develop normal depth perception (Held and Hein, 1963).

Experiments with human beings have also shown that active involvement in one's environment is important for accurate perception. People who have been blind from birth and who have had their sight restored by

FACT OR FICTION

By feeling people's faces, blind people can visualize how they look.

Fiction. Visualization is based on the memory of things we have seen. If a person has been blind since birth, he or she has no such memories.

Depth perception develops in infancy.

an operation (which is possible in only a few cases) have visual sensations, but initially they cannot tell the difference between a square and a circle or see that a red cube is like a blue cube (Valvo, 1971). In fact some had difficulty making such simple distinctions six months after their vision was restored.

Not all such cases end happily. Gregory (1978) tells the story of S. B., a man who had his sight restored at the age of fifty-two. Before the operation this man had lived an active and productive life. He liked making things in a shed in his garden, and sometimes rode a bicycle with a friend holding his shoulder to guide him. Immediately after the cornea transplant, he could only see a blur, but his sight improved rapidly. He had some trouble judging distance—for example, he thought his hospital window was about 6 feet from the ground when it was really about 60. But he recognized objects by sight that he had learned by touch. He had little trouble learning to tell time—for years he had used a watch with large raised numerals.

But S. B. never learned to completely trust his new sense. When he was blind, he would blithely cross the busiest streets with only his cane to guide him. Later, he was terrified by traffic and never felt comfortable crossing the street. After the initial thrill wore off, S. B. gradually became rather depressed by how drab the world was. Flaking paint and blemishes on things disturbed him. His depressions gradually became deeper and more general, and he died a few years after the operation.

Depth Perception

Depth perception—the ability to recognize distances and three-dimensionality—develops in infancy. If you place a baby on a large table, he or she will not crawl over the edge. The baby is able to perceive that it is a long distance to the floor. Psychologists test depth perception in infants with a device called the visual cliff, shown in Figure 5.14 (Gibson and Walk, 1960).

People use many cues to perceive depth. One is the information provided by retinal disparity, as discussed earlier in the chapter. Another is **motion parallax**—the apparent movement of objects that occurs when you move your head from side to side or when you walk around. You can demonstrate motion parallax by looking toward two objects in the same line of vision, one near you and the other some distance away. If you move your head back and forth, the near object will seem to move more than the far object. In this way, motion parallax gives you clues as to which objects are closer than others.

You are probably familiar with many other cues to distance. Nearby objects sometimes obscure parts of objects that are farther away. The more distant an object is, the smaller its image. Continuous objects such as railroad tracks, roads, rows of trees, and the walls of a room form converging lines, another cue to distance.

Constancy

When we have learned to perceive certain objects in our environment, we tend to see them in the same way, regardless of changing conditions. You probably judge the whiteness of the various portions of these pages to be fairly constant, even though you may have read the book under a wide range of lighting conditions. The light, angle of vision, distance, and, therefore, the image on the retina all change, but your perception of the object does not. Thus despite changing physical conditions, people are able to perceive objects as the same by the processes of size, shape, and brightness **constancy** (Figure 5.16).

An example of size constancy will illustrate how we have an automatic system for perceiving an object as being the same size whether it is far or near. A friend walking toward you does not seem to change into a giant even though the images inside your eyes become larger and larger as she approaches. To you, her appearance stays the same size because even though the size of your visual image is increasing, you are perceiving an additional piece of information: distance is decreasing. The enlarging eye image and the distance information combine to produce a perception of an approaching object that stays the same size.

Distance information compensates for the enlarging eye image to produce size constancy. If information about distance is eliminated, your perception of the size of the object begins to correspond to the actual size of the eye image. For example, it is difficult for most people to estimate the size of an airplane in the sky because they have little experience judging such huge sizes and distances. Pilots, however, can determine whether a flying plane is large and far away or small and close because they are experienced in estimating the sizes and distances of planes.

Illusions

Illusions are perceptions that are misrepresentations of reality. For example, look at the lines in Figure 5.17. Which lines are longer? Measure the

Figure 5.16
This figure can be used to demonstrate two striking features of vision. Stare steadily at the lowest right-hand star for about forty-five seconds, or until the colors start to shimmer. Then stare at a blank piece of paper. After a second or two you should see a *negative afterimage* of this figure in which the flag shows the normal colors. This occurs because the receptors for green, black, and yellow become fatigued, allowing the complementary colors of each to predominate when you stare at the white paper. Since these complements are, respectively, red, white, and blue, you see a normal American flag. Now shift your glance to a blank wall some distance away. Suddenly the flag will appear huge. This happens because of the principle of constancy—the brain interprets the same image as large when it is far away (apparently on the wall) and small when it is close (apparently on a piece of paper in your hand).

a   b   c

Figure 5.17
The Muller-Lyer illusion (a) and the Ponzo illusion (b) are two of the most famous illusions in psychology. The lines between the arrow heads in (a) are exactly the same length, as are the heavy black lines in (b). Some psychologists believe that the reason these lines appear to be different in length is that the brain interprets the diagrams in (a) and (b) as though they are scenes such as that in (c).

Figure 5.18
These two women appear to be a giant and a midget in an ordinary room. In fact, they are ordinary-sized women in a very peculiar room. This room, the true design of which is shown in the accompanying diagram, was constructed by psychologist Adelbert Ames. Again, the illusion is produced by tricking the brain into accepting an unusual situation as usual.

lengths of the pairs of lines with a ruler, then look again. Do the lines *look* as long now that you *know* they are the same? For most people, the answer is no.

A possible explanation of this type of illusion is that even though the patterns are two-dimensional, your brain treats them as three-dimensional. These illusions have features that usually indicate distance in three-dimensional space. The top line in Figure 5.17a, for example, can be thought of as the far corner of a room; the bottom line is like the near corner of the building. In Figure 5.17b and c the converging lines create the illusion of distance so that the lower bar looks nearer and shorter than the upper bar. This "perceptual compensation" seems to be unconscious and automatic.

Figure 5.18 shows two women in a room. The sizes of the women look dramatically different because you perceive the room as rectangular. In fact, the ceiling and walls are slanted so that the back wall is both shorter and closer on the right than on the left. But even when you know how this illusion was achieved, you still accept the peculiar difference in the women's sizes because the windows, walls, and ceiling appear rectangular. Your experience with rectangular rooms overrides your knowledge of how this trick is done.

EXTRASENSORY PERCEPTION

In this chapter, we have discussed the perception of tangible and measurable aspects of our environment. But humans are rarely content with un-

Figure 5.19
Dr. J. B. Rhine of Duke University administering an ESP test to two subjects using a special deck of cards.

derstanding only what can be seen and directly measured. We are fascinated by things that can't be seen, easily explained, or often even verified—flying saucers, atoms, genes, and extrasensory perception.

Extrasensory perception (ESP)—receiving information about the world through channels other than the normal senses—is a hotly debated topic. Many people are convinced that ESP exists because of an intense personal experience that can never be scientifically validated. For instance, we all have some fears before traveling, and we imagine the worst: our plane will crash, our train will be derailed, or we will have an automobile accident. These events almost never happen, and we easily forget about our frightening premonitions. However, if the improbable should actually take place, our premonitions turn into compelling evidence for the existence of precognition. Such coincidences sometimes become widely publicized evidence supporting paranormal phenomena, and we may quickly forget all the occasions when our premonitions were completely wrong. However, if we are truly interested in validating the existence of ESP, we must keep track of the frequency of its failures as well as its successes.

Scientists have been investigating ESP since the turn of the century. Probably the most famous **parapsychologist** (as these researchers into the supernatural are called) is J. B. Rhine. Around 1930, Rhine began a series of precise statistical tests of ESP. In tests of telepathy, for example, a "sender" focuses one at a time on each of twenty-five cards in a special deck. (The deck includes five cards for each of five different symbols.) A "receiver" locked in a distant room states which card he thinks the sender is focusing on. With luck alone, the receiver will guess about five cards correctly, sometimes a few more, sometimes a few less. Yet thousands of tests have shown that some people consistently respond above the average.

Some ESP researchers have concluded that these people are receiving information through senses or other channels we do not know about.

The results found in these studies are indeed statistically unlikely, but in other ways they are not nearly as impressive. For example, in one recent study (described in Chance, 1976), Charles Tart screened 1,500 college students and found 25 who seemed to have ESP. The students were shown a machine that randomly turned on one of four lights. They had to guess which light would come on next. They guessed nearly 7,500 times, and were right 26.8 percent of the time. Since one would expect people without ESP to be right only 25 percent of the time (one out of four), and since they guessed so many times, the result was statistically significant: the odds were more than 2,500 to 1 against this performance occurring by chance. These are impressive odds, but they are not particularly impressive results. This minimal ESP would not be particularly useful for playing the stock market or a football pool.

And there is one more problem with Tart's experiment. Unsupervised undergraduates collected the data. Many studies have shown that experimenters who believe in ESP tend to make errors supporting their belief, just as skeptics make errors showing that it does not exist. Another problem is that of intentional fraud. It would not be the first time a student falsified data to please his professor or get a good grade. And there have been several rather spectacular cases of fraud in ESP research.

Another reason many scientists do not accept the results of experiments supporting ESP is that the findings are highly unstable. One of the basic principles of scientific research is that one scientist should be able to replicate another scientist's results. Not only do different ESP experiments yield contradictory findings, but the same individual seems to show ESP on one day but not on the next. Proponents of ESP argue that this type of research cannot be consistently replicated because the special abilities are stifled in a laboratory situation. They say that ESP responses are best generated in highly emotional or relevant situations. Laboratory experiments that test people's ability to sense which symbols appear on cards are irrelevant to most people's lives and far from being highly emotional, and are usually a boring way to spend an afternoon. According to this viewpoint, it is remarkable that ESP has been reported to appear in the laboratory setting at all.

Although ESP may indeed be a very fragile phenomenon, the inability to replicate results and the difficulty of verifying ESP events are crucial problems. Many will remain skeptical about the existence of ESP until these problems are solved. However, such skepticism has often been overcome in the past. For example, just a century or so ago, the suggestion that many diseases were caused by invisible organisms was greeted with disbelief. Only after the work of Pasteur and other researchers proved that a clear relationship existed between these organisms and illness, was the "germ theory" of disease accepted. Perhaps the development of appropriate techniques for testing ESP could similarly lead to establishing the existence of paranormal phenomena—and perhaps they won't.

SUMMARY

Use the following outline as a tool for reviewing this chapter. Copy the outline onto your own paper, leaving spaces between headings to make notes about key concepts.

I. Sensation

   A. Threshold

   B. Sensory Differences and Ratios

   C. Sensory Adaptation

   D. Motivation and Signal-Detection Theory

II. The Senses

   A. Vision

   B. Hearing

   C. Smell and Taste

   D. The Skin Senses

   E. Balance

   F. Body Sensations

III. Perception

   A. Principles of Perceptual Organizations

   B. Figure-Ground Perception

   C. Perceptual Inference

   D. Learning to Perceive

   E. Depth Perception

   F. Constancy

   G. Illusions

IV. Extrasensory Perception

CONCEPTS AND VOCABULARY

1. What is a stimulus? Give several examples.

2. What field of psychology tries to quantify the relationship between stimuli from the world and the sensory experiences produced by them?

3. What is the difference between an absolute threshold and a difference threshold?

4. What is the current view of the ability of subliminal advertising to influence a person's behavior?

5. What psychological principle explains why you are more likely to notice when a single light bulb burns out in a room with three lamps than when a single light bulb burns out in a sports arena?

6. What are several possible explanations for phantom limb pain?

7. Which sense has received the most research? Why?

8. What is believed to be the cause of color blindness?

9. What cues do we use to determine distance and depth in vision? What cues do we use to determine direction of sounds?

10. Why are the senses of taste and smell known as the chemical senses?

11. What four kinds of information do we receive from our skin?

12. What sensory system results in dizziness? How does it work?

13. What sources of sensory information would a person use when dancing?

14. Gestalt psychologists have identified several principles that we use in organizing our perceptions. What are some of these principles?

15. If you took two books of the same size and placed one at the far end of the room and the other on a table in front of you, you would conclude that they are the same size, even though the farther one creates a smaller image on your retina. Why do you perceive them as the same size?

16. How do psychologists currently feel about the available evidence for the existence of ESP?

1. **Analyze.** To appreciate the importance of visual sensations in your daily life, try doing some of your daily activities while blindfolded. You will need the help of a friend, who can serve as your watchdog to prevent injury. While you are blindfolded, notice your sensations of taste, sound, and touch. How is your use of these sensations different from what it normally is? What cues do you use to guide your walking? How do you rely on your past experiences to help you "see" while blindfolded?

2. **Evaluate.** One of the objections to the use of subliminal advertising techniques is that it could be used to manipulate or influence large numbers of people without their knowing it. Evaluate whether you think this is an important objection. How do you feel about the use of subliminal advertising techniques?

3. **Apply.** Close your eyes and gently press on your eyeballs. What sensation do you experience? Do you "see" anything? How can you explain the visual experience in the absence of light rays?

4. **Synthesize.** Sensory adaptation refers to the ability of the senses to adjust themselves to a constant level of stimulation. A sense gets used to a new level and responds only to changes from it. Create a simple experiment to test for sensory adaptation.

APPLYING KNOWLEDGE

1. Have a friend stand with his or her back to you. Touch various parts of the friend's back with one pencil or with two pencils held close together. Each time you touch the back, ask how many points he or she felt. Now touch the points to the friend's hand and arm, again asking how many points he or she feels. What are the results? What accounts for the results?

2. To demonstrate the information shown in Figure 5.9, prepare solutions of salt water (salty), lemon juice (sour), baking soda (bitter), and sugar water (sweet). Dab each solution on various points on your tongue, and see if you can verify which area of the tongue is predominately sensitive to each of these major tastes.

3. Perform the following experiment to test one kind of sensory adaptation. Write a sentence while looking at your writing in a mirror. Do this until it begins to feel natural. Then write the sentence normally. Does normal writing now feel strange?

4. Try the following experiment to demonstrate an illusion of the sense of touch. Stretch a foot-square piece of chicken wire tautly over a frame. Blindfold your subject and ask him or her to hold the thumb and forefinger of his or her hand to lightly touch each side of the chicken wire. Slide the wire rapidly back and forth between his or her fingers. Ask your subject to report the sensation he or she feels. Most people report feeling a continuous slippery or oily surface. This illusion will probably be stronger if the subject does not know in advance the actual nature of the material he or she is feeling.

5. Station yourself behind a window or glass door (to eliminate sounds and smells that you might give off) and stare intently at someone who has his or her back toward you. Pick someone who is within a ten-yard range and who is not engaged in any particular activity at the moment. Does the person turn around and look at you? If so, how long does it take him or her to "sense" your presence? How can you explain this phenomenon? Can you develop a "control" procedure to see how long it takes someone to turn around when you are not looking at his or her back?

6. Hold a pencil about 12 inches in front of your face. Look at it with your left eye closed, then with your right eye closed. Notice how the pen-

cil seems to jump around. What happens when you look at the pencil with both eyes? What principle does this experiment demonstrate?

7. Fill three bowls with water—hot tap water in one, cold in another, and lukewarm in the third. Put one hand in the cold water and the other in the hot water and leave them there for thirty seconds. Now put both hands in the lukewarm water at the same time. What do you feel? How does this demonstrate the principle of sensory adaptation?

8. Get a fresh potato and peel it. Do the same with an apple. Now have a friend close his eyes and smell a fresh onion while he takes a bite of each one. Can he tell which food is which without his sense of smell? Try this experiment with various people, using different foods that have similar textures.

9. To illustrate the importance of two retinal images for depth perception, try out the following demonstration with the help of a friend. You will need to construct a pendulum using a 3- to 4-foot piece of string with a weight attached. Secure your pendulum to the middle of the top part of a door frame. With the door open, set the pendulum in motion swaying back and forth parallel to the door frame. Now have your friend stand in front of the doorway wearing a patch over one eye. Ask your friend to describe the motion of the pendulum. In what direction does it move? Now have your friend switch the patch from one eye to the other and describe the pendulum movement again. What differences are there in the two descriptions?

10. Put on a backpack that has been filled with ten pounds of materials. Arrange a series of objects that differ in weight from very light (a piece of paper) to medium weight (a paperback book) to heavy (a pound of candy or a 2-pound weight). Have a friend insert these objects into the backpack one at a time, in increasing order of weight. Be sure you cannot

see which object is being placed in the pack. After each object is placed in the pack, give a report of the perceived difference in weight. At what point do you notice the difference in the weight of the pack? Explain your experience by referring to the concept of difference thresholds.

ANALYZING VIEWPOINTS

1. If sensation consists entirely of electrical signals in the brain that are subject to interpretation by perception, does everyone experience the world differently? Write an essay that argues that everyone experiences the world differently. Then, write an essay that argues that everyone experiences the world as the same. Use what you have learned from the chapter.

2. Does extrasensory perception exist? Many people believe that it does, but the scientific community has strong doubts. Write a paper that presents a case for both sides of this issue. Use what you learned from the chapter.

BEYOND THE CLASSROOM

1. Arrange to watch a movie with your parents or grandparents. As soon as the film is over, ask each person to write a paragraph describing the last scene in the movie. (You should also write a paragraph.) After the paragraphs have been written, read each one aloud. Did everyone have the same perception of the scene, or did some people perceive it differently? If there are differences, ask people to talk about what they perceived. How could you explain these differences? Talk to your class about your findings.

CHAPTER 6

Motivation and Emotion

Key Terms:

Cannon-Bard theory
drive reduction theory
fundamental needs
homeostasis
innate behavior
James-Lange theory
lateral hypothalamus (LH)
motivation
polygraph
psychological needs
self-actualization needs
ventromedial hypothalamus (VMH)

Why do people climb Mount Everest and cross the Atlantic in a balloon? Why do some people spend every waking moment memorizing batting averages while others don't know the difference between the New York Red Sox and the Boston Yankees? And, as the song asks, why do fools fall in love?

Although all psychology is concerned with what people do and how they do it, research on motivation and emotion focuses on the underlying why of behavior.

BIOLOGICAL MOTIVES

We see Ruth studying all weekend while the rest of us hang out, and since we know she wants to go to law school, we conclude that she is "motivated" by her desire to get good grades. We see Harold working after classes at a job he doesn't like, and since we know he wants to buy a car, we conclude that he is "motivated" to earn money for the car. Conceptions of motivation in psychology are in many ways similar to those expressed in everyday language; since motivation cannot be observed directly, psychologists, like the rest of us, infer motivation from goal-directed behavior.

Some behavior is determined by the physiological state of the organism. Like other animals, human beings have certain survival needs. The nervous system is constructed in such a way that dramatic variations in blood sugar, water, oxygen, salt, or essential vitamins lead to changes in

Objectives:

After studying this chapter, you should be able to

- give reasons for the physiological basis of motivation.
- discuss drive reduction theory and the critiques of drive reduction theory.
- summarize the study of social motives.
- explain Maslow's hierarchy of needs.
- give examples of the physiological theories of emotion.
- give reasons for the cognitive theorists' approach to the study of emotions.

Figure 6.1 Motivation—why we do things—cannot be observed directly; it can only be inferred from goal-directed behavior.

Anorexia Nervosa and Bulemia. Anorexia nervosa and bulimia are serious eating disorders. Both syndromes are found mostly in young females. They very rarely occur in males.

A person suffering from anorexia nervosa stops eating to the point of starvation. The disorder is typically associated with extreme dieting. Symptoms of anorexia include body weight at least 15 percent below normal, an extreme fear of gaining weight, and a perception that one's body is too heavy or out of shape. Psychologists estimate that 1 out of 250 women between 12 and 18 years of age are anorexic. Up to 10 percent of anorexics die within 10 years.

Bulimia is a more common eating disorder. It is characterized by alternating periods of uncontrolled eating followed by purging—self-induced vomiting, taking of laxatives, or fasting. This is why bulimia is also referred to as binge–purge syndrome. Bulimia can result in ulcers, tooth decay, and electrolyte imbalance, which may cause heart problems. It has been estimated that about 4.5 percent of female college students suffer from bulimia.

behavior designed to return the body to a condition of chemical balance. The first part of this section discusses the role of such physiological factors in motivating behavior.

But many human motives, such as Ruth's desire to get into law school or Harold's desire to buy a car, do not have a simple physiological basis. Although not all psychologists would be able to agree on an explanation of these behaviors, none would say that they were the result of physiological deficits. The rest of this section discusses some approaches to analyzing the motivational bases of these kinds of human activities.

The Physiology of Motivation

All organisms, including humans, have built-in regulating systems that work like thermostats to maintain body temperature, the level of sugar in the blood, the production of hormones, and so on. As we saw in Chapter 4, when the level of thyroxin in the bloodstream is low, the pituitary gland secretes a thyroxin-stimulating hormone. When the thyroxin level is high, the pituitary gland stops producing this hormone. Similarly, when your body temperature drops below a certain point, you start to shiver, your blood vessels constrict, and you put on more clothes. All these activities reduce heat loss and bring body temperature back to the correct level. If your body heat rises above a certain point, you start to sweat, your blood vessels dilate, and you remove clothes. These processes cool you.

The tendency of all organisms to correct imbalances and deviations from their normal state is known as **homeostasis.** Several of the drives that motivate behavior are homeostatic—hunger, for example.

Hunger.   What motivates people to seek food? Often you eat because the sight and smell of, say, pizza tempts you into a store. Other times you eat out of habit (you always have lunch at 12:30) or to be sociable (a friend invites you out for a snack). But suppose you are working frantically to finish a term paper. You don't have any food in your room, so you ignore the fact that it is dinner time and you keep working. But at some point your body will start to demand food. You'll feel an aching sensation in your stomach. What produces this sensation? What makes you feel hungry?

Your body requires food to function. When you miss a meal, your liver releases stored sugar into your bloodstream to keep you going. After a time, however, this supply runs out and the hypothalamus begins to act.

The hypothalamus, as indicated above, is a structure at the base of the brain that regulates food intake. It not only tells us when we need to eat, it also tells us when to stop eating. How does it work? The hypothalamus is laced with blood vessels that make it extremely sensitive to levels of sugar in the blood. It also has numerous connections to the brain that are capable of raising or lowering the level of certain chemicals in the brain (Ahlskog and Hoebel, 1973). Experiments have shown that this is what makes us crave food or feel too full to eat more.

If the portion of the hypothalamus called the **lateral hypothalamus (LH)** is stimulated with electrodes, a laboratory animal will begin eating, even if it has just finished a large meal. Conversely, if the LH is removed

a

b

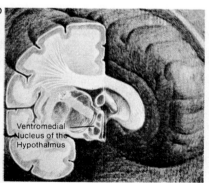

Ventromedial
Nucleus of the
Hypothalmus

Figure 6.2
(left) The fat rat. (right) A drawing
showing the part of the human
brain that corresponds to the part
lesioned in the rat. The view is
from the front of the brain, with one
half shown in cross section. (See
Figure 4.5, page 84.)

surgically, an animal will stop eating and eventually die of starvation if it is not fed artificially. Thus the LH provides the "go" signals: it tells you to eat.

If a different portion of the hypothalamus called the **ventromedial hypothalamus (VMH)** is stimulated, an animal will slow down or stop eating altogether, even if it has been kept from food for a long period. However, if the VMH is removed, the animal will eat everything in sight until it becomes so obese it can hardly move (Figure 6.2). This indicates that the VMH provides the "stop" signals: it tells you when you have had enough food.

The level of sugar in the blood is not the only thing that causes the hypothalamus to act. If your stomach is empty, the muscles in the stomach walls contract periodically (producing hunger pangs). These contractions activate the LH, which sends "go" or "eat" signals to other areas of your brain. When your stomach is full, the VMH sends "stop" signals, even though the energy from the food you have just eaten has not yet reached your bloodstream (digestion takes time). In addition, the hypothalamus responds to temperature. The LH, or "go" signal, is more active in cold temperatures; the VMH, or "stop" signal, more active in warm temperatures (presumably because people and other animals need to eat more in cold weather).

In summary, the hypothalamus "interprets" at least three kinds of information: the level of sugar in the blood, the amount of food in the stomach, and body temperature. These determine whether the hypothalamus will tell you (via chemical changes in the brain) to eat or stop eating.

Obesity.   Like the rats whose VMHs are destroyed, many people have trouble keeping their hips from looking like the Goodyear blimp. Stanley Schachter (1971) and his colleagues at Columbia University have done a number of ingenious studies which show that obese people respond to external cues—they eat not because they are hungry, but because they see something good to eat or their watches tell them it's time.

> Obese people eat not because they are hungry, but because they see something tempting or their watches say it's time.

To prove this, Schachter first set up a bogus taste test in which people were asked to rate five kinds of crackers. He was really not interested in how these people rated the crackers on his elaborate questionnaires. Schachter simply wanted to see how many crackers normal and overweight people would eat. Each person was asked to skip lunch, so they all came to the test hungry. Some were told that the taste test required a full stomach; they were given as many roast beef sandwiches as they wanted. The rest stayed hungry. Schachter's theory predicted that normal people eat because they're hungry while obese people eat whether they are hungry or not. This was true. People of normal weight ate more crackers than overweight people did when both groups were hungry, and fewer crackers after they had eaten the roast beef.

In another study, Schachter put out a bowl of peanuts which people could eat while they sat in a waiting room. Sometimes the nuts were still in their shells, and sometimes they weren't. Fat people ate the nuts only when they didn't have to bother taking the shells off. Thus, again, they ate simply because food was there. People of normal weight were equally likely to try a few nuts whether they were shelled or not. In still another study, Schachter found that fat college freshmen were more likely to cancel dormitory food contracts than normal freshmen. Why? The overweight were more concerned with the taste of their food, and they simply couldn't stand the institutional fishcakes and spaghetti.

In summary, Schachter argues that overweight people respond to external cues (for example, the smell of cookies hot from the oven) while normal people respond to internal cues (the stomach contractions of hunger). His work shows that, for people, even physiological needs like hunger are influenced by complex factors.

Drive Reduction Theory

Drive reduction theory, which dominated psychological thinking in the 1940s and early 1950s, emerged from the work of experimental psychologist Clark Hull and his associates (1943). Hull traced motivation back to basic physiological needs. According to Hull, when an organism is deprived of something it needs (such as food, water, or sex) it becomes tense and agitated. To relieve this tension it engages in more or less random activity. Thus biological needs *drive* an organism to act.

If one of these random behaviors reduces the drive, the organism will begin to acquire a habit; that is, when the drive is again felt, the organism will first try the same response again. Habits channel drives in certain directions. In short, **drive reduction theory** states that physiological needs drive an organism to act in either random or habitual ways until its needs are satisfied.

Hull and his colleagues suggested that all human motives—from the desire to acquire property to striving for excellence and seeking affection or amusement—are extensions of basic biological needs. For example, people develop the need for social approval because as infants they were fed and cared for by a smiling mother or father. Gradually, through generalization and conditioning, the need for approval becomes important in itself. Approval becomes a learned drive.

Losing Weight

If you want to lose weight, begin by keeping detailed records of everything you eat for a week or two. Get a good book on nutrition and analyze your eating habits, particularly the number of calories you consume on an average day. Forget about miracle diets that promise you can have as many cheesecakes as you want. The only people who benefit from miracle diets are the writers who get rich from books about them.

Once you figure out what you are eating and what you should be eating, all that's left is the hard part—doing something about it. Set up a system of rewards for sticking to your diet and punishments for sneaking off for hot fudge sundaes. Continue to monitor what and when you eat and chart your progress.

Some therapists believe you should not start a major weight-reduction program when the rest of your life is a mess. Of course, if your life is always a mess, this may be one place to start.

For more details, see R. L. Williams and J. D. Long, *Toward a Self-Managed Life Style*, 2nd ed. Boston: Houghton Mifflin. 1979.

Drive reduction theory dominated psychologists' thinking for over a decade. However, the results of experiments conducted in the late 1950s suggested that Hull and his colleagues had overlooked some of the more important factors in human—and animal—motivation.

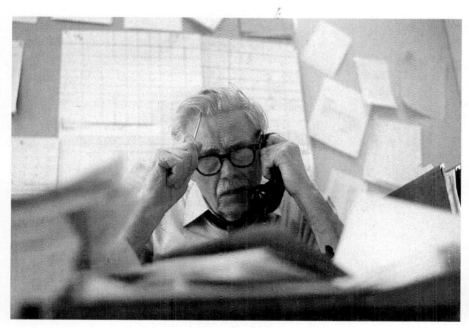

Figure 6.3
What motivates a hard-driven executive? Researchers suggest a variety of factors may be involved, including the desire to lead others, to earn more money, and to gain recognition and praise.

Figure 6.4
The monkeys in Harlow's classic experiment on the determinants of mother love spent most of their time with the terrycloth mother even though they fed from the wire mother. The terrycloth mother was also a security base when they were frightened.

Figure 6.5
This monkey worked hard for the privilege of watching an electric train, but it would be difficult to say what drive is reduced as a result.

According to drive reduction theory, infants become attached to their mothers because mothers usually relieve such drives as hunger and thirst. Harry Harlow (among others) doubted that this was the only or even the main source of an infant's love for its mother. Harlow decided to challenge drive reduction theory with an experiment. He took infant monkeys away from their mothers and put them alone in cages with two surrogate "mothers" made of wire (Figure 6.4). One of the wire mothers was equipped with a bottle. If drive reduction theory were correct, the monkeys would become attached to this figure, because it was their only source of food. The other wire mother was covered with soft cloth but could not provide food and relief from hunger. In test after test, the small monkeys preferred to cling to the cloth mother, particularly when strange, frightening objects were put into their cages (Harlow and Zimmerman, 1959).

Thus one of the factors that many drive theorists overlooked is that some experiences (such as hugging something or someone soft) are inherently pleasurable. Although they do not seem to reduce biological drives, these experiences serve as incentives or goals for behavior. Another factor that drive theorists overlooked was the pleasure humans and related animals derive from stimulation or arousal (Figure 6.5). Just think about how dogs love to be petted or how children love horror movies and rides at amusement parks that are designed to terrify them. In the end, then, a drive *for* stimulation looked as plausible as a drive to *reduce* stimulation.

Many psychologists concluded that there could be no general theory of motivation of the type Hull suggested. Instead of a drive reduction theory, we are left with a list of unlearned, innate drives that include hunger and thirst, but also curiosity, contact with soft things, and many others.

What Motivates People To Take Unnecessary Risks?

Fifty . . . forty-nine . . . forty-eight . . . forty-seven. . . . The skydiver counted the seconds till it would all be over. There was no chance he would get out of this fall alive . . . no chance his chute would open. As he pulled the cord and felt the chute snap open above his head, only one thought ran through his mind: he would live to try it again.

What motivates skydivers and others to take such risks? Psychologists Richard Solomon and John Corbit believe the answer lies in the emotional responses the risk-taker experiences before, during, and after the feat:

1. The skydiver is terrified the first time he jumps. When he lands, his terror is quickly replaced by a stunned feeling that lasts only a few minutes. This in turn is replaced by normal composure.
2. After several jumps, the skydiver is no longer terrified; instead he feels anxious before the jump. But the main change is in the way he feels afterward. The exhilaration lasts for many hours.
3. This "afterglow" motivates the skydiver to jump again.

According to Solomon and Corbit, another response pattern may also be working at the same time. They propose that the central nervous system automatically opposes highly emotional responses in order to reduce the intensity of these feelings. Thus, after we've taken part in a risky activity for a while, we do not experience the extreme highs and lows we did at first. And we are more willing to take risks we found nearly impossible to take in the beginning.

For more details, see Richard L. Solomon and John D. Corbit, "An Opponent-Process Theory of Motivation," *Psychological Review*, 81 (1974): 119–145.

Figure 6.6
Needs identified by Henry Murray in his formulation of a theory of human personality. Murray distinguishes between a class of primarily physical needs and a—much larger—class of psychological needs.

n Acquisition
(to gain possessions and property)

n Conservance
(to collect, repair, clean, and preserve things)

n Order
(to arrange, organize, put away objects)

n Construction
(to organize and build)

n Achievement
(to overcome obstacles, to exercise power, to strive to do something difficult as well and as quickly as possible)

n Recognition
(to excite praise and commendation)

n Defendance
(to defend oneself against blame or belittlement)

n Dominance
(to influence or control others)

n Autonomy
(to resist influence or coercion)

n Aggression
(to assault or injure)

n Affiliation
(to form friendships and associations)

n Rejection
(to snub, ignore, or exclude)

n Nurturance
(to nourish, aid, or protect)

n Succorance
(to seek aid, protection, or sympathy)

n Play
(to relax, amuse oneself, seek diversion and entertainment)

n Cognizance
(to explore)

SOCIAL MOTIVES

Many psychologists have concentrated their research on social motives rather than on the unlearned, biological motives we have been discussing. Social motives are learned from our interactions with other people.

In Chapter 11 we will discuss the theories of several psychologists who sought to explain the development of personality. One such psychologist was Henry Murray, whose theory of personality identifies sixteen basic needs (see Figure 6.6). Note that most of these are social motives rather than biological needs (see Murray *et al.*, 1934). Lists such as these are sometimes forgotten shortly after they appear in print, because in itself such a list is not very useful. Murray's list has not been forgotten, however. In fact, hundreds of studies have been performed on just one of these needs, the need for achievement.

McClelland and the Need for Achievement

One reason the achievement motive has been so well researched is that David McClelland became interested in finding some quantitative way of measuring social motives (McClelland *et al.*, 1953). Once he did this, he believed he could search for a technique of changing motivation, because he could then have a method of measuring whether a change had occurred. McClelland concentrated his research on the need for achievement because he felt that techniques for increasing this motive might be very useful in improving the lives of millions of people.

McClelland's main tool for measuring achievement motivation was the Thematic Apperception Test (TAT). This test consists of a series of pictures. Subjects are told to make up a story that explains each picture. Tests of this sort are called projective tests, and we will describe them in detail in Chapter 12. At this point, it is only important to know that there are no right

Figure 6.7
A picture of the sort that might be used in the measurement of the need for achievement. Examples of stories that would be scored from fairly high to low are given below. The portions of the stories printed in italics are the kinds of themes considered to reflect the need for achievement.

This guy is just getting off work. These are all working guys and they don't like their work too much either. The younger guy over on the right knows the guy with the jacket.

Something bad happened today at work—*a nasty accident that shouldn't have happened.* These two guys don't trust each other *but they are going to talk about it. They mean to put things to rights. No one else much cares,* it seems.

The guy with the jacket is *worried.* He feels that *something has to be done. He wouldn't ordinarily talk to* the younger man *but now he feels he must.* The young guy is ready. He's *concerned* too but doesn't know what to expect.

They'll both realize after talking that you never know where your friends are. *They'll both feel better* afterward because they'll feel they have someone they can rely on next time there's trouble.

Harry O'Silverfish has been working on the Ford assembly line for thirteen years. Every morning he gets up, eats a doughnut and cup of coffee, takes his lunch pail, gets in the car, and drives to the plant. It is during this morning drive that his mind gets filled with *fantasies of what he'd like to be doing* with his life. Then, about the same time that he parks his car and turns off his ignition, he also *turns off his mind*—and it remains turned off during the whole working day. In the evenings, he is *too tired and discouraged to do much* more than drink a few beers and watch TV.

But this morning Harry's mind didn't turn off with the car. He had witnessed a car accident on the road—in which two people were killed—soon after leaving home. Just as he reaches the plant gate, Harry suddenly turns. Surprised, he discovers that he has made *a firm decision* never to enter that plant again. He knows that *he must try another way* to live before he dies.

These are hard-hats. It's the end of the shift. There is a demonstration outside the plant and the men coming out are looking at it. Everyone is just walking by. They are not much interested. One person is *angry and wants to go on strike,* but this does not make sense to anyone else. He is out of place. Actually he is not really angry, he is just bored. He looks as though he might do a little dance to amuse himself, which is more than the rest of them do. *Nothing will happen* at this time *till more people join* this one man in his needs.

or wrong answers. Since the test questions are ambiguous, the answers a person gives are believed to reflect his or her unconscious desires. Each story is "coded" by looking for certain kinds of themes and scoring these themes according to their relevance to various types of needs, such as achievement. Coding has by now been refined to the point where trained coders agree about 90 percent of the time.

McClelland noted first that hungry subjects tended to include more stories about getting food than subjects who were not hungry. Next he performed an analogous test for the need for achievement: he created a group of subjects who were "deprived" of achievement. He did this by giving them a series of tests designed so that they did poorly and knew it. They were allowed to try again and still did poorly. Then he administered the TAT, saying that it was being used to look for creative, intelligent group leaders. As a control, he gave the TAT to another group with a "relaxed" set of instructions, encouraging them to write stories that pleased them. Then he analyzed the stories to see how they differed. In addition, the TAT stories of all kinds of known successful achievers were studied and compared to those of control groups. (Figure 6.7 shows an example of how need for achievement might be measured.)

Based on these tests, McClelland developed a scoring system for the TAT. For example, a story would be scored high in achievement imagery if the main character was concerned with standards of excellence and a high level of performance, with unique accomplishments (such as inventions and awards), or with the pursuit of a long-term career or goal.

In later studies, people who scored high and low in achievement on the TAT were compared in a variety of situations. For example, it was found that high achievers were able to solve anagrams (unscrambling and rearranging letters into meaningful words) faster than those less interested in achievement (Kolb, 1973). More significantly, McClelland followed up the careers of some students at Wesleyan University who had been tested with the TAT in 1947. He wanted to see which students had chosen entrepreneurial work—that is, work in which they had to initiate projects on their own. He found that eleven years after graduation, 83 percent of the entrepreneurs (business managers, insurance salesmen, real estate investors, consultants, and so on) had scored high in achievement, but only 21 percent of the nonentrepreneurs had scored that high (McClelland, 1965).

Next, McClelland checked to see whether the achievement motive had any real effects on society (1961). He and his associates studied the children's literature of England, Spain, and ancient Athens, scoring it for achievement in the same manner as they would a TAT story. They found that, in general, high levels of achievement motivation appeared fifty to one hundred years before improvements in the economic situation of each country.

Encouraged by this finding, McClelland and others then set about devising a training course in achievement motivation. The trainees in this course learned to score their own TAT stories and to recognize achievement themes in them. They also rewrote their stories again and again, attempting to include more achievement themes in them. Then they discussed everyday life situations and case histories with other members of the group, focusing on achievement themes. Group members also played a business game designed to give them quick feedback for decision making and problem solving.

Success with this program has been reported after applying it in such diverse places as Spain, Mexico, Italy, India, and poverty areas of Kentucky (McClelland and Winter, 1969). For example, a group of seventy-six men running small businesses in Indian villages was given the training and was later compared to a similar group not given the training. The trained groups showed significant and large increases in entrepreneurial activity (such as starting new businesses or gaining large increases in salary), while the untrained group did not change.

McClelland does not believe we should all train ourselves as high achievers. In fact, he has said that such persons are not always the most interesting, and they are usually not artistically sensitive (McClelland and Harris, 1971). They would also be less likely to value intimacy in a relationship. Studies have shown that high achievers prefer to be associated with experts who will help them achieve instead of with more friendly people.

One interesting feature of the research on achievement motivation is that virtually all of the major studies used males as their subjects. The generalizations regarding the factors that influence the desire for achievement apply to men but not to women. Research has revealed that women have a more complex set of motives for achievement and success.

Fear of Success.   McClelland's work has inspired a wide variety of research on other aspects of motivation. Matina Horner (1970, 1972) asked eighty-nine men to write a story beginning with the line, "After first term finals, John finds himself at the top of his medical school class." Substituting the name Anne for John in the opening line, she also asked ninety women to write a story. Ninety percent of the men wrote success stories. However, over sixty-five percent of the women predicted doom for Anne.

Some of the women feared for Anne's social life. They described her as undatable or unmarriageable, and suggested that she would be socially isolated if she excelled in her studies and career. Some wrote about the guilt and despair she would experience if she continued to succeed. And some refused to believe the opening line. It was impossible for Anne to be first in her class; there must be some mistake.

On the basis of this study Horner identified another dimension of achievement motivation, the *motive to avoid success.* Females in our society are (or were) raised with the idea that being successful in all but a few careers is odd and unfeminine. Thus a woman who is a success in medicine, law, and other traditionally male occupations must be a failure as a woman. It might have been all right for Anne to pass her exams, but the fact that she did better than all the men in her class made the female subjects anxious.

Horner discovered that bright women, who had a very real chance of achieving in their chosen fields, exhibited a stronger fear of success than did women who were average or slightly above average. (Expecting success made them more likely to avoid it, despite the obvious advantages of a

Being a mother might be quite satisfying for one woman, but not for another.

rewarding career.) This seemed to confirm Horner's belief that success involves deep conflicts for women (see Figure 6.8).

Many other researchers then set out to verify Horner's findings. They quickly found that the picture was more complicated than Horner's study seemed to suggest. For one thing, it's very hard to define success. Being a mother might be quite satisfying for one woman, but a sign of failure for someone who would have preferred a career. Also, it is often hard to tell whether a person who doesn't try something is more afraid of success or failure.

It is important to remember that much of the earlier research into people's need for achievement or fear of success was done at a time when traditional sex role stereotypes were more accepted than they are now. In the 1970s, we began to see a change in the way males and females were treated. These changes have resulted in a different set of learned motives for men and women. In any case, many different tests of people's attitudes toward success have been invented as a result of Horner's work, and psychologists are beginning to understand the many issues involved in getting ahead in our society. Tresemer (1976b: 215) wrote that researchers are now asking: "When does a person avoid success, and, by the way, what do you mean by success?"

Maslow's Hierarchy of Needs

Abraham Maslow, one of the pioneers of humanistic psychology, believes that *all* human beings need to feel competent, to win approval and recognition, and to sense that they have achieved something. He places achievement motivation in the context of a hierarchy of needs all people share.

Maslow's scheme, shown in Figure 6.9, incorporates all the factors we have discussed so far in this chapter, and goes a step further. He begins with biological drives, including the need for physical safety and security. In order to live, people have to satisfy these **fundamental needs.** If people are hungry, most of their activities will be motivated by the drive to acquire food, and they will not be able to function on a higher level.

Figure 6.9
Maslow's hierarchy of needs. According to Maslow, it is only after satisfying the lower levels of needs that a person is free to progress to the ultimate need of self-actualization.

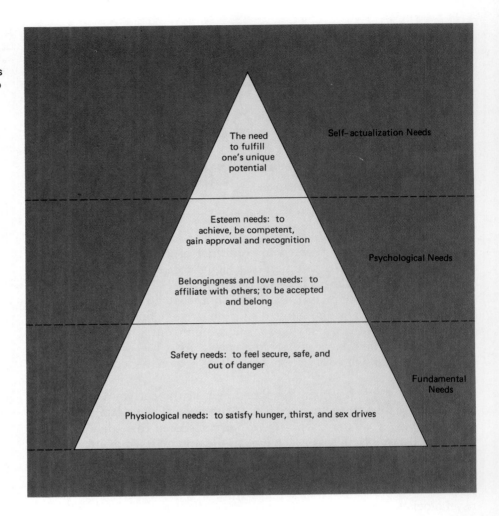

The second level in Maslow's hierarchy consists of **psychological needs:** the need to belong and to give and receive love, and the need to acquire esteem through competence and achievement. Maslow suggests that these needs function in much the same way that biological needs do, and that they can be filled only by an outside source. A lack of love or esteem makes people anxious and tense. There is a driven quality to their behavior. They may engage in random, desperate, and sometimes neurotic or maladaptive activities to ease their tensions. Unless these needs are satisfied, a person will be unable to move on. Most of his or her behavior will be motivated by unfulfilled psychological needs. Thus an unusually intelligent woman who does not feel loved may avoid success in the hope of being accepted as one of the crowd.

Self-actualization needs are at the top of Maslow's hierarchy. These may include the pursuit of knowledge and beauty, or whatever else is required for the realization of one's unique potential. Maslow believes that although relatively few people reach this level, we all have these needs. To be creative in the way we conduct our lives and use our talents, we must first satisfy our fundamental and psychological needs. The satisfaction of these needs motivates us to seek self-actualization.

Maslow thus adds to motivation theory the idea that some needs take precedence over others and the suggestion that achieving one level of satisfaction releases new needs and motivations. (We discuss Maslow's theory in more detail in Chapter 11.)

EMOTION

It is difficult to draw a clear line between motives and emotions. We saw that when a person needs food, the stomach contracts, the level of sugar in the blood drops, neural and endocrine systems are thrown slightly off balance, and taste buds become more sensitive. We saw that when a person is frightened, heart and breathing rates quicken, energy level rises, the senses mobilize, and blood rushes away from the stomach into the brain, heart, and other muscles. Of course, a poet might diagnose a pounding heart, loss of appetite, and heightened awareness of the moonlight and scented breezes as love. Why, if all three involve identifiable physiological changes, do we call hunger a biological drive, and fear and love emotions?

It depends on whether we are describing the source of our behavior or the feelings associated with our behavior. When we want to emphasize the needs, desires, and mental calculations that lead to goal-directed behavior, we use the word "drive" or "motivation." When we want to stress the feelings associated with these decisions and activities, we use the word "emotion" or "affect."

Clearly, the two are intertwined. We frequently explain our motives in terms of emotions. Why did you walk out of the meeting? I was angry. Why do you go to so many parties? I enjoy meeting new people and love to dance. Why did you lend your notes to someone you don't particularly like? I felt guilty about talking behind her back. Why did you apply for a summer job overseas? The idea of flying to Saudi Arabia excites me—and so on.

As these examples demonstrate, emotions push and pull us in different directions. Sometimes emotions function like biological drives: our feelings energize us and make us pursue a goal. Which goal we pursue may be determined by our social learning experiences. Other times we do things because we think they will make us feel good: anticipated emotions are the incentive for our actions. The consequences of striving for one goal or another also evoke emotions.

Expressing Emotions: Innate and Learned Behavior

In *The Expression of the Emotions in Man and Animals* (1872), Charles Darwin argued that all people express certain basic feelings in the same ways. Without knowing a person's language, you can tell whether he or she is amused or infuriated just by looking at that person's face.

Recent studies indicate that Darwin was right. One group of re-

FACT OR FICTION

A person who is in a good mood is more likely to be helpful.

Fact. Positive emotional states are associated with greater helping. It has been found that the "glow of good will" occurs even when being in a good mood is caused by a minor event. Thus, people who find change left in phone booths or have cookies placed on their study tables in the library are more generous when asked for help.

Photograph Judged						
Judgment	Happiness	Disgust	Surprise	Sadness	Anger	Fear
Culture			**Percent Who Agreed with Judgment**			
99 Americans	97	92	95	84	67	85
40 Brazilians	95	97	87	59	90	67
119 Chileans	95	92	93	88	94	68
168 Argentinians	98	92	95	78	90	54
29 Japanese	100	90	100	62	90	66

Figure 6.10
The data in this table show that there is substantial agreement among the members of different cultures about the meaning of various facial expressions. The muscular movements that produce these expressions are probably innate human responses. (After Ekman, Friesen, and Ellsworth, 1972)

searchers selected a group of photographs they thought depicted surprise, anger, sadness, and happiness. Then they showed the photographs to people from five different cultures and asked them to say what the person in each photograph was feeling. The results of this experiment are shown in Figure 6.10. The overwhelming majority of the subjects identified the emotions as the researchers expected they would. Was this simply because they had met Americans, or at least seen American television shows and movies, and so learned how to "read" our facial expressions? Apparently not. A second study was conducted in a remote part of New Guinea, with people who had had relatively little contact with outsiders and virtually no exposure to mass media. They too were able to identify the emotions being expressed (Ekman, Friesen, and Ellsworth, 1972).

These studies imply that certain basic facial expressions are **innate**— that is, part of our biological inheritance. Observations of children who were born blind and deaf lend support to this view. These youngsters could not have learned how to communicate feelings by observing other people. Still, they laugh like other children when they're happy, pout and frown to express resentment, clench their fists and teeth in anger (see Goodenough, 1932).

Psychologist Carroll Izard and his colleagues (Trotter, 1983) developed a coding system for assessing emotional states in people. By noticing changes in different parts of the face, such as the eyebrows, eyes, and mouth, they have been able to identify ten different emotional states. For example, anger is indicated when a person's eyebrows are sharply lowered and drawn together, and the eyes narrowed or squinted. Izard has used his coding system to study emotional expressions in infants. Trained coders watching videotaped segments of an infant's face assess the emotional state of the baby. This technique is especially useful for studying emotions in young children who cannot verbally report what they are feeling. Izard's work also enables psychologists to study how effectively parents are able to read their babies' faces and figure out what they are feeling. Not only are parents watching their babies, but the reverse is also true. Babies spend a lot of time watching their parents. Infants have many opportunities to learn about and express emotions by using the parents' faces as models.

Learning is an important factor in emotional expression. James Averill (1983) believes that many of our everyday emotional reactions are the result of social expectations and consequences. He believes that emotions are responses of the whole person and that we cannot separate an individual's physical or biological experience of emotions from that person's thoughts or actions associated with those emotions. We learn to express and experience emotions in the company of other people and we learn that emotions can serve different social functions. Parents, for example, modify their children's emotions by responding angrily to some outbursts, by being sympathetic to others, and on occasion by ignoring their youngsters. In this way, children are taught which emotions are considered appropriate in different situations and which emotions they are expected to control.

Learning explains the differences we find among cultures once we go beyond such basic expressions as laughing or crying. For example, in Victorian English novels, women closed their eyes, opened their mouths with a gasp, and fainted when they were frightened or shocked. In Chinese novels, men fainted when they became enraged. Medical records from the period indicate that Chinese men did indeed faint from anger (Klineberg, 1938). What these findings suggest is that all of us are born with the capacity for emotion and with certain basic forms of expression, but that when, where, and how we express different feelings depend in large part on learning.

Analyzing facial expressions helps us to describe emotions, but it does not tell us where emotions come from. Some psychologists believe emotions derive from physical changes, others, that emotions result from mental processes.

Physiological Theories

In *Principles of Psychology*, a classic work published in 1890, William James attempted to summarize the best available literature on human behavior, motivations, and feelings. When it came to drawing up a catalogue of human emotions, James gave up; he felt there were too many subtle variations, too many personal differences. But he was struck by the fact that nearly every description of emotions he read emphasized bodily changes. James's observations of his own and other people's emotions confirmed this point. We associate feelings with sudden increases or decreases in energy, muscle tension and relaxation, and sensations in the pit of our stomach.

The James-Lange Theory.   After much thought James concluded that we use the word "emotion" to describe our visceral or "gut" reactions to the things that take place around us. In other words, James (1890) believed that emotions are the perception of certain internal bodily changes.

> My theory . . . is that *the bodily changes follow directly the perception of the exciting fact, and that our feeling of the same changes as they occur IS the emotion.* Commonsense says, we lose our fortune, are sorry and weep; we meet a bear, are frightened and run; we are insulted by a rival, are angry and strike. . . . [T]he more rational statement is that we feel sorry because we cry, angry because we strike, afraid because we tremble. . . . Without the bodily states following on the perception, the latter would be . . . pale, colorless, destitute of emotional warmth.

In a sense, James was putting the cart before the horse. Other psychologists had assumed that emotions trigger bodily changes; James argued that the reverse is true. Because Carl Lange came to the same conclusion about the same time, this position is known as the **James-Lange theory** (Lange and James, 1922). Izard's (1972) theory of emotions bears a striking resemblance to the James-Lange theory. He believes that our conscious experience of emotion results from the sensory feedback we receive from the muscles in our faces. You can check this out by noticing the difference in your emotional experience when you smile for two minutes as opposed to when you frown for two minutes. According to Izard's view, if you continue to frown, you will experience an unpleasant emotion.

The Cannon-Bard Theory.   Techniques for studying bodily changes improved over the next three decades, and evidence that contradicted the James-Lange theory began to grow. For example, the physiological changes that occur during emotional states also occur when people are not feeling angry or sad—or anything. In fact, injecting a drug that produces physiological arousal of the body does not necessarily produce changes in emotions. (If James and Lange had been correct, such physiological changes would always produce emotions.) Also the internal state of the body changes only slowly. "Gut" reactions could not produce the rushes of emotion we all experience from time to time. Indeed, if bodily changes were the seat of emotion, we would all be rather dull.

In 1929, Walter B. Cannon published a summary of the evidence against the James-Lange theory. Cannon argued that the thalamus (part of the lower brain) is the seat of emotion—an idea Philip Bard (1934) expanded and refined. According to the **Cannon-Bard theory,** certain experiences activate the thalamus, and the thalamus sends messages to the cortex (or

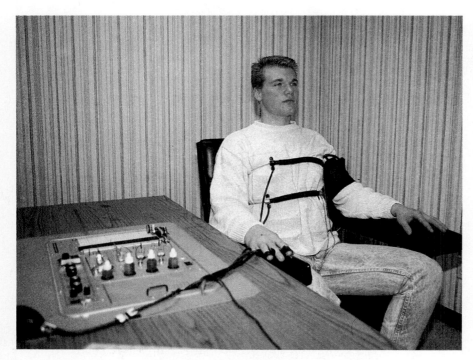

Figure 6.11
Taking a lie detector test: the polygraph measures sweating of the skin, breathing, blood pressure, and heart rate.

higher brain) and to the body organs. (More sophisticated experiments showed that the thalamus is not involved in emotional experience, but the hypothalamus is.) Thus, when we use the word "emotion," we are referring to the *simultaneous* burst of activity in the brain and "gut" reactions. In Cannon's words, "The peculiar quality of emotion is added to simple sensation when the thalamic processes are aroused" (1929).

Cannon also emphasized the importance of physiological arousal in many different emotions. He was the first to describe the "fight or flight" reaction of the sympathetic nervous system that prepares us for an emergency. Some of the signs of physiological arousal are measured in one of the most famous applications of psychological knowledge: lie detection.

USING PSYCHOLOGY

Lie Detection

Most of us associate lie detection with shifty-eyed criminals accused of murdering their grandmothers. But in reality, American industry uses the lie detector far more often than the police do. No one knows exactly how many polygraph tests (**polygraph** is another name for a lie detector) are given each year, but one psychologist (Lykken, 1974) places the number at several million. Companies use these tests for everything from finding out whether a job applicant has ever

MORE about. . .

Men, Women, and Lying. A psychologist who has conducted research on conflict between men and women has found that many women get upset about men's lack of emotional expression.

Women seem to express emotions more often than men. This may explain another research finding: Men are better liars than women. One study found that videotapes of male college students instructed to lie were seen as sincere. However, women's lies were more easily detected.

Why are women worse liars than men? One possibility has to do with women being better at expressing their emotions than men. Since women appear to be better at expressing themselves and do so more often than men, they may find it more difficult when required to hide what they truly feel. Men, on the other hand, tend to limit their emotional expressions. They also believe that the expression of most emotions is controllable. Thus, expressing an emotion that one does not feel may come more easily for many males.

been in trouble to seeing who's got his or her hand in the till at the local hamburger stand.

The first modern "lie detector" was invented by Leonarde Keeler, a member of the Berkeley, California, police force in the 1920s. As you can see in Figure 6.11, a polygraph includes electrodes for measuring the electrical resistance of the skin (often called the GSR, this is a measure of sweating), a tube that is tied around the chest to measure breathing, and an inflatable cuff that measures blood pressure and heart rate. There is no single physiological change that always goes along with a lie. Rather, the lie-detection expert looks for general signs of the activation of the sympathetic nervous system: an irregular breathing pattern, high heart rate and blood pressure, and increased sweating (indicated by decreases in the electrical resistance of the skin). Lie detection is an art rather than a science, so the technique is only as good as the man who uses it (Hassett, 1978).

Surprisingly, almost all of the people who become lie-detection experts have backgrounds not in psychology but in law enforcement. The way they cross-question a person is at least as important as the machine itself. To illustrate this point, polygraphers sometimes tell an old tale about a medieval prince who wanted to find out which of his servants had stolen some food. He called all his servants together and announced that he had a sacred donkey in the next room. The donkey would bray only when the guilty man pulled his tail. One by one, the servants went by themselves into a dark room with the donkey, pulled his tail, and returned to the prince. Finally, the last man returned and still the ass had not made a sound. The prince then told the servants to hold out their hands. He had covered the donkey's tail with soot. Only the guilty man had been afraid to pull the tail, and so only his hands were clean (Sternbach, Gustafson, and Colier, 1962). Similarly, some experts say that if a person believes in the lie detector, it can be used to make him or her tell the truth. Indeed, many people confess during an hour-long interview that usually takes place before the machine is even plugged in.

The polygrapher tries to develop three different kinds of questions for the actual tests. Some are nonemotional (for example "Is your name Richard Nixon?"); some are emotional but not relevant to the investigation ("Have you ever lied to your parents?"); a few are related specifically to the investigation. The theory is that everyone will react emotionally to the last two categories, but only the guilty party will respond *more* to questions about the crime. It is important that the questions be as specific as possible. A polygrapher would not ask "Did you ever steal anything?" but rather "Did you ever steal more than one hundred dollars from the E-Z Credit Furniture Store?"

How effective are lie detectors? It's hard to say. Like all good businesspeople, polygraph experts advertise their successes and forget about their failures. In one review of many criminal cases (Orlansky, 1965), the lie detector was proved wrong about 2 percent of the time. But this figure is misleading. If a lie detector test says a suspect is innocent, the police often won't bother to look for more evidence. So it's very hard to know when it's wrong. And even if the figure were as low as 2 percent, that's not going to help you if you're one of the people the lie detector lies about.

Overall, the ability of polygraphs to detect the arousal often associated with lying is quite impressive. But lie detectors do make mistakes. For this reason, the results of polygraph tests are not ordinarily allowed as evidence in a court of law. When, if ever, they should be used in industry is a political question rather than one that psychologists are specially qualified to answer.

Cognitive Theories

Cognitive theorists believe that bodily changes and thinking *work together* to produce emotions. Physiological arousal is only half of the story. What you feel depends on how you interpret your symptoms. And this, in turn, depends on what is going on in your mind and in your environment.

The Schachter-Singer Experiment. Stanley Schachter and Jerome Singer designed an experiment to explore this (1962). They told all their subjects they were testing the effects of vitamin C on eyesight. In reality, most received an adrenalin injection. One group was told that the "vitamin" injection would make their hearts race and their bodies tremble (which was true). Another group was deliberately misinformed: the injection would make them numb. A third group was not told anything about how their bodies would react to the shot. And a fourth group received a neutral injection that did not produce any symptoms. Like the third group, these subjects were not given any information about possible side effects.

After the injection, each subject was taken to a reception room to wait for the "vision test." There they found another person who was actually part of the experiment. The subjects thought the stooge had had the same injection as theirs. With some subjects, the stooge acted wild and crazy—dancing around, laughing, making paper airplanes with the questionnaire they'd been asked to fill out. Other subjects had to fill out a long and

Cognitive theorists believe bodily changes and thinking work together to produce emotions.

offensive questionnaire that asked, for example: "With how many men (other than your father) has your mother had extramarital relationships? 4 and under ____; 5–9 ____; 10 and over ____." The stooge for this group acted quite angry.

Subjects from the first group, who had been told how the injection would affect them, watched the stooge with mild amusement. So did subjects who had received the neutral injection. However, those from the second and third groups, who either had no idea or an incorrect idea about the side effects, joined in with the stooge (Figure 6.12). If the stooge was euphoric, so were they; if he was angry, they became angry.

What does this experiment demonstrate? That internal components of emotion (such as those adrenalin produces) affect a person differently, depending on his or her interpretation or perception of the social situation. When people cannot explain their physical reactions, they take cues from their environment. The stooge provided cues. But when people knew that their hearts were beating faster because of the adrenalin shot, they did not feel particularly happy or angry. The experiment also shows that internal changes are important—otherwise the subjects from the neutral group would have acted in the same way as those from the misinformed groups. Perception and arousal *interact* to create emotions.

Arnold's Theory.   According to Magda Arnold, everyday emotions can be analyzed into a series of stages (Figure 6.13). In the first, you *perceive* a person, object, or event. It may take place in your imagination, as when you think about something you expect to happen in the future or replay a scene from your past.

The next stage is *appraisal.* You decide whether what is happening will

Figure 6.12
Two of the conditions in Schachter and Singer's experiment on emotion. (a) A subject is misled about the effects he should expect from an adrenalin injection. Placed with a stooge who joyfully flies airplanes around the room, he attributes his state of arousal to a similar mood in himself and joins in. (b) A subject is told exactly what to expect from the injection. Although placed in the same situation as the first subject, he recognizes his physical sensations as the product of the injection and is not affected by the actions of the stooge.

1. Observation: "There are fighter planes coming up."
2. Appraisal: "There is danger; they may catch up with me and hit the plane."
3. Fear (not attended to because the pilot is fully occupied evading the fighter planes).
4. Physiological changes: increase in heart rate; tremor; and fatigue, which becomes cumulative until the mission is finished.
5. Awareness of these changes (will be delayed until the necessity for action is past and attention is free to notice the physiological state).
6. Secondary estimate: "I am chronically tired, trembling, irritable--I must be ill."
7. Secondary emotion: fear of illness, heart disease, and so on.
8. Physiological changes: reinforcement of fatigue, tremor, and so on, increasing the malaise.

Figure 6.13
Magda Arnold's theory of emotion describes a continuous process of reaction and appraisal. This figure shows how a person may respond immediately and effectively in a dangerous situation and later misinterpret the aftereffects.

help you, hurt you, or have no effect on you. Suppose you see one of your instructors walking toward you. If you have nothing special to gain and nothing to fear from her, you do not react emotionally. You say hello, chat for a moment, and walk on.

However, if you have been cutting class and suspect that the instructor is going to ask for an explanation, or if you know that she was impressed with a term paper you wrote and will probably compliment you, you will react—physiologically and emotionally. Your heart begins to beat a little faster, and you feel nervous or excited (depending on whether you cut classes or wrote an excellent paper). These are the third and fourth stages: *bodily change* and *emotion.*

In most cases, emotion and bodily change occur at the same time. However, in some situations you skip from stage three (bodily changes) to stage five, which is *action.* You see a car rushing toward you, adrenalin pours into your system, and you jump back without stopping to think. Only after you've leaped to safety do you sense your heart pounding and experience the emotion of fright (Arnold, 1960, 1970). (See also the discussion of stress in Chapter 13.)

In fact, other emotion researchers believe that emotion may play an important role in our survival as human beings and in our ability to achieve goals, precisely because it spurs us to action. Take the example of the car rushing toward you. If you do not jump out of the way, you may not live to see another day. On less extreme levels, emotions may serve to help us achieve difficult goals. Suppose you want your own car, but your parents say no. You may feel angry with them, or embarrassed because all your friends have cars. These emotions may spur you to get a job to earn money for a car, or to explore other options with your parents. Either way, you are responding to an emotion by acting to achieve a goal.

Emotions and physical changes are interwined. It will probably be many years before we understand all the complex ways in which the two interact in human behavior.

CHAPTER 6 REVIEW

SUMMARY

Use the following outline as a tool for reviewing this chapter. Copy the outline onto your own paper, leaving spaces between headings to make notes about key concepts.

I. Biological Motives

    A. The Psychology of Motivation

    B. Drive Reduction Theory

II. Social Motives

    A. McClelland and the Need for Achievement

    B. Maslow's Hierarchy of Needs

III. Emotion

    A. Expressing Emotions: Innate and Learned Behavior

    B. Physiological Theories

    C. Cognitive Theories

CONCEPTS AND VOCABULARY

1. What physiological processes determine whether or not we "feel hungry"? How do normal-weight and overweight people differ in their sensitivity to these cues?

2. Explain why each of the following is or is not consistent with Hull's drive reduction theory: hunger, curiosity, the need for oxygen, taking risks.

3. Which theory of motivation suggests that all human motives are extensions of basic biological needs?

4. How did Harlow's experiment challenge drive reduction theory?

5. How does McClelland measure a person's need for achievement? What kind of person has a high need for achievement?

6. What explanation is given for the finding that women have a greater motive to avoid success? Why might this difference disappear in the future?

7. What are the five levels of needs in Maslow's hierarchy?

8. According to Maslow's hierarchy of needs, which needs must be satisfied first? Which needs are satisfied after all others?

9. How do psychologists try to distinguish between motivation and emotion?

10. What research evidence suggests that our expression of emotions is universal across different societies and cultures and may be innate? What evidence suggests that emotions are affected by learning?

11. How does the Cannon-Bard theory of emotion differ from the James-Lange theory?

12. What did Schachter and Singer's experiment demonstrate?

13. You are driving a car and a small child steps into the street a third of a block in front of the car's path. Use Arnold's theory of emotion to explain your response.

CRITICAL THINKING

1. **Evaluate.** Try going without bread in your meals for several days a week. Do you find that you are beginning to think about bread more often, even dream about it? Are you becoming more aware of advertisements for bread? Compare your experience with the description of drive reduction behavior in this chapter.

2. **Analyze.** Write down several activities or behaviors you do when your time is your own. In which level of Maslow's hierarchy of needs would you place each of these activities or behaviors; that is, what really motivates you to engage in each of them? Perhaps you will discover

a different kind of motive, one that doesn't seem to fit in with Maslow's set. Check the chapter on personality and the Maslow readings to see whether or not it might fit. If none of the activities on your list seems to be motivated by self-actualization, can you imagine activities that would be, and that you might enjoy doing?

3. **Analyze.** To gain a clearer understanding of the range of emotional reactions you experience, keep an "emotion diary" for one day. Try to jot down what you felt, how you interpreted your feelings, and what brought on your reaction. At the end of the day, analyze your diary to determine the differences in physiological reactions that you experienced in response to each situation. What conclusions can you draw about your emotional responses on that day?

APPLYING KNOWLEDGE

1. With a partner or as a group, select ten emotions to express. Then play a variation of charades, with one person attempting to convey each of these emotions by facial expression alone. Are some emotions harder to convey than others? Are there consistent differences in interpretation between individuals? How important do you think context (the social situation in which the facial expression occurs) is in perceiving other people's emotions?

2. Collect the fantasies of people in your class. Each person should write several stories or fantasies, possibly around a set of ambiguous pictures. Names should not be placed on fantasies (so as to ensure privacy), but each person should mark male or female on the fantasy. Then compare the fantasies of males and females for the achievement motive. Are there differences? Do you think there have been changes in this factor in the last few years?

3. If you are interested in the achievement motive, you might try the story-writing techniques described in this chapter. Try writing stories with and without achievement themes. Include themes related to the three aspects of achievement motivation. After you have written several stories, think about whether this exercise has made you more aware of achievement. Do you think doing the exercise increased your ability to achieve?

ANALYZING VIEWPOINTS

1. Lie detectors are being used increasingly by businesses to determine whether candidates for employment are being honest about their qualifications. As you know from reading the chapter, lie detectors, while usually accurate, can make mistakes. Should lie detectors be used by businesses as part of interviewing prospective job candidates? Write a paper that argues both sides of the issue. Include both psychological and ethical reasons in your report.

BEYOND THE CLASSROOM

1. Attend a sporting event at your school or in your community. Observe the event for at least thirty minutes. Watch for evidence of achievement motivation in the participants. Do some players appear to be more motivated than others? How can you tell? If possible, talk with the coach after the game. Ask the coach what techniques he or she uses to motivate the players. Does one technique work for all the players, or does the coach use different techniques for different players? What suggestions would you make for increasing the players' motivation? Interpret your observations in light of the theories of motivation presented in the chapter. Report to the class on your findings.

CHAPTER 7

Altered States of Consciousness

Key Terms:

biofeedback
consciousness
hallucination
hallucinogens
hypertension
hypnosis
LSD
marijuana
meditation
posthypnotic suggestion
REM sleep

As you read this sentence you are conscious of the words on this page. Or maybe your awareness is drifting to that attractive classmate sitting across from you in the library. In either case, everything you think and feel is part of your conscious experience.

You might expect, then, that normal states of **consciousness** would be one of the most active areas of research in psychology. But this is not the case. Although some of the earliest researchers defined psychology as the study of conscious experience, consciousness proved to be a difficult topic to analyze scientifically. Behaviorism—with its emphasis on studying only what people do, not what they think or feel—became popular partly because studying consciousness had proved to be so difficult. Even today, psychobiologist Roger Sperry (1976: 9) has called consciousness "one of the most truly mystifying unknowns remaining in the whole of science."

But a related area that *has* been the subject of a great deal of research in recent years is the study of altered states of consciousness. An altered state of consciousness involves a change in mental processes, not just a quantitative shift (such as feeling more or less alert). Sensations, perceptions, and thought patterns actually change. The most obvious and familiar example is sleep. People spend about a third of their lives in this altered state of consciousness. Other examples include daydreams, hallucinations, delirium, hypnotic states, being drunk or "high" on drugs, and the heightened awareness people experience during various forms of meditation (Tart, 1972).

In the past twenty years, psychologists have begun to examine altered states of consciousness by having people sleep, undergo hypnosis, or take drugs during laboratory experiments. In the laboratory, researchers can observe changes in behavior and measure changes in breathing, pulse rate, body temperature, and brain activity. (Brain activity, or "waves," can be recorded with a device known as an electroencephalograph, or EEG.) The

Objectives:

After studying this chapter, you should be able to

- describe the research related to sleep and dreaming.
- define altered states of consciousness.
- give reasons for the research of biofeedback and meditation.

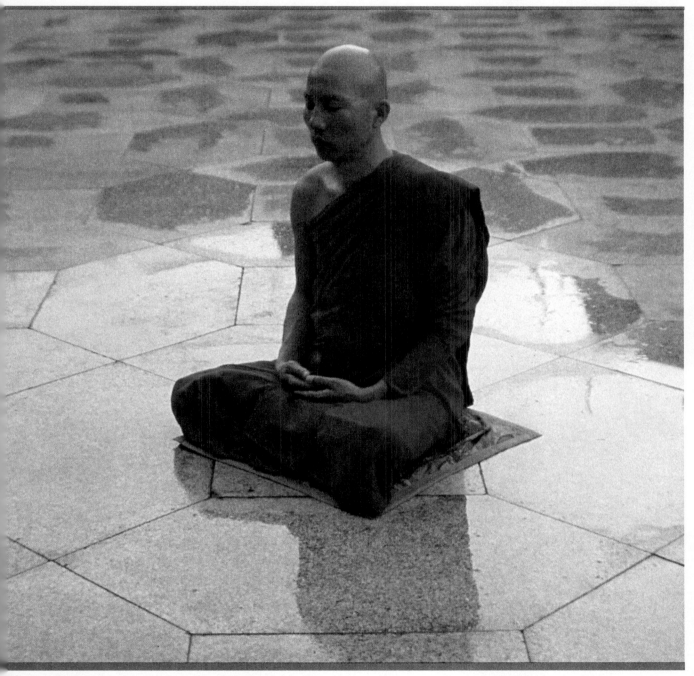

Figure 7.1 An altered state of consciousness, like meditation, involves a change in mental processes. Sensations, perceptions, and thought patterns actually change.

Figure 7.2
Everything we think and feel is part of our conscious experience. This girl, for instance, may be conscious of several things—the sound of the rain on the window, the look of a tree bending in the wind, her mother standing next to her, and voices in a nearby room.

Figure 7.3
This woman is doing a yoga exercise. Yoga stretches and tones muscles, but it is also a mental discipline that allows practitioners to achieve an altered state of consciousness.

subjects' own reports of how they feel or what they remember supplement these data. What have psychologists learned about these phenomena? We begin with sleep.

SLEEP AND DREAMS

Most people think of sleep as a state of unconsciousness, punctuated by brief periods of dreaming. This is only partially correct. Sleep is a state of *altered* consciousness, characterized by certain patterns of brain activity.

Although sleep is a major part of human and animal behavior, it has been extremely difficult to study until recently. A researcher cannot ask a sleeping person to report on the experience without first waking the person. This problem was solved with the development of the EEG machine for recording the electrical activity of the brain. By observing sleeping subjects and by recording their brain and body responses, researchers have discovered two different types of sleep patterns—*quiet sleep* and *active sleep*. There are four different stages of quiet sleep.

Stages of Sleep

As you begin to fall asleep, your body temperature declines, your pulse rate drops, and your breathing grows slow and even. Gradually, your eyes close and your brain briefly emits alpha waves, as observed on the EEG, which are associated with the absence of concentrated thought and with relaxation (Figure 7.4). Your body may twitch, your eyes roll, and brief visual images flash across your mind (although your eyelids are shut) as you enter Stage I sleep, the lightest level of sleep.

In Stage I sleep, your muscles relax and your pulse slows a bit more, but your breathing becomes uneven and your brain waves grow irregular. This phase lasts for about ten minutes. At this point, your brain waves begin to fluctuate between high and low voltages—a pattern that indicates you have entered Stage II sleep. Your eyes roll slowly from side to side. Some thirty minutes later, you drift down into a deeper level of Stage III sleep, and low voltage waves (called delta waves) begin to sweep your brain every second or so.

Stage IV is the deepest sleep of all; it is difficult to waken a sleeper in this stage. Large, regular delta waves indicate you are in a state of oblivion. If you are awakened by a loud noise or sudden movement, you may feel disoriented. Talking out loud, sleepwalking, and bed wetting—all of which may occur in this stage—leave no trace on memory. Deep sleep is important to your physical and psychological well-being. Perhaps this is why people who are able to sleep only a few hours at a time descend rapidly into Stage IV and remain there for most of their nap.

On an average night, however, Stage IV sleep lasts only an hour or an hour and a half. You then climb back through Stages III and II to Stage I. At this point, something curious happens. Although your muscles are even more relaxed than before, your eyes begin to move rapidly. You have

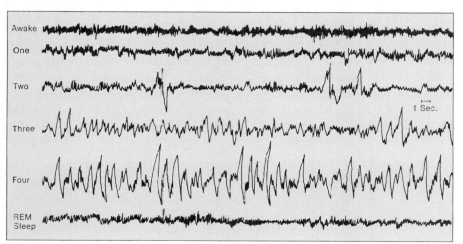

Figure 7.4
(top) A diagram showing the passage of a sleeper through the various stages of sleep over a seven-hour period. (bottom) The patterns of electrical activity (EEGs) in the brain that correspond to the various stages of sleep. The EEG pattern shown for being awake is one that occurs when the person is resting quietly with eyes closed.

entered a more active type of sleep characterized by rapid eye movement. This is called **REM sleep.** Your pulse rate and breathing become irregular, and the levels of adrenal and sexual hormones in your blood rise—as if you were in the middle of an intensely emotional or physically demanding activity. Often, your face or fingers twitch and the large muscles in your arms and legs are paralyzed. Your brain sends out waves that closely resemble those of a person who is fully awake. For this reason, REM sleep is called active sleep. Stages I through IV are sometimes referred to as NREM (non REM) or quiet sleep because of the absence of rapid eye movement and because of the slower pattern of brain waves. It is during REM sleep that almost all dreaming normally takes place.

REM sleep lasts for about ten minutes, after which you retrace the descent to Stage IV. You go through this cycle every ninety minutes or so. Each time the period of Stage IV sleep decreases and the length of REM sleep increases—until you eventually wake up. But at no point does your brain become inactive.

How Much Sleep?

The amount of sleep a person needs in order to function effectively varies considerably from individual to individual and from time to time within a person's life. Sixteen-year-olds spend an average of ten to eleven hours asleep each night. Students in graduate school average eight hours a night.

MORE about...

The Function of Dreams. Contrary to the view that dreams serve no function, a new theory suggests that dreams are the brain's way of "unlearning" or removing certain unneeded memories. In other words, dreams are a form of mental housecleaning.

Such mental housecleaning might be necessary because it is not useful to remember every single detail of your life. Instead we tend to remember *important* things and somehow forget the rest. If the theory is correct, then those things that need to be forgotten are included in dreams, and the very act of dreaming somehow helps to erase them.

This idea has been proposed by Francis Crick, Nobel Prize winner and co-discoverer of DNA. Crick believes that if it were not for the helpful effects of dreams, evolution could not have produced the highly refined human brain. He theorizes that a brain so complex as ours could not work properly without a cleaning-up mechanism.

Newborns spend an average of sixteen to eighteen hours a day sleeping, almost half of it in REM sleep (Dement, 1976). Unless deprived of REM sleep, adults average about 25 percent of their time in REM sleep, and 75 percent in NREM sleep. Although the amount of sleep a person needs may vary, it does appear that everyone sleeps and that both types of sleep are important to normal functioning.

Dreams

We call the mental activity that takes place during sleep dreaming. Everybody dreams, although most people are able to recall only a few, if any, of their dreams. Sleep researchers sometimes make a point of waking subjects at regular intervals during the night to ask them about their dreams. The first few dreams are usually composed of vague thoughts left over from the day's activities. A subject may report that she was watching television, for example. As the night wears on, dreams become longer and more vivid and dramatic, especially dreams that take place during REM sleep. Since the amounts of time spent in REM sleep increase during the night, the last dream is likely to be the longest and the one people re-

Insomnia

Everyone has had a sleepless night at one time or other—a night where nothing you do brings the calm, soothing peace you want. Some people have sleep problems like this all the time, and they rarely get more than an hour or two of uninterrupted sleep a night. To help these insomniacs, psychologists Richard R. Bootzin and Perry M. Nicassio have developed a behavior modification program to strengthen the bed as a cue for sleep and weaken it as a cue for sleep-interfering activities.

They suggest that insomniacs follow these instructions:

1. Lie down to sleep only when you feel sleepy.
2. Don't use the bed for any activity other than sleep. That means no eating, reading, watching television, listening to the radio, or worrying in bed. The only exception is sexual activity.
3. If after you're in bed for about ten minutes you find that you can't sleep, get up and go into another room. This will help you associate your bed with falling asleep quickly and dissociate it with tossing and turning. Return to your bed when you feel sleep coming on.
4. Repeat step 3 if you still can't sleep. Get out of bed as many times as necessary during the night.
5. Get up at the same time every morning no matter how little sleep you had the night before. This will help you develop a consistent sleep pattern.
6. Don't nap during the day.

Laboratory studies have shown the effectiveness of these techniques in helping insomniacs fall asleep and stay asleep. If you have a problem, they may work for you.

For more details, see Richard R. Bootzin, *Behavior Modification and Therapy: An Introduction.* Cambridge, Mass.: Winthrop, 1975.

member when they wake up. Researchers have found that, after people have been deprived of REM sleep, they subsequently increase the amount of time they spend in REM sleep. Thus it appears that a certain amount of dreaming each night is necessary (Dement, 1976).

The Content of Dreams.   When people are awakened randomly during REM sleep and asked what they had just been dreaming, the reports generally are commonplace, even dull (Hall and Van de Castle, 1966). The dreams we remember and talk about "are more coherent, sexier, and generally more interesting" than those collected in systematic research (Webb, 1975: 140).

Researchers who have recorded the contents of thousands of dreams have found that most—even the late-night REM adventures—occur in such commonplace settings as living rooms, cars, and streets. Most dreams involve either strenuous recreational activities or passive events such as sitting and watching, not work or study. A large percentage of the emotions experienced in dreams are negative or unpleasant—anxiety, anger, sadness, and so on. Contrary to popular belief, dreams do not occur in a split second; they correspond to a realistic time scale.

Often we incorporate our everyday activities and some night events into our dreams. Some sleep researchers have attempted to manipulate the content of a person's dreams by exposing the dreamer to either a light water spray, or a flashing light, or a five-second tone. They found that the water was incorporated into 42 percent of the dreams, the light into 23 percent, and the tone into 9 percent (Dement and Wolpert, 1958). Some people maintain that their creative ideas or inspiration come from dreaming. Samuel Taylor Coleridge, for example, is said to have composed his poem *Kubla Khan* while dreaming.

Only a small proportion of dreams are negative enough to be consid-

> **Everybody dreams, but most people can recall very few of their dreams.**

Figure 7.5
A sleep experiment. In recent years psychologists have done much research on sleep in order to increase our knowledge of the various states of consciousness.

Anxious people have more nightmares.

Fiction. Anxious people have about the same number of nightmares as emotionally stable people.

Dreams are not meaningless, they are not absurd. . . . On the contrary, they are psychical phenomena of complete validity— fulfillments of wishes. . . .

If I eat anchovies or olives in the evening . . . I develop thirst during the night which wakes me up. But my waking is preceded by a dream . . . That I am drinking.

Dreams which can only be understood as fulfillments of wishes and which bear their meaning upon their faces without disguise are to be found under the most frequent and various conditions. They are mostly short and simple dreams. . . .

But in cases where the wish-fulfillment is unrecognizable, where it has been disguised, there must have existed some inclination to put up a defense against the wish; and owing to this defence the wish was unable to express itself except in a distorted shape. . . .

A young physician had sent in his income tax return, which he had filled in perfectly honestly, since he had very little to declare. He then had a dream that *an acquaintance of his came to him from a meeting of the tax commissioners and informed him that, while no objection had been raised to any of the other tax returns, general suspicion had been aroused by his and a heavy fine had been imposed on him.* The dream was a poorly disguised fulfilment of his wish to be known as a doctor with a large income. . . .

Before Freud wrote his treatise on dreams in 1900, there had been no modern attempt to investigate dreams. Freud saw dreams as "the royal road to the unconscious."

Freud believed that dreams often represented disguised fulfillment of repressed wishes. In Freudian dream interpretation, every dream has a *manifest content* that comes from the events of the day, sensations during sleep, and early memories, and a *latent content* that comes from the person's unconscious wishes. Freud was particularly interested in wishes involving childhood psychosexual conflicts.

Very few psychologists still use Freud's system of dream interpretation, but it opened the door for the scientific study of dreams.

From Sigmund Freud, *The Interpretation of Dreams.* Translated from the German and edited by James Strachey. Third English edition. New York: Avon Books, 1965.

Figure 7.6
Freud on dreams.

ered nightmares. Nightmares often have such a frightening quality that we awaken in the middle of them. The sense of dread in nightmares may be related to the intensity of brain activity and to the stimulation of those parts of the brain responsible for emotional reactions. The emotional reaction of dread may then influence the content of the dream. For example, you may dream that you are about to open a door and you experience a sense of dread. Once you are emotionally aroused in the dream, you may create images in the dream to justify your feelings.

Dream Interpretation

Although dreams may contain elements of ordinary, waking reality, these elements are often jumbled in fantastic ways. The dreamer may see people in places they would never go, wander through strange houses with endless doors, find her- or himself transported backward in time. The dreamer may be unable to speak—or able to fly. What do these distortions mean?

Dream interpretations have been discovered dating back to 5,000 years before Christ. Sigmund Freud was the first in the modern era to argue that dreams are an important part of our emotional lives (see Figure 7.6).

Freud believed that no matter how simple or mundane, dreams may contain clues to thoughts and desires the dreamer is afraid to acknowledge or express in his or her waking hours. Indeed, he maintained that dreams are full of hidden meanings and disguises.

Freud believed that the symbolism of dreams is a private language that each individual has invented for himself or herself. These symbols vary greatly from person to person. Suppose that a dreamer sees herself standing naked among fully clothed strangers. For one person, this dream may symbolize a desire to show her true self to people, without pretense. For another person, the dream may symbolize a fear of having her inadequacies exposed in public. In his work with patients, Freud tried to break through the disguise of dream imagery and discover the true desires and wishes of the dreamer.

However, some social scientists are skeptical of dream interpretations. Nathaniel Kleitman, one of the pioneers who discovered REM sleep, wrote in 1960: "Dreaming may serve no function whatsoever." According to this view, the experience of a dream is simply an unimportant by-product of stimulating certain brain cells during sleep. McCarley (1978), for example, argues that the common experience of feeling paralyzed in a dream simply means that brain cells that inhibit muscle activity were randomly stimulated.

HYPNOSIS

Hypnosis is a form of altered consciousness in which a person becomes highly suggestible and does not use his critical thinking ability. By allowing the hypnotist to guide and direct him, a person can be made conscious of things he is usually unaware of and unaware of things he usually notices. (The subject may recall in vivid detail an incident he had forgotten, or feel no pain when his hand is pricked with a needle.)

Hypnosis does not put the subject to sleep, as many people believe. A hypnotic trance is quite different from sleep. In fact, the subject becomes highly receptive and responsive to certain internal and external stimuli. He is able to focus his attention on one tiny aspect of reality and ignore all other inputs. The hypnotist induces a trance by slowly persuading the subject to relax and to lose interest in external distractions. Whether this takes a few minutes or much longer depends on the purpose of the hypnosis and the method of induction.

Figure 7.7
A hypnotist, drawn by Daumier, a famous nineteenth-century French painter and caricaturist.

A subject must cooperate in order to be hypnotized; he or she is not under the hypnotist's "power."

Psychologists who use hypnosis stress that the relationship between the hypnotist and subject involves cooperation, not domination. The subject is not under the hypnotist's "power" and cannot be forced to do things against his will. Rather, the person is simply cooperating with the hypnotist by becoming particularly responsive to the hypnotist's suggestions. *Together* they try to solve a problem or to learn more about how the subject's mind works. Anyone can resist hypnosis by simply refusing to open his or her mind to the hypnotist, and people under hypnosis cannot be induced to do things they would not do when "awake" unless they want to.

Hypnotists can also suggest things for their subjects to remember when the trance is over, a phenomenon known as **posthypnotic suggestion**. For example, the hypnotist might suggest that after the person is awakened she will be unable to hear the word "psychology." When she comes out of the trance, the subject may report that some people around her are speaking strangely. They seem to leave out some words occasionally, especially when they are talking about topics involving the taboo word "psychology." The subject is not aware that part of her consciousness has been instructed to block out that word. Posthypnotic suggestion has been found to be particularly helpful in changing unwanted behaviors, such as smoking or overeating.

Psychologists do not agree about the nature of hypnosis. Some, like Theodore Barber (1965), argue that hypnosis is not a special state of consciousness. If people are simply given instructions and told to try their hardest, they will be able to do anything that hypnotized people can do. Barber has shown that unhypnotized people can hold a heavy weight at arm's length for several minutes; they can lie stiff as a board with only one chair under their shoulders and another under their feet to support them; they can even stick needles through their hands.

Others, like Ernest Hilgard (1977), believe that there is something special about the hypnotic state. People who are hypnotized are very suggestible; they go along with the hypnotist and do not initiate activities themselves; and they can more easily imagine and remember things. Hilgard believes that consciousness includes many different aspects that may become separated, or dissociated, during hypnosis. This view is called neo-dissociation theory.

Another explanation of hypnosis is based on the importance of suggestibility in the hypnotic induction. According to some theorists (Sarbin and Coe, 1972, 1979), hypnotized people behave as they do because they have accepted the role of a hypnotized subject. We expect that hypnotized individuals will forget certain things when told, or will recall forgotten material, and we play the role. Many stage hypnotists entertain their audiences with dramatic hypnotic demonstrations by carefully selecting volunteers who appear most willing to play the role (Bowers, 1976).

Whether hypnosis is a special state of consciousness or not, it does reveal that people often have potential abilities that they don't use. Continued study may help us to understand where these abilities come from and how to use them better.

HALLUCINATIONS

Hallucinations are sensations or perceptions that have no direct external cause—seeing, hearing, smelling, tasting, or feeling things that do not exist.

Hypnosis, meditation, certain drugs, withdrawal from a drug to which one has become addicted, and psychological breakdown may produce hallucinations. (We discuss the hallucinations associated with drug withdrawal and mental breakdowns in Chapter 15.) But they also occur under "normal" conditions. People hallucinate when they are dreaming and when they are deprived of the opportunity to sleep. Periods of high emotion, concentration, or fatigue may also produce false sensations and perceptions. For example, truck drivers on long hauls have been known to swerve suddenly to avoid stalled cars that do not exist. Even daydreams involve mild hallucinations.

Interestingly enough, it seems that hallucinations are very much alike from one person to the next. Soon after taking a drug that causes hallucinations, for example, people often see many geometric forms in a tunnellike perspective. These forms float through the field of vision, combining with each other and duplicating themselves. While normal imagery is often in black and white, hallucinations are more likely to involve color.

When Seigel (1977) traveled to Mexico's Sierra Madre to study the reactions of Huichol Indians who take peyote, he found that their hallucinations were much like those of American college students who took similar drugs. Seigel believes that these reactions are similar because of the way such drugs affect the brain: portions of the brain that respond to incoming stimuli become disorganized while the entire central nervous system is aroused.

SENSORY DEPRIVATION

In 1951, Donald Hebb began a series of experiments on the effects of boredom. As one of the researchers (Heron, 1957: 52) later described it: "The aim of this project was to obtain basic information on how human beings would react in situations where nothing at all was happening."

Male college students were paid to lie all day on a comfortable bed—they would get up only for meals and to go to the bathroom. Plastic visors over their eyes kept them from seeing anything but diffuse light; U-shaped foam-rubber pillows around their heads and the hum of a small air conditioner kept out any sounds; and cotton gloves and long cardboard cuffs restricted the sense of touch (see Figure 7.8). In short, the subjects could not see, hear, or touch anything—they were in a state of sensory deprivation.

Most people had signed up for the experiment hoping to catch up on their work—planning term papers, lectures, and so on. But under these conditions they quickly became irritable and found that they had trouble concentrating. After a while, some of them even began to hallucinate.

Many other studies of sensory deprivation have been performed since (Zubeck, 1969). They have used a variety of techniques for restricting sensory input, including lying in a tub of warm water for several days and submerging completely in a pool heated to body temperature while wearing nothing but a diving helmet to supply oxygen. Not all techniques and conditions had the same effects. Hallucinations were generally not as common in later experiments, but sensory deprivation consistently did lead to irritability, restlessness, and emotional upset.

DRUG STATES

The drugs of interest for the study of consciousness are those that interact with the central nervous system to alter a person's mood, perception, and behavior. Such drugs range from the caffeine in coffee and in cola drinks to powerful consciousness-altering substances like marijuana, alcohol, amphetamines, and LSD (see Table 7.1).

Marijuana

Marijuana has been used as an intoxicant among Eastern cultures for centuries. In some societies it is legally and morally acceptable whereas alcohol is not. Before 1960, marijuana use in the United States was common only among members of certain subcultures, such as jazz musicians and artists in big cities. By 1960, however, college students had discovered marijuana, and since then its rate of use has increased by a factor of perhaps ten thousand. According to government figures, about one out of every seven Americans over the age of fifteen uses marijuana in any given week.

Figure 7.8
Experimenting on the effects of boredom. Gloves and cotton cuffs prevented input to the hands and fingers; a plastic visor diffused the light coming into the eyes; a foam pillow and the continuous hum of the air conditioner and fan made input to the ears low and monotonous. Except for eating and using the bathroom, the subjects did nothing but lie on the bed. (After ''The Pathology of Boredom,'' by Woodburn Heron. © 1957 by Scientific American, Inc. All rights reserved.)

Figure 7.9
The effects of crack, like other drugs, vary from person to person.

Table 7.1 / Drugs Used for Mind-Alteration

Name of Drug or Chemical	Duration of Action (hours)	Habituation Potential (Psychological Dependence)	Tolerance Potential (Leading to Higher Dose)	Addiction Potential (Physical Dependence)
Alcohol	2–4	High	Yes	Yes
Nicotine	1–2	High	Yes	Yes
Depressants Barbiturates (Amytal, Nembutal, phenobarbital, Seconal) Quaaludes	4–6	High	Yes	Yes
Valium/Librium	4–6	Moderate	Yes	Yes
Narcotics (opium, heroin, morphine, codeine, percodan, demerol, cough syrup)	4–6	High	Yes	Yes
Stimulants (amphetamines, Benzedrine, Methedrine, Dexedrine, Ritalin, preludin)	4–8	High	Yes	Yes
Caffeine	2–4	Moderate	Yes	Yes
Hallucinogens LSD	10–12	Degree unknown	Unknown	Unknown
Psilocybin	6–8	Degree unknown	Unknown	Unknown
Mescaline	12–14	Degree Unknown	Unknown	Unknown
PCP	Variable	High	Yes	Yes
Inhalants (hydrocarbons, nitrous oxide, chlorohydrocarbons)	1–2	Moderate	Unknown	Unknown
Cocaine (crack)	1–2	High	Yes	Yes
Antidepressants Lithium Dibenzapines (tofranil, elavil) MAO inhibitors	8–12	Low	No	No
Marijuana (cannabis)	2–4	Moderate	Possible	Possible
Hashish	2–4	Moderate	Possible	Possible
Caffeine	2–4	Moderate	Yes	Yes

Usual Short-Term Effects	Usual Long-Term Effects
CNS depressant; relaxation (sedation); sometimes euphoria; drowsiness; impaired judgment, reaction time, coordination, and emotional control; frequent aggressive behavior	Diversion of energy and money from more creative and productive pursuits; habituation; possible obesity with chronic excessive use; irreversible damage to brain and liver; addiction; DTs; death
CNS stimulation; relaxation; constriction of blood vessels; impaired breathing.	Cancer; heart and blood vessel disease; respiratory diseases; habituation
CNS depressants; sleep induction; relaxation (sedation); sometimes euphoria; drowsiness; impaired judgment, reaction time, coordination, and emotional control; relief of anxiety-tension; lethargy; suppression of hallucinations	Irritability, weight loss, addiction with severe withdrawal illness; drowsiness; blurred vision; jaundice; habituation; possible death
CNS depressants; sedation; euphoria; relief of pain; apathy; impaired intellectual functioning and coordination	Constipation; loss of appetite and weight; temporary impotence or sterility; habituation; addiction with unpleasant and painful withdrawal illness; death
CNS stimulants; increased alertness, reduction of fatigue; loss of appetite; insomnia; sometimes euphoria; increased respiration and heart rate	Restlessness, insomnia, irritability, weight loss; paranoia; gastric irritation; habituation; death
Effects are unpredictable but can include intense visual imagery; increased sensory awareness; feeling of consciousness expansion; anxiety; rapid mood changes; nausea; increased pulse rate, and blood pressure; very violent behavior with PCP.	Sometimes precipitates or intensifies an already existing psychosis. Other effects include panic reaction; distorted judgment and perception; flashbacks; possible brain damage and genetic damage
Euphoria, shortness of breath, nausea, headache, dizziness, fainting	Unknown
CNS stimulant; often elevates mood; increased heart rate and respiration; drying of the nose; laxative; depression and fatigue after effects wear off	Restlessness; irritability; destruction of nasal walls; habituation; diversion of energy and money; weight loss; paranoia; death
Relief of depression (elevation of mood); stimulation	Basically the same as tranquilizers
Distortion of thoughts and perception; short-term memory loss; impaired coordination; panic reaction; increased appetite; hallucination in larger doses	Impaired judgment; apathy; temporary sterility and infertility; brain damage; lung cancer; possible genetic damage; habituation
CNS stimulant; increased alertness; reduction of fatigue; increased pulse rate	Sometimes insomnia, restlessness, gastric irritation; habituation

The active ingredient in marijuana is a complex molecule called tetra-hydrocannabinol (THC), which occurs naturally in the common weed *Cannabis sativa*, or Indian hemp. Marijuana is made by drying the plant; hashish is a gummy powder made from the resin exuded by the flowering tops of the female plant. Both marijuana and hashish are usually smoked, but they can also be cooked with food and eaten.

The effects of the drug vary somewhat from person to person and also seem to depend on the setting in which the drug is taken. But, in general, most sensory experiences seem greatly augmented—music sounds fuller; colors look brighter; smells are stronger; foods have stronger flavors; and other experiences are more intense than usual. Users may feel elated, the world may seem somehow more meaningful, and even the most ordinary events may take on an extraordinary significance. A person who is high on marijuana may, for example, suddenly become aware of the mystical implications of a particular painting. The sense of time is greatly distorted. A short sequence of events may seem to last for hours. Users may become so obsessed with an object that they sit and stare at it for many minutes. A musical phrase of a few seconds' duration may seem to stretch out in time until it becomes isolated from the rest of the composition.

As many users of marijuana have discovered, however, the drug can heighten unpleasant as well as pleasant experiences. If a person is in a frightened, unhappy, or depressed mood to begin with, the chances are excellent that taking the drug will blow the negative feelings out of proportion, so that the user's world, temporarily at least, becomes very upsetting. Cases have been reported in which marijuana appears to have helped bring on psychological disturbances in people who were already unstable before they used it.

Despite the obvious need for careful research on marijuana, the first well-controlled scientific studies of its effects did not appear until the late 1960s. Some of these studies have suggested that heavy and prolonged use of marijuana may impair reproductive functioning. Other studies suggest that marijuana use is more damaging to the lungs than cigarette use. Although there is no direct evidence that marijuana use causes lung cancer, the tar in marijuana smoke has been shown to produce tumors in laboratory animals.

Hallucinogens

Hallucinogens—so-called because their main effect is to produce hallucinations—are found in plants that grow throughout the world, and have been used for their effects on consciousness since earliest human history (Schultes, 1976). These drugs are also called "psychedelic" ("mind-manifesting") because they are seen as demonstrating the ways in which the mind has the potential to function.

Among the more common hallucinogenic plants are belladonna, henbane, mandrake, datura (jimson weed), one species of morning-glory, peyote, many kinds of mushrooms, and also cannabis. While we still do not

Figure 7.10
South American Indian in a drug trance during a religious ceremony. In this culture, hallucinogens are used to heighten the religious experience.

know the exact chemical effects of hallucinogens on the brain, some contain chemical compounds that seem to mimic the activity of certain neurotransmitters, the chemical messengers that regulate brain-cell activity.

LSD (lysergic acid diethylamide), the best-known and most extensively studied of the hallucinogens, is also the most potent; in fact, it is one of the most powerful drugs known. LSD, which is a synthetic substance, is 100 times stronger than psilocybin, which comes from certain mushrooms, and 4,000 times stronger than mescaline, which comes from the peyote. A dose of a few millionths of a gram has a noticeable effect; an average dose of 100 to 300 micrograms produces a "trip" that lasts from six to fourteen hours.

During an LSD trip a person can experience any number of mood states, often quite intense and rapidly changing. The person's "set"—expectations, mood, beliefs—and the circumstances under which he or she takes LSD can affect the experience, making it euphoric or terrifying. Perceptual hallucinations are very common with LSD. A typical hallucinatory progression begins with simple geometric forms, progresses to complex images, and then to dreamlike scenes (Seigel, 1977). The user may encounter such distortions in form that familiar objects become almost unrecognizable. A wall, for example, may seem to pulsate or breathe. One's senses, too, seem to intermingle; sounds may be "seen" and visual stimuli may be "heard." A person may experience a dissociation of the self into one being who observes and another who feels. Distortions of time, either an acceleration or a slowing down, are also common. A single stimulus may become the focus of attention for hours, perceived as ever-changing or newly beautiful and fascinating.

As measured by the ability to perform simple tasks, LSD impairs thinking, even though users may feel they are thinking more clearly and logically than ever before. Panic reactions are the most common of LSD's unpleasant side effects. Those who experience panic and later describe it often say that they felt trapped in the experience of panic and were afraid that they would never get out or that they would go mad.

Alcohol

The most widely used and abused mind-altering substance in the United States is alcohol. The consumption of alcohol is encouraged by advertisements and by social expectations and traditions. The immediate effect of alcohol is a general loosening of inhibitions. Despite its seeming stimulating effect, alcohol is actually a depressant that serves to inhibit the brain's normal functions. When people drink, they often act without the social restraint or self-control they normally apply to their behavior.

In small doses, alcohol use can have a temporarily pleasant effect. The effects of alcohol consumption, however, depend on the amount and frequency of drinking. As the amount consumed increases within a specific time, the drinker's ability to function diminishes. The person experiences slurred speech, blurred vision, and an impairment in judgment and memory. Permanent damage to the brain and liver and a change in personality can result from prolonged heavy use of alcohol.

Recent studies have suggested that not all of the early effects of drinking are the result of the alcohol alone. People expect to feel a certain way when they drink. In one study, men who were led to believe they were drinking alcohol when they were, in fact, drinking tonic water, became more aggressive. They also felt more sexually aroused and were less anxious in social situations (Marlatt and Rohsenow, 1981).

BIOFEEDBACK

Biofeedback involves learning to control your internal physiological processes with the help of feedback from these physiological states. For example, you can be hooked up to a biofeedback machine so that a light goes on every time your heart rate goes over 80 (Figure 7.11). You could then learn to keep your heart rate below 80 by trying to keep the light off. How would you do it? When researcher David Shapiro (1973) asked a participant in one of his experiments how he changed his heart rate, the subject asked in return, "How do you move your arm?"

Figure 7.11
Subject practicing biofeedback.

However people do it, biofeedback has been used to teach people to control a wide variety of physiological responses, including brain waves (EEG), heart rate, blood pressure, skin temperature, and sweat-gland activity (Hassett, 1978a). The basic principle of biofeedback is simple: feedback makes learning possible. Imagine trying to learn to play the saxophone if you were deaf. If you couldn't hear all the squeals and honks you made by mistake, your version of "The Star-Spangled Banner" would probably cause all your neighbors to move. It is only through the feedback of hearing your errors that your playing improves.

But our bodies are not designed to provide subtle feedback about internal physiological states. I have no idea whether my heart rate is now 60, 80, or 100 unless I take my pulse. Biofeedback involves using machines to tell people about very subtle, moment-to-moment changes in the body. People can then experiment with different thoughts and feelings while they watch how each affects their bodies. In time, most people can learn to change their physiological processes.

One of the most widely publicized uses of biofeedback was "alpha training." Alpha refers to a certain type of brain-wave activity, typically seen in the EEG when a person relaxes. Alpha has also been observed in the brain waves of some people when they meditate. As a result, a few years ago alpha biofeedback was widely advertised as a quick and easy way to achieve an altered state of consciousness—a sort of instant medita-

Biofeedback has more potential for treating physical disease than for spiritual well-being.

tion. Most researchers are very skeptical of such claims. These days, most people feel that biofeedback has more potential for treating physical disease than for spiritual well-being.

Before biofeedback, scientists believed that responses like heart rate and sweat-gland activity were involuntary, that people could not consciously control them. When researchers in the 1960s began to find that people could, there was a great deal of excitement about these newly discovered potentials of the nervous system. Many began experimenting with biofeedback to cure medical and stress-related conditions like high blood pressure, migraine headaches, and tension headaches. At first, many biofeedback cures were reported in the press. But psychologists were suspicious that these miraculous cases had more to do with the power of suggestion than with biofeedback itself. (Doctors are very familiar with the fact that patients often improve when they believe in a treatment, even if it's only a sugar pill.)

Therefore, more careful studies were started to see what medical conditions could be helped by biofeedback. Some of the best-documented biofeedback cures involve special training in muscular control. Tension headaches often seem to result from constriction of the frontalis muscle in the forehead. Thomas Budzynski and others (1973) used biofeedback to teach people to relax this specific muscle. The practice went on for several weeks while other people were given similar treatments without biofeedback. Only the biofeedback group improved significantly.

Migraine headaches have been successfully treated by a more controversial process—biofeedback for hand warming. People watch a meter that gives a very precise reading of the temperature of their fingers and gradually learn to warm up their hands slightly. Some researchers believe that this works because it changes the pattern of blood flow in the body, decreasing circulation to arteries in the forehead. Others think that the technique simply relaxes people. A third group continues to wonder whether the power of suggestion isn't the most important element in this particular cure.

Using biofeedback to treat conditions from partial paralysis to epilepsy is a very active area of research; but it will take at least several years to discover the problems for which biofeedback is the best solution medical science can offer.

MEDITATION

In the 1960s, psychologists began to study **meditation,** focusing attention on an image or thought with the goal of clearing one's mind and producing an "inner peace." In one of the first experiments, people were simply asked to concentrate on a blue vase.

The participants soon reported that the color of the vase became very vivid and that time passed quickly. The people could not be distracted as easily as they normally might. Some people felt themselves merging with the vase. Others reported that their surroundings became unusually beautiful, filled with light and movement. All the meditators found the experience pleasant. After twelve sessions they all felt a strong attachment to the vase and missed it when it was not present during the next session (Deikman, 1963).

Other researchers went on to show that when people meditated, their physiological state changed. The most famous of these studies was done by Robert Keith Wallace at UCLA (1970). He measured the brain waves (EEG), heart rate, oxygen consumption, and sweat-gland activity of fifteen people as they practiced Transcendental Meditation. (Transcendental Meditation is a Westernized version of yoga meditation techniques that was developed by the Maharishi Mahesh Yogi.) For two twenty-minute periods each day, meditators sit in a comfortable position and repeat a special word—called a *mantra*—over and over again. Wallace found that when people did this, electrical measurements of their bodies proved that they were deeply relaxed.

Further studies suggested that the regular practice of meditation was not only physically relaxing (Woolfolk, 1975), but also led to changes in behavior such as decreased drug use (Benson and Wallace, 1972). Dr. Leon Otis recently warned that a few people who meditate develop anxiety, depression, and other problems (Hassett, 1978c). But researchers generally agree that most people can benefit from the sort of systematic relaxation that meditation provides.

There is some controversy over how meditation techniques differ and what their specific effects are. In his best-selling book *The Relaxation Response*, Herbert Benson (1975) argues that most forms of meditation produce the same result, which he called the "relaxation response." Benson believes that all through recorded history, people have been using various techniques to elicit the relaxation response. He cites many examples, including the contemplative practices of St. Augustine and Martin Luther's instructions for prayer.

Figure 7.12
The *mandala* is a symbol of the universe used as an aid to meditation. This one is Tibetan and is now in the Newark Museum.

The opposite of Walter Cannon's famous "fight or flight" response, the relaxation response is said to be physiologically distinct from more casual states of relaxation or sleep. Four basic elements are required to elicit the relaxation response: a quiet environment, a comfortable position, a "mental device" (such as a word that is repeated over and over again, or a physical object that the meditator concentrates on), and a passive attitude. Although not all psychologists agree that the relaxation response is entirely different from sleep or that all relaxation yields the same physical pattern, most do believe that Benson's technique can be helpful for many people. It is described in detail in his book.

USING PSYCHOLOGY

Lowering Blood Pressure

One out of every three American adults has high blood pressure. More than 90 percent of these cases are diagnosed as essential **hypertension**—a euphemism that means nobody really knows what is causing it. Traditionally, physicians have treated this problem with pills. But now doctors are shifting their emphasis from pills to people. Patients with high blood pressure are being taught to relax, often with the help of meditation and biofeedback (Hassett, 1978b).

Blood pressure is the force of the blood moving away from the heart, pushing against the artery walls. It changes from instant to instant, peaking as the heart beats and blood spurts through the arteries, and gradually decreasing to a minimum just before the next beat. Blood pressure is expressed as two numbers: systolic pressure (the maximum value when the heart beats) over diastolic pressure (the minimum pressure between beats). It is measured in millimeters of mercury (abbreviated mmHg), a standard unit of force. Normal blood pressure is somewhere around 120/80 mmHg.

Blood pressure varies constantly and increases under stress. Visiting the dentist, taking an examination, thinking about trying out skydiving with the new friend you're trying to impress, even drinking a cup of coffee (a mild stimulant) will increase your blood pressure temporarily. Strong emotions, particularly suppressed anger, will also raise blood pressure.

When blood pressure goes up and stays up, the medical condition is called hypertension. Definite hypertension refers to a blood pressure greater than 160/95. Hypertension is called the silent killer because it usually produces no pain, no other symptoms or warnings before causing severe damage to the cardiovascular system or other organs. But a killer it is. It is a primary cause of stroke (blood-vessel damage in the brain) and, like smoking and high cholesterol levels, increases the risk of suffering heart attacks and coronary-artery disease.

After researchers discovered that normal people could raise and lower blood pressure with the help of biofeedback, it was but a small step to the idea that hypertensives could be taught to lower their blood pressure. In 1971, Harvard researchers Herbert Benson, David Shapiro, Bernard Tursky, and Gary Schwartz reported in *Science* that they had done just that. Five essential hypertensives had learned to lower their systolic pressure over the course of several weeks of training. Since then, others have found that biofeedback can be used to reduce both systolic and diastolic blood pressure.

Even in the first study, however, there were hints that biofeedback's effects don't always last after the subject leaves the laboratory. Gary Schwartz, for example, noticed that one man had a puzzling pattern of successes and failures. Five days a week, this hypertensive man faithfully attended training sessions, collecting $35 every Friday for his success in lowering his systolic pressure. When he returned each Monday morning, however, he again had high blood pressure. After several weeks of this, Schwartz took the patient aside and asked for an explanation. It seemed that Saturday nights the man took his biofeedback earnings to the race track, gambled, and lost both his money and his controlled level of blood pressure.

So it was clear from the start that biofeedback was not a magical cure, only part of the answer. Since blood-pressure biofeedback requires complex and expensive equipment, it wasn't practical to use it with large numbers of patients. Other researchers therefore experimented with teaching hypertensives to relax their muscles, using a simpler form of biofeedback. This too led to lower blood pressure, at least temporarily.

Herbert Benson has experimented with meditation as a partial treatment for high blood pressure, and again it has been successful. Finally, one group of researchers (Surwit, Shapiro, and Good, 1978) directly compared the effects of blood-pressure biofeedback, muscle-tension biofeedback, and meditation. All three reduced blood pressure, and there were no significant differences among the groups. Since biofeedback requires elaborate instruments and meditation does not, it seems likely that the latter will be more widely used (Hassett, 1978).

SUMMARY

Use the following outline as a tool for reviewing this chapter. Copy the outline onto your own paper, leaving spaces between headings to make notes about key concepts.

   I. Sleep and Dreams

     A. Stages of Sleep

     B. How Much Sleep?

     C. Dreams

     D. Dream Interpretation

  II. Hypnosis

 III. Hallucinations

 IV. Sensory Deprivation

  V. Drug States

     A. Marijuana

     B. Hallucinogens

     C. Alcohol

 VI. Biofeedback

VII. Meditation

CONCEPTS AND VOCABULARY

1. Describe each of the four stages of sleep. During which stage is it most difficult to awaken someone? During which stage do we dream and display REM?

2. What percentage of sleep time do adults usually spend in REM sleep?

3. What techniques can insomniacs use to help them fall asleep and stay asleep?

4. What is one possible explanation for the sense of dread people usually experience during a nightmare?

5. What is Freud's view of the meaning of dreams? What is Kleitman's view of dreams?

6. What happens when someone is hypnotized? What does Barber say about hypnosis being an altered state of consciousness? How does Hilgard view hypnosis?

7. What is the phenomenon of posthypnotic suggestion?

8. What is the definition of hallucination? What are some possible causes of hallucination?

9. What are some of the typical effects of sensory deprivation on people?

10. Which consciousness-altering drugs have a high potential for psychological dependence?

11. What are the typical reactions caused by LSD?

12. What are possible consequences of prolonged heavy use of alcohol?

13. What are some health problems that biofeedback can potentially help?

14. What are the basic elements of the relaxation response?

15. What is the most widely used and abused mind-altering substance in the United States?

CRITICAL THINKING

1. **Analyze.** What behaviors do you perform automatically? Pick one of your automatic behaviors and pay close attention to how you perform it. What are the individual parts that make up the behavior? How does consciously thinking about the behavior affect your performance of it?

2. **Evaluate.** Keep track of your dreams for at least a week. Dreams are difficult to remember, so keep a paper and pencil by your bed. When you wake up after a dream, keep your eyes closed and try to remember it in your mind. Then write it down, including as much detail as you can. Also write down any ideas you may have about what the dream means and any feelings you may have about the dream. After you

have kept track of your dreams for several days, ask yourself: Am I able to consciously control my dreams in any way? Am I better able to understand myself by examining my dreams?

3. **Analyze.** One way of becoming aware of your consciousness is through meditation. Meditation is not concentration in the normal sense of the word. It is opening up one's awareness to the world at the present. Try the following for ten to fifteen minutes a day. Find a quiet spot without distractions. Listen quietly without making any generalizations on what you hear. Listen for the sounds without naming them. After each period, write down your observations. Which sounds did you "hear" for the first time?

4. **Synthesize.** Have you ever hallucinated a sight or sound—perhaps when you were very tired or upset? What did you experience? Why do you suppose you created this particular hallucination?

APPLYING KNOWLEDGE

1. Hypnosis is a form of suggestibility. You may discover which of your friends is susceptible to hypnosis by doing the following test in hypnosis. Have your subjects place a coin in their open palm. Repeatedly suggest to them that they feel the palm slowly turning over, until the coin falls out of the palm. You may be surprised at the results.

2. Pick any word and say it one hundred times. What happens?

3. Some of the mind-altering chemicals that people use during the day are not ordinarily thought of as drugs. These include caffeine, cough syrup, and nicotine. Observe your family and/or friends for a twenty-four-hour period. Which drugs or chemicals did you see used? In what quantities were they used? Did you notice any changes in the person's mood or behavior? What do your observations tell you about the effects of these drugs or chemicals on people's behavior and moods?

ANALYZING VIEWPOINTS

1. Since Freud's pioneering work on dreams, many psychologists have theorized that by interpreting the content of our dreams, we can better understand our unconscious desires. Other social scientists have maintained a more commonplace view of dreams. They suggest that our dreams reflect more about what we were thinking about or doing on a particular day than what our unconscious desires may be. Write an article that presents a case for both viewpoints. You may want to look for recent magazine articles on dreams. If possible, use a recent dream that you remember as an example to support one of the viewpoints.

BEYOND THE CLASSROOM

1. In recent years, efforts to send an anti-drug message to teenagers have taken many forms. One strategy is to place anti-drug ads in magazines teenagers are likely to read, such as *Rolling Stone* or *Seventeen*. Look through recent magazines for advertisements against the use of drugs. Photocopy or cut out any ads you find. Bring the ads to class and ask class members to react to each ad. Ask your classmates which ads they think are effective. Then ask your classmates which ads they think are ineffective. Using the feedback you received from your classmates, come up with several ideas for new ads that would effectively convey an anti-drug message to teenagers. Present these ads to the class for additional feedback.

UNIT 3

The Life Span

CHAPTER 8

Infancy and Childhood

Key Terms:

accommodation
anal stage
assimilation
conservation
critical period
developmental psychology
genital stage
grasping reflex
identification
imprinting
internalization
latency stage
maturation
object permanence
Oedipal conflict
oral stage
phallic stage
representational thought
role taking
rooting reflex
separation anxiety
socialization
sublimation
telegraphic speech

The young child lives in a strange world of wonders and delights. A doorknob or the leg of a table is a mysterious object that an infant will fondle and taste for hours. Mommy and Daddy are the source of all life's great pleasures, and many of its pains. Each day there is something new to be learned.

It is hard to believe that less than twenty years ago we were only two feet tall and were taking our first step. Just a year or two after that, we spent our days intently playing house, cops and robbers, and doctor. Most of the events from our early lives are long forgotten, but we changed faster and learned more in childhood than we ever will again.

Developmental psychology is the study of the changes that occur as people grow up and grow old. It covers the entire life cycle, from conception to death. What does the newborn know? How does the infant respond in the early years of life? How do people learn to walk and talk, to think and feel? How do people develop their unique personalities? These are some questions developmental psychologists seek to answer.

In this chapter we describe the many different psychological processes we experience from infancy through childhood. In the next chapters we will look at adolescence, adulthood, and old age.

THE BEGINNING OF LIFE

Development begins long before an infant is born. Expectant mothers can feel strong kicking and sometimes hiccuping inside them during the later stages of pregnancy, and it is common for a fetus (an unborn child) to suck its thumb, even though it has never suckled at its mother's breast or had a bottle.

Objectives:

After studying this chapter, you should be able to

- describe the processes of intellectual development and Piaget's theory.
- discuss the development of language.
- compare the theories of social development.
- summarize the cognitive-developmental theory and Kohlberg's stages of moral reasoning.

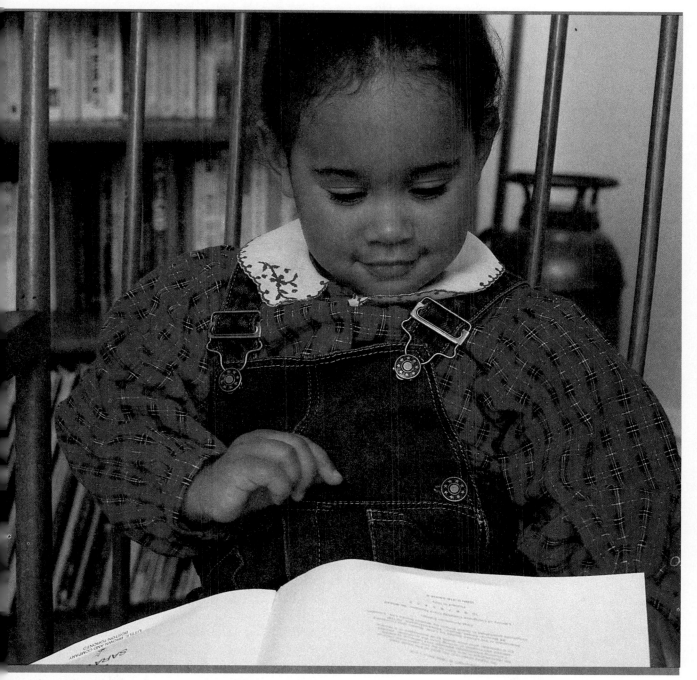

Figure 8.1 Childhood is a time of rapid learning. We change faster and learn more in these years than we ever will again.

Figure 8.2
(a) The strength of the grasping reflex is demonstrated in a baby only a few days old (b) This infant is responding to a touch on the cheek by opening his mouth and turning his head. The response is called the rooting reflex.

a   b

Birth puts staggering new demands on a baby's capacity to adapt and survive. He goes from an environment in which he is totally protected from the world to one in which he is assaulted by lights, sounds, touches, and extremes of temperature. The newborn is capable of certain coordinated movement patterns, called reflexes, that can be triggered by the right stimulus (Figure 8.2). The **grasping reflex,** for example, is a response to a touch on the palm of the hand. Infants can grasp an object, such as a finger, so strongly that they can be lifted into the air. We suspect this reflex is left over from an earlier stage in human evolution, when babies had to cling to their apelike mothers' coats while their mothers were climbing or searching for food.

Also vital is the **rooting reflex.** If an alert newborn is touched anywhere around the mouth, he will move his head and mouth toward the source of the touch. In this way the touch of his mother's breast on his cheek guides the baby's mouth toward her nipple. The sucking that follows contact with the nipple is one of the baby's most complex reflexes. The baby is able to suck, breathe air, and swallow milk twice a second without getting confused. This is at least as difficult as learning to walk and chew gum at the same time.

Besides grasping and sucking, the newborn looks at his body and at his surroundings. From birth, unless he is sleeping, feeding, or crying, the baby is directing his gaze toward bright patterns and faces, tracing the outlines of those patterns with his eye movements.

How do newborn infants, lying in a hospital nursery, perceive the world? Do they see a roomful of stable objects and hear distinct sounds? Or is the sensory world of newborns an ever-changing chaos of meaningless shapes and noises—as William James put it, "one great booming, buzzing confusion"?

These are difficult questions to answer. How does one measure the capabilities of newborn infants who cannot speak or understand the questions of curious psychologists? One reasonable approach is to take advantage of the things babies *can* do. And what they can do is suck, turn their heads, look at things, cry, smile, and show signs of surprise or fright. The vigor of a baby's sucking, the patterns of eye movements, and expressions of pleasure and displeasure are all closely tied to how the baby is being stimulated. By measuring these behaviors while stimulating the baby in different ways, it is possible to infer how the infant perceives the world. For example, infants spend less time looking at out-of-focus movies than they do looking at the same movies in focus. Moreover, infants quickly learn to suck vigorously on a pacifier attached to the focusing mechanism of a movie projector in order to cause an out-of-focus picture to become more sharply defined (Figure 8.3). This suggests that babies are attuned to distinct edges; if the visual world were a blurry confusion for infants, they would not care that a movie was slightly blurry (Kalmis and Bruner, 1973). Studies like this have refuted the notion that the world is essentially disorganized and chaotic to a baby.

HOW DO BABIES GROW?

In the space of two years this grasping, rooting, searching infant will develop into a child who can walk, talk, and feed herself or himself. This transformation is the result of both maturation and learning.

Maturation

To some extent a baby is like a plant that shoots up and unfolds according to a built-in plan. Unless something is wrong with an infant, she will begin to lift her head at about three months, smile at four months, and grasp objects at five to six months. Crawling appears at eight to ten months. By this time the baby may be able to pull herself into a standing position, although she will fall if she lets go. Three or four months later she will begin to walk, tentatively at first, but gradually acquiring a sense of balance.

Figure 8.3
Inferring how an infant perceives the world: the four-month-old baby sucks on the pacifier to keep the pattern in focus.

Psychologists call internally programmed growth **maturation.** Maturation is as important as learning or experience, especially in the first years. Unless a child is persistently underfed, severely restricted in her movements, or deprived of human contact and things to look at, she will develop more or less according to this schedule. Conversely, no amount of coaching will push a child to walk or speak before she is physiologically ready.

This was demonstrated in an experiment with identical twins (Gesell and Thompson, 1929). One twin, but not the other, was given special training in climbing stairs, building with blocks, and the like. This child did acquire some skill in these areas. But in a short time the second child learned to climb and build just as well as his twin—and with much less practice. Why? Because he had matured to the point where he could coordinate his legs and hands more easily.

Ethnic Differences in Infants

It probably won't surprise you to learn that different breeds of puppies show striking differences in temperament and behavior. Young beagles, for example, are irrepressibly friendly; wire-haired terriers are tough and aggressive. But it probably will raise both your eyebrows to discover that newborn infants belonging to different ethnic groups start out life with different sets of responses that seem to relate more to their genes than to their individual personalities.

To learn just how important ethnic differences are in the way we respond, psychologist Daniel G. Freedman studied the responses of newborn Chinese and Caucasian babies. His results show that in many ways Chinese and Caucasian babies behave like two different breeds.

Here are some examples of the differences Dr. Freedman found. The Chinese babies were far more adaptable than the Caucasians. They cried less easily and were easier to console. In addition, they seemed comfortable in almost any position they were placed while the Caucasian infants tossed and turned until they were satisfied. When a cloth was briefly placed against the babies' noses, the Caucasian infants responded with a fight; they immediately turned their faces or swiped at the cloth with their hands. The Chinese babies adapted to the cloth's presence in the simplest possible way—by breathing through their mouths. As Dr. Freedman points out, "It was as if the old stereotypes of the calm, inscrutable Chinese and the excitable, emotionally changeable Caucasian were appearing spontaneously in the first 48 hours of life."

For more details, see Daniel G. Freedman, "Ethnic Differences in Babies," *Human Nature,* January 1979.

No two babies are exactly alike, and no two mature according to the same schedule.

The process of maturation becomes obvious when you think about walking. An infant lacks the physical control walking requires. However, by the end of the first year the nerves connected to the child's muscles have grown. He or she is ready to walk.

By recording the ages at which thousands of infants first began to smile, to sit upright, to crawl, and to try a few steps, psychologists have been able to draw up an approximate timetable for maturation (Figure 8.4). This schedule helps doctors and other professionals to spot problems and abnormalities. If a child has not begun to talk by the age of two and a half, a doctor will recommend tests to determine if something is wrong.

However, one of the facts to emerge from this effort is that the maturational plan inside each child is unique. On the average, babies start walking at twelve to thirteen months. However, some are ready at nine months, and others delay walking until eighteen months. And each baby has his or her own temperament. Some infants are extremely active from birth and some quiet. Some are cuddly and some stiff. Some cry a great deal while others hardly ever whimper. No two babies are exactly alike, and no two mature according to the same timetable.

Figure 8.4
The sequence of motor development. The age given for the appearance of each skill is approximate; there is a wide range of individual differences. (Adapted from Shirley, 1933)

Learning

Maturation is only part of the process of growing up. Infants and small children are exceptionally responsive. Each experience changes the child, teaches him something, pushes him in some direction. The child learns to make associations, to expect certain events—such as mother and food—to come together. Children learn to do things that produce rewards and to avoid doing things that produce punishments. They also learn by imitating other people.

Recent experiments indicate that infants too are able to learn new behaviors. Even newborn babies change their behavior in response to the environment—which, as you will recall from Chapter 2, is the basic definition of "learning." One team of psychologists taught two- and three-day-old infants to turn their heads at the sound of a buzzer by rewarding them with a bottle each time they did so.

Another researcher built a small theater for four- to five-week-old babies. The infants were placed in a well-padded seat opposite a blank wall that served as a movie screen, and were given pacifiers. The pacifiers were connected to the projector. As we described earlier, the infants had to suck on the pacifiers to focus the picture. Soon the babies had learned the trick and sucked hard, pausing for only a few seconds to catch their breath. When the researcher reversed the procedure, so that sucking blurred the picture, they quickly learned to lengthen the pause to eight seconds (Pines, 1970). We can assume that infants are just as responsive to everyday events as they are to experiments.

Clearly, then, learning is an important part of the process of growing up. In the pages that follow we will show how inner plans and outside influences—maturation and learning—work together in the development of intellect, language, love, and morality.

INTELLECTUAL DEVELOPMENT

If you have a younger brother or sister, you may remember times when your parents insisted that you let the little one play with you and your friends. No matter how often you explained hide-and-seek to your four-year-old brother, he spoiled the game. Why couldn't he understand that he had to keep quiet or he'd be found right away?

This is a question Swiss psychologist Jean Piaget set out to answer more than fifty years ago. Of the several theories of intellectual development, Piaget's is the most comprehensive and influential. Common sense told him that intelligence, or the ability to understand, develops gradually, as the child grows. The sharpest, most inquisitive four year old simply cannot understand things a seven year old grasps easily. What accounts for the dramatic changes between the ages of four and seven?

Piaget spent years observing, questioning, and playing games with babies and young children—including his own. He concluded that younger children aren't "dumb" in the sense of lacking a given *amount of informa-*

tion. Rather they think in a different *way* than older children and adults; they use a different kind of logic. A seven year old is completely capable of answering the question "Who was born first, you or your mother?" but a four year old isn't (Chukovsky, 1963). Intellectual development involves quantitative changes (growth in the *amount* of information) as well as qualitative changes (differences in the *manner* of thinking).

In time Piaget was able to detail the ways in which a child's thinking changes, month by month, year by year. Although the rate at which different children develop varies, every child passes through the same predictable stages. Each stage builds on the last, increasing the child's ability to solve more complex problems.

How Knowing Changes

Understanding the world involves the construction of *schemes,* or plans for knowing. Each of us is an architect and engineer in this respect, constructing intellectual schemes, applying them, and changing them as necessary. When we put a scheme into action, we are trying to understand something. In the process of **assimilation,** we try to fit the world into our scheme. In that of **accommodation,** we change our scheme to fit the characteristics of the world.

According to Piaget, newborns have a set of ready-made responses. They respond to bright lights by blinking, to objects in their hands by grasping, to a sudden loss of support by throwing out their arms and legs, and to an object in the mouth by sucking. These reflexes let babies understand things. In grasping a block, babies assimilate it to their grasping scheme after accommodating it—changing their grasp to fit it.

Assimilation and accommodation work together to produce intellectual

Figure 8.5
(from left to right and top to bottom) This child possesses a scheme for grasping objects and pulling them to her that does not adequately match the features of the environment she is now trying to assimilate. Her scheme will not get the toy through the bars of the playpen. An accommodation—the addition of turning to grasping and pulling—achieves a state of equilibrium.

a   b

Figure 8.6
This infant of about six months cannot yet understand that objects have an existence of their own, away from her presence. (a) The infant gazes intently at a toy elephant. (b) When the elephant is blocked from view, she gives no indication that she understands the toy still exists. This thinking pattern changes by age two, as shown in Figure 8.7.

growth. When events do not fit into existing schemes, new and grander schemes have to be created. The child begins to see and understand things in a new light. Progressive changes in the way a baby conceives objects illustrate this.

Object Permanence.   A baby's understanding of things lies totally in the here and now. The sight of a toy, the way it feels in her hands, the sensation it produces in her mouth are all she knows. She does not imagine it, picture it, think of it, remember it, or even forget it. How do we know this?

When an infant's toy is hidden from her, she acts as if it had ceased to exist (Figure 8.6). She doesn't look for it; she grabs whatever else she can find and plays with that. Or she may simply start crying. At ten to twelve months, however, this pattern begins to change. When you take the baby's toy and hide it under a blanket—while she is watching—she will search for it under the blanket. However, if you change tactics and put her toy behind your back, she will continue to look for it under the blanket—even if she was watching you the whole time.

You can't fool a twelve- to eighteen-month-old baby quite so easily. A child this age watches closely and searches for the toy in the last place she saw you put it. But suppose you take the toy, put it under the blanket, conceal it in your hands, and then put it behind your back. A twelve month old will act surprised when she doesn't find the toy under the blanket—and keep searching there. An eighteen or twenty-four month old will guess what you've done and walk behind you to look (Figure 8.7). She knows the toy must be somewhere (Ginsburg and Opper, 1969: 50–56).

This is a giant step in intellectual development. The child has progressed from a stage where she apparently believed that her own actions created the world, to a stage where she realizes that people and objects are independent of her actions. This new scheme, **object permanence,** might be expressed: "Things continue to exist even though I cannot see or touch them." The child now conceives of a world of which she is only a part.

Representational Thought.   The achievement of object permanence suggests that a child has begun to engage in what Piaget calls **representational thought.** The child's intelligence is no longer one of action only. Now, children can picture (or represent) things in their minds. At fourteen months of age, Piaget's daughter demonstrated this. When she was out visiting another family, she happened to witness a child throwing a temper tantrum. She had never had a tantrum herself, but the next day she did—screaming, shaking her playpen, and stamping her feet as the other child had. She had formed so clear an image of the tantrum in her mind that she was able to create an excellent imitation a day later (Ginsburg and Opper, 1969: 65). To Piaget, this meant that his daughter was using symbols. Soon she would learn to use a much more complex system of symbols—spoken language. Where the infant is limited to solving problems with his or her actions, the older child can mentally represent the problem and use language to think it through. Thinking with actions, in other words, comes before thinking with language.

The Principle of Conservation. More complex intellectual abilities emerge as the infant grows into childhood. Somewhere between the ages of five and seven, most children begin to understand what Piaget calls **conservation,** the principle that a given quality does not change when its appearance is changed. For example, if you have two identical short, wide jars filled with water and you pour the contents of one of these jars into a tall, thin jar, a child under five will say that the tall jar contains more water than the short one. If you pour the water back into the short jar to show the amount has not changed, the child will still maintain that there was more water in the tall container. Children under five do not seem to be able to think about two dimensions (height and width) at the same time. That is,

Figure 8.7
By the age of two, a child realizes that the disappearance of an object does not mean that it no longer exists. In fact, if an object is concealed, a child will search for it because he or she knows it still exists somewhere.

Figure 8.8
The girl taking part in this demonstration thinks there is more water in the tall beaker; she has not yet acquired conservation. Although she has seen the liquid poured from one beaker to another, she bases her decision on the height of the column of water and ignores its diameter.

they do not understand that a change in width is made up for by a change in the height of the tall glass (Figure 8.8).

Within two years, the same child will tell you that the second jar contains the same amount of water as the first. If you ask why, he may say because the short jar is fatter than the tall jar—indicating that he is able to coordinate his perceptions of height and width. Or he may point out that if you poured the water back into the short jar, it would be the same—indicating that he is able to think in reverse, to retrace the steps of the experiment. Younger children generally cannot do this.

Another type of conservation experiment begins when a child is shown two identical balls of clay. Then, the child watches the experimenter flatten one ball and roll it into the shape of a sausage. Again, the young child believes that the amount of clay has changed. The older child conserves. That is, she recognizes that the amount of clay is unaffected by the change in appearance.

Many such cognitive advances take place between the years of five and twelve. This is the stage when children develop a working knowledge of the world. They develop skills in the trial-and-error approach to problem solving. But in general, their thinking is extremely concrete. They need to try solutions out; they cannot work through problems in their heads, and have difficulty thinking about hypothetical situations or abstract concepts.

Piaget described the changes that occur in children's understanding in four stages of cognitive development (Table 8.1). During the *sensorimotor stage*, the young infant uses schemes that primarily involve his body and sensations. The *preoperational stage* emerges when the child begins to use mental images or symbols to understand things. By the third, *concrete operational stage*, children are able to use logical schemes, but their understanding is limited to concrete objects or problems. In the *formal operational stage*, the person is able to solve abstract problems. According to Piaget, a person's development through these four stages depends on both the maturation of his or her nervous system and on the

---

Table 8.1 / Piaget's Stages of Cognitive Development

SENSORIMOTOR STAGE (birth to two years): Thinking is displayed in action, such as the grasping, sucking, and looking schemes. Child gradually learns to discover the location of hidden objects at about eighteen months, when the concept of object permanence is fully understood.

PREOPERATIONAL STAGE (two to six years): Beginning of symbolic representation. Language first appears; child begins to draw pictures that represent things. Child cannot represent a series of actions in his or her head in order to solve problems.

CONCRETE OPERATIONAL STAGE (six to twelve years): Ability to understand conservation problems. Ability to think of several dimensions or features at same time. Child can now do elementary arithmetic problems, such as judging the quantity of liquid containers and checking addition of numbers by subtraction.

FORMAL OPERATIONAL STAGE (twelve years to adulthood): Thinking becomes more abstract and hypothetical. The individual can consider many alternative solutions to a problem, make deductions, contemplate the future, and formulate personal ideals and values.

---

kinds of experiences he or she has had. Everyone goes through the stages in the same order, but not necessarily at the same age.

Some Implications of Intellectual Development

A clear picture of the development of cognitive abilities sheds light on some of the other areas of child behavior. For example, at about ten or twelve months, many children go through a period of **separation anxiety.** They become extremely upset when their mothers take them to a friend's or relative's house and leave without them. A five-month-old baby does not react this way. Why does a one year old?

Perhaps the answer is that the older child is more confused by Mom's disappearance. One study consistent with this view found that infants were not particularly upset when their mothers left a room through a familiar exit, like the nursery door. But when Mom left in a surprising way—for example, by stepping into a closet—the baby became upset. Thus, separation anxiety arose when the mother's disappearance led to uncertainty.

Piaget's theory also helps explain why seven and eight year olds are more conscious of sexual identity than younger children are. If you've worked with children, you will know that four- or five-year-old boys object loudly to playing baseball with girls—and vice versa. Why?

Four-year-old children can tell you whether they are boys or girls, and many are fully informed about anatomical differences. Yet if you question children this age, you'll find that they believe people can change their sex by wearing clothes designed for the opposite sex, changing their haircut, playing games associated with the opposite sex, and the like. In other words, if you pour a boy into a female container, he'll change. Only when they understand conservation do they realize that one's sex is permanent. It is at this point that children become concerned about their own sexual identity.

USING PSYCHOLOGY

Children and Television

Today, more than 95 percent of American families have at least one television set—some have two or more—and children spend a significant amount of time watching TV. One estimate is that children under two spend an average of two and a half hours a day in front of the television. This amount increases to four hours a day for children eight to ten years old (Liebert, Sprafkin, and Davidson, 1982). By the time you graduate from high school, you will have spent an estimated 15,000 hours in front of the TV. Clearly, television is an important force in children's lives. In what specific ways does television viewing affect children's development? This question has generated much debate and numerous research studies.

Perhaps the most controversial and studied issue is the effect of watching television violence and aggression on children's behavior. The results of research studies support the view that violence on television leads to aggressive behavior in children. By observing highly attractive models engaging in a variety of aggressive and physically violent behaviors, children are encouraged to act in a similar way.

The extent to which children imitate aggressive acts on TV is influenced by the age of the child. The most sensitive time for children to learn aggressive behaviors from TV is when they are eight to nine years old (Eron, *et al.*, 1983). Also, if children are already predisposed to aggressive behaviors, they are more likely to imitate aggression seen on TV. When parents watch aggressive or violent shows with their children and discuss the events afterwards, the negative effects seem to be reduced and the positive effects enhanced.

When children watch television, they are forming beliefs about what the world is like. Their views of reality, including their views of how people act toward one another, are influenced by the characters they see portrayed on television. Often, adult TV themes include negative motives, such as jealousy, revenge, corruption, and violence. While adults may view these programs as entertainment and not base conclusions about their social world on them, children do not have the cognitive sophistication to separate television "reality" from everyday experience.

Another potent way in which television affects social behavior is through the presentation of sex role models and ethnic stereotypes. Girls who consistently see women por-

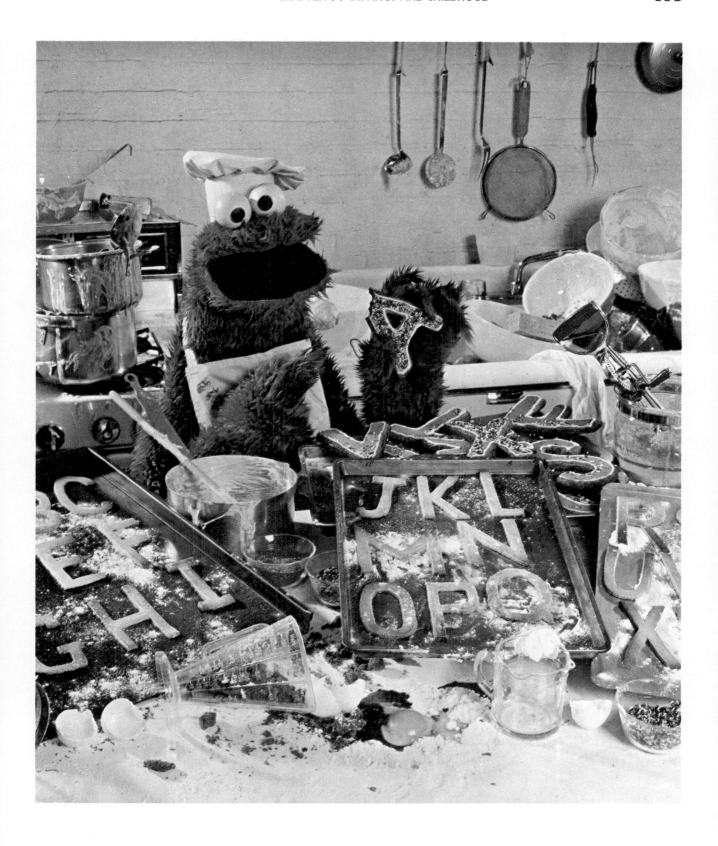

trayed as helpless victims or housewives are likely to accept this view of women as part of their sex role. Recent concerns over the racial, ethnic, and sex role stereotypes on television have resulted in a more representative depiction of people on television. However, commercials still seem flagrantly to reinforce limiting social stereotypes.

Special attention has been given to the format of children's television programs. Programs are carefully produced to capture and hold the viewer's attention. The format of commercial television programs, particularly children's shows, contains rapid-fire, action-packed sequences that are highlighted by audio and visual special effects. Children's attention is especially guided by the television format of cartoons (Wright and Huston, 1983). Children spend countless hours, particularly on Saturday morning, watching the humorous (and often violent and aggressive) adventures of cartoon characters. The faster the pace of the program, the more receptive children are to it.

On the positive side, TV has a rich and largely untapped potential for educating and enhancing children's development (Singer and Singer, 1983). Television is an excellent vehicle for presenting new information about the world beyond the child's or adult's immediate experience. Also, some of the more recent children's programs have attempted to help children deal more effectively with their fears. For example, by watching a television character overcome a fear of animals, children are able to deal more effectively with similar fears of their own.

In 1982, the United States government conducted a review of studies on the impact of television on social behavior (Pearl, *et al.*, 1982). On the basis of over twenty years of research and 3,000 scientific studies, the reviewers concluded:

> Television can no longer be considered a casual part of daily life, an electronic toy. Research findings have long since destroyed the illusion that television is merely innocuous entertainment. While the learning it provides is mainly incidental rather than direct and formal, it is a significant part of the total acculturation process (Pearl, 1982, 1:87).

The use of educational programs is an important issue for psychologists, educators, and parents. Recently, the American Psychological Association issued a statement supporting the view that exposure to violence on television promotes aggressive behavior. With more responsible attitudes toward TV programs, we can use them as an important vehicle for education.

MENTAL RETARDATION

The term "mentally retarded" is applied to people who have since child-hood been less able to learn and understand things than most people of the same age. Retarded children have difficulty learning to tie their shoes, find it impossible to keep up in school, and cannot join in the games that other children their age enjoy.

Mental retardation is an intellectual disability rather than an emotional one. But it is possible for retarded people to find the world so unpleasant that they withdraw from it in a neurotic or psychotic manner. Retarded people are often made worse by the way other people treat them. Most retarded people are capable of living relatively normal lives if given the chance. They must, however, be given special attention, affection, and understanding if they are to reach their full potential as human beings.

Unfortunately, retardates are often treated as if they were unseeing, unhearing, uncomprehending "objects." The presence of a retarded child in a household may cause a great deal of friction and resentment among members of the family. This situation does not go unnoticed by the re-tarded child. Despite his intellectual handicaps, the child is a sensitive human being who understands the meaning of anger and resentment as well as of love and acceptance. Conflict and rejection can rob the child of the supportive environment necessary for his maximum development.

Only about one-fourth of the six million people who are called retarded in the United States actually have something physically wrong with their brains. Their retardation is due to diseases contracted before birth or dur-ing early infancy, to brain injuries, to poor nutrition in childhood, or to some other physical factor.

The majority of people who are called retarded are people who seem never to have learned to use their minds. They may have been brought up in lonely, dull, or frightening environments in which there was no oppor-tunity or reward for thinking. This situation occurs most often with chil-dren born into poor or unstable families and reared in slums or orphan-ages. If such children are given the opportunity and the encouragement to use their minds early enough, they are often able to live normal lives.

THE DEVELOPMENT OF LANGUAGE

Language and thought are closely intertwined. Both abilities involve using symbols, as we saw in Chapter 3. We are able to think and talk about objects that are not present and about ideas that are not necessarily true. A child begins to think, to represent things to himself, before he is able to speak. But the acquisition of language propels the child into further intel-lectual development (see Piaget, 1926). We have been able to learn a good deal about the acquisition of language from our nearest relative in the animal kingdom, the chimpanzee.

Figure 8.10
Washoe at about five years of age. She is shown here using the American Sign Language sign for "hat."

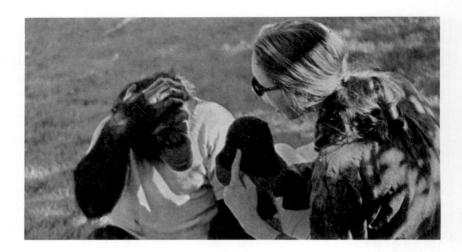

Can Animals Use Language?

Psychologists believe that chimpanzees must develop at least as far as two-year-old humans because, like two year olds, they will look for a toy or a bit of food that has disappeared. They can represent the existence of that toy or bit of food in their minds. Can they be taught to "talk" about it?

Many psychologists have tried to teach chimpanzees to use language, but only recently have such efforts been successful. One husband-and-wife team, the Gardners, raised a baby chimp named Washoe in their home and taught her to use the American Sign Language for deaf people (Figure 8.10). At three-and-one-half years of age, Washoe knew eighty-seven signs for words like "food," "dog," "toothbrush," "gimmee," "sweet," "more," and "hurry."

Making these signs at the appropriate times would not be enough to be called language, though. A dog or a parrot might make signs that its owner could interpret as demands for a walk or for food. Washoe's remarkable achievement was that some of her signs had abstract meanings and that she could put signs together in new ways to produce new meanings. For example, she learned the sign for "more" (putting her fingertips together over her head) because she loved to be tickled and wanted more. But she was not simply doing something like a dog does when it rolls over to be tickled; she was able to use the same sign later in entirely new circumstances—asking for more food or more hair brushing.

Since the original experiments with Washoe, several chimpanzees have been taught to "talk" in other ways. Lana the chimpanzee was trained on a special typewriter connected to a computer. The machine has fifty keys, each marked with a different symbol which stands for a word in Yerkish, a special monkey language devised just for this study. When Lana presses a key, the symbol appears on the screen in front of her. Lana has learned to type out sentences and thus converse with the experimenters. Sometimes, she types a word out of order, reads the sentence on the screen, and erases it (by pressing the erase key) before she has been corrected. In other cases, Lana has made up phrases to describe objects she's never seen before. For example, the first time Lana saw a ring, she identified it as a "finger bracelet."

The ability to arrange symbols in new combinations to produce new meanings is especially well developed in the human brain. The rules for such organization of symbols are called *grammar*. Grammatical rules are what make the sentence "the rhinoceros roared at the boy" mean the same thing as "the boy was roared at by the rhinoceros." On the surface, these sentences appear different because the word position is changed. But on a deeper level, we know that the first is an active sentence and the second a passive transformation of it. It may be in our ability to use such grammatical rules that we surpass the simpler language of the chimpanzee.

How Children Acquire Language

The example of Washoe shows that there are several steps in learning language. First, one must learn to make the signs; then, one must give them meaning; and finally, one must learn grammar. Each child takes these steps at his or her own rate. During the first year of life, the "average child" makes many sounds. Crying lessens, and the child starts making mostly cooing sounds, which develop into a babble that includes every sound humans can make—Chinese vowels, African clicks, German rolled *r*'s, and English *o*'s.

Late in the first year, the strings of babbles begin to sound more like the language that the child hears. Children imitate the speech of their parents and their older brothers and sisters, and are greeted with approval whenever they say something that sounds like a word. In this way children learn to speak their own language, even though they could just as easily learn any other.

The leap to using sounds as symbols occurs some time in the second year. The first attempts at saying words are primitive, and the sounds are

Figure 8.11
A two-year-old's telegraphic speech: the two-word phrases leave out words but still get the message across.

incomplete: "Ball" usually sounds like "ba," and "cookie" may even sound like "doo-da." The first real words usually refer to things the infant can see or touch. Often they are labels or commands ("dog!" "cookie!").

By the time children are two years old, they have a vocabulary of at least fifty words. Toward the end of the second year, children begin to express themselves more clearly by joining words into two-word phrases (Figure 8.11).

But at age two, a child's grammar is still unlike that of an adult. Children use what psychologists call **telegraphic speech**—for example, "Where my apple?" "Daddy fall down." They leave out words but still get the message across. As psychologists have discovered, two year olds already understand certain rules (Brown, 1973). They keep their words in the same order adults do. Indeed, at one point they overdo this, applying grammatical rules too consistently. For example, the usual rule for forming the past tense of English verbs is to add "ed." But many verbs are irregular: "go"/ "went," "come"/"came," "swim"/"swam," "fall"/"fell." At first children learn the correct form of the verb: "Daddy went yesterday." But once children discover the rule for forming past tenses, they replace the correct form with sentences like "Daddy *goed* yesterday." Although they have never heard adults use this word, they construct it in accordance with the rules of grammar that they have extracted from the speech they hear.

By the age of four or five children have mastered the basics of the language. Their ability to use words will continue to grow with their ability to think about and understand things.

EMOTIONAL DEVELOPMENT

While the child is developing his ability to use his body, to think and to express himself, he is also developing emotionally. He begins to become attached to specific people and to care about what they think and feel. In most cases, the child's first relationship is with his mother.

Experiments with Animals

The early attachment of a child to his mother and the far-reaching effects of this attachment provide a good example of the way in which maturation and learning work together in development. Experiments with baby birds and monkeys have shown that there is a maturationally determined time of readiness for attachment early in life. If the infant is too young or too old, the attachment cannot be formed. But the attachment itself is a kind of learning. If the attachment is not made, or if an unusual attachment is made, the infant will develop in an unusual way as a result.

Imprinting.   Konrad Lorenz, a student of animal behavior, was a pioneer in this field. Lorenz discovered that infant geese become attached to their mothers in a sudden, virtually permanent learning process called **imprinting.** A few hours after they struggle out of their shells, goslings are ready to

Figure 8.12
Konrad Lorenz and the baby geese imprinted on him instead of a mother goose.

start waddling after the first thing they see. Whatever it is, they stay with it and treat it as though it were their mother from that time on. Usually, of course, the first thing they see is the mother goose, but Lorenz found that if he substituted himself or some moving object like a green box being dragged along the ground, the goslings would follow that (Figure 8.12). Goslings are especially sensitive just after birth, and whatever they learn during this **critical period** makes a deep impression that resists change. From this early experience with their mother—or mother substitute—the goslings form their idea of what a goose is. If they have been imprinted with a human being instead of a goose, they will prefer the company of human beings to other geese and may even try to mate with humans later in life.

Figure 8.13
An infant rhesus monkey in one of Harry Harlow's experiments.

Surrogate Mothers.   Lorenz's experiments showed how experience with a mother—whether real or a substitute—can determine an infant bird's entire view of itself and others. An American psychologist, Harry Harlow, went on to study the relationship between mother and child in a species closer to humans, the rhesus monkey. His first question was: What makes the mother so important? He tried to answer this question by taking baby monkeys away from their natural mothers as soon as they were born, as described in Chapter 6. To review: Harlow raised the monkeys with two surrogate, or substitute, mothers. Each monkey could choose between a mother constructed of wood and wire and a mother constructed in the same way but covered with soft, cuddly terry cloth. In some cages, the cloth mother was equipped with a bottle; in others, the wire mother was.

The results were dramatic. The young monkeys became strongly attached to the cloth mother, whether she gave food or not, and for the most part ignored the wire mother (Figure 8.13). If a frightening object was placed in the monkey's cage, the baby monkey would run to the terry-cloth mother for security, not to the wire mother. It was the touching that mattered, not the feeding.

Effects Later in Life.   In another set of experiments, Harlow discovered that monkeys raised without real mothers grew up with serious emotional problems. As adults they did not seem to know how to play or defend themselves or even mate, although they tried. In fact, when frightened by a strange human they often attacked their own bodies instead of making threatening signs of aggression as normal monkeys do.

The monkeys who had cloth mothers with bottles grew up more normally than the others, but even they were not well adjusted to normal monkey life. A partially adequate substitute for a mother turned out to be peers—other baby monkeys. Infant monkeys who played with other monkeys like themselves grew up fairly normally even if they never saw their mothers. To grow up completely normally, however, both mother *and* peers were necessary (Figure 8.14). Why were real mothers and other infant monkeys so essential?

One possible answer is that no matter how much contact comfort the cloth mother could provide, "she" could not encourage independence. A normal mother, brother, or sister often becomes annoyed at an infant's

Figure 8.14
One of Harry Harlow's series of
experiments with monkeys showed
the importance of early peer
contact for normal development.

clinging as he gets older, forcing him to stand on his own two feet. The cloth mother, however, is always available. The encouragement of independence is only one factor. Interactions with mother and peers also allow the baby to see and learn from the behavior of other monkeys. The silent surrogate provided no such opportunities.

Human Babies

Can these findings be applied to human babies? Is there a critical period when infants need to become attached to a mothering person, as Lorenz's experiments suggest? Do children who are temporarily or permanently separated from their mothers or raised in institutions without benefit of a single mothering person develop abnormally, as Harlow's monkeys did?

Some psychologists would answer these questions with a firm "yes." Babies begin to form an attachment to their mothers (or to a surrogate mother) at about six months, when they are able to distinguish one person from another and are beginning to develop object permanence. This attachment seems to be especially strong between the ages of six months and three years. By three years, the child has developed to the stage where he is able to remember and imagine his mother and maintain a relationship with her (in fantasy) even if she is absent.

According to one psychologist, children who are separated from their mothers during this period may never be able to form attachments to other people. Suppose a child is hospitalized for an extended period. At first she will show signs of intense distress, crying and fussing as if she were trying to bring her mother back. When this fails, she will lapse into a state of apathy, which may last for several days. If the separation continues, she will begin to respond to attention and to act cheerfully, but her relations with others take on a superficial quality. She does not become attached to any one person (Bowlby, 1960–1961).

Some psychologists believe that institutionalization causes intellectual as well as psychological damage. Their studies indicate that children who are deprived of a stable mothering person at an early age are retarded in their ability to use words and solve problems. Restless and unable to concentrate, they do poorly in school. Their aggressiveness makes them unpopular with their schoolmates (Spitz and Wolff, 1946).

However, new research suggests that inadequate care and lack of learning opportunities, not mother deprivation, cause these problems. Orphanages and other institutions vary considerably in the care they give children, and so do the children who enter them. One team of psychologists found that although infants in an orphanage were slow to develop, they caught up with children raised at home by the age of four or five. Other researchers were unable to detect any difference in intelligence or emotional development between institutionalized and noninstitutionalized children. Indeed, a few psychologists believe that children raised in well-run orphanages are friendlier, more inquisitive, and in general develop faster than children raised in the average home. It depends on the child and the institution (see Thompson and Grusec, 1970: 606–607).

Imaginary Playmates

There's nothing new about polka dot elves, pink teddy bears, and other imaginary playmates; children have had them since childhood began. But there's a lot new in our understanding of the role these invisible, mysterious friends play in the normal development of children.

When Dr. Jerome L. Singer and Dr. Dorothy G. Singer studied a group of three- and four-year-olds, they found a number of striking differences between children with imaginary playmates and those without. Here are some of their results:

- Imaginary playmates are more common than you might think; more than half the children had them.
- Children with imaginary playmates are less aggressive and more cooperative than other children.
- They are rarely bored and have a rich vocabulary, far advanced for their age.
- They watch fewer hours of television than other children, and the programs they watch have fewer cartoons and violence.
- They have a greater ability to concentrate than other children.

Above all, imaginary playmates are true companions to children. They are always there to listen and talk, to be supportive and forever loyal. They seem to fill a gap in children's lives and are especially important to children who are first-born or who have no brothers or sisters. They are an adaptive mechanism that helps children get through the boring times of life.

Instead of worrying that imaginary playmates are a sign of insecurity and withdrawal, we should all look in wonderment at how creative and adaptive a healthy child can be.

For more details, see Maya Pines, "Invisible Playmates," *Psychology Today*, September 1978.

The debate over this issue is likely to continue for some time. What we do know is that up to six or seven months, most infants are indiscriminate. They respond to strangers as readily as they respond to their mothers and other familiar people; they will coo or whine at just about anyone. At six months, however, they begin to develop a strong attachment to their mother (or whoever is caring for them). In fact, at about eight months many babies rather suddenly develop an intense fear of strangers—crying, hiding against their mothers, and showing other signs of distress when someone they do not know or remember approaches them. Separation anxiety, which appears at ten to twelve months, is further proof of attachment. Children do not remain exclusive for long, however. By eighteen months nearly all babies have developed attachments to their father, siblings, grandparents, or other people who play an active role in their lives (Maccoby and Masters, 1970).

An infant begins to develop a strong attachment to its mother by the age of six months.

Figure 8.15
A year-old infant clings to his mother: at this age, attachment to the mother is strong and exclusive.

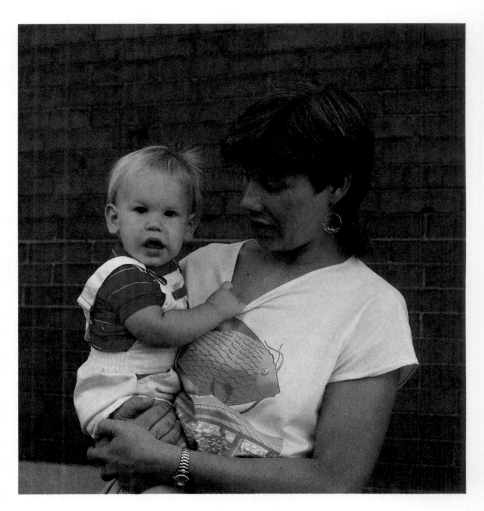

SOCIALIZATION

Learning the rules of behavior of the culture in which you are born and grow up is called **socialization.** To live with other people, a child has to learn what is considered acceptable and unacceptable behavior. This is not as easy as it sounds. Some social rules are clear and inflexible. For example, you are not permitted to have sexual relations with members of your immediate family.

Most social rules leave room for individual decisions, so that sometimes there seems to be a "gray area" between right and wrong. Some rules change from situation to situation. Some apply to certain categories of people. For example, the rules for boys in our society are different from the rules for girls. We tend to encourage boys to express aggression but not· fear; traditionally, girls have been raised to express emotions but not ambitions. Of course the rules for feminine behavior change over the years. We do not expect adolescent girls to act like little girls, or middle-aged women to act like adolescents. To complicate matters, we require different behavior from single and married women, housewives and career women, female executives and female secretaries.

Learning what the rules are, when to apply and when to bend them, is only part of socialization. Every society has ideas about what is meaningful, valuable, beautiful, and worth striving for. Every society classifies people according to their family, sex, age, skills, personality characteristics, and other criteria. Every culture has notions about what makes individuals behave as they do. In absorbing these notions, a child acquires an identity as a member of a particular society, a member of different social categories (such as male or female), a member of a family—and an identity as an individual. This is a second dimension of socialization.

Finally, socialization involves learning to live with other people and with yourself. Anyone who has seen the shock on a two year old's face when another child his age takes a toy he wants, or the frustration and humiliation a four year old experiences when she discovers she can't hit a baseball on the first try, knows how painful it can be to discover that other people have rights and that you have limitations.

In the pages that follow we examine several theories about how the child becomes socialized. We begin with Freud's theory of psychosexual development, which has been a major influence on our understanding of socialization.

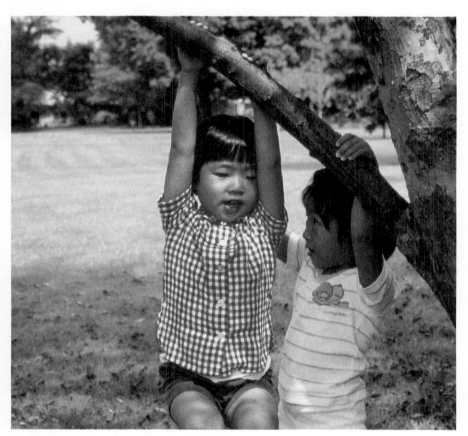

Figure 8.16
Learning the difference between acceptable and unacceptable behavior is part of socialization.

Freud's Theory of Psychosexual Development

Freud believed that all children are born with powerful sexual and aggressive urges that must be tamed. In learning to control these impulses, children acquire a sense of right and wrong. They become "civilized." The process—and the results—are different for boys and girls.

In the first few years of life boys and girls have similar experiences. Their erotic pleasures are obtained through the mouth, sucking at their mother's breast. Weaning is a period of frustration and conflict—it is the child's first experience with not getting what he wants. Freud called this the **oral stage** of development. Later the anus becomes the source of erotic pleasure, giving rise to what Freud called the **anal stage.** The child enjoys holding in or pushing out his feces until he is required, through toilet training, to curb this freedom.

The major conflict comes between the ages of three and five, when children discover the pleasure they can obtain from their genitals. As a consequence, they become extremely aware of the differences between themselves and members of the opposite sex. In this **phallic stage,** according to Freud, the child becomes a rival for the affections of the parent of the opposite sex. The boy wants to win his mother for himself and finds himself in hostile conflict with his father. The girl wants her father for herself and tries to shut out her mother. These struggles take place on an unconscious level; generally the child and the parents do not have any clear awareness that it is going on.

Freud called this crisis the **Oedipal conflict,** after Oedipus, the king in Greek tragedy who unknowingly killed his father and married his mother. Freud believed that the boy's feelings for his mother create intense conflicts. The boy finds that he hates his father and wishes him gone or dead. But his father is far stronger than he is. The boy fears that his father will see how he feels and punish him, perhaps by castrating him. (A parent telling the child that masturbation is nasty, or perhaps that it will make him sick, merely confirms his fears.) To prevent this horrible punishment, the boy buries his sexual feelings and tries to make himself "good." He tries to become as much like his father as possible so that his father will not want to hurt him. He satisfies himself with becoming *like* the person who possesses mother, instead of trying to possess her himself. In this process, which is called **identification** with the aggressor, the boy takes on all his father's values and moral principles. Thus, at the same time that he learns to behave like a man, he **internalizes** his father's morality. His father's voice becomes a voice inside him, the voice of conscience.

Freud believed that in girls the Oedipal conflict takes a different form. The girl finds herself in the similarly dangerous position of wanting to possess her father and to exclude her mother. To escape punishment and to possess the father vicariously, she begins to identify with her mother. She feels her mother's triumphs and failures as if they were her own, and she internalizes her mother's moral code. At the same time, the girl experiences what Freud called penis envy. Whereas the boy is afraid of being castrated, the girl suspects that her mother has removed the penis she once

Figure 8.17
Socialization is a process that begins almost immediately after birth. Through it, children learn how to behave with others and how to use certain behaviors to get their own way.

had. To make up for this "deficiency," she sets her sights on marrying a man who is like her father and develops the wish to have babies.

Freud believed that at about age five children enter a **latency stage.** Sexual desires are pushed into the background, and children busy themselves with exploring the world and learning new skills. This process of redirecting sexual impulses into learning tasks is called **sublimation.** Although children this age often avoid members of the opposite sex, sexual interest reappears in adolescence. The way in which a person resolves the Oedipal conflict in childhood influences the kind of relationships he or she will form with members of the opposite sex throughout life. Ideally, when one reaches the **genital stage,** one derives as much satisfaction from giving pleasure as from receiving it.

Today relatively few psychologists believe that sexual feelings disappear in childhood, that all young girls experience penis envy, or that all young boys fear castration. Freud was attempting to set off a revolution in our thinking about childhood. Like many revolutionaries, he probably overstated the case. Yet the idea that children have to learn to control powerful sexual and aggressive desires, and the belief that such early childhood experiences can have a long-term effect on adult personality and behavior, would be difficult to deny. (We shall return to Freud in the chapter on personality theories.)

Erikson's Theory of Psychosocial Development

To Erik Erikson, socialization is neither so sudden nor so emotionally violent. Erikson takes a broader view of human development than Freud in

---

Table 8.2 / Erikson's Stages of Psychosocial Development

Approximate Age	Crisis
0–1	TRUST VS. MISTRUST: If an infant is well cared for, she will develop faith in the future. But if she experiences too much uncertainty about being taken care of, she will come to look at the world with fear and suspicion.
1–2	AUTONOMY VS. DOUBT: Here the child learns self-control and self-assertion. But if he receives too much criticism, he will be ashamed of himself and have doubts about his independence.
2–5	INITIATIVE VS. GUILT: When the child begins to make her own decisions, constant discouragement or punishment could lead to guilt and a loss of initiative.
5–Puberty	INDUSTRY VS. INFERIORITY: The child masters skills and takes pride in his competence. Too much criticism of his work at this stage can lead to long-term feelings of inferiority.
Adolescence	IDENTITY VS. ROLE CONFUSION: The teen-ager tries to develop her own separate identity while "fitting in" with her friends. Failure leads to confusion over who she is.
Early Adulthood	INTIMACY VS. ISOLATION: A person secure in his own identity can proceed to an intimate partnership in which he makes compromises for another. The isolated person may have many affairs or even a long-term relationship, but always avoids true closeness.
Middle Age	GENERATIVITY VS. STAGNATION: A person who becomes stagnated is absorbed in herself and tries to hang onto the past. Generativity involves a productive life which will serve as an example to the next generation.
Later Adulthood	INTEGRITY VS. DESPAIR: Some people look back over life with a sense of satisfaction, and accept both the bad and the good. Others face death with nothing but regrets.

---

terms of both time and scope. Although he recognizes the child's sexual and aggressive urges, he believes that the need for social approval is just as important (hence his term, psychosocial development). And although he believes that childhood experiences have a lasting impact on the individual, he sees development as a lifelong process.

We all face many "crises" as we grow from infancy to old age, as we mature and people expect more from us. Each of these crises represents an issue that everyone faces. The child—or adolescent or adult—may develop more strongly in one way or another, depending on how other people respond to his or her efforts.

For example, the two year old is delighted with his new-found ability to walk, to get into things, to use words, and to ask questions. The very fact that he has acquired these abilities adds to his self-esteem. He's eager to use them. If the adults around him applaud his efforts and acknowledge his achievements, he begins to develop a sense of autonomy, or independence. However, if they ignore him except to punish him for going too far or being a nuisance, the child may begin to doubt the value of his achievements. He may also feel shame because the people around him act as if his new desire for independence is bad.

This is the second of eight stages in Erikson's theory. Each stage builds on the last. A child who has learned to trust the world is better equipped to seek autonomy than one who is mistrustful; a child who has achieved autonomy takes initiative more readily than one who doubts himself; and so on. The basic question in each stage is whether the individual will find ways to direct his needs, desires, and talents into socially acceptable channels and learn to think well of himself.

Erikson's eight crises are outlined in Table 8.2. We will refer to this theory as we continue our discussion of the life cycle in the next chapter.

Learning Theories of Development

Both Freud and Erikson stress the emotional dynamics of social development. Their theories suggest that learning social rules is altogether different from learning to ride a bicycle or to speak a foreign language. Many psychologists disagree. They believe children learn the ways of their social world because they are rewarded for conforming and because they copy older children and adults in anticipation of future rewards. In other words, social development is simply a matter of conditioning and imitation.

Conditioning.   Adults—especially parents and teachers—have the power to reward and punish. Consciously and unconsciously they use praise, smiles, and hugs to reward a child for behaving in ways they consider good and for expressing attitudes that support their own. They tend to ignore or to be hostile toward the expression of opinions that are contrary to their own and toward behavior of which they disapprove.

Sex-role training provides obvious examples of this. At home and in school, boys are encouraged to engage in athletics and to be assertive. Girls are discouraged from doing these things, but are rewarded for being helpful and nice, looking neat, and acting cute. Even the rewards children receive are usually sex-typed. How many girls receive footballs or tool kits as presents? How many boys get dolls or watercolor sets?

These are some of the ways in which adults use conditioning to shape a child's development. Children gradually learn to behave in the way that leads to the greatest satisfaction, even when no one is watching. To avoid punishment and gain rewards from those around them, they learn to reward and punish themselves. A child may criticize herself for making a mistake that has led to punishment in the past. The mistake may be a moral one—lying, for example. A boy may learn to be hard on himself for showing sensitivity, because in the past his tears and blushes were met with humiliating laughter.

This is not to say that children always do as they are told. Adults also teach youngsters how to get away with misbehavior—for example, by apologizing or by giving a present to someone they have wronged. In this way, some children learn that they may receive praise instead of punishment for bad conduct.

Figure 8.18
Imitation of aggression in children. (top row) Frames from one of the films psychologist Albert Bandura showed to children. (bottom two rows) Behavior of children who watched the film and were given a chance to play with similar objects.

Imitation.   A second way in which children learn social rules is by observing other people. When youngsters see another child or an adult being congratulated for behaving in certain ways or expressing certain attitudes, they are likely to imitate that person in the hope of obtaining rewards themselves.

Albert Bandura's experiments indicate that children are very quick indeed to imitate other people's behavior (Bandura and Walters, 1963). Bandura's basic technique is to show children movies of a person reacting to a situation. He then puts the children in the same situation to see how they behave.

In one experiment Bandura showed a film of a frustrated adult taking out her anger on a "Bobo" doll (Figure 8.18). The woman assaulted the doll—yelling, kicking, and punching it with all her might. After the film, children who had been deliberately frustrated with broken promises and delays were led to a room that contained an identical doll. Taking their cue from the film, they launched furious attacks—imitating the actress's behavior down to the last kick.

Later Bandura added two different endings to the film. In one the actress was praised and given candy and soft drinks after she had attacked the doll. In the other she was severely scolded for her behavior. Most of the children who saw the second version learned from the actress's experience and did not attack the doll so they would not be punished. What this suggests is that conditioning and modeling work together. Children do not imitate everything they see, only the behavior that seems to bring rewards.

The Cognitive-Developmental Approach

Theorists who emphasize the role of cognition or thinking in development view the growing child quite differently. Learning theory implies that the child is essentially passive—a piece of clay to be shaped. The people who administer rewards and punishments and serve as models do the shaping. Cognitive theorists see the *child* as the shaper. Taking their cue from Piaget, they argue that social development is the result of the child's acting on the environment and trying to make sense out of his experiences. The games children play illustrate this.

Play. Children's games are serious business. When left to their own devices, youngsters spend a great deal of time making up rules. This enables them to learn for themselves the importance of agreeing on a structure for group activities. A child can relax and enjoy himself without fear of rejection as long as he does not break the rules. The world of play thus becomes a miniature society, with its own rules and codes.

Another function of most games is to teach children about aspects of adult life in a nonthreatening way. In young children's games, it is the experience of playing, not winning, that counts. Children can learn the

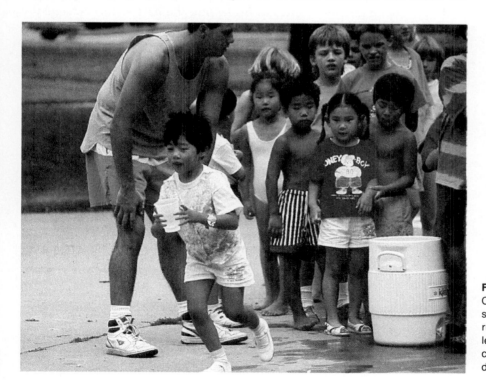

Figure 8.19
Children's games are not just fun: seeing the need for and making rules, trying on adult roles, and learning the dimensions of competition are all part of the developmental process.

dimensions of competition of various kinds, including testing themselves against their outer limits, but they will not be hurt by comparison as they may be in win-or-lose situations.

Much of children's play involves **role taking.** Youngsters try on such adult roles as mother, father, teacher, storekeeper, explorer, and rock star. Role taking allows them to learn about different points of view firsthand. Suppose a child plays a mother opposite another child who plays a whiny, disobedient baby. When she finds herself totally frustrated by the other child's nagging she begins to understand why her mother gets mad. You can't cook even a pretend meal when the baby keeps knocking over the pots and pans.

Moral Development.   Lawrence Kohlberg's studies show just how important being able to see other people's points of view is to social development in general and to moral development in particular. Kohlberg (1968) studied the development of moral reasoning—deciding what is right and what is wrong—by presenting children of different ages with a series of moral dilemmas. For example:

> In Europe, a woman was near death from cancer. One drug might save her, a form of radium that a druggist in the same town had recently discovered. The druggist was charging $2,000, ten times what the drug cost him to make. The sick woman's husband, Heinz, went to everyone he knew to borrow the money, but he could only get together about half of what it cost. He told the druggist that his wife was dying and asked him to sell it cheaper or let him pay later. But the druggist said "No." The husband got desperate and broke into the man's store to steal the drug for his wife. Should the husband have done that? Why?

At every age, some children said that the man should steal, some that he should not. What interested Kohlberg, however, was how the children arrived at a conclusion. He wanted to know what sort of reasoning they used. After questioning about a hundred children, Kohlberg identified six stages of moral development. He then replicated his findings in several different cultures.

In stage one, children are totally egocentric. They do not consider other people's points of view and have no sense of right and wrong. Their main concern is avoiding punishment. A child in this stage will say that the man should steal because people will blame him for his wife's death if he does not, or that he should not steal because he might get caught and go to prison.

Children in stage two have a better idea of how to "work the system" to receive rewards as well as to avoid punishment. Kohlberg calls this the "marketplace orientation." Youngsters at this level interpret the Golden Rule as "help someone if he helps you, and hurt him if he hurts you." They are still egocentric and premoral, evaluating acts in terms of the consequences, not in terms of right and wrong.

In stage three, children become acutely sensitive to what other people want and think. A child in this stage will say that the man in the story should steal because people will think he is cruel if he lets his wife die, or that he should not steal because people will think he is a criminal. In other words, children want social approval in stage three, so they apply the rules other people have decreed literally and rigidly.

In stage four, a child is less concerned with the approval of others. The key issue here is "law and order"—a law is seen as a moral rule and is obeyed because of a strong belief in established authority. Many people remain at the fourth stage of moral development for their whole lives. Moral thinking here, as at stage three, is quite rigid.

In the remaining two stages, people begin to broaden their perspective. The stage-five person is primarily concerned with whether a law is fair or just. He believes that laws must change as the world changes, and they are never absolute. The important question is whether a given law is good for society as a whole. Stage six involves an acceptance of ethical principles that apply to everyone, like the Golden Rule: "Do unto others as you would have them do unto you." Such moral "laws" cannot be broken; they are more important than any written law.

To reach the highest levels of moral development, a child must first be able to see other people's points of view. But this understanding is no guarantee that a person will respect the rights of others. Thus, cognitive abilities influence moral development, but there is far more to morality than simple understanding.

USING PSYCHOLOGY

Child Abuse

While many parents cope with their life stresses and provide a warm and safe environment for their children, there are an alarming number of cases reported in which children are physically, sexually, or psychologically abused or neglected by their parents or stepparents (Parke and Lewis, 1980). *Child abuse* includes the physical or mental injury, sexual abuse, negligent treatment, or mistreatment of children under the age of eighteen by adults entrusted with their care.

Accurate statistics are difficult to compile, since many incidents of child abuse go unreported. One estimate, however, is that in 1982 one out of every forty-three American children under the age of fourteen was abused (*New York Times*, 1983). Abuse can range from such hideous acts as beating, burning, and scalding to less intense but equally damaging violent spankings and verbal abuse.

Child abuse is viewed as a social problem resulting from a variety of causes. Many abusive parents were themselves mistreated as children, suggesting that these parents may have learned an inappropriate way of caring for children.

MORE about...

Kohlberg and Bias. Not everybody agrees with Kohlberg. Critics accuse him of being overly influenced by Western culture. They say that he sees moral reasoning through the eyes of someone brought up in Europe or America. Children from other cultures, they say, would not necessarily follow Kohlberg's six stages of moral development.

For example, we are raised to believe that we are responsible for ourselves and for our families, and that we must make our own decisions. Other cultures, in contrast, place the community first, and the individual second. Thus, a child from an Israeli kibbutz, or from a Chinese village, would look at Heinz's situation in a different way. The child might say that Heinz should consult his community before making a decision. Or the child might ask why the community is not helping Heinz in the first place.

Although it seems that children throughout the world go through Kohlberg's first stages, their later stages may be influenced by their particular culture.

Abusive parents abuse all their children.

Fiction. Studies indicate that abusive parents often focus on only one child. That child usually has had physical or behavioral problems from an early age. And while that one child may be grossly maltreated, more "normal" siblings may not be abused by the parents at all.

Some parents still believe in "spare the rod and spoil the child" (if you do not spank children they will be spoiled). Such parents tend to use the harsh physical discipline that they saw their own parents using. Many abusive parents have little patience with their children. Often they have unrealistic expectations for them.

Overburdened and stressed parents are more likely to abuse their children, particularly children who are troublesome. Low-birthweight infants and hyperactive or mentally retarded children have a higher than normal incidence of abuse. One reason for this higher incidence may be that such children are less responsive and more difficult to care for, thus making greater demands on the parents (Belsky, 1980). Social-cultural stresses such as unemployment and lack of contact with family, friends, and groups in the community are associated with child abuse.

The most effective way of treating child abuse is to prevent future incidents. Parent education for abusive parents allows them to learn new ways of dealing with their children. Many state social welfare agencies not only provide assistance to abusive parents in managing their children, but also have programs to identify families at risk for child abuse. Families that are experiencing severe economic, psychological, or marital strains are viewed as high-risk families. By providing information about resources and a support system for these families, communities may reduce the incidence of child abuse. Such support services as employment and educational opportunities for both parents and children, support groups for parents, child care facilities, homemaker services, and hotlines help reduce child abuse (Parke and Slaby, 1983).

One especially troubling form of child abuse is sexual abuse. While more than 90 percent of those who abuse children are men, women have also been known to participate in individual or organized sexual abuse of children. Perhaps the most devastating effect of sexual abuse is that the child is often tricked into participating in the activity but later believes the act to be his or her fault. If the offender is someone the child knows well, the child not only experiences the trauma and stress of abuse, but is also forced to keep the incident a secret for fear of getting the grownup in trouble. Often, parents and other usually responsible adults unintentionally dismiss the sexually abused child's attempts to tell about the incident because the idea of sexual abuse is too horrifying for them to accept.

SUMMARY

Use the following outline as a tool for reviewing this chapter. Copy the outline onto your own paper, leaving spaces between headings to make notes about key concepts.

I.   The Beginning of Life

II. How Do Babies Grow?

   A. Maturation

   B. Learning

III. Intellectual Development

   A. How Knowing Changes

   B. Some Implications of Intellectual Development

IV. Mental Retardation

V.   The Development of Language

   A. Can Animals Use Language?

   B. How Children Acquire Language

VI. Emotional Development

   A. Experiments with Animals

   B. Human Babies

VII. Socialization

   A. Freud's Theory of Psychosexual Development

   B. Erikson's Theory of Psychosocial Development

   C. Learning Theories of Development

   D. The Cognitive-Developmental Approach

CONCEPTS AND VOCABULARY

1. What behaviors do newborn babies display?

2. What is maturation? How does it explain why a four-month-old baby cannot be taught to walk?

3. What evidence is there that a young baby can learn to do some things?

4. According to Piaget, what two processes are the basis for intellectual development in children?

5. What are the stages that a child goes through when developing object permanence?

6. What is the principle of conservation, and when do children acquire it?

7. How do children learn to talk?

8. How are the first six months of life different from the second six months in terms of a child's emotional and interpersonal development?

9. What is socialization? Why is it so important to development?

10. How do Freud's and Erikson's theories of development differ?

11. What role does play assume in the development of children?

12. What are Kohlberg's stages of moral development?

CRITICAL THINKING

1. **Analyze.** What happens when a boy plays with Rambo dolls? How does this behavior fit into the concept of modeling? Is this behavior liberating to boys, or does it feminize their behavior? Explain your answer. What would be the effect of girls playing football? Explain the difference(s) between your answers about boys and girls.

2. **Synthesize.** How are sex roles communicated to people in American society? Look carefully through magazines and newspapers, watch television commercials, and listen to the radio. What activities, interests, worries, virtues, weaknesses, physical characteristics, and mannerisms are presented as attributes of typical men and women? Are sex roles portrayed differently in different media? Are there various stereotypes within each sex?

3. **Evaluate.** What are the events that you feel have been the most significant in your life? What

have been the main influences on your social and emotional development?

4. **Analyze.** Do you and your parents share the same religious beliefs? Political orientation? Feelings about violence? Attitudes toward sex? Goals for living? Opinions about money? Views on drugs? Do you have similar tastes in clothing colors and styles? Music? Pets? Housing? Furniture? Foods? Cars? Entertainment? After asking yourself these questions, determine how well your beliefs, opinions, and tastes agree with those of your parents. How important do you think your early social training was for what you believe, think, and like?

APPLYING KNOWLEDGE

1. Observe an infant under eighteen months of age, keeping a log of the baby's activities. Compare your notes with the developmental descriptions in this chapter. How closely does the baby follow the norm? What differences did you note?

2. Talk with children who are under five years old, paying particular attention to their grammar. What kinds of errors do they make? What kinds of grammatical rules do they already seem to know?

3. If you have an infant brother or sister, or a pet dog or cat, perform a simple experiment to test for object permanence. Be sure to use several different objects for your test, and be certain that the baby or animal is not afraid of, or uninterested in, the object. Most dogs or cats will probably search for vanished objects.

4. Ask children of different ages the following questions: Where does the sun go at night? Could you become a girl (a boy) if you wanted to? Does your brother (sister) have any brothers (sisters)? What makes leaves fall off trees? If you find some of their theories interesting, it is easy to think of many other questions.

5. Observe a father with an infant one or two years old for signs of emotional attachment. An infant day care center, a church nursery, a pediatri-

cian's waiting room, or a play area in a shopping mall are good places to locate a father-child pair. Ideally, you want to find a place where the toddler is allowed some freedom to move about while in the presence of the father. How often does the child make contact with his or her father? Does the child move away and explore? How does the infant respond to unfamiliar people or objects? Besides physical contact, in what ways do the father and child stay in contact with each other? If the father happens to leave for a moment, what is the infant's reaction?

6. Child abuse is a growing concern in our culture; everyday examples of the problem can be found in your local newspapers, in magazines, or on television news reports. Keep a record of these accounts for a period of time. What kinds of abuse are being reported? How old are the children involved? Who are the abusers? What legal action was taken? How was the abuse detected? What state or local agencies are involved with the care of the children?

7. Watch children's television programs on a Saturday morning. Pay attention to both the programs and the commercials. What kinds of behavior do the characters model for the children? What do the children learn about how to get along with others, about aggression, sex roles, and food? What are the differences between the television characters and real people? In what ways do you think television is good for children? In what ways do you think television is a negative influence on children?

8. List ten events or behaviors that you think are important in the first few years of a child's life. Examine the list and differentiate between maturational and learned developmental behaviors. Do you think maturational or learned behaviors are the most important for early childhood? Explain your answer.

9. Observe a group of two-year-old children. Record the two-word sentences you hear. What sorts of words are used and in what contexts? Can you specify the grammatical rules children of this age use in combining words?

10. Recall several early learning experiences such as learning to tie shoes, ride a bicycle, read, whistle, etc. How did you feel about these accomplishments? How did you learn? Who helped you learn? Write a one-page paper describing your experiences.

11. Give three examples of how children learn on their own through everyday experiences.

12. Make a list of ten concepts. Which three would be easiest for a child to learn? Which three would be most difficult? Why?

13. If you were watching a three-year-old, what activities might you use to encourage the child to use his or her imagination?

14. Explain how the ways adults and other children speak to a child can affect the child's language development.

ANALYZING VIEWPOINTS

1. Since 1950 the number of employed mothers with preschool children has more than tripled. These mothers regularly place their children in the care of others. The effects of this day care are hotly debated by psychologists. Some say that children in day care are as healthy and soundly developed as children raised at home. Others say that day care causes emotional and behavioral problems in children. Write an essay supporting each viewpoint. Use what you have learned from the chapter about child development and attachment. Read recent magazine and newspaper articles for more information on the day care issue.

2. Your text discusses the effects of television on children. More recently there has been great controversy over children's use of interactive video games such as Nintendo. Supporters say that this is the age of technology and the games help sharpen children's skills. Others say that children become addicted to these games; they stop interacting with friends and engaging in more creative activities. Have you had any experience with these games? Write down the pros and cons on this issue. Use your own experience, survey adults for their opinions, and read recent articles in newspapers and magazines.

3. Some communities from time to time pass ordinances that ban the sale of toy guns because they feel that violence is provoked in large part by what we learn in the environment. Do you agree or disagree with this type of ordinance? Why? Explain your answer.

4. Tanya is a mother who works outside the home. She argues that she spends at least two to three hours of quality time with her child every evening. Her friend, Stephanie, is a mother who is not employed outside the home. She argues that these two to three hours may be quality time for Tanya, but not necessarily for her child. She thinks there are many times when two to three hours of morning time (or afternoon time) would be the time when the child is most open to quality interaction. In other words, maybe the two to three hours in the evening are an irritable time for the child, and the child benefits little from the interaction. Who do you agree with? What are your reasons for your position?

BEYOND THE CLASSROOM

1. Spend some time observing children at a park or central play area. Which children share? Which children fight over toys? Do some children play alone? Are there children playing games together? What kinds of games are being played? Are boys more aggressive than girls? Can you associate types of play with age or gender? Report your findings to the class.

2. While shopping (or in any situation where there are young children and parents), look for signs of children trying to learn. Record the children's comments and questions as well as their parents' responses. Then, in writing, give examples of parents encouraging learning and of parents discouraging learning.

3. Find out how your school system identifies and helps children with learning disabilities. Identify other sources of help for children and parents.

CHAPTER 9

Adolescence

Key Terms:

androgynous
asynchrony
authoritarian families
conformity
democratic families
identity crisis
laissez-faire families
menarche
permissive families
puberty
rationalization
self-fulfilling prophecy
sex identity
sex role
social learning theory

Adolescence is the transition period between childhood and adulthood during which people reach a new stage of their psychosocial development. In some societies adolescence is not recognized as a separate stage of life; individuals move directly from childhood to adulthood (see Mead, 1961). In our own society, however, adolescence is looked upon as a time of preparation for adult responsibilities (Hall, 1904). These new burdens must be assumed just at the time when young people are undergoing complex physical and emotional changes that affect them both personally and socially.

Because so much is happening in these years, psychologists have focused a great deal of attention on the period of adolescence. Though we cannot report on all of that research here, we can highlight some important psychological findings concerning the personal and social development of teenagers and the difficulties they may experience. But first we will turn our attention to some widely held views of the adolescent years.

VIEWS OF ADOLESCENCE

What is it like to be adolescent? Are the years between late childhood and early adulthood the best that life has to offer—a carefree time to act on ideals unburdened by practical concerns? Or is that period a time of crisis, rebellion, and unhappiness? The answer seems to depend on whom you ask. Adults, adolescents themselves, and psychologists give different answers.

Objectives:

After studying this chapter, you should be able to

- define adolescence.
- describe the physical, cognitive, and idealogical changes that characterize adolescence.
- describe research related to the sexual attitudes and roles of adolescents.
- discuss the social development of the adolescent and the role of peers and family.

Figure 9.1 In our society, adolescence is regarded as a period of transition in which young people are expected to assume more and more adult responsibilities.

How Adults View Adolescence

Every adult has lived through the experience of adolescence. However, the past teenage years of most adults do not always help them understand the concerns and difficulties of today's adolescents. Adults vary in their attitudes toward teenagers in general and certain adults have conflicting feelings about them.

Many adults admire and even idealize young people. Youth is valued in our culture. The values, music, fashions, and activities of young people are heavily promoted in the mass media. Through dress, cosmetics, consumer purchases, and a variety of physical activities, adults attempt to look and feel as healthy and active as adolescents. Adults who love sports admire young athletes. Studies have shown that adults dedicated to such social issues as nuclear disarmament, world hunger, and improving the environment admire young people who are active in trying to achieve progress in these areas (Rice, 1978).

Older people who live and work directly with teenagers often value the influence young people have in their lives. Teenagers help keep them connected to a larger world outside their own experience.

On the other hand, many studies have shown that some adults feel threatened by youth. Most parents are in their forties when they watch their teenage children develop physically into maturity and are themselves beginning to see the decline of their own bodies. This situation can produce negative feelings, particularly when the adults see themselves outperformed by younger people. They may regret the loss of their own youth and envy those who are still young.

While advertising contributes to a "cult of youth," the news and popular press often portray teenagers in a negative light. Young people are often depicted as disruptive or disturbed—the stories of teenage crime and misconduct are the most sensational and thus the ones the average person is likely to notice. In truth, most adolescents go through their teenage years without extreme storm and stress.

One of the reasons that negative images of adolescents surface is that different generations sometimes hold different ideas of morality. On controversial issues such as sexual activity or the use of nuclear weapons, the views of younger people may contrast with those of their parents, whose experiences have been different.

Also, adolescents may provoke a negative reaction from their parents by displaying traits that their parents see as a reflection of themselves that they would prefer not to see. For example, parents who are insecure about their academic abilities may feel uncomfortable if they see the same pattern emerging in their teenage children.

For one reason or another, some adults do view adolescents in an exaggerated light—either good or bad. Some idealize youth by remembering only its positive aspects. Others look on adolescence with horror, seeing only its burdens of stress, tension, conflict, or dependency. Studies have shown that some adults can see younger people only as antisocial, destructive, dirty, and unreliable (Majeras, 1976). However, most adults probably do not hold extreme views, just as most young people do not fit into either extreme stereotype.

How Adolescents View Themselves

Does the overly idealized view of adolescence on the one hand and the overly negative view on the other affect the way the young see themselves? According to many psychologists, the answer is yes. Adolescents tend to regard themselves the way they think others see them. Adult stereotypes serve as a mirror for them, and they take society's reflections as authentic models for their own behavior (Anthony, 1969). Therefore, depending on the views of the adults with whom he or she interacts, an adolescent will tend to either overidealize or hold a negative image of himself or herself.

Theories of Adolescence

The contradictory views of society at large are reflected not just in the behavior of adolescents but in the theories of psychologists. Controversy concerning the nature of adolescent experience has raged ever since 1904, when G. Stanley Hall presented his pioneering theory of adolescence. Hall, who thought in evolutionary terms, saw the adolescent as representing a transitional stage in our evolutionary development from beast to human. Being an adolescent for Hall was something like being a fully grown animal in a cage, an animal who sees freedom but doesn't know quite when he or she will be freed or how he or she will handle it. Thus, the adolescent was portrayed as existing in a state of great "storm and stress," as a marginal being, confused, troubled, and highly frustrated.

Through the years many psychologists and social scientists have supported Hall's theories, but there have been others who strongly disagreed. The latter theorists regard adolescence as a relatively smooth period of growth that is in no way discontinuous with the period of childhood that precedes and the period of young adulthood that follows.

Figure 9.2
The experience of adolescence varies widely among different cultures. These boys in New Guinea are undergoing the last stage of a puberty rite. When they complete the ritual and emerge from this hut, they will be adults of their tribe.

One major proponent of this theory was Margaret Mead. In a series of classic anthropological studies in the late 1920s and early 1930s, Mead (1961) found that in some cultures adolescence is a highly enjoyable time of life and not at all marked by storm and stress.

Other studies conducted since then have tended to support Mead. They point to a relative lack of conflict in the lives of adolescents and a smooth, continuous development out of childhood.

Though adolescence may not be as crisis-ridden as some psychologists think, few would deny that there is at least some stress during that period. Great physical, mental, and emotional changes occur during adolescence. As psychologist Robert Havighurst (1972) has pointed out, every adolescent faces challenges, in the form of developmental tasks that must be mastered. Among the tasks that Havighurst lists are the following:

1. Accepting one's physical make-up and acquiring a masculine or feminine sex role
2. Developing appropriate relations with agemates of both sexes
3. Becoming emotionally independent of parents and other adults
4. Achieving the assurance that one will become economically independent
5. Deciding on, preparing for, and entering a vocation
6. Developing the cognitive skills and concepts necessary for social competence
7. Understanding and achieving socially responsible behavior
8. Preparing for marriage and family
9. Acquiring values that are harmonious with an appropriate scientific world picture

Though the tasks present a challenge, adolescents generally handle it well. Most face some stress but find ways to cope with it.

There are, of course, exceptions. A small percentage of young people experience storm and stress throughout their adolescent years. Another small group confronts the changes all adolescents experience with no stress at all. Perhaps the only safe generalization is that development through adolescence is a highly individual and varied matter.

The pattern of development a particular adolescent displays depends upon a great many factors. The most important of these include the individual's adjustment in childhood, the level of adjustment of his or her parents and peers, and the changes that occur during adolescence. It is to these changes that we now turn.

PERSONAL DEVELOPMENT

Becoming an adult involves much more than becoming physically mature, though that is an important part of the process. The transition from childhood to adulthood also involves changes in patterns of reasoning and moral thinking, and adjustments in personality and sexual behavior. Though the process is complex, most adolescents cope reasonably well with their changing circumstances.

Physical Changes

Physical Growth. **Puberty,** or sexual maturation, is the biological event that marks the end of childhood. Hormones trigger a series of internal and external changes. These produce different growth patterns in boys and girls.

At about the age of ten, girls rather suddenly begin to grow. Before this growth spurt fat tissue develops, making the girl appear chubby. The development of fat tissue is also characteristic of boys before their growth spurt. But whereas boys quickly lose it, progressing into a "string bean" or lean and lanky phase, girls retain most of this fat tissue as they begin to spurt, and even add to it (Faust, 1977).

Once their growth spurt begins, females can grow as much as two or three inches a year. During this period, a girl's breasts and hips begin to fill out, and she develops pubic hair. Between ten and seventeen she has her first menstrual period, or **menarche.** Another year or so will pass before her periods become regular and she is capable of conceiving a child. Yet most societies consider menarche the beginning of womanhood.

At about twelve, boys begin to develop pubic hair and larger genitals. Within a year or two they become capable of ejaculation. Though their growth spurt begins later than that of girls, it lasts about three years longer. Once their growth spurt begins, boys grow rapidly and fill out, developing the broad shoulders and thicker trunk of an adult man. They also acquire more muscle tissue than girls and develop a larger heart and lungs. Their voices gradually deepen. Hair begins to grow on their faces and later on their chests.

The rate and pattern of sexual maturation varies so widely that it is difficult to apply norms or standards to puberty. In general, however, girls begin to develop earlier than boys and for a year or two may tower over male agemates.

The period of adolescent growth can be an awkward one for both boys and girls because of **asynchrony**—the condition of uneven growth or maturation of bodily parts. For example, the hands or feet may be too large or small for the rest of the body. As the adolescent grows older, however, the bodily parts assume their correct proportions.

Reactions to Growth. In general young people today are better informed than they were two or three generations ago. Most do not find the signs of their sexual maturation upsetting. Nevertheless, the rather sudden bodily changes that occur during puberty make all adolescents somewhat self-conscious. This is particularly true if they are early or late to develop. Adolescents desperately want to be accepted by their peers, to conform to ideals of how a male or female their age should act, dress, and look. In one study, over half of the adolescent girls and a third of the boys spontaneously expressed concern about their appearance (Dwyer and Mayer, 1968–1969).

Studies also suggest a relation between the way young men and women see their bodies and the way they feel about themselves (McCandless, 1960). Most adolescents, and especially girls, tend to evaluate themselves in terms of their culture's body ideal. For example, in our culture, long legs, a

Figure 9.3
The physiological changes of puberty bring a new kind of self-awareness that did not exist in childhood.

sleek figure, and well-developed breasts are thought of as desirable for women, and girls are very concerned about approximating this ideal (Wiggins, Wiggins, and Conger, 1968).

Youths of both sexes are particularly sensitive about any traits they possess that appear to be sex-inappropriate. For example, boys tend to be very shy about "underdeveloped" genitalia, lack of pubic hair, or "fatty breasts," whereas girls are likely to be disturbed by "underdeveloped" breasts, dark facial hair, or visible muscles.

Individual differences in growth significantly affect the personality of young adolescents. For example, research indicates that boys who mature early have an advantage. They become heroes in sports, leaders in formal and informal social activities. Other boys look up to them; girls have crushes on them; adults tend to treat them as more mature. As a result they are generally more self-confident and independent than other boys. Late-maturing boys, whose high-pitched voices and less-than-ideal physiques may make them feel inadequate, tend to be withdrawn or rebellious (Dwyer and Mayer, 1968–1969).

Variations in the rate of development continue to have an effect on males even into their thirties. Those who matured earlier have been found to have a higher occupational and social status than those who matured later (Ames, 1957). The correlation weakens, however, as males enter their forties (Jones, 1965).

With girls the pattern is somewhat different. Girls who mature early may feel embarrassed rather than proud of their height and figure at first. Some begin dating older boys and become bossy with people their own age. Late-maturing girls tend to be less quarrelsome and to get along with their peers more easily. In their late teens, girls who matured early may be more popular and have a more favorable image of themselves than girls who matured slowly. However, the differences between early maturers and late maturers do not seem to be as pronounced among girls as they are among boys (Dwyer and Mayer, 1968–1969).

Why does physical growth have such powerful psychological effects, especially for boys? According to one widely held theory, the psychological reactions to physical growth may be the result of a **self-fulfilling prophecy.** For example, the boy who believes he does not meet his culture's physical ideal may think less of himself and not pursue success as doggedly as the next person. His belief actually helps bring about the failure he feared.

Changes in Thinking

During adolescence, the thinking patterns characteristic of adults emerge. Jean Piaget has described this as "formal operational" thinking (Piaget and Inhelder, 1969). From about age eleven or twelve, most people's thinking becomes more abstract and less concrete. For example, the adolescent can consider the answer to a hypothetical question like, "What would the world be like if people lived to be 200?" He or she can entertain such hypothetical possibilities in a way that a young child cannot. This ability expands the adolescent's problem-solving capacity. A teenage boy who discovers that his car's engine has a knock can consider a number of possible causes and systematically test out various auto parts until he finds the root of the problem. This is the same ability that a scientist must have to conduct experiments.

With comprehension of the hypothetical comes the ability to under-stand abstract principles. Not only is this capacity important for studying higher-level science and mathematics, but it leads the adolescent to deal with such abstractions in his or her own life as ethics, conformity, and phoniness. It allows for introspection—examining one's own motives and thoughts. One adolescent is quoted as saying, "I found myself thinking about my future, and then I began to think about why I was thinking about my future, and then I began to think about why I was thinking about why I was thinking about my future."

These new intellectual capacities also enable the adolescent to deal with overpowering emotional feelings through **rationalization.** After failing a test, for example, an individual may rationalize that it happened "because I was worried about the date I might be going on next week." An eight-year-old is too tied to concrete reality to consider systematically all the reasons why he or she might have failed.

Do all adolescents fully reach the stage of formal operational thinking at the same age? As you might suspect, just as there are variations in sexual maturity, so there are variations in cognitive maturity. In general, the rate of mental growth varies greatly both among individual adolescents and among social classes in this country. One study showed that less than half of the seventeen-year-olds tested had reached the stage of formal operational thinking (Higgins-Trenk and Gaite, 1971). Another study indicated that this type of thinking was more common among upper- and middle-class adolescents than working- and lower-class youth (Dulit, 1972).

Differences have also been noted among nations. Formal operational thinking is less prevalent in some societies than in others, probably because of differences in the amount of formal education available. People who cannot read and write lack the tools to separate thought from concrete reality and hence never reach a more advanced level of thinking (Greenfield and Bruner, 1966).

For those who do reach that level, the change in thinking patterns is usually accompanied by changes in personality and social interactions as well. For example, adolescents tend to become very idealistic. This is related to the fact that, for the first time, they can imagine the hypothetical—how things might be. When they compare this to the way things are, the world seems a sorry place. As a result, they can grow rebellious. Some adolescents even develop a "messianic complex" and believe they can save the world from evil. In addition, they typically become impatient with what they see as the adult generation's failures. They don't understand why, for example, a person who feels a job compromises his or her principles doesn't just quit. In other words, adolescents tend to be somewhat unrealistic about the complexities of life. But at the same time, their idealism can help keep older adults in touch with ways in which the world could be improved.

Moral Development

Besides experiencing physical and cognitive changes, some adolescents, though by no means all, also go through important changes in their moral thinking. You'll recall that, according to Lawrence Kohlberg (whose theory was reviewed in Chapter 8), moral reasoning develops in stages. Young children in the early stages of their moral development are very egocentric. They consider an act right or wrong depending on whether or not it elicits punishment (Stage 1) or on whether it has positive or negative consequences for themselves (Stage 2). At later stages they judge an action by whether or not it is socially approved (Stage 3) or is sanctioned by established authority (Stage 4).

Many people never get beyond the last stage, and their moral thinking remains quite rigid. But for those who do, adolescence and young adulthood are usually the periods of the most profound development. Individuals who progress to Stage 5 become concerned with whether a law is fair or just. They believe that the laws must change as the world changes and are never absolute. Individuals who reach Stage 6, on the other hand, accept absolute ethical principles, such as the Golden Rule, that they have worked through for themselves. Such moral laws apply to everyone, cannot be broken, and are more important than any written law.

Reaching higher levels of moral thinking involves the ability to abstract—to see a situation from another's viewpoint. That is why such moral development tends to occur in adolescence, when individuals gain the capacity for formal operational thinking. But not all adolescents who display such thinking simultaneously show higher levels of moral reasoning. In fact, only about one in ten do (Kohlberg and Gilligan, 1971). Thus, formal thought, while necessary for higher moral development, does not guarantee it.

Overall, psychologists agree that a person's moral development depends on many factors, especially the kind of relationship the individual has with his or her parents. Evidence shows that during high school, adolescent moral development does not progress much. However, during college, when the individual is away from home more and therefore less under the influence of parents, more pronounced changes in moral development occur.

Personality Changes and Identity Formation

The changes adolescents undergo affect many facets of their existence, so it is hardly surprising that cumulatively they have a shaping influence on personality. Psychologists who have studied personality changes in adolescence have focused on the concept of identity. One psychologist in particular, Erik Erikson, has shown that the establishment of identity is key to adolescent development. His theory of how individuals arrive at an integrated sense of self has inspired a great deal of argument, both pro and con. Because his views have been so influential, we turn our attention now to his theory and the studies that support and challenge it.

Erikson's Theory of the Identity Crisis. According to Erikson, building an identity is a task that is unique to adolescence. Children are aware of what other people (adults and peers) think of them. They know the labels others apply to them (good, naughty, silly, talented, brave, pretty, and the like). They are also aware of their biological drives and of their growing physical and cognitive abilities. Children may dream of being this or that person and act these roles out in their play. But they do not brood about who they are or where they are going in life. Children live in the present; adolescents begin to think about the future.

To achieve some sense of themselves, adolescents must go through what Erikson termed an **identity crisis**—a time of storm and stress during which they worry intensely about who they are (1968). Several factors contribute to the onset of this crisis, including the physiological changes and cognitive developments we have described as well as awakening sexual drives and the possibility of a new kind of intimacy with the opposite sex. Adolescents begin to see the future as a reality, not just a game. They know they have to confront the almost infinite and often conflicting possibilities and choices that lie ahead. In the process of reviewing their past

Children live in the present; adolescents begin to think about the future.

and anticipating their future, they begin to think about themselves. The process is a painful one, full of inner conflict, because they are torn by the desire to feel unique and distinctive on the one hand and to "fit in" on the other. Only by resolving this conflict do adolescents achieve an integrated sense of self.

Erikson's theory finds support in the work of another psychologist, James Marcia. According to Marcia (1966), Erikson is correct in pointing to the existence of an adolescent identity crisis. That crisis arises because individuals must make commitments on such important matters as occupation, religion, and political orientation. Using the categories of "crisis" and "commitment," Marcia distinguished four adolescent personality types: (1) *identity moratorium adolescents*, who have not experienced a crisis or made a commitment on any of the important matters facing them; (2) *identity foreclosure adolescents*, who have not had a crisis but have made a commitment based not on their own choice, but on the suggestion of others; (3) *identity confused* or *diffused adolescents*, who are in a continual search for meaning, commitment, and self-definition and thus experience life as a series of ongoing crises, and (4) *identity achievement adolescents*, who have experienced crises, considered many possibilities, and freely committed themselves to occupations and other important life matters.

These categories must not be too rigidly interpreted. It is possible for an individual to make a transition from one category to another, and it is also possible for the same individual to belong to one category with respect to religious commitment and to another with regard to political orientation or occupational choice. Marcia's main contribution is in clarifying the sources and nature of the adolescent identity crisis.

Criticism of Erikson's Theory.   Although Erikson and Marcia insist that all adolescents experience an identity crisis, not all psychologists agree. The term "crisis" suggests that adolescence is a time of nearly overwhelming stress. It also implies that the adolescent transition to maturity requires a radical break with childhood experience. As we noted earlier, many psychologists believe that adolescence is not so strife-ridden and constitutes a relatively smooth transition from one stage of life to the next.

One of the reasons Erikson may have arrived at his view is that he focused his study on disturbed adolescents who sought clinical psychiatric treatment. When adolescents attending school are selected at random and studied, critics point out, most show no sign of crisis and appear to be progressing rather smoothly through adolescence (Haan and Day, 1974).

Other Viewpoints.   Psychologists and social scientists seeking an alternative to Erikson's theory have offered several other explanations of adolescent identity formation. Albert Bandura (1964), for example, starts with the premise that crisis is not the normal state of affairs for adolescents. When crises develop—as they do in only about 10 percent of all adolescents—the cause is generally a change in the external circumstances of an individual's life rather than a biological factor. Thus, a divorce in the family or a new set of friends may trigger teen-age rebellion and a crisis, but no internal biological clock dictates those events.

Human development, in Bandura's view, is one continuous process. At all stages, including adolescence, individuals develop by interacting with others. Because of Bandura's emphasis on interaction in understanding adolescence and all other phases of human development, his approach is usually referred to as the **social learning theory** of development (Bandura, 1977).

Margaret Mead, mentioned earlier in this chapter, also stresses the importance of the social environment in adolescent identity formation. On the basis of her studies in Samoa (1961), for example, she concluded, like Bandura, that human development is more a continuous process than one marked by radical discontinuity. In that remote part of the world, adolescents are not expected to act any differently than they did as children or will be expected to act as adults. The reason is that children in Samoa are given a great deal of responsibility: They do not suddenly go from being submissive in childhood to being dominant later in life. Mead also points out that in Samoa, as in other non-industrial societies, children have sex roles similar to those of adults and therefore do not experience the onset of sexuality as a traumatic experience or an abrupt change. The identity crisis, then, is by no means a universal phenomenon.

Personality development in adolescence is a complex phenomenon. No one theory can do justice to all that is involved in the process. Erikson's emphasis on the adolescent's need for his or her own identity is an important contribution to understanding adolescent development. By focusing on individual psychology, however, he tended to ignore the influence of society and culture on the young. The studies of Bandura and Mead provide needed correctives. Thus, to arrive at a balanced picture of personality change and identity formation in adolescence, we must call upon all viewpoints.

Sexuality: Attitudes and Roles

As we noted earlier, adolescence is accompanied by puberty, when individuals mature sexually. The physical changes that occur are accompanied by changes in behavior. Adolescence is also the time when an individual develops attitudes about sex and expectations about the sex role he or she will fill.

Sexual Attitudes.   Most of us have heard the term "sexual revolution" but has one actually occurred in the last decade or so? In terms of behavior, the answer is "probably not." Although middle- and upper-class girls who attend college seem to be more sexually active than college girls were twenty years ago, sexual behavior in other social categories is about the same today as it was then. In terms of attitudes, however, there has been a change. For example, the majority of young people believe it is morally acceptable for an engaged couple to have sexual intercourse; the majority of adults do not.

Attitudes affect the way we feel about sex and the way we respond sexually. Around the world there are wide variations in what youngsters are told about sex and how they respond. In some societies children are kept in the dark about sex until just before they are married, whereas in

Figure 9.4
While the sexual behavior of adolescents has not changed significantly over the past twenty years, there has been a major shift in their sexual attitudes.

others preadolescent children are encouraged to engage in sexual play, even intercourse, in the belief that such play will foster mature development.

In the United States, because of our "Puritan" past, many people still identify sex with sin except within marriage and with the intent of reproducing. This view is being challenged, however, by those who view sex as a source of pleasure as well as a means of perpetuating the species.

Today, girls' attitudes toward such sexual matters as premarital intercourse and pornography are still more conservative than boys', though this gap between the sexes is smaller than originally thought (Zubin and Money, 1973). Other variations among adolescents today with respect to attitudes have been noted. For example, older adolescents are less conservative than younger ones, and, in recent years, more affluent and educated adolescents (especially girls) have become more "liberated" in their attitudes (and behaviors) than their less affluent and educated counterparts.

Sex Roles.   Sex identity and sex role are two different, though closely related, aspects of our sexual lives. **Sex identity** results from biological inheritance. Thus, if one has a vagina, one's sex identity is female; if a penis, male. Sex identity includes genetic traits we have inherited, and may include perhaps some sex-linked behaviors as well. An obvious example of a sex-linked behavior is the erection of the penis during sexual excitement.

A person's **sex role,** in contrast, is defined partly by genetic makeup but mainly by the society and culture in which the individual lives. The sex role is a standard of how a person with a given sex identity is supposed to behave. For example, in the United States, men were traditionally viewed as dominant, competitive, and emotionally reserved; women were viewed as submissive, cooperative, and emotionally responsive. These traits were considered appropriate for the different sexes.

Sex roles tell us how we are expected to behave, look, think, and feel in order to be considered by others, and to consider ourselves, "masculine" or "feminine." For example, in the past, a woman who repaired telephone lines might be considered by many people to be "unfeminine." Why? Because she does not conform to the traditional sex role requirement that women are not supposed to perform physical labor.

Sex roles vary from one society to another, and they can change over time within a given society. Sex roles give social meaning to sex identity. However, not all societies agree on the roles the sexes should assume. Indeed, anthropologists have found that some societies reverse the roles that we traditionally give to men and women, while others assign to both sexes what we might consider "masculine" or "feminine" roles. Not only do sex roles vary among societies, but they may change radically within a society, as we are witnessing today in America.

Characteristics that have been encouraged in American men are ruggedness, forcefulness, independence, strength, dominance, and aggressiveness—traits necessary to be the breadwinner in the family. In contrast, women have been encouraged to be meek, passive, sensitive, dependent, and affectionate—characteristics suitable for being a helpmate and child rearer. These sex-role stereotypes have their roots deep in a time in our history when a division of labor was necessary for survival. Today, however, modern technology and birth control have freed women from duties associated with child rearing and childbearing for a large part of their lives. Sharp sex role divisions are no longer necessary or appropriate, especially in the labor force. New concepts of what it means to be "masculine" and "feminine" are becoming more widely accepted.

Partly because of the changing technology and partly as a result of affirmative action and other social and political movements, young people today have a much broader definition of what is appropriate behavior for men and women. Many people not only accept men who are to be emotionally and physically involved in the care of their children and take responsibility for other domestic duties, but expect these behaviors from them. Likewise, many women today are involved in occupations that, in the past, were reserved for men. Some of the symbols used to distinguish the sexes such as "wearing the pants" are completely obsolete. Similarly, many traditionally feminine symbols such as hair dyes and cosmetics are available to men.

Given these changing standards of acceptable sex roles, psychologist Sandra Bem argues that people should accept new **androgynous** roles—that is, roles that involve a flexible combination of traditionally male and female characteristics. She began her research by asking college students how desirable they considered various characteristics for a man and for a woman. Not surprisingly, she found that traits such as ambition, self-reliance, independence, and assertiveness were considered to be desirable for men. It was desirable for women to be affectionate, gentle, understanding, and sensitive to the needs of others.

These and other traits were then listed in a questionnaire called the

Bem Sex Role Inventory. Bem asked people to rate how each of these traits applied to them on a scale from one (never or almost never true) to seven (always or almost always true). In one early report (Bem, 1975), she described the results for 1,500 Stanford undergraduates: about 50 percent stuck to "appropriate" sex roles (masculine males or feminine females), 15 percent were "cross-sex typed" (women who described themselves in traditionally male terms, or men who checked feminine adjectives), and 36 percent were androgynous people who checked off both male and female characteristics when they described themselves.

In later studies, Bem found that the androgynous people were indeed more flexible. Such women were able to be assertive when it was required (so could traditional males, but traditional females could not). Such people were also able to express warmth, playfulness, and concern (as could traditional females, but traditional males could not). In our complex world, Bem argues, androgyny should be our ideal: there is no room for an artificial split between "woman's work" and "a man's world."

Androgyny is becoming an accepted ideal in our culture. One consequence of this shift is that adolescents who are developing into adults have more choices in the way they define themselves in life. In some ways, this shift toward more freedom in sex roles has resulted in greater personal responsibility. No longer limited by rigid sex role stereotypes, young people are challenged to define themselves according to their talents, temperaments, and values. At the same time, not all people within the culture accept the more androgynous sex roles. Older people, especially, may still define themselves and others in terms of more traditional and rigid sex role standards.

USING PSYCHOLOGY

Teenage Depression and Suicide

Each year more than one million teenagers run away from home. More than a million teenage girls in the United States get pregnant each year. It is estimated that more than 1.3 million American teenagers have serious drinking problems. These statistics highlight the seriousness of teenage depression. Many teenagers who feel helpless and hopeless use alcohol or other drugs, run away, become pregnant, or kill themselves. Suicide is second only to accidents as a cause of death among adolescents. Many accidents may, in fact, be disguised suicides.

According to Kathleen McCoy (1982), the phenomenon of teenage depression is much more widespread than most parents or educators suspect. To many grownups who see adolescence as the best years of life, depression and youth may seem incongruous.

What events trigger depression in adolescents? One major event is the loss of a loved one through death, divorce, separation, or family relocation. The adolescent may experience grief, guilt, panic, and anger as a reaction to a loss. If the youth is not able to express these feelings in a supportive atmosphere, depression may result.

Another related source of teenage depression is the breakdown of the family unit, often as a result of separation and divorce. Family members may be in conflict with each other and thus unable to communicate well. Adolescents may be thus deprived of the emotional support they need.

Unlike depressed adults, who usually look and feel sad or "down," depressed teenagers may appear to be extremely angry. They often engage in rebellious behavior such as truancy, running away, drinking, using drugs, or being sexually promiscuous. Often, depressed teenagers appear intensely hyperactive and frantic, traits that are often mistaken for normal behavior in teenagers. McCoy urges parents and educators to be aware of the warning signals of teenage depression and suicide. One warning signal is a change in the intensity and frequency of rebellious behavior. Others are withdrawal from friends, engaging in dangerous risk-taking, talking about suicide, and excessive self-criticism. Often the greatest danger of suicide occurs after a depression seems to be lifting.

The best way to deal with teenage depression is to communicate with the teenager about his or her problems. Sometimes, a caring, listening parent can help the youth deal with his or her concerns. In other cases, parents and their teenage child may need professional help. This is particularly true when few channels of communication have been established within the family.

Suicide attempts are made more frequently among females, but are more often fatal among males. One of the reasons that males more often "succeed" in committing suicide is that they are apt to use more violent means such as shooting, stabbing, or hanging themselves. Females are more likely to take a drug overdose, which is a slower process and can be more readily reversed if the person is found in time.

Some teenagers attempt suicide as a cry for help or attention or as a way of manipulating others rather than out of a desire to die. A suicide attempt may be designed to punish a former boyfriend or girlfriend or to call attention to a drug problem the teenager cannot deal with alone.

? FACT OR FICTION

Publicizing teenage suicides helps prevent more suicides.

Fiction. In the mid-1980s, leaders in communities around the country believed that talking publicly about teenage suicides as they occurred would stop other teens from taking their own lives. Unfortunately, the opposite occurred. Publicizing suicides seems to encourage more. Psychologists are trying to understand why this happens.

SOCIAL DEVELOPMENT

Adolescent development is multifaceted. In addition to the personal development just described, the adolescent also experiences changes in his or her social relationships. No longer a child though not yet an adult, the teenager must find a new role in the family—one that parents are not always ready to accept. He or she must also adjust to new, often more intense relationships with peers. The influence of family and peers on adolescent development has been the subject of much research, which is worth reviewing here.

The Family

One of the principal developmental tasks for adolescents is becoming independent of their families. Unfortunately, the means of achieving this status are not always clear, either to the adolescents or to their parents. First, there are mixed feelings on both sides. Some parents have built their life styles around the family and are reluctant to let the child go. Such parents know they will soon have to find someone else on whom to shift their emotional dependence. Also, parents whose children are old enough to leave home sometimes have to wrestle with their own fears of advancing age. Many parents worry about whether their children are really ready to cope with the harsh realities of life—and so do adolescents. At the same time that young people long to get out on their own and try themselves against the world, they worry a lot about failing there. This internal struggle is often mirrored in the adolescent's unpredictable behavior, which parents may interpret as "adolescent rebellion." Against this background of uncertainty, which is almost universal, there are various family styles of working toward autonomy.

The way in which adolescents seek independence and the ease with which they resolve conflicts about becoming adults depend in large part on the parent-child relationship.

In **authoritarian families** parents are the "bosses." They do not feel that they have to explain their actions or demands. In fact, such parents may feel the child has no right to question parental decisions.

In **democratic families** adolescents participate in decisions affecting their lives. There is a great deal of discussion and negotiation in such families. Parents listen to their children's reasons for wanting to go somewhere or do something, and make an effort to explain their rules and expectations. The adolescents make many decisions for themselves, but the parents retain the right to veto plans of which they disapprove.

In **permissive** or **laissez-faire** families children have the final say. The parents may attempt to guide the adolescents, but give in when the children insist on having their own way. Or the parents may simply give up their child-rearing responsibilities—setting no rules about behavior, making no demands, voicing no expectations, virtually ignoring the young people in their house.

What Adolescents Need and Want from Their Parents

Much as teenagers may wish it, the perfect parents probably do not exist. Every family's circumstances and personalities practically guarantee that there will be at least occasional clashes between parents and their adolescent offspring. Yet both parents and teenagers can benefit from having a general idea of the qualities adolescents need and want from their parents. This knowledge can help parents meet their children's needs, and it provides a yardstick against which teenagers can measure their expectations of their parents to see how realistic those expectations are. Several studies have revealed a number of qualities that adolescents most need and want in their parents.

1. Teenagers want parents to take an interest in their activities and to be available when they need help and support. One disappointed high school basketball player expressed this view very clearly:

   I'm the star player on the school basketball team, but never once has either parent come to see me play. They're either too busy or too tired or can't get a baby sitter for my younger sister. The crowds cheer for me, the girls hang around my locker, some kids even ask me for my autograph. But it doesn't mean much if the two most important people in my life don't care.

2. Parents should listen to what their teenaged children say, and should try to understand their point of view.
3. Similarly, parents should communicate with their children, exchanging ideas and talking *with* their teenagers, not *at* them.
4. Parents should love and accept adolescents as they are. Too often, teenagers feel rejected and worthless because they cannot meet their parents' too-high expectations of them.
5. Parents should trust their children and respect their privacy. Teenagers especially resent parents who open their mail, read their diaries, or eavesdrop on their phone conversations.
6. Parents should allow their children to learn to be independent by giving them leeway in such areas as choice of friends and clothing. Teenagers especially want their parents to grant them autonomy in gradually increasing amounts as they learn to handle it.
7. Parents should be neither too strict nor too permissive. Once family rules are established—preferably in a democratic way—parents should be consistent in enforcing them.
8. Parents should do their best to provide a positive emotional climate in the home. A prevailing mood of affection, cheerfulness, and optimism is much more beneficial to all family members than an atmosphere of marital unhappiness, fear, depression, and hostility.
9. Parents should set a good example for their adolescent children. By this teenagers mean that parents should "practice what they preach" and not be afraid to admit it when they make mistakes.

For more details, see F. P. Rice, *The Adolescent: Development, Relationships, and Culture*, 2nd ed. Boston: Allyn and Bacon, 1978, pp. 410–419.

Figure 9.5
The style of parent-child relationship—authoritarian, democratic, or permissive—plays a large part in determining how adolescents gain independence and make the transition to adulthood.

Numerous studies suggest that adolescents who have grown up in democratic families are more autonomous, in the sense of having more confidence in their own values and goals than other young people do. They are also more independent, in the sense of wanting to make their own decisions (with or without advice). There are several reasons for this.

First, the child is able to assume responsibility gradually. He or she is not denied the opportunity to exercise judgment (as in authoritarian families) or given too much responsibility too soon (as in permissive families). Second, the child is more likely to identify with parents who love and respect him or her than with parents who treat him or her as incompetent or who seem indifferent. Finally, through their behavior toward the child, democratic parents present a model of responsible, cooperative independence for the growing person to imitate.

Children raised in authoritarian families lack practice in negotiating for their desires and exercising responsibility. They tend to resent all authority, to rebel without cause. Children raised in permissive families tend to feel unwanted and to doubt their own self-worth. They often do not trust themselves or others (Conger, 1973: 208–215).

Although the style parents adopt in dealing with their children influences adolescent development, it would be wrong to conclude that parents are solely responsible for the way their children turn out. Adolescents themselves may contribute to the style parents embrace, with consequences for their own personal development. Parents may adopt a laissez-faire attitude simply because they find that style the easiest way to cope with a teenager who insists on having his or her own way. Adolescents experiencing rapid physical and emotional changes may force their parents to make major adjustments to them.

Conflict between adolescents and parents, even in democratic families, is not uncommon. Quarrels can arise over many issues, including church attendance, choice of friends, performance of home chores, use of time, and attitude toward studies. In general, the more authoritarian a family, the more frequent such conflicts tend to be. But other factors affect the frequency of arguments. The sex of the adolescent is one such factor, with girls reporting more conflict with family members than boys. The size of the family is another. Large middle-class families, for example, experience more conflict than smaller ones (Edwards and Branberger, 1973: 105).

Despite the sometimes strained relations in families, the home environment does have a shaping influence on such important decisions as occupational choice. Sociologists have found, for example, that adolescents from high-status families tend to select high-status occupations much more frequently than those from lower-class families (Elder, 1968). This fact may be explained in large part by the kind of feedback parents in different social classes tend to give their children. The parents of the high achievers may have fostered in their children the kind of self-confidence necessary for success (Rosenberg and Simmons, 1972).

Thus far in this section we have emphasized the relationship between the adolescent and his or her parents, but there is also a flow of influence between the adolescent and other family members, especially siblings. Older siblings, for example, serve as role models for the adolescent. Younger siblings allow the adolescent to assume the role of surrogate parent, and thus to learn an array of adult roles and responsibilities. In general, siblings learn from one another—through play, sharing secrets and experiences, and through fighting—how to negotiate relationships with others and thereby to get along better in the larger world.

The Peer Group

The people all adolescents can trust not to treat them like children are their peers. Teenagers spend much of their time with friends—they need and use each other to define themselves.

High schools are important as places for adolescents to get together. And they do get together in fairly predictable ways. Most schools contain easily recognizable and well-defined sets, or crowds. And these sets are arranged in a fairly rigid hierarchy—everyone knows who belongs to which set and what people in that set do with their time. Early in adolescence the sets are usually divided by sex, but later the sexes mix. Sets usually form along class lines. Some school activities bring teenagers of different social classes together, but it is the exception rather than the rule that middle-class and lower-class adolescents are close friends, though recent evidence suggests that interclass friendships may be increasing (Hraba and Grant, 1970; Proshansky and Newton, 1968).

Besides class, what determines whether an adolescent will be accepted by a peer group? Many studies have shown that personal characteristics are very important. Well-liked peers tend to be well-groomed, good-looking, outgoing, neat, fun, and adept at making others feel accepted. Unpopular peers are seen by others as irresponsible, sloppy, childish, shy, and lonely, among other negative characteristics (Hartup, 1970; Harrocks and Benimoff, 1967).

Belonging to a *clique* (a group within a set) is very important to most adolescents and serves several functions. Most obviously, perhaps, it ful-

Adolescents need and use the peer group to define themselves.

fills the need for closeness with others. But, in addition, it gives the adolescent a means of defining himself or herself, a way of establishing an identity. The group does this by helping the individual achieve self-confidence, develop a sense of independence from family, clarify values, and experiment with new roles (Rogers, 1977). By providing feedback, clique members not only help define who an individual is but also who he or she is not: group membership separates an adolescent from others who are not in his or her set.

Of course, there are drawbacks to this kind of social organization. One of the greatest is the fear of being disliked, which leads to **conformity**—the "glue" that holds the peer group together. A teenager's fear of wearing clothes that might set him or her apart from others is well known. But group pressures to conform may also lead young people to do more serious things that run contrary to their better judgment.

Despite their tendency to encourage conformity, peer groups are not always dominant in an adolescent's life. Both parents and peers exercise considerable influence in shaping adolescent behavior and attitudes. Peers tend to set the standards on such matters as fashion and taste in music (Munns, 1972). Their advice on school-related issues may also be considered more reliable than parental counsel (Brittain, 1963, 1969).

When it comes to basic matters, however, involving marriage, religion, or educational plans, adolescents tend to accept their parents' beliefs and to follow their advice (Chand, Crider, and Willets, 1975; Kandel and Lesser, 1969). Only in a few areas touching basic values—for example, drug use or

Figure 9.6
Most adolescents spend much of their time with a peer group, which is a source of self-identity as well as a source of social pressure to conform.

sexual behavior—are there differences. Even here the differences are not fundamental and represent only a difference in the strength with which the same basic belief is held (Lerner and Knapp, 1975).

Peer groups, then, do not pose a threat to parental authority. Even though parents spend less time with their adolescent children as the latter mature, their influence is still strong. Adolescents of both sexes tend to choose friends with values close to those of their parents (Bandura, 1964; Douvan and Adelson, 1965). Thus, generational conflict is not nearly so pronounced as some would have us believe.

DIFFICULTIES IN THE TRANSITION FROM LATE CHILDHOOD TO EARLY ADOLESCENCE

As we have seen in this chapter, adolescence is a time of transition. There are many developmental tasks to be mastered, but adolescence is not distinct from other periods of life in this respect. As Havighurst (1972) has pointed out, every stage of life brings with it unique challenges specific to that stage, be it old age, early childhood, or adolescence.

When a person has mastered the tasks of adolescence, he or she is an adult, but not a "mature" adult, for the developmental stage of adulthood spans many years and the end of adolescence is just the beginning of this long journey. The graduate-adolescent is a "young" adult heading toward "middle" adulthood, the phase before mature adulthood. The young adult will find that he or she now has new tasks to master unique to this stage of life.

Given the great array of profound changes the adolescent must cope with involving his or her mind, body, emotions, and social relationships, it is natural and normal that most adolescents should experience some *temporary* psychological difficulties. The great majority, however, adjust fairly quickly. Mental illness and suicide are relatively rare among adolescents (though the rates of both have been increasing over the past several decades). Thoughts about mental illness and death, however, are quite common among otherwise healthy adolescents.

Research shows that only about 20 percent of adolescents have problems so severe that they can't function well in social situations or at school (Masterson, 1967). This troubled minority often "acts out" problems in one of several ways. Acts of juvenile delinquency, running away from home, unwanted pregnancies, alcohol and drug abuse, and underachievement at school are typical.

Unfortunately, troubled adolescents do not simply "outgrow" their problems, but carry them into later life if they are not treated (Jones, 1974; Masterson, 1967). Adults, therefore, should be concerned about troubled teenagers. It is important to note, however, that abnormal behavior should be seen as a more intense form, or a more extreme degree, of normal behavior. It should not be considered a different *kind* of behavior. For example, teenagers who experiment with drugs—or even become drug abusers—need understanding; by not labeling the teenaged drug abuser "strange" or "different," we can better meet his or her psychological needs.

PSYCHOLOGY and YOU

Teenagers and Work. By high school graduation, more than 80 percent of students have had some kind of job. Most take low-skilled jobs that provide an opportunity to make some extra money. While most people tend to believe that any kind of job experience is good, research indicates that such work can, in fact, be harmful.

One reason for this is that students who work evenings or weekends have less time to study. If you work, you need to set time aside for school work. Another is that students might gain a false impression of the workplace from their work experience. The jobs they take tend to be low-paying, boring, and unchallenging. You need to remember that while you are still in high school you have few skills to offer. A higher education, and some training, will open doors to better jobs.

Finally, working while still in school can create false ideas about money. Most students work to pay for luxury items such as brand-name clothes or concert tickets. There's a danger that they will experience "premature affluence" because what they earn is spending money; they don't have to pay for necessities such as food and rent. Realizing that spending money may, in fact, be less available when you take a full-time job will help you avoid this trap.

Use the following outline as a tool for reviewing this chapter. Copy the outline onto your own paper, leaving spaces between headings to make notes about key concepts.

I. Views of Adolescence

    A. How Adults View Adolescence

    B. How Adolescents View Themselves

    C. Theories of Adolescence

II. Personal Development

    A. Physical Changes

    B. Changes in Thinking

    C. Moral Development

    D. Personality Changes and Identity Formation

    E. Sexuality: Attitudes and Roles

III. Social Development

    A. The Family

    B. The Peer Group

IV. Difficulties in the Transition from Late Childhood to Early Adolescence

CONCEPTS AND VOCABULARY

1. What are two views that adults have toward adolescents?

2. What are four reasons that may explain why some adults view adolescents in a negative light?

3. What is Stanley Hall's theory of adolescence? Does the research of Margaret Mead support his position?

4. Do early-maturing adolescent boys have a more positive view of themselves than late maturers? Is this difference the same for early- and late-maturing girls? Why does physical growth affect how persons feel about themselves?

5. What does Piaget mean by "formal operational" thinking? How does this change in cognitive ability affect an adolescent?

6. According to Kohlberg, what are the fifth and sixth stages of moral development? What other change is necessary in order for persons to achieve these advanced stages of moral development?

7. Based on Erikson's concept of identity crisis, what are the four adolescent personality types presented by Marcia? According to Bandura, what percentage of adolescents go through an identity crisis and what is its cause?

8. How does sex role differ from sexual identity? When Sandra Bem discusses androgyny, is she talking about sex role or sexual identity?

9. What are the three types of family interaction patterns? Which style would you use if you wanted your children to act independently and have confidence in their personal decisions?

10. In what areas do adolescents tend to follow the beliefs and advice of their parents?

11. What percentage of adolescents have a very difficult time mastering the developmental tasks of this period in their lives? Are these persons "different" from other adolescents who have less difficulty?

CRITICAL THINKING

1. **Evaluation.** Write five words or phrases that, in your opinion, characterize adolescence. Ask an adult (for example, a parent) to write five words or phrases, also. What are the similarities and differences? In your opinion, what are some reasons for the differences?

2. **Analyze.** Erikson and Marcia insist that all adolescents experience an identity crisis. Do you agree? What identity crises have you experienced?

APPLYING KNOWLEDGE

1. Pretend you are a high school psychology teacher. Tell what you would plan to teach in the course, reasons for your selections, and how you would plan to teach this material. Would you use an experiential or a cognitive approach? Which topics of importance to adolescents would you specifically include?

2. If you were a parent, which family structure would you choose to have in your home—authoritarian, laissez-faire, or democratic? What behaviors would you engage in to ensure that family structure actually existed?

3. It has often been said that American culture is preoccupied with youthfulness and remaining young. The values, music, fashion, and activities of young people are heavily publicized in the mass media. Find as many examples as you can of America's fascination with youth. Be sure to examine newspapers, magazines, radio, television, and popular music when you search for examples. Pay particular attention to advertising that emphasizes the marketing of youthful values. Report your findings to the class.

4. Some psychologists believe that men and women should accept androgynous sex roles. Androgynous sex roles consist of a combination of characteristics that are both masculine and feminine. Think of some traits that you consider to be masculine or feminine. Then think of people who possess mostly all masculine or all feminine traits. Next, think of people who possess both masculine and feminine characteristics. Your examples can be people you know, or they can be people from television, movies, or music. Do people with either mostly masculine or mostly feminine characteristics behave differently from people with both masculine and feminine traits? If so, in what type of situation? Do you think someone with an androgynous sex role is healthier than someone with a traditional sex role? Explain your reasoning.

5. Belonging to a clique is often a very important part of adolescence. Identify three different cliques in your school. How would you characterize the people who belong to each clique? What keeps cliques together? Are you part of any clique? Why or why not?

ANALYZING VIEWPOINTS

1. According to Erikson, building an identity is a task that is unique to adolescence. Other social scientists have suggested that building an identity is a lifelong process, and that changes to the identity occur at different times. Write an essay that argues in favor of Erikson's point of view. Then write an essay that argues that building an identity is a lifelong experience. Support your arguments with evidence from the chapter as well as evidence from your own experience.

BEYOND THE CLASSROOM

1. Many communities and mental health centers sponsor suicide hot lines. Ask your guidance counselor or school nurse if he or she knows of a hot line in your area. If possible, contact someone at the hot line and ask the person to come to your school and speak about how the hot line works. Have the person explain what type of training is required to become a phone counselor; how many calls come in on a typical night; what is the busiest time of day, day of the week, and time of year. If you are unable to find a hot line in your area, look for articles on teen suicide and what is being done to prevent it. Report your findings to the class.

CHAPTER 10

Adulthood and Old Age

Key Terms:

ageism
closed awareness
decremental model of aging
generativity
menopause
mutual pretense awareness
open awareness
stagnation
suspected awareness
thanatology

In the preface to *The Seasons of a Man's Life* (1978), Yale researcher Daniel Levinson wrote: "Young adults often feel that to pass 30 is to be 'over the hill,' and they are given little beyond hollow clichés to provide a fuller sense of the actual problems and possibilities of adult life at different ages. The middle years, they imagine, will bring triviality and meaningless comfort at best, stagnation and hopelessness at worst. . . . Adults hope that life begins at 40—but the great anxiety is that it ends there. The result of this pervasive dread about middle age is almost complete silence about the experience of being adult."

As much as middle age is dreaded, old age is looked on with even greater fear and misunderstanding. Whereas in some cultures reaching old age is thought of as a blessing, in ours it is awaited with anxiety. Everyone wants to look and act young. Gray hair must be dyed, faces lifted.

Much of our fear of aging is rooted in stereotypes of what it is to grow older. Middle age, it is thought, is a time of deterioration, both physically and mentally. Many believe that sexual life declines markedly. In old age the process of deterioration only accelerates.

But these are not true pictures of aging. Indeed, the positive side of adult life is one of the best-kept secrets in our society. By undermining some of the stereotypes about growing older, we hope to convey a true image of adult life.

ADULTHOOD

What is middle age like? For one thing, it is a period of great paradox. There is change and sameness, success and failure, crisis and stability, joy and sadness. Middle age can be a time when a person matures fully into what

Objectives:

After studying this chapter, you should be able to

- describe the physical, sexual, and intellectual changes that occur during adulthood.
- identify recent research related to older adults.
- identify and describe the stages of dying.

Figure 10.1 Because of stereotypes that encourage us to fear aging, many of us tend to overlook the positive aspects of adulthood.

MORE about...

The Cohort Effect. Suppose you were asked to measure the performance of trains at various points along a busy route. How would you go about it?

You might adopt a *longitudinal* approach. You would board a train and stay with it for its entire journey, recording your observations along the way. Alternatively, you might employ a *cross-sectional* strategy. You would ask observers stationed at key points to report on the performance of various trains that pass by.

Psychologists who study the behavior of people as they progress through adulthood and old age face a similar task. Since this "journey" can last decades, few researchers adopt a purely longitudinal approach. Instead, most conduct cross-sectional studies in which they can measure different age groups, or *cohorts*, together at one time.

Unfortunately, people from different cohorts usually have different experiences in a number of important areas, including access to education, nutrition, career opportunities, and social values. Their different backgrounds make it difficult to determine how age affects human abilities, attitudes, and even health.

he or she is. Or it can be a time when life closes in and what was once possibility is now limitation. How each person reacts depends on circumstances and one's general outlook on life.

Until quite recently psychologists knew little about adulthood. In the past, more emphasis was placed on childhood and adolescence, and relatively little attention was given to the study of middle age. Freud, for example, felt that the personality was set during childhood and adolescence, and he did not consider the later development of the individual. As we saw in Chapter 8, Erikson does view development as a lifelong process. But his work, too, concentrates more on childhood and adolescence than on adulthood and old age.

Today, however, a growing number of psychologists are studying adult psychology. (That it is a recent field of study is ironic, for both young and old agree that adulthood is the prime of life. Certainly, it is the longest period of our lives.) Much of what they are learning emphasizes that adulthood is a period of changes and transitions. Among these changes are the new developmental tasks that adults must meet. These tasks include helping teenage children become responsible and satisfied adults; taking on adult social and civic responsibility; performing well in an occupation; finding satisfying leisure activities; relating to one's husband or wife as a person; adjusting to the physical changes of middle age; and relating to one's aging parents (Havighurst, 1972).

If you recall the developmental tasks of adolescence discussed in Chapter 9 (and some of your own experiences) you may recognize similarities between the years of adulthood and the adolescent years. During both periods bodily changes require psychological adjustments, relating well to others is an important goal (whether to parents, peers, or spouses), and meeting new responsibilities requires a good deal of effort. Teenagers often think they have nothing in common with their parents. But the tasks of adolescence and adulthood are similar enough that they can form the basis for improved communication between generations. In addition, understanding the problems and changes that accompany growing older can be good preparation for a time of life we all must enter.

Physical Changes

In general, human beings are at their physical peak between the ages of eighteen and twenty-five. This is the period when we are strongest, healthiest, and have the quickest reflexes. One has only to think of the average age of professional athletes or dancers to verify this.

For most adults, the process of physical decline is slow and gradual. Strength and stamina begin to decline in the late twenties. A twenty year old manages to carry four heavy bags of groceries; a forty year old finds it easier to make two trips. In middle age appearance changes. The hair starts to turn gray and perhaps to thin out. The skin becomes somewhat dry and inelastic; wrinkles appear. In old age, muscles and fat built up over the years break down, so that people often lose weight, become shorter, and develop more wrinkles, creases, and loose skin.

With time the senses require more and more stimulation. During their forties most people begin having difficulty seeing distant objects, adjusting to the dark, and focusing on printed pages, even if their eyesight has always been good. Many experience a gradual or sudden loss of hearing in their later years. In addition, reaction time slows. If an experimenter asks a young person and an older person to push a button when they see a light flash on, the older person will take longer to do so.

Health Problems.   Some of the changes we associate with growing older are the result of the natural processes of aging. Others result from diseases and from simple disuse and abuse. Two of the most common health problems of middle age—heart disease and cancer—are related to obesity and smoking. Obesity can cause heart attacks and lead to hypertension and diabetes. In fact, for someone who is 30 percent overweight, the chance of dying during middle age is increased by 40 percent (Turner and Helms, 1979). Heavy smoking is related to cancer of the mouth, throat, and lungs, and to respiratory and heart problems. It increases the possibility of cardiovascular disease, which is the leading cause of death during middle age (U.S. Department of Health, Education, and Welfare, 1971). The nonsmoker, on the other hand, encounters only half the health problems of the heavy smoker. A person who eats sensibly, exercises, avoids cigarettes, drugs, and alcohol, and is not subjected to severe emotional stress will look and feel younger than someone who neglects his or her health.

Menopause.   Between the ages of forty-five and fifty, a woman's production of sex hormones is sharply reduced. This biological event is called **menopause.** The woman stops ovulating (producing eggs) and menstruating, and therefore cannot have any more children. However, menopause does not cause any reduction in a woman's sexual drive or sexual enjoyment.

Many women experience some degree of discomfort during menopause. However, the irritability and severe depression some women experience with "the change of life" appear to have an emotional rather than physical origin.

A recent study shows that the negative effects of menopause are greatly exaggerated. Half of the women interviewed said they felt better, more confident, calmer, and freer after menopause than they had before. They no longer had to think about their periods or getting pregnant. Their relations with their husbands improved; they enjoyed sex as much as or more than they had before. Many said the worst part of menopause was not knowing what to expect (Neugarten *et al.*, 1963).

Men do not go through any biological change equivalent to menopause. The number of sperm a man's body produces declines gradually over the years, but men have fathered children at an advanced age.

Sexual Behavior.   Is there sex after forty? According to one recent study, most college students believe their parents have intercourse no more than once a month and one-fourth of the students believed that their parents had had intercourse only once or not at all in the last year (Pocs et al., 1977). In general, young people are uncomfortable with the idea that older people have sexual lives.

Despite younger people's beliefs, studies have shown that sexual activ-

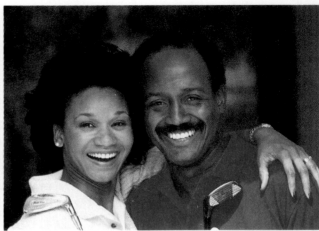

Figure 10. 2
Sexual interest and activity do not suddenly cease at a certain age: as more and more studies show, those who have partners and remain active, productive people also continue to enjoy active sex lives.

ity does not automatically decline with age. Indeed, as sex researchers William Masters and Virginia Johnson point out, there is no physiological reason for stopping sexual activity with advancing age (1970). Most older people who have an available partner maintain quite vigorous sex lives. Those who are inactive cite boredom with a partner of long standing, poor physical condition or illness (such as heart disease), or acceptance of the stereotype of loss of sex drive with aging.

It is true that there are changes in sexuality during adulthood. A man reaches his sexual peak in his late teens. From that time on, his sexual responsiveness declines. But the decline is very gradual and, except for the self-doubt it sometimes causes, does not usually interfere with normal sexual functioning. Kinsey measured this gradual decline of frequency of orgasm per week for males from sixteen on, but found even at age seventy almost 70 percent of the males were still sexually active (Kinsey et al., 1948). Women reach their sexual peak later than men; in addition, the decline in their sexual responsiveness occurs later. When it does occur, it is probably less than in men (Botwinick, 1978).

Psychological factors may be a greater hindrance to a man's sexual activity than are physical factors. Preoccupation with his job and with making money may decrease a man's sexual drive. In addition, the decline in sexual responsiveness may arouse a "fear of failure" in some men that in turn affects their sexual responsiveness even more.

More so than age, then, good physical and mental health seem to be the key factors affecting sexual activity. Adults can and do continue to enjoy a healthy sex life. Sex after forty is not only possible, it is a fact of life.

Intellectual Changes

People are better at learning new skills and information, solving problems that require speed and coordination, and shifting from one problem-solving strategy to another in their mid-twenties than they were in adolescence (Baltes and Schaie, 1974). These abilities are considered signs of intelligence; they are the skills intelligence tests measure.

At one time many psychologists thought that intellectual development reached a peak in the mid-twenties and then declined. The reason was that people do not score as high on intelligence tests in middle age as they did when they were younger. Further investigation revealed that some parts of these tests measure speed, not intelligence (Bischof, 1969). As indicated above, a person's reaction time begins to slow after a certain age. Intelligence tests usually "penalized" adults for this fact.

One intelligence test, the Wechsler, takes this into account by testing two very different sorts of abilities. On the verbal portion, which measures facility with words and stored information, older people show little decline. However, on the performance parts of the test, which measure speed of reaction in performing tasks, their scores are lower. On the basis of such tests researchers have concluded that overall decline in abilities is not great and is hardly apparent until about age fifty or later (Botwinick, 1978).

Even with a decline in speed, people continue to acquire information and to expand their vocabularies as they grow older. The ability to comprehend new material and to think flexibly improves with the years. This is particularly true if a person has had higher education, lives in a stimulating environment, and works in an intellectually demanding career. One researcher studied over seven hundred individuals who were engaged in scholarship, science, or the arts. Although the patterns varied from profession to profession, most of the subjects reached their peaks of creativity and productivity in their forties (Dennis, 1966).

Social and Personality Development

As we mentioned earlier, studies have just begun to focus on middle age. Until recently, psychologists commonly applied theories of childhood and adolescent development to the middle years (Botwinick, 1973). Only now are they beginning to find out how age affects personality. There is evidence to suggest that an individual's basic character—his or her style of adapting to situations—is relatively stable over the years. But researchers are also convinced that personality is flexible and capable of changing as an individual confronts new tasks.

Many studies support the first point. A number of researchers have given the same attitude and personality tests to individuals in late adolescence and again ten or fifteen years later. Many of the subjects believed that they had changed dramatically. But the tests indicated they had not. The degree of satisfaction they expressed about themselves and about life in general in their middle years was consistent with their earlier views. Confident young people remained confident; self-haters, self-hating; passive individuals, passive—unless something upsetting had happened to them, such as a sudden change in economic status (see Kimmel, 1974).

Despite the stability of character, people do face many changes in their lifetimes and adjust accordingly. Adults encounter new developmental tasks, just as adolescents do. They too must learn to cope with problems and deal with new situations. Learning the skills needed to cope with change seems to occur in stages for both adult males and females. One researcher who has studied personality development in males, Daniel Levinson, has developed a theory concerning the cycle of changes men go through.

Like adolescents, adults must cope with new situations and developmental tasks.

Levinson's Theory of Male Development.   The work of Daniel Levinson and his colleagues at Yale was not well known until 1976 when it was popularized in a national best seller by Gail Sheehy entitled *Passages: Predictable Crises of Adult Life.* During his research, Levinson interviewed four groups of men between the ages of thirty-five and forty-five: ten were executives, ten were hourly workers in industry, ten were novelists, and ten were university biologists.

A life structure was developed for each man based on these interviews. Each life structure was an account of the major periods of the man's life as determined by his activities, his associations, and his relationships. A careful analysis of these life structures revealed a pattern that seemed to apply to almost all the men sampled.

The model of adult development for men that Levinson and his colleagues proposed is shown in Figure 10.3. The three major eras are early adulthood (from about age seventeen to about age forty), middle adulthood (forty to sixty), and late adulthood (beginning at about sixty). Between these eras are important transition periods at ages thirty, forty, fifty, and sixty, which last approximately five years. Levinson's research focused on the early adult era and the mid-life transition. The following discussion concentrates on what he learned about these stages.

Entering the adult world. From about age twenty-two to age twenty-eight, the young man is considered, both by himself and by society, to be a novice in the adult world—not fully established as a man, but no longer an adolescent. During this time he must attempt to resolve the conflict between the need to explore the options of the adult world and the need to establish a stable life structure. He needs to sample different kinds of relationships, to keep choices about career and employment open, to ex-

Figure 10.3
A model of the developmental sequence of a man's life proposed by Levinson. The scheme emphasizes that development is an ongoing process that requires continual adjustment.

plore the nature of the world now accessible to him as an adult. But he also needs to begin a career and to establish a home and family of his own. The first life structure, then, may have a tentative quality. The young man may select a career or a job but not be committed to it. He may form romantic attachments and may even marry during this period; but the life structure of early adulthood often lacks a full sense of stability or permanence.

The age-thirty crisis. A few years ago the motto of the rebellious, politically oriented young people who sought to change American society was "Never trust anyone over thirty." Levinson's data reveal that the years between twenty-eight and thirty-three are indeed often a major transition period. The thirtieth birthday can truly be a turning point; for most men in Levinson's sample, it could be called "the age-thirty crisis." During this transitional period the tentative commitments that were made in the first life structure are reexamined, and many questions about the choices of marriage partner, career, and life goals are reopened, often in a painful way. The man feels that any parts of his life that are unsatisfying or incomplete must be attended to now, because it will soon be too late to make major changes.

Settling down. The questioning and searching that are part of the age-thirty crisis begin to be resolved as the second adult life structure develops. Having probably made some firm choices about his career, family, and relationships, the man now begins actively carving out a niche in society, concentrating on what Levinson calls "making it" in the adult world. The man attempts to move up the ladder of prestige and achievement in his chosen career or profession and to be a full-fledged member of adult society.

Levinson found that near the end of the settling-down period, approximately between the ages of thirty-six and forty, there is a distinctive phase that he has labeled "becoming one's own man." Whereas earlier the young man had looked to an older, more experienced man as a mentor, someone who would share his experience and wisdom, the relationship with the mentor is often fundamentally changed, or even broken off, in the process of becoming one's own man. Now it is time to become fully independent. During this period the man strives to attain the seniority and position in the world that he identified as his ultimate goal at the beginning of the settling-down period.

The mid-life transition. At about age forty the period of early adulthood comes to an end and the mid-life transition begins. From about age forty to age forty-five, the man begins again to ask questions, but now the questions concern the past as well as the future. He may ask: "What have I done with my life?" "What have I accomplished?" "What do I still wish to accomplish?" At age thirty the man had primarily looked ahead toward goals, but at the mid-life transition he is in a position to assess his accomplishments and to determine whether or not they have been satisfying. During this transition he begins to develop yet another life structure that will predominate during the period of middle adulthood.

During this period, the man often experiences a resurgence of interest in sex. In part this may be a result of his general reevaluation of his life to this point. In addition, he and his wife may have more time together alone, without the pressures of caring for small children. At the same time, how-

Figure 10.4
Mentor and protégé: the desire to transmit one's knowledge and experience to the next generation is a sign of what Erikson calls the "generativity" resolution of the crisis of middle age. The opposite resolution—stagnation—results in self-absorption, bitterness, and looking backward.

ever, his marriage may be at a low point (Rollins and Feldman, 1970) if he and his wife have developed different interests over the years of their marriage. Thus, the man's relationship with his wife—whether good or bad—is likely to be an important factor in the mid-life transition.

This may also be an important period in the relationship between the man and his adolescent children, since each is going through a period of transition. The man plays an important part in his children's lives as do the children in their father's (Vaillant, 1977). Some of the teenager's own experiences may, in addition, rekindle feelings the parent had long forgotten. For example, a father may be reminded of his own youthful political ideals by a son who is active in protests against nuclear power plants.

Often a successful mid-life transition is accompanied by the man's becoming a mentor for a younger man. This event signals the attainment, in Erik Erikson's terms, of generativity. By **generativity**, Erikson means the desire to use one's accumulated wisdom to guide future generations—directly, as a parent, or indirectly. The opposite—**stagnation**—can also occur. A man may choose to hang on to the past, perhaps by having an affair with a younger woman to recapture his youth. Or he may become preoccupied with his health or bitter about the direction his life has taken.

The mid-life transition has been the most discussed aspect of Levinson's work. About 80 percent of the men in his sample experienced the mid-life transition as a moderate to severe crisis, characterized by the questioning of virtually every aspect of their lives. But it is a period of questioning from which a new life structure must emerge.

Middle adulthood. The late forties is a time when true adulthood can be achieved. The man who finds satisfactory solutions to his life crisis reaches a period of stability. He understands and tolerates others; he displays a sensitivity and concern for other people as people. He is able to strike a balance between the need for friends and the need for privacy.

For the man who is not as fortunate, this period can be a time of extreme frustration and unhappiness. Instead of generativity, there is stagnation; instead of change and improvement, there is a mood of resignation to a bad situation. The job is only a job. The individual may feel cut off from family and friends. The future holds no promise. By avoiding this life crisis, he is only inviting a later appearance of it, at age fifty, with more crushing force (Rogers, 1979).

Those who successfully adjust to middle age can find it a most gratifying period. The difficult early adulthood years are behind them; now they are looked to for leadership and expertise. In their work, marriage, and personal lives, they are happier than ever before. They are in the prime of life—a time that will someday be looked back upon as the best years of their lives (Stevens-Long, 1979).

Female Development.   While there have been far more studies conducted among men than among women, some researchers have focused their attention on women's mid-life development. Sheehy's best-selling book, mentioned earlier, is one of them. Working with Levinson's basic theories, Sheehy interviewed 115 people who described their experiences as adults. The author discovered a major difference between men and women in how they can best rebuild their lives at mid-life. Throughout their lives, most women have traditionally served others in their roles as wife and mother. So although generativity may be a goal for many men, it may not be the ideal solution for some women who have reached mid-life.

Career versus family. Until recently, both men and women in industrial societies felt that women had to make an either-or choice between home and career. Most women chose the former. The traditional role of wife and mother, while satisfying for many, proved to be unfulfilling for others. For some women, staying at home to care for the children makes it difficult to feel involved in the world. Other women sense a loss of self-worth in being defined by their husband's role. They want to be thought of as more than simply "the wife of an attorney."

To solve this problem, Sheehy believes, women must overcome their dependency on their spouses. Returning to work or to school may give a woman the missing sense of personal identity. Today, more and more women are realizing that they do not have to choose between career and family. Women now have more opportunities than ever to become independent and self-fulfilled human beings.

Physical attractiveness in mid-life. Women have traditionally been more conscious of the aging process than men. This is perhaps because the male selection of a partner for courtship and marriage depended to a great extent on the physical attractiveness of the woman. Also, as a woman comes to be considered less attractive with age, she often faces the problem of adjusting to a different image of herself. It has been shown that physical attractiveness eases social adjustment for college women but actually makes adjustment more difficult for them twenty years later (David Campbell, as reported in Berscheid and Walster, 1974: 200–201). Perhaps this reflects the fragile nature of self-esteem that is based on only one aspect of identity such as physical attractiveness.

The "empty nest" syndrome. A significant event in many women's lives is the departure from home of the last child. Contrary to popular belief, this event need not be traumatic. In fact, many women find that the period after the children are grown is one of the happiest of their lives. If they have not already done so, they may return to an interrupted career or start a new one (Stevens-Long, 1979).

Of course, not all women experience the same sense of new freedom. Psychologists have found that a stable marriage makes a difference. If a woman has a warm relationship with her husband, she may find the adjustment easier because of his support. Conversely, if the woman is widowed or divorced, the transition can be much more difficult. How well her children adjust to their new independence can also affect a mother's happiness at this time (Harkins, 1978).

Depression in mid-life. In her book *Unfinished Business,* Maggie Scarf (1980) draws attention to another difference between men and women in their mid-life development. Statistically, women are from two to six times more likely than men to suffer from depression. Depression can affect people of all ages, but it is most common among middle-aged women. In a survey conducted in New Haven (Boyd and Weissman, 1981), 7 percent of the women compared with 2.9 percent of the men aged forty to sixty-five years old suffered from depression. Scarf believes that the reason for this difference in rate of depression is cultural. She views depression as the byproduct of a traditional feminine sex-role stereotype. Early in life, young girls have been taught and encouraged to define themselves as worthwhile through their relationships with other people. They feel good when they establish connections with people and are taught to look to others for approval and to be dependent.

Thus, during the early years of a woman's life, she may derive a sense of personal worth from her roles of daughter, lover, wife, and mother. These relationships change as children grow, parents die, or marriages fail. Some women begin to experience a sense of loss and personal worthlessness. They may see themselves as failures compared with their husbands, who have experienced successes in their careers. The onset of menopause can trigger depression in some women. Those who have defined themselves as childbearers now view themselves as useless when they lose their ability to produce and care for children. On the other hand, many women welcome this time of life. Some women in their fifties find that the nature of their marriage changes when they no longer have to focus their attention on the needs of their children. The prospect of giving up the traditional roles of a dependent wife for a more independent role may be unsettling for a while, especially for those women who have spent a lifetime living according to a sex-role stereotype. Once those women become accustomed to their new role, however, many find that they enjoy the freedom that middle adulthood brings.

Figure 10.5
Many women experience what is called the "empty nest" syndrome when grown children leave home and the twenty-four-hour-a-day job in which they have been absorbed for probably two decades is suddenly over. Some women find new careers; others return to those they gave up when the children were born. For many, however, this is a period of stress and readjustment.

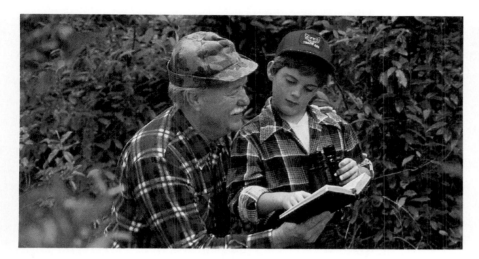

Figure 10.6
Many of our society's stereotyped attitudes about the elderly are not valid. Old people do not always become senile; they are not necessarily resistant to change; and they are not useless.

OLD AGE

Recently in one big-city newspaper, the photograph of a man celebrating his ninetieth birthday was placed on the obituary page. Is this only the view on aging of one newspaper editor? Perhaps, but unfortunately, many people tend to regard old age as being just one step away from the grave. Indeed, some would rather die than grow old.

The fear of growing old is probably one of the most common fears in our society. We are surrounded with indications that aging and old age are negative—or at best something to ridicule. Birthday cards make light of aging; comedians joke about it. Advertisements urge us to trade in older products for the newer, faster model. We retire older workers—whether or not they want to retire—and replace them with younger people. Many of us do not even want to use the word *old*; instead we refer to "golden agers," "senior citizens," and the like.

Many of our attitudes about aging are based on the **decremental model of aging,** which holds that progressive physical and mental decline is inevitable with age. In other words, chronological age is what makes people "old." In fact, there are great differences in physical condition among the elderly, depending on their genetic makeup and environment. Many of us know people who are eighty and look and act fifty, and vice versa. The prevalence of the decremental view in our society can be explained in part by ignorance and a lack of contact with older people. The result is a climate of prejudice against the old. One researcher, Butler, has coined the word **ageism** to refer to this prejudice. As with racism and sexism, ageism feeds on myths rather than facts.

Young people tend to believe that the old suffer from poor health, live in poverty, and are frequent victims of crime. But the elderly seldom see these as personal problems, though, interestingly, they tend to think of them as problems for other older people (Harris, 1975).

The notion that the aged tend to withdraw from life and sit around doing nothing is also very common. But this too is a false picture. George

? FACT OR FICTION

The elderly need more sleep than younger adults.

Fiction. Studies show that as people progress from adulthood to old age, their need for sleep generally decreases. However, sleep efficiency declines rapidly with age. Sleep in elderly people is more disrupted and fragmented, so they need to spend more time in bed and take naps to get their required sleep. To the casual observer, the elderly appear to sleep longer.

PSYCHOLOGY
UPDATE

Alzheimer's Disease. Alzheimer's disease is an affliction more commonly seen among the elderly. Although extremely rare in people under 50, Alzheimer's strikes roughly 2 percent of those over 65 and more than 10 percent of those over 80.

Alzheimer's is a neurological disease marked by a gradual deterioration of cognitive functioning. Early signs of the disease include frequent forgetting, poor judgment, increased irritability, and social withdrawal. Eventually Alzheimer's patients lose their ability to comprehend simple questions and to recognize friends and loved ones. Ultimately they require constant supervision and custodial care. Rarely do patients die from the disease itself, but their weakened state leaves them vulnerable to a variety of other potentially fatal problems.

Little is known about the cause of Alzheimer's. Some recent research suggests a genetic component, though this is not conclusive.

At present there is no cure for the disease. Many patients and their caretakers (usually their families) are offered supportive therapy that helps them learn to accept the relentless progression of the disease and the limitations it imposes on its victims.

Burns, Ronald Reagan, and Helen Hayes are good examples of active older Americans, and many less well-known older people follow their lead. In fact, the majority of older Americans work or wish to work either for pay or as volunteers.

Related to the idea that the elderly are unproductive is the notion that older people are inflexible or senile. In actuality, rigidity is more a lifelong habit than a response to aging. The older person who tends to be rigid was probably rigid as a young adult. Senility, which affects only 10 percent of the aged, usually results from some disease rather than from the natural process of aging.

The opposite notion that old age is a time not of slippage but of stress-free bliss is also untrue (Butler, 1974). The aged are, in fact, subject to more stress than any other group, though many endure crises with remarkable strength.

Older people, however, do not think of themselves in terms of the myths mentioned above. They feel they are just as able as when they were younger. Most older people find their lives are as interesting as ever. Health, activities, and money have more to do with the happiness of the elderly than does their chronological age.

Changes in Health

Most people over sixty-five are in reasonably good health. Physical strength and the five senses do decline, of course, but 80 percent of the elderly are able to carry out their normal activities. (Fifteen percent are unable to do so, and five percent are in institutions.) For the most part, the health of an older person is related to his or her health when younger. Good health in adolescence and adult life carries over into old age.

All people, young and old, are subject to disease, though. About 40 percent of the elderly have at least one chronic disease (a permanent disability as opposed to an acute or temporary disability more common with younger people). The four most prevalent chronic diseases—heart disease, hypertension, diabetes, and arthritis—tend to afflict women more than men. In general, the major causes of death among the old are heart disease, strokes, and cancer.

The quality of health care for the elderly remains by and large inferior to that of the general population. The reasons for this are numerous. The elderly in the lower socioeconomic class tend not to take care of themselves or to seek out treatment when needed. Many doctors prefer to administer to younger patients with acute diseases rather than to older patients with long-term chronic conditions that can only be stabilized, not cured. Some doctors hold stereotypical views of the aged that can lead to misdiagnosis and improper treatment.

For the one million old people who are no longer able to care for themselves, there are institutions. However, too many of these nursing homes have inadequate facilities. As more and more people each year reach late adulthood, it is paramount that there be a general overhaul of health care treatment and facilities for the elderly.

Changes in Life Situation

For younger people transitions in life—graduation, marriage, parent-hood—are usually positive and create a deeper involvement in life. In late adulthood, transitions—retirement, widowhood—are often negative and reduce responsibilities and increase isolation. Perhaps the most dev-astating transition is the loss of a spouse. Over 50 percent of women and 20 percent of men are widowed by the age of fifty-six. And by the age of eighty, one-third of men and seven out of ten women are alone (Stevens-Long, 1979). All too often, the person loses not just a spouse but the support of friends and family, who cannot cope with the widowed person's grief or feel threatened by the survivor's new status as a single person.

The loss of self-esteem that comes with retirement and a diminished role in the community, or the grief over the loss of a spouse, can bring on a deep depression. One of every four suicides in the country is a person over sixty-five, and older men commit suicide far more frequently than do women (Butler and Lewis, 1973). Unfortunately, the elderly receive only two percent of the available psychiatric services. To some extent, this is a result of societal attitudes toward old people. The adjustment and emotional problems of the old are often viewed by mental health personnel as natural and unavoidable results of aging. The same symp-toms in younger people would more likely receive attention and treatment (Butler, 1963).

Financial Resources.   Most of the elderly have incomes of only half their preretirement income. Although the public believes that the lack of money is a major problem for the old, only 15 percent of the elderly find it a personal problem (Kalish, 1977). Yet even though the percentage is smaller than many of us may have thought, it still indicates that lack of money is a problem for many of the elderly. Those who are living alone and without family are in the most precarious position. Of course, many old people do not stop working because they want to; quite frequently workers who are forced to retire would rather continue working. Societal prejudice against hiring and retaining people over the normal retirement years will no doubt change as the life span of the general population increases.

Changes in Sexual Activity

Just as young people tend to think sexual activity diminishes at mid-life, they often believe it ceases altogether in old age. But the majority of people over the age of sixty-five continue to be interested in sex, and healthy partners enjoy sexual activity into their seventies and eighties. The reasons some do not engage in sexual activity apparently are related to poor health or the death of a spouse, rather than to a lack of interest or to sexual physiology and functioning. Societal attitudes are another factor that discourages sexual expression by the elderly. Old people are not supposed to be interested in sex or be sexually active. Sexual relationships in old age—and even displays of affection—are often considered silly, improper, or even morally wrong. People who grow old in this atmosphere may give up sexual activity because they are "supposed to." On a more personal level, older people often encounter opposition from family and friends if they want to remarry after the death of a spouse. Children and family, too, find the idea of love and sex in old age ridiculous or even vaguely disgusting. A change in our ideas may enable a large segment of our population to continue to enjoy a healthy sex life in old age.

Adjusting to Old Age

Many of the changes the elderly face make their adjustment to everyday life more difficult because they represent a loss of control over the environment. And when older people are unable to maintain what they value most—good health, recognition in the community, visits from family and friends, privacy, leisure and work activities—the quality of their life suffers dramatically, along with their self-image.

The loss of control is usually gradual, and it may involve both physical changes (becoming sick or disabled) and external circumstances (moving to a nursing home). It is most devastating when it is cumulative (Schwartz and Proppe, 1970). Losing a husband is terrible enough, but the burden is only made worse by the further losses of friends and one's house. Those who experience a loss of control often develop a negative self-concept. They can regain their sense of control and a more positive self-image if they are helped to make the best of the options available to them. People with assertive personalities are often better at coping with life changes than more passive individuals because they are better able to demand and get the attention they need.

In order to help old people adjust, society must make some basic changes. Older people are beginning this process themselves by forming organizations such as the Gray Panthers and the American Association of Retired Persons to speak out on social issues of importance to them. Since the population over sixty-five is constantly growing, social policy will have to take the elderly into consideration more and more. Attitudes toward old people are already slowing changing. Eventually a time will come when old age will be considered the culmination of life, not simply the termination.

Changes in Mental Functioning

As people age, there are also changes in many of the mental functions they use, although there is much less decline in intelligence and memory than people think. If you compare measures of intellectual ability for a group of elderly people with similar measures for younger people, you might see a difference—namely that older people do not score as well on intellectual tests. However, the older group of people will most likely be less educated and less familiar with test-taking than younger people. Furthermore, there are many different types of mental skills and abilities that combine to produce intellectual functioning, and these abilities do not develop at the same rate or time across the life span.

John Horn (1979) has proposed two types of intelligence, *crystallized* and *fluid* intelligence. Crystallized intelligence refers to the ability to use accumulated knowledge and learning in appropriate situations. This ability increases with age and experience, showing no decline in older adulthood. Fluid intelligence is the ability to solve abstract relational problems and to generate new hypotheses. This ability is not tied to schooling or education and gradually increases in development as the nervous system matures. As people age and their nervous systems decline, so does their fluid intelligence. Thus, older people may not be as good at problems that require them to combine and generate new information or ideas. A decline in the nervous system affects reaction time, visual motor flexibility, and memory. Elderly people have difficulty retrieving information from memory. If they are asked to recognize a familiar name or object, they cannot do so as well as younger people.

The ability of older people to remember and think clearly may also vary with their environment. B. F. Skinner has maintained that older people do not receive as much reinforcement from the environment for their mental and verbal behaviors as younger people and so decline in their performance (Skinner and Vaughn, 1983). As their abilities to hear, taste, and see decline, as friends and relatives die, and as younger people become less responsive to their ideas, elderly people become less motivated to use their mental faculties. Recognizing the ways in which one's thinking is influenced by the circumstances of aging is a necessary first step toward changing these circumstances.

At age 79, Skinner wrote a book entitled *Enjoy Old Age* in which he suggests some practical ways to change one's environment to increase mental performance. One technique he uses to improve his memory of new ideas is to carry a pocket notebook in which he can write down a thought as he has it. Later, he does not have to search his memory, but merely flip open his notebook for recall. To avoid the embarrassment and unpleasantness of not remembering a person's name, he suggests appealing graciously to age and accepting this shortcoming. He recommends that to avoid getting sidetracked in a discussion by an interruption, the older person should rehearse or make mental notes of what is to be said. Just as physical abilities decline with physical fatigue, mental abilities decline with mental fatigue. Skinner suggests that older people protect themselves from mental fatigue by taking leisurely breaks in their mental activity and by working fewer hours a day on thought-related tasks.

DEATH AND DYING

Should terminally ill patients be told they are going to die? What are the consequences for the family, the hospital staff, and the patient if the patient is informed? What if the patient is not informed? In their book *Awareness of Dying* (1965), Barney Glaser and Anselm Strauss have looked at these issues and their effects on dying patients, their families, and

Growing Old in Japan

Like the United States, Japan is a highly industrialized and urbanized society. But the Japanese view of aging is markedly different from that in the United States. In contrast to the old in America, the elderly in Japan occupy a position of honor. In part, this respect for age is based on ancient social and religious traditions not readily adaptable to our culture. But there are specific Japanese programs and practices that we might well import.

A fundamental problem for the elderly in this country is that they receive very little respect and as a result often have very little self-respect. The Japanese show their respect for old people in several ways: by bowing and honorific language, by celebrating Respect for Elders Day each year, and by making an occasion of an individual's sixty-first birthday. In our society, which values equality, it is highly unlikely that bowing would be accepted. But we could take other actions to encourage better treatment of the elderly—for example, reserving a certain number of seats for older people on buses and trains. Since we already have a tradition of holidays and honorary occasions to recognize the contributions of certain groups—such as Veterans Day, Father's Day, and Mother's Day—we could establish a similar day to honor the elderly.

America's old people may not be given much respect because they often lack status. Stripped of their jobs at sixty-five, many then occupy the lower rungs of the economic ladder and go without adequate medical care. In Japan that situation rarely develops because the able-bodied continue to work or to help their families in the home. In addition, they are guaranteed a minimum income, receive free annual health examinations, and are eligible for completely free medical care after age seventy. We could benefit by following Japan's lead here, especially in providing more job opportunities for the aged.

We Americans might also profit by copying the Japanese example of fully integrating the elderly in our daily lives. In Japan 75 percent of the old live with their children, as opposed to only 25 percent in the United States. For those who do live alone, the Japanese have established programs to assure that they receive daily visits or calls. To encourage the active involvement of all older citizens in social activities, the government subsidizes Elders Clubs and sports programs. Through these programs the aged supply each other with mutual support and gain a sense of self-pride.

Another reason the old are so well-off in Japan is that they are politically organized. Older people in this country could probably profit by studying the tactics of their Japanese counterparts in winning strong governmental support for programs for the elderly.

For more details, see Erdman Palmore, "What Can the USA Learn from Japan about Aging?" in S. H. Zarit (ed.), *Readings in Aging and Death: Contemporary Perspectives*. New York: Harper & Row, 1977.

hospital staffs. Very often physicians decide not to tell patients that they are dying. Glaser and Strauss have called this **closed awareness;** the staff and family are aware of a patient's condition but the patient is not. Doctors often prefer this alternative because it minimizes demands on them. The patient's family and friends frequently support this decision because they are unable to confront the fact of death. Even when they are not informed, however, some patients begin to suspect that their illness is terminal. At this point, **suspected awareness,** they try to find out from the staff or their families whether their suspicions are correct.

If the patient does discover the seriousness of the illness, the hospital staff has two alternatives. They may pretend with the patient that neither knows that the disease is terminal **(mutual pretense awareness),** or they may openly acknowledge its gravity and perhaps even discuss the condition with the patient **(open awareness).** Nurses often prefer to be completely frank with patients from the start to avoid the distrust that sometimes develops when patients suspect they are dying but cannot discover the truth. The trend today is to inform patients of their condition, with the hospital staff given some discretion as to how much information to reveal.

Once patients have been informed of their condition, they must then cope with a truth that few of us want to face. Elizabeth Kubler-Ross (1969) has done some pioneer work on how the terminally ill react to their impending death. Her investigations have made a major contribution to the new field of **thanatology**—the study of death and dying. Based on interviews with 200 dying patients, she has identified five stages of psychological adjustment. The first stage is *denial.* People's most common reaction to learning that they have a terminal illness is shock and numbness, followed by denial. They react by saying, "No, it can't be happening to me." They may assert that the doctors are incompetent or the diagnosis mistaken. In extreme cases, people may refuse treatment and persist in going about business as usual. Most patients who use denial extensively throughout their illness are people who have become accustomed to coping with difficult life situations in this way. Indeed, the denial habit may contribute to the seriousness of a condition. For example, a person might refuse to seek medical attention at the onset of the illness, denying that it exists.

During the second stage, *anger,* the reaction of dying people is "Why me?" They feel anger—at fate, at God, at the powers that be, at every person who comes into their life. They resent the healthy, particularly those who must care for them. They are angry at others for perceiving them as dying. At this stage, they are likely to alienate themselves from others, for no one can relieve the anger they feel at their shortened life span and lost chances.

During the stage of *bargaining,* people change their attitude and attempt to bargain with fate. For example, a woman may ask God for a certain amount of time in return for good behavior. She may promise a change of ways, even a dedication of her life to the church. She may

USING PSYCHOLOGY

Hospices

Death is one of the few taboos left in twentieth-century America. The breakdown of extended families and the rise of modern medicine have insulated most people in our society from death. Many people have no direct experience with death, and, partly as a result, they are afraid to talk about it. In 1900, two-thirds of those who died in the United States were under fifty, and most of them died at home in their own beds. Today, most Americans live until at least sixty-five, and they die in nursing homes and hospitals. Elaborate machines may prolong existence long after a person has stopped living a normal life.

Figure 10. 7
A hospice patient during a visit
with his family.

A new movement to restore the dignity of dying revolves around the concept of the hospice—usually a special place where terminally ill people go to die. The hospice is designed to make the patient's surroundings pleasant and comfortable—less like a hospital and more like a home. Doctors in hospices do not try to prolong life but to improve the quality of life. A key component of hospice care is the use of tranquilizers and other drugs to ease discomfort and relieve pain.

The patient in a hospice leads the most normal life he or

she is able to, and is taken care of as much as possible by family members. If it can be arranged, a patient may choose to die at home.

The first and most famous hospice facility was St. Christopher's Hospice in London, England, established in 1967 to treat terminally ill cancer patients. In 1974, the first hospice was established in New Haven, Connecticut, and the numbers have grown since.

Currently in the United States, there are more than 440 operational hospice programs (Butterfield-Picard and Magno, 1982). Unfortunately, the availability of these programs is limited. Most medical insurance plans do not provide coverage for hospice care: this limits access to these programs to the more affluent. Furthermore, most programs depend on the help of a family member or friend to provide for the daily care of the dying person. Nonetheless, the hospice movement has helped to change many Americans' attitudes toward death.

announce that she is ready to settle for a less threatening form of the same illness and begin to bargain with the doctor over the diagnosis. For example, if she submits gracefully to some procedures, might she be rewarded by being spared the next stage of the illness? This stage is relatively short and is followed by the stage of *depression*.

During depression dying people are aware of the losses they are incurring (for example, loss of body tissue, loss of job, loss of life savings). Also, they are depressed about the loss that is to come: they are in the process of losing everything and everybody. Kübler-Ross suggests that it is helpful to allow such people to express their sadness and not to attempt to cover up the situation or force them to act cheerfully.

Finally, patients *accept* death. The struggle is over and they experience a sense of calm. At this point, they are tired and weak and sleep often. In some cases, the approach of death feels appropriate or peaceful. Patients may limit the number of people they will see and may not have much interest in matters of the world. They seem to become detached intentionally so as to make death easier.

Not all terminal patients progress through the stages Kübler-Ross describes. For example, a person may die in the denial stages because he or she is psychologically unable to proceed beyond it or because the course of the illness does not grant the necessary time to do so. Kübler-Ross notes that patients do not limit their responses to any one stage; a depressed patient may have recurring bursts of anger. She notes, too, that all patients in all stages persist in feeling hope. Even the most accepting and realistic patients leave open the possibility that they may live after all.

SUMMARY

Use the following outline as a tool for reviewing this chapter. Copy the outline onto your own paper, leaving spaces between headings to make notes about key concepts.

I. Adulthood

   A. Physical Changes

   B. Intellectual Changes

   C. Social and Personality Development

II. Old Age

   A. Changes in Health

   B. Changes in Life Situation

   C. Changes in Sexual Activity

   D. Adjusting to Old Age

   E. Changes in Mental Functioning

III. Death and Dying

CONCEPTS AND VOCABULARY

1. In what ways are adulthood and adolescence similar stages of development?

2. What physical changes occur during adulthood? What are the more common health problems of adulthood?

3. What changes occur in intellectual abilities during adulthood? On what types of mental activities do adults perform more poorly? In what ways are adults better able to perform mental activities?

4. What are Levinson's stages of adulthood? What occurs in each?

5. What is the "mid-life transition?" What problems do men face during this transition?

6. What does Erikson mean by generativity? What is stagnation?

7. List and summarize three mid-life problems faced by adult women.

8. Describe how the "decremental model of aging" leads to prejudiced attitudes toward the aged ("ageism").

9. What health problems are faced by the elderly? How many are able to lead normal lives? How many have a chronic illness? How does their sexual behavior change?

10. What kinds of life transitions or changes do the elderly face?

11. What is crystallized intelligence? What is fluid intelligence? Which type of intelligence increases with age?

12. What is the field that studies death and dying called?

13. Describe the different levels of awareness at which terminally ill persons can view their condition? Which do you think is the best approach?

14. What are Kübler-Ross's five stages of psychological adjustment to death?

15. What is a hospice? How does a hospice differ from a typical hospital? What is one of the key components of hospice care?

CRITICAL THINKING

1. **Analyze.** In this chapter, it is suggested that self-esteem is vulnerable when it is based on only one aspect of identity—physical attractiveness. List other aspects of identity on which one could base his or her self-esteem in order to strengthen it. What do you think your self-esteem is based on? Can you think of any ways you could strengthen your self-esteem?

2. **Synthesize.** If someone were to ask you, "What can I do to stay mentally, emotionally, and physically young as long as possible," what would you tell this person?

3. **Synthesize.** Death and dying have only recently become topics that are discussed openly. Given this growing openness, what changes do you see being made to make the adjustment to the prospect of dying less severe? What kinds of programs could hospitals and homes for the aged implement to help people make this adjustment?

4. **Analyze.** List several controversial questions, such as "Do you believe in fighting for your country no matter what the circumstances?" Ask people of different age groups to respond to your questions. Do you notice differences in the levels of reasoning? Use the explanations contained in this chapter and your own thoughts to account for the differences.

APPLYING KNOWLEDGE

1. Interview an adult who is over fifty years old. Ask this person to describe himself or herself physically, socially, intellectually, and emotionally at the ages of twenty, thirty, forty, and fifty. Before the interview, list specific questions that would elicit this information. Ask which age was his or her favorite and why.

2. Arrange to interview a man and a woman who are middle-aged. Interview them separately. Before you do the interviews, prepare a list of questions about work and family experiences. After you finish the interviews, think about how each person answered the questions. Did you find any differences between the man and the woman in attitudes or feelings about work? About attitudes toward the family? Do you think that men and women go through different stages of adult development? What are the dangers of generalizing from one set of interviews?

ANALYZING VIEWPOINTS

1. You have probably heard the saying, "you can't teach an old dog new tricks." This saying could mean that it is difficult to get adults to learn new ways of doing things. Think about this statement in light of adult development and learning. What evidence is there that this statement is correct? What evidence is there that this statement is incorrect? Using what you have learned, write a paper that presents evidence supporting both sides of the issue.

2. In some communities, elderly adults have the option of living in separate housing provided for senior citizens. Along with the benefits of this type of living arrangement go certain disadvantages. What are the benefits of separate housing for elderly adults? What disadvantages do you see? Write an article that makes the case that separate housing is the best solution for senior citizens. Then write an article that argues that senior citizens should live in the community, not in separate housing.

BEYOND THE CLASSROOM

1. Find out what services your community offers to its elderly adults. Look in the phone book to see if there are any special phone numbers for information on services for the elderly. You may want to ask at the town hall or at your local library. Once you know what services are offered, try to visit a senior citizens' center or retirement home. If possible, tour the facility and talk with some of the senior citizens. How do you think these services could be improved to make the experience of old age a more fruitful and happier time? What services could the elderly provide to your community? Prepare a report describing your experiences.

UNIT 4

Personality and Individuality

CHAPTER 11

Personality Theory

Key Terms:

archetype

behaviorism

collective unconscious

conditions of worth

contingencies of reinforcement

defense mechanisms

displacement

ego

extrovert

factor analysis

fully functioning person

humanistic psychology

id

inferiority complex

introvert

organism

positive regard

projection

reaction formation

regression

repression

self

self-actualization

superego

trait

unconditional positive regard

unconscious

Nancy and Ruth both failed their midterm examinations in psychology, but they reacted in very different ways. When Nancy saw her grade, she felt sick to her stomach and had to fight back tears. She cut her next class, rushed home, and shut herself up in her room to lie in bed, stare at the ceiling, and feel inadequate. Ruth, on the other hand, was all bluster. She too cut her next class after learning her grade, but she ran to the cafeteria to join her friends and make loud jokes about her stupid psychology professor.

Why did Nancy and Ruth act so differently in similar situations? Speaking loosely, there is something inside people that makes them think, feel, and act differently. And that "something inside" is what we mean by personality. It accounts for both the differences among people and for the consistencies in an individual's behavior over time and in different situations.

A theory of personality is an attempt to explain human nature in all its complexity and contradictions. While other psychologists confine their studies to more limited problems (like how the eye works, or why we remember some situations better than others), personality theorists face the most complex problem of all: Why do we do the things we do? The psychologists and psychiatrists whose insights we will be describing based their theories on what they learned from their own lives; from patients whose emotional difficulties they helped to ease; and from literature, philosophy, science, and the theories of other psychologists. Directly and indirectly, these theorists have changed the way we think about ourselves.

Objectives:

After studying this chapter, you should be able to

- identify the nature and aims of personality theory.
- compare and contrast the personality theories discussed in this chapter.

Figure 11.1 Psychologists who study personality explore whatever it is that makes one person think, feel, and act differently from another—what causes one person to like the spotlight and another to hate it.

WHAT PERSONALITY THEORIES TRY TO DO

You might assume that a theory of personality is little more than one person's philosophy of life and speculations about human nature. In fact, personality theories serve a number of very practical functions.

First, personality theories provide a way of organizing the many facts you know about yourself and other people. You know people may be outgoing or shy, bossy or meek, quick-tempered or calm, witty or dull, fun-loving or gloomy, responsible or lazy.

All these words describe *personality traits,* or general ways of behaving that characterize an individual. Personality theorists try to determine whether certain traits go together and why, why a person has some traits and not others, and why a person might exhibit different traits in different situations. There is a good deal of disagreement among theorists as to which traits are significant, and whether personality traits are stable over time or represent the individual's response to specific circumstances. Nevertheless, all theorists share one common goal: to discover patterns in the ways people behave.

A second purpose of any personality theory is *to explain the differences* between individuals. In so doing, theorists probe beneath the surface. Suppose a man you know is humble to the point of being self-effacing. When the conversation turns to him, he seems embarrassed. He is much happier bustling about, making people comfortable, and asking about their lives than he is talking about himself. A woman you know is just the opposite. She enjoys nothing better than talking about the work she is doing, the people she's met, her plans for the future. When she asks about your life you suspect it's either because she's being polite or because you might be useful to her. You explain their different behaviors in terms of motives: the man's primary goal in life is to please other people; the woman is extremely ambitious. But these explanations are little more than descriptions. How did these two individuals come to have different motives in the first place? Here, too, personality theorists disagree. One might suggest that the man had parents who discouraged any aggressive behavior while the woman's parents encouraged achievement and aggressive behavior. Another might seek less obvious causes—arguing, for example, that the roots of these differences could be traced back to toilet training.

A third goal of personality theory is to explore how people conduct their lives. It is no accident that most personality theorists began as psychotherapists, attempting to help people overcome emotional problems. In working with people who experienced considerable psychological pain and had difficulty coping with the everyday problems of life, they inevitably developed ideas about what it takes to live a relatively happy, untroubled life. Personality theorists try to explain why problems arise, and why they are more difficult for some people to manage than for others.

In addition, personality theorists are concerned with determining how life can be improved. It seems obvious that many people are dissatisfied with themselves, their parents, their husbands or wives and children, their home lives. People resign themselves to unrewarding jobs, and there is a widespread feeling that much is wrong with society and the world. Almost

Instant Personality Analysis and Astrology

Suppose someone handed you an astrological reading and told you it was specially written for you. Would you believe it? According to several studies, you probably would.

Subjects who were shown general personality assessments, which could have been written for almost anyone, readily believed they were prepared just for them. Believers—both men and women alike—rated the accuracy of the description at approximately 4.5 on a scale of 1 to 5, with 5 being the highest rating.

Researchers also found that the more personal facts an individual believes are used to compile a personality description, the greater his or her faith in its accuracy. Thus, an individual who thinks a horoscope is based on the year, month, and day of birth is more likely to believe its description than someone who thinks no personal information was used at all.

Our willingness to accept general descriptions of ourselves as accurate may be due to the universal human failing of being a bit too gullible. This is especially true when the words we hear are filled with praise.

For more details, see C. R. Snyder and Randee Jane Shenkel, "The P. T. Barnum Effect," *Psychology Today,* March 1975.

everyone recognizes that we need to grow and change, individually and collectively. But what are the proper goals of growth and change? How can we cope with the inevitable conflicts of life?

Personality psychologists attempt to answer these questions with systematic theories about human behavior. These theories are used to guide research; and research, in turn, can test parts of a theory to see whether they are right or wrong. Thus, while we all have our pet theories about why people act certain ways, formal personality theories try to make such ideas more scientific by stating them very precisely and then testing them.

Psychology is still a very young science, and these tests have just begun. There are now many conflicting theories of personality, each with its friends and foes. In this chapter, we will describe four major schools of thought among personality theorists.

Psychoanalytic theories, developed by Sigmund Freud and his followers, emphasize the importance of motives hidden deep in the unconscious. B. F. Skinner and the behaviorists study the way rewards and punishments shape our actions. Humanistic theorists, like Abraham Maslow and Carl Rogers, emphasize human potential for growth, creativity, and spontaneity. Finally, trait theorists, like Gordon Allport and Raymond Cattell, stress the importance of understanding basic personality characteristics such as friendliness and aggression.

Each of the theorists we will discuss has a different image of human nature. What they have in common is a concern with understanding the differences among people.

PSYCHOANALYTIC THEORIES

Charming, spacious, homelike 1 rm. apts. Modern kitchenette. Hotel service. Weekly rats available.
—from classified advertisement, *New York Times*

This advertisement was received and typeset by someone at the *Times*. The person who set the ad probably did not leave the "e" out of "rate" deliberately, but was it just an innocent mistake?

Slips like these are common. People usually laugh at them, even if they are meaningful. But sometimes they are disturbing. Everyone has had the experience of making some personal remark that hurt a friend and has later asked himself, "Why did I say that? I didn't mean it." Yet, when he thinks about it, he may realize that he was angry at his friend and wanted to "get back" at him.

Sigmund Freud: Psychosexuality and the Unconscious

It was Sigmund Freud who first suggested that the little slips that people make, the things they mishear, and the odd misunderstandings they have are not really mistakes at all. Freud believed there was something behind these mistakes, even though people claimed they were just accidental and quickly corrected themselves. Similarly, when he listened to people describe their dreams, he believed the dreams had some meaning, even though the people who dreamed them did not know what they meant.

Freud was a physician who practiced in Vienna in the early 1900s. Since he specialized in nervous diseases, a great many people talked to him about their private lives, their conflicts, fears, and desires. At that time most people thought, as many still do, that we are aware of all our motives and feelings. But Freud reasoned that if people can say and dream things without knowing their meaning, they must not know as much about themselves as they think they do. After years of study he concluded that some of the most powerful influences on human personality are things we are *not* conscious of.

Freud was the first modern psychologist to suggest that every personality has a large **unconscious** component. Life includes both pleasurable and painful experiences. For Freud, experiences include feelings and thoughts as well as actual events. Freud believed that many of our experiences, particularly the painful episodes of childhood, are forgotten or buried in the unconscious. But although we may not consciously recall these experiences, they continue to influence our behavior. For example, a child who never fully pleases his demanding mother or father may feel unhappy much of the time and will doubt his abilities to succeed and to be loved. As an adult, the person may suffer from feelings of unworthiness and low self-esteem, despite his very real abilities. Freud believed that unconscious motives and the feelings people experience as children have an enormous impact on adult personality and behavior.

> **Freud concluded that some of the most powerful influences on human personality are things we are not conscious of.**

The Id, Ego, and Superego

Freud tried to explain human personality by saying that it was a kind of energy system—like a steam engine or an electric dynamo. The energy in human personality comes from two kinds of powerful drives, the life drives and the death drives. Freud theorized that all of life moves toward death, and that the desire for a final end shows up in human personality as destructiveness and aggression. But the life instincts were more important in Freud's theory, and he saw them primarily as erotic or pleasure-seeking urges.

By 1923 Freud had described what became known as the structural components of the mind: id, ego, and superego (Figure 11.2). Though Freud often spoke of them as if they were actual parts of the personality, he introduced and regarded them simply as a *model* of how the mind works. In other words, the id, ego, and superego do not refer to actual portions of the brain. Instead, they explain how the mind functions and how the instinctual energies are regulated.

In Freud's theory the id is the reservoir or container of the instinctual urges. It is the lustful or drive-ridden part of the unconscious. The id seeks immediate gratification of desires, regardless of the consequences.

The personality process that is mostly conscious is called the **ego.** The ego is the rational, thoughtful, realistic personality process. For example, if

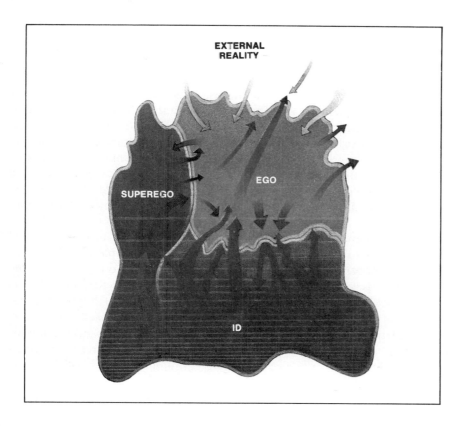

Figure 11.2
A visual interpretation of the Freudian theory of personality structure. The ego tries to balance the id's desires against the superego's demands and the realities of the world. In doing this it sometimes suppresses the irrational tendencies of the id, but it may also be able to deflect the id's energy into channels acceptable to both the superego and the outside world. These interactions and conflicts are represented by arrows in the figure.

a person is hungry, the id might drive her to seek immediate satisfaction by dreaming of food or by eating all the available food at once instead of keeping some of it for a later time. The ego would recognize that the body needs real food and that it will continue to need food in the future; it would use the id's energy to preserve some of the food available now and to look for ways of finding more.

Suppose you thought of stealing the desired food from someone else. The part of the personality that would stop you is called the **superego.** The id is concerned with what the person *wants* to do and the ego is concerned with planning what she *can* do; the superego is concerned with what she *should* do. It is the moral part of the personality, the source of conscience and of high ideals. But the superego can also create conflicts and problems. It is sometimes overly harsh, like a very strict parent. The superego, then, is also the source of guilt feelings which come from serious as well as mild deviations from what it defines as "right."

The id and the superego frequently come into conflict with each other. Because neither is concerned with reality, they may both come into conflict with the outside world as well. Freud saw the ego as part of the person that must resolve these conflicts. Somehow, the ego must find a realistic way to satisfy the demands of the id without offending the superego. If the id is not satisfied, the person feels an intolerable tension of longing or anger or desire. If the superego is not obeyed, the person feels guilty and inferior. And if outside reality is ignored, the person suffers such outcomes as starvation or dislike by other people (Freud, 1943).

Defense Mechanisms

The ego's job is so difficult that unconsciously all people resort to psychological defenses. Rather than face intense frustration, conflict, or feelings of unworthiness, people deceive themselves into believing nothing is wrong. If the demands of the id and the ego cannot be resolved, it may be necessary to distort reality. Freud called these techniques **defense mechanisms** because they defend the ego from experiencing anxiety about failing in its tasks (Figure 11.3). Freud felt that these defense mechanisms stem mainly from the unconscious part of the ego, and only ordinarily become conscious to the individual during a form of psychotherapy called psychoanalysis.

To some degree, defense mechanisms are necessary to psychological well-being. They relieve intolerable confusion, help people to weather intense emotional crises, and give individuals time to work out problems they might not be able to solve if they allowed themselves to feel all the pressures at work within them. However, if a person resorts to defense mechanisms all or most of the time, continually deceiving himself and others about his true feelings and aspirations, he will avoid facing and solving his problems realistically. A few of the defense mechanisms Freud identified are discussed below.

Displacement. Displacement occurs when the object of an unconscious wish provokes anxiety. This anxiety is reduced when the ego unconsciously

Figure 11.3
Some of the defense mechanisms in Freud's theory. Projection is a person seeing ridiculous attributes of his own personality as though they were possessed by others. Repression is shown by a woman who is not only concealing and restraining a monstrous impulse but also trying to conceal from herself the fact that she is doing so. The displacement of a widow's love from her lost husband and family onto her pets is another common mechanism.

shifts the wish to another object. The energy of the id is **displaced** from one object to another, more accessible, object. For example, if you wanted to hit your father but were afraid to, you might hit your kid brother instead. Your poor brother gets slapped around partly because he reminds you of your father and partly because he's not as likely to hit back.

Repression.   When a person has some thought or urge that causes the ego too much anxiety, she may push that thought or urge out of consciousness down into the unconscious. This process is called **repression.** The person simply "forgets" the thing that disturbs her, or pushes it out of awareness without ever realizing it. For example, a grown woman whose father is meddling in her life may have the impulse to say "I hate you, Dad." But the woman may feel so anxious and afraid about having such an impulse that she will come to believe—without realizing what she is doing—that what she feels is not hatred. She replaces the feeling with apathy, a feeling of not caring at all. She says, "I don't hate you. I have no special feelings at all about you." Nevertheless, the feelings of anger and hostility remain in the unconscious and may show themselves in cutting remarks or sarcastic jokes, slips of the tongue, or dreams.

Reaction Formation.   **Reaction formation** involves replacing an unacceptable feeling or urge with its opposite. For example, a divorced father may resent having his child for the weekend. Unconsciously, he feels it is terribly wrong for a father to react that way, so he showers the child with expressions of love, toys, and exciting trips. A woman who finds her powerful ambitions unacceptable may play the role of a weak, helpless, passive female who wants nothing more than to please the men in her life—unconsciously covering up her true feelings.

Projection.   Another way the ego avoids anxiety is to believe that impulses coming from within are really coming from other people. For example, a boy who is extremely jealous of his girl friend but does not want to admit to himself that he is threatened by her independence may claim, "I'm not jealous—she's the one who's always asking where I've been, who was that girl I was talking to . . ." This mechanism is called **projection** because inner feelings are thrown, or projected, outside. It is a common mechanism, which you have probably observed in yourself from time to time. Many people, for example, feel that others dislike them, when in reality they dislike themselves.

Regression.   **Regression** means going back to an earlier and less mature pattern. When a person is under severe pressure and his other defenses are not working, he may start acting in ways that helped him in the past. For example, he may throw a temper tantrum, make faces, cry loudly, or revert to eating and sleeping all the time the way he did as a small child. If you have ever been tempted to stick out your lower lip and pout when you know that you should really accept the fact that you cannot have your own way, you have experienced regression.

The recognition of the tremendous forces that exist in human personality and the difficulty of controlling and handling them was Freud's great contribution to understanding human life. After Freud, it became easier to understand why human life contains so much conflict. It is a matter, Freud thought, of a savage individual coming to terms with the rules of society. The id is the savage part, and the superego, the representative of society. In a healthy person the ego, the "I," is strong enough to handle the struggle (see Hall, 1954).

Freud was also the first psychologist to claim that infancy and childhood were critical times for forming a person's basic character structure. He felt that personality was well formed by the time the child entered school and that subsequent growth consisted of elaborating this basic structure. (We described Freud's theory of the stages of development in Chapter 8.)

Evaluating Freud's Contribution

Freud was the first major social scientist to propose a unified theory to understand and explain human behavior. No theory that has followed has been more complete or more complex. But his ideas were controversial when they were proposed at the turn of the century, and they are controversial today. Some psychologists treat Freud's writings as a sacred text—if Freud said it, it must be so. At the other extreme, many have accused Freud of being unscientific—of proposing a theory that is too complex ever to be proved true or false.

In 1977, Seymour Fisher and Roger Greenberg published a book *(The Scientific Credibility of Freud's Theories and Therapy)* that summarized more than fifty years of research on Freud's ideas. Some parts of his theory held up well. For example, Freud believed that the male homosexual had an unusually close and intense involvement with his mother, while his relationship with his father was more likely to be characterized by distance, coldness, and conflict. To test this idea one psychologist (Ullman, 1960) asked groups of heterosexual and homosexual prisoners to describe their parents. He found that homosexuals were more likely to say that their mothers gave them "too much" love and affection while their fathers gave "too little." Many other studies of homosexuals pointed in the same direction.

Other Freudian beliefs were not supported by evidence. For example, psychoanalysis (a form of therapy Freud proposed in which a person spends years examining the unconscious basis of his problems) seems to be no more effective than other forms of psychotherapy that are simpler, cheaper, and less time-consuming.

Fisher and Greenberg concluded: "When we add up the totals from our research, balancing the positive against the negative, we find that Freud has fared rather well. But like all theorists, he has proved in the long run to have far from a perfect score. He seems to have been right about a respectable number of issues, but he was also wrong about some important things" (396).

In Freud's Footsteps: Jung and Adler

Freud's revolutionary ideas attracted many followers, and a number of these psychoanalysts came to develop important theories of their own.

At one time, Carl Jung was Freud's closest associate. But when Freud and Jung started to argue about psychoanalytic theory, their personal relationship became strained. Finally, they stopped speaking to each other entirely, a mere seven years after they met.

Jung disagreed with Freud on two major points. First, he took a more positive view of human nature, believing that people try to develop their potential as well as to handle their instinctual urges. Second, he distinguished between the personal unconscious (which was similar to Freud's idea of the unconscious) and the **collective unconscious,** which is a storehouse of instincts, urges, and memories of the entire human species down

Figure 11.4
Carl G. Jung. One of the most mystical and metaphysical of the pioneer theorists, Jung has had, until recently, a wider acceptance in Europe than in America.

Figure 11.5
Alfred Adler. Adler's writings on psychotherapy offer more optimism and practicality than those of Freud or Jung. His intuitive and common-sense approach to human life has greatly affected the thinking of psychologists throughout this century.

through history. He called these inherited, universal ideas **archetypes.** The same archetypes are present in every person. They reflect the common experiences of humanity with mothers, fathers, nature, war, and so on.

Jung went on to identify the archetypes by studying dreams and visions, paintings, poetry, folk stories, myths, and religions. He found that the same themes—the "archetypes"—appear again and again. For example, the story of Jack and the Beanstalk is essentially the same as the story of David and Goliath. Both tell how a small, weak, good person triumphs over a big, strong, bad person. Jung believed such stories are common and easy to understand because the situations they describe have occurred over and over again in human history and have been stored as archetypes in the unconscious of every human being (Jung, 1963).

Like Jung, Alfred Adler was an associate of Freud who left his teacher in the early part of this century to develop his own approach to personality. Adler believed that the driving force in people's lives is a desire to overcome their feelings of inferiority. Classic examples are Demosthenes, who overcame a speech impediment by practicing speaking with pebbles in his mouth and became the greatest orator of ancient Greece; Napoleon, a short man who conquered Europe in the early 1800s; and Glenn Cunningham, an Olympic runner who lost his toes in a fire as a child and had to plead with doctors who wanted to amputate his legs because they thought he would never be able to use them again.

Everyone struggles with inferiority, said Adler. He describes a person who continually tries to cover up and avoid feelings of inadequacy as having an **inferiority complex** (a term he introduced). Children first feel inferior because they are so little and so dependent on adults. Gradually they learn to do the things that older people can do. The satisfaction that comes from even such simple acts as walking or learning to use a spoon sets up a pattern of overcoming inadequacies, a pattern that lasts throughout life. Adler called these patterns *"life styles."*

Adler believed that the way parents treat their children has a great influence on the styles of life they choose. Overpampering, in which the parents attempt to satisfy the child's every whim, tends to produce a self-centered person who has little regard for others and who expects everyone else to do what he or she wants. On the other hand, the child who is neglected by his or her parents may seek revenge by becoming an angry, hostile person. Both the pampered and the neglected child tend to grow up into adults who lack confidence in their ability to meet the demands of life. Ideally, said Adler, a child should learn self-reliance and courage from his or her father and generosity and a feeling for others from his or her mother (Adler, 1959).

Although Jung and Adler were the first major figures to break with Freud, many others followed. Erich Fromm's theory centered around the need to belong and the loneliness freedom brings. Karen Horney stressed the importance of basic anxiety, which a child feels because she is helpless, and basic hostility, a resentment of one's parents that generally accompanies this anxiety (Figure 11.6). She also attacked several basic beliefs of Freud, including his emphasis on the importance of penis envy in the development of women. Erik Erikson accepted Freud's basic theory, but

Horney on Basic Anxiety and Hostility

The typical conflict leading to anxiety in a child is that between dependency on the parents . . . and hostile impulses against the parents. Hostility may be aroused in a child in many ways: by the parents' lack of respect for him; by unreasonable demands and prohibitions; by injustice; by unreliability; by suppression of criticism; by the parents dominating him and ascribing these tendencies to love. . . . If a child, in addition to being dependent on his parents, is grossly or subtly intimidated by them and hence feels that any expression of hostile impulses against them endangers his security, then the existence of such hostile impulses is bound to create anxiety. . . . The resulting picture may look exactly like what Freud describes as the Oedipus complex: passionate clinging to one parent and jealousy toward the other or toward anyone interfering with the claim of exclusive possession. . . . *But the dynamic structure of these attachments is entirely different from what Freud conceives as the Oedipus complex. They are an early manifestation of neurotic conflicts rather than a primarily sexual phenomenon.*

From Karen Horney, *The Neurotic Personality in Our Time.* New York: Norton, 1939.

Figure 11.6
Karen Horney on basic anxiety and hostility.

outlined eight psychosocial stages (described in Chapter 8) that every person goes through from birth to old age. These and other neo-Freudians have helped to keep psychoanalytic theory alive and growing.

BEHAVIORAL THEORIES

American psychology has long been dominated by the study of human and animal learning. In the 1940s, Yale psychologists John Dollard and Neal Miller used learning theory to analyze Freud's ideas, but behaviorists did not endorse Freud. **Behaviorism** holds that the proper subject matter of psychology is objectively observable behavior. Behaviorists believe that as individuals differ in their learning experiences, they acquire different behaviors and hence different personalities.

B. F. Skinner: Radical Behaviorism

Although his radical behaviorism was not proposed as a theory of personality, B. F. Skinner has had a major impact on personality theory. Skinner sees no need for a general concept of personality structure. He focuses instead on precisely what is causing a person to act in a specific way. It is a very pragmatic approach, one that is less concerned with understanding behavior than with predicting it and controlling it.

Consider the case of Fred, a college sophomore who has been rather depressed lately. Freud might seek the roots of Fred's unhappiness in events in his childhood. Skinner's approach is more direct. First of all, Skinner would reject the vague label "depressed." Instead he would ask, exactly how does Fred behave? The answer may be that Fred spends most

Figure 11.7
B. F. Skinner. Skinner's pioneering work in behavioral psychology has resulted in a number of new therapeutic techniques that have been markedly successful in treating certain kinds of problems.

of the day in his room, cuts all his classes, and rarely smiles or laughs.

Next, Skinner would try to understand the **contingencies of reinforcement.** What conditions are maintaining these behaviors? What reinforces Fred for never leaving his room? One hypothesis is that Fred's girlfriend Ethel has unintentionally reinforced this behavior by spending a lot of time with Fred, trying to cheer him up. Perhaps she didn't pay much attention to him before he was depressed. Note that Skinner's approach immediately suggests a hypothesis that can be proved true or false. If paying attention to Fred encourages his moroseness, then ignoring him should decrease the likelihood of this behavior. So Ethel might try ignoring Fred for a few days. If he then starts leaving his room, she has discovered the contingencies of reinforcement that govern Fred's behavior. If not, she will know that the hypothesis is wrong and can try something else. Perhaps Fred is glued to the TV in his room all day and has become a game-show addict. Take away the TV and you will find out whether that is the reinforcer.

At first, radical behaviorism may seem to imply that Fred is somehow faking his depression so that he can watch "Hollywood Squares," see more of his girlfriend, or whatever. Skinner does not make this assumption. Fred may be entirely unaware of the rewards that are shaping his behavior. In any case, Fred's feelings are beside the point. What matters is not what's going on inside Fred's head, but what he is doing. The point is to specify his behavior and then find out what causes it.

Skinner's approach has become very popular among psychologists, partly because it is so pragmatic. It is a very action-oriented, very American approach: don't get all agitated about what's wrong; just jump in and try to fix it. It is true that radical behaviorism often works. Skinnerians have applied the techniques to a wide range of behaviors, from teaching pigeons to play Ping-Pong to teaching severely retarded people to dress themselves and take part in simple activities once believed beyond their abilities.

Normal people's behavior, too, can be changed with rewards and punishments, as every parent knows. The success of radical behaviorists with normal people has been more limited, partly because our reinforcers are so complex. For example, in several studies juvenile delinquents have been placed in rehabilitation communities in which they are rewarded (with special privileges or food) for behaving in certain ways—taking classes, cleaning up their rooms, and so on. In one such study, Buehler, Patterson, and Furness (1966) found that delinquent girls reinforced each other for breaking the rules and talking back. Sometimes, peer approval can be a more powerful reinforcer than any reward a psychologist can offer.

Albert Bandura: Social Learning Theories

Skinner emphasizes operant conditioning in his description and explanation of personality. However, Albert Bandura and his late colleague Richard Walters (1963) believe that personality is acquired not only by direct reinforcement of behavior but also by *observational learning*, or imitation. In observational learning, a person acquires a new behavior by watching the actions of another person. For example, to teach a child how to hit a baseball with a bat, you could hand the child the bat and ball and reinforce him every time he used the bat and ball correctly (operant conditioning). However, you would probably demonstrate the correct way to hold the bat and swing at the ball instead because this way the child would acquire the behavior more quickly. Bandura and Walters believe that much of a young child's individual behavior and personality is acquired by exposure to specific everyday models.

Bandura found that the consequences to a model engaging in a particular behavior influence the observer's willingness to perform (but not necessarily acquire) that behavior. In one study (Bandura, 1965), three groups of children watched models engaging in behavior that was either rewarded, punished, or had no consequences. In a free play session afterward, the children imitated the rewarded model most and the punished and no-consequence models least. When the same children were later offered a reward for reproducing the behavior they had seen in the films, all three groups imitated the behaviors equally well.

In Bandura's view, people are capable of directing their own behavior by their choice of models. In part, when your parents object to the company you keep, they are trying to change the models you use. The most effective models are those who are the most similar to and most admired by the observer. Thus, you are more likely to learn new behaviors from your friends than from your parents' friends.

HUMANISTIC PSYCHOLOGY

One might look at **humanistic psychology** as a rebellion against the rather negative, pessimistic view of human nature that dominated personality theory in the first part of this century. As we have seen, psychoanalysts emphasized the struggle to control primitive, instinctual urges on the one hand, and to come to terms with the authoritarian demands of the superego or conscience on the other. The behaviorists, too, saw human behavior in mechanistic terms: our actions are shaped by rewards and punishments. Humanistic psychologists object to both approaches on the grounds that they demean human beings—Freud by emphasizing irrational and destructive instincts, Skinner by emphasizing external causes of behavior. In contrast, the humanists stress our relative freedom from instinctual pressures (compared to other animals) and our ability to create and live by personal standards.

Humanistic psychology is founded on the belief that all human beings strive for **self-actualization**—that is, the realization of their potentialities as unique human beings. Self-actualization involves an openness to a wide range of experiences; an awareness of and respect for one's own and other people's uniqueness; accepting the responsibilities of freedom and commitment; a desire to become more and more authentic or true to oneself; and an ability to grow. It requires the courage, in Kipling's words, "to trust

MORE about . . .

Interpersonal Theories of Personality. Most theories of personality consider the person as an individual. Some psychologists, however, regard personality as a function of a person's social environment. One of the first of these thinkers was Harry Stack Sullivan.

Sullivan's theories have been organized into a two-dimensional model. One dimension is *power*, which ranges from dominance at one end of the scale to submissiveness at the other. The second dimension is *friendliness*, which ranges from friendliness to hostility. Most behaviors can be described as a combination of these two dimensions. For example, "helpfulness" is a combination of dominance and friendliness; "trusting" is a combination of submissiveness and friendliness.

Researchers also noticed that a person's actions tend to elicit specific responses from other people. A behavior and its most likely response are said to be *complementary*. For example, most people will respond to a request for help (trusting) by offering advice (helping), regardless of how "helpful" they are as individuals. Thus, many behaviors result not simply from a person's personality but also from that person's social environment.

Improving Your Self-image

If your self-image can stand a boost, try taking these steps toward greater self-confidence. As you're reading this list, remember what humanistic personality theorists believe: a positive self-image is at the heart of successful adjustment.

- Base your personal goals on an honest appraisal of your strengths and weaknesses. Trying to be something you're not can only weaken your self-image.
- Don't let guilt and shame determine your goals. Let positive thinking guide your decision-making.
- Don't blame everything that goes wrong on yourself. Sometimes external events can play an equally important role.
- When others dismiss your views, keep in mind that events are interpreted in different ways by different people.
- When things go wrong, don't be too hard on yourself. Never think of yourself as a failure, stupid, or ugly.
- Accept criticism of the things you do, but don't allow people to criticize you as a person.
- Use your failures in a constructive way. They may be telling you to readjust your goals and start over in a new direction.
- Don't stay in a situation that makes you feel inadequate. If you can't change the situation, move on to something new.

Try these suggestions and you'll soon see that there's no better feeling than feeling good about yourself.

For more details, see Philip Zimbardo, *Shyness*, Reading, Mass.: Addison-Wesley, 1977.

Figure 11.8
Abraham Maslow. Maslow's work, as well as that of Carl Rogers and others, helped create a humanistic orientation toward the study of behavior by emphasizing growth and the realization of an individual's potential.

yourself when all men doubt you. . . ." Humanists view this striving as a basic human instinct and the essence of human dignity.

Abraham Maslow: Growth and Self-Actualization

Abraham Maslow was one of the guiding spirits of the humanistic movement in psychology. He deliberately set out to create what he called "a third force in psychology" as an alternative to psychoanalysis and behaviorism. Maslow tried to base his theory of personality on studies of healthy, creative, self-actualizing people who fully utilize their talents and potential, rather than on studies of disturbed individuals. He criticized other psychologists for their pessimistic, negative, and limited conceptions of human beings. Where is the psychology, he asked, that deals with gaiety, exuberance, love, and expressive art to the same extent that it deals with misery, conflict, shame, hostility, and habit?

When Maslow decided to study the most productive individuals he could find—in history as well as in his social and professional circles—he was breaking new ground. The theories of personality we discussed earlier

---

Table 11.1 / Characteristics of Self-Actualized Persons

They are realistically oriented.

They accept themselves, other people, and the natural world for what they are.

They have a great deal of spontaneity.

They are problem-centered rather than self-centered.

They have an air of detachment and a need for privacy.

They are autonomous and independent.

Their appreciation of people and things is fresh rather than stereotyped.

Most of them have had profound mystical or spiritual experiences although not necessarily religious in character.

They identify with mankind.

Their intimate relationships with a few specially loved people tend to be profound and deeply emotional rather than superficial.

Their values and attitudes are democratic.

They do not confuse means with ends.

Their sense of humor is philosophical rather than hostile.

They have a great fund of creativeness.

They resist conformity to the culture.

They transcend the environment rather than just coping with it.

Source: Abraham Maslow, *Motivation and Personality* (New York: Harper & Row, 1954).

in this chapter were developed by psychotherapists after years of working with people who could not cope with everyday frustrations and conflicts. In contrast, Maslow was curious about people who not only coped with everyday problems effectively, but who also created exceptional lives for themselves, people like Abraham Lincoln, Albert Einstein, and Eleanor Roosevelt.

Maslow found that, although these people sometimes had great emotional difficulties, they adjusted to their problems in ways that allowed them to become highly productive. Maslow also found that such self-actualized individuals share a number of traits (Table 11.1). First, they *perceive reality accurately*, unlike most people who, because of prejudices and wishful thinking, perceive it rather inaccurately. Self-actualized people also *accept themselves*, other people, and their environments more readily than "average" people do. Without realizing it, most of us project our hopes and fears onto the world around us. Often we become upset with people whose attitudes differ radically from our own. We spend a good deal of time denying our own shortcomings and trying to rationalize or change things we do not like about ourselves. Self-actualizing individuals accept themselves as they are.

Secure in themselves, healthy individuals are more *problem-centered* than self-centered. They are able to focus on tasks in a way that people concerned about maintaining and protecting their self-image cannot. They are more likely to base decisions on ethical principles than on calculations of the possible costs or benefits to themselves. They have a strong sense of *identity with other human beings*—not just members of their family, ethnic group, or country, but all humankind. They have a strong *sense of humor*, but laugh with people, not at them.

Maslow also found that self-actualizing people are exceptionally *spontaneous*. They are not trying to be anything other than themselves. And they know themselves well enough to maintain their integrity in the face of opposition, unpopularity, and rejection. In a word, they are *autonomous*. They *value privacy* and frequently seek out solitude. This is not to say that they are detached or aloof. But rather than trying to be popular, they focus on deep, *loving relationships with the few people* to whom they are truly close.

Finally, the people Maslow studied had a rare ability to appreciate even the simplest things. They approached their lives with a *sense of discovery* that made each day a new day. They rarely felt bored or uninterested. Given to moments of intense joy and satisfaction, or "peak experiences," they got high on life itself. Maslow believed this to be both a cause and an effect of their creativity and originality (Maslow, 1970).

As indicated in Chapter 6, Maslow believed that to become self-actualizing a person must first satisfy his or her basic, primary needs—for food and shelter, physical safety, love and belonging, and self-esteem. Of course, to some extent the ability to satisfy these needs depends on factors beyond the individual's control. Still, no amount of wealth, talent, beauty, or any other asset can totally shield someone from frustration and disappointment. The affluent as well as the poor, the brilliant as well as the slow, have to adjust to maintain themselves and to grow.

Many psychologists have criticized Maslow's work. His claim that human nature is "good," for example, has been called an intrusion of subjective values into what should be a neutral science. His study of self-actualizing people has been criticized because the sample was chosen on the basis of Maslow's own subjective criteria. How can one identify self-actualized people without knowing the characteristics of such people? But then, if one knows these characteristics to begin with, what sense does it make to list them as if they were the results of an empirical study?

Despite such criticism, Maslow's influence has been great. He has inspired many researchers to pay more attention to healthy, productive people and has led many group leaders and clinicians to seek ways to promote the growth and self-actualization of workers, students, and clients in therapy.

Figure 11.9
Carl Rogers. Rogers's theories have had a considerable impact on modern psychology and on society in general. He has emphasized personal experience rather than drives and instincts.

Carl Rogers: Your Organism and Yourself

The people Carl Rogers counsels are "clients," not "patients." The word "patient" implies illness, a negative label that Rogers rejects. As a therapist, Rogers is primarily concerned with the roadblocks and detours on the path to self-actualization (or "full functioning," as he calls it). Rogers believes that many people suffer from a conflict between what they value in themselves and what they learn other people value in them. He explains how this conflict develops this way: There are two sides or parts to every person. One is the **organism**, which is the whole of a person, including his or her body. Rogers believes that the organism is constantly struggling to become more and more complete and perfect. Anything that furthers this end is good: The organism wants to become everything it can possibly be. For example, children want to learn to walk and run because their bodies are built for these activities. People want to shout and dance and sing because their organisms contain the potential for these behaviors. Different people have different potentialities, but every person wants to realize them, to make them real, whatever they are. It is of no value to be able to paint and not to do it. It is of no value to be able to make witty jokes and not to do so. Whatever you can do, you want to do—and to do as well as possible. (This optimism about human nature is the essence of humanism.)

Each individual also has what Rogers calls a **self.** The self is essentially your image of who you are and what you value—in yourself, in other people, in life in general. The self is something you acquire gradually over the years by observing how other people react to you. At first, the most significant other person in your life is your mother (or whoever raises you). You want her approval or **positive regard.** You ask yourself, "How does she see me?" If the answer is, "She loves me. She likes what I am and what I do," you begin to develop positive regard for yourself.

But often this does not happen. The image you see reflected in your mother's eyes and actions is mixed. Whether or not she approves of you often depends on whether or not you spit up your baby food or do your homework on time. In other words, she places conditions on her love: *if* you do what she wants, she likes you. Young and impressionable, you accept these verdicts and incorporate **conditions of worth** into yourself. "When I use obscene language at the dinner table, I am bad." You begin to see yourself as good and worthy only if you act in certain ways. You've learned from your parents and from other people who are significant to you that unless you meet certain conditions you will not be loved.

Rogers's work as a therapist convinced him that people cope with conditions of worth by rejecting or denying parts of their organism that do not fit their self-concept. For example, if your mother grew cold and distant whenever you became angry, you learned to deny yourself the right to express or perhaps even feel anger. Being angry "isn't you." In effect, you are cutting off a part of your organism or whole being; you are allowing yourself to experience and express only part of your being.

The greater the gap between the self and the organism, the more limited and defensive a person becomes. Rogers believes the cure for this situation is **unconditional positive regard.** If significant others (parents, friends, a mate, perhaps a therapist) convey the feeling that they value you for what you are, in your entirety, you will gradually learn to grant yourself the same unconditional positive regard. The need to limit yourself declines. You will be able to accept your organism and become open to *all* your feelings, thoughts, and experiences—and hence to other people. This is what Rogers means by **fully functioning.** The organism and the self are one: the individual is free to develop all his or her potentialities. Like Maslow and other humanistic psychologists, Rogers believes that self-regard and regard for others go together, and that the human potentials for good and for self-fulfillment outweigh the potentials for evil and despair (Rogers, 1951, 1961).

TRAIT THEORIES

Betsy spends many hours talking to other people, circulates freely at parties, and strikes up conversations while she waits in the dentist's office. Carl, though, spends more time with books than with other people and seldom goes to parties. In common-sense terms, we say that Betsy is friendly and Carl is not. Friendliness is a personality **trait** and some theorists have argued that studying such traits in detail is the best approach to solving the puzzle of human behavior.

One psychologist has defined a trait as "any relatively enduring way in which one individual differs from another" (Guilford, 1959). A trait, then, is a predisposition to respond in a certain way in many different kinds of situations—in a dentist's office, at a party, or in a classroom. More than any other personality theorists, trait theorists emphasize and try to explain the consistency of an individual's behavior in different situations.

Trait theorists generally make two basic assumptions about these underlying sources of consistency: every trait applies to all people (for example, everyone can be classified as more or less dependent) and these descriptions can be quantified (for example, we might establish a scale on which an extremely dependent person scores 1 while a very independent person scores 10).

Thus, every trait can be used to classify people. Aggressiveness, for example, is a continuum: a few people are extremely aggressive or extremely unaggressive, and most of us fall somewhere in the middle. We understand people by specifying their traits, and we use traits to predict people's future behavior. If you were hiring someone to sell vacuum cleaners, you would probably choose Betsy over Carl. This choice would be based on two assumptions: that friendliness is a useful trait for salespeople and that a person who is friendly in the dentist's office and at parties will be friendly in another situation—namely, in the salesroom.

Trait theorists go beyond this kind of common-sense analysis to try to discover the underlying sources of the consistency of human behavior. What is the best way to describe the common features of Betsy's behavior? Is she friendly, or socially aggressive, or interested in people, or sure of herself, or something else? What is the underlying *trait* that best explains her behavior?

Most (but not all) trait theorists believe that a few basic traits are central for all people. An underlying trait of self-confidence, for example, might be used to explain more superficial characteristics like social aggressiveness and dependency. If this were true, it would mean that a person would be dependent because he or she lacked self-confidence. Psychologists who accept this approach set out on their theoretical search for basic traits with very few assumptions.

Most trait theorists believe a few basic traits are central for all people.

This is very different from the starting point of other personality theorists we have considered. Freud, for example, began with a well-defined theory of instincts. When he observed that some people were stingy, he set out to explain this in terms of his theory. Trait theorists would not start by trying to understand stinginess. Rather, they would try to determine whether stinginess was a trait. That is, they would try to find out whether people who were stingy in one type of situation were also stingy in others. Then they might ask whether stinginess is a sign of a more basic trait like possessiveness: Is the stingy person also very possessive in relationships? Thus, the first and foremost question for the trait theorists is: What behaviors go together?

Instead of theories telling them *where* to look, trait theorists have complex and sophisticated methods that tell them *how* to look. These methods begin with the statistical technique of correlation (discussed in Chapters 19 and 20)—using one set of scores to predict another. If I know that someone talks to strangers in line at the supermarket, can I predict that he will be likely to strike up conversations in a singles bar? Such predictions are never perfect. Perhaps the reason Betsy is so outspoken in the dentist's office is that she's terrified, and jabbering to strangers is the only way she can distract herself from the image of a sixteen-foot drill. Sometimes, actions that look like manifestations of one trait may really reflect something else entirely.

Gordon Allport: Identifying Traits

Gordon W. Allport was one of the most influential psychologists of his day. Many of his ideas of personality are similar to those of humanistic psychology. For example, Allport emphasizes the positive, rational, and conscious reasons why we act the way we do. But he is most famous for his pioneering work on traits (Allport, 1961).

A trait, Allport said, makes a wide variety of situations "functionally equivalent"; that is, it enables a person to realize that many different situations call for a similar response. Thus, traits are responsible for the relative consistency of every individual's behavior.

Allport provided a number of classification schemes for distinguishing among kinds of traits. For example, he was concerned with emphasizing the differences between two major ways of studying personality. In the nomothetic approach, researchers study large groups of people in the search for general laws of personality. This can be contrasted with the idiographic approach, in which one studies a particular person in detail, emphasizing his or her uniqueness. On the basis of this distinction, Allport defined common traits as those that apply to everyone and individual traits as those that apply more to a specific person.

An example of the latter is found in Allport's book *Letters from Jenny* (1965), which consists of 172 letters a woman whom Allport calls Jenny Masterson wrote to a friend. Jenny reveals herself in these letters (which she wrote between the ages of fifty-eight and seventy) as a complex and fiercely independent woman. In his preface to the book, Allport writes:

> To me the principal fascination of the Letters lies in their challenge to the reader (whether psychologist or layman) to "explain" Jenny—if he can. Why does an intelligent lady behave so persistently in a self-defeating manner?

PSYCHOLOGY
UPDATE

The Robust Five. Over the years, trait theorists have devised a number of ways to measure personality. Each involves a different number of traits or factors.

For example, the Eysenck Personality Inventory (EPI) describes personality using three traits: extroversion (sociability, being outgoing), neuroticism (emotional stability), and psychoticism (the ability to deal with real-life tasks). The California Personality Inventory (CPI) uses over 400 items to measure 20 distinct factors.

Recently, trait psychologists have shown that five traits appear repeatedly in different research studies. Known as the five robust factors, they are (1) neuroticism, (2) extroversion, (3) openness (creativity, originality), (4) agreeableness (warmth), and (5) conscientiousness (motivated, directed).

Do these five factors seem to describe all aspects of your personality? If not, what other factors describe you?

Allport's own attempt to understand Jenny Masterson began with a search for the underlying traits that would explain the consistency of her behavior.

Raymond B. Cattell: Factor Analysis

More recent theorists have concentrated on what Allport called *common traits*, which they try to quantify in a precise, scientific manner. Their primary tool in this task has been an extremely sophisticated mathematical technique called **factor analysis** which describes the extent to which different personality variables are related.

Raymond B. Cattell has used factor analysis extensively to study personality traits. Cattell defines a trait as a tendency to react to related situations in a way that remains more or less stable. He distinguishes between two kinds of tendencies: surface traits and source traits. *Surface traits* are clusters of behavior that tend to go together. An example of a surface trait is altruism, which involves a variety of related behaviors such as helping a neighbor who has a problem or contributing to an annual blood drive. Other examples of surface traits are integrity, curiosity, realism, and foolishness. *Source traits* are the underlying roots or causes of these behavioral clusters—for example, ego strength, dominance, and submissiveness. Cattell believes that measuring surface and source traits will enable us to identify those characteristics that all humans share and those that distinguish one person from another.

Cattell (1965) discovered these traits by studying large numbers of people, using three basic kinds of data: life records, questionnaires, and objective tests. Life records include everything from descriptions of an individual (by people who have known him or her for some time) to school grades to records of automobile accidents. Questionnaire data are the individual's answers to a series of questions, whether or not these answers are truthful. (The fact that someone underrates himself or herself or tries to create a highly favorable impression may be significant.) Objective test data are a person's responses to tests designed to detect or prevent this type of "cheating."

Hans Eysenck: Two Dimensions of Personality

Using factor analysis of personality data similar to the type used by Cattell, Hans Eysenck (1970), an English psychologist, concluded that there are two basic dimensions of personality. The first dimension refers to the degree to which people have control over their feelings. At the emotionally stable end of the personality spectrum is a person who is easy-going, relaxed, well adjusted, and even-tempered. At the neurotic end of the spectrum is the moody, anxious, and restless person.

Eysenck's second dimension was actually identified years earlier by Carl Jung as *extroversion versus introversion*. **Extroverts** are sociable, outgoing, active, lively people. They enjoy parties and seek excitement. On the other end of the dimension are **introverts**, who are more thoughtful, reserved, passive, unsociable, and quiet.

Use the following outline as a tool for reviewing this chapter. Copy the outline onto your own paper, leaving spaces between headings to make notes about key concepts.

I. What Personality Theories Try to Do

II. Psychoanalytic Theories

   A. Sigmund Freud: Psychosexuality and the Unconscious

   B. The Id, Ego, and Superego

   C. Defense Mechanisms

   D. Evaluating Freud's Contribution

   E. In Freud's Footsteps: Jung and Adler

III. Behavioral Theories

   A. B. F. Skinner: Radical Behaviorism

   B. Albert Bandura: Social Learning Theories

IV. Humanistic Psychology

   A. Abraham Maslow: Growth and Self-Actualization

   B. Carl Rogers: Your Organism and Yourself

V. Trait and Theories

   A. Gordon Allport: Identifying Traits

   B. Raymond B. Cattell: Factor Analysis

   C. Hans Eysenck: Two Dimensions of Personality

1. What functions do personality theories serve? Can you list the four major schools of thought among personality theorists?

2. According to Freud, what two factors have enormous impact on adult personality and behavior? What are the sources of the energy in the human personality? What are Freud's three structures of the personality? Can you match the words *can*, *want*, and *should* to these three structures?

3. What techniques do people use to defend against anxiety and to distort reality? What technique are you likely to be using if you pout? What technique might you be using if you think a teacher is angry at you because he or she gave a hard test but the teacher is not actually angry?

4. Who was the first major social scientist to propose a unified theory of human behavior? Who were two of his followers? How did they differ from him?

5. What name did Jung give to inherited, universal ideas? What term did Adler introduce?

6. What psychologist has had a major impact on personality theory without actually proposing a theory of personality? What was his approach called? Was he concerned about understanding behavior?

7. Why was B. F. Skinner's approach to personality popular among psychologists?

8. How do Bandura and Walters believe personality is acquired?

9. What branch of psychology developed in reaction to psychoanalytic theory and behaviorism? This theory was founded on what belief? Who were the men who founded this approach?

10. List five characteristics of a self-actualized person.

11. According to Rogers there are two parts to every person. What are they? What situation creates a gap between these two parts? What is the cure for this situation?

12. Why does Rogers object to the use of the term "patient" to refer to a person who seeks counseling?

13. What does Rogers mean by the term "fully functioning"?

14. What are the two basic assumptions behind trait theories?

15. What are Allport's two major ways of studying personality?

16. What tool did Cattell use to study personality?

17. Cattell distinguished two kinds of traits. What are they?

CRITICAL THINKING

1. **Analyze.** List the qualities and traits that you think comprise the "healthy" or "actualized" person. If this is done in class, you can see how your ideas of health and actualization differ from those of the other class members.

2. **Evaluate.** What are the key features of your own personality? What are the key features of the personalities of each of your parents? Compare your personality with those of your parents. There will be both similarities and differences. Because one's parents are necessarily such highly influential forces in a child's development, it may be of greater interest to note the chief differences in personalities. Then try to identify the factors responsible for those differences. For example, what key individuals or events have influenced or redirected the course of your life or changed your habits of living? How have society's institutions affected you?

3. **Synthesize.** Develop your own theory of personality by answering the following questions. How does a person acquire a personality? What are the most important motivations for people? Why are people different? How can people change their personalities?

4. **Evaluate.** Read a weekly magazine that describes people and their lives and underline the adjectives used to describe the personalities of the people featured in the articles. Then make a list of these traits, noting how many times each trait or adjective was used in all of the magazine's articles. Are there some traits that appear more frequently than others? How important would you say these traits are in your own life? Are there characteristics that seem to be important to you but are not included in your list?

5. **Analyze.** Think of a person you know well, someone you have had a chance to observe in a variety of social settings over a period of time. Describe that person in terms of his or her characteristic way of interacting with people. How do other people respond to this person? Does the person's behavior change depending on the setting? Explain your observations using a behavioral model of personality. What would you say are important reinforcers for this person?

APPLYING KNOWLEDGE

1. The text contains a list of characteristics that Maslow found to be representative of people whom he described as "self-actualized." From among your acquaintances, choose a few whom you especially respect or admire for "doing their own thing," people who achieve satisfaction by being who and what they are. Ask them to list what they see as their distinguishing personality characteristics. Compare their answers and your observations with Maslow's list. In addition, compare this information with Jung's idea of individuation and Rogers's fully functioning person. Do the theories adequately describe the characteristics you admire? Are they consistent with them?

2. Make a collage that depicts your particular personality, using pictures and words from magazines and newspapers. For example, include your likes, dislikes, hobbies, personality traits, appearance, and so on.

3. Listen to conversations of several friends, relatives, teachers, and so on. Try to identify their

use of defense mechanisms and write down the circumstances surrounding their use. Try to listen to your own conversations and do the same for yourself. Why do you think people use defense mechanisms?

4. Select a newspaper or news magazine article that describes the activities or accomplishments of a person—for example, a popular sports figure, convicted criminal, politician, or business person. Then select a particular personality theory to describe the person's behavior and outlook on life. You may have to go beyond the material in the article to make a convincing argument for the theoretical view you have selected. Then, enter into a classroom discussion with other students who have selected different personality theories to explain the same individual's personality. How do these theoretical views of the person differ? Decide which view best explains the person's actions.

5. Look and listen for "Freudian slips." Write them down and try to determine the reasons for each slip.

6. Imagine that you have a friend who is having problems in school. He is failing several subjects and spends very little time doing homework or studying for tests. He prefers to watch television. Your friend's parents do not understand why he is this way. Based on your knowledge of personality theories, answer these questions: How would Skinner explain your friend's behavior? How would Bandura explain his behavior?

ANALYZING VIEWPOINTS

1. Despite the many theories of personality developed by psychologists, many people rely more on a reading of their horoscope to interpret their personality. Are horoscopes any less valid than personality theories? How do the two differ? Is classifying someone as friendly or aggressive much different than classifying someone as an Aquarian? Write a paper that debates the merits of trait theories of personality versus horoscopes. In formulating your answer, consider how well each approach fulfills the four functions of personality theory discussed in the chapter.

2. Jung believed that people are unconsciously linked to their ancestral past. What evidence can you think of for or against the "collective unconscious" Jung described? Prepare a paper summarizing this evidence, pro and con. Be sure to use your own experiences as well as what you have learned from the chapter to develop your arguments.

BEYOND THE CLASSROOM

1. Go to your local library and do additional reading on two different personality theories. Arrange a class debate in which one group supports one theory and the other group supports the other theory. One lively debate would be between the behaviorists' position and the humanistic approach.

2. Both Jung and Eysenck talk about extroversion versus introversion as being a basic part of personality. Choose five people—include friends, acquaintances, or family members—and observe their behavior. If possible, observe them in public situations and in family situations. Classify each person as either extroverted, introverted, or unable to determine. Keep a record of your observations, including evidence for your classifications. Next, ask these five people whether they would say they are extroverted or introverted. What do the results tell you about extroversion/introversion as a personality trait? Is someone extroverted or introverted in all situations, or does it vary depending on the situation? Did you learn anything interesting about how people see themselves as compared to how others see them? Report your findings to the class.

CHAPTER 12

Psychological Testing

Key Terms:

achievement test
aptitude test
intelligence quotient (IQ)
interest test
norms
objective personality tests
percentile system
projective personality tests
reliability
situational test
validity

As students, you are quite familiar with the use of tests to evaluate your academic performance. Testing has become an ever-present part of people's lives in our culture. In order to apply for a job as mail carrier, firefighter, lawyer, or electrician, a person must take a standard civil service or licensing exam. In these cases, the tests are designed to measure what skills and knowledge the person has acquired. Other tests are designed to assess more general characteristics of personality. For example, a psychologist may want to assess your personality to help you select a suitable career or deal with an emotional problem.

Whether the test is designed to measure mental abilities or personality characteristics, its use and interpretation depend on how well it is constructed and the extent to which scores are related to actual performance. What does it mean when a person scores high on standardized written intelligence tests but earns poor grades in school? Can you actually select a mate by a computerized matching of your personality? Is it acceptable to screen job applicants by using personality tests or to place children in special programs on the basis of intelligence testing? What strategies are most useful in taking tests?

Over the years, psychologists have developed a wide range of tools for measuring individual differences in intelligence, interests, skills, achievements, knowledge, and personality patterns. Their use by educators, the military, industry, and mental health practitioners has raised some concerns. This chapter will describe the major types of tests in current use and discuss ways of dealing with them.

Objectives:

After studying this chapter, you should be able to

- describe the concept of IQ and list several IQ tests.
- explain the application of aptitude tests, achievement tests, and personality tests.

Figure 12.1 Americans rely heavily on psychological testing because such tests promise to reveal a great deal about a person in a very short time.

BASIC CHARACTERISTICS OF TESTS

The lure of tests is that they promise to make it possible to find out a great deal about a person in a very short time.

All tests have one characteristic in common that makes them both fascinating and remarkably practical: they promise to make it possible to find out a great deal about a person in a very short time. Tests can be useful in predicting how well a person might do in a particular career; in assessing an individual's desires, interests, and attitudes; and in revealing psychological problems. One great virtue of standardized tests is that they can provide comparable data about many different individuals. Further, psychologists can use some tests to help people understand things about themselves more clearly than they did before.

One of the great dangers of testing, however, is that we tend to forget that tests are merely *tools* for measuring and predicting human behavior. We start to think of test results (for example, an IQ) as things in themselves. The justification for using a test to make decisions about a person's future depends on whether a decision based on test scores would be fairer and more accurate than one based on other criteria. The fairness and usefulness of a test depend on several factors: its reliability, its validity, and the way its norms were established.

Test Reliability

The term **reliability** refers to a test's consistency—its ability to yield the same result under a variety of different circumstances. There are three basic ways of determining a test's reliability. First, if a person retakes the test, or takes a similar test, within a short time after the first testing, does he or she receive approximately the same score? If, for example, you take a mechanical aptitude test three times in the space of six months and score 65 in January, 90 in March, and 70 in June, then the test is unreliable. It does not produce a measurement that is stable over time (Figure 12.3).

Figure 12.2
Two examples of group testing. Both school exams and aptitude tests can be considered psychological tests because both are intended to measure psychological variables (knowledge and skills).

The second measure of reliability is whether the test yields the same results when scored by different people. If both your teacher and a teaching assistant score an essay test that you have written, and one gives you a B while the other gives you a D, then you have reason to complain about the test's reliability. The score you receive depends more on the grader than on you. On a reliable test, your score would be the same no matter who graded your paper.

One final way of determining a test's reliability is to find out whether, if you divide the test in half and score each half separately, the two scores are approximately the same. If a test is supposed to measure one quality in a person (for example, reading comprehension or administrative ability), then it should not have some sections on which the person scores high and others on which he or she scores low.

In checking tests for reliability, psychologists are trying to prevent chance factors from influencing a person's score. All kinds of irrelevant matters can interfere with a test. If the test taker is depressed because his pet goldfish is sick or angry that he had to miss his favorite "I Love Lucy" rerun to take the exam, or if a broken radiator has raised the temperature in the testing room to 114 degrees, he will probably score lower than if he is reasonably relaxed, comfortable, and content. No test can screen out all interferences, but a highly reliable test can do away with a good part of them.

Test Validity

A test may be reliable but still not be valid. **Validity** is the ability of a test to measure what it is supposed to measure (Figure 12.4). For example, a test that consists primarily of vocabulary lists will not measure aptitude for engineering. A history test will not measure general learning ability.

Determining the validity of a test is more complex than assessing its reliability. One of the chief methods for measuring validity is to find out how well a test *predicts* performance. For example, a group of psychologists design a test to measure management ability. They ask questions about management systems, attitudes toward employees, and so on. Will the people who score high on this test really make good managers?

Suppose the test makers decide that a good way to check the validity of the test is to find out how much a manager's staff improve in productivity in one year. If the staffs of those managers who scored high on the test produce more than the staffs of those managers who scored low on the test, the test may be considered valid. Corporations may then adopt it as one tool to use in deciding whom to hire as managers.

What if managers who are good at raising productivity are poor at decision making? It may be that this test measures talent for improving productivity, not general management ability. This is the kind of difficulty psychologists encounter in trying to assess the validity of a test. As the example shows, nothing can be said about a test's validity until the *purpose* of the test is absolutely clear.

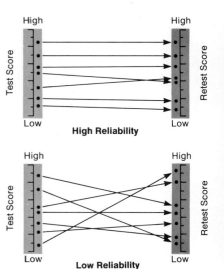

Figure 12.3
Test reliability. On the left, the test scores obtained by seven individuals are ordered on a scale. On the right, the corresponding scores on a second version of the same test, given at a later time, are ordered. In the upper diagram the two sets of scores correspond very closely. This pattern means the test is highly reliable. In the lower diagram, there is little relationship between the two. This scrambled pattern means the test has low reliability.

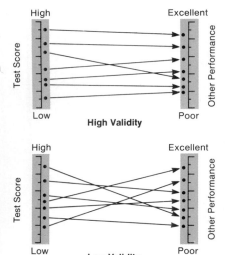

Figure 12.4
Test validity. Reliability and validity are assessed in exactly the same way, except that assessment of validity requires that test scores be compared to some other measure of behavior. The lower diagram might represent the comparison of scores on the "head size" test of intelligence (on the left) with school grades (on the right). The upper diagram might represent the result of comparing Stanford-Binet scores with school grades. The Stanford-Binet is a valid test for predicting school grades; the head size measurement is not.

Establishing Norms

Once a test result is obtained, the examiner must translate the score into something useful. Suppose a child answers thirty-two of fifty questions on a vocabulary test correctly. What does this score mean? If the test is reliable and valid, it means that the child can be expected to understand a certain percentage of the words in a book at the reading level being tested. In other words, the score predicts how the child will *perform* at a given level.

But a "raw" score does not tell us where the child stands in relation to other children at his or her age and grade level. If most children answered forty-five or more questions correctly, 32 is a low score. However, if most answered only twenty questions correctly, 32 is a very high score.

The method psychologists generally use to transform raw scores into figures that reflect comparisons with others is the **percentile system,** which bears some resemblance to what is called "grading on the curve." In the percentile system the scores actually achieved on the test are written down in order, ranging from the highest to the lowest. Each particular score is then compared with this list and assigned a percentile according to the percentage of scores that fall at or below this point. For example, if half the children in the above example scored 32 or below, then a score of 32 is at the fiftieth percentile. If 32 were the top score, it would be at the one-hundredth percentile. In the example given in figure 12.5, a score of 32 puts the child in the seventy-fifth percentile, since only 25 percent of the children scored higher than she did.

When psychologists are designing a test to be used in a variety of schools, businesses, clinics, or other settings, they usually set up a scale for comparison by establishing norms. The test is given to a large representative sample of the group to be measured—for example, sixth graders, army privates, engineers, or perhaps the population as a whole. Percentiles are then established on the basis of the scores achieved by this standardization group. These percentiles are called the test's **norms.** Most of the intelligence, aptitude, and personality tests you will encounter have been pro-

Figure 12.5
The meaning of percentile scores. The range of possible raw scores on a test is shown in relation to an idealized curve that indicates the proportion of people who achieved each score. The vertical lines indicate percentiles, or proportions of the curve below certain points. Thus, the line indicated as the 1st percentile is the line below which only 1 percent of the curve lies; similarly, 99 percent of the curve lies below the 99th percentile.

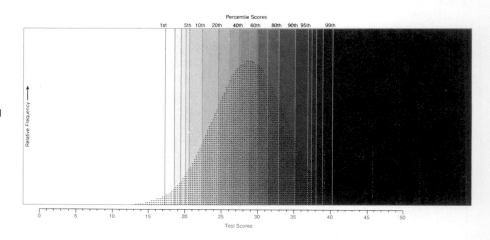

vided with norms in this way. Your percentile on an aptitude test such as the SAT, for example, reflects your standing among people of your age and grade who have taken these exams.

It should be remembered, however, that norms are not really standards—even though a norm group is sometimes misleadingly referred to as a "standardization group." Norms refer only to what has been found normal or average for some group of people. If Johnny can read at the fiftieth percentile level, that does not mean he has met some absolute standard for ability to read. It only means that he reads better than half the population (50 percent), and worse than the other half.

In summary, when you take a test and obtain your score, you should consider the following questions in evaluating the results. (1) Do you think that if you took the same test or a similar test again, you would receive a similar score? (2) Does your performance on this test reflect your normal performance in the subject the test is designed to measure? (3) If you were to compare your score with those of your classmates, would it reflect your general standing within that group of people?

INTELLIGENCE TESTING

Among the most widely used and widely disputed tests in America today are those that are designed to measure "intelligence" and yield an "IQ" score. This section will describe some of the major intelligence tests and present some of the issues that surround them.

The Development of Intelligence Tests

Alfred Binet, a French psychologist, was the first to develop a useful intelligence test. In 1904 Binet was asked by the Paris school authorities to devise a means of picking out "slow learners" so they could be placed in special classes from which they might better profit. Binet was unable to define intelligence, but he believed it was reflected in such things as the ability to make common-sense judgments, to tell the meanings of words, and to solve problems and puzzles. Binet assumed that whatever intelligence was, it increased with age; that is, older children had more intelligence than younger children. Therefore, in selecting items for his test he only included items on which older children did better than younger children. By asking the same questions of many children, Binet was able to determine the average age at which a particular question could be answered. For example, he discovered that certain questions could be answered by most twelve year olds but not by most eleven year olds. If a child of eleven, or even nine, could answer these questions, he or she was said to have a *mental age* of twelve. If a child of twelve could answer the nine-year-old-level questions but not the questions for ten year olds and eleven year olds, he or she was said to have a mental age of nine. Thus a slow learner was one who had a *mental age* that was less than his or her *chronological age*.

MORE about. . .

Multiple Intelligences?
Many people believe that intelligence is primarily the ability to think logically. Psychologist Howard Gardner considers this view of intelligence to be inadequate, however, because it omits many other important skills. Gardner argues for a broader perspective that includes seven types of intelligence. The seven are: (1) verbal ability; (2) logical-mathematical reasoning skills; (3) spatial ability, or the ability to find your way around an environment and to form mental images; (4) musical ability, or the ability to create and perceive pitch and rhythm patterns; (5) body-kinesthetic ability, or skill at fine motor movements required for tasks such as gem cutting and surgery; (6) interpersonal skills, involving understanding the feelings of others; and (7) intrapersonal skills, or knowledge of oneself.

Gardner's research on the results of brain disease convinced him that humans possess these seven different and often unrelated intellectual capacities or "intelligences." Moreover, he argues that the biological organization of the brain affects one's strength in each of the seven areas.

Figure 12.6
Two tests on the Stanford-Binet being administered to a little boy. (top) The examiner has built a tower of four blocks and has told the child, "You make one like this." (bottom) The examiner shows the child the card with six small objects attached to it and says, "See all these things? Show me the dog," and so on.

The Stanford-Binet.   Binet's intelligence test has been revised many times since he developed it. The Binet test currently in widespread use in the United States is a revision created at Stanford University: the Stanford-Binet Intelligence Test (Terman and Merrill, 1973). The Stanford-Binet, like the original test, groups test items by age level. To stimulate and maintain the child's interest, a variety of tasks are included, ranging from defining words to drawing pictures and explaining events in daily life. Children are tested one at a time. The examiner must carry out standardized instructions—at the same time putting the child at ease, getting him to pay attention, and encouraging him to try as hard as he can (Figure 12.6).

In the final scoring, the mental age indicates how high a level the person has reached. If his performance is as high as the average twelve year old's, he has a mental age of twelve. The **IQ,** or **intelligence quotient,** is called a quotient because it was originally computed by dividing mental age by actual (chronological) age and multiplying the result by 100 to eliminate decimals. (A nine year old with a mental age of twelve would have an IQ of 133.) Although the term IQ has stuck, the actual computation is now made on a basis similar to the percentile system.

The Wechsler Tests.   Two other frequently used intelligence tests are the Wechsler Intelligence Scale for Children, or WISC, and the Wechsler Adult Intelligence Scale, or WAIS (Wechsler, 1958). The Wechsler tests differ from the Stanford-Binet in several important ways. For example, the Wechsler tests place more emphasis on performance tasks (such as doing puzzles) than does the Stanford-Binet, so that individuals who are not particularly skilled in the use of words will not be as likely to receive low IQ scores (Figure 12.7).

Moreover, in addition to yielding one overall score, the Wechsler tests yield percentile scores in several areas—vocabulary, information, arithmetic, picture arrangement, and so on. These ratings are used to compute separate IQ scores for verbal and performance abilities. This type of scoring provides a more detailed picture of the individual's strengths and weaknesses than a single score does.

Group Tests.   The Wechsler and Stanford-Binet tests, because they are given individually, are costly and time-consuming to administer. During World War I, when the United States Army found that it had to test nearly two million men, and quickly, individual testing was a luxury the army could not afford. Thus paper-and-pencil intelligence tests, which could be given to large groups of people at the same time, were developed. Current group IQ tests, such as the Army Alpha and Beta tests, have proved to be convenient and effective and are used extensively in schools, employment offices, and many other institutions.

The Uses and Meaning of IQ Scores

In general, the norms for intelligence tests are established in such a way that most people score near 100. Out of one hundred people, seventeen will score above 115 and seventeen will score below 85. About three in one hundred score above 130, and three score below 70. This means that a

General Information

1. How many wings does a bird have?
2. How many nickels make a dime?
3. What is steam made of?
4. Who wrote "Paradise Lost"?
5. What is pepper?

General Comprehension

1. What should you do if you see someone forget his book when he leaves his seat in a restaurant?
2. What is the advantage of keeping money in a bank?
3. Why is copper often used in electrical wires?

Arithmetic

1. Sam had three pieces of candy and Joe gave him four more. How many pieces of candy did Sam have altogether?
2. Three men divided eighteen golf balls equally among themselves. How many golf balls did each man receive?
3. If two apples cost 15¢, what will be the cost of a dozen apples?

Similarities

1. In what way are a lion and a tiger alike?
2. In what way are a saw and a hammer alike?
3. In what way are an hour and a week alike?
4. In what way are a circle and a triangle alike?

Vocabulary

"What is a puzzle?"
"What does 'addition' mean?"

Figure 12.7
Test items similar to those included in the various Wechsler intelligence scales. (a) A sampling of questions from five of the verbal subtests. (b) A problem in block design, one of the performance subtests. (c) Another example of a performance subtest. The subject is asked to put together puzzle pieces to form a familiar object, such as a duck. (Test items courtesy The Psychological Corporation, New York)

score of 130 places a person in the ninety-seventh percentile; a score of 70, in the third percentile.

What do these scores mean? What do the tests measure? IQ scores seem to be most useful when related to school achievement: they are quite accurate in predicting which people will do well in schools, colleges, and universities. Critics of IQ testing do not question this predictive ability. They do wonder, however, whether such tests actually measure "intelligence." Most psychologists agree that intelligence is the ability to acquire new ideas and new behavior. Is success in school or the ability to take a test a real indication of such ability? Generally, IQ tests measure the ability to solve certain types of problems. But they do not directly measure the ability to pose those problems or to question the validity of problems set by others (Hoffman, 1962). This is only part of the reason why IQ testing is so controversial.

The Controversy over IQ

Much of the debate about IQ testing centers around one question: Do genetic differences or environmental inequalities cause two people to receive different scores on intelligence tests? It has been shown that some of the questions on these tests clearly give middle-class people an advantage. One intelligence test, for example, includes the following question as a test of reasoning ability:

A symphony is to a composer as a book is to what?
paper   sculptor   author   musician   man

A. Davis (1951) found that 81 percent of children from well-off families, but only 51 percent of children from lower-classs families, answered this correctly. When Davis rephrased the question in less "highbrow" terms, using everyday words and common experiences, the gap closed.

A baker goes with bread, like a carpenter goes with what?
a saw   a house   a spoon   a nail   a man

Fifty percent of the children from both income groups answered this question correctly. The first question measured experience in middle-class culture as well as reasoning; the second, reasoning alone.

In addition, there is mounting evidence that poor children do not try as hard as middle-class children on intelligence tests. Why? Because the test itself makes them uncomfortable. They tend to see tests as punishments, as situations designed to make them look bad. Many rush through a test, choosing responses almost at random—just to get it over with. In contrast, middle-class children tend to see tests as an opportunity to prove themselves and to win praise. They work more slowly, making fewer wild guesses and scoring higher. Thus the differences among groups reflect motivation as well as intelligence.

TEST-TAKING STRATEGIES

The difference in scores achieved by middle-class and poor children on IQ tests has been shown to reflect not only a difference in accumulated knowledge, but also a difference in skills for taking tests. Several researchers have coached disadvantaged children in test taking—with good results. It seems that many do not fully understand the tasks they are required to perform on the tests. They have not learned the strategies to solve test problems. When they do, their scores improve. This suggests that a person's IQ score also reflects his or her skill and experience in taking tests. In short, IQ tests are far from perfect measures of intelligence, because a variety of factors irrelevant to intelligence affect results.

Many educators and psychologists have studied the way people prepare themselves for tests and the way they respond in a testing situation. These strategies can be useful in preparation for any kind of test, whether it is a mid-term exam in biology, a civil service test, or a college entrance exam.

Figure 12.8
Psychologist Adrian Dove developed the Counterbalance Intelligence Test to stress the fact that cultural background can influence performance on an intelligence test. People from certain cultural backgrounds would get high scores on this test, whereas people from other cultural backgrounds would probably get very low scores.

The Dove Counterbalance Intelligence Test
by Adrian Dove

If they throw the dice and "7" is showing on the top, what is facing down?
(a) "Seven"   (b) "Snake eyes"
(c) "Boxcars"   (d) "Little Joes"
(e) "Eleven"

Jazz pianist Ahmad Jamal took an Arabic name after becoming really famous. Previously he had some fame with what he called his "slave name." What was his previous name?
(a) Willie Lee Jackson
(b) LeRoi Jones
(c) Wilbur McDougal
(d) Fritz Jones   (e) Andy Johnson

In "C. C. Rider," what does "C. C." stand for?
(a) Civil Service
(b) Church Council
(c) County Circuit, preacher of an old-time rambler
(d) Country Club
(e) "Cheating Charley" (the "Boxcar Gunsel")

Cheap "chitlings" (not the kind you purchase at the frozen-food counter) will taste rubbery unless they are cooked long enough. How soon can you quit cooking them to eat and enjoy them?
(a) 15 minutes   (b) 2 hours
(c) 24 hours
(d) 1 week (on a low flame)
(e) 1 hour

If a judge finds you guilty of "holding weed" (in California), what's the most he can give you?
(a) Indeterminate (life)   (b) A nickel
(c) A dime   (d) A year in county
(e) $100.00.

A "Handkerchief Head" is
(a) A cool cat   (b) A porter
(c) An "Uncle Tom"   (d) A hoddi
(e) A "preacher"

Studying for a Test

One of the differences between people who do well on tests or exams and those who do poorly is in the type and amount of studying they do. People who have developed good study habits often earn high grades and derive a general sense of accomplishment from their efforts. Knowing that they are adequately prepared for a test also reduces their anxiety. Like other skills, studying skills are acquired through practice and instruction.

Psychologists who study how people learn verbal or written material have shown that people master material better when they practice or rehearse the material several times. What this means is that the student who reads the assigned chapters for an exam several times will remember more of the material than the student who studies by reading the assigned chapters only once. In terms of studying then, practice does make perfect. Furthermore, peoples' performance on a test will most likely improve if they space their study time over several intervals rather than cram all the studying into one session. It would be better to study an hour a night for five nights than to cram all of the studying into five hours on the night before the exam. Cramming can sometimes be useful, but only when it is used as a reminder of what has previously been studied during spaced or distributed study sessions. When cramming is used as a substitute for planned study, test performance is not as good.

Psychological research also suggests that people should plan their study time so that they avoid studying materials that are similar to each other. Suppose, for example, that a student is studying for a French exam and at the same time she has Spanish and geometry homework to do. Since French and Spanish are more similar than French and geometry, she should space her Spanish and French study time so that she reduces the possibility of one interfering with the other. She could do her Spanish homework early in the day, and set aside several short blocks of time in the late afternoon and evening to prepare for the French exam. In between the times set aside for studying French, she could do her geometry home- work, since this material is less likely to interfere with her memory of the French material.

Reducing Test Anxiety

One of the biggest problems that people have in preparing for or taking an exam or test is anxiety. As the time draws near to the test, people generally experience an increase in tension. While some people are able to keep their anxiety to a reasonable level, others are so panic stricken that they cannot perform well. Actually, a moderate amount of tension improves performance. A person who feels no tension at all is not as alert or attentive to details as he or she could be. When a person experiences a high level of tension, however, panic and disorganization set in and performance declines. Thus, a person who is too tense will need to calm down, while the noninvolved person may need to motivate himself or herself in order to do well on tests. Adequate preparation for a test helps reduce some of the anxiety people have. Beyond that, a person can learn specific techniques for reducing tension and relaxing before an exam. For example, allowing plenty of time to get to the testing setting and having a good night's sleep beforehand will help reduce anxiety.

Some people may be relatively relaxed when they enter an exam room but then suddenly find that they can't remember anything they had learned for the exam. Mental blocks occur when people temporarily panic. If you ever experience such a block, close your eyes and slowly take a few deep breaths and let your body relax. Sometimes, this quick technique will be enough to free you from your mental block.

Since most tests are timed and many tests are designed to assess performance under pressure, one way you can reduce the stress of test-taking is to manage the time you have during the exam. Know how much time you will have beforehand and be sure to have a watch so that you can keep track of the time. Divide your time so that you don't take too long on any one part. If you don't manage your time, you might discover that you have ten minutes left to complete the second half of the test.

Another way to reduce your level of anxiety is to believe in yourself and tell yourself that you *can* do well on the test. Having a plan of action or a strategy for taking the test will increase your confidence in test-taking. Knowing how to take a test involves some familiarity with the different kinds of tests and questions you will be asked.

Preparing Yourself for a Test

With the increase in the use of tests for job and college selection, a number of courses and books have been developed to help people prepare for specific exams. These courses usually have two goals: one is to familiarize the individual with testing strategies and to help the test-taker develop a knowledge of testing procedures. The second goal is to provide specific instruction or coaching in the subject matter of the test.

If you have had no experience at all with machine-scored multiple choice exams, you may not be as confident as a more experienced test-taker. Thus, a familiarity with the question format and with the special answer sheets can be useful. Many courses offer sample items on which you can practice. Sometimes, the answer sheets can be confusing to the inexperienced test-taker because of the various codes that are required to identify the person taking the test. Marking your answer correctly may also mean using a specific type of pencil, selecting an answer row, and completely filling in the space between two parallel lines or inside circles. When you do have to mark your answers in rows of circles or squares, make sure you are in the correct row. It's easy to skip one row accidentally and then place all subsequent answers in the wrong rows.

In addition to the actual mechanics of taking tests, you can learn how to read and answer multiple-choice items. For example, it is important to know ahead of time whether there is a penalty for guessing. Some exams are scored only for correct answers ("rights only" scoring), in which case you would do better to guess an answer than to leave a blank. Other exams are scored by subtracting the number of wrong answers, or some proportion of the number of wrong answers, from the number of correct answers (formula scoring). Follow the test publisher's advice on guessing. You should also learn to read all of the multiple-choice options, not just the first one that seems right. You will probably improve your score if you don't spend too much time on puzzling items, especially since most tests are timed. Later, if time permits, you can go back to difficult items and apply more specific strategies for deciding on the best answers. (See Test-Taking Tips box in this chapter.)

Some organizations offer courses that provide coaching for specific tests. They vary in cost and quality. Some are very expensive and very intensive, sometimes involving daily study for a period of up to six months. There is debate among educators about the benefit of such courses. Often, the focus of coaching courses is on increasing a person's vocabulary and refreshing his or her knowledge of specific subjects such as geometry or algebra. If a person has been out of school for a while, these courses may be helpful, but for a student who is currently taking English and mathematics courses, these programs may not prove beneficial.

Figure 12.9
The General Aptitude Test Battery (GATB) consists of a number of different kinds of tests. Samples of items testing verbal and mathematical skills (top) and manual skills (bottom) are shown here.

Family Size and IQ

It wasn't that long ago that nearly everyone came from a large family. Now most couples have just one, two, or three children.

Instead of bemoaning the loss of the large family, psychologists tell us we should be happy it's gone, for according to studies, large families produce children with lower IQs. Psychologists also point to evidence that keeping a family small may increase the likelihood of having smart children and that a child's intelligence is affected by where in the birth order he or she was born.

The classic study of family size and IQ was conducted in the Netherlands. It was based on the military examinations of more than 386,000 Dutchmen. Researchers found that the brightest subjects came from the smallest families and had few, if any, brothers and sisters when they were born. Thus, the first-born child in a family of two was usually brighter than the last child in a family of ten.

The effects of family size on intelligence may be explained by what a house full of children does to the home environment. It increases the amount of time a child spends with other children and decreases the amount of parental attention he or she receives. When this happens, and children have limited contact with adults, development of intelligence has been known to suffer.

For more details, see R. B. Zajonc and G. B. Markus, "Birth Order and Intellectual Development," Psychological Review, 1975, vol. 82.

1. Which two words have the same meaning?
   (a) open **(b)** happy **(c)** glad **(d)** green

2. Which two words have the opposite meaning?
   (a) old **(b)** dry **(c)** cold **(d)** young

3. A man works 8 hours a day, 40 hours a week. He earns $1.40 an hour. How much does he earn each week?
   (A) $40.00 **(C)** $50.60
   (B) $44.60 **(D)** $56.00

4. At the left is a drawing of a flat piece of metal. Which object at the right can be made from this piece of metal?

USING PSYCHOLOGY

The SAT

The tremendous success of mass testing to screen people for the army in World War I encouraged the College Board (a nonprofit membership association of schools and colleges) to develop objective tests to screen students for college admission. It developed a number of college entrance examinations, including the SAT (Scholastic Aptitude Test). This test, along with achievement and other tests, makes up the College Board's Admissions Testing Program. The American College Testing Program (ACT) offers another, similar series of admissions tests. The results of standardized tests are among several criteria that colleges use for selecting students.

More than one million high school students take SATs every year. Juniors take the PSAT (Preliminary Scholastic Aptitude Test) to prepare them for the kinds of questions they will encounter on SATs, for early admission to college, and for scholarship applications.

The three-hour SAT is a multiple-choice test divided into six parts: two verbal parts, two parts on mathematics, a part on standard written English, and a part made up of "equating" questions. The verbal parts measure your ability to use words. They include questions on vocabulary, sentence completions, word relationships (analogies and antonyms), and reading comprehension. The math parts measure your grasp of elementary mathematical principles and determine how well and fast you can solve problems. The Test of Standard Written English requires you to recognize mistakes in English grammar and usage. The "equating" questions are either new questions being tested for difficulty, or old questions from former tests that are used to standardize scores so that students are not penalized if their particular SAT is more difficult than former SATs.

You do not pass or fail SATs. Your score is compared with those of others who took similar tests over the years. Most colleges use these relative values, based on a national rather than a local standard, as part of their assessment of your academic ability.

The average scores of students taking the SATs dropped gradually over the first ten years that national averages were recorded (beginning in 1972). There are many theories explaining this. One theory is that some schools lacked the traditionally strong emphasis on the basic academic skills. Another theory is that teachers were giving students higher grades than in the past for comparable work, so that students with lower capabilities were advancing through the grades.

In 1982, an upward trend in the national scores began. A shift back to a more rigorous curriculum is credited, in part, for this improvement.

The fact that different teachers and schools grade comparable work differently is a major rationale for nationally standardized tests such as the SATs. Many studies have shown that SATs are a more accurate gauge of student ability than the subjective opinions of the students' teachers (Stanley, 1976: 313).

MEASURING ABILITIES AND INTERESTS

Intelligence tests are designed to measure a person's overall ability to solve problems that involve symbols such as words, numbers, and pictures. Psychologists have developed other tests to assess special abilities and experiences. These include aptitude tests, achievement tests, and interest tests.

Aptitude Tests

Aptitude tests attempt to discover a person's talents and to predict how well he or she will be able to learn a new skill. The General Aptitude Test Battery (GATB) is the most widely used of these tests (Figure 12.9). Actually, the GATB comprises nine different tests, ranging from vocabulary to manual dexterity. Test results are used to determine whether a person meets minimum standards for each of a large number of occupations. In addition to the GATB there are aptitude tests in music, language, art, mathematics, and other special fields.

Achievement Tests

Whereas aptitude tests are designed to predict how well a person will be able to learn a new skill, **achievement tests** are designed to measure how much a person has already learned in a particular area. Such tests not only enable an instructor to assess a student's knowledge, they also help students to assess their progress for themselves.

The distinction between achievement and aptitude tests has become somewhat blurred in recent years. What psychologists had at first thought were tests of aptitude—defined as *innate* ability or talent—turned out to measure experience as well, so that in part they were achievement tests. On the other hand, achievement tests often turned out to be the best predictors of many kinds of occupational abilities, so that they were in some sense aptitude tests. Because of this overlap, psychologists have agreed that the distinction between the two types of tests rests more on purpose than on content. If a test is used to predict future ability, it is considered to

PSYCHOLOGY UPDATE

Adaptive Testing. Computers are often used to administer ability tests. One computer-based method is called "adaptive testing." To understand adaptive testing, recall that in a standard test everyone gets the same questions in the same order. With an adaptive test, however, the order of questions is changed by the computer as it *adapts* the test to the individual's performance.

If you are taking the test and answer several problems correctly, the computer will begin to challenge you with harder problems. If you miss a question, the computer will follow it with an easier problem, and so on. The purpose of this testing method is to measure your ability by finding the difficulty level where you correctly answer most but not all of the problems (70 percent, for example). Adaptive testing is more accurate than standard testing, especially when test takers are either very high or very low in ability.

Figure 12.10
Taking a test: A number of factors, including the individual's mood and the physical setup of the room, can influence the results. A person can easily do poorly on one day in one setting and well on another day in different circumstances.

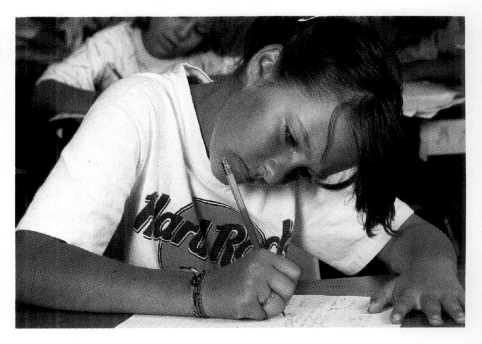

be an aptitude test; if it is used to assess what a person already knows, it is an achievement test.

Interest Tests

The instruments for measuring interests are fundamentally different from the instruments for measuring abilities. Answers to questions on an intelligence test indicate whether a person can, in fact, do certain kinds of thinking and solve certain kinds of problems. There are right and wrong answers. But the answers to questions on an interest or a personality test cannot be right or wrong. The question in this type of testing is not "How much can you do?" or "How much do you know?" but "What are you like?"

The essential purpose of an **interest test** is to determine a person's preferences, attitudes, and interests. The test taker's responses are compared to the responses given by people in clearly defined groups, such as professions or occupations. The more a person's answers correspond to those of people in a particular occupation, the more likely that person is to enjoy and succeed in that profession.

In constructing the widely used Strong Vocational Interest Inventory, for example, psychologists compared the responses of people who are successfully employed in different occupations to the responses of "people in general." Suppose most engineers said they liked the idea of becoming astronomers but would not be interested in a coaching job, whereas "people in general" were evenly divided on these (and other) questions. A

Admissions Test Scores

Every spring and winter, high school students go through an American rite of passage: they take their college entrance exams. How well they do influences what happens in their lives from that point on. The colleges they attend, the jobs they get, the people they marry are all affected, to some degree, by their scores.

Little wonder, then, that most students try to do everything they can to do well on the exams. Although no one has discovered a magic formula for getting the top grades, many students repeat exams such as the SAT, usually taking it first in the spring of their junior year and then in the winter of their senior year. According to Educational Testing Service, the writers of this test, one student in twenty will gain 100 points or more and about one in a hundred will lose 100 points or more. Generally speaking, the odds are with students to improve their scores. College admissions committees take this into account when they interpret the results.

Experts attribute this score gain to several factors. Students' intellectual capacities have increased between their junior and senior years, and a round of practice helped take the jitters out of exam time. In sum, the students taking the test for the second time are a little older, a little smarter, and more experienced.

person who responded as the engineers did would rank high on the scale of interest in engineering. The Kuder Preference Record, part of which is shown in Figure 12.11, is based on the same principle. The purpose of these measures is to help people find the career that is right for them.

		Most	Least
G.	Read a love story	● G. ●
H.	Read a mystery	● H. ●
I.	Read science fiction	● I. ●
J.	Visit an art gallery	● J. ●
K.	Browse in a library	● K. ●
L.	Visit a museum	● L. ●
M.	Collect autographs	● M. ●
N.	Collect coins	● N. ●
O.	Collect butterflies	● O. ●
P.	Watch television	● P. ●
Q.	Go for a walk	● Q. ●
R.	Listen to music	● R. ●

Figure 12.11
Items from the Kuder Preference Record (KPR), a test that works like the Strong Vocational Interest Inventory. The person taking the test is asked to pick from among three possible activities the one he or she would most like to do and the one he or she would least like to do. The test provides numerous sets of such alternatives.

PERSONALITY TESTING

Psychiatrists and psychologists use **personality tests** to assess personality characteristics and to identify problems. Some of these tests are **objective,** or forced choice—that is, a person must select one out of a small number of possible responses. Others are **projective**—they encourage test takers to respond freely, giving their own interpretations of various test stimuli.

Objective Personality Tests

The most widely used objective personality test is the Minnesota Multiphasic Personality Inventory (MMPI). Like other personality tests, the MMPI has no right or wrong answers. The test consists of 550 statements to which a person can respond "true," "false," or "cannot say." Items include "I like tall women"; "I wake up tired most mornings"; "I am envied by most people"; "I often feel a tingling in my fingers."

The items on the MMPI reveal habits, fears, delusions, sexual attitudes, and symptoms of mental problems. Although the statements that relate to a given characteristic (such as depression) are scattered throughout the test, the answers to them can be pulled out and organized into a single depression scale. There are ten such clinical scales to the MMPI.

In scoring the MMPI, a psychologist looks for patterns of responses, not a high or low score on all the scales. This is because the items on the test do not, by themselves, identify personality types. In creating the MMPI, the test makers did not try to think up statements that would identify depression, anxiety, and so on. Rather, they invented a wide range of statements about all sorts of topics; gave the test to groups of people already known to be well adjusted, depressed, anxious, and so on; and retained for the test those questions that discriminated among these groups—questions, for example, that people suffering from depression or from anxiety neurosis almost always answered differently from normal groups (Hathaway and McKinley, 1940). Many of the items on the MMPI may sound like sheer nonsense. But they work, and for many psychologists that's all that counts. One unique aspect of the MMPI is that it has a built-in "lie detector." If an individual gives a false response to one statement, he or she may be caught by a rephrasing of the same question at a later point.

The MMPI has proved useful in helping to diagnose various forms of mental disturbance and in providing data for personality research (Dahlstrom and Welsh, 1960). It has also been used—and misused—in employment offices to screen job applicants. A person who is trying to get a job is likely to give answers he or she thinks the employer would like to see—thereby falling into some of the traps built into the test. Administering the MMPI under such circumstances can produce misleading, even damaging results. Innocently trying to make a good impression, the job applicant ends up looking like a liar instead. As an aid to counseling and therapy, however, it can be a valuable tool.

Projective Personality Tests

Projective tests are open-ended examinations that invite people to tell stories about pictures, diagrams, or objects. The idea is that because the

Figure 12.12
Inkblots similar to those used on the Rorschach test. In interpretations of a person's responses to the inkblots, as much attention may be paid to the style of the responses as to their content.

test material has no established meaning, the story a person tells must say something about his needs, wishes, fears, and other aspects of his personality. In other words, the subject will project his feelings onto the test items.

Perhaps the best-known and most widely discussed projective measure is the Rorschach ink-blot test, developed by Swiss psychiatrist Hermann Rorschach. Rorschach created ten ink-blot designs and a system for scoring responses to them. To administer the test, a psychologist hands the ink blots, one by one, to the subject, asking the person to say what he or she sees. The person might say that a certain area represents an airplane or an animal's head. This is the free-association period of the test. The psychologist then asks certain general questions in an attempt to discover what aspects of the ink blot determined the person's response (Figure 12.12).

There are a number of systems for scoring Rorschach responses. Some are very specific and concrete. For example, according to one system a person who mentions human movement more often than color in the ink blots is probably introverted while an extrovert will mention color more than movement. Other systems are far more intuitive—for example, simply noting whether the person taking the test is open or hostile. Many researchers have criticized the Rorschach, charging that scoring systems are neither reliable nor valid. But it continues to be widely used by therapists.

The second most widely used projective measure was developed by Henry Murray. The Thematic Apperception Test (TAT) consists of a series of twenty cards containing pictures of vague but suggestive situations. The individual is asked to tell a story about the picture, indicating how the situation shown on the card developed, what the characters are thinking and feeling, and how it will end (Figure 12.13).

As with the Rorschach, there are many different scoring systems. The interpreter usually focuses on the themes that emerge from the story and the needs of the main characters. Are they aggressive? Do they seem to have needs for achievement, love, or sex? Are they being attacked or criticized by another person, or are they receiving affection and comfort?

Figure 12.13
Three cards similar to those used in the Thematic Apperception Test (TAT). The scenes depicted in the drawings allow a variety of interpretations, and the person taking the test is assumed to project his or her own needs, wishes, defenses, and other personality factors into the story.

SITUATIONAL TESTING

The use of psychological tests for such things as job placement has become extremely controversial in recent years. Is there any direct relation between a person's responses to statements on the MMPI and his everyday behavior? Do a person's perceptions of an ink blot really tell whether she will be able to remain calm under pressure or to give and take orders efficiently? Many psychologists think not. They believe that the closer a test is to the actual situation the examiner wants to know about, the more useful the results will be. A test that measures an individual's performance in terms of emotional, attitudinal, and behavioral responses to "true life" situations is called a **situational test**. (An example is a test for a driver's license, requiring that the person actually drive.)

One of the first situational tests for job placement was developed by the Office of Strategic Services (OSS) during World War II (Office of Strategic Services Assessment Staff, 1948). The OSS wanted to evaluate candidates for assignment to military espionage, which requires a high degree of self-control and frustration tolerance. In order to judge the candidates, the OSS set up a three-day session of intensive testing during which candidates were required to live together in close quarters and were confronted with a number of complicated and frustrating problems.

In one procedure, a staff member instructed the candidate to build a certain type of cube with the help of two assistants. The helpers were actually psychologists who played prearranged roles. One was extremely lazy and passive, engaged in projects of his own, and offered no advice. The other interfered with the work by making impractical suggestions, harassing the candidate, and asking embarrassing questions. The "assistants" succeeded so well in frustrating the candidates that not one finished the construction. But by placing the candidates in situations similar to those they would encounter as agents, the examiners were able to predict how these men might respond to military intelligence work. Court decisions and federal regulations now stipulate that job-placement tests in many professions must be work-related.

Figure 12.14
Using this airplane flight simulator, pilots are trained and tested before they are given the responsibility of flying a real airliner. None of the standard tests described in this chapter could predict accurately whether a pilot would panic in such a situation. (United Air Lines photo)

Ethical Problems of Testing

The widespread use of testing raises numerous ethical questions. We would all probably agree it is appropriate for the law to require that people pass driving tests before taking the wheel alone. But is it appropriate for a business organization to pry into an individual's fundamental beliefs and private fantasies before offering that person a job? Is it right for colleges to use attitude questionnaires in order to select their freshman classes? What does a student's attitude toward her mother or the opposite sex or freedom of the press have to do with whether or not she will be able to pass French 1A or Anthropology 1B?

Such considerations lead to doubts about the use of tests in making major decisions about individual lives. Should people be denied a college education or be confined to a mental institution on the basis of test results? Should people be required to take tests at all, when many find it a traumatic, demanding experience of questionable value? The answers to these questions are not easy. Psychological tests, like other technological advances, have their uses and their limitations. Like automobiles, tranquilizers, and nuclear power, tests can be overused and badly used. But, as is the case with other technologies, they can be used well if people understand them.

FACT OR FICTION

?

It is good practice to review and change your answers on a multiple-choice test if you disagree with your first responses.

Fact. Although students often believe that their "first impression" is correct, this may not be the case. Studies show that students are likely to benefit from changing answers, especially if they are fairly confident that the new answer is the correct one.

USING PSYCHOLOGY

Test-Taking Tips

The following tips will help you perform better on tests. Some of them have to do with studying for the test, some with taking the test, and some with your answers on particular types of tests.

1. Outline a plan to decide how much and how long you will study. Use any practice material that is available for the test.
2. Make yourself familiar with the format of standardized tests—multiple choice, verbal analogy, and so on.
3. When preparing for an essay question, review the major ideas. For short answer tests, memorize material such as dates, events, and formulas.
4. Get plenty of sleep the night before the test. Always arrive at the testing place on time. Bring a watch, but try not to focus on it.
5. Sit in a place where you will not be distracted by friends.
6. Read the instructions carefully and, if you are allowed to mark on the test, underline or circle key phrases in the directions. In essay questions, these might include "compare and contrast," "trace," "define," and "illustrate." Also underline important elements of a reading comprehension passage such as names, numbers, and dates so that you can locate them quickly. If the directions are not clear, ask any questions before the timing period begins.
7. Make sure you know what the penalty is for guessing.
8. Go through the test and plan how much time you will spend on each part. Answer the questions that are easy for you first, then concentrate on the harder ones if time permits.
9. In essay questions, always write an outline before you begin writing. Spend one-third to one-half of your time on the outline and the rest on the actual writing. If you run out of time, hand in the rest of the outline.
10. In a multiple-choice test, read every possible answer before making your choice. In rankings, one of the answers in the middle is usually right. In true-false questions, answers with absolute qualifiers, such as "always" or "never" are often wrong. In an "all of the above" question, if you know that at least two answers are correct, choose "all of the above."

SUMMARY

Use the following outline as a tool for reviewing this chapter. Copy the outline onto your own paper, leaving spaces between headings to make notes about key concepts.

I. Basic Characteristics of Tests

   A. Test Reliability

   B. Test Validity

   C. Establishing Norms

II. Intelligence Testing

   A. The Development of Intelligence Tests

   B. The Uses and Meaning of IQ Scores

   C. The Controversy over IQ

III. Test-Taking Strategies

   A. Studying for the Test

   B. Reducing Test Anxiety

   C. Preparing Yourself for a Test

IV. Measuring Abilities and Interests

   A. Aptitude Tests

   B. Achievement Tests

   C. Interest Tests

V. Personality Testing

   A. Objective Personality Tests

   B. Projective Personality Tests

VI. Situational Testing

   A. Ethical Problems of Testing

CONCEPTS AND VOCABULARY

1. What is one characteristic that all tests have in common?

2. What are several uses of psychological tests?

3. What is test reliability? Describe three ways of assessing reliability.

4. What is test validity? How is the validity of a test determined?

5. What are norms?

6. An IQ test score is a poor predictor of musical ability. Does this mean the IQ test is not valid? Explain your answer.

7. How do psychologists compare scores obtained by different individuals?

8. Who was the first psychologist to develop an intelligence test? What is the test he developed called?

9. How was the first IQ test developed? How was the "intelligence quotient" calculated by Binet? How is it calculated now?

10. How does the Stanford-Binet IQ test differ from the Wechsler IQ tests?

11. What are some ways you can prepare for taking a test besides studying a text and your notes? Give examples of ways to improve your general test-taking behavior.

12. What was the main finding of the study of family size and IQ in the Netherlands?

13. What is the difference between an aptitude test and an achievement test? Give an example of each type of test.

14. In what ways do interest tests differ from achievement tests? When are interest tests used?

15. What are the two basic types of personality tests? What are some of the differences between the types? Give an example of each type of test.

16. What distinguishes situational tests from other forms of tests previously discussed? What is the advantage of a situational test?

17. What are the advantages and disadvantages of using tests to make decisions?

CRITICAL THINKING

1. **Analyze.** The chapter discusses a wide range of devices used to measure intelligence, aptitudes, personality traits, and so on. Think about and write down the criteria by which you "test" others. How crucial are these "tests" in determining whether or not you decide to pursue a friendship? Think about the ways in which you "test" yourself. Are the criteria you use for yourself the same as those you use for others? If not, what are the differences?

2. **Synthesize.** If you were asked to rate people on an intelligence scale of your own making, what criteria would you use, and how would you make your decision? What roles would such factors as memory, emotional maturity, creativity, morality, and intuition play in formulating your intelligence scale? How would you "test" for these factors?

3. **Synthesize.** One criticism of many tests is that they favor one particular segment of the population: usually white, middle- and upper-class, well-educated individuals. Is it possible to design a test that is truly objective, a test that favors no one group over another? What types of factors would you need to consider in the design of the test? How would you assess its reliability? Its validity? Assume you have been asked to design a test to measure athletic ability. How would you answer each of these questions?

4. **Evaluate.** Tests are widely used in education to assess student's intelligence and to predict future academic success. But only a small number of tests have been used to predict how happy people will be with their lives or how successful they will be in their careers. Explain why you think this may be the case. Are there certain things that testing cannot access or predict? Think of several examples.

APPLYING KNOWLEDGE

1. Can intelligence be learned? Try the following with two groups of subjects. For one group, give a series of problems like the following example: "Is this statement true or false? If gyuks are jogins and kuulls are jogins, then gyuks are kuulls." For the other group, give the same instructions, but also explain the first example by translating gyuks, jogins, and kuulls as cats, animals, and dogs. Then the statement will read, "If cats are animals and dogs are animals, then cats are dogs." The statement is obviously false. You can make up other examples, like "If some chairs are made of wood, and some tables are made of wood, then chairs are tables." Experiment with a variety of these statements. Make some true and some false. Compare the results of the two groups. This is a question from an intelligence test. Can people learn to improve their scores on intelligence tests? Explain your answer.

2. Do you believe that test-taking strategies can make a major difference in how well a student performs on a test? Develop a ten-minute presentation on how to improve your test-taking skills. Give the presentation to your class. Be sure to include the following issues: how to study more effectively; how to reduce test anxiety; and how to take the test itself. How will you know if your course has been successful? Suggest different methods for assessing the success of your presentation.

3. Ask one of your academic teachers if you can spend some time after class talking about how he or she makes up a test. How does the teacher decide the number and type of questions? Does he or she prefer objective or subjective questions? Does the teacher consider the validity or reliability of the test? How is the test scored? Are the tests ever graded on a curve?

4. Choose several adults you know—they may be relatives, teachers, or acquaintances. Interview them about the types of tests they have taken in their lives. Classify the various types of tests (e.g., intelligence, personality, job-related). Ask whether they considered the test(s) fair. How do they feel about tests in general? After talking with several adults, present your findings to the class. Lead a discussion about whether we rely too much on testing in our society.

5. Suppose you were asked to select the best person to be your teacher from among a group of applicants for the job. How would you go about making the selection? Devise a situational test to use in your assessment. What behaviors would you most want to evaluate in the applicants? Involve your classmates in your development of the situational test.

6. Imagine that you work for an insurance company and are trying to find out how likely it is for people of different ages to be involved in accidents. What criterion do you use? The number of accidents per year? Accidents per thousand miles of driving? Discuss what is right or wrong with these and other criteria.

7. Call or write for one of the questionnaires available from a computer dating service (they usually place advertisements in the classified sections of newspapers). Fill out or just look over the questionnaire. What general categories do the questions seem to fall into? What does the questionnaire seek to measure? Do you think it might be a useful way to obtain meaningful information about people?

ANALYZING VIEWPOINTS

1. Intelligence tests, such as the SAT, are supposed to measure a student's abilities gained over a lifetime of schooling. Many students, however, take advantage of one of the SAT preparatory courses that help students prepare for the test.

These courses often "guarantee" higher scores for participating students. Because these courses often cost a good deal of money, not every student is able to take advantage of them. Are these SAT prep courses fair? Should they be allowed? Write an essay debating each side of the issue. Be sure to address the issue of how these courses affect the validity of the SAT test.

2. Psychological testing has been considered an invasion of privacy by some people. Others maintain that psychological tests are an important means of gathering information. Write an essay that describes the pros and cons concerning the use of psychological testing.

3. In some cultures, people are assigned to jobs and provided educational opportunities based on their scores on IQ tests. Develop a list of the pros and cons of using IQ scores for job assignment and educational placement.

BEYOND THE CLASSROOM

1. Call a local business and set up an appointment with someone who hires new employees, such as a member of the personnel department or the owner of a small business. Tell the person you see that you are doing a project for a psychology class, and you would like to find out more about the use of tests in hiring. Find out if tests are used and, if so, what kinds of information the tests provide. Present your findings to the class.

2. Invite a representative from your school guidance or counseling office to talk to the class about the tests used to measure people's interests or abilities. Ask him or her to explain what different tests are used in your school and how they are used. Suggest that the speaker bring samples of different types of tests to circulate among students.

UNIT 5

Adjustment and Breakdown

CHAPTER 13

Stress and Conflict

Key Terms:

anger
anxiety
approach-approach conflict
approach-avoidance conflict
avoidance-avoidance conflict
biofeedback
conflict situation
cognitive appraisal
cognitive preparation
denial
depressant
distress
double approach-avoidance conflict
eustress
fear
frustration
intellectualization
learned helplessness
meditation
social support
stress
stressor
stress reaction
progressive relaxation

Roger Leary, an ambitious high school junior, fails his final exam in French; he is terrified that his chances of getting into college have been ruined, and a day or two later he develops an unsightly rash. Janet Olson, Roger's classmate, learns that her parents cannot afford to pay her tuition for her freshman year of college; her friends wonder why she has suddenly become so bad-tempered. Angela Ferris gets her first leading role in a high school play; while running to call her boyfriend, she realizes that she cannot remember his phone number. Roger, Janet, and Angela may all suffer from **stress**.

What exactly is stress? There are many definitions, and even researchers in the field use the term in several ways. To some experts, stress is an *event* that produces tension or worry—failing a final exam, for instance. Others describe it as a person's physical or psychological *response* to such an event. Still other researchers regard stress as a person's *perception* of the event: a perceived difference between a demand placed upon a person and his or her ability to handle it or previous experience in coping with it (Mechanic, 1974; Wild and Hanes, 1976). This is the definition we shall use in this chapter—that is, we shall use the term stress to refer to a person's perception of his or her inability to cope with a certain tense event or situation.

To refer to the stress-producing event or situation, we shall use the term **stressor,** which is widely used in the field. It is important to note that an event that is a stressor for one person may not be for another. For example, traveling in an airplane may be a stressor for someone who has never flown, but not for a flight attendant. To discuss the body's response to a stressor, we shall use the term **stress reaction.**

Objectives:

After studying this chapter, you should be able to

- give examples of the psychological, physica , and behavioral reactions to stress.
- discuss research related to coping with stress.

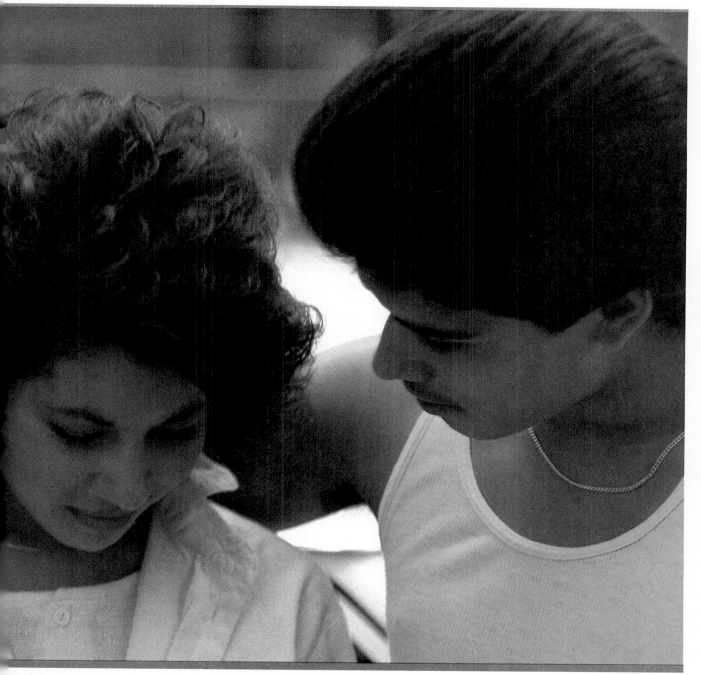

Figure 13.1 Stress is our perception of an inability to cope with a difficult situation or event—a serious fight for instance.

Many people think of stress only as a condition to be avoided. However, Hans Selye, the dean of stress researchers, has distinguished between two types of stress: negative stress, or **distress,** which stems from acute anxiety or pressure and can take a harsh toll on the mind and body; and positive stress, or **eustress,** which results from the strivings and challenges that are the spice of life (Selye and Cherry, 1978).

Stress, then, is a normal—even essential—part of life that goes hand in hand with working toward any goal or facing any challenge. In fact, as athletes gearing up for a game, executives meeting a deadline, and students cramming for an exam can testify, stress can spur us on to greater effectiveness and achievement. And whether we like it or not, we cannot escape stress; "complete freedom from stress," notes Selye (1974), "is death." But we can learn to cope with stress, so that it makes our lives interesting without overwhelming us.

Conflict Situations

In our daily lives, we often have to make difficult decisions between two or more options—for example, going to a movie with friends or staying home to study for tomorrow's exam. These alternatives tend to result from conflicting motives—say, the desire to socialize versus the desire to do well in school—and they are a major source of stress. Psychologists call these dilemmas **conflict situations** and divide them into four broad categories.

In an **approach-approach conflict,** the individual must choose between *two attractive alternatives.* For example, a high school senior has been accepted at two excellent colleges, and she must decide which one to attend. Such a conflict is generally easy to resolve. The student in this situation will find some reason to attend one college rather than the other—perhaps better climate or more courses in her intended major field. An approach-approach conflict normally does not produce a great deal of stress, since both choices are satisfying.

An **avoidance-avoidance conflict** occurs when an individual confronts *two unattractive alternatives.* Consider the case of a college graduate who has been unable to find a job after many months of searching. He is finally offered a position that has no future and does not pay well. Should he accept it, or should he continue to look for something better? Either course of action will be frustrating, and there is usually a high level of indecision and stress. The young man in this example may decide that one option is "the lesser of two evils," or he may try to escape the decision; for instance, he may register with a temporary-employment agency until he gets the "right" job, or he may apply to graduate school.

An individual who wants to do something but fears it at the same time is experiencing an **approach-avoidance conflict.** For example, a man wants to ask for a raise, but he is afraid he will be fired if he does. In cases like this, the degree of stress depends on the intensity of the desire or of the perceived threat. Resolution of this type of conflict is often very difficult and generally depends on the person's finding added reasons to choose one alternative over the other. The man in this example may learn that his boss thinks his work has been excellent, so he feels there is little risk of being fired if he asks for more money.

Probably the most common conflict situation is a **double approach-avoidance conflict,** in which the individual must choose between *two or more alternatives, each of which has attractive and unattractive aspects.* To use a simple illustration, **a** young woman working in Chicago cannot decide whether to spend her vacation in Paris or at her parents' home in North Carolina. She has never been to Paris, but the air fare and hotel bills will be more than she can really afford. Visiting her parents will be inexpensive and relaxing, but not very exciting. As in an approach-avoidance conflict, the degree of stress generated depends on the intensity of the attractions and repulsions. A double approach-avoidance conflict may be resolved in one of three ways: (1) finding new factors that make one option preferable—the young woman may hear about a reduced air fare to Paris; (2) finding a third alternative—she may decide to go to Quebec, which is closer and less expensive than Paris but still French in character; (3) choosing one of the alternatives in order to stop having to worry about the problem. In this last case, the person usually rationalizes his or her choice by emphasizing its good points and downplaying its drawbacks as well as the advantages of the other option; thus, the young woman may rationalize her decision to go to Paris by emphasizing that the trip will probably cost even more next year.

Life Changes

Among the most important sources of stress are major life changes—marriage, serious illness, a new job, moving away, and death in the family, for example. Common to most of these events is the separation of an individual from familiar friends, relations, or colleagues. Even marriage may involve breaking free from many longstanding ties.

Many stress researchers have concentrated on these life changes to determine how much stress they are likely to cause. One study (Thoits, 1978) differentiated between "isolating" events—death, divorce, and loss of job, for example—and "integrating" events, such as marriage, a new job, or birth of a child. It also analyzed events that involve a gain or a loss of prestige. This study found that isolating events and those that reduce prestige lead to higher levels of distress among all groups of people.

Two of the foremost life-change researchers are Thomas H. Holmes and Richard H. Rahe (1967), who developed a scale to measure the effects of forty-three common events, ranging from the death of a spouse to going on a vacation. Holmes and Rahe asked a cross-section of the population to rate each of these events on a scale of 1 to 100, with marriage randomly assigned a value of 50, on the basis of how much adjustment the event required. The figures they obtained form the basis of their Social Readjustment Rating Scale, which is shown in Table 13.1.

It is important to note that one life change can trigger others, thus greatly increasing the level of stress. For example, marriage (50 units) may be accompanied by a change in financial status (38 units), a change in living conditions (25 units), revision of personal habits (24 units), and a change in residence (20 units)—a combined total of 157 units.

Life changes are among the most important sources of stress.

Table 13.1 / Social Readjustment Rating Scale

Rank	Life Event	Mean Value
1	Death of spouse	100
2	Divorce	73
3	Marital separation	65
4	Jail term	63
5	Death of close family member	63
6	Personal injury or illness	53
7	Marriage	50
8	Fired at work	47
9	Marital reconciliation	45
10	Retirement	45
11	Change in health of family member	44
12	Pregnancy	40
13	Sex difficulties	39
14	Gain of new family member	39
15	Business readjustment	39
16	Change in financial state	38
17	Death of close friend	37
18	Change to different line of work	36
19	Change in number of arguments with spouse	35
20	Mortgage over $10,000	31
21	Foreclosure of mortgage or loan	30
22	Change in responsibilities at work	29
23	Son or daughter leaving home	29
24	Trouble with in-laws	29
25	Outstanding personal achievement	28
26	Wife begin or stop work	26
27	Begin or end school	26
28	Change in living conditions	25
29	Revision of personal habits	24
30	Trouble with boss	23
31	Change in work hours or conditions	20
32	Change in residence	20
33	Change in schools	20
34	Change in recreation	19
35	Change in church activities	19
36	Change in social activities	18
37	Mortgage or loans less than $10,000	17
38	Change in sleeping habits	16
39	Change in number of family get-togethers	15
40	Change in eating habits	15
41	Vacation	13
42	Christmas	12
43	Minor violations of the law	11

Reprinted with permission from T. H. Holmes and R. H. Rahe, "The Social Readjustment Rating Scale," *Journal of Psychosomatic Research*, 1967, Table 3, p. 216. © 1967, Pergamon Press Ltd.

Rahe (1975) administered this scale to thousands of naval officers and enlisted men and found that the higher a man's score, the more likely he was to become ill. Men with scores below 150 tended to remain healthy, while about 70 percent of those with scores over 300 became sick. Researchers have since given the Holmes-Rahe scale to other groups of people and have found a relationship between high scores and a number of diseases.

The value assigned to a life change on the Holmes-Rahe scale is only a general indicator of its relative impact; it will not be true for every individual. Liem and Liem (1976) found that other factors can modify the effects of life-change stressors. In their study, psychological disturbances were lower among subjects who felt close to friends and received emotional support from them; physical symptoms were lower among subjects who had more money.

Some investigators (Hough, Fairbanks, and Garcia, 1976) have questioned the accuracy of the Holmes-Rahe scale. They point out that it examines only a small percentage of the enormous number of stressors and that it does not take into account cultural differences in what are regarded as stressors. Nevertheless, in spite of these problems and variations in individual stress reactions, the Holmes-Rahe scale is a useful guideline for measuring stress.

Figure 13.2
The birth of a child is a happy event, but it also creates stress for the baby's parents and siblings.

Work

Most people spend more time at work than they do at any other activity. Not surprisingly, then, work can be a prime source of stress, and there is a great deal of evidence to show that on-the-job stress affects the physical and mental health of many employees. The statistics are staggering: one study (Cooper and Marshall, 1976) estimated that cardiovascular disease, which is often linked to stress, accounts for 12 percent of worker absenteeism in the United States and adds up to an average loss of about $4 billion a year. Other physical and mental health problems that often stem from stress—migraine headaches, for example—resulted in a loss of 22.8 million work days in just one year.

What causes stress on the job? Researchers have identified more than forty factors that can be occupational stressors. We can group these factors into seven general categories.

1. *The nature of the job.* A worker may suffer stress reactions as a result of *working conditions* (temperature, humidity, noise, vibration, and lighting, for example) or *work overload* (a workload that is too heavy or too difficult); *underload* (too little work) can also be a stressor.
2. *Role in the organization.* An employee may suffer from *role ambiguity* or *role conflict*. Role ambiguity arises when the worker is unclear about what is expected of him or her. Role conflict occurs when the job demands that the worker do things that (a) he or she dislikes or disapproves of or (b) he or she thinks are beyond the scope of the job description. *Responsibility for other people* is another important role-related stressor. People in "white-collar" (managerial and professional) positions seem most likely to be victims of this type of stress.

Figure 13.3
Feeling responsible for other people is one source of on-the-job stress. In a hospital, where one wrong decision could mean the difference between life and death, this particular stressor may affect many employees.

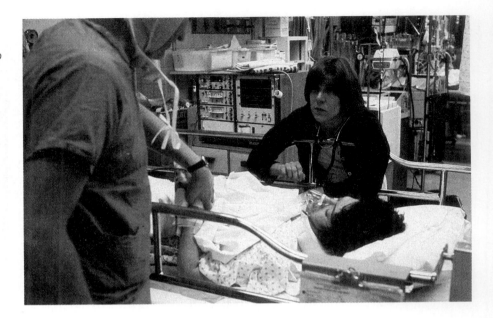

3. *Interpersonal relationships.* Research suggests that poor relationships between a worker and his or her superiors, subordinates, and colleagues may be stressful.

4. *Career development.* For many workers, especially those in the early phase of their careers, the desire to advance rapidly may be a stressor. For other workers, usually older ones, fear and frustration can result when they reach a "career ceiling," the point at which they can no longer advance within the organization.

5. *Organizational structure and climate.* An organization that does not encourage a sense of belonging, worker participation in decision making, and good communication within its ranks is likely to generate stress. Margolis *et al.* (1974) found that lack of participation is the most important and consistent signal of on-the-job stress and subsequent stress reactions.

6. *Family and outside activities.* The worker's life away from the job can cause stress on the job. Burke and Weir (1977) found that a close, supportive marriage—in which an employee can informally discuss job problems with his or her spouse—is likely to prevent or reduce on-the-job stress and increase both occupational and marital satisfaction. In contrast, a less successful marriage can intensify, if not create, stress at work.

7. *Miscellaneous.* As we have seen, life changes can be significant stressors. Many life changes are work-related—a change of jobs, unemployment, and retirement, for example (Cooper and Payne, 1979).

Everyday Sources of Stress

Some stressors—notably the life changes we have discussed—are major events. However, there are many minor sources of stress that we must confront and cope with either on an everyday basis (rush-hour traffic, for example) or only once in a while (say, running out of gas).

Frustration.   **Frustration** is a common source of everyday stress. It is the feeling of bafflement or disappointment that results when a person's progress toward a goal is blocked. It has a wide variety of causes—delays (a long checkout line at the supermarket), lack of resources (not enough money to buy a new record or clothes), physical limitations (running for a bus and missing it), accidents (breaking a glass), other people (someone breaks a date at the last minute), or institutional regulations (an overdue fine for returning a library book a day late).

Frustration is a daily occurrence; in fact, it would be possible for *all* of the examples given above to happen to one person in one day. Frustration is especially stressful when we feel that it has been caused by unreasonable circumstances (say, saving just enough money to buy a certain Father's Day present, only to learn that the store has raised its prices) or when the circumstances are unexpected. Constant frustration has been shown to cause stress reactions such as aggression, fantasy, and withdrawal.

Environmental Stressors.   As we have seen, environmental conditions such as noise may cause stress on the job, and these factors can have similar effects on the public at large. In fact, surveys have shown that Americans regard noise as one of the foremost irritants in their lives. Noise is particularly aggravating when it is loud, irregular, or uncontrollable. Constant exposure to unpleasant noise levels can lead to hearing loss and can interfere with learning. One study, for example, showed that children who lived in the lower, noisier floors of an apartment house built over a highway had a lower reading ability than did children living in the upper, quieter floors (Cohen *et al.*, 1973).

It has long been assumed that crowding is an environmental stressor, and indeed most people dislike certain high-density situations and can feel stress when other people get too close. Recent research on the long-term effects of crowding indicates, however, that its negative impact may have been overestimated.

For one thing, there is a positive side to crowding. Imagine, for example, that you and a friend go to a football game and find you are the only spectators in the stadium. You would probably feel quite peculiar, since we expect—and enjoy—the excitement of a cheering crowd in such a situation. The relationship between the actual density of a crowd and a person's feeling unpleasantly crowded is complex (Stokols, 1972). It depends largely on our ability to maintain a degree of privacy and distance from others. You may enjoy being part of a crowd at a rock concert, for example, but you may hate it when everyone shoves to get out.

Jonathan Freedman (1975) has concluded that the effects of crowding depend on the situation. If the situation is pleasant, crowding makes people feel better; if the situation is unpleasant, crowding makes them feel worse. In other words, being packed together *intensifies* people's reactions, but it does not *create* them.

Although there is overcrowding in many urban areas where there is also a high crime rate, we cannot state that crowding causes crime; other factors may be responsible. In fact, our modern urban life style is an extremely important stressor.

PSYCHOLOGY UPDATE

Hassles and Uplifts. In addition to the impact that major stressful events such as a divorce or death in the family can have, psychologists have studied the effects that relatively minor, day-to-day stressors can have on health. These more common stressors are called *hassles*. Examples of hassles include losing your car keys, being caught in a crowded elevator with a smoker, or being late for work because you were stuck in a traffic jam. Research has found a connection between hassles and health problems. It may be that hassles gradually weaken the body's defense system, making it harder to fight off potential health problems.

It has also been suggested that small, positive events—called *uplifts*—can protect against stress. Uplifts are things that make a person feel good, such as winning a few dollars in a lottery or doing well on an exam. Some psychologists claim that uplifts can have the opposite effect of hassles—they can reduce stress and protect a person's health.

The United States is now an urban nation, and more than one-half of our population lives on only 1 percent of the land. Not only are our cities crowded, but they also are nuclei of noise, soot, traffic, crime, and fear—all of which are stressors. Stanley Milgram (1970) describes urban living as "stimulus overload"; the individual is barraged by more inputs than he or she can deal with. As a result, Milgram says, people in cities tend to deal with each other more quickly, they ignore stimuli that do not directly concern them (a blind person trying to cross a busy street, for example), and they identify others only as roles (the tailor who does not have your suit ready, rather than Mr. Jones whose wife was rushed to the hospital last night). The result of these behaviors is a fast-paced, alienating, impersonal, and lonely environment. A steady push to achieve, another stressor, often stems from the pace and pressure of city life.

REACTIONS TO STRESS

A person who encounters a stressor that is intense or prolonged will react to it. There is a wide variety of stress reactions, and their effects range from beneficial to harmful. Many of these responses—physiological ones in particular—are inborn methods that our ancestors probably evolved to cope with stress effectively. And many responses to stress are automatic. Just as the body reacts to a cut by producing new tissue, it has means to heal the wounds of stress—crying, for example.

Coping mechanisms that worked for our remote ancestors are not necessarily successful in our modern technological society. But human beings are often slow to give up anything that is well established. We are more likely to depend solely on these ancient stress responses than to make conscious attempts to modify them or adopt others that we now know are more appropriate to our twentieth-century life style.

The ways in which different people react to stress vary considerably; each person's response is the product of many factors, some of which we shall discuss later in this section. Stress reactions may be physical, psychological, or behavioral, but these categories are not clear-cut. The human body is a *holistic* (integrated) organism; our physical well-being affects how we think and behave, poor mental health can trigger physical illness, and so on.

Regardless of the stressor, the body reacts with immediate arousal. The adrenal glands are stimulated to produce (a) hormones that increase the amount of blood sugar for extra energy and (b) adrenalin, which causes rapid heartbeat and breathing and enables the body to use energy more quickly. These responses are designed to prepare a person for self-defense. However, if stress persists for a long time, the body's resources are used up. The person becomes exhausted and, in extreme cases, dies.

Selye (1956) has identified three stages in the body's stress reaction: alarm, resistance, and exhaustion. In the *alarm* stage, the body mobilizes its "fight-or-flight" defenses: heartbeat and breathing quicken, muscles tense, the pupils dilate, and hormones that sustain these reactions are secreted. The person becomes exceptionally alert and sensitive to stimuli in

b

c

a

d

Figure 13.4
Our reactions to various events depend on our own personalities and attitudes as well as on the severity of the event itself. The man coping with the terminal illness of a loved one, the family facing the destruction of their home, the father facing a financial crisis at home, and the high school senior waiting for her college admissions interview are all experiencing various levels of stress.

the environment and tries to keep a firm grip on his or her emotions. For example, a hiker who confronts a rattlesnake on a mountain trail freezes in his tracks, is suddenly aware of every sound around him, and tries not to panic. If the alarm reaction is insufficient to deal with the stressor, the person may develop symptoms such as anxiety or gastrointestinal disturbance.

In the *resistance* stage, the person often finds means to cope with the stressor and to ward off, superficially at least, adverse reactions. Thus an airline passenger who recovers from the shock and frustration of losing her luggage may tell herself to keep calm when reporting its disappearance to airline officials, calling her insurance company, and so on. At this stage, the person may suffer psychosomatic symptoms, which result from strain that he or she pretends is nonexistent.

If exposure to the stressor continues, the individual reaches the stage of *exhaustion*. At this point, the adrenal and other glands involved in the "fight-or-flight" response have been taxed to their limit and become unable to secrete hormones. The individual reaches the breaking point: he or she becomes exhausted and disoriented and may develop delusions—of persecution, for example—in an effort to retain some type of coping strategy. A classic example of exhaustion is a mother who sits in the ruins of a bombed-out house rocking a dead baby as if nothing has happened. Soldiers in this condition have been known to wander aimlessly or fall asleep under fire (Toffler, 1970: 344–346).

Let us now examine some of the major psychological, behavioral, and physical reactions to stress. We shall discuss both short-term and long-term responses in each category.

Figure 13.5
A soldier subjected to extreme and prolonged stress may reach the stage that Hans Selye calls exhaustion and be unable to think clearly or act decisively.

Psychological Reactions

Short-term Reactions.   Short-term psychological stress reactions may be either emotional or cognitive. The most common response to a sudden and powerful stressor is **anxiety,** which is a feeling of imminent but unclear threat. An employee whose boss passes by in the hall without saying hello may develop anxiety about her future on the job. **Anger** is likely to result from frustration. A college student who does not make the lacrosse team may fly into a rage when he puts his favorite record on the turntable and it skips. **Fear** is usually the reaction when a stressor involves real danger—a fire, for example. Fear directs the individual to withdraw or flee, but in severe cases he or she may panic or freeze and be unable to act. Common examples of short-term emotional stress reactions are overreacting to minor irritations, getting no joy from the daily pleasures of life, feeling hemmed in, and doubting one's own abilities.

Cognitive reactions include difficulty in concentrating or thinking clearly. A student who must give an oral presentation may worry about it but find himself unable to sit down and prepare for it. Another student wants to visit her father at work to surprise him with the news that she has been admitted to her first-choice college, but cannot recall where his office is. Another type of cognitive stress reaction is unjustified suspicion or distrust of others.

Long-term Reactions.   Prolonged stress, in combination with other factors, affects mental health. It does not necessarily cause mental illness, but it may contribute to the severity of mental illness. There is an increased likelihood of psychiatric disorder following a major life change, for example. Among attempted suicides, depressives, schizophrenics, and neurotics there seems to be quite a definite link between stress and subsequent symptoms.

Behavioral Reactions

Short-term Reactions.   There are many short-term behavioral changes that result from stress. A person may develop nervous habits (trembling or pacing, for example), gulp meals, smoke or drink more, or feel tired for no reason. There may be changes in his or her posture. He or she may temporarily lose interest in eating, grooming, bathing, and so on.

Some behavioral reactions are positive, however. In a tornado, for example, some people will risk their lives to help others. Such stressors often create attitudes of cooperation that override individual differences and disagreements.

Escape is another behavioral stress reaction, and it is often the best way to deal with frustration. For example, a woman who is on a bus that is caught in snarled traffic may get off and walk to her destination.

Long-term Reactions.   While many people can endure great amounts of stress without marked behavioral responses, others may be seriously affected. Severe stress can be significant to the development of escapist personality styles—alcoholism, chronic unemployment, and attempted suicide, for example. It has also been noted as a contributing cause of aggressive personalities, delinquency, and criminal behavior. And people with high scores on the Holmes-Rahe scale appear to be more accident-prone than average.

Physical Reactions

Short-term Reactions.   As we have mentioned, the physiological "fight-or-flight" response—accelerated heart rate and so on—is the body's immediate reaction to stress. This response is geared to prepare human beings to fight or run from an enemy such as a savage animal or a band of warriors, and it was probably useful earlier in human history. But we cannot deal with most modern stressors—a financial problem, for instance—in this manner, and physical responses to stress are now generally inappropriate. In fact, prolonged physical arousal can cause health problems including difficulty in breathing, insomnia, migraine headaches, urinary and bowel irregularities, muscle aches, sweating, and dryness of mouth.

Research is confirming that stress is a major cause of disease today.

Long-term Reactions.   The evidence is mounting up to confirm that stress is a major cause of illness today. We have already discussed the study by Rahe (1975), which found that most subjects who scored 150 or less on the Holmes-Rahe scale reported good health for the following year, while 70 percent of those with scores over 300 became sick. And one estimate (Schmale, 1972) holds that up to 80 percent of all disease today may have its origin in stress.

Emotional stress is very clearly related to such illnesses as peptic ulcers, hypertension, certain kinds of arthritis, asthma, and heart disease. Those who work in high-stress occupations may pay a high price. Air-traffic controllers, for example, who spend their days juggling the lives of hundreds of people on air routes where a minor error can mean mass death, are said to suffer from the highest incidence of peptic ulcers of any professional group (Cobb and Rose, 1973). Similarly, a student may come down with flu on the day before an important exam, or a director may have an asthma attack on the opening night of a play.

Stress can be at least partly responsible for almost *any* disease, as shown by the scope of illnesses associated with high Holmes-Rahe scores. And stress can contribute to disease in several ways. Sometimes it can be the direct cause of illness; a migraine headache, for example, is usually a physical reaction to stress. Stress may also contribute to illness indirectly. It may reduce our resistance to infectious disease by tampering with the immune defense system. Furthermore, stress can lower our resistance to disease if we react by neglecting our diet, not exercising, or smoking or drinking too much.

Animal studies suggest that psychological stress may contribute to some forms of cancer. One study involved a group of mice known to be vulnerable to cancer. Some of the mice were kept for 400 days in housing that exposed them to stressful noises made by people and animals. Other mice were kept in quieter housing. At the end of the period, 92 percent of the high-stress mice had developed cancer compared with only 7 percent of the low-stress animals (Anderson, 1982).

Some people smoke in order to reduce tension, but smoking increases their risk of lung and mouth cancer. Having any form of cancer is in itself a highly stressful occurrence. The degree to which a person is able to cope with this stress can be an important factor in his or her recovery (Taylor, 1983).

Factors Influencing Reactions to Stress

Personality Differences.   In some cases, the individual's personality may make him or her more vulnerable to stress. For example, two researchers have suggested that persons who exhibit a behavior pattern they call "Type A" are very likely to have coronary artery disease, often followed by heart attacks, in their thirties and forties. Those who do not have this pattern (Type B people) almost never have heart attacks before the age of seventy (Friedman and Rosenman, 1974).

The Type A person's body is in a chronic state of stress, with an almost constant flow of adrenalin into the bloodstream. This adrenalin apparently interacts with cholesterol or other chemical agents to block the coronary arteries, which lead to the heart. (It may be that high levels of adrenalin prevent the normal chemical breakdown of cholesterol in the blood.)

Type A people are always prepared for fight or flight. They have a great deal of "free-floating" hostility—that is, anger that has no real object or focus. They are extremely irritable, and one of the things that irritates Type A people most is delay of any kind. They become impatient waiting in line, always move and eat rapidly, often try to do two or three things at once (such as reading while eating), and feel guilty when they aren't doing *something.* They are also extremely competitive. In short, Type A people are always struggling—with time, other people, or both. Note that we have been describing an extreme version of the Type A personality. Most people respond to the world with Type A behavior at some times, but are not in a constant state of stress. According to Friedman and Rosenman, about half of the American white male population exhibits enough Type A behavior to bring on the high adrenalin and cholesterol levels that precede coronary disease.

Ray Rosenman has noted that modern society generally favors those who can achieve rapidly and aggressively; it therefore encourages Type A behavior. Thus, he believes, Type A behavior results from the interplay between personality and environmental conditions (Rosenman, in Dembroski, 1978).

Another personality trait that can affect the strength of a stress reaction is emotional expressiveness. Some recent research suggests that people who neither express nor admit to strong feelings of despair, depression, and anger are more likely to develop cancer than those who can give vent to their emotions. One study of cancer victims, for example, found that only 30 percent confessed to feeling discouraged about the future, even though many of these patients had tumors that were incurable (Plumb and Holland, 1977). However, the findings in this area have been mixed; some

MORE about . . .

Stress and Natural Disasters. A very stressful life event was experienced by the victims of the 1980 Mount Saint Helens volcanic eruption in the state of Washington.

One study looked at the effects of the eruption on the residents of Othello, Washington. The researchers compared data gathered from community records for a six-month period after the disaster with the same time the previous year. The records indicated large increases in alcohol abuse, domestic violence, and physical illnesses. The death rate increased by nearly 19 percent.

The long-lasting impact of the Mount Saint Helens disaster can be seen from the results of a three-year study that compared the residents of Castle Rock, Washington, which had been greatly affected by the volcano, with those living in another town that was not affected by the disaster. The adult residents of Castle Rock were nearly twelve times as likely to suffer from a psychiatric disorder. Many of the Castle Rock residents were suffering from posttraumatic stress, depression, and severe anxiety.

Are You Type A?

Are you high-strung, tense, always concerned about time? Then you might have a Type A personality. To find out for sure, ask yourself the following questions. Your answers will tell you whether you're giving your heart a hard time.

- Are you continually aware of time? Type A people live by the clock and measure their day in terms of how much they accomplish each minute.
- Are you always in a rush? Type A people do everything very quickly. They eat, move, walk, and talk at a speeded-up pace.
- Do you lose your patience when things take too long? Type A people get outraged when a sales clerk spends an extra minute ringing up a sale.
- Do you always try to do more than one thing at the same time? Type A people feel that one of the best ways to get more accomplished is to do two or more things at once.
- Do you tend to use nervous gestures to emphasize your point? Type A people express their tension by clenching their fists, pointing their fingers, and banging on the desk.
- Do you evaluate your life in terms of how much you accomplish rather than what you accomplish? Type A people emphasize such quantitative measures as the number of A's they got in school and the number of sales they made during the month.

If you answered yes to most of these questions, it may be time to slow down. Not because slower is better, but because slower is less taxing on your heart.

For more details, see Meyer Friedman and Ray Rosenman, *Type A Behavior and Your Heart.* New York: Knopf, 1974.

studies have found no strong connection between cancer and personality. The link remains an intriguing possibility that warrants further research.

Perceived Control over Stressors. In the late 1950s, psychologist Joseph Brady and his colleagues (1958) published the results of their classic (but now questioned) experiment on the effects of controlling stressful events. They linked two monkeys to a machine that gave them an equal number of shocks. One could prevent the shocks by pushing a lever and the other could not (Figure 13.6). The monkey who could control the shocks—later named the "executive monkey"—developed ulcers. Brady theorized that constant worry about when to press the lever produced higher levels of stress for the executive monkey than inability to act did for the powerless one.

Later attempts to achieve similar results with other animals were not successful. According to J. M. Weiss (1972), when Brady's research team

Figure 13.6
The "executive monkey" experiment. The monkey at the left, which could prevent shocks by pushing a lever, was the one that developed ulcers. The results of this study could not be duplicated, however. The accepted view today is that control over stressors helps to *prevent* physical disorders.

set up the original study, there was a bias in the selection of subjects. The monkeys who were selected to be the "executive monkeys" had shown themselves to be more likely to push the lever than the monkeys who were selected for the no-control situation. Thus, these monkeys may have been more reactive and hence possibly more prone to develop ulcers.

The accepted view today is that physical disorders are more likely when we do *not* have control over stressors. Most evidence to support this theory comes from experiments on animals. Weiss (1972), for example, gave two groups of rats identical electric shocks. In one group, a rat could avoid the shock by touching its nose to a panel; the other group had no control over the shocks. The group that could regulate the shocks developed far fewer ulcers than those that could not.

Subsequent experiments showed that feedback is also an important factor. Animals that responded to avoid shock and then heard a tone to signal that they had done the "right" thing suffered fewer ulcers than those that responded to avoid the shock but were given no feedback.

Weiss (1971) found that lack of feedback can harm human beings as well. His research showed that people develop ulcers when they have to make a very great many responses but receive no feedback about their effectiveness. This lack of feedback is a factor in role ambiguity, which we discussed earlier in the chapter.

Another study that used human subjects (Hokanson *et al.,* 1963) punished errors on cognitive tasks with mild electric shocks. Subjects who

Stress on the Home Front. War creates tremendous stresses not only on soldiers in the field, but also on loved ones back home. The Persian Gulf war was particularly stressful on military families because more than 25,000 of the armed forces sent to Saudi Arabia were women.

The women soldiers were forced to leave their children behind with their husbands, parents, or other family members. Husbands had to take leave of absence from their jobs or arrange for day care for their children. Many children of troops in the Gulf suffered from nightmares and loss of appetite.

One way that the husbands and wives of combat troops coped with wartime stresses was to form support groups among themselves so they could talk about their problems and fears. Military bases offered family members various kinds of help, such as psychological counseling and financial support. Schools with large numbers of military children also provided counseling and special programs to help students cope.

were allowed to take breaks when they wanted to showed less increase in blood pressure than did those who were assigned times for breaks. Such research supports the conclusion that we respond to a stressor more intensely when we cannot control it.

Social Support. Sidney Cobb (1976) has defined **social support** as information that leads someone to believe that he or she is cared for, loved, respected, and part of a network of communication and mutual obligation. He has found that social support can reduce both the likelihood and the severity of stress-related diseases.

Cobb's conclusion has been backed up by many other studies. A study of pregnant women (Nuckolls, Cassel, and Kaplan, 1972), for example, noted that 91 percent of those with high Holmes-Rahe scores and low social support experienced complications in pregnancy, as compared with only 33 percent of those with high Holmes-Rahe scores and high social support. (In fact, it is interesting to note that the high-stress and high-support group suffered fewer complications than did women who reported *low* Holmes-Rahe scores.) Another research team (Webb and Collette, 1975) showed that people who live alone are more likely to suffer serious illness or behavioral disorders due to stress than are people who live in families. As mentioned in Chapter 8, parents who physically abuse their children tend to be socially isolated. During periods of stress, they do not have a network of friends, co-workers, or church members to turn to. One of the preventive approaches to treating child abuse is to develop social support groups for people under financial, emotional, or psychological stress. In some communities, hot lines and volunteer family aides are available.

Some sources of social support can be especially helpful. One study of male blue-collar workers (Wells, 1977) reported that social support from wives and supervisors counteracted the health consequences of stress more effectively than did support from co-workers, friends, or relatives.

Amount of Stress. Throughout this chapter, we have emphasized that high amounts of stress can have serious effects on physical and mental health. However, as we noted earlier, *low* stress at work—underload—may trigger similar reactions. One group of researchers (Caplan *et al.*, 1975) studied more than 2,000 men in many different occupations. They found that as on-the-job boredom increases, so does the probability of psychological and physical complaints and illnesses. Assembly-line workers rated their jobs as most boring and suffered the most stress-related disorders. Accountants, engineers, and computer programmers reported average amounts of boredom. Professors and physicians expressed the lowest levels of boredom and had the fewest stress-related health problems.

Another study (Harrison, 1976), however, drew different conclusions. Work overload corresponded to greater job dissatisfaction in all the occupations under consideration. Underload, however, caused discontent mostly among white-collar workers; it had little effect on the job dissatisfaction of assembly-line workers. One possible explanation is that on-the-job gratification is more important to white- than to blue-collar workers, and underload does not allow for much job gratification (House, 1972).

a

b

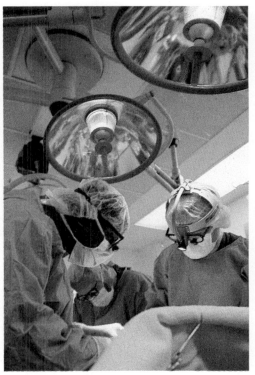

c

Figure 13.7
Low stress and boredom on the job can damage
health as much as high stress can. One study
found that assembly-line workers rated their jobs
as most boring and suffered the most stress-
related disorders. Computer programmers reported average levels of boredom. Physicians noted
the least boredom and had the fewest stress-related complaints.

In spite of these somewhat inconsistent findings, we can basically describe the relationship between stress and health as a bell curve. At both
extremes of the curve—very low and very high stress—illness is most probable. At the center of the curve, a person feels challenged without being
overwhelmed; this is the point at which he or she is most likely to be
healthy and effective.

COPING WITH STRESS

The best overall recommendation for coping with stress is to bring it under
control before it is too late. Richard Rahe and Ransom J. Arthur (1968)
have divided the process by which stress can cause disease into six stages:

1. *Perception of the situation.* The person is aware that something is challenging him or her.
2. *Psychological responses.* The person denies or minimizes the situation or represses its effects.
3. *Physiological responses.* The person undergoes the "fight-or-flight" reaction, which we have discussed.
4. *Protective behavior.* The person tried to deal with the situation.
5. *Signs of illness.* The person begins to act sick—staying home from work or school, for example.
6. *Frank disease.* A doctor confirms the illness, and the person is officially sick.

Rahe and Arthur believe that dealing with stress during the first four stages can generally—and relatively easily—prevent disease. If a person has reached the final two stages, though, the process is hard to stop or reverse.

To break the chain of events that can cause a stress-related disease, it is necessary for a person either to alter his or her awareness of the problem and of the potential consequences or, if stress is unavoidable, to modify its physical and psychological effects. Let us now look at some specific coping strategies that people use to combat stress.

Psychological Coping Strategies

Our interpretation or evaluation of an event—a process psychologists call **cognitive appraisal**—helps to determine its stress impact. Drugs can affect cognitive appraisal. For example, drinking may help to convince a man who has been fired that his troubles are not serious, or that he will enjoy unemployment, or that getting drunk is the best solution for the time being.

We can also try to influence our cognitive appraisals by means of psychological coping strategies, and stress reactions are more likely to occur when these strategies fail. Common coping mechanisms are **denial,** in which a person decides that the event is not really a stressor, and **intellectualization,** in which the person watches the situation from an emotionally detached standpoint.

Both denial and intellectualization can prevent physical reactions to stress. In one study (Lazarus *et al.,* 1965), three groups of subjects viewed a film that showed gruesome accidents at a sawmill. One group was told that the injuries were not real, but were staged by the actors (denial); a second group was advised that they were seeing an educational film about the importance of safety measures (intellectualization); the third group was told nothing. The levels of physical reaction were lower in the first two groups than in the third. Thus, if a person does not evaluate an event or situation as stressful, a stress reaction will not occur.

When a person knows that stress is unavoidable, though, **cognitive preparation** can be the most successful coping strategy. Irving Janis (1958) studied patients before and after surgery—which is a major stressor—to analyze the relationship between fear before the event and coping afterward. He found that patients who expressed a moderate amount of fear recovered most successfully; those who showed extreme fear or little or no fear before surgery did not cope as well following their operations. Janis believes that cognitive preparation, which he terms "the work of worrying," enables a person to rehearse possible outcomes mentally. In this way, he or she is better prepared for whatever does happen than is someone who has used denial or intellectualization beforehand.

Modifying Physical Reactions to Stress

Drugs.   Many people use drugs—both legal and illegal—as a way to reduce stress and the physical symptoms, as well as the tension, boredom, and depression, that accompany it. Physicians often prescribe mild sedatives (Valium, for example) for people who complain of stress. Some of these drugs may indeed relieve stress temporarily, but most do not. In addition, all of these drugs carry a risk of dangerous side effects, including physical dependence. If you must use drugs to cope with stress, do so only as a temporary measure to help you through a crisis. *Do not* use them to deal with normal, everyday stress.

Alcohol is the most widely used and abused drug today. It is a **depressant,** which means that it reduces the activity of the central nervous system. As a result, drinking will reduce tension quickly. However, research (for example, Miller, 1976) has demonstrated that the more often a person drinks to escape stress, the more dependent he or she will become on alcohol. Among chronic alcoholics in particular, drinking may actually *increase* depression or anxiety (Nathan and O'Brien, 1971). Alcoholism is a critical health problem in the United States; the National Institute on Alcohol Abuse and Alcoholism estimates that between nine and ten million adults in America are alcoholics or problem drinkers.

Tobacco is the second most commonly used drug. Many smokers claim that cigarettes relieve various stressors; they will smoke more at work, at parties, or when anxious or nervous. Studies (Silverstein, 1976; Perlick, 1977) indicate that smoking does not reduce anxiety or irritability; *not* smoking, however, tends to aggravate the smoker's stress reaction. Not only are cigarettes useless against stress, but they greatly increase the risk of lung cancer and a host of other major illnesses.

As we saw in Chapter 7, marijuana is a widely used drug, especially among young people. It produces a mild sense of relaxation, but research is still being conducted to determine how serious its side effects are.

Relaxation.   Many techniques of relaxation have been developed specifically to cope with stress. More than half a century ago, Dr. Edmond Jacobson devised a method called **progressive relaxation** to reduce muscle tension. This involves lying down comfortably and tensing and relaxing each major muscle group in turn. Jacobson later added exercises for mental relaxation in which a person conjures up images and then lets them go. **Meditation** is a relaxation technique that has been shown to counteract both physical and psychological responses to stress (see Chapter 7). Experienced meditators quickly reach an alpha-wave mental state identical to that of Stage I sleep and are able to resume their activities feeling refreshed.

Biofeedback.   As Chapter 7 explained, **biofeedback** is a technique for bringing specific body processes—blood pressure and muscle tension, for example—under a person's conscious control. The subject is hooked up to an electronic device that measures the process he or she wants to regulate and plays that process back, in the form of either sounds or visual patterns. This feedback somehow enables many, though not all, people to learn to control various bodily responses. Biofeedback has been used most successfully to train tense people to relax.

Behavioral Coping Strategies

Controlling Stressful Situations.   There are several ways in which we can control our exposure to stressful events and thereby reduce levels of stress. As we have mentioned, escape or withdrawal, when possible, can be an effective coping strategy. A young woman who is not enjoying herself at a party, for example, can leave. When avoiding an event is not practical, controlling its timing may be helpful; you can try to space out stress-producing events so they do not occur at the same time. A couple who are planning to have a baby in the summer, for instance, may postpone looking for a new house until the following year.

Problem Solving.   Sometimes neither avoiding nor spacing events is possible. A high school senior may face a deadline for a college application and an important exam on the same day. In cases like this, problem solving, or confronting the matter head-on, can be the best way to cope. We often regard frustrations or conflicts as problems to be solved; in this way, the situation becomes a positive challenge rather than a negative setback. Problem solving involves a rational analysis of the situation that will lead to an appropriate decision. The student in our example may map out the remaining days to allocate specific times to work on the application and others to study for the test; he may also decide that he can gain more time for these activities by skipping band practice or post-poning a date until the following weekend. Problem solving is a very healthy strategy that tends to sharpen insights and attention to detail and develop flexibility.

Exercise.   Physical exercise is another constructive way to reduce stress. It stimulates and provides an outlet for physical arousal, and it may burn off stress hormones. Continuous rhythmic exercise—running or swim-ming, for example—is not only effective against stress but also ideal for respiratory and cardiovascular fitness. One study of longshoremen (Paffenbarger and Hale, 1975) found that a high level of physical activity serves to protect against heart disease.

Support Groups and Professional Help.   We have discussed the positive role that social support plays in reducing stress. There are groups that operate beyond ordinary personal networks to help people with specific stress-related problems—Alcoholics Anonymous, Weight Watchers,

Figure 13.8
Physical exercise reduces stress, so find a way of introducing a regular exercise program into your schedule. You don't need to become an athlete: this man gets his exercise by walking to and from work every day.

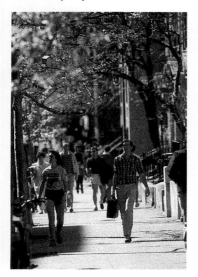

crisis intervention centers, and so on. Professionals such as doctors, ministers, psychologists, and social workers can also be consulted when help is necessary.

Training.   A situation can be stressful because we are unsure of our ability to deal with it; it may be new, unfamiliar, or dangerous. Training to prepare for such a situation can ease the stress. For instance, a student who is nervous about going to a friend's country club because she does not play tennis might take a few tennis lessons. Exposure to moderate stressors in a relatively safe but challenging environment allows a person to gain experience as well as confidence in his or her coping abilities; the Outward Bound program that trains young people in wilderness survival illustrates this strategy.

Improving Interpersonal Skills.   A great deal of the stress we undergo today results from interpersonal relations. Developing skill in dealing with other people—family, friends, co-workers—is thus one of the best ways to manage stress. There are several advantages to being able to interact well with others: increased self-confidence and self-esteem, less chance of loneliness or interpersonal conflict, and development of social support systems.

A Lifelong Challenge

Although we have emphasized the problems and difficulties that stress can cause, we should not forget that stress is not necessarily "bad." As we have seen, too little stress can be as harmful as too much stress under some circumstances.

Throughout our lives, stress is a challenge that we will inevitably and repeatedly encounter. It is thus best to develop a range of coping strategies that we can apply to different situations, and it is important to learn when each strategy is most suitable. Coping strategies that are used inappropriately can actually increase stress.

Some people respond to setbacks in coping by learning *not* to try to cope at all. Psychologists call this condition **learned helplessness** (Seligman, 1975; see Chapter 2). In learned helplessness, a person suffers from an event or situation so severely or so often that he or she comes to believe that it is uncontrollable and that any effort to cope will fail. The person also begins to apply the same attitude to other situations; for example, a man who feels continually frustrated and thwarted on the job may give up trying to cope with difficulties in other areas of his life as well.

We *can* learn to cope if we try. Albert Ellis (1978) sums up perhaps the most positive way to deal with stress:

I feel determined to strive to use whatever power I have to change the unpleasant stresses of life that I can change, to dislike but realistically accept those that I cannot change, and to have the wisdom to know the difference between the two.

SUMMARY

Use the following outline as a tool for reviewing this chapter. Copy the outline onto your own paper, leaving spaces between headings to make notes about key concepts.

I. Sources of Stress
   A. Conflict Situations
   B. Life Changes
   C. Work
   D. Everyday Sources of Stress

II. Reactions to Stress
   A. Psychological Reactions
   B. Behavioral Reactions
   C. Physical Reactions
   D. Factors Influencing Reactions to Stress

III. Coping with Stress
   A. Psychological Coping Strategies
   B. Modifying Physical Reactions to Stress
   C. Behavioral Coping Strategies
   D. A Lifelong Challenge

CONCEPTS AND VOCABULARY

1. What is the most common conflict situation? In what ways can this conflict be resolved?

2. In what ways have researchers differentiated among life events?

3. What are two criticisms of the Holmes-Rahe scale?

4. Who identified three stages in the body's response to stress? What are the three stages?

5. To what illnesses is emotional stress clearly related? To what illnesses is stress at least partly related?

6. What are the negative effects of "Type A" behavior? Why do people exhibit "Type A" behavior?

7. How can emotional expressiveness affect the development of cancer? Are the research findings conclusive in this area?

8. What is the accepted view on the relationship between degree of control over stressors and its effect on physical disorders? Brady's famous study does not agree with the accepted view. How is this difference reconciled?

9. What is the best overall recommendation for coping with stress? When stress is unavoidable, what is the most successful coping strategy? Is worrying beneficial when a person faces an *unavoidable* stress?

10. What are five behavioral ways to cope with stress?

11. If a person does not learn to cope with stress, what condition may result?

CRITICAL THINKING

1. **Analyze.** Some studies have found that high levels of stress can lead to both physical and mental illness. Do you believe this is true? What evidence do you have? Are all individuals equally susceptible to stress-related illnesses? Are some people better able to cope with stress than others? What does this say about stress as a *cause* of illness?

2. **Evaluate.** What are the major sources of stress in school? Can you pinpoint specific occasions, times, and events when many students seem to feel stressed? Do students seem more stressed prior to tests or exams? Can you discover any common elements among these sources of stress? What might be done to alleviate stress in

school? Would stress be reduced or eliminated if there were no grades? What if there were no tests? What would school be like without stress? Should stress in school be eliminated?

APPLYING KNOWLEDGE

1. Study your own family, and try to identify stressors affecting each family member. Do these stressors result from the roles that family members have, from their ages, from their contacts with the outside world, from the ways that family members relate to each other, or from some other sources? Are there ways in which you contribute to family stress? Are there ways in which you do (or could) help reduce stress?

2. The Holmes-Rahe "Social Readjustment Rating Scale" lists life events deemed to be stressful to adults. Assume your job is to develop a similar scale for teenagers only. In what ways would your scale be different? What would you add to or delete from the list?

3. Short-term reactions to stress often include physical responses—in other words, illnesses and other health problems. Ask a variety of people to give you examples of times when they have suffered from short-term health problems that they believe were associated with stress. You may have to prompt them with specific questions—for example: "Did you or your spouse get sick on your honeymoon?" "How did you feel on the first day of school this year?" "The last time you stayed home from school (or work) because of illness, was there anything stressful happening in your life?" Try to list a number of examples of stresses and corresponding health problems.

4. Try a systematic program of relaxation to see if physical relaxation helps you deal with stress. For example, try to deliberately relax your muscles for a minute or two between each of your classes, at lunch time, and during other breaks. Do this consistently for a week. At the end of the week, evaluate your mental attitude. Do you feel less stressed?

5. Go to a local shopping center or mall and observe a few cigarette smokers. Many smokers claim that smoking cigarettes relieves stress. Do the smokers you observe seem to smoke more in stressful situations, such as waiting on a line? Do the smokers seem relaxed? Do you believe that smoking relieves tension and stress?

ANALYZING VIEWPOINTS

1. Is stress always "bad"? Can stress ever be positive? Write a paper that presents both viewpoints. To gather additional information on this topic, you may want to read books and recent magazine articles on stress. Be sure to give examples in support of both positions.

BEYOND THE CLASSROOM

1. The Holmes-Rahe "Social Readjustment Rating Scale" is designed to measure the effects of various stressful life events, ranging from the death of a family member to changes at work or school. Holmes and Rahe assigned relative values to each event with the idea that the higher the value, the more stressful the event. Interview five people you know, asking each person how stressful the past year has been. Ask them to rate the past year's stress on a 1-to-10 scale, with 1 being least stressful and 10 being most stressful. When they tell you what rating they would assign to the past year's stress, write it down. Then, using the list that appears on page 320, ask these same people to look at the list of stressful events. Ask them to circle the events that have occurred in their lives over the past year. Study the five lists. Compare the results of the list with the person's 1-to-10 rating of how stressful the past year has been. What do the results say about the relationship between stress and major life events?

CHAPTER 14

Adjustment in Society

The McCaslins and their five children live in a rural area of eastern Kentucky. The father is a tall, gangly man who broke his back several years ago while working in a local coal mine. He is not able to perform any kind of physical labor and has been unable to find any other kind of work. The coal company refused to give him a disability pension, and probably because he is living at home, his family has been denied welfare. Consequently, the family is forced to survive on garden vegetables and what little food they can buy with some assistance from relatives.

In spite of this hard, meager existence, they all work to maintain a close, loving relationship with one another. The father has strong ideas, talks a lot, and involves himself with his wife and children. The parents do not touch each other very much in front of strangers or their children, but "they give each other long looks of recognition, sympathy, affection, and sometimes anger or worse. They understand each other in that silent, real lasting way that defies . . . labels," writes psychiatrist Robert Coles (1971). Because they have learned to cope with the stresses of disability and poverty, we can say that the McCaslins are well adjusted.

By **adjustment,** psychologists mean the process of adapting to, as well as actively shaping, one's environment. When psychologists call a person well adjusted, they do *not* mean that he or she has managed to avoid stress, problems, and conflicts; as we saw in Chapter 13, such escape is impossible. They *do* mean that the person has learned to deal with frustration, disappointment, and loss and makes the most of himself or herself and available opportunities.

Psychologists who study adjustment try to understand not only how people cope with extreme hardship but also how they handle more ordinary experiences of life—for example, love and marriage, parent-child re-

Objectives:

After studying this chapter, you should be able to

- describe the styles and types of marriages.
- define the nature of parental-child interactions and conflicts.

Figure 14.1 Adjustment is adapting to as well as actively shaping one's environment. It is coping with the ordinary experiences and stresses of life as well as with the moments of extreme hardship.

lationships, college, and work—that are potential sources of stress. Adjusting to each of these experiences involves unique challenges and difficulties, which we shall study in this chapter.

LOVE AND MARRIAGE

The idea of love without marriage is no longer shocking. The fact that a couple is developing a close and intimate relationship, or even living together, does not necessarily mean that they are contemplating marriage. Still the idea of marriage without love remains heresy in Western thought. Marrying for convenience, companionship, financial security, or *any* reason that doesn't include love strikes most of us as immoral or at least unfortunate.

And this, according to psychologist Zick Rubin (1973), is one of the main reasons why it is difficult for many people to adjust to love and marriage. Exaggerated ideas about love may also help to explain the growing frequency of divorce. Fewer couples who have "fallen out of love" are staying together for the sake of the children or to avoid gossip than did in the past. But let us begin at the beginning, with love.

Love

Some years ago Rubin (1973) covered the University of Michigan campus with requests for student volunteers. The top line of his posters—"Only dating couples can do it!"—attracted hundreds of students, so many that he had to turn most away. Those who remained—couples who had been going together for anywhere from a few weeks to six or seven years—filled out questionnaires about their feelings toward their partners and their same-sex friends. Their answers enabled Rubin to distinguish between liking and loving (see Figure 14.1).

Liking is based primarily on respect for another person and the feeling that he or she is similar to you. Loving is rather different. As Rubin writes, "There are probably as many reasons for loving as there are people who love. In each case there is a different constellation of needs to be gratified, a different set of characteristics that are found to be rewarding, a different ideal to be fulfilled" (228–229). However, looking beyond these differences, Rubin identified three major components of romantic love: *need, the desire to give,* and *intimacy.*

People in love feel strong desires to be with the other person, to touch, to be praised and cared for by their lover. Whether men and women look to their partners to fill leftover needs that were never satisfied in childhood, as many psychologists suggest, is debatable. But the fact that love is so often described as a longing, a hunger, a desire to possess, a sickness that only one person can heal, suggests the role need plays in romantic love.

Equally central is the desire to give. Love goes beyond the cost-reward level of human interaction. It has been defined as "the active concern for the life and growth of that which we love" (Fromm, 1956: 26), and as "that state in which the happiness of another person is essential to our own"

Figure 14.2
Distinguishing between liking and loving: a portion of Rubin's questionnaire.

Liking

1. *Favorable evaluation.*
   I think that _____ (my boyfriend or girlfriend) is unusually well adjusted.
   It seems to me that it is very easy for _____ to gain admiration.

2. *Respect and confidence.*
   I have great confidence in _____'s good judgment.
   I would vote for _____ in a class or group election.

3. *Perceived similarity.*
   I think that _____ and I are quite similar to each other.
   When I am with _____, we are almost always in the same mood.

Loving

1. *Attachment.*
   If I could never be with _____, I would feel miserable.
   It would be hard for me to get along without _____.

2. *Caring.*
   If _____ were feeling badly, my first duty would be to cheer him (her) up.
   I would do almost anything for _____.

3. *Intimacy.*
   I feel that I can confide in _____ about almost anything.
   When I am with _____, I spend a good deal of time just looking at him (her).

(Heinlein, in Levinger and Snoek, 1972: 10). Without caring, need becomes a series of self-centered, desperate demands; without need, caring is charity or kindness. In love, the two are intertwined.

Need and caring take various forms, depending on individual situations. What all people in love share is intimacy—a special knowledge of each other derived from uncensored self-disclosure. Exposing your "true self" to another person is always risky. It doesn't hurt so much if a person rejects a role you are trying to play. But it can be devastating if a person rejects the secret longings and fears you ordinarily disguise, or if he or she uses private information to manipulate you. This is one of the reasons why

Figure 14.3
It is easy to think of love in a narrow context and consider only the sexual relationship that exists between a man and a woman. But this view omits the kinds of love that exist between children and grandparents, between people and their pets, between members of the same sex—particularly twins, and between parents and their children.

MORE about . . .

Triangular Theory of Love.
Love comes in many sizes and shapes. A theory that accounts for the many forms of love has been proposed by psychologist Robert Sternberg. Sternberg's triangular theory of love contends that love is made up of three parts: intimacy, passion, and commitment. The various combinations of these parts account for why love is experienced in many different ways.

Intimacy refers to the feeling part of love—as when we feel close to another. Passion is love's motivating aspect, which drives us to seek romance. Commitment is the thinking component of love—when we realize that a relationship is love and we desire to maintain the relationship over time.

Using Sternberg's model, we can see how different kinds of love are made up of different degrees of intimacy, passion, and commitment. The "love at first sight" felt on a first date has lots of passion but little commitment, whereas the love felt by a couple celebrating their fiftieth wedding anniversary has much intimacy and commitment but probably less passion.

love so often brings out violent emotions—the highs and lows of our lives.

Rubin conducted a number of experiments to test common assumptions about the way people in love feel and act. He found that couples who rated high on his "love scale" did, indeed, spend more time gazing into each other's eyes (while waiting for the experimenter) than other couples did. However, he was unable to prove that lovers sacrifice their own comfort for that of their partners.

Perhaps the most interesting discoveries in "love research" concern the differences between men and women. Rubin found that most couples were equal on the love scale: the woman expressed the same degree of love for her partner as he did for her. However, women tended to *like* their boy friends—to respect and identify with them—more than their boy friends liked them. Women also tended to love and share intimacies with their same-sex friends more often than men did with theirs.

This is not surprising. As Rubin suggests, women in our society tend to specialize in the social and emotional dimensions of life. However, the revelation that men are significantly more romantic than women is surprising. Men tended to agree with statements like "As long as they love each other, two people should have no difficulty getting along together in marriage," but disagree with unromantic statements like "One should not marry against the serious advice of one's parents." Women tended to take practical and social considerations more seriously. A full 72 percent of the women in the study were undecided about whether they would marry someone who possessed all the qualities they looked for in a mate but whom they did not love. In contrast, 65 percent of the men answered this question with a flat no.

A follow-up questionnaire, sent a year after Rubin's original study, indicated that when both a man and a woman are romantic, the relationship is likely to progress—that is, they become more intimate and committed to each other. The implication of this finding? That love is not something that happens *to* you; it is something you seek and create.

Marriage

A couple decides to make a formal and public commitment to each other. They marry. Will they "live happily ever after"? Their chances are good if they come from similar cultural and economic backgrounds, have about the same level of education, and practice (or fail to practice) the same religion. Their chances are better still if their parents were happily married, they had happy childhoods, and they maintain good relations with their families. All of these are good predictors of marital success. Study after study has shown that marital success tends to run in families, and particularly in families whose members marry "their own kind." This is the principle of homogamy: like marrying like (Arkoff, 1968: 467–474). What the statistics do not tell us is *how* couples who report they are satisfied with their marriages adjust to each other's hopes and demands, moods and quirks.

J. F. Cuber and Peggy Harroff (1965) found a wide range of adjustments in the upper-middle-class community they studied. Cuber and Harroff chose to study affluent families for two reasons: first, because they be-

Figure 14.4
Healthy adjustment to marriage seems to depend on whether the couple's needs are compatible, on whether their images of themselves coincide with their images of each other, and on whether they agree on what the roles of husband and wife should be.

lieved that too many marital studies focus on families in crisis; second, because such families represent the American ideal in many respects.

About one in six of the marriages they studied did in fact live up to the ideal. The couple enjoyed each other's company and spent a good deal of time together. At the same time, both husband and wife had a strong sense of individual identity and participated in separate activities. Cuber and Harroff called this a **vital marriage.** In a smaller number of **total marriages,** the husband and wife were deeply involved in each other's careers and hobbies, spent most of their time together, and seemed to live for each other.

More common were what the researchers labeled devitalized and passive-congenial marriages. **Devitalized marriages** had begun with passionate love affairs and high hopes for a life of marital bliss. Over the years the couple had drifted apart, but they still got along well enough to stay together. The couples who had worked out **passive-congenial marriages** had never been deeply involved with each other. For these individuals, marriage was a convenience. Living together and sharing responsibilities made it easier for both husband and wife to pursue individual interests. They had not been looking for a lifelong honeymoon and were content with their relationship.

Cuber and Harroff used the term **conflict-habituated marriage** to describe husbands and wives who spent most of their time fighting. These couples were always at each other's throats. But they did not see their battles as a reason for divorce. Indeed, the fighting seemed to bind them together.

Mirra Komarovsky's study of blue-collar marriages (1964) provides an interesting contrast. Nearly all the couples Komarovsky studied saw marriage as a utilitarian arrangement and had settled into passive-congenial relationships. In general these couples believed that males and females have different needs and interests. They thought it natural for a woman to feel closer to her female friends and relatives than to her husband; a husband closer to his male friends and relatives than to his wife. So long as the husband filled his role as breadwinner and the wife her role as home-maker and mother, both felt satisfied. There were some exceptions, some vital marriages, in the group studied. Komarovsky notes that the couples who enjoyed each other's company and shared leisure activities had higher levels of education and higher incomes than the other couples she inter-viewed (see Skolnick, 1973: 238–246).

Statistics on the reasons why couples file for divorce reveal a similar pattern. Lower-class couples are more likely to complain of lack of finan-cial support, physical cruelty, or drinking; middle-class couples, of mental cruelty or incompatibility (Levinger, 1966).

Marital Problems and Divorce

In general, healthy adjustment to marriage seems to depend on three factors: whether the couple's needs are compatible; whether the hus-band's and wife's images of themselves coincide with their images of each other; and whether they agree on what the husband's and wife's roles in marriage are.

Conflict is likely to develop if the husband or wife has a deep need for achievement but the spouse is content with a leisurely, comfortable, un-distinguished life. If a husband sees himself as sensitive and compassion-ate but the wife considers him crude and unfeeling, they are not likely to get along very well. Problems may erupt when a wife discovers that her husband expects her to quit her job when he finishes school and estab-lishes himself in his career (something they may never have discussed). Similarly, a marriage may founder when a husband finds his wife devoting to their children the attention she once gave to him.

External factors may make it impossible for one or both to live up to their own role expectations. A man who is unemployed cannot be the good provider he wants to be and may take his frustrations out on his family, who constantly remind him of this. A woman trying to raise a family in a slum tenement cannot keep the kitchen with a broken sink clean, provide good meals for her family, or keep her children safe.

And often couples just grow apart: the husband becomes totally en-grossed in his work or in a hobby; the wife, in her career, children, or community affairs. One day they wake up and realize that they stopped communicating years ago (see Arkoff, 1968: 469–487).

Let us suppose they are unable or unwilling to fill each other's needs and role expectations through accommodation or compromise. Perhaps they cannot face their problems. For example, many people have a taboo about discussing—much less seeking help for—sexual problems. Perhaps they have sought professional help, talked their difficulties out with each other and with friends, and come to the conclusion that they want more from life than their current marriage allows. For whatever reasons, they decide on divorce. What then?

In many ways, adjusting to divorce is like adjusting to death—the death of a relationship. Almost inevitably, divorce releases a torrent of emotions: anger (even if the person wanted a divorce), resentment, fear, loneliness, anxiety, and above all the feeling of failure. Both individuals are suddenly thrust into a variety of unfamiliar situations. A man may find himself cooking for the first time in years; a woman, fixing her first leaky faucet. Dating for the first time in five or ten years can make a formerly married person feel like an adolescent. Friends may feel they have to choose sides. Some divorcing people may find it unsettling to think of giving up on a marriage or being unattached and free to do whatever they like. One of the biggest problems may be time—the free time a person desperately wanted but now has no idea what to do with.

All of this adds up to what Mel Krantzler calls "separation shock." The shock may be greatest for individuals who saw divorce as liberation and did not anticipate difficult times. But whatever the circumstances, most divorced people go through a period of mourning that lasts until the person suddenly realizes that he or she has survived. This is the first step toward adjustment to divorce. Resentment of his or her former spouse and of the opposite sex in general subsides. The pain left over from the past no longer dominates the present. The divorced person begins calling old friends, making new ones, and enjoying the fact that he or she can base decisions on his or her own personal interests. In effect, the divorcee has begun to construct a new identity as a single person (Krantzler, 1973: 94–95).

Children and Divorce

Adjusting to divorce is usually far more difficult for children than for their parents. First, rarely do the children want the divorce to occur: the conflict is not theirs, but their parents'. Second, while the parents may have good reasons for the separation, the children (especially very young children) are unlikely to understand those reasons. Third, the children themselves rarely have any control over the outcome of the divorce. Such decisions as whom they will live with and how frequently they will be able to see the separated parent are out of their hands. Finally, children, especially young ones, can't muster as much emotional maturity as their parents to help them through such an overwhelming experience.

Adolescents experience special problems as a result of their parents' divorce, for their developmental stage already involves the process of breaking family ties. When that separation takes place before the adolescent is ready to play his or her own hand in it, the experience can be terribly unsettling. As one young person said, "[It was] like having the rug pulled out from under me" (Wallerstein and Kelly, 1974: 486).

Like their parents, most children do eventually come to terms with divorce. They learn to put some distance between themselves and their parents' conflict, and they learn to be realistic about the situation and make the best of it. Adjustment is made easier when parents take special care to explain the divorce and give children plenty of freedom to ask questions and express their feelings.

As common as divorce is in our society, luckily it is still a problem that

> **Adjusting to a divorce tends to be harder for children than for their parents.**

the majority of children don't have to cope with. But marital problems are not the only area of family conflict. Just as there are discrepancies between expectations and reality for husbands and wives, disillusionments and disagreements also exist between children and parents. Parents expect certain behaviors and attitudes from their children, but these expectations sometimes are not met. Children and their parents do often disagree. However, unlike married couples, children and parents cannot divorce. They must find other ways of resolving their conflicts.

PARENT-CHILD RELATIONSHIPS

The scene: Son enters living room, bouncing a basketball.

Mother: Get out of here with that. You'll break something!
Son: No, I won't!

(The ball hits a lamp.)

Mother: For crying out loud, you never listen to anything I say. You had to break something, didn't you? You're so stupid sometimes.
Son: You broke the washing machine. What does that make you?
Mother: Floyd, you know better than to be rude.
Son: You were rude first. You called me stupid.
Mother: I don't want to hear another word from you. Go to your room this minute!
Son: Quit trying to boss me around. I'm not a kid anymore.
Mother: To your room this instant!
Son: Go ahead, make me.

—Adapted from Haim G. Ginott, *Between Parent and Teenager* (1971).

As the scene above illustrates, conflict, whether between husband and wife or child and parent, is a process that can escalate with surprising quickness from contradictory desires to a bitter power struggle complete with name-calling. In our society, parent-child conflict is particularly common and explosive during adolescence. Adolescence is a period of inner struggles—goals versus fear of inability to accomplish them, desire for independence versus continued need for dependence, and idealized image of parents versus the realization that they are "only human." The adolescent thus needs parents who are sure of themselves, their identities, and their values. Such parents serve not only as models to follow or reject but also as sources of stability in a world that, to the adolescent, has become complicated and full of choices.

Sources of Parent-Adolescent Conflict

"The generation gap" is an expression we have all heard and used. It refers to a simple fact: adolescents and their parents tend to think differently about things. Some of the specific issues may change from one generation to the next. For example, in the days of World Wars I and II, many parents

Figure 14.5
Conflict and power struggles between parents and children are inevitable, especially when expectations of behavior or desires differ.

were upset and frightened because their sons wanted to run off and join the armed forces. But during the Vietnam War, parents were hurt and angered because some of their sons refused to "serve their country."

One of the most frequently discussed areas of disagreement between adolescents and their parents is sex. Parents accustomed to thinking of sex as something for married people are likely to find their children in active disagreement. In part as a result of the Pill, more young people are having sexual relations at a younger age than in the past. Equally significant, young people today tend to view premarital sex as equally acceptable for both men and women—a shift away from the old double standard (Smigel and Seiden, in LeFrancois, 1976: 316).

Another common area of disagreement is drugs. A survey conducted in 1977 for the National Institute on Drug Abuse found that 28 percent of its high school sample had tried marijuana and 4.6 percent had tried LSD at least once. Many parents may remember run-ins with their own parents over the use of alcohol (indeed, 52 percent of the same high school sample also reported drinking at least once). But the much-publicized arrival of drugs on the national scene is something new. In the past the use of drugs was restricted to the lower class; now drug use is acceptable behavior in peer groups regardless of social class.

The list of issues on which adolescents and parents can disagree could go on for pages, for it is seemingly endless. But there are other sources of conflict between parents and children of all ages.

Parental Expectations

In her book *Peoplemaking*, Virginia Satir describes a case from her experience as a family therapist:

> . . . [J]ust after Christmas . . . a young mother whom I will call Elaine came to see me. She was in a rage at her six-year-old daughter, Pam. It seems that Elaine had scrimped and saved many months to buy Pam a very fancy doll. Pam reacted with indifference to the doll her mother had worked so hard to get. Elaine felt very crushed and disappointed, inside. Outside she acted angry (1972: 205).

Elaine had done something many parents do. She had taken a childhood dream of her own (she never had a fancy doll when she was growing up) and projected it onto her daughter—who already had several dolls and really would have preferred a sled.

It is easy for parents to take their own unfulfilled dreams—not just for a little girl to have a doll but for a grown daughter or son to be a doctor or go to college—and wish for their child to fulfill them instead. It is also easy for parents to expect children to share their own interests and goals. Many fathers, for example, just assume that their sons will want to continue in the family business, whether or not the young man has ever expressed any such interest. But is is not always easy for parents to remember that because of different circumstances, different times, and different personalities, children frequently don't have the same dreams as their parents. If parents can't accept the difference between their own goals and those of their children, the result is likely to be hurt feelings and anger, leaving the child with the choice of either submission or rebellion.

The Power Struggle: Escalating Conflict

There is no question that there are many potential sources of conflict within the family. Fathers and mothers play different roles and have different expectations for themselves and each other. They also have values, goals, and expectations that they try to instill in their children—even though the effort may sometimes be reminiscent of putting a shoe on the wrong foot. Both children and adults may become stuck in their roles: parents sometimes forget how it felt to be a child, and children often have difficulty imagining what it is like to be a parent. Each family member experiences personal stresses, too, that relate to life outside the family, in jobs, school, or dating. All these pressures demand some understanding or at least tolerance from other members of the family.

As differences between family members persist, it may be difficult for individuals to keep trying to listen and understand each other's point of view. A father and son can argue the point of whether the motorcycle belongs in the garage or on the street just so many times before their words become a monotonous dialogue that no one listens to.

Instead of making a constructive effort to work out a solution to differences, parents and children, or wives and husbands, may take an easier but counterproductive route—that of blaming the other person, placing the entire responsibility for a problem on his or her shoulders. There are several ways of doing this. One is *judging*, or *criticizing*, accusing the other person of being at fault ("You're being selfish!"); another is *diagnosing*, or *psychoanalyzing*, by commenting on a person's possible psychological motives for an action ("You're taking it out on me because you had a rough day at work"). Other common tactics include teaching ("We don't put our elbows on the dinner table"); and *name-calling*, or *shaming*, humiliating another, thus making him or her feel ashamed, embarrassed, or guilty ("Don't you feel like a baby for storming around like that?") (Gordon, 1975: 113). In each instance, when one person tries to avoid responsibility for the conflict, the result is likely to be its escalation rather than its resolution.

In parent-child conflict the general pattern of family interactions also has a great deal to do with whether disagreements and disappointments reach the stage of war we witnessed earlier in the basketball episode. We saw in Chapter 9 that parents and children tend to relate to one another according to three general patterns. *Authoritarian parents* deal with their children (actually, deal *at* them) by making decisions for them. As one father put it, "You have to start early letting them know who's boss" (Gordon, 1975: 151). *Permissive parents* do just the opposite: they enforce only the guidelines their children will let them enforce. *Democratic parents* try to interact with their children in a way that will provide guidance but do not attempt to dominate the relationship.

Both dominant and permissive parents have good chances of develop-

Figure 14.6
When real communication is achieved in the family, family members are able to trust and be open with each other. They can be secure in the knowledge that they are understood.

ing a conflict-ridden relationship with their children. In the first case, as we have seen, children are bound to rebel as they grow up and learn to think for themselves; and in the second case, parents themselves may eventually feel like rebelling as their children keep testing their parents' limits. In democratic families, though, the chances for conflict to escalate are not so great. That is because these families try to depend on communication instead of power as a means of making decisions.

COLLEGE LIFE

We have been talking about the things that happen within the family, when children, wives, and husbands live together in the same household. But families don't stay together forever. Children grow up and leave home to set up new households and start their own families.

Growing up involves gaining a sense of autonomy (the ability to take care of oneself) and independence. Each person learns to make decisions, develop a value system, be responsible, and to care for himself or herself. Growing up is a process that starts long before an individual leaves home to live as a self-sufficient adult. But ultimately, it means separating from the family, both physically and emotionally.

For millions of young Americans, college is one of the first big steps toward this separation. College students are freer than they ever have been or may ever be again. This can be a personally liberating and stimulating

Figure 14.7
College life makes many demands on students away from home for the first time. Organizing one's time, meeting new people, and confronting ideas that challenge old assumptions all require adjustment.

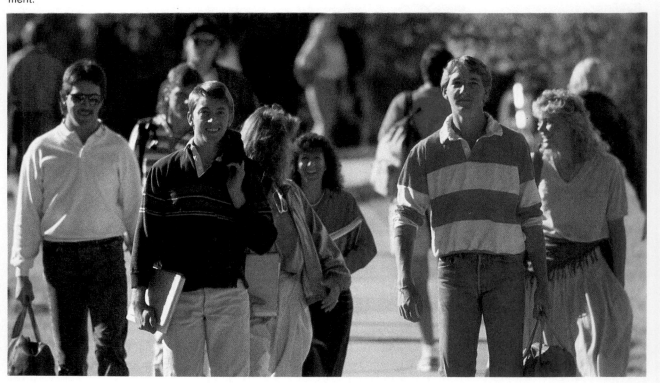

experience. But it also requires adjustment. The emotional upheaval many freshmen feel has been called "college shock."

Peter Madison (1969) spent close to ten years collecting data on how several hundred students adjusted to college. Each student provided a detailed life history and kept a weekly journal. Madison had classmates write descriptions of some of the students, and tested and retested some at various points in their college careers. The results?

Madison found that many students approach college with high, and often unrealistic, aspirations. For example, Joan wanted to be an astronomer. She liked the idea of being different, and she considered astronomy an elite and adventuresome field. But she didn't know how many long, hard, unadventuresome hours she would have to spend studying mathematics to fulfill her dream. Sidney planned to become a physician for what he described as "humanitarian" reasons. But he had never thought about working in a hospital or watching people sicken and die.

These two students, like many others, based their goals on fantasy. They didn't have the experience to make realistic choices or the maturity to evaluate their own motives and needs. Their experiences during the first semesters of college led them to change both their minds and their images of themselves.

Many students approach college with unrealistically high expectations.

Sources of Change

How does going to college stimulate change? First, college may challenge the identity a student has established in high school. A top student who does extremely well on the College Boards is likely to go to a top college. Nearly everyone there is as bright and competitive as she is. Within a matter of weeks the student's identity as a star pupil has evaporated; she may have to struggle to get average grades. Young people who excelled in sports, drama, or student politics may have similar experiences. The high school student-body president discovers two other high school presidents in his dormitory alone.

Second, whether students come from small towns or big cities, they are likely to encounter greater diversity in college than they ever have before—diversity in religious and ethnic backgrounds, family income levels, and attitudes. During his first quarter, Bob dated a Catholic woman, a Jewish woman, and an Oriental woman; a history major, a music major, an English major, and a math major. Fred found that the students living in his house ranged from "grinds," who did nothing but study, to "liberals," who were involved in all sorts of causes; from athletes, who cared more about physical than intellectual competition, and business types, who saw college as a place to get vocational training and make contacts for future use, to guys who just wanted to have a good time.

A student who develops a close relationship with another, then discovers that the person holds beliefs or engages in behavior he or she has always considered immoral, may be badly shaken. If you come from a strict fundamentalist background, how do you reconcile the fact that a woman you have come to admire drinks heavily on occasion and thinks nothing of going to bed with a man on their first date? You are faced with a choice between abandoning deeply held values and giving up an important

Figure 14.8
After completing a year or two of college, students may find that the career goals they had as high-school seniors no longer suit their interests.

friendship. Madison (1969) calls close relationships between individuals who force each other to reexamine their basic assumptions **developmental friendships.** He found that developmental friendships in particular and student culture in general have more impact on college students than professors do.

However, if instructors and assigned books clarify thoughts that have been brewing in a student's mind, they can make all the difference. This was true of Sidney. Sidney did extremely well in the courses required for a pre-med student, but found he enjoyed his literature and philosophy classes far more. He began reading avidly. He felt as if each of the authors had deliberately set out to put all his self-doubts into words. In time Sidney realized that his interest in medicine was superficial. He had decided to become a doctor because it was a respected profession that would give him status, security, and a good income—and would guarantee his parents' love. The self-image Sidney had brought to college was completely changed.

Coping with Change

Madison found that students cope with the stress of going to college in several different ways. Some "tighten up" when their goals are threatened by internal or external change. They redouble their efforts to succeed in the field they have chosen and avoid people and situations that might bring their doubts to the surface. Bob, for example, stuck with a chemical-engineering program for three years, despite a growing interest in social science. By the time he realized that this was not the field for him, it was too late to change majors. He got his degree, but left college with no idea where he was heading.

Others avoid confronting doubt by frittering away their time, going through the motions of attending college but detaching themselves emotionally.

And some students manage to keep their options open until they have enough information and experience to make a choice. Sidney is an example. In June of his freshman year he wrote in his diary,

> I must decide between philosophy and medicine. If I have enough confidence in the quality of my thought, I shall become a philosopher; if not, a comfortable doctor. (quoted in Madison, 1969: 58)

By June of the following year he had decided.

> Sitting on a tennis court I had the very sudden and dramatic realization that my life was my own and not my parents', that I could do what I wanted and did not necessarily have to do what they wanted. I think I correlated this with dropping out of the pre-med program. Material values became less and less important from then on. (58)

Madison calls this third method of coping **resynthesis.** For most students this involves a period of vacillation, doubt, and anxiety. The student tries to combine the new and old, temporarily abandons the original goal, retreats, heads in another direction, retreats again—and finally reorganizes his or her feelings and efforts around an emerging identity. Thus Joan changed her major to psychology and found that she was now able to combine her desire to be a scientist with her interest in people.

THE WORK EXPERIENCE

For one person work means loading 70,000 pounds on his five-axle truck, driving alone for several hours a day, perhaps for several days, with only a few stops for food and fuel, talk, relief, and sleep. While he is alone in the cab, tension is constant: it is hard to brake suddenly carrying thousands of pounds, so he must always think ahead. The work is wearing, yet he likes the odd hours and the opportunity to be outside.

For another person work means spending eight or nine hours a day at an advertising agency, dealing with clients and supervising commercial writers. She earns good money, spends a great deal of time talking with people, and has plenty of opportunities to exercise her talents as a manager. All three are qualities she likes about her job. But she must also deal with deadlines and worry about whether millions of dollars worth of ads will sell the products or not—and, subconsciously, whether it's worth the effort if they do.

For a third person work means training severely handicapped children to use their muscles to grasp a spoon, to gesture in sign language, and perhaps to take a few steps. The job is often depressing and frustrating, but there are also moments of intense personal satisfaction when a child makes progress.

The point is, each person's work experience is different. Jobs are performed in different settings: offices, stores, schools, hospitals, mines, trucks. Some occupations have structured time schedules; others are more flexible. Some workers are self-employed; most must answer to one or

Figure 14.9
Each person's work experience is different; for some, work provides a means of self-expression. Few careers offer as much personal satisfaction as that of creative or performing artist. This photo shows the celebrated cellist and conductor Pablo Casals rehearsing with his orchestra.

more higher-ups. Some workers are "in it for the money"; for others the job is a vehicle for more important personal satisfactions. Some workers do an entire task from beginning to end; others, like factory workers and copy editors, are only part of a larger process. And each person reacts differently to a job as a result of his or her own personality.

The First Job

For most people, getting their first full-time job is the major step into adulthood. It is exciting but frightening. Most students have vague notions about the world of work, pieced together from hearsay, brief glimpses during interviews, and the employer's sales pitch. The new secretary in publishing does not know what proofreaders and editors actually do. More important, she does not know what will be expected of her. Will the other workers accept her? The unknown is always frightening, and the first days and weeks on a job are often stressful. The ex-student finds herself completely exhausted at the end of the day.

Although some individuals receive training in job skills in school, few are taught all they will need to know in their first job: how to handle office politics, for instance, or cope with trivial problems, such as getting a typewriter repaired. Work also involves "psychological skills," such as common sense, an ability to deal with people, and an ability to cope with minor crises on a day-to-day basis. Few students are prepared for this.

In addition, the actual tasks a new employee is required to perform may be unexpected and disappointing. In school a student may have been writing papers about the world food crisis and the symbolist poets. At work in a publishing house she may find herself typing letters, filling out forms, and taking messages. She may get little or no feedback on her perform-

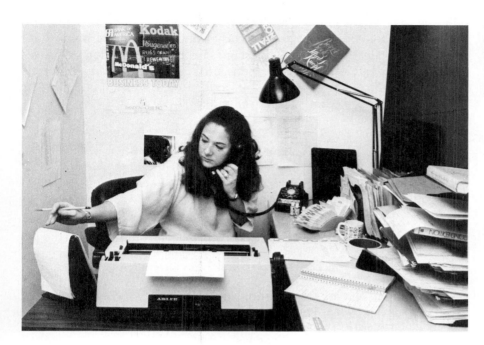

Figure 14.10
A young person's first job often requires a long period of adjustment. Hopes for an exciting, interesting job may have to be deferred until after serving an apprenticeship.

ance. A memo she spent hours writing may lie unread on her boss's desk. She dreamed of guiding young authors through their first novel, but in reality she rarely even meets an author. In short, she finds she is neither growing personally nor making a meaningful contribution to literature. The job falls considerably short of her expectations, in part because they were unrealistic to begin with (Coleman and Hammen, 1974: 351).

The "come-down" experience is common for almost any new worker, especially when he or she must start at the bottom of a job hierarchy. What kind of effect does it have? E. H. Schein (1968) found that half of one class of MIT graduates left their first jobs within three years—in part because they were not prepared for the work, in part because they were disillusioned.

Work Satisfaction and Dissatisfaction

The Ability to Adjust. As a rule people do not become stars, editors, or company vice-presidents overnight. A young employee may know he could handle some things better than his boss does three weeks after taking a job. But if he becomes too impatient or if he makes the boss look foolish, he is likely to lose the opportunity to put his ideas into practice in the future. The emphasis here is on compromise: long-term personal goals should not be forsaken, but patience and an ability to tolerate frustration and delay are needed. A young woman may dream of becoming an actress, but waiting on tables may be the best job she can get. In this case, she will be happiest if she accepts waitressing as a short-term solution and uses her free time to come closer to achieving long-term goals.

Adjusting to work also means being able to take the good with the bad. No job, whether it be high-fashion model, corporation vice-president, or major-league baseball player, is all glamor. A model may have to pose in a bathing suit in 40-degree weather; a corporation vice-president may have to deal with distasteful office politics and boring correspondence; a baseball player must attend practice sessions and stay away from liquor. As one chemist has stated: "Most of my job I do for free, because I enjoy it. The parts I don't like are what I do for the money."

Sources of Work Satisfaction. Some workers may seek high salaries, pleasant working conditions, and low-pressure jobs; others may be concerned only with finding personal fulfillment at work. Most workers, however, have both economic and personal goals. One study (Quinn *et al.*, 1971) has identified five major sources of work satisfaction.

1. *Resources.* The worker feels that he or she has enough available resources—help, supplies, and equipment, for example—to do the job well.
2. *Financial reward.* The job pays well, offers good fringe benefits, and is secure.
3. *Challenge.* The job is interesting and enables the worker to use his or her special talents and abilities.
4. *Relations with co-workers.* The worker is on good terms professionally and socially with colleagues.
5. *Comfort.* Working conditions and related factors—hours, travel to and from the job, work environment, and so on—are attractive.

Changing Careers

The Bureau of Labor reported recently that in one twelve-month period, about one-third of all American workers (excluding farm workers and household workers) changed their occupations. Some theorists predict that in the future, people will change their **career** (by which they mean a vocation in which a person works at least a few years) several times in their lifetime.

As we saw earlier, people live longer today than ever before, and so they have a longer work life. It is not uncommon for a person to retire from one job at the age of sixty or sixty-five, then embark on a whole new career as a real-estate salesperson, travel broker, writer, or consultant. Some employers (especially some local governments) have early-retirement programs that allow people to leave jobs with partial pay at a relatively young age; alumni of these programs have been especially good candidates for "second wind" careers. Many women also split their careers by stepping out of the job market to raise children, then reentering the working world for a second full career.

There is some evidence that people are changing careers because they are not so easily satisfied as they once were. There have been periods in our history, like the Great Depression, when work of any sort could attract and hold steady workers simply because of the great need for money. But times have changed. As we have seen, people want work that is psychologically as well as financially rewarding. If a person is unhappy at a job, changing careers may provide the answer, through better pay, better working conditions, or more interesting tasks. "Job shopping," or trying out several careers, is most common among people who have recently entered the

Figure 14.11
Many people continue to work after their retirement, but they are likely to change the kind of work they do. Someone who has worked in an office for many years, for instance, may relish the chance to work outdoors.

labor force and are still trying to get a feel for the work that suits them best. This is one reason why most of the people who change occupations are under the age of thirty-five (Byrne, 1975: 54).

Does this mean you should forget about career training, since you probably will not stick with your first job? Not at all. You should acquire as many abilities and interests as you can—in and out of school; you should work to develop your interpersonal skills; and you should look at change as desirable and challenging. In these ways, more occupations will be open to you, and the better your chances of employment will be, both now and in the future.

Comparable Worth

Consider the following two cases. Susan is employed as a day-care supervisor for a state government. In order to qualify for this job, she needed three years of experience as well as college credit. In her job, she is responsible for not only the care and well-being of the children but also the supervision of several subordinates. Harry, also a state worker, is in charge of a storeroom and is responsible for supplying goods to various departments in his building as well as supervising several subordinates. In order to qualify for his job, Harry needed four years of experience. In terms of actual job demands, Harry's and Susan's jobs might seem to be quite comparable. However, Harry is paid more than Susan, despite the fact that Susan's job requires college credit. In theory, jobs of comparable training, skill, and importance should be compensated at the same rate. In practice, however, the market value of many jobs traditionally held by females is considerably lower than that of comparable jobs traditionally held by males. Moreover, as Juanita Kreps, Secretary of Labor in the Carter Administration, pointed out, "Many of the occupational groups in which women are concentrated pay low wages while requiring higher-than-average educational achievement" (Kreps, 1971: 40).

Many groups have been working hard to achieve equal pay for comparable work. The National Organization for Women has made the upgrading of traditionally female jobs one of its highest priorities. Labor unions have also been addressing the issue of pay equity. Delegates at the 1981 national convention of the AFL-CIO were urged to press for equal pay for comparable work in all future contract negotiations.

It may seem surprising that such demands were necessary. After all, the Civil Rights Act, passed by Congress in 1964, had included Title VII, which prohibits discrimination on the basis of sex in hiring, firing, terms of compensation, and work conditions. Moreover, the Equal Employment Opportunity Commission (EEOC) had been set up to enforce Title VII. The fact is that, for economic reasons, many employers are unwilling to raise salaries, especially if they are able to find workers who will accept the low wages that they do offer. It is up to the workers, therefore, to demand the wages to which they are entitled.

A 1981 Supreme Court decision has opened the door for workers to bring lawsuits for equal pay for comparable work under Title VII. However, it may be a while before standards of worth and job comparability are established.

SUMMARY

Use the following outline as a tool for reviewing this chapter. Copy the outline onto your own paper, leaving spaces between headings to make notes about key concepts.

I. Love and Marriage

   A. Love

   B. Marriage

   C. Marital Problems and Divorce

   D. Children and Divorce

II. Parent-Child Relationships

   A. Sources of Parent-Adolescent Conflict

   B. Parental Expectations

   C. The Power Struggle: Escalating Conflict

III. College Life

   A. Sources of Change

   B. Coping with Change

IV. The Work Experience

   A. The First Job

   B. Work Satisfaction and Dissatisfaction

   C. Changing Careers

   D. Comparable Worth

CONCEPTS AND VOCABULARY

1. What do psychologists mean by "adjustment"? Give an example of an adjustment you have recently made.

2. In what ways are liking and loving different? What are three major components of liking and loving? How do males and females differ in their feelings of love?

3. What types of upper-middle-class marriages are described by Cuber and Harroff? What types of marriage did Komarovsky find in blue-collar workers?

4. What factors does marital happiness depend upon? What leads to marital conflict?

5. How do spouses react to divorce? How are children affected by divorce?

6. What are some common sources of parent-adolescent conflict?

7. How can parental expectations result in parent-child conflict? What are some of the counterproductive reactions to conflict displayed by parents and children?

8. How do authoritarian parents deal with their children? How about permissive parents? Democratic parents?

9. What are some of the new experiences and challenges that a student faces when entering college? How do students cope with stress at college?

10. What new challenges are faced in work? What factors determine how satisfied a person is with his or her work? What leads to career changes?

CRITICAL THINKING

1. **Synthesize.** The divorce rate has increased over the past several years. Some experts believe that one out of two marriages today will end in divorce. How do you account for this recent trend? What do you think could be done to slow the rise in the divorce rate?

2. **Analyze.** Write a short paper entitled "My Most Difficult Adjustment in Life." Relate an experience that required an adjustment. What were your feelings at the time? How did you eventually make the adjustment? How did you feel once you made the adjustment? What did you learn from this experience that could help you adjust to future changes in your life?

3. **Synthesize.** Pretend someone has just asked you, "How do I know if I'm in love?" How would you respond?

APPLYING KNOWLEDGE

1. The idea of "romantic love" is fostered in fairy-tales like "Cinderella" and "Sleeping Beauty" and in popular songs, novels, short stories, and TV commercials. Take examples from one or two of these areas, and discuss how they express the romantic ideal of falling in love with the perfect stranger.

2. Cuber and Harroff (1965) classify marriages as vital, total, devitalized, passive-congenial, or conflict-habituated. Study your family, neighbors, or friends, and discuss why you think their marriages fall into one of these five categories.

3. If any of the marriages of people you know have ended in divorce, make some notes on why you think this occurred. If some of these people are available, ask them how they adjusted to being divorced and what kind of problems they had. What did they do to help their children adjust to the divorce?

4. The chapter mentions two potential sources of parent-adolescent conflict (drugs and sex). Ask several adults that you know what conflicts they had with their parents when they were adolescents. Were the conflicts ever resolved, or did they just go away over time? Ask several of your friends what conflicts they have with their parents. Are any of their conflicts the same as the conflicts mentioned by the adults you talked to? Do you think there are certain parent-adolescent conflicts that every generation experiences?

ANALYZING VIEWPOINTS

1. For many young adults, college is the first major step toward gaining a sense of autonomy. The separation from the family often provides the young adult with opportunities for growth and personal development. In recent years, however, many young adults have been moving back home after they graduate from college. How do you think this might affect their developing sense of autonomy? Write a paper that argues both sides of the issue. Include reasons why moving back home should have little impact on the young adult's sense of autonomy, and reasons why the move home may hinder the young adult's development into adulthood.

2. One of the enduring myths involving love and marriage is the idea of "love at first sight." Psychologists often do not take the idea seriously, pointing out that most people learn to love and cherish another person over a period of time. Is there such a thing as love at first sight? Or is this just a romantic myth perpetuated by images from the movies and television? Write an essay debating both sides of the issue. Use what you have learned from the chapter, as well as any magazine articles you can find on the topic of love. Be sure to give examples. You may include people you know or people who are public figures.

BEYOND THE CLASSROOM

1. Talk to several adults about their first job. What were their expectations? Were these expectations met? Did they enjoy the job? How long did they work at this particular job? What did they learn from their first job about the world of work? What did they learn about themselves? Did this job lead to a career in the same field? Go to the library and read any of Studs Terkel's books on working. (Ask your teacher or librarian for a reference.) Compare the experiences of the adults you talked to with several of the adults you read about in Terkel's book. Report to the class on what you now know about individuals' experiences in their first jobs.

CHAPTER 15

Disturbance and Breakdown

A man living in the Ozark Mountains has a vision in which God speaks to him. He begins preaching to his relatives and neighbors, and soon he has the whole town in a state of religious fervor. People say he has a "calling." His reputation as a prophet and healer spreads, and in time he is drawing large audiences everywhere he goes. However, when he ventures into St. Louis and attempts to hold a prayer meeting, blocking traffic on a main street at rush hour, he is arrested. He tells the policemen about his conversations with God, and they hurry him off to the nearest mental hospital.

A housewife is tired all the time, but she has trouble sleeping. The chores keep piling up because she has no energy. Applications for evening courses and "help wanted" clippings from the classified ads lie untouched in a drawer. She consults the family doctor, but he says she's in perfect health. One night she tells her husband that she's thinking of seeing a psychotherapist. He thinks this is ridiculous. According to him, all she needs is to get up out of her chair and get busy.

Who is right? The "prophet" or the policemen? The housewife or her husband? It is often difficult to draw a line between "sanity" and "madness," normal and abnormal behavior. Behavior that some people consider normal seems crazy to others. Many non-Western peoples, along with religious fundamentalists in our own country, feel that having visions and hearing voices is an important part of a religious experience. Other people believe these are symptoms of mental disturbance. The man in the example above was interviewed by psychiatrists, diagnosed as "paranoid schizophrenic," and hospitalized for mental illness. Had he stayed home, he could have been considered perfectly okay. Indeed, more than okay—special (Slotkin, 1955).

Objectives:

After studying this chapter, you should be able to

- distinguish between the concepts of normalcy and abnormality.
- identify the behavioral patterns psychologists label neurotic.
- describe the concept of psychosis and give possible explanations for its origin.
- describe how a personality disorder differs from neurosis and psychosis.

Figure 15.1 For psychologists, defining abnormality is neither simple nor sure. Much depends on the approach one uses and on the cultural setting in which the behavior takes place.

WHAT IS ABNORMAL BEHAVIOR?

Behavior some people consider normal seems crazy to others.

In our example, the man was classified as mentally troubled because his behavior was so different from what other people felt was "normal." Yet the fact that a person is different does not necessarily mean that he or she is insane. Indeed, going along with the crowd may at times be self-destructive. Most readers—and most psychologists—would agree that a teen-ager who uses heroin because nearly everyone in his social circle does has problems.

In the case of the housewife, she was the one who decided she was psychologically troubled, simply because she was so unhappy. Yet unhappiness and even genuine depression are certainly not foolproof signs of psychological disturbance or of impending breakdown. Everyone feels low from time to time.

How, then, do psychologists distinguish the normal from the abnormal?

There are a number of ways to define abnormality, none of which is entirely satisfactory. We will look at the most popular ways of drawing the line between normal and abnormal: the deviance approach, the adjustment approach, and the psychological-health model. Then we will look at the application of these principles in legal definitions of abnormality. Finally, we will consider the criticism that in all these models people are arbitrarily labeled mentally ill.

Deviation from Normality

One approach to defining abnormality is to say that whatever most people do is normal. Abnormality, then, is any deviation from the average or from the majority. It is normal to bathe periodically, to express grief at the death of a loved one, and to wear warm clothes when going out in the cold, because most people do so. Because very few people take ten showers a day, or laugh when a loved one dies, or wear bathing suits in the snow, those who do so may be considered abnormal.

However, the deviance approach, as commonly used as it is, has serious limitations. If most people cheat on their income-tax returns, are honest taxpayers abnormal? If most people are noncreative, was Shakespeare abnormal? Because the majority is not always right or best, the deviance approach to defining abnormality is not a generally useful standard.

Adjustment

Another way to distinguish normal from abnormal people is to say that normal people are able to get along in the world—physically, emotionally, and socially. They can feed and clothe themselves, work, find friends, and live by the rules of society. By this definition, abnormal people are the ones who fail to *adjust*. They may be so unhappy that they refuse to eat or so lethargic that they cannot hold a job. They may experience so much anxiety in relationships with others that they end up avoiding people, living in a lonely world of their own.

Figure 15.2
The line between normal and abnormal is a fine one and depends very much on the observer and the standard being used. What some people consider deviant, others may see as just a little odd.

Figure 15.3
The Madwoman, painted by Chaim Soutine in 1920. Many people believe that those who are mentally ill are always recognizable by their bizarre appearance and behavior—that they are somehow fundamentally different from the rest of us.

Psychological Health

The terms "mental illness" and "mental health" imply that psychological disturbance or abnormality is like a physical sickness—such as the flu or tuberculosis. Although many psychologists are beginning to think that "mental illness" is different from physical illness, the idea remains that there is some ideal way for people to function psychologically, just as there is an ideal way for people to function physically. Some psychologists feel that the normal or healthy person would be one who is functioning ideally or who at least is striving toward ideal functioning. Personality theorists such as Carl Jung and Abraham Maslow (see Chapter 11) have tried to describe this striving process, which is often referred to as *"self-actualization."* According to this line of thinking, to be normal or healthy involves full acceptance and expression of one's own individuality and humanness.

One problem with this approach to defining abnormality is that it is difficult to determine whether or not a person is doing a good job of actualizing him- or herself. How can you tell when a person is doing his or her best? What are the signs that he or she is losing the struggle? Answers to such questions must often be arbitrary.

USING PSYCHOLOGY

Legal Definitions of Sanity

When John Hinckley was tried for shooting President Ronald Reagan in 1981, he was found "not guilty by reason of insanity" and sent to a mental hospital. This widely publicized case raised some concern among psychiatrists and lawyers about the legal definition of sanity. The terms "sane" and "insane" are legal, rather than psychological, terms.

While there is no single definition of criminal insanity, the most widely used set of guidelines was developed by the American Law Institute in 1962. It emphasized that people are not responsible for their criminal acts if "as a result of mental disease or defect" they do not know that what they did was wrong or if they were unable to act differently. The guidelines also noted that "the terms 'mental disease or defect' do not include an abnormality manifested only by repeated criminal . . . conduct."

Figure 15.4
President Reagan waving to the crowd moments before he was shot by John Hinckley. Hinckley's attorney argued that his client was insane and could not be held responsible for the shooting.

It is often difficult to apply these guidelines to real people. As in the Hinckley case, expert witnesses are usually called on both sides. The defense lawyer maintains that his or her client is insane, and the prosecutor tries to prove the defendant sane. The jurors decide which set of expert witnesses is correct. A person who is judged insane may spend more time in a mental hospital than he or she would have spent in prison if judged sane.

Although an insanity defense generates publicity, this plea is used rarely and is usually unsuccessful. The courts judge people insane much more often for purposes of commitment to mental institutions.

Laws vary from state to state, but generally a person can be committed to a mental hospital if he or she is judged to be (1) mentally ill and (2) in need of treatment or dangerous to himself or herself or others.

In *formal commitment* proceedings, a friend or relative usually asks a judge to order a mental health examination. *Informal commitment* occurs when, for example, the police bring in a person who is acting wildly. In most states, a person can be held against his or her will for a specified period of time if two physicians (not necessarily psychiatrists) sign a certificate ordering the commitment.

In recent years, many mental patients have formed groups to protect their legal rights. As a result, the legal status of involuntary commitment procedures and patients' rights for treatment is likely to continue to change in the 1980s (Davison and Neale, 1978).

Is Mental Illness a Myth?

The current definitions of abnormality are somewhat arbitrary. And this fact has led some theorists to conclude that labeling a person as "mentally ill" simply because his or her behavior is odd is cruel and irresponsible. The foremost spokesman of this point of view is the American psychiatrist Thomas Szasz (1961).

Szasz argues that most of the people whom we call mentally ill are not ill at all. They simply have "problems in living"—serious conflicts with the world around them. But instead of dealing with the patient's conflict as something that deserves attention and respect, psychiatrists simply label him as "sick" and shunt him off to a hospital. The society's norms remain unchallenged, and the psychiatrist remains in a comfortable position of authority. The one who loses is the patient, who is deprived both of responsibility for his behavior and of his dignity as a human being. As a result, Szasz claims, the patient's problems intensify. Szasz's position is a minority stand. Most psychologists and psychiatrists would agree that a person who claims to be God or Napoleon is truly abnormal and disturbed.

The fact that it is difficult to define abnormality does not mean that no such thing exists. What it does mean is that we should be very cautious about judging a person to be "mentally ill" just because he or she acts in a way that we cannot understand. It should also be kept in mind that mild psychological disorders are extremely common. It is only when a psychological problem becomes severe enough to disrupt everyday life that it is thought of as "abnormality" or "illness."

THE PROBLEM OF CLASSIFICATION

For years psychiatrists have been trying to devise a logical and useful method for classifying emotional disorders. This is a difficult task, for psychological problems do not lend themselves to the same sort of categorizing that physical illnesses do. The causes and symptoms of psychological disturbances and breakdowns, and the cures for those breakdowns, are rarely obvious or clearcut.

All of the major classification schemes have accepted the medical model—they assume that abnormal behavior can be described in the same manner as any physical illness. The physician diagnoses a specific disease when a person has certain specific symptoms.

In 1952, the American Psychiatric Association agreed upon a standard system for classifying abnormal symptoms, which it published in the *Diagnostic and Statistical Manual of Mental Disorders*, or DSM. This has been revised twice as the **DSM-II** (1968) and the **DSM-III** (1980).

The DSM-II was criticized as too vague: two psychologists often gave different diagnoses for the same patient. The DSM-III system requires more concrete and specific symptoms for a diagnosis. As a result, its diagnoses are far more reliable. In DSM editions prior to DSM-III, disorders were classified not only by symptoms but also by assumed causes. This made consistent diagnoses difficult. Also, before the publication of DSM-III, it was difficult to assign multiple diagnoses.

Before 1980, the two most commonly used diagnostic distinctions were neurosis and psychosis. **Neurosis** is a disorder in which severe anxiety reduces a person's ability to deal effectively with reality. **Psychosis** is a disorder in which a person is often unable to deal with reality at all and withdraws into a private world. Psychosis is not an advanced stage of neurosis. It is a distinct type of psychological disturbance. These two diagnostic terms were dropped in the new diagnostic classification scheme because it was felt that the range of disorders they described was too wide.

Even though the terms *neurosis* and *psychosis* have been replaced by more specific ones, they are still used by many psychologists and lay people. Thus, this chapter will discuss symptoms and possible causes of several forms of neurosis and psychosis, as well as personality disorders and addiction to alcohol and other drugs.

As you read, you will probably feel that some of the descriptions could be applied to you at times. They probably could, but remember, a psychologically disturbed person is one who turns normal human quirks into extreme and distorted *patterns* of thought and behavior. When we speak of psychologically disturbed individuals we are not talking about people who have their normal share of difficulties, but rather about people who are hopelessly unhappy, whose minds are confused and chaotic, who have a difficult time doing the simple things in life, or who act in ways that are truly harmful to themselves or to other people.

NEUROSIS

The general term *neurosis* is used to refer to a variety of disorders that share certain characteristics, including feelings of anxiety and personal inadequacy and an avoidance of dealing with problems. Neurotic people often have unrealistic images of themselves. They are plagued by self-doubt and seem unable to free themselves of recurring worries and fears. Their emotional problems may be expressed in constant worrying, sudden mood swings, or a variety of physical symptoms (for example, headaches, sweating, muscle tightness, weakness, and fatigue). Neurotics often have difficulty forming stable and satisfying relationships. Even though their behavior may be self-defeating and ineffective in solving problems, neurotic people often refuse to give up their neurotic behaviors in favor of more effective ways of dealing with anxiety. In the DSM-III, neurotic disorders are classified under three main headings: *anxiety disorders* such as *phobias, obsessions,* and *compulsions; somatoform disorders;* and *dissociative disorders.*

Anxiety

Once in a while, everyone feels nervous for reasons he or she cannot explain, but a severely neurotic person almost always feels this way. Neurotic **anxiety** is a generalized apprehension—a vague feeling that one is in danger. Sometimes, this anxiety blossoms into full-fledged panic attacks, which may include choking sensations, chest pain, dizziness, trembling, and hot flashes. Unlike fear, which is a reaction to real and identifiable threats, anxiety is a reaction to vague or imagined dangers.

Some people experience a continuous, generalized anxiety. Fearing unknown and unforeseen circumstances, they are unable to make decisions or enjoy life. They may become so preoccupied with their internal problems that they neglect their social relationships. People who experience neurotic anxiety often have trouble dealing with their family and friends and fulfilling their responsibilities, and this adds to their anxiety. They are trapped in a vicious cycle. The more they worry, the more difficulty they have; the more difficulty they have, the more they worry.

Often, the experience of generalized anxiety is accompanied by physical symptoms: muscular tension; an inability to relax; a furrowed brow; and a strained face. Poor appetite, indigestion, diarrhea, and frequent

Figure 15.5
A person suffering from
agoraphobia would fear going into
a crowded shopping center such
as this one.

urination are also commonly present. Because anxious people are in a constant state of apprehension, they may have difficulty sleeping or, once asleep, may wake up suddenly in the night. As a result, they may feel tired when they wake up in the morning.

Why are some people so anxious? According to Freudian psychoanalytic theory, anxiety is caused by unconscious desires and conflicts that are so disturbing that those who are affected cannot find any satisfying solution. These unresolved conflicts often persist on an unconscious level. Neurotically anxious people are more or less constantly afraid of emotions that they do not feel capable of handling. When something happens to bring the emotions closer to the surface, the fear becomes intense. For example, people who are unable to face or express feelings of anger may become tense and fearful when they see other people arguing or when hostile images flash into their minds, because they are reminded of emotions they are trying to deny.

Hans Eysenck (1957) has proposed a biological explanation of the origins of anxiety. Eysenck believes that some people are born with very excitable nervous systems. They tend to overreact to "threatening" stimuli and gradually come to associate anxiety with many different situations. Other theorists stress the role of learning. If a man feels very anxious on a date, for example, even the thought of another date may make him nervous, so he learns to avoid having dates and there is never a chance to unlearn the anxiety. His anxiety may then generalize to other situations and become a worse problem.

Phobias

When severe anxiety is focused on a particular object or situation, it is called a **phobia.** A phobia can focus on almost anything, including high places (acrophobia), enclosed spaces (claustrophobia), and darkness (nyctophobia). A person with a phobia has an intense, persistent, irrational fear of something.

Phobic individuals develop elaborate plans to avoid the situations they fear. For example, people suffering from an extreme fear of crowds (agoraphobia) may stop going to movies or shopping in large, busy stores. Some reach the point where they will not leave their houses at all.

Phobias range in intensity from mild to extremely severe. Most people deal with their phobias by avoiding the thing they are frightened of. Thus the phobias are learned and maintained by the reinforcing effects of avoidance. One common form of treatment for phobias involves providing the phobic person with opportunities to experience the feared object under conditions in which he or she feels safe.

Some psychologists explain certain phobias in terms of projection. What the people really fear is an impulse inside themselves. To avoid this fear, they unconsciously project it onto something outside themselves. For example, a woman who is terrified of heights may really be afraid of losing control and "letting go" to other wishes or feelings. By concentrating on avoiding heights, she is able to control other disturbing urges and push them out of her consciousness.

Obsessions and Compulsions

A person suffering from acute anxiety may find himself thinking the same thoughts over and over again. Such an uncontrollable pattern of thoughts is called an **obsession.** Or someone may repeatedly perform irrational actions. This is called a **compulsion.** The neurotic person may experience both these agonies together—a condition called *obsessive-compulsive neurosis.*

A compulsive person may feel compelled to wash her hands twenty or thirty times a day, or to avoid stepping on cracks in the sidewalk when she goes out. An obsessive person may be unable to rid herself of unpleasant thoughts about death, or of a recurring impulse to make obscene remarks in public. And the obsessive-compulsive may wash her hands continually *and* torment herself with thoughts of obscene behavior.

Everyone has obsessions and compulsions. Love might be described as an obsession; so might a hobby that occupies most of a person's spare time. Striving to do something "perfectly" is often considered to be a compulsion. But if the person who is deeply engrossed in a hobby or who aims for perfection enjoys this intense absorption and can still function effectively, he or she is usually not considered neurotic. Psychologists consider it a problem only when such thoughts and activities interfere with what a person wants and needs to do. Someone who spends so much time double-checking every detail of her work that she can never finish a job is considered more neurotic than conscientious.

Why do people develop obsessions and compulsions? Possibly because they serve as diversions from a neurotic person's real fears and their origins and thus may reduce anxiety somewhat. In addition, compulsions provide a disturbed person with the evidence that she is doing something well, even if it is only avoiding cracks on a sidewalk. Thus there is some logic in this apparently illogical behavior.

Somatoform Disorders

Neurotic anxiety can create a wide variety of physical symptoms for which there is no apparent physical cause. This phenomenon is known as a

Figure 15.6
An artist's representation of three phobias: (a) fear of heights, called acrophobia; (b) fear of enclosed spaces, called claustrophobia; and (c) fear of dirt, called mysophobia. (After Vassos, 1931)

Figure 15.7
A still from the film *The Caine Mutiny,* in which Humphrey Bogart played Captain Queeg, an individual who was obsessed with order. Any disruption of Queeg's routine sent him into panic and produced the compulsive behavior of continually rolling ball bearings in his hand. Queeg's behavior led his officers to label him "mentally ill" and to mutiny against him.

Figure 15.8
A patient who complained to a doctor that his right hand had become numb might be diagnosed as a neurotic suffering from a conversion reaction, depending on the exact pattern of the numbness. The skin areas served by different nerves in the arm are shown in (a). The "glove" numbness shown in (b) could not result from damage to these nerves.

somatoform disorder, or hysteria. The term *hysteria* was more commonly used in Freud's time to refer to unexplainable fainting, paralysis, or deafness. Today the term *somatoform disorder* is preferred. There are two major types of somatoform disorders: *conversion reactions* and *hypochondriasis*.

Conversion Reactions. A **conversion reaction** is the conversion of emotional difficulties into the loss of a specific physiological function. Many people occasionally experience mild conversion reactions, as when someone is so frightened he or she cannot move, but a neurotic disorder is not simply a brief loss of functioning due to fright. It persists.

A conversion reaction results in a real and prolonged handicap—the person literally cannot hear or speak or feel anything in his left hand or move his legs or exercise some other normal physical function (Figure 15.8). For example, a man might wake up one morning and find himself paralyzed from the waist down. The normal reaction to this would be panic. If the man is neurotic, however, he might accept the loss of function with relative calm. (This is one sign that a person is suffering from a psychological rather than a physiological problem.) Most psychologists believe that people suffering from conversion reactions unconsciously invent physical symptoms to gain freedom from unbearable anxiety. For example, a woman who lives in terror of blurting out things that she does not want to say may lose the power of speech. This "solves" the problem. Conversion reactions are comparatively rare.

Hypochondriasis. Conversion reactions must be distinguished from **hypochondriasis,** in which a person who is in good health becomes preoccupied with imaginary ailments. The hypochondriac spends a lot of time looking for signs of serious physical illness and often misinterprets minor aches, pains, bruises or bumps as early signs of a fatal illness. Despite negative results in medical tests and physical evaluations, the hypochondriac typically continues to believe that a disease or malfunction exists.

Dissociative Disorders

Another form of neurotic behavior may take the form of a **dissociative reaction** in which the person experiences either a loss of memory or identity or exhibits two or more identities. These psychological phenomena fascinate many people, so we hear a good deal about amnesia and "split personalities." Actually, they are very rare.

Loss of memory, or *amnesia*, may be an attempt to escape from problems by blotting them out completely. Amnesiacs remember how to speak and usually retain a fund of general knowledge, but they may not know who they are, where they live and work, or who their family is (Levant, 1966). Other types of amnesia are caused by brain damage.

In **fugue,** another type of dissociative reaction, amnesia is coupled with active flight to a different environment. For example, a woman may suddenly disappear and "wake up" three days later in a restaurant 200 miles from home. She may actually establish a new identity—assume a new name, marry, take a job, and so forth—in a new place. She may repress all knowledge of a previous life. A fugue state may last for days or for decades. However long it lasts, the individual, when she comes out of it, will have no memory of what she has done in the interim. Fugue, then, is a sort of traveling amnesia, and it probably serves the same psychological function as amnesia: escape from unbearable conflict or anxiety.

In multiple personality, a third type of dissociative reaction, someone seems to have two or more distinct identities. Eve White, a young woman who sought psychiatric treatment for severe headaches and blackouts, has become a famous example. Eve White was a conscientious, self-controlled, rather shy person. However, during one of her therapy sessions, her expression—and her personality—suddenly changed. Eve Black, as she now called herself, was childlike, fun-loving, and irresponsible—the opposite of the woman who originally walked into the psychiatrist's office. Eve Black was conscious of Eve White's existence, but considered her a separate person. Eve White did not know about Eve Black, however, and neither was she conscious of Jane, a third personality that emerged during the course of therapy. (This case served as the basis for the book and film *The Three Faces of Eve.*) Some psychologists believe that this dividing up of the personality is the result of the individual's effort to escape from a part of himself or herself that he or she fears. The "secret self" then emerges in the form of a separate personality.

While cases like Eve and Sybil (a woman whose sixteen personalities were also described in a book and a movie) are fascinating, they are extremely rare and somewhat controversial. One researcher (Abse, 1966) reviewed the entire psychological literature and was able to find published accounts of only two hundred people who supposedly suffered from any dissociative reaction.

Depression

Depression is a pattern of sadness, anxiety, fatigue, agitated behavior, and reduced ability to function and interact with others. It may also interfere with sleep patterns and the ability to concentrate. It ranges from mild feelings of uneasiness, sadness, and apathy to intense suicidal despair. Occasional depression is a common experience. Most of us feel depressed when someone we love dies, for example. And, from time to time, everyone feels "blue" for no apparent reason. However, when depression is chronic (that is, the person never seems to "snap out of it") or especially intense, it is considered a serious psychological problem.

According to Freudian theory, severe depression may reflect guilt and the need for self-punishment. For example, a person may feel that he or she neglected someone who just died and may unconsciously hold himself or herself responsible for that person's death. In this case, depression acts as a self-imposed jail term: the person does not allow himself or herself to be happy.

In recent years, the cognitive theories of Aaron Beck and Martin Seligman have often served as the basis for research on depression. Beck (1967) believes that depressed people draw illogical conclusions about themselves—they blame themselves for normal problems and consider every minor failure a catastrophe. A depressed man who failed his driver's test,

Figure 15.9
The pattern of chronic depression is a familiar one to therapists, but its causes are still a matter of debate. There is the Freudian theory of guilt and the need for self-punishment; the cognitive theories of Beck and Seligman; and a theory of chemical imbalance in the brain.

Figure 15.10
A "suicide hotline." The man shown here is one of many trained volunteers who work at suicide prevention centers throughout the country.

for example, might consider himself a hopeless nerd as a result, and conclude that he will never be able to get a car of his own. As described in Chapter 2, Martin Seligman (1975) believes that depression is caused by a feeling of learned helplessness. The depressed person learns to believe that he has no control over events in his life, that nothing he does makes any difference, and that it is useless to even try.

Another theory explains depression as a chemical imbalance in the brain. According to this view, some people are more likely to become depressed because they are born with low levels of a specific brain chemical. (According to one current theory, the chemical is the neurotransmitter serotonin. This predisposing factor influences other brain chemicals. Low levels of the neurotransmitter norepinephrine are associated with depression; high levels with mania.)

Suicide

Not all people who commit suicide are depressed, and not all depressed people attempt suicide. But many depressives do think about suicide, and some of them translate these thoughts into action.

People may take their lives for any number of reasons: to escape from physical or emotional pain (perhaps a terminal illness or the loneliness of old age); to end the torment of unacceptable feelings (such as homosexual fantasies); to punish themselves for wrongs they feel they have committed; to punish others who have not perceived their needs (Mintz, 1968). In many cases we simply do not know why the suicide occurred.

But we do know that every year between 20,000 and 30,000 Americans end their lives—about one every thirty minutes. More women than men attempt suicide, but more men than women succeed. Suicide is most common among the elderly, but also ranks as the third most common cause of death among college students. Contrary to popular belief, people who threaten suicide or make an unsuccessful attempt usually *are* serious. Studies show that about 70 percent of people who kill themselves threaten to do so within the three months preceding the suicide, and an unsuccessful attempt is often a trial run (Alvarez, 1970).

Anxiety, phobias, obsessions, compulsions, somatoform disorders, depression, and suicide—all are ways people use, in various combinations, to escape problems in themselves or the world in which they live. With the obvious exception of suicide, these neurotic reactions do not shut people off completely from daily life. Psychosis does.

PSYCHOSIS

A neurotic person is one who is emotionally crippled by anxiety but continues to slug it out with life as best he or she can. A psychotic person is one whose distorted perceptions and behavior reach such an irrational, fantastic, and fear-laden level that he or she withdraws completely from normal life. One might say that a neurotic dreams in an unreal way about life, whereas a psychotic lives life as an unreal dream.

Like neurosis, psychosis is not a single problem; it has no single cause or cure. Rather, it is a collection of symptoms that indicates an individual has serious difficulty trying to meet the demands of life. Two major categories of psychosis are *schizophrenia* and *affective reactions*. *Autism* is a psychosis found in children.

Schizophrenia

Approximately half the patients in United States mental hospitals have been diagnosed as schizophrenic (Taube and Rednick, 1973). What distinguishes this disorder from other types of psychological disturbance? **Schizophrenia** involves confused and disordered thoughts and perceptions.

Suppose a psychiatrist is interviewing a patient who has just been admitted to a hospital. The individual demonstrates a wide assortment of symptoms. He is intensely excited, expresses extreme hostility toward members of his family, and at the same time claims that he loves them, showing conflicting feelings. One minute he is extremely aggressive, questioning the psychiatrist's motives and even threatening her. The next minute he withdraws and acts as if he does not hear anything she says. Then he begins talking again. "Naturally," he says, "I am growing my father's hair." Although all of the person's other behavior indicates psychological problems, this last statement would be the "diagnostic bell ringer." It reveals that the man is living in a private disordered reality.

Many schizophrenics experience **delusions** (false beliefs maintained in

Figure 15.11
These paintings were done by a male patient diagnosed as schizophrenic with paranoid tendencies. Both illustrations are characterized by the symbolism of watchful eyes, grasping hands, and the self as subject matter.

the face of contrary evidence) and **hallucinations** (sensations in the absence of appropriate stimulation). For example, a paranoid schizophrenic generally believes that others are plotting against him—contriving ways to confuse him, make him look ridiculous, perhaps to get rid of him. People are watching him constantly. His thoughts are being monitored. When he goes to the movies to escape, he finds—to his horror—that the film is all about him. The ticket taker and the man in the next row are in on the plot. These delusions are usually supported by hallucinations, in which his five senses detect the evidence of the plot. He may taste poison in his food, smell gas in his bedroom, or hear voices telling him why he has been singled out or what lies in store for him.

Often, schizophrenics withdraw from other people into a private world of fantasy. In *simple schizophrenia* individuals gradually lose interest in what happens around them, becoming increasingly apathetic, listless, and noncommunicative. Such individuals may be able to hold menial jobs or may survive as "drifters," but their interpersonal contacts are few. *Catatonia* is an extreme form of withdrawal in which the person becomes totally unresponsive. She may maintain the same posture for hours, mute and seemingly oblivious to physical discomfort. Periodic flare-ups, when the person becomes violent toward herself or others, may be the only sign of emotional life in a catatonic person.

Other schizophrenics are active and busy, but their behavior and speech are incomprehensible to others. The person may repeat a bizarre gesture, whose meaning is known only to him, over and over. He may express inappropriate emotions—for example, giggling uncontrollably as he relates violent and morbid fantasies. He may invent words or repeat phrases as if they were magical incantations—for reasons known only to himself (Maher, 1972). The result is sometimes what psychologists call "word salad": a jumble of unconnected, irrational phrases.

It is as if the gears in the schizophrenic's mental machinery had slipped and the connections had gone haywire. One patient described the experience as losing the ability to focus his thoughts.

"I can't concentrate. It's diversion of attention that troubles me. I am picking up different conversations. It's like being a transmitter. The sounds are coming through to me but I feel my mind cannot cope with everything. It's difficult to concentrate on any one sound."

Another told of being unable to organize his perceptions.

"Everything is in bits. You put the picture up bit by bit into your head. It's like a photograph that's been torn to bits and put together again.

Figure 15.12
A portrait of a "suicidal melancholic" done in England in the nineteenth century. This woman, only thirty-four when the portrait was made, suffered from the delusion that she would be murdered and eventually began to attempt suicide in order to escape the danger.

You have to absorb it again. If you move it's frightening. The picture you had in your head is still there but it's broken up" (McGhie and Chapman, 1961).

Affective Reactions

Another common type of psychosis is one in which individuals are excessively and inappropriately happy or unhappy. These **affective reactions** (from the word "affect," meaning mood) may take the form of high elation, hopeless depression, or an alternation between the two.

In a **manic reaction,** a person experiences elation, extreme confusion, distractibility, and racing thoughts. Often, the person has an exaggerated sense of self-esteem and engages in irresponsible behavior such as shopping sprees, insulting remarks,   or the following type of behavior:

> On admission she slapped the nurse, addressed the house physician as God, made the sign of the cross, and laughed loudly when she was asked to don the hospital garb. This she promptly tore to shreds. . . . She sang at the top of her voice, screamed through the window, and leered at the patients promenading in the recreation yard (Karnash, 1945).

In the **depressive reaction,** the individual is overcome by feelings of failure, sinfulness, worthlessness, and despair. We have already described depression as a form of neurosis. Psychotic depression differs from neurotic depression—just as psychosis in general differs from neurosis in general—in that the psychotic has lost contact with reality. The neurotic depressive may feel chronically dejected, but she still knows how to get to the bank, how old her children are, and how to differentiate between fantasy and reality. The psychotic depressive has left reality behind and has moved into a bleak fantasy world constructed out of her despair. She is likely to claim that her children are dead, that she killed them, that the world is coming to an end, that it is all her fault. Furthermore, the psychotic depressive may stop functioning altogether and descend into a stupor, not eating, not speaking, and not moving.

> The patient lay in bed, immobile, with a dull, depressed expression on his face. His eyes were sunken and downcast. Even when spoken to, he would not raise his eyes to look at the speaker. Usually he did not respond at all to questions, but sometimes, after apparently great effort, he would mumble something about the "Scourge of God" (Coleman, 1976).

In some cases, referred to as *manic-depressive* psychosis, a patient will alternate between frantic action and motionless despair. Some theorists have speculated that the manic periods serve as an attempt to ward off the underlying hopelessness. Others believe that mania can be traced to the same biochemical disorder responsible for depression.

Autism

Autism is a childhood psychosis that seems to be present at birth. From an early age, autistic children are aloof and noncommunicative. Often they do not even cry or coo like other babies. They act as if other people do not exist. Speech patterns are very peculiar, and some of these children never learn to communicate with language at all. They become very upset over any change in their environment. They want things to remain the same. They sometimes develop bizarre attachments to physical objects, like the autistic child who went everywhere wrapped in a shower curtain.

These children are usually physically healthy—in fact, they are often quite beautiful. Psychologists do not really know what causes autism. Are these children born this way, or are they reacting to rejection by their parents? Do they have some mysterious brain defect? Do their bodies produce too much or too little of certain vital chemicals? Have their families given them some insoluble problem that causes overpowering anxiety?

Causes of Psychosis

There are many theories but very few facts about what causes psychosis. Psychologists think that their problems result from the interaction of several factors, but none of these factors is at all clearly understood.

Hereditary Factors. There is some evidence that people may inherit a predisposition or tendency to become psychotic. Close relatives of schizophrenics, for example, are much more likely to become schizophrenic than are other people, even if they never come into contact with their schizophrenic relative (Rosenthal *et al.,* 1971; Kety *et al.,* 1971). Just how this predisposition might be transmitted from generation to generation is a matter of speculation. According to one theory, some people are born with a nervous system that gets aroused very easily and takes a long time to recover to normal (Figure 15.14). People like this might be particularly

> **Some people may inherit a predisposition or tendency to become psychotic.**

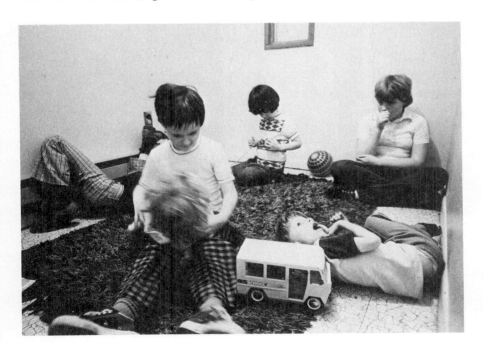

Figure 15.13
Autistic children. Though they are all in the same place, each child is in his own world, and there is no interaction.

likely to get upset when they are stressed (Zubin and Spring, 1977). Thus a situation that might be only mildly upsetting to one person might cause a psychotic reaction in an acutely sensitive person. However, if this person is raised in a relatively simple, pressure-free environment, he might never develop psychological problems.

Biochemical Factors. The proper working of the brain depends on the presence of the right amounts of many different chemicals, from oxygen to proteins. Some psychologists believe that psychosis is due largely to chemical imbalances in the brain. With depression, for example, abnormally low amounts of certain chemicals may disturb the transmission of electrical impulses from one brain cell to another.

Chemical problems may also be involved in schizophrenia. A number of researchers think that the basic problem in schizophrenia is that too much or too little of certain chemicals has "knocked out of kilter" the brain's mechanisms for processing information. As a result, the schizophrenic cannot organize his thoughts. When he tries to keep one thought at the center of his awareness, other thoughts—irrelevant ones—keep pushing in and interfering with his concentration (Wynne, Cromwell, and Matthyssee, 1978). In short, he experiences the kind of thought disturbance reported by the schizophrenic patients quoted earlier in this chapter.

Unusual concentrations of certain chemicals have in fact been found in the bodies of many schizophrenics. However, it is hard to tell whether these chemicals are the cause of schizophrenia or the result of it. They may even be caused by the fact that schizophrenics tend to live in hospitals, where they get little exercise, eat institutional food, and are generally given daily doses of tranquilizers. Living under such conditions, anyone—not just the schizophrenic person—might begin to show chemical imbalances.

The Double Bind. Some theorists believe that many mental problems,

Figure 15.14
A child born with a biochemically unusual nervous system that reacts very strongly to stimulation may have pronounced hallucinations during an early childhood illness that has no lasting effect on most children. As he grows older, he may try to discuss his memories of that time with his parents. Being insecure themselves, they may become uneasy and respond in ways that make him feel he is wrong or bad in some way. His unusual biochemistry causes him to react very strongly to this rebuff, and he now has further troubling experiences he needs to make sense of. He then feels a conflict between his need to talk to his parents about these experiences and his fear of their cold response. He is well on the way to becoming psychologically disordered unless the links in this chain are somehow broken.

particularly those that involve confused thoughts and isolation from other people, result from conflicts in communication. These psychologists believe that a child's ability to think and to communicate with others can be undermined if his or her parents repeatedly communicate contradictory messages. For example, a mother may resent her child and feel uncomfortable around him, yet also feel obligated to act lovingly toward him. She tells the child how much she loves him, but at the same time she stiffens whenever he tries to hug her. Thus the child is given one message in words and another in action.

As a result, the child is placed in an impossible situation. If he reaches out to his mother, she shows him (in her actions) that she dislikes this. If he avoids her, she tells him (in words) that she dislikes that. He wants very much to please her, but no matter what he does, it is wrong. He is caught in a *double bind*.

According to **double-bind theory,** a childhood full of such contradictory messages results in people perceiving the world as a confusing, disconnected place and believing that their words and actions have little significance or meaning. Consequently they may develop the kind of disordered behaviors and thoughts we have been describing.

Which of these theories is correct? At this point, we do not know. It may be that each is partially true. Perhaps people who inherit a tendency toward psychological disorders react more strongly to a double bind than others would. Perhaps people who are caught in a double bind are especially vulnerable to chemical imbalances. Or perhaps it takes a combination of all three factors—heredity, biochemical disorders, and conflict—to produce psychotic behavior (Meehl, 1962). Only further research will give us the answer.

PERSONALITY DISORDERS

Personality disorders are different from the problems we have been discussing. People with personality disorders generally do not suffer from acute anxiety; nor do they behave in bizarre, incomprehensible ways. Psychologists consider these people "abnormal" because they seem unable to establish meaningful relationships with other people, to assume social responsibilities, or to adapt to their social environment. This diagnostic category includes a wide range of self-defeating personality patterns, from painfully shy, lonely types to vain, pushy show-offs. In this section we focus on the **antisocial personality,** sometimes called the sociopath or psychopath.

Antisocial individuals are irresponsible, immature, emotionally shallow people who seem to court trouble. Extremely selfish, they treat people as objects—as things to be used for gratification and to be cast coldly aside when no longer wanted. Intolerant of everyday frustrations and unable to save or plan or wait, they live for the moment. Seeking thrills is their major occupation. If they should injure other people along the way or break social rules, they do not seem to feel any shame or guilt. It's the other

Figure 15.15
Many psychologists would classify these gang members as antisocial individuals. Gangs are frequently dedicated to violence and destruction.

person's tough luck. Nor does getting caught seem to rattle them. No matter how many times they are reprimanded, punished, or jailed, they never learn how to stay out of trouble. They simply do not profit from experience.

Many antisocial individuals can get away with destructive behavior because they are intelligent, entertaining, and able to mimic emotions they do not feel. They win affection and confidence from others whom they then take advantage of. This ability to charm while exploiting helped Charles Manson to dominate the gang of runaways whom he eventually led into the gruesome Tate-LaBianca murders in 1969.

If caught, antisocial individuals will either spin a fantastic lie or simply insist, with wide-eyed sincerity, that their intentions were utterly pure. Guilt and anxiety have no place in the antisocial personality. A fine example is that of Hugh Johnson, a con man recently caught after having defrauded people out of thousands of dollars in sixty-four separate swindles. When asked why he had victimized so many people, "he replied with some heat that he never took more from a person than the person could afford to lose, and further, that he was only reducing the likelihood that other more dangerous criminals would use force to achieve the same ends" (Nathan and Harris, 1975: 406–407).

How do psychologists explain such a lack of ordinary human decency and shame? According to one theory, the psychopath has simply imitated his or her own antisocial parents. Others point to lack of discipline or inconsistent discipline during childhood. Finally, some researchers believe that psychopaths have a "faulty nervous system." While most of us get very aroused when we do something that we've been punished for in the past, psychopaths never seem to learn to anticipate punishment.

DRUG ADDICTION

In American society, drug abuse has become a major psychological problem. Millions of Americans depend so heavily on drugs that they hurt themselves physically, socially, and psychologically.

Abuse of drugs invariably involves **psychological dependence.** Users come to depend so much on the feeling of well-being they obtain from the drug that they feel compelled to continue using it. People can become psychologically dependent on a wide variety of drugs, including alcohol, caffeine, nicotine (in cigarettes), opium, marijuana, and amphetamines. When deprived of the drug, a psychologically dependent person becomes restless, irritable, and uneasy.

In addition to psychological dependence, some drugs lead to physiological **addiction.** A person is addicted when his system has become so used to the drug that the drugged state becomes the body's "normal" state. If the drug is not in the body, the person experiences extreme physical discomfort, just as he would if he were deprived of oxygen or of water.

Just as dependence causes a psychological need for the drug, addiction causes a physical need. Furthermore, once a person is addicted to a drug,

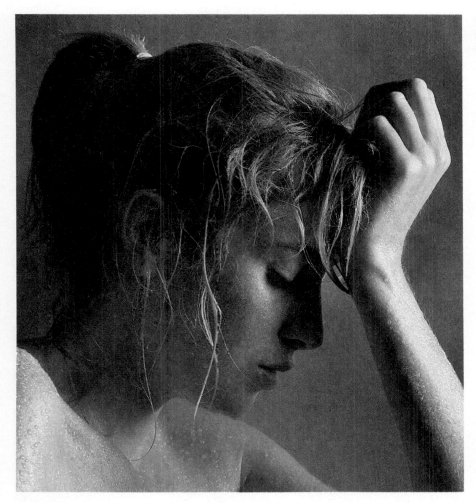

Figure 15.16
A drug addict during one of the stages of withdrawal.

he develops **tolerance;** that is, his body becomes so accustomed to the drug that he has to keep increasing his dosage in order to obtain the "high" that he achieved with his earlier doses. With certain sleeping pills, for example, a person can rapidly develop a tolerance for up to fifteen times the original dose. Further, an addict must have his drug in order to retain what little physical and psychological balance he has left. If he does not get it, he is likely to go through the dreaded experience of withdrawal.

Withdrawal is a state of physical and psychological upset during which the body and the mind revolt against, and finally get used to, the absence of the drug. Withdrawal symptoms vary from person to person and from drug to drug. They range from a mild case of nausea and "the shakes" to hallucinations, convulsions, coma, and death.

Alcoholism

Although heroin addiction seems to receive more attention in the media, this country's most serious drug problem is alcoholism. Somewhere between 8 and 12 million Americans are alcoholics. According to one recent estimate, 1.3 million teen-agers and preteen-agers have a serious drinking problem (Ray, 1978). Fifty percent or more of the deaths in automobile accidents each year can be traced to alcohol; in half of all murders either the killer or the victim has been drinking; and some 13,000 people die of liver damage caused by alcohol every year. In addition, the cost in human suffering to the alcoholic and his or her family is impossible to measure.

In small doses, alcohol might be called a social wonder drug. The first psychological function that it slows down is our inhibitions. Two drinks can make a person relaxed, talkative, playful, even giggly. (It is for this reason that many people consider alcohol a stimulant—it is really a depressant.)

As the number of drinks increases, the fun decreases. One by one, the person's psychological and physiological functions begin to shut down. Perceptions and sensations become distorted, and behavior may become obnoxious. The person begins to stumble and weave, speech becomes slurred, and reactions—to a stop sign, for example—become sluggish. If

Figure 15.17
This chart shows the effects of alcohol on a 150-pound person. Because alcohol is diluted in the blood, a 200-pound man can usually tolerate more liquor than a 110-pound woman.

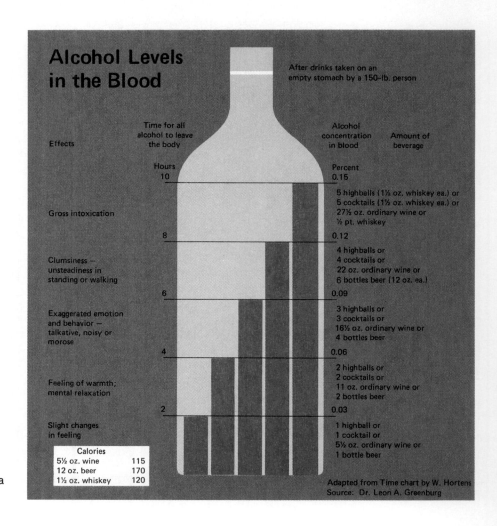

enough alcohol accumulates in the body, it leads to unconsciousness—and in some cases coma and death. It all depends on how much and how rapidly alcohol enters the bloodstream—which, in turn, depends on a person's weight, body chemistry, and how much he or she drinks how quickly (Figure 15.15).

Alcohol can produce psychological dependence, tolerance, and addiction. One researcher has outlined three stages of alcoholism. In the first stage, the individual discovers that alcohol reduces her tensions, gives her self-confidence, and reduces social pressures. Drinking makes her feel better. In the second stage, the beverage becomes a drug. The individual begins to drink so heavily that she feels she has to hide her habit. Thus she begins "sneaking" drinks. In this stage she may also begin to suffer from blackouts—she is unable to recall what happened during a drinking episode. In the final stage, she drinks compulsively, beginning in the morning. She becomes inefficient at work and tends to go on drinking sprees that may last for weeks. She is now an alcoholic, drinking continuously, eating infrequently, and feeling sick when deprived of her drug. Her health deteriorates rapidly (Jellinek, 1960).

The first step in treating the alcoholic is to see her through the violent withdrawal typical of alcohol addiction, and then to try to make her healthier. She may be given a variety of treatments—from drugs to psychotherapy. Alcoholics Anonymous, an organization for alcoholics, run by people who have had a drinking problem, has been more successful than most organizations. There is no certain cure for alcoholism. As many alcoholics return to the bottle as heroin addicts return to the needle. One problem is that our society tends to encourage social drinking and to tolerate the first stage of alcoholism.

> **? FACT OR FICTION**
>
> *Alcoholism can lead to permanent memory loss.*
>
> Fact. Some alcoholics suffer from Korsakoff's syndrome, a form of amnesia in which the person is unable to remember any newly acquired information. For example, even after years of treatment, one patient did not recognize his therapist and introduced himself whenever they met.

DSM-III: NEW WAYS TO CATEGORIZE MENTAL ILLNESS

As mentioned earlier, there were several problems with the DSM-II classification scheme, including use of such general terms as neurosis and psychosis.

The DSM-III solves some of these by emphasizing behavior patterns that have been found to occur in particular clusters rather than emphasizing the causes of various disorders. Furthermore, each diagnostic disorder is distinguished from other, similar diagnoses that a psychiatrist or psychologist may be considering.

Within each diagnostic category, the following descriptions are included:

1. essential features of the disorder—those that "define" the disorder;
2. associated features—features that are usually present;
3. diagnostic criteria—a list of symptoms (taken from the lists of es-

PSYCHOLOGY UPDATE

DSM-III-R. Psychiatrists, psychologists, and other researchers conduct studies called clinical trials to see whether the DSM classification system is helpful and useful. However, clinical trials take several years to design, run, and report. For this reason the organizers of the DSM system try not to change the system too often.

In 1987, the American Psychological Association published a revised manual called DSM-III-R. However, since relatively little time had elapsed since the publication of DSM-III, most changes were minor. For example, *affective disorders* are now called *mood disorders*, to be consistent with popular usage. The personality disorders now include two additional categories (sadistic and self-defeating) as "proposed personality disorders."

DSM-IV, scheduled to be published in 1994, promises few major changes from DSM-III-R. One controversial addition is the inclusion of premenstrual syndrome (PMS) as a distinct category. Overall, the greater specificity that came with DSM-III was well received by most practitioners, and refinements to make descriptions of diagnostic categories even more specific are expected in DSM-IV.

Table 15.1 / DSM-III AXIS I AND II CATEGORIES

AXIS I CATEGORIES

1. **Disorders usually first evident in infancy, childhood, or adolescence**
   Mental retardation
   Attention deficit disorder
   Conduct disorder
   Anxiety disorders of childhood or adolescence
   Eating disorders (for example, anorexia, bulimia)
   Stereotyped movement disorder (for example, tics)
   Pervasive development disorder (for example, autism)
   Other physical disorders (for example, stuttering, bedwetting)

2. **Organic mental disorders**
   Senile and presenile dementia
   Substance-induced organic disorder

3. **Substance-use disorder**

4. **Schizophrenic disorders**
   Disorganized
   Catatonic
   Paranoid
   Chronic undifferentiated

5. **Paranoid disorders**

6. **Affective disorders**
   Dysthymic disorder
   Bipolar disorder
   Major depression

7. **Anxiety disorders**
   Phobic disorders
   Anxiety states
   Post-traumatic stress disorder

8. **Somatoform disorders**
   Somatization disorder
   Conversion disorder
   Psychogenic pain disorder
   Hypochondriasis

9. **Dissociative disorders**
   Psychogenic amnesia
   Psychogenic fugue
   Multiple personality
   Depersonalization disorder

10. **Psychosexual disorders**
    Gender identity disorders
    Paraphilias
    Psychosexual dysfunctions

11. **Factitious disorders**

12. **Disorders of impulse control** (for example, kleptomania, pyromania, pathological gambling)

13. **Adjustment disorder**

AXIS II CATEGORIES (PERSONALITY DISORDERS)

Paranoid
Schizoid
Schizotypal
Histrionic
Narcissistic
Antisocial
Borderline
Avoidant
Dependent
Compulsive
Passive-aggressive

sential and associated features) that must be present for the patient to be given this diagnostic label; and
4. information on differential diagnosis—that is, how to distinguish this disorder from other disorders with which it might be confused.

These more precise diagnostic criteria reduce the chances that the same patient will be classified as schizophrenic by one doctor and manic-depressive by another. Since researchers often rely on diagnostic labels

Being Sane in an Insane Place

The doors slam shut. The hospital attendant turns the key. You are locked in a room with insane people. And they think you're insane too. They'll find out in no time, you tell yourself, but they don't. They keep you behind bars for your own good.

Despite our perception that psychiatric diagnosis is a science, it is quite possible for sane people to be institutionalized. The fact that it happened in the experiment we are about to describe suggests that psychiatric diagnosis is as much in the mind of the observer as it is in the behavior of the observed.

Eight people, including three psychologists, a pediatrician, and a housewife, called twelve different psychiatric hospitals complaining that they heard voices. Beyond this symptom, the pseudopatients presented the facts of their lives as they actually were. Once they were admitted to the hospital, they went back to their ordinary behavior. They dropped their claims of hearing voices, spoke to other patients and staff as they would to people outside the hospital, and told everyone they were feeling fine.

The hospital staff was not at all suspicious of these changes. They never suspected that the pseudopatients were sane. When these people were finally released, they were given the diagnosis of schizophrenia in remission. In the hospital's view they were not sane nor had they ever been sane. Interestingly, many legitimate patients detected the experimenters' sanity and told them that they didn't belong.

For more details, see D. L. Rosenhan, "On Being Sane in Insane Places," *Science*, 179, January 1973.

to study underlying factors that may cause disorders, it is particularly important for their work that patients with similar symptoms be classified in the same diagnostic category.

The DSM-III also recognizes the complexity of classifying people on the basis of mental disorders. Often, a person may exhibit more than one disorder or may be experiencing other stresses that complicate the diagnosis. In early classification systems, it was difficult to give a patient more than one label. The DSM-III overcame this problem by using five major dimensions, or *axes*, to describe a person's mental functioning. Each axis reflects a different aspect of a patient's case. Because the DSM-III uses five axes to evaluate individuals, it is referred to as a multiple-axial system.

Axis I is used to classify current symptoms into explicitly defined categories. These categories range from disorders that are usually first evident in infancy, childhood, or adolescence (such as conduct disorders or autism) to substance-use disorders (such as alcoholism), to schizophrenic disorders. (See Table 15.1 for a more detailed listing of the Axis I and II categories.)

Axis II is used to describe personality disorders or maladaptive traits such as compulsiveness, over-dependency, or aggressiveness. Axis II is also used to describe specific developmental disorders for children, adolescents, and, in some cases, adults. Examples of developmental problems that would be classified under Axis II are language disorders, reading difficulties, and speech problems.

It is possible for an individual to have a disorder on both Axis I and Axis II. For example, an adult may have a major depression noted on Axis I and a compulsive personality disorder noted on Axis II. A child may have a conduct disorder noted on Axis I and a developmental language disorder on Axis II. In other cases, a person may be seeking treatment primarily for a condition noted on Axis I or Axis II alone. The use of both Axes I and II permits multiple diagnoses and allows the clinician flexibility in making provisional diagnoses when there is not enough information available on the patient to make a firm diagnosis.

Axis III is used to describe physical disorders or conditions that are potentially relevant to understanding or managing the person. In some cases, a physical disorder may be causing the syndrome diagnosed on either Axis I or II. In other cases, the physical disorder may be important in the overall management of the individual, as in the case of a diabetic child with a conduct disorder.

Axis IV is a measurement of the current stress level at which the person is functioning. The rating of stressors is based on what the person has experienced within the past year. An eight-point code is used to describe stressors ranging from no apparent stressors to catastrophic levels of stress. The prognosis may be better for a disorder that develops following a severe stressor than for one that develops after no stressor or a minimal stressor.

Axis V is used to describe the highest level of adaptive functioning present within the past year. Adaptive functioning refers to three major areas: social relations, occupational functioning, and the person's use of leisure time. Social relations refer to the quality of a person's relationships with family and friends. Occupational functioning involves functioning as a worker, student, or homemaker and the quality of the work accomplished. Use of leisure time includes recreational activities or hobbies and of the degree of involvement and pleasure a person has in them.

With DSM-II, a patient's diagnosis might have been simply "alcohol addiction." Under the new system, however, he or she might be diagnosed as follows:

Axis I:	alcohol dependence;
Axis II:	avoidant personality disorder;
Axis III:	diabetes;
Axis IV:	loss of job, one child moved out of house, marital conflict;
Axis V:	fair.

This offers a good deal more information about the patient—information that may be useful in devising a treatment program. Furthermore, this five-part diagnosis may be extremely helpful to researchers trying to discover connections among psychological disorders and other factors such as stress and physical illness.

CHAPTER 15 REVIEW

SUMMARY

Use the following outline as a tool for reviewing this chapter. Copy the outline onto your own paper, leaving spaces between headings to make notes about key concepts.

I. What is Abnormal Behavior?

    A. Deviation from Normality

    B. Adjustment

    C. Psychological Health

    D. Is Mental Illness a Myth?

II. The Problem of Classification

III. Neurosis

    A. Anxiety

    B. Phobias

    C. Obsessions and Compulsions

    D. Somatoform Disorders

    E. Dissociative Disorders

    F. Depression

    G. Suicide

IV. Psychosis

    A. Schizophrenia

    B. Affective Reactions

    C. Autism

    D. Causes of Psychosis

V. Personality Disorders

VI. Drug Addiction

    A. Alcoholism

VII. DSM-III: New Ways to Categorize Mental Illness

CONCEPTS AND VOCABULARY

1. Describe three ways of defining abnormality. Describe one shortcoming of each definition.

2. What is the legal definition of insanity? Is pleading insanity highly successful as a means of defense in criminal cases?

3. What does Szasz mean by the phrase "problems in living?"

4. What system do psychologists use to classify abnormal behavior? In what ways is this system different from the one that preceded it? What are some of the advantages of the new system?

5. What are some differences between neurosis and psychosis? What is the difference between symptoms (for example, depression) that a psychologically healthy person might experience from time to time and the symptoms of a psychologically disturbed person?

6. Describe the symptoms associated with anxiety. Give two explanations for the cause of anxiety.

7. How do phobias differ from normal fears? Give one explanation for the causes of phobias.

8. What is an obsession? What is a compulsion? Why do people develop obsessions and compulsions?

9. What do psychologists mean when they refer to someone as having a somatoform disorder?

10. What is a conversion reaction? What do psychologists believe causes a conversion reaction?

11. How do conversion disorders and hypochondriasis differ?

12. What is a fugue? What psychological function might it serve?

13. What is multiple personality? How common a disorder is it? What do psychologists think multiple personality may come from?

14. What is Freud's explanation for neurotic depression? Describe the more contemporary theories that explain the causes of depression.

15. What is schizophrenia? What are two common experiences of schizophrenics? Summarize two types of schizophrenic reactions.

16. What is a manic reaction? What is a depressive reaction? What is manic-depressive psychosis? All three can be classified as what type of reaction?

17. Do psychologists know what causes autism? What avenues are they exploring?

18. What are the three major causes given for psychotic reactions?

19. How do personality disorders differ from neuroses and psychoses?

20. How would you describe someone who is classified as having an antisocial personality disorder?

21. What are the differences between drug dependency, drug addiction, and drug tolerance?

22. What evidence is there that heavy drinking is a serious problem in America? Is alcohol a stimulant or a depressant? What are the stages of alcoholism? What can be done to help alcoholics?

2. **Analyze.** It is thought that one of the conditions that produces mental disorders is overexposure to double-bind situations. Everyone has faced these situations at various times. How many examples from your own experiences can you think of that illustrate various forms of the double-bind situation? How did you resolve the conflicts? Can you see patterns of behavior responses developing?

3. **Evaluate.** Whenever you dismiss certain people as "creeps," for example, you are really saying more about yourself than about the people you are labeling. For example, people who are nervous in social gatherings usually cannot stand other people who are nervous in social gatherings. For a good indication of your own problems, make a list of people you don't like and the reason(s) why you don't like them. Take a hard, honest look at those traits you have written down and see how many of them apply to you as well.

4. **Analyze.** What are you afraid of? Do you fear high places, or water, or maybe snakes or spiders? Try to think back to when you first had these fears. Can you state rationally why you have each of your fears?

5. **Analyze.** What makes you anxious? Consider the times you have experienced a general apprehension and try to list the particular settings or situations in which you are most likely to feel this way. What ways have you developed to help you cope with anxiety? Are there times when anxiety has hindered your behavior? Are there times when anxiety has helped your behavior? If you answered the last two questions in the affirmative, how do you explain the difference?

CRITICAL THINKING

1. **Synthesize.** Develop your own definition of mental illness. Is your definition free of social values, or are values a necessary part of every definition of mental illness?

APPLYING KNOWLEDGE

1. Watch television for a week. Keep a journal of programs which have some psychological theme. What examples of mental breakdown

are described? How common are they made to appear? Are simple solutions given? How is the psychologist or psychiatrist shown? Does this person have ready answers? What are they?

2. Cut out about fifteen pictures of people from magazines and paste them on a large piece of paper. Include among the pictures several of people with long or mussed up hair and untidy clothes. Ask several friends or classmates if they can determine which of the people in the pictures are mentally ill. How many select the people with unkempt appearances? What conclusions can you draw from this experiment?

3. Study a book of paintings and drawings by Vincent Van Gogh. Can you tell which were done when he was mentally healthy and which were done when he was suffering from severe psychological disorder? How?

4. Read newspapers and news magazines for articles dealing with mental illness. Keep a record of the maladaptive behavior that is identified and who makes the diagnosis. In what contexts is mental illness discussed? Do the articles address legal issues? What can you learn about treatment of mental illness from your collection of articles?

ANALYZING VIEWPOINTS

1. In many states, temporary insanity can be used as a defense in a criminal trial. As the chapter mentions, John Hinckley was found not guilty by reason of insanity of attempting to assassinate then President Reagan. Write a paper that argues for and against the legitimacy of the insanity defense in criminal cases. Before you begin writing, spend some time researching the insanity defense at your local library. Look for

books, magazine articles, and newspaper articles on the topic. Find information concerning a particular case in which the insanity defense was used. Use the information you find as the basis for your paper.

2. Individuals who are defined as mentally incompetent or as dangers to themselves or society can, in many states, be held in an institution against their will for up to 72 hours. Is this a reasonable policy? Does it matter who is classifying the individuals? Is there any potential for abuse? In an essay, debate both sides of the issue: yes, there is a need for authorities to be able to confine individuals who may do themselves or others harm; and no, confining an individual based on someone's subjective judgment violates the individual's freedom and personal rights.

BEYOND THE CLASSROOM

1. Find out more about the treatment and care of mental health patients in your community. First ask your school nurse or school psychologist to give you a list of places in the community that provide treatment for mental health problems. Possibilities are a community mental health center, a halfway house, or a local hospital. Choose one of the places, then call and explain that you are doing a project for a high school psychology class and ask if someone could come to your class and talk about mental health services in your community. Work with other students to prepare a list of questions you can ask the speaker. Questions might focus on the most common types of problems; the duration of treatment programs; and the effectiveness of different kinds of treatment.

CHAPTER 16

Therapy and Change

Key Terms:

behavior therapy
client-centered therapy
contingency management
encounter groups
family therapy
free association
gestalt therapy
group therapy
human potential movement
placebo effect
psychoanalysis
psychotherapy
rational-emotive therapy
resistance
systematic desensitization
transactional analysis
transference
unconditional positive regard

At certain times of transition and crisis in life, we may feel an urgent need to find someone trustworthy to share our doubts and problems with. A parent, relative, or close friend is often helpful in such times of need. But many psychological problems are too bewildering and complex to be solved in this way. When people become dissatisfied or distraught with life and suspect that the reason lies inside themselves, they are likely to seek help from someone with training and experience in such matters. People who have been trained to deal with the psychological problems of others include social workers, psychologists, and psychiatrists. The special kind of help they provide is called **psychotherapy.**

This chapter will present some of the major approaches to therapy and will describe what it is like to undergo therapy. It will explore various types of group therapy, probe the current situation in America's mental institutions, and touch on the trend toward community mental health.

WHAT IS PSYCHOTHERAPY?

Psychotherapy literally means "healing of the soul," and in early times psychological disturbances were often thought to represent some sort of moral or religious problem. Madmen were sometimes viewed as being inhabited by devils or demons, and treatment consisted of exorcism—the driving out of these demons by religious ceremonies or by physical punishment. Within the last two hundred years, however, views of psychological disorders have changed. Mental disorders have slowly come to be thought of as diseases, and the term "mental illness" is now popularly applied to many psychological problems.

Objectives:

After studying this chapter, you should be able to

- explain the nature of psychotherapy and trace its historical development.
- describe psychoanalysis and its aims.
- give examples of various forms of group therapy.

Figure 16.1 Each of the many different kinds of therapy is based on varying theories about human personality, but the primary goal of each lies in strengthening the person's control over his or her life.

Figure 16.2
Therapist and patient. Many people have a mental picture of therapy as taking place with the person lying on a couch while a middle-aged, bearded man sits taking notes in a chair. Nowadays therapists are more likely to talk to their patients in a face-to-face position and to use a variety of techniques rather than just a strict psychoanalytic approach.

The fact that psychological disturbance is seen as the symptom of a disease has helped to reduce the stigma associated with such problems, and it has done much to convince society that troubled people need care and treatment. Nevertheless many psychotherapists feel that the term "mental illness" has outlived its usefulness and that, in fact, it may now be doing more harm than good.

The trouble with letting a person think of herself as mentally ill is that she sees herself in a passive, helpless position. She sees her troubles as being caused by forces over which she has no control. By thinking of herself in this way, the person can avoid taking responsibility for her own situation and for helping herself change.

One of the functions of psychotherapy is to help people realize that they are responsible for their own problems and that, even more importantly, they are the only ones who can really solve these problems. This approach does not imply that people become disturbed on purpose or that no one should need outside help. People often adopt certain techniques for getting along in life that seem appropriate at the time but that lead to trouble in the long run. Such patterns can be difficult for the individual to see or change. The major task of the therapist, therefore, is to help people examine their way of living, to understand how their present way of living causes problems, and to start living in new, more beneficial ways. The therapist can be thought of as a guide who is hired by the individual to help her find the source of her problems and some possible solutions.

Characteristics of Psychotherapy

There are many different kinds of therapy, only a few of which will be described in this chapter. Each one is based on different theories about how human personality works, and each one is carried out in a different style. Some psychotherapists stick rigorously to one style and consider the others useless. Other psychotherapists pick and choose methods from many different kinds of therapy and use whatever works best. But whatever the style or philosophy, all types of psychotherapy have certain characteristics in common.

The primary goal of psychotherapy is to strengthen the patient's control over his or her life. People seeking psychotherapy feel trapped in behavior patterns. Over the years they have developed not only certain feelings about themselves, but behaviors that reinforce those feelings. Such people lack the freedom to choose the direction their lives will take. Their behavior and feelings make it impossible for them to reach their goals. For example, a man who is severely critical of himself may feel others are equally harsh in their judgments of him. Rather than risk feelings of rejection, he avoids social gatherings. A person who is uncomfortable meeting other people will, no doubt, feel lonely and rejected. His critical feelings about himself will be strengthened, and he may come to feel that he will remain unloved for life.

The aim of psychotherapy for such a person would be to free him of his burden of self-hate. With a more positive self-image, the man would not be locked into the cycle of avoidance, rejection, and despair. For perhaps the

How to be Assertive

It's hard to be assertive all the time in every situation. You may find it easy to ask a favor of a friend but impossible to make a similar request of a stranger. If you want to spread your assertiveness over more situations, try following these simple suggestions:

- Begin your attempts at developing assertiveness in the least threatening situations. Start with your brother, not your boss.
- Increase your nonverbal assertiveness. Stand erect, look a person straight in the eyes during conversation, eliminate nervous habits, smile.
- Work up to a difficult task in a series of gradual steps. If you're afraid to ask someone for a date, start by saying hello. Then gradually increase the time you spend talking to that person until you're comfortable enough to pop the question.
- If you're afraid to tell people how you feel when you disagree, start by expressing your opinion when you're asked. Once you feel confident in your ability to disagree, you're ready to volunteer your feelings.
- If you find it hard to begin a conversation with a person you've just met, try asking open-ended questions, listening carefully for any additional information the person gives and commenting on it, volunteering information about yourself, and giving compliments.

By following these suggestions, you probably won't increase your assertiveness overnight. But each day will bring you closer to your goal.

For more details, see R. L. Williams and J. D. Lang, *Toward a Self-Managed Life Style,* 2nd ed. Boston: Houghton Mifflin, 1979.

first time, he could feel in control of his life. His behavior would be based on *choice,* and not on the necessity that goes with fixed behavior patterns.

In order to change, it is necessary for the patient to achieve some *understanding* of his troubles. One of the first tasks of therapy, therefore, is to examine the patient's problem closely.

The man in our example will, in the course of his therapy, discover the origin of his self-critical, despairing feelings. He may also realize that, although these feelings developed from real situations, perhaps during his childhood, they no longer apply to his adult capabilities. Gradually the patient's view of himself will become more realistic.

Another major task of therapy is to help the patient find meaningful *alternatives* to his present unsatisfactory ways of behaving. The patient we have been discussing may look for ways to meet new people rather than avoid them.

One of the most important factors in effective treatment is the patient's belief or hope that he *can* change. The influence that a patient's hopes and expectations have on his improvement is often called the **placebo effect.** This name comes from giving medical patients *placebos*—harmless sugar

---
Table 16.1 / Kinds of Therapists

Psychiatrists are medical doctors who specialize in the treatment of mental illness. They generally take a post-M.D. residency in a mental institution. Because of their medical background, psychiatrists are the only group licensed to prescribe drugs.

Psychoanalysts are psychiatrists who have taken special training in the theory of personality and techniques of psychotherapy of Sigmund Freud, usually at a psychoanalytic institute. They must themselves be psychoanalyzed before they can practice.

Lay analysts are psychoanalysts who do not have degrees in medicine but who have studied with established psychoanalysts.

Clinical psychologists are therapists with a Ph.D. degree. They are the product of a three-to-four-year research-oriented program in the social sciences, plus a one-year predoctoral or postdoctoral internship in psychotherapy and psychological assessment.

Counselors generally have a master's or doctor's degree in counseling psychology. They usually work in educational institutions, where they are available for consultation about personal problems. They customarily refer clients with serious problems to psychiatrists or psychologists.

Psychiatric social workers are people with a graduate degree in psychiatric social work. They generally receive supervised practical training coupled with two years of courses in psychology.

Nonprofessionals include clergy, physicians, teachers, and others who dispense a great deal of advice despite the fact that they have had no formal training in therapy or counseling. Nevertheless, more troubled people turn to nonprofessionals than to professionals.

---

pills—when they complain of ailments that do not seem to have any physiological basis. The patients take the tablets and their symptoms disappear.

The placebo effect does not imply that problems can be solved simply by fooling the patient. It does demonstrate, however, the tremendous importance of the patient's attitude in finding a way to change. A patient who does not believe she can be helped probably cannot be. A patient who believes she can change and believes she has the power to change will find a way. Therapy goes beyond the placebo effect. It combines the patient's belief that she can change with hard work and professional guidance

What Makes a Good Therapist?

In American society, there are many people who practice psychotherapy. Some, like psychiatrists, are trained in psychology and medicine; others, like counselors and clergy, have considerably less formal training. The different kinds of professional therapists and the training that each goes through before practicing psychotherapy are shown in Table 16.1.

Before going to a professional therapist, most people first turn to a friend or other nonprofessional for help and advice. Sometimes, this is exactly what's needed. But professional therapists are likely to be more skillful in encouraging the person to examine uncomfortable feelings and problems. In the process of therapy, the patient may feel frustrated because he cannot push the burden of responsibility onto someone else the way he can with a friend.

The process of therapy is always difficult and upsetting, and patients often become heavily dependent on the therapist while they are trying to make changes. A patient may become angry or hurt, for example, if his therapist suddenly goes on vacation. The therapist, therefore, has to be careful not to betray the trust that the patient has placed in her. On the other hand, she must not let the patient lean on her or take out his problems on her. Patients often try to avoid their problems by using the therapist as a substitute parent or by blaming her for their misfortunes.

Whether psychotherapy will be beneficial to a person depends on both the patient and the therapist. Patients who get the most out of psychotherapy are people with high intelligence, a good education, and a middle-class background. Such people have much in common with most therapists, and this similarity seems to help. In addition, the people who benefit most from psychotherapy are those who have relatively mild problems about which they have considerable anxiety or depression. Severely disturbed, apathetic patients are much more difficult to change. Therapy will also be more effective with people who are introspective and who can withstand frustration. Therapy is neither easy nor fast; it demands as much from the patient as it does from the therapist.

There are three characteristics that are found in effective therapists. First, a therapist needs to be reasonably *healthy*. A therapist who is anxious, defensive, and withdrawn will not be able to see his patient's problems clearly. A second important characteristic is a capacity for *warmth* and *understanding*. Troubled people are usually fearful and confused about explaining their problems. The therapist needs to be able to give the patient confidence that he is capable of caring and understanding. Finally, a good therapist must be *experienced* in dealing with people—in understanding their complexities, seeing through the games they play to trick the therapist and themselves, and judging their strengths and weaknesses. Only by having worked with many people can a therapist learn when to give support, when to insist that the patient stand on his own feet, and how to make sense of the things people say.

KINDS OF PSYCHOTHERAPY

Although there are many approaches to psychotherapy (several are included in the "Suggested Readings" at the end of this chapter), only the three most influential approaches will be discussed here: psychoanalysis, the human potential movement, and behavior therapy. In addition to these types of individual therapy, several kinds of group therapy will be described.

Psychoanalysis

For a long time **psychoanalysis** was the only kind of psychotherapy practiced in Western society. It was this type of therapy that gave rise to the classic picture of a bearded Viennese doctor seated behind a patient who is lying on a couch.

Psychoanalysis is based on the theories of Sigmund Freud. According to Freud's views, psychological disturbances are due to anxiety about hidden conflicts between the unconscious components of one's personality. (Freud's theory of personality is described in Chapters 8 and 11.) One job of the psychoanalyst, therefore, is to help make the patient aware of the unconscious impulses, desires, and fears that are causing the anxiety. Psychoanalysts believe that if the patient can understand her unconscious motives, she has taken the first step toward gaining control over her behavior and freeing herself of her problems. Such understanding is called *insight.*

Psychoanalysis is a slow procedure. It may take years of fifty-minute sessions several times a week before the patient is able to make fundamental changes in her life. Throughout this time, the analyst assists his patient in a thorough examination of the unconscious motives behind her behavior. This task begins with the analyst telling the patient to relax and talk about everything that comes into her mind. This method is called **free association.** The patient may consider her passing thoughts too unimportant or too embarrassing to mention. But the analyst suggests that she express everything—the thought that seems most inconsequential may, in fact, be the most meaningful upon closer examination.

As the patient lies on the couch, she may describe her dreams, talk about her private life, or recall long-forgotten experiences. The psychoanalyst sits out of sight behind the patient and often says nothing for long periods of time. He occasionally makes remarks or asks questions that guide the patient, or he may suggest an unconscious motive or factor that explains something the patient has been talking about, but most of the work is done by the patient herself.

The patient is understandably reluctant to reveal painful feelings and to examine lifelong patterns that need to be changed, and as the analysis proceeds, she is likely to try to hold back the flow of information. This phenomenon—in fact, any behavior that impedes the course of therapy—is called **resistance.** The patient may have agreed to cooperate fully, yet she finds at times that her mind is blank, that she feels powerless and can no longer think of anything to say. At such times the analyst will simply point out what is happening and wait for the patient to continue. The analyst may also suggest another line of approach to the area of resistance. By analyzing the patient's resistances, both the therapist and the patient can understand how the patient deals with anxiety-provoking material.

Sooner or later, the analyst begins to appear in the patient's associations and dreams. The patient may begin feeling toward the analyst the way she feels toward some other important figure in her life. This process is called **transference.**

If the patient can recognize what is happening, transference may allow

Figure 16.3
The phenomena of resistance and transference. Here the patient's resistance is shown in the fact that he is seeing the therapist as a menacing dentist. At the same time, he is transferring: the "dentist" seems to him like an impersonal, frightening mother.

her to experience her true feelings toward the important person. But often, instead of experiencing and understanding her feelings, the patient simply begins acting toward the therapist in the same way she used to act toward the important person, usually one of her parents.

The therapist does not allow the patient to resort to these tactics. He remains impersonal and anonymous. He always directs the patient back to herself. The therapist may ask, for example, "What do you see when you imagine my face?" The patient may reply that she sees the therapist as an angry, frowning, unpleasant figure. The therapist never takes this personally. Instead, he may calmly say, "What does this make you think of?" Gradually, it will become clear to both patient and therapist that the patient is reacting to the neutral therapist as though he were a threatening father.

Through this kind of process, the patient becomes aware of her real feelings and motivations. She may begin to understand, for example, why she has trouble with her boss at work—she may be seeing her boss, her therapist, and indeed any man in a position of authority, in the same way that as a child she saw her father.

The Human Potential Movement

Humanistic psychology has given rise to several new approaches to psychotherapy, known collectively as the **human potential movement.** We discussed these schools of psychology in Chapter 11. To review, humanistic psychologists stress the actualization of one's unique potentials through personal responsibility, freedom of choice, and authentic relationships.

Client-centered Therapy.   **Client-centered therapy** is based on the theories of Carl Rogers (1951; see Chapter 11). The use of the term "client" instead of "patient" gives one an insight into the reasoning behind Rogers's method. "Patient" may suggest inferiority, whereas "client" implies an equal relationship between the therapist and the person seeking help.

Client-centered therapists assume that people are basically good and

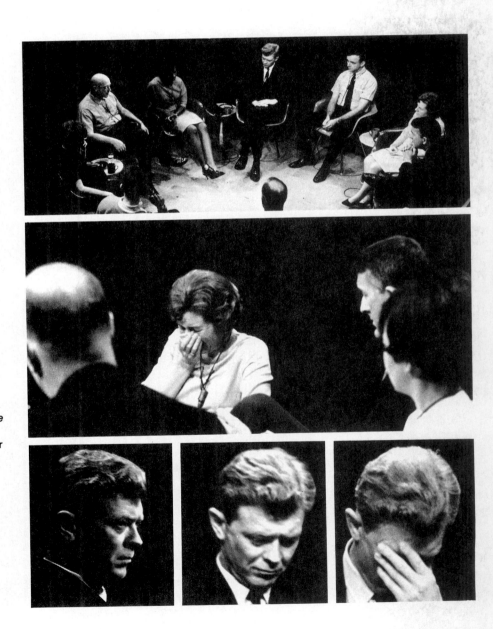

Figure 16.4
Carl Rogers is shown here *(on the left, top photograph)* leading an encounter group. Many encounter group leaders, including Rogers, feel that their role in the group is the same as that of any other member. Only if the group as a whole or any one of its members gets into trouble will the leader intervene to rescue the situation. Typically, other group members will exhibit leadership or therapeutic skills and the designated leader will remain in the background.

that they are capable of handling their own lives. Psychological problems arise when the true self becomes lost and the individual comes to view himself according to the standards of others. One of the goals of therapy, therefore, is to help the client to recognize his own strength and confidence so that he can learn to be true to his own standards and ideas about how to live effectively.

In the course of an interview, the client is encouraged to speak freely about intimate matters that may be bothering him. He is told that what he talks about is up to him. The therapist listens and encourages conversation but tries to avoid giving opinions. Instead, she tries to echo back as clearly as possible the feelings the client has expressed. She may try to extract the main points from the client's hesitant or rambling explanations. For example, a male client may tell a long story about an incident with his father, and the therapist may respond by saying, "This kind of thing makes you feel very stupid." The client may in turn say, "No, not stupid, angry. It's really he who is being stupid." And the therapist will say, "Oh, I see, you really feel angry at him when he acts this way." Between them, they form a clearer and clearer picture of how the client really feels about himself, his life, and the people around him.

Client-centered therapy is conducted in an atmosphere of emotional support that Rogers calls **unconditional positive regard.** As in psychoanalysis, the therapist never says that she thinks the client or what the client has said is good or bad. But she shows the client that she will accept anything that is said without embarrassment, reservation, or anger. Her primary responsibility is to create a warm and accepting relationship between herself and her client.

This acceptance makes it easier for the client to explore thoughts about himself and his experiences. He is able to abandon old values without fear of disapproval, and he can begin to see himself, his situation, and his relationships with others in a new light.

As he reduces his tensions and releases his emotions, the client feels that he is becoming a more complete person. He gains the courage to accept parts of his personality that he had formerly considered weak or bad, and, by recognizing his self-worth, he can set up realistic goals and consider the steps necessary to reach them. The client's movement toward independence signals the end of the need for therapy—he can assume the final steps to independence on his own.

Existential Therapy. Like Rogers, all therapists in the human potential movement see their role as helping individuals to achieve self-determination. Existential therapists believe that for most people, freedom and autonomy are threatening. To acknowledge that you are a unique and independent person is to acknowledge that you are alone. Unconsciously many people avoid this realization, burying their feelings and desires. Therapists like Rollo May (1969) attempt to help patients overcome the fear of freedom, get in touch with their true feelings, and accept responsibility for their lives.

Viktor Frankl (1970) is also an existentialist, but approaches therapy

MORE about . . .

Carl Rogers and Unconditional Positive Regard. One of the fundamental aspects of Carl Rogers's client-centered therapy (also called "*person-centered therapy*") is to show the client unconditional positive regard. However, this ideal is difficult to reach in practice.

Rogers was not content merely to theorize about psychological processes. He believed in conducting research to verify his hypotheses. To that end he often recorded therapy sessions he conducted (with the client's permission, of course), so that his methods could be studied scientifically. One of his students, Charles Truax, did just that.

Truax analyzed Rogers's responses to a client during the course of therapy. He found that Rogers displayed frequent verbal and nonverbal reinforcements to statements that indicated optimism or self-assuredness. He provided relatively few reinforcements after the client complained of symptoms and frustrations.

It seems that there is a strong pull to support ideas we agree with and to ignore those we disagree with. Apparently, even the master of unconditional positive reinforcement is not immune from this motive.

somewhat differently. After listening to a patient express despair, he might ask, "Why don't you commit suicide?" Frankl is not being cruel or sarcastic. He is trying to help the individual find meaning in life. The patient's answer (whether it is "my husband and children," "my religion," or "my work") provides clues about what the person values.

In Frankl's view, feelings of emptiness and boredom are the primary source of emotional problems.

> Mental health is based on a certain degree of tension between what one has already achieved and what one still ought to accomplish, or the gap between what one is and what one should become. Such a tension is inherent in the human being and is therefore indispensable to mental well-being. . . . What people actually need is not a tensionless state but rather the striving and struggling for some worthy goal (1970: 165–166).

Frankl believes a therapist should help to open the patient's eyes to the possibilities in life and guide him or her toward challenges.

Gestalt Therapy

Developed by Fritz Perls in the 1950s and 1960s, **gestalt therapy** emphasizes the relationship between the patient and therapist in the here and now (Perls, Hefferline, and Goodman, 1965). Suppose that toward the middle of a session a patient runs out of problems to discuss and sits mute, staring blankly out the window. Instead of waiting for the patient to speak up, a gestalt therapist would say what he feels. "I can't stand the way you just sit there and say nothing. Sometimes I regret ever becoming a therapist. You are impossible. . . . There, now I feel better" (Kempler, 1973: 272). The therapist is not blowing off steam in an unprofessional way. He does this to encourage (by example) the patient to express his feelings, even if it means risking a relationship.

Gestalt therapy is based on the belief that many individuals are so concerned with obtaining approval that they become strangers to themselves. For example, an individual may always defer to authority figures, but he may be detached from the part of himself that has fantasies of rebelling. Neither part acknowledges the other. Gestalt therapists attempt to help a person fit the pieces together. (The word "gestalt" comes from the German word for "configuration.")

Rational-Emotive Therapy

Rational-emotive therapy (RET) is a form of therapy developed by Albert Ellis in the late 1950s (Ellis, 1973). Ellis believes that people behave in deliberate and rational ways, given their assumptions about life. Emotional problems arise when an individual's assumptions are unrealistic.

Supppose a man seeks therapy when a woman leaves him. He cannot stand the fact that she has rejected him. Without her his life is empty and miserable. She has made him feel utterly worthless. He must get her back. An RET therapist would not look for incidents in the past that are making the present unbearable for this man, as a psychoanalyst would. RET therapists do not probe; they reason. Like a spoiled child, the man is demanding that the woman love him. He expects—indeed, insists—that things will always go his way. Given this assumption, the only possible explanation for her behavior is that something is dreadfully wrong, either with him or with her.

What is wrong, in the therapist's view, is the man's thinking. By defining his feelings for the woman as need rather than desire, he—not she—is causing his depression. When you convince yourself that you need someone, you will in fact be unable to carry on without that person. When you believe that you cannot stand rejection, you will in fact fall apart when you encounter rejection.

The goal of rational-emotive therapy is to correct these false and self-defeating beliefs. Rejection is unpleasant, but it is not unbearable. The woman may be very desirable, but she is not irreplaceable. To teach the individual to think in realistic terms, the RET therapist may use a number of techniques: role playing (so that the person can see how his beliefs affect his relationships); modeling (to demonstrate other ways of thinking and acting); humor (to underline the absurdity of his beliefs); and simple persuasion. The therapist may also make homework assignments to give the man practice in acting more reasonably. For example, the therapist may instruct him to ask women who are likely to reject him out on dates. Why? So that he will learn that he can cope with things not going his way.

Ellis believes that the individual must take three steps to cure or correct himself. First, he must realize that some of his assumptions are false. Second, he must see that he is making *himself* disturbed by acting on false beliefs. Finally, he must work to break old habits of thought and behavior. He has to practice, to learn self-discipline, to take risks.

Transactional Analysis

Introduced by Eric Berne (1964) in the early 1950s, **transactional analysis** is both a theory of personality and a method of therapy. The central assumption of transactional analysis (often referred to as TA) is that people function and experience their world from one of three perspectives, or ego states. *Ego states* represent the ways people organize their thoughts, feelings, and actions. Sometimes adults think, feel, and act from a *child ego* state. For example, a man who has been stopped by a police officer for speeding may feel and act as he did when he was a boy and was caught doing something wrong by his parents. Other times, people may act, think, and feel like one of their parents, close friends, or teachers—from a *parent ego* state. For example, a person who acts in a judgmental and opinionated way is most likely functioning from the parent ego state.

The *adult ego* state represents people's thoughts, feelings, and behaviors that are rationally related to their experience of the present. Unlike reactions in the child or parent ego states (reactions that are shaped and sometimes distorted by past experiences with other people) reactions in the adult ego state allow people to deal effectively and responsibly with their everyday problems.

If a friend tells you "you should carry an umbrella today—it might rain," he or she is probably speaking from a parent ego state. If you say or think "Mind your own business," you are probably reacting from a child ego state. An adult ego state reaction would be to look around and see whether it looks like rain and act accordingly.

Berne believed that these three personality parts develop through people's interactions with significant people in their lives. Furthermore, he believed that while people are growing up they develop specific plans that define how they will act toward other people and how other people are expected to act toward them. People learn to "play games" or engage in predictable exchanges with other people to fit their life plan.

The goal of the TA therapist is to help people identify maladaptive transactions or strategies for living (usually from the parent or child ego state) and to help them develop more effective adult ego state responses. The TA therapist usually begins therapy by establishing a contract with the client. The contract states what the client wants to change and what the therapist will or will not do to help the client achieve his or her goal.

One woman sought TA therapy to help her deal with her relations with men. She found that on a first date with someone, she would always make a point of saying that she just wanted to be friends, but then she would act in a flirtatious way that gave the opposite impression. If the man made a pass at her, she would be outraged. By exploring and discussing her behavior with her therapist, she discovered that she had been playing games from her child ego state. This insight helped her recognize what she wanted in her relationships, and helped her learn how to behave. In most cases, transactional analysis focuses on the individual's assuming responsibility for his or her actions (see Holland, 1973).

Behavior Therapy

Behavior therapists believe a disturbed person has learned to behave in the wrong way.

Psychoanalysis and the human potential movement have sometimes been criticized for being "all talk and no action." In **behavior therapy** there is much more emphasis on action. Rather than spending large amounts of time going into the patient's past history or the details of his or her dreams, the behavior therapist concentrates on finding out what is specifically wrong with the patient's current life and takes steps to change it.

The idea behind behavior therapy is that a disturbed person is one who has *learned* to behave in the wrong way. The therapist's job, therefore, is to "reeducate" the patient. The reasons for the patient's undesirable behavior are not important; what is important is to change the behavior. To bring about such changes, the therapist uses certain conditioning techniques first discovered in animal laboratories. (The principles of conditioning are explained in Chapter 2.)

One technique used by behavior therapists is **systematic desensitization.** This method is used to overcome irrational fears and anxieties the patient has learned. The goal of desensitization therapy is to encourage people to imagine the feared situation while relaxing, thus extinguishing the fear response. For example, suppose a student is terrified of

Figure 16.5
The behavior therapy approach to the treatment of autism involves the use of contingency management, also known as operant conditioning (see Chapter 2). The therapist is rewarding the child with affection (left) and with food (top right) for performing such desirable behaviors as coming toward the therapist and eating and drinking at the table . (bottom right) The therapists are introducing two autistic children to the experience of holding hands.

speaking in front of large groups of people—that, in fact, his stage fright is so tremendous that he is unable to speak when called upon in class. How would desensitization therapy effectively change this person's behavior?

The therapist might have the student make a list of all the aspects of talking to others that he finds frightening. Perhaps the most frightening aspect is actually standing before an audience, whereas the least frightening is speaking to a single other person. The patient ranks his fears in order, from the most frightening on down. First, the therapist begins teaching the patient to relax. As he relaxes, the patient tries to imagine as vividly as possible the least disturbing scene on his list. As he thinks about speaking to a single stranger, the student may feel a mild anxiety. But because the therapist has taught him how to relax, the patient is soon able to think about the experience without feeling afraid. The basic logic is that a person cannot feel anxious and relaxed at the same time. The therapist attempts to replace anxiety with its opposite, relaxation.

This procedure is followed step by step by the list of anxiety-arousing events. The patient finally reaches a point where he is able to imagine the situations that threaten him the most without feeling anxiety. Now the therapist starts to expose the person to real-life situations that have previously frightened him. Therapy finally reaches the point where the student is able to get up and deliver an unrehearsed speech before a full auditorium.

Another form of behavior therapy is called **contingency management.** In this method the therapist and patient decide what old, undesirable behavior needs to be eliminated and what new, desirable behavior needs to appear (Figure 16.5). Arrangements are then made for the old behavior to go unrewarded and for the desired behavior to be reinforced. In its simplest form, contingency management consists of the therapist agreeing with the patient, "If you do X, I will give you Y." This form of agreement is similar to systems of reward that people often use on themselves. For instance, a college student may say to himself, "If I get a good grade on the exam, I'll treat myself to a great dinner." The reward is *contingent* (dependent) upon getting a good grade.

Contingency management is used in prisons, mental hospitals, schools, and army bases, as well as with individual patients. In these situations it is possible to set up whole miniature systems of rewards, called token economies. For example, psychologists in some mental hospitals select behavior they judge desirable. Patients are then rewarded for these behaviors with "hospital," or token, money. Thus if a patient cleans his room or works in the hospital garden, he is rewarded with token money. The patients are able to cash in their token money for things they want, such as candy or cigarettes, or for certain privileges, such as time away from the ward. These methods are successful in inducing mental patients, who often sit around doing nothing day after day, to begin leading active lives. They learn to take care of themselves and to take on responsibility instead of having to be cared for constantly.

In the past few years, behavior therapists have started experimenting with procedures to help people gain control over their own thoughts and actions. Chapter 2 describes some of these new techniques for cognitive behavior modification.

Group Therapies

In the forms of therapy described thus far, the troubled person is usually alone with the therapist. In **group therapy,** however, she is in the company of others. There are several advantages to this situation. Group therapy gives the troubled person practical experience with one of her biggest problems—getting along with other people. A person in group therapy also has a chance to see how other people are struggling with problems similar to her own, and she discovers what other people think of her. She, in turn, can express what she thinks of them, and in this exchange she discovers where she is mistaken in her views of herself and of other people and where she is correct.

Another advantage to group therapy is the fact that one therapist can help a large number of people. Most group-therapy sessions are led by a trained therapist who makes suggestions, clarifies points, and keeps activities from getting out of hand. In this way, her training and experience are used to help as many as twenty people at once.

Family Therapy.   Recently therapists have begun to suggest, after talking to a patient, that the entire family unit should work at group therapy. This method is particularly useful because the members of the group are all people of great importance in one another's lives. In **family therapy** it is

Figure 16.6
A group therapy session. Therapists use various techniques to get the members of the group to help one another see themselves and others more clearly.

Figure 16.7
A family therapy session. Here the therapist observes the interactions in a family in order to discern, describe, and treat the patterns that contribute to the disturbance of one or more of its members.

possible to untangle the twisted web of relationships that have led one or more members in the family to experience emotional suffering.

Often family members are unhappy because they are mistreating or are being mistreated by other family members in ways no one understands or wants to talk about. The family therapist can point out what is going wrong from an objective viewpoint and can suggest ways of improving communication and fairness in the family.

Not all group therapies are run by professionals, however. Some of the most successful examples are provided in nonprofessional organizations, such as self-help groups.

Self-Help Groups.   An increasing number of self-help groups have emerged in recent years. These voluntary groups, composed of people who share a particular problem, are conducted without the active involvement of a professional therapist. During regularly scheduled meetings, members of the group come together to discuss their difficulties and to provide support and possible solutions.

Self-help groups have been formed to deal with problems ranging from alcoholism, overeating, and drug addiction, to child abuse, widowhood, single parenting, adjusting to cancer, and gambling. The best known self-help group is Alcoholics Anonymous (AA) which was founded in 1930. Many self-help groups have based their organizations on the AA model in which individual members can call on other members for help and emotional support.

The purpose of Alcoholics Anonymous is "to carry the AA message to the sick alcoholic who wants it." According to AA, the only way for alcoholics to change is to admit that they are powerless over alcohol and that their lives have become unmanageable. Alcoholics must come to believe that only some power greater than themselves can help them. Those who think they can battle out the problem alone will not be successful.

Members of AA usually meet at least once a week to discuss the meaning of this message, to talk about their experiences with alcohol, and to

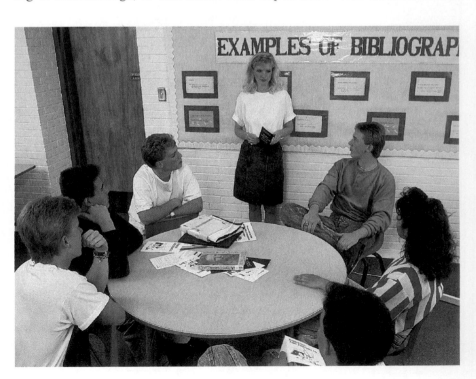

Figure 16.8
An encounter group session. The purpose of these groups is to provide experiences that will help people to live more intense lives; the methods used are intended to increase sensitivity, openness, and honesty.

describe the new hope they have found with AA. Mutual encouragement, friendship, and an emphasis on personal responsibility are used to keep an individual sober.

Encounter Groups.   The power of group interaction to affect and change people has given rise to the controversial **encounter group.** Encounter groups are primarily for people who function adequately in everyday life but who, for some reason, feel unhappy, dissatisfied, or stagnant.

The purpose of encounter groups (which are also known as T-groups or sensitivity training) is to provide experiences that will help people live more intense lives. Being in a small group (between five and fifteen people) for this express purpose is bound to teach an individual something about interpersonal relations. Techniques are often used in groups to overcome the restrictions people live by in everyday life. A typical exercise requires each person to say something to every other person and at the same time to touch him or her in some way. Such methods are intended to increase sensitivity, openness, and honesty.

Role playing is another common encounter-group technique. It is a form of theater in which the goal is to help people expose and understand themselves. A person may try acting out the role of a character in one of his dreams; another person may pretend to be herself as a child talking to her mother, played by another member. By switching roles and placing themselves in each other's situation, group members are better able to see themselves as others see them. Acting out a past experience or playing the role of another person can do much to bring out a person's hidden and true feelings (Back, 1972).

Regardless of the type of therapy, all groups require experienced leaders who are qualified to take responsibility for the group. In a few cases, people who have been unprepared for the intense emotional exposure that occurs in such groups have suffered long-lasting psychological distress from the experience.

DOES PSYCHOTHERAPY WORK?

In 1952 Hans Eysenck published a review of five studies of the effectiveness of psychoanalytic treatment and nineteen studies of the effectiveness of "eclectic" psychotherapy, treatment in which several different therapeutic approaches are combined. Eysenck concluded that psychotherapy was no more effective than no treatment at all. According to his interpretation of these twenty-four studies, only 44 percent of the psychoanalytic patients improved with treatment, while 64 percent of those given eclectic psychotherapy were "cured" or had improved. Most startling, Eysenck argued that even this 64-percent improvement rate did not demonstrate the effectiveness of psychotherapy, since it has been reported that 72 percent of a group of hospitalized neurotics improved *without* treatment. If no treatment at all leads to as much improvement as psychotherapy, the obvious conclusion is that psychotherapy is not effective. Eysenck (1966) vigorously defended his controversial position, which generated a large number of additional reviews and a great many studies of the effectiveness of psychotherapy.

One of the most thoughtful and carefully reasoned reviews was written by Allen Bergin (1971). Bergin made the following points in reply to Eysenck. First, he demonstrated that when some different but equally reasonable assumptions about the classification of patients were made, the effectiveness of psychoanalytic treatment was much greater than Eysenck had reported; perhaps as many as 83 percent of the patients improved or recovered. Second, he reviewed a number of studies which showed that the rate of improvement without treatment was only about 30 percent.

Bergin's review leads one to question the validity of Eysenck's sweeping generalization that psychotherapy is no more effective than no treatment at all. But much of Bergin's argument is based on differences of opinion about how patients should be classified. Precise criteria for "improvement" are difficult to define and to apply. The nature of "spontaneous remission" (sudden disappearance) of symptoms in persons who have not received formal psychotherapy is difficult to assess, for these people may have received help from unacknowledged sources—friends, relatives, religious advisers, family physicians. And if, as some researchers believe, the prime ingredient in therapy is the establishment of a close relationship, then "spontaneous remission" in people who have received continuing help from such sources is not spontaneous at all.

A recent analysis of nearly 400 studies of the effectiveness of psychotherapy, conducted by Mary Lee Smith and Gene V. Glass (1977), used elaborate statistical procedures to estimate the effects of psychotherapy. They found that therapy is generally more effective than no treatment, and that on the average most forms of therapy have similar effects.

Will any therapy do for any client? Probably not. Smith and Glass (1977) were able to show that for some specific clients and situations, some forms of therapy would be expected to have a greater effect than others (Figure 16.9). For example, if the client is a thirty-year-old neurotic of average

Figure 16.9
Is psychotherapy effective? Researchers Lee and Glass think the answer is yes. People receiving each of the types of psychotherapy shown in this graph were compared with untreated control groups. The bars indicate the percentile rank the average treated person attained on outcome measures when compared to control subjects for each type of therapy. (Adapted from Smith and Glass, 1977)

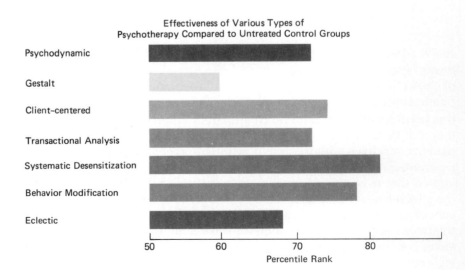

Effectiveness of Various Types of Psychotherapy Compared to Untreated Control Groups

Psychodynamic
Gestalt
Client-centered
Transactional Analysis
Systematic Desensitization
Behavior Modification
Eclectic

50   60   70   80

Percentile Rank

intelligence seen in individual sessions by a therapist with five years of experience, psychodynamic therapy would be expected to have a greater effect than systematic desensitization. But in the case of a highly intelligent twenty-year-old with a phobia, systematic desensitization would be expected to have greater impact. However, these are educated guesses based on the interpretation of some complex statistical manipulations. Studies designed to answer these kinds of specific questions are now needed.

ORGANIC THERAPY

The various "talking" and "learning" therapies we have described so far in this chapter have been aimed primarily at patients who are still generally capable of functioning within society. But what of those people who are not capable of clear thinking or who are dangerous to themselves or others? For a long time the most common method of keeping dangerous or overactive psychotic patients in check was physical restraint—the strait jacket, wet-sheet wrapping, isolation. The patient was also calmed down by means of psychosurgery (see Chapter 5) and electroconvulsive shock. From the mid-1950s on, however, the use of drugs made it possible virtually to eliminate these forms of restraint.

Antipsychotic drugs (also known as major tranquilizers) are used in the treatment of schizophrenia. The most popular of these drugs are the phenothiazines, which include Thorazine (chlorpromazine) and Stelazine (trifluoperazine). Schizophrenic patients who take these drugs improve in a number of ways: they become less withdrawn, become less confused and agitated, have fewer auditory hallucinations, and are less irritable and hostile (Cole, 1964). Studies directly comparing phenothiazines with other forms of therapy suggest that these drugs are the most effective form of treatment now available for schizophrenia (May, 1968).

Although the patient who takes antipsychotic drugs is often improved enough to leave the hospital, he or she may have trouble adjusting to the outside world. Many patients now face the "revolving door" syndrome of going to a mental hospital, being released, returning to the hospital, being released again, and so on. Phenothiazines also have a number of unpleasant side effects, including a dry mouth, blurred vision, grogginess, constipation, and muscle disorders.

Another class of drugs, called *antidepressants* (including Elavil, Tofranil, and Parnate), make some depressed patients happier. Interestingly, they do not affect the mood of normal people. It is almost as if these drugs supply a chemical that some depressed people lack. Some of the antidepressants have such severe side effects that they can lead to death, so they must be given under close medical supervision.

Lithium is now widely used to return manic-depressive patients to a state of equilibrium in which extreme mood swings disappear. While all of the other drugs described here are synthetic, lithium is a natural chemical element. It, too, can lead to severe problems if it is not taken under proper medical supervision.

All About Valium

Valium is one of the most frequently prescribed brands of the drug diazepam. More than 25 million Americans use this minor tranquilizer to help them cope with the pressures in their lives. Approximately 80 percent of the Valium prescribed is consumed by ordinary people who have trouble dealing with today's fast-paced society. Only about 20 percent is taken by patients in hospitals and institutions.

Valium acts as a central nervous system depressant to reduce the amount of anxiety and arousal a person feels. It is also used for such varied purposes as the relief of muscle spasms, the emergency control of seizures, the control of hypertension, and the relief of anxiety and unwanted muscle spasms during labor. Most doctors believe that Valium serves these functions in a way that no other minor tranquilizer can.

Doctors who have analyzed the use and overuse of Valium agree, however, that it is a drug that can never be taken for granted and that it needs careful watching. Many people who use it could probably deal with their anxiety more effectively by determining and eliminating the source of the anxiety. If this is not effective, they might try other ways of handling stress, such as counseling, support groups, and exercise programs.

Commonly known as sedatives or mild tranquilizers, *anti-anxiety drugs* are used to reduce excitability and cause drowsiness. The most extensively used drugs of this kind are Miltown (meprobamate), Librium (chlordiazepoxide), and Valium (diazepam). Although these drugs came into widespread use in the 1970s, fewer people are using them now. Valium, however, continues to be one of the most widely prescribed drugs in the United States (see box).

While these drugs are effective for helping normal people cope with difficult periods in their lives, they are also prescribed for the alleviation of various neurotic symptoms, psychosomatic problems, and symptoms of alcohol withdrawal. The major effect of Valium, Librium, and Miltown is to depress the activity of the central nervous system. If the drugs are taken properly, the side effects are few and consist mainly of drowsiness. However, prolonged use may lead to dependency, and heavy doses taken along with alcohol can result in death.

"Shock treatment," as *electroconvulsive therapy* is commonly called, has proved extremely effective in the treatment of depression, though no one understands exactly how it works (Kalinowsky, 1975). It involves administering, over several weeks, a series of brief electrical shocks of approximately 70 to 130 volts. The shock induces a convulsion similar to an epileptic seizure. As it is now applied, electroconvulsive therapy entails very little discomfort for the patient. Prior to treatment, the patient is given a sedative and injected with a muscle relaxant to alleviate involuntary muscular contractions and prevent physical injury. Even with these improvements, however, electroconvulsive therapy is a drastic treatment and must be used with great caution. It is now used far less frequently than it was in the past.

MENTAL INSTITUTIONS

When the demands of everyday life cannot be met, the mentally disturbed person may face the prospect of institutionalization. There are institutions to handle many different social problems: prisons for criminals, hospitals for the physically ill, and mental institutions for people who are considered unable to function in normal society.

Commitment

The process of placing a person in a mental hospital is called *commitment*. It is estimated that two out of five mental patients are committed against their will. Involuntary commitment is a controversial legal and ethical issue. It has been argued that a committed mental patient has fewer rights than a convicted criminal.

Whether a person ends up in a mental hospital depends on a number of factors beyond his or her mental state. People with family and friends who are willing to care for them are less likely to be institutionalized. Money is also a factor. With budget cutbacks leading to more limited public facilities, it is now getting harder for a person to stay in a mental hospital for any length of time.

Conditions

The quality and cost of care in mental institutions vary greatly. There are more than 4,000 mental health facilities in the United States. About half of them offer inpatient care. Among these, private institutions offer more concentrated care and a better environment, but many of them are very expensive. The majority of people go to state mental hospitals or cheaper private institutions. The quality of treatment in these hospitals varies tremendously. It is possible, in fact, for a patient's condition to worsen or remain unchanged because the patient comes to depend on the hospital environment and loses social and vocational skills. When patients fail to improve, they remain institutionalized year after year. This situation exists because most public hospitals lack funds for adequate nursing staffs, equipment, and trained therapists. In many cases, the patients' day-to-day care is left to attendants who do little more than clean and feed the patients and keep order.

Ideally, a mental hospital should be a place where the patient is temporarily freed from social pressures he or she cannot bear. Limited and carefully planned demands should be made by a staff capable of under-

PSYCHOLOGY and YOU

The Mentally Ill Homeless: The Legacy of Deinstitutionalization. Homelessness is an increasing problem in the United States, and it is likely that you come into contact with the homeless at least occasionally. When you do, chances are good that you may be observing a person with a psychiatric disorder.

Recent surveys indicate that 30 to 40 percent of the homeless are mentally ill. This seems to be a direct result of deinstitutionalization.

Since the introduction of psychoactive drugs in the 1950s, the number of patients confined to mental institutions has steadily dropped. Unfortunately, most psychoactive drugs do not cure disorders. Rather, they merely control the more obvious symptoms of mental illness so that patients are no longer dangerous. Thus, there is no longer any reason to keep these people institutionalized.

A majority of mental inmates have been released from institutions, but they often find it impossible to hold steady jobs or to live on their own. In this way, the noble goal of deinstitutionalization has contributed to the problem of homelessness and has affected all our lives.

Figure 16.10
The traditional custodial mental hospital setting: a bare room, barred windows, a hospital gown. Such a setting contributes to the person's isolation and feeling of separation from the everyday world and can actually decrease the chances of recovery.

A mental hospital should be a place where a person is temporarily freed from social pressures he or she cannot bear.

standing and concern for the individual. Unfortunately, the reality of many state hospitals does not fit this ideal. Patients can become molded into a pattern of obedience, dependence, and conformity by a deadening routine of sleep, meals, Ping-Pong, and other ways of filling time (see Goffman, 1961).

As the patients become increasingly apathetic and resigned, they lose all ties with the outside world. In order to survive the boredom of each day, they rely on fantasy, dreams, and sleep, and they stop thinking about returning to outside life. Nevertheless, many patients welcome this routine—they prefer to be taken care of and to avoid the responsibilities of the outside world.

Individual and group psychotherapy are provided in mental hospitals, but this type of therapy is slow and expensive, and it does not work well with hospital patients, who are often beyond caring whether they improve or not. Partly as a result, mental hospitals tend to stress the organic treatments described above.

There are certain dangers inherent in the use of psychiatric drugs. They are often administered to make up for the lack of staff at mental hospitals. In many institutions it is common policy to administer a tranquilizer to every patient early in the morning, so that throughout the day there is very little activity among patients, thus reducing the workload required of an already overworked staff.

Most psychiatric drugs, when given in high doses over long periods, have undesirable side effects, such as extreme lethargy or peculiar losses of coordination. For such reasons, it is not uncommon for mental patients to flush some of their drugs down the toilet.

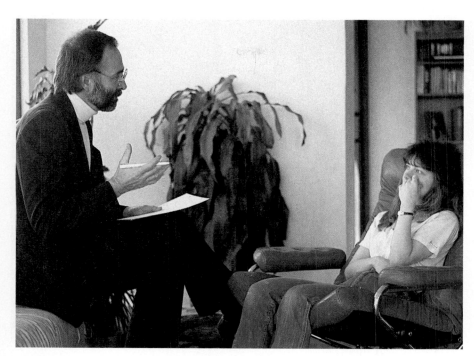

Figure 16.11
In a hospital where the goal is to re-store the person to normal function-ing, every effort is made to duplicate real settings and real situations and to involve the person in his or her treatment. This patient is meeting with her doctor to discuss her treat-ment and evaluate how she is doing and what should happen next.

COMMUNITY MENTAL HEALTH

Since the nineteenth century, extremely deviant behavior has been viewed as an illness to be treated by medical personnel in a hospital setting. Large mental hospitals were built in rural areas, where space could be obtained cheaply and patients could be concealed from the public, who thought them unsightly and dangerous. But the social isolation of patients, their removal from familiar surroundings and family life, often made later re-adjustment to society even more difficult. Released patients found them-selves too far from the hospital for any supplementary care and too fragile to cope independently with the pressures of the outside world. Eventually it became apparent that if these patients were to make a successful return to the community, the community was going to have to provide some support.

Community Mental Health Centers

The Community Mental Health Centers Act of 1963 was designed to solve some of the problems faced by patients trying to reenter society. One mental health center was required for every 50,000 members of the U.S. population, to supply needed psychological services for the ex-patient at-tempting to function within the community. These centers were also sup-posed to educate community workers such as police, teachers, and clergy in the principles of preventive mental health, to train paraprofessionals, and to carry out research. A countrywide system of mental health centers

Figure 16.12
Halfway houses and community centers are part of a new movement to return as many people as possible to the community. This group of ex-hospital patients meets to discuss problems and help one another make the adjustment from inmate to functioning member of a community.

has not yet been achieved, and funding for existing centers has been cut back in many cities; but those centers that are in operation supply important services.

Outpatients can walk into a clinic and receive therapy once, twice, or several times a week, without leaving school, job, or family, and without feeling stigmatized as institutionalized mental patients. The centers also serve as a bridge between hospitalization and complete independence by giving care to patients after they are released from hospitals.

For the more severely disturbed, hospitalization can be provided within the community. Friends and family have easy access to patients, who feel less isolated and more accepted. Many centers have arrangements for day hospitals, in which patients take advantage of the hospital during the day and go home at night. Night hospitals work in a similar manner: patients may work or go to school during the day and spend the night at the hospital.

Many community mental health centers also maintain storefront clinics that are open around the clock to deal with such emergencies as acute anxiety attacks, suicide attempts, and bad drug trips. The centers may have teams of psychologically trained personnel on call to go to city hospital emergency rooms to deal with psychological traumas.

Mental health centers provide qualified personnel to serve as consultants to other community workers, such as teachers, police, and clergy, advising them on how to handle psychological problems in the classroom and within the community. Sensitivity workshops give instruction on such matters as how to intervene in potentially violent family quarrels, how to talk potential suicides out of jumping off a bridge, and how to keep truants from dropping out of school.

Halfway Houses. There are thousands of people who spend time in mental hospitals, prisons, and homes for delinquents and who, when finally released, are psychologically unprepared to return to life in society. They may be able to behave well under structured conditions, but they find the freedom and immensity of society confusing and overwhelming. Such people can ease back into society through halfway houses.

Halfway houses give their inhabitants the support they need in order to build enough confidence to reenter society. Unwritten rules and informal social pressures guide the members in their efforts to readjust to the larger world (Raush and Raush, 1968).

USING PSYCHOLOGY

Crisis Intervention Programs

A fairly new approach to mental health is the development of community-based crisis intervention programs, which help individuals and families deal with emergencies or highly stressful situations. Typically, during a period of emotional turmoil, people feel overwhelmed and cannot deal with their everyday affairs. The crises may be the death of a loved one, the loss of a job, a rape or mugging, a family breakup, or an attempted suicide. The intervention is generally short-term, lasting for no more than five or six sessions. It is like psychological first aid.

Crisis intervention counselors use four approaches. First, they provide general support by listening to the person's concerns and by providing encouragement and hope that the crisis will pass. Second, counselors help people assess their situation realistically; identify what they can do to help themselves; and look directly into their emotions, thoughts, and behavior to gain a clearer assessment of the problem. Third, counselors help individuals work out adaptive ways of coping with present and future crises. Fourth, counselors help people make some permanent changes in their lives. They may, for example, help people change jobs, move to a safer neighborhood, or establish stable friendships and support groups.

Crisis intervention may take the form of a telephone hot line. People who are in trouble can telephone at any time and receive immediate counseling, sympathy, and comfort. The best known of these systems is the Los Angeles Suicide Prevention Center, which was established in 1958. Similar hot lines have been set up for alcoholics, rape victims, battered women, runaway children, gamblers, sexually abused people, and lonely people who just need a shoulder to cry on or someone to listen to them. In addition to providing sympathy, hot line volunteers give information on community services that can help callers with their problems.

One type of hot line that has become available in recent years responds to issues and problems concerning AIDS (*Ac*quired *I*mmune *D*eficiency *S*yndrome). The National AIDS Hot Line is affiliated with the Centers for Disease Control in Atlanta. Its phones are answered twenty-four hours a day by information specialists who are trained to answer callers' questions and to use crisis intervention techniques. There are also many state AIDS hot lines. Some are staffed by medical personnel including physicians, nurses, and pharmacists. The reason for this is that some of the people who call in ask about symptoms they are experiencing. Counselors need to be able to answer effectively.

AIDS hot lines are not only for people who suspect they have AIDS. Since AIDS is an infectious and terminal disease, many people are confused and frightened about its spread. Hot lines encourage such people to call and ask questions about the disease. Can I get infected just by sitting next to someone with AIDS? If I do not know anyone with AIDS, should I still be concerned about the disease? These and other questions are answered by information specialists at the hot lines. The hot lines also provide referrals to treatment and assessment centers, counseling facilities, and support groups. People who call are not asked for their names. All callers remain anonymous. The National AIDS Hot Line number is 1-800-342-AIDS.

Figure 16. 13
Crisis intervention counselors are trained to deal with people who are going through critical periods in their lives. This counselor works in a shelter for battered women.

Hot lines are usually staffed by volunteers. After dealing with the immediate emotional turmoil over the telephone, the volunteer urges the caller to go to a community facility and meet with a crisis intervention counselor who can provide more assistance. If necessary, long-term help (more than five or six sessions) is set up so the person can develop more effective ways of coping.

Many of the people who staff the crisis intervention hot lines or community centers are not mental health specialists but have been trained to provide help to people who are going through crises. Even trained counselors and therapists require specialized skills to deal with their clients' emotional turmoil during an emergency.

Crisis intervention workers are taught to listen to and understand what people are saying, even when the situation may be highly emotional or chaotic. The skilled attention of a concerned listener sometimes helps a person in crisis become aware of feelings that contribute to his or her sense of panic.

In order to be effective in their helping role, crisis workers must learn how to deal with their own emotional reactions to common crisis situations through role-playing and other methods. By practicing their reactions beforehand, the trainees become more relaxed and less anxious in real-life crises. In addition, role playing allows the workers to become aware of their own feelings and biases.

The Rise of the Paraprofessional

Professionals who traditionally treat mental disorder have always been in short supply. Moreover, they tend to be white and middle class, which may inhibit free communication with nonwhite or poorly educated patients. To overcome both problems, increasing numbers of mental health workers called paraprofessionals are being trained. In a classic study, Margaret Rioch (1967) showed that housewives with no previous psychological training but with well-balanced and sympathetic natures made excellent mental health counselors after two years of intensive training. In recent years, paraprofessionals have been providing a wide variety of mental health services, including interviewing, testing, counseling, and making home visits. When they are carefully screened and trained, and because they often are close in ethnic background to their clients, they have been effective.

Community mental health centers are now in a time of change. Community resistance, budgetary cutbacks, and controversy over the effectiveness of certain programs are all major forces that will shape the future of community psychology.

Use the following outline as a tool for reviewing this chapter. Copy the outline onto your own paper, leaving spaces between headings to make notes about key concepts.

 I. What Is Psychotherapy?

  A. Characteristics of Psychotherapy

  B. What Makes a Good Therapist?

 II. Kinds of Psychotherapy

  A. Psychoanalysis

  B. The Human Potential Movement

  C. Gestalt Therapy

  D. Rational-Emotive Therapy

  E. Transactional Analysis

  F. Behavior Therapy

  G. Group Therapies

 III. Does Psychotherapy Work?

 IV. Organic Therapy

 V. Mental Institutions

  A. Commitment

  B. Conditions

 VI. Community Mental Health

  A. Community Mental Health Centers

  B. The Rise of the Paraprofessional

CONCEPTS AND VOCABULARY

1. What is psychotherapy and what is its goal? What two goals should the client achieve during therapy?

2. What kinds of professionals see persons with behavioral problems? What characteristics of the therapist have been found to increase effectiveness? What client characteristics are associated with favorable outcomes in therapy?

3. What is the goal of psychoanalysis? What does the therapist do to achieve this goal?

4. What is the goal of humanistic psychotherapy? What similarities are there between this type of therapy and psychoanalysis?

5. What is the goal of rational-emotive therapy (RET)? What steps does RET expect the client to take to solve the problem?

6. How does behavior therapy differ from the previously discussed therapies in its approach to correcting an individual's problem? Describe the behavioral therapeutic techniques of systematic desensitization and contingency management.

7. Describe three types of group therapy.

8. Describe the results of studies that have attempted to evaluate the effectiveness of psychotherapy.

9. What are the effects of antipsychotic drugs, antidepressants, and antianxiety drugs? When is each used? What are the side effects and dangers of each?

10. What are community mental health centers and how do they operate? What is a halfway house?

CRITICAL THINKING

1. **Synthesize.** Recommend a treatment for the following problems: compulsive overeating, inability to finish work, severe depression. Think of real examples as much as possible. How do the techniques you suggest resemble the therapies described in this chapter?

2. **Analyze.** On a sheet of paper draw a large thermometer ranging from 0 to 100 degrees. Think

of the most fearful thing you can imagine, and write it down at the 100-degree mark. Write down the least fearful thing you can think of at the 0-degree mark. Continue to list your fears on the thermometer according to their severity. Have several friends make similar lists of their fears. Compare lists, looking for differences and similarities. Do you think any of your fears are based on conditioning? Can you think of a method of reconditioning that would remove the fear or make it less intense?

3. **Evaluate.** Transactional analysis distinguishes between three different ways of experiencing ourselves: parent, adult, and child ego states. Think back to a recent crisis or difficult time you experienced. Then imagine your parents in the same situation. What would your mother or father do in that same situation? This represents a possible parent ego state reaction. Imagine how you would have reacted to the situation as a six year old. Your response to this reflects your child ego state reactions. How do you feel about the situation now? Your answer will most likely reflect your adult ego state. Which ego state helps you deal with the crisis most effectively?

APPLYING KNOWLEDGE

1. Ask several people in different businesses if they would hire someone they knew had undergone psychotherapy. Do their responses indicate to you that society has matured to where it now understands and accepts emotional problems in the same way it accepts medical problems? Do you believe a person should be barred from high public office because he or she has sought psychotherapy?

2. Begin assertiveness training by trying the following exercise. Engage a friend in a casual conversation. During part of the conversation, raise or lower your voice. Experiment with the amount of eye contact you have during the conversation. Try staring at your friend, then not

making any eye contact at all. Change the rate of your speaking from very fast to very slow. What kind of reactions in your friend do you notice with each change? What new insights about yourself did you gain by doing this exercise?

ANALYZING VIEWPOINTS

1. Within the field of psychology there is conflicting evidence about the effectiveness of psychotherapy. Some studies have concluded that psychotherapy is really no more effective than no treatment at all. Other studies have found just the opposite—that psychotherapy *is* generally more effective than no treatment at all. What do you think? Does psychotherapy work? Write a paper that presents a sound argument for both sides of the issue. Use what you have learned from the chapter and look for additional information in magazine articles and books on the topic.

BEYOND THE CLASSROOM

1. Make plans to attend an open meeting of one of the following self-help support groups: Alcoholics Anonymous, Alanon, Alateen, Smokenders, Narcotics Anonymous, Weight Watchers, or Overeaters Anonymous. Go with a classmate so that you can share your observations and experiences. At the meeting, notice the ways in which the group provides support for people. Present your observations to the class.

2. Go to your local library or video store to find a movie that portrays life in a mental institution, such as "One Flew over the Cuckoo's Nest" or "Awakenings." Watch the film carefully. How do these portrayals match with your text's description? In a paper, describe some of the patients' symptoms and how you would classify them. What kind of treatment(s) are being administered?

UNIT 6

Human Relations

Chapter 17
Human Interaction

Chapter 18
Attitudes and Social Influence

CHAPTER 17

Human Interaction

Key Terms:

attribution theory
body language
charisma
complementarity
diffusion of responsibility
ego-support value
group
ideology
implicit personality theory
nonverbal communication
norms
personal space
physical proximity
social functions
social leader
social rule
sociogram
stereotype
stimulation value
task functions
task leader
utility value

People vary considerably in their need for social contact and in their desire and ability to be alone. You have probably heard tales of hermits and recluses who voluntarily isolate themselves, but most people would not welcome a solitary life. What is so important about being around other people? And what do psychologists know about human interaction?

NEEDING OTHER PEOPLE

From infancy we depend on others to satisfy our basic needs. In this relationship we learn to associate close personal contact with the satisfaction of basic needs. In later life we seek personal contact for the same reason, even though we can now care for ourselves.

Being around other human beings, interacting with others, has become a habit that would be difficult to break. Moreover, we have developed needs for praise, respect, love and affection, the sense of achievement, and other rewarding experiences. And these needs, acquired through social learning, can only be satisfied by other human beings (Bandura and Walters, 1963).

Anxiety and Companionship

Social psychologists are interested in discovering what circumstances intensify our desire for human contact. It seems that we need company most when we are afraid or anxious, and we also need company when we are unsure of ourselves and want to compare our feelings with other people's.

Objectives:

After studying this chapter, you should be able to

- describe the basic human need for interaction with others.
- discuss the ways individuals form impressions of one another.
- describe the interactive patterns within groups.

Figure 17.1 How much we need other people varies, but interaction with others is a way of satisfying the needs we all have for praise, respect, love, and affection.

Low Anxiety   High Anxiety

● Women who chose to be alone
   or did not care
● Women who chose to affiliate

Figure 17.2
The results of Schachter's 1959 experiment about the effects of anxiety on affiliation.

Psychologist Stanley Schachter (1959) decided to test the old saying "Misery loves company." His experiment showed that people suffering from a high level of anxiety are more likely to seek out company than those who feel less anxious. He arranged for a number of college women to come to his laboratory. One group of women was greeted by a frightening-looking man in a white coat who identified himself as Dr. Gregor Zilstein of the medical school. Dr. Zilstein told each woman that she would be given electric shocks in order to study the effect of electricity on the body. He told the women, in an ominous tone, that the shocks would be extremely painful. With a devilish smile, he added that the shocks would cause no permanent skin damage. For obvious reasons, this group of women was referred to as the high-anxiety group.

The doctor was friendly to the other group of women, and told them that the shocks would produce only ticklish, tingling sensations, which they might even find pleasant. These women formed the low-anxiety group.

Zilstein told each subject that she would have to leave the laboratory while he set up the equipment. He then asked each woman to indicate on a questionnaire whether she wished to wait alone in a private room or with other subjects in a larger room. Most women in the low-anxiety group chose to wait alone. However, the overwhelming majority of high-anxiety women preferred to wait with others. Thus, the experiment demonstrated that high anxiety produces a need for companionship (Figure 17.2).

Comparing Experiences and Reducing Uncertainty

People also like to get together with one another to reduce their uncertainties about themselves. For example, when you get exams back, you probably ask your friends how they did. You try to understand your own situation by comparing it to other people's. You learn your strengths and weaknesses by asking: Can other people do it, too? Do they do it better or worse? Many individuals use the performance of others as a basis for self-evaluation. According to this theory, one of the reasons why the women in the shock experiment sought company was to find out how they should respond to Dr. Zilstein. Should they feel fear or anger, or should they take the whole thing in stride? One way to get this information was to talk to others.

Schachter conducted another experiment to test this idea. It was essentially the same as the Dr. Zilstein experiment, but this time *all* the women were made anxious. Half of them were then given the choice between waiting alone and waiting with other women about to take part in the same experiment. The other half were given the choice between waiting alone and passing the time in a room where students were waiting to see their academic advisers.

As you might expect, the women who had a chance to be with other women in the same predicament seized the opportunity. These women wanted to compare their dilemma with others. But most of the women in the second group chose to spend the time alone rather than with the unconcerned students. As the experimenter put it, "Misery doesn't love just any kind of company, it loves only miserable company."

Other researchers have shown that the more uncertain a person is, the more likely he or she is to seek out other people. Like Schachter, Harold Gerard and J. M. Rabbie recruited volunteers for an experiment. When the volunteers arrived, some of them were escorted to a booth and attached to a machine that was suppose to measure emotionality. The machine was turned on, and the subjects were able to see not only their own ratings but the ratings of three other participants as well. In each case the dial for the subject registered 82 on a scale of 100; the dials for the other participants registered 79, 80, and 81. (As you've undoubtedly guessed, the machine was rigged.) A second group of subjects was attached to a similar machine and was shown their own ratings but not those of other participants. A third group was not given any information about themselves or other participants in the experiment. When asked whether they wanted to wait alone or with other subjects, most of the people in the first group chose to wait alone. They had seen how they compared to others and felt they were reacting appropriately. However, most of the subjects in the other two groups, who had no basis for evaluating themselves, chose to wait with other people (Gerard and Rabbie, 1961).

Seeking company when you are frightened or uncertain about your feelings seems to work. People who choose to be in a group when they are afraid of an experimental procedure or lack information about how they compare to others are less anxious than those who "tough it out" and wait alone (Wrightsman, 1960).

CHOOSING FRIENDS

Most people feel they have a great deal of latitude in the friends they choose. Easy transportation, telephones, and the spare time available to most Americans would all seem to ease communication among them and, therefore, to permit them a wide range of individuals from whom to choose companions, friends, and lovers. But in fact, we rarely venture beyond the most convenient methods in making contact with others.

Proximity

Would it surprise you to learn that the most important factor in determining whether two people will become friends is **physical proximity**—the distance from one another that people live or work? In general, the closer two individuals are geographically to one another, the more likely they are to become attracted to each other. And it is more than just the opportunity for interaction that makes the difference.

Psychologists have found that even in a small two-story apartment building where each resident was in easy reach of everyone else, people were more likely to become close friends with the person next door than with anyone else (Figure 17.3). Psychologists believe that this is a result of the fears and embarrassments most people have about making contact with strangers. When two people live next door to one another, go to the same class, or work in the same place, they are able to get used to one

The single most important factor in choosing friends is physical proximity.

Figure 17.3
A set of apartments such as this one was used in a study of friendship choice. It was found that the fewer doors there were between people, the more likely they were to become friends.

another and to find reasons to talk to one another without ever having to seriously risk rejection. To make friends with someone whom you do not see routinely is much more difficult. You have to make it clear that you are interested and thus run the risk of making a fool of yourself—either because the other person turns out to be less interesting than he or she seemed at a distance or because that person expresses no interest in you. Of course, it may turn out that both of you are very glad someone spoke up.

Reward Values

Proximity helps people make friends, but it does not ensure lasting friendship. Sometimes people who are forced together in a situation take a dislike to one another that develops into hatred. Furthermore, once people have made friends, physical separation does not necessarily bring an end to their relationship. What are the factors that determine whether people will like each other once they come into contact?

One reward of friendship is stimulation. A friend has **stimulation value** if she is interesting or imaginative or if she can introduce you to new ideas or experiences. A friend who is cooperative and helpful, who seems willing to give his time and resources to help you achieve your goals, has **utility value.** A third type of value in friendship is **ego-support value:** sympathy and encouragement when things go badly, appreciation and approval when things go well. These three kinds of rewards—stimulation, utility, and ego support—are evaluated consciously or unconsciously in every friendship. A man may like another man because the second man is a witty conversationalist (stimulation value) and knows a lot about gardening (utility value). A woman may like a man because he values her opinions (ego-support value) and because she has an exciting time with him (stimulation value).

Who Is Shy?

If you would rather disappear into the wallpaper than go to the class dance, you're shy. If you prefer to spend evenings at home instead of risking the possibility of meeting new people, you're shy too. But contrary to what you probably think, you are not alone. More than 80 percent of people questioned in one survey on shyness said they had been shy at some time in their lives. Out of this number, 40 percent said they felt shy now.

This does not mean that everyone is equally shy: There are degrees of shyness ranging from slight discomfort in some situations to sheer panic in all situations. Only 25 percent of the sample approached the far end of the scale, considering themselves to be chronically shy. An even smaller group—4 percent—said they were shy all the time in all situations.

If you are shy, it may give you some comfort to know that shyness is not a purely American trait. It is found to differing degrees in cultures throughout the world. In fact, right at this moment, 60 percent of Orientals would say they were shy too.

For more details, see Philip G. Zimbardo, *Shyness*. Reading, Mass.: Addison-Wesley, 1977.

By considering the three kinds of rewards that a person may look for in friendship, it is possible to understand other factors that affect liking and loving.

Physical Appearance.   A person's physical appearance greatly influences others' impressions of him or her. People feel better about themselves when they associate with people others consider desirable. This is true of same-sex as well as opposite-sex relationships. Physical attractiveness influences our choice of friends as well as lovers.

In one study (Dion, Berscheid, and Walster, 1972), subjects were shown pictures of men and women of varying degrees of physical attractiveness and were asked to rate their personality traits. The physically attractive people were consistently viewed more positively than the less attractive ones. They were seen as more sensitive, kind, interesting, strong, poised, modest, and sociable, as well as more sexually responsive. It seems, therefore, that although we have all heard that "beauty is only skin deep," we act as if it permeates one's entire personality.

Homely people are generally viewed in an unfavorable light. Research has shown that obese adults, who in our culture are considered unattractive, are often discriminated against when they apply for jobs. Even homely children are targets of prejudice (Figure 17.4). An unattractive child is far more likely to be judged "bad" or "cruel" for a particular act of misbehavior than is a more attractive peer (Dion, Berscheid, and Walster, 1972).

Interestingly, psychologists have found that both men and women pay

How to Relate to People

If you're like most people, you want others to like you, but knowing exactly how to make them like you is not always that easy. Most psychologists believe that the principle of *reciprocal reinforcement* has a lot to do with how you get along with others. In simple terms, this principle states that people will like you if your behavior makes them feel good about themselves.

Here are some reinforcement techniques you can use to get a head start on winning and keeping friends:

- When you're talking to another person, try to spend at least 50 percent of the time listening to what the other person says. That may mean cutting down on your chatter, but the results will be well worthwhile.
- Be an active rather than a passive listener. By commenting directly on what the other person says, you will show that you are really interested in his conversation.
- Instead of focusing on your own accomplishments, ask questions about the person you are with. This tells him in no uncertain terms that you care about what he has done. The best time to talk about yourself is when the other person asks.
- Approval is one of the best reinforcers if it is used correctly, but another person is easily turned off if it is not sincere. Be sure to praise only those things the other person considers important and don't use an overlavish or repetitive approach.

For more details, see Robert L. Williams and James D. Long, *Toward a Self-managed Life Style,* 2nd ed. Boston: Houghton Mifflin, 1979.

much less attention to physical appearance when choosing a marriage partner or a close friend than when inviting someone to go to a movie or a party. But neither men nor women necessarily seek out the most attractive member of their social world. Rather, people usually seek out others whom they consider their equals on the scale of physical attractiveness (Levinger and Snoek, 1972).

Approval.   Another factor that affects a person's choice of friends is approval. All of us tend to like people who say nice things about us because they make us feel better about ourselves—they provide ego-support value.

The results of one experiment suggest that other people's evaluations of oneself are more meaningful when they are a mixture of praise and criticism than when they are extreme in either direction. No one believes that he or she is all good or all bad. As a result, one can take more seriously a person who sees some good points and some bad points. But when the good points come first, hearing the bad can make one disappointed and angry at the person who made them. When the bad points come first, the effect is opposite. One thinks, "This person is perceptive and honest. At

Figure 17.4
In one experiment, adult women were shown reports about and photographs of children participating in a variety of antisocial behaviors. The adults tended not only to see the behaviors committed by the unattractive children as more generally antisocial, but to attribute a more inherently negative moral character to these children than to the attractive ones. (Adapted from Dion, 1972)

first she was critical but later she saw what I was really like" (Aronson and Linder, 1965).

Similarity. People tend to choose friends whose backgrounds, attitudes, and interests are similar to their own. Nearly always, husbands and wives have similar economic, religious, and educational backgrounds.

There are several explanations for the power of shared attitudes. First, agreement about what is stimulating, worthwhile, or fun provides the basis for sharing activities. People who have similar interests are likely to do more things together and to get to know one another better.

Figure 17.5
These two men obviously enjoy each other's company. In addition to having stimulation value for each other, they probably provide considerable utility value: they may be able to give each other advice about business problems and opportunities.

Second, most of us feel uneasy around people who are constantly challenging our views, and we translate our uneasiness into hostility or avoidance. We are more comfortable around people who support us. A friend's agreement bolsters your confidence and contributes to your self-esteem. In addition, most of us are self-centered enough to assume that people who share our values are basically decent and intelligent (unlike others we know).

Finally, people who agree about things usually find it easier to communicate with each other. They have fewer arguments and misunderstandings; they are better able to predict one another's behavior and thus feel at ease with each other.

Complementarity—an attraction between opposite types of people—is not unusual, however. For example, a dominant person might look for a submissive mate. Still, most psychologists agree that similarity is a much more important factor. Although the old idea that opposites attract seems reasonable, researchers have not been able to verify it (Berscheid and Walster, 1978: 78–81).

PERSONAL RELATIONSHIPS

Your personal relationships with others bring meaning and substance to your everyday experiences. Knowing that you have loved ones who care about you and are willing recipients of your affection contributes to the quality of your life and your overall sense of well-being. Throughout life, you establish different kinds of personal relationships. Your first meaningful relationships were established within the family.

Parent-Child Relationships

Noted psychologist Erik Erikson, among others, believed that early and persistent patterns of parent-child interaction can influence people's later adult expectations about their relationships with the significant people in their lives. If a young infant's first relationship with a caregiver is loving, responsive, and consistent, the child will develop a trust in the ability of other people to meet his or her needs. This trusting, in turn, will encourage the person to be receptive to people. On the other hand, a child who has experienced unresponsive, inconsistent, or unaffectionate care in infancy will most likely be more wary or mistrustful of other people. Within the parent-child relationship, we learn how to manipulate others to have our needs met. A parent is likely to satisfy the wishes of a child who acts "good," that is, who does what the parent asks. The child may also learn to get attention by pouting or having temper tantrums.

As children develop and form relationships with people outside their family, they apply what they have learned about relationships. As a result of childhood experiences, an individual might, for example, believe that the only way to establish and maintain good relationships with friends is always to say what pleases them rather than speak the truth.

Your parents influence the quality of your adult relationships in other ways. They provide you with your first model of a marital relationship. As you watched your mother and father interacting with each other as husband and wife, you were most likely forming some tentative conclusions about the nature of relationships. Later on, you might use their example as a guide in selecting a future mate or in evaluating your relationships. If your parents have a happy marriage, you will most likely seek to duplicate it by imitating their patterns. If you believe their lives are unhappy or unfulfilled as a result of the nature of their relationship, you may try to create a very different type of relationship with a mate.

Love Relationships

While most people say that they love their parents, their friends, and maybe even their brothers and sisters, they attach a different meaning to *love* when referring to a boyfriend, girlfriend, or spouse. Love means different things to different people and within different relationships.

Psychologist Zick Rubin (1973) has distinguished between *like* and *love*. According to Rubin, liking usually involves respect or high regard for another person. Love usually involves liking plus three other elements: great attachment to and dependency on the person; a caring for or desire to help the person; and the desire for an exclusive, intimate relationship with the person. Other researchers (Berscheid, 1983; Davis, 1985; and Hatfield and Walster, 1981) have distinguished between two types of love. *Passionate love* is an intensely emotional and sexual fascination with a mate and a strong desire for exclusiveness. Feelings of excitement, anxiety, tenderness, and jealousy are all common in passionate love. Passionate love is what is commonly referred to as "romantic love" in which lovers long for their partners and seek to capture their affection. In contrast to the relatively short-lived passionate love is *companionate love*, which is defined as the affection we feel for those with whom our lives are deeply intertwined. People who share a mutual concern and care for each other and who have strong, frequent, and long-term interactions are likely to experience companionate love. Friendship, understanding, and the willingness to make sacrifices for each other are characteristic of companionate love.

Falling in Love.   The differences between passionate and companionate love can be further examined by reviewing the development of each type of love. Psychologists Ellen Berscheid and Elaine Walster (1974) maintain that three criteria must be met for passionate love to occur. First, there must be a culturally held expectation that one will fall in love or be smitten by passionate desire for a person. People who believe in "love at first sight" or "falling head over heels in love" are likely to experience it. Second, there must be an appropriate "love object," someone who is "right."

The third criterion is the presence of an emotional arousal, which the person interprets as love. This emotional arousal can be experienced in a number of different ways, ranging from sexual arousal to anxiety or anger. In fact, the source of a person's emotional arousal or love feelings

Figure 17.6
What makes people fall in love? Is there such a thing as love at first sight? Does romantic love endure? Romance has inspired poets, painters, and playwrights through the ages. Psychologists are also interested in learning more about what causes people to fall in and out of love.

Love and Separation. Suppose you were involved in a serious romance and your partner had to move away. What would happen to your relationship?

Psychologists have studied couples who endure many different types of separation: college students who separate during vacations, college students who attend different schools, traveling executives and their spouses, military couples separated by active tours of duty, and prisoners of war and their families. Two findings consistently emerge from these studies: (1) all separations are stressful; and (2) strong relationships generally endure separations, whereas weak relationships generally do not. In fact, some college students report that they use separations (during the summer break or a semester abroad) specifically to test the strength of their relationships. On the other hand, people dissatisfied with their relationships often seek separations by accepting jobs requiring frequent travel or requesting transfers to new locations.

Will your relationship survive a separation? The answer depends more on the strength of your relationship than on the separation itself.

may not even be the loved one, but another source. Suppose, for example, you have a frightening or unsettling experience. To calm yourself down, you think about your boyfriend or girlfriend. According to Berscheid and Walster's theory, the emotional arousal you have experienced from the fright will channel itself into what feels like romantic love. Similarly, if you are going on a date and are anxious or excited about going to a new place, you may interpret the emotional arousal you feel as love for your date.

The onset of romantic or passionate love is fairly swift and sudden. It is quite fragile compared with companionate love. Passionate love, marked by strong, emotional upswings, rarely lasts long. Some passionate love relationships turn into longer lasting companionate love relationships.

The development of companionate love is less dramatic than that of passionate love. It begins as a mutual attraction between two people and changes as they build their relationship together. The development of a more intimate relationship may be stable and uneventful, stable but increasingly satisfying, or unstable and conflict-ridden. There are many variations in relationship patterns. Relationships that seem unstable often find stability, and seemingly unchanging relationships sometimes deteriorate into separation.

The development of a close companionate relationship is influenced by the degree to which each person is willing to reveal personal and private information about himself or herself. Couples who are willing to trust each other and who communicate their feelings and ideas freely are likely to have a close relationship that endures. Ordinarily, the more personal information a person discloses to a companion, the more personal information the companion is likely to disclose in return. This mutual disclosure serves to deepen the relationship.

Nonverbal Communication

Central to the development and maintenance of a relationship is the willingness to communicate aspects of yourself to others. Communication involves at least two people: a person who sends a message and a person who receives it. The message sent consists of an idea and some emotional component. Messages are sent verbally and nonverbally. "I like to watch you dance" is a verbal message; a warm smile is an example of **nonverbal communication.**

Although most people are aware of what they are saying verbally, they are often unaware of their nonverbal messages. They are more aware of the nonverbal messages when they are on the receiving end of them. You have probably heard someone say, "It doesn't matter," speaking in a low voice and looking away; the unspoken message is "My feelings are hurt." You do not need to be told in so many words that a friend is elated or depressed, angry or pleased, nervous, or content. You sense these things. People communicate nonverbally not only through facial expressions but also through their use of space and body language (posture and gestures).

Personal Space. Anthropologist Edward T. Hall became acutely aware of the importance people attach to space when he found himself backing away from a colleague he particularly liked and respected. The associate was not an American, which led Hall to wonder whether people from different cultures had different ideas about the proper distance at which to hold an informal conversation. He decided to pursue the question.

After much observation, Hall concluded that Americans carry a two-foot "bubble" of privacy around them. If another person invades this bubble, we feel slightly threatened, imposed upon, and generally uncomfortable. For Germans, the bubble of privacy is much larger; for Arabs, much smaller (Hall, 1959). Thus, an Arab man talking to a German man, for example, may try to establish his accustomed talking distance and move closer. The German may conclude that the Arab is "pushy." When the German moves back to what he feels is a normal distance, the Arab may take this as a sign of coldness and conclude that the man is aloof.

Hall observed Americans to see how we use space to communicate our feelings about other people and to define relationships. He found that Americans usually allow only intimates (husbands and wives, other family members, and close friends) to come closer than two feet, a point at which touching is almost inevitable. When we are forced to stand very close to non-intimates, as in a crowded elevator, we try to hold our bodies immobile and avoid eye contact.

When we maintain a distance of four feet or so, we are essentially putting the other person "at arm's length." People who work together generally observe this boundary. When we want to hold people off, consciously or unconsciously, we create a four- to seven-foot bubble between us and them. Sometimes, we use social distance to show status. An executive of a large corporation may put visitors' chairs nine feet from his or her desk to create the impression of status, but many executives are aware of this form of communication and will try to counter the impression by placing the chairs closer than four feet.

If you go to an uncrowded beach, you will probably settle down between twelve and twenty-five feet from other people (Figure 17.7). If you arrange a room for a speaker, you will probably leave this same twelve- to twenty-five feet of space between the podium and the first row of seats. Hall calls this "public distance" and suggests it provides a sense of safety. At twelve feet, an alert person can take defensive action if threatened. At the same time, twelve feet or more does not invite personal communication. To talk, two people would have to move closer (Hall, 1966). The ways in which people use space to communicate will become clear if you keep this scheme in mind. If you put your beach towel five feet from another person's when there is plenty of empty space, you're issuing an invitation. If you step back when someone at a party comes within two feet, you're discouraging further intimacy even though you may not be aware of the nonverbal message you're sending.

Body Language.   The way you carry your body also communicates information about you. This is your **body language.** If you stand tall and erect, you convey the impression of self-assurance. If you sit and talk with your arms folded and legs crossed, you communicate that you are protecting yourself. When you unfold your arms and stretch out, you may be saying that you are open to people.

Figure 17.7
"Public distance" at the beach. People place themselves between 12 and 25 feet apart, a signal that no direct personal communication is desired.

Figure 17.8
Body language: The postures we adopt and the gestures we make convey messages. Like all other kinds of behavior, how we use our bodies is governed by social rules.

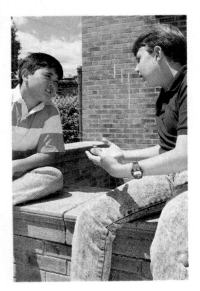

One group of researchers found that women who adopt an open body position are better liked and are listened to more closely than women who assume a closed position. A number of students were given a questionnaire that measured their opinions on everything from the legalization of marijuana to the custom of tipping. A few weeks later, they were invited back and asked to evaluate a certain other student's responses to the same questions. Some subjects were shown a slide of this female student sitting in a closed position; others saw a slide of her sitting in a neutral or open position. A high percentage of those who saw the open-looking picture indicated that they liked her and changed many of their opinions to agree with hers when they filled out the questionnaire a second time. On the other hand, the group that saw the closed-looking picture tended to stick with their original responses (McGinley, LeFevre, and McGinley, 1975).

Although the use of body language is often unconscious, many of the postures we adopt and gestures we make are governed by **social rules** (Figure 17.8). These rules are very subtle. For example, your teacher or boss is much more likely to touch you than you are to touch him or her. Touching is considered a privilege of higher status.

There are cultural differences in body language, just as there are in the use of space. For example, Americans move their heads up and down to show agreement and shake them back and forth to show disagreement. The Semang of Malaya thrust their heads sharply forward to agree and lower their eyes to disagree, while the Dayak of Borneo agree by raising their eyebrows and disagree by bringing them together.

You do not have to go to Borneo to observe cultural variations in nonverbal communication. In a field study conducted in hospitals, airports, and fast-food restaurants, LaFrance and Mayo (1976) found that American blacks and whites use eye contact in very different ways. Although people of both races looked at each other for the same proportion of time during a conversation, the timing was different. Blacks tend to look at their partner when they are speaking, and to look away while listening; whites do just the opposite. These unconscious differences may sometimes make blacks and whites uncomfortable when they talk to each other.

HOW PEOPLE PERCEIVE ONE ANOTHER

It takes people very little time to make judgments about one another. From one brief conversation, or even by watching a person across a room, you may form an impression of what someone is like. And first impressions influence the future of a relationship. If a person *seems* interesting, he or she becomes a candidate for future interaction. A person who seems to have nothing interesting to say—or much too much to say—does not. We tend to be sympathetic toward someone who seems shy; to expect a lot from someone who impresses us as intelligent; to be wary of a person who strikes us as aggressive.

Forming an impression of a person is not a passive process in which certain characteristics of the individual are the input and a certain impression is the automatic outcome. If impressions varied only when input varied, then everyone meeting a particular stranger would form the same impression of him or her. This, of course, is not what happens. One individual may judge a newcomer to be "quiet," another may judge the same

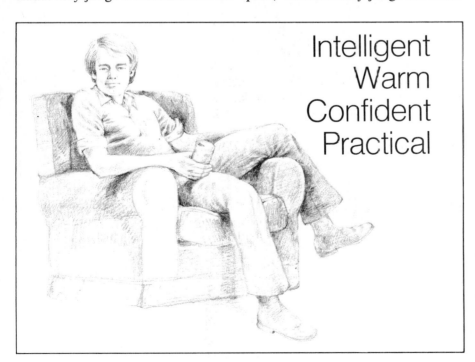

Intelligent
Warm
Confident
Practical

Figure 17.9
What is your impression of this person? Do you think you would like him? What do you think of the way he is dressed? What sort of expression does he have on his face? When you have formed an impression, turn to the drawing in Figure 17.10 and do the same.

person to be "dull," and still another person may think the person "mysterious." These various impressions lead to different expectations of the newcomer and to different patterns of interaction with him or her.

Implicit Personality Theory

One reason different people tend to develop different impressions of the same stranger is that we each have our own **implicit personality theory**— our own set of assumptions about how people behave and what traits or characteristics go together. When you meet someone who seems unusually intelligent, you may assume she is also active, highly motivated, conscientious, and so on. Another person in the group may have an altogether different "theory" about highly intelligent people—that they are unrealistic, boastful, insensitive, and the like. Whatever the person does provides "evidence" for both theories. You are impressed by how animated she becomes when talking about her work; the other person is impressed by how little attention she pays to other people. Both of you are filling in gaps in what you know about the person, fitting her into a type you carry around in your head.

Experiments indicate that our impressions are strongly influenced by a few traits (Figures 17.9, 17.10). For example, one researcher invited a guest lecturer to a psychology class. Beforehand all the students were given a brief description of the visitor. The descriptions were identical in all traits but one. Half the students were told that the speaker was cold, the other half that he was warm. After the lecture the researcher asked all the students to evaluate the lecturer. Reading their impressions, you would hardly

Figure 17.10
If your impressions of this person are different from your impressions of the person in Figure 17.9, the difference must be due to the change in a single word—the illustrations are otherwise identical.

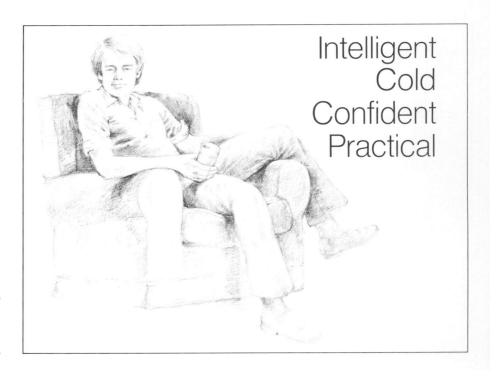

Intelligent
Cold
Confident
Practical

know that the two groups of students were describing the same person. The students who had been told he was cold saw a humorless, ruthless, self-centered person. The other students saw a relaxed, friendly, concerned person. Changing one word—substituting "warm" for "cold"—had a dramatic impact on the audience's perception of the lecturer. It also affected their behavior. Students in the "warm group" were warm themselves, initiating more conversations with the speaker than did the students in the other group (Kelley, 1950).

Stereotypes. The line between applying implicit personality theories to people (as the students did) and thinking in stereotypes is a very thin one. A **stereotype** is a set of assumptions about people in a given category. The belief that Jews are clannish or that students who wear suits are not to be trusted are examples. Stereotypes are based on half-truths and nontruths, and tend to blind us to differences among people and to the way individuals actually behave.

Implicit personality theories are useful because they help us to predict with *some* degree of accuracy how people will behave. Without them, we would spend considerable energy observing and testing people to find out what they are like, whether we want to pursue a relationship with them, and so on. Like stereotypes, the assumptions we make about people from our first impressions tend to weaken as we get to know them better.

Personality Versus Circumstance: Attribution Theory

First impressions and the decision to pursue or abandon a relationship depend in large part on the situations in which we observe people. Suppose you walk into a library and find a man pacing back and forth. You sit down. He continues to pace for what seems like hours. The chances are you would want to avoid this man. He seems like an extremely unhappy and nervous person. But suppose the setting is the waiting room for a maternity ward. Your feelings about him would be entirely different (Rubin, 1973: 100–101).

The conclusions we draw about people thus vary according to whether we attribute their actions to personal qualities (such as general nervousness) or to the situation or role in which they find themselves (such as an expectant father). In recent years, many social psychologists have become interested in **attribution theory**—the attempt to understand how we interpret people's actions (Shaver, 1975). One key step involves deciding, as we did in the case of the pacing man, whether behavior is a result of personal qualities or external pressure (Figure 17.11).

Another important issue involves motive and intent: "What did he hope to accomplish by that?" If a new friend, for example, starts off your day by telling you that the sweater you just bought is hideous, you can interpret that as an attempt to be helpful or as an act of hostility. Your opinion of this person will depend on the motive you accept.

Of course, some actions are more revealing than others. Some behavior is so common that it reveals very little about personality. If a bank teller cashes your check without comment and gives you a half smile, you prob-

PSYCHOLOGY UPDATE

Stereotyping Bias in Psychiatric Diagnosis. Psychiatric professionals are trained to be objective observers of human behavior, but they are not immune to stereotyping their patients. Researchers have identified biases involving several groups, including the mentally retarded, the elderly, and people of low socioeconomic status (SES).

Mentally retarded people were consistently *underdiagnosed*; that is, they were not given a diagnosis when their symptoms indicated that a disorder in fact existed. Specifically, retarded patients frequently showed symptoms of depression, anxiety, and other disorders, but these problems were rarely diagnosed.

Frequently people of low SES and elderly patients were *overdiagnosed*, that is, given diagnoses that were not warranted by their behavior. In the absence of clear symptoms, some low-SES patients were falsely labeled as schizophrenic. Often physical and cognitive deterioration expected of elderly patients was labeled depression or dementia (disorganized thinking).

These findings have prompted psychiatric professionals to take a closer look at the symptoms of these patients and the conditions that may contribute to their problems.

Figure 17.11
Who attributes what to whom? In this first part of an experiment, actors A and B were talking while observers C and D watched B and A, respectively. Both actors later rated their own behavior in terms of personal characteristics about themselves or characteristics of the situation. Observers C and D similarly rated each of their target actors. The results showed that actors attributed their own behavior more to situational factors than to enduring personality factors. Observers, however, saw the actors' behavior more in terms of personality factors. (Adapted from Storms, 1973)

> **How we interpret another's behavior depends just as much on how we perceive it as on what it is.**

ably will not be able to tell much about her personality. But if she greets you with a warm hello (even though you've never laid eyes on this person in your life) and proceeds to get you in a long discussion of the weather, politics, and football, you might infer a great deal more about her personality. According to one theory (Jones and Davis, 1965), behavior that is unexpected or unusual and that can most plausibly be explained by only one motive provides the most important clues to a person's real nature.

In one study investigating attribution theory, a group of researchers asked subjects to watch three individuals take a test, and to evaluate their intelligence at various points during the test and after it was finished. *All* three individuals answered fifteen of thirty questions correctly. However, one started out well but then did poorly; the second did poorly at first but then improved; the third alternated between right and wrong answers, showing no pattern. Most subjects indicated that they thought the first individual was more intelligent than the others, although they all received the same score (Jones *et al.*, 1968). Why? Because once you have committed yourself to a judgment about a person (as subjects were required to do), changing your evaluation means admitting you made a mistake. Most of us find this somewhat hard to do. The subjects in this experiment clung to their original evaluation rather than admit a mistake.

The point is that we all actively perceive other people's actions. And what we conclude about other people depends not just on what they do, but also on our interpretations. This is true not just when we deal with individuals, but also when we react to groups.

WHAT ARE GROUPS?

What do the Rolling Stones, the St. Stanislaus Parish Bowling Team, the National Association for Retired Midgets, and Argentina have in common?

Each can be classified as a **group.** In general, the features that distinguish a group from a nongroup are interdependence and shared goals.

Interdependence

All the people in the world who have red hair and freckles make up a category of people, but they are not a group. The people in this collection are not interdependent. Interdependence occurs when any action by one of them will affect or influence the other members or when the same event will influence each one. For instance, in groups of athletes, entertainers, or roommates, each member has a certain responsibility to the rest of the group; if he or she does not fulfill his or her responsibility, the other members will be affected. For the athletes, the consequence may be losing the game; for the entertainers, a bad show; for the roommates, a messy apartment.

In small groups, members usually have a direct influence on one another: one person yells at another, smiles at him, or passes him a note. In larger groups, the influence may be indirect. The interdependence between you and the president of the United States is not a result of personal contact. Nevertheless, one of the things that make the people of the United States a group is the fact that the president's actions affect you and that your actions, together with those of many other Americans, affect him.

Common Goals

Group members become interdependent because they see themselves as sharing certain common goals. Groups are usually created to perform tasks

Figure 17.12
A task-oriented group. Whether or not the doctors and nurses in this surgical team are friendly outside the operating room does not matter; their main purpose as a group is to do a certain job.

or to organize activities that no individual could handle alone. Members of a consumer group, for example, share the common goal of working for consumer protection. Members of ethnic and religious groups desire to perpetuate a common heritage or set of beliefs.

The purposes groups serve are of two general kinds: **task functions,** those directed toward getting some job done; and **social functions,** those directed toward filling the emotional needs of members. In most groups, task and social functions are naturally combined and cannot easily be separated.

Political parties, teams of surgeons, and crews of construction workers are all task-oriented groups (Figure 17.12). Although social interactions occur within each of these groups, their main purpose is to complete a project or achieve some change in the environment. Social functions are emphasized in more informal, temporary groups. When people take walks together, attend parties, or participate in conversations, they have formed a group to gain such social rewards as companionship and emotional support. But again, every group involves both task and social functions, at least to some degree.

HOW GROUPS ARE HELD TOGETHER

The factors that work to hold groups together—that increase cohesiveness—include the attitudes and standards they share, and their commitment to them.

Norms

One way in which groups keep their members going in the same direction is by developing group norms. **Norms** are rules for the behavior and attitudes of group members. These rules are not necessarily rigid laws. They may be more like tendencies or habits. But group members are expected to act in accordance with group norms and are punished in some way if they do not. If a college student shaved her hair off, her friends would not hesitate to say something about it. And strangers might point and giggle—simply because she violated the norm that hair should be a certain length and style. Thus, the punishment may take the form of coldness or criticism from other group members. If the norm is very important to the group, a member who violates it may receive a more severe punishment or may be excluded from the group.

Ideology

For a group to be cohesive, members must share the same values. In some cases, people are drawn together because they discover they have common ideas, attitudes, and goals—that is, a common **ideology.** In other instances, people are attracted to a group because its ideology provides them with a new way of looking at themselves and interpreting events, and a new set of goals and means for achieving them. The civil-rights movement of the sixties, for example, provided, among other things, an explanation of black oppression in America and the hope that something could be done to change things. Similarly, the women's movement of the seventies focused on women's rights. Leaders, heroes and heroines, rallies, books and pamphlets, slogans, and symbols all help to popularize an ideology, win converts, and create feelings of solidarity among group members.

Commitment

Cohesiveness will be high if members are committed to their group. One factor that increases individual commitment is the requirement of personal sacrifice. If a person is willing to pay money, endure hardship, or undergo humiliation to belong to a group, he or she is likely to stick with it. For example, college students who undergo embarrassing initiation rites to join sororities or fraternities tend to develop a loyalty to the group that lasts well beyond their college years.

Another factor that strengthens group commitment is participation. When people actively participate in group decisions and share the rewards of the group's accomplishments, their feeling of membership increases— they feel that they have helped make the group what it is. For example, social psychologists have compared groups of workers who participate in decisions that affect their jobs with other workers who elect representatives to decision-making committees or workers who are simply told what to do. Those who participate have higher morale and accept change more readily than the other workers (Coch and French, 1948).

The processes that hold a group together must work both ways. The individual must be responsive to the norms of the group, subscribe to its ideology, and be prepared to make sacrifices in order to be a part of it. But the group must also respond to the needs of its members. It cannot achieve cohesiveness if its norms are unenforceable, if its ideology is inconsistent with the beliefs of its members, or if the rewards it offers do not outweigh the sacrifices it requires.

INTERACTIONS WITHIN GROUPS

Providing an individual with values and a sense of identity is only one aspect of the group's meaning to him or her. The particular part he or she plays in the group's activities is also important. Each group member has certain unique abilities and interests, and the group has a number of different tasks that need to be performed. The study of the parts various members play in the group, and of how these parts are interrelated, is the study of *group structure*.

There are many different aspects to group structure: the personal relationships between individual members, such as liking relationships and trusting relationships; the rank of each member on a particular dimension, such as power, popularity, status, or amount of resources; and the roles

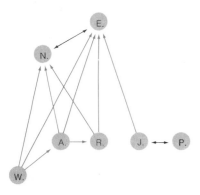

Figure 17.13
Sociograms showing patterns of friendship choices within two groups. The blue arrows indicate liking that is not returned; the black arrows indicate a two-way friendship. The more a person is liked, the higher in the pattern he or she appears. The pattern of the bottom group shows a hierarchical structure, with E and N clearly the leaders. The sociogram of the top group indicates strong group cohesiveness, with even D and T, the two least-liked members, clearly tied in to the group and having friends who like them.

various members play. (A few typical group roles are leader, joker, and the silent member.)

Communication Patterns

One technique psychologists use to analyze group structure is the **sociogram.** All members of a group are asked to name those people with whom they would like to interact on a given occasion or for a specific purpose, those they like best, and so on. For example, the members may be asked with whom they would like to go to a party, to discuss politics, to spend a vacation, or to complete an organizational task. Their choices can then be diagramed, as shown in Figure 17.13. Sociograms can help psychologists predict how that individual is likely to communicate with other group members.

Another way to discover the structure of a group is to examine the communication patterns in the group—who says what to whom, and how often.

One experiment on communication patterns was done by Harold Leavitt in 1951. He gave a card with several symbols on it to each person in a group of five. (Leavitt put each person in a separate room or booth and allowed the members to communicate only by written messages.) In this way he was able to create the networks shown in Figure 17.14. Each circle represents a person; the lines represent open channels. Subjects placed in each position could exchange messages only with the persons to whom they were connected by channels.

The most interesting result of this experiment was that the people who were organized into a "circle" were the slowest at solving the problem but the happiest at doing it. In this group everyone sent and received a large number of messages until someone solved the problem and passed the information on. In the "wheel," by contrast, everyone sent a few messages to one center person, who figured out the answer and told the rest what it was. These groups found the solution quickly, but the people on the outside of the wheel did not particularly enjoy the job.

Following the experiment, the members in each group were asked to identify the leader of their group. In the centralized groups (wheel, Y, and chain), the person in the center was usually chosen as the group leader. But in the circle network half the group members said they thought there was no real leader, and those who did say there was a leader disagreed on who that leader was. Thus a centralized organization seems more useful for task-oriented groups, whereas a decentralized network is more useful in socially oriented groups.

Leadership

All groups, whether made up of gangsters, soldiers, workers, or politicians, have leaders. A leader embodies the norms and ideals of the group and represents the group to outsiders. Within the group, a leader initiates action, gives orders, makes decisions, and settles disputes. In short, a leader is one who has a great deal of influence on the other members of the group.

Most of us think of leadership as a personality trait. To an extent this is true. Leaders tend to be better adjusted, more self-confident, more energetic and outgoing, and slightly more intelligent than other members of their group (Gibb, 1969). However, the nature of the group in part determines who will lead. Different circumstances call for different kinds of leaders. A group that is threatened by internal conflict requires a leader who is good at handling people, settling disputes, soothing tempers, and the like. A group that has a complex task to perform needs a leader with special experience to set goals and plan strategies for achieving them (Fiedler, 1969).

Within a group there may be two kinds of leaders, then. They are easy to tell apart by the things they say. One kind, the **social leader,** tends to make encouraging remarks, to break any tension with a joke, to solicit the reactions of others to whatever is going on. The other, the **task leader,** takes over when it is time to convey information, give opinions, or suggest how to do something. This leader is bossier and is not reluctant to disagree and press for a particular idea or course of action even if it creates tension in the group. A task leader usually has special knowledge or skills, and so different people may fill this role, depending on what the group is doing. The social leader is likely to be the same person, whatever the group does, because the need for promoting cohesion is always there. The social leader usually commands the loyalty of the group (Bales, 1958).

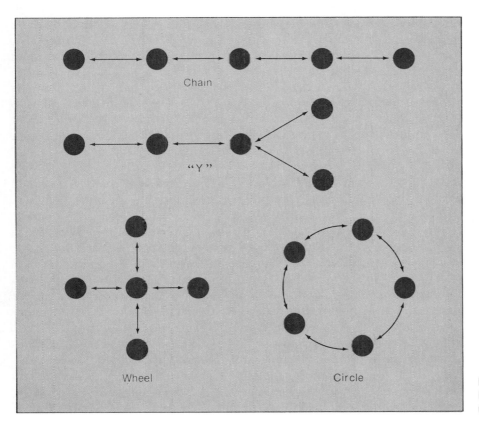

Figure 17.14
Harold Leavitt's communication network.

Figure 17.15
Lee Iacocca was fired from his job at one automobile company, yet he went on to become the Chairman of the Board of the Chrysler Corporation. Iacocca's leadership skills were put to the test at Chrysler, and he is widely credited with having steered his company away from bankruptcy to success.

There are many ways in which a person can acquire enough influence to become the leader of a group. Three of the most common are expertise, charisma, and power.

An expert directs the group's activity because he or she has the knowledge that the group needs to achieve its goals. For example, a ship's captain must know how to run a ship and how to meet an emergency at sea. Many leaders also possess a strong emotional appeal, or **charisma.** President John F. Kennedy was a striking example of a political leader with a charisma that aroused strong feelings among both followers and enemies. Influence can also come from the power to control rewards and punishments. A president of a company can give raises and promotions; he can also fire or demote people. He is a leader not because members like him, but because he owns the most shares in the company or because he has been appointed by those who own shares.

For whatever reason a member becomes a leader, the way he or she leads will affect the structure of his or her group and the roles other members play. A powerful leader may make all the important decisions for the group and assign relatively unimportant tasks to other members. A more democratic leader may try to involve as many members as possible in the decision-making process.

Diffusion of Responsibility

Sometimes, several people are faced with a common problem although they have no leader and may not even see themselves as a group. There have been many famous examples of muggings, rapes, and murders that were committed in public while a large group of people watched without intervening or calling for help.

Psychologists have tried to find out why these people didn't act by studying artificial crises. In one experiment, college students were asked to participate in a discussion of personal problems. They were asked to wait in separate rooms. Some were told that they would be communicating with only one other person; others were given the impression that they would be talking with five other people. All communication, the psychologist told each student, was to take place over microphones so that everyone would remain anonymous and thus would speak more freely. Each person was to talk in turn.

In reality, there were no other people—all the voices the subjects heard were on tape. As the discussion progressed, the subject heard one of the participants go into what sounded like an epileptic fit. The victim began to call for help, making choking sounds. The experimenters found that most of the people who thought they were alone with the victim came out of their room to help him. But of those who believed there were four other people nearby, less than half did anything to help.

The experimenters suggested that this behavior was the result of **diffusion of responsibility.** In other words, because several people were present, each subject assumed someone else would help. The researchers found that in experiments where people could see the other participants, the same pattern emerged. In addition, bystanders reassured one another that it would not be a good idea to interfere. These findings on diffusion of responsibility suggest that the larger the crowd or group of bystanders, the more likely any given individual is to feel that he or she is not responsible for whatever is going on (Darley and Latané, 1968).

Another influence that inhibits action is the tendency to minimize the *need* for any response. To act, you must admit that an emergency exists. But you may not know exactly what is going on when you hear screams or loud thumps upstairs. You are likely to wait before risking the embarrassment of rushing to help where help is not needed or wanted. It is easier to persuade yourself that nothing needs to be done if you look around and see other people behaving calmly. Not only can you see that they think nothing is wrong, but you can see that not doing anything is entirely proper. You are able to minimize the need to act and shift any responsibility to those around you.

USING PSYCHOLOGY

The Peer Group

In the early years of a child's life, parents play an important and influential role. As children grow older, however, the influence of their peers becomes increasingly strong. Peer groups are made up of people who have similar interests, frequent contact, and a mutual influence on each other. Peer interactions are different from parent-child or teacher-student interactions in that peer interactions are usually initiated for companionship and amusement, whereas parent or teacher interactions are more often based on a need for protection, care, or instruction (Damon, 1983). People generally choose their peer groups, whereas they do not choose their parents, siblings, or teachers.

Research on infants and preschool children indicates that peer interactions through play help children develop important social skills. By the time children reach school age, they spend almost as much of their time with peers as they do with their parents. By the second grade, most children have at least three or four good friends among their same-sex peers (Reisman and Shorr, 1978). During the transition from childhood to adolescence, peers become the central focus of attention. The peer group remains a major source of socialization during adolescence and young adulthood. Unlike peer groups in grade school, which are made up primarily of same-sex friends of the same age, adolescent and adult peer groups consist of members of both sexes and include a wider range of ages.

The peer group serves a number of important functions in a person's life. To begin with, peers provide companionship—people to spend time with and talk to. The way peers provide this closeness changes with development.

Sociologist Dexter Dunphy (1963) has observed the changes in the way teenagers in an urban setting spend time with each other. In early adolescence, teenagers spend most of their time with same-sex friends in cliques of three or four people. Then, these friendships expand to include additional same-sex friends. By the mid-teens, these friendships have evolved into organized crowds in which cliques engage in group-to-group interaction. The crowds soon include both sexes and include social activities such as dances and parties. By late adolescence, people begin to date within these crowds and to form more intimate relationships. By young adulthood, the peer crowd has disintegrated, to be replaced by loosely organized groups of couples.

Another important psychological feature of peer groups is peer acceptance. Peer friendships and peer group acceptance are compelling forces. The extent to which you are liked and accepted by your peers can affect the way you feel about yourself as well as the way your peers treat you. In an effort to be accepted and admired, members of peer groups conform to the standards and values of the group.

In adolescence, conformity to peer group standards generally increases with age, but the level of conformity depends on the tasks or behavior demanded. If a person is uncertain about an issue or has mixed feelings, he or she is more likely to go along with the group opinion. In matters involving a firm personal conviction, however, the older adolescent is more likely to take an individual stand, even when the opinion conflicts with peer group standards.

Peer group influence is generally strongest in matters of personal preference and taste. Peers shape a teenager's preference for music, hairstyles, clothes, recreation, and choice of friends. Peers are also much more influential than parents or teachers in shaping sexual attitudes and behavior. The use of drugs and alcohol is heavily influenced by peer group activities.

While parents, older adults, and teachers are more likely than peers to influence a person's political views and academic and career choices, the socioeconomic status of the peer group does influence an adolescent's vocational plans. For example, lower-class teenagers with middle-class friends generally aspire to higher-status careers. One reason for this influence may be that people seek out others who share their goals and values. Parents of any class who encourage their

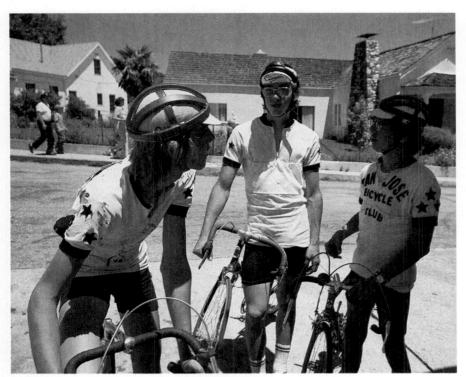

Figure 17.16
Peer groups are an important part of a teenager's life. Group members are likely to dress alike, talk alike, and share similar interests and goals.

children to do well in school and to aspire to high-status careers also influence their children's choice of friends based on these values.

Peer group affiliation can encourage adolescents to become more independent of their parents. Peers provide an opportunity for people to try out or discuss new behaviors that are not encouraged or are discouraged by parents. For example, most parents do not discuss or encourage adolescents' sexuality, but peers readily exchange ideas and information on this subject. Family ties become less intense as adolescents identify with their peer group and try out new behaviors and ideas.

The shift in interest toward the peer group helps to encourage a separateness between parent and adolescent. Sometimes, the pressure to conform to peer group standards instead of parental standards results in overt rebellion and antisocial behavior. For most people, however, independence from parents is achieved without extreme disruption. Most adolescents and young adults accept their parents' values as their own once they establish independence.

The influence of peers can sometimes produce unpleasant effects. While almost everyone wants to be accepted and liked by peers, not everyone is. Some people experience peer rejection or neglect. Usually the people who achieve high peer status (those liked by a number of peers) are friendlier, more physically attractive, more socially outgoing, cooperative, and do better in school (Dodge, 1983). As a rule, the unpopular people lack the social skills necessary for acceptance and often engage in socially undesirable actions such as aggressive and antagonistic behavior. People who are neglected or rejected by their peers may withdraw and feel very lonely and isolated. Frequently they are shy and unhappy and lack self-confidence. Some individuals go to extreme lengths to please a group in order to earn acceptance or avoid rejection. This desire to please can, in turn, lead to further disruptive behavior. Adolescents who try to adjust to a peer group whose views oppose those held by their families may also face considerable conflict and stress (Newman, 1982).

Adolescents derive more than just "fun" from participating in their peer group activities. Peer groups satisfy an emotional need—the need to belong. The members of a peer group feel a bond that distinguishes "us" from "them." It is somewhat paradoxical that this way of finding out who "we" are helps the individual find out who he or she is.

The negative aspect of peer group unity is the prejudicial nature of the "in group" and the tendency to discredit members of the "out group." The positive side of this unity is the security and strength that it gives, for example, to minorities dealing with prejudices from a majority. In this way, peer groups serve the same psychological function as support groups.

GROUP CONFLICT VERSUS COOPERATION

Conflicts between groups are a fact of everyday life: some level of hostility exists between women and men, young and old, workers and bosses, blacks and whites, Catholics and Protestants, students and teachers. Why do these conflicts exist, and why do they persist? In the next chapter, we discuss prejudice, discrimination, and related issues. But first let us consider the findings of a group of psychologists who created a boys' camp in order to study intergroup relations. The camp at Robber's Cave offered all the usual activities, and the boys had no idea that they were part of an experiment.

From the beginning of the experiment, the boys were divided into two separate groups. The boys hiked, swam, and played baseball only with members of their own group, and friendships and group spirit soon developed. After a while the experimenters (working as counselors) brought the groups together for a tournament. The psychologists had hypothesized that when these two groups of boys were placed in competitive situations, where one group could achieve its goals only at the expense of the other, hostility would develop. They were right.

Figure 17.17
Scenes from the Robber's Cave experiment. (a) The boys in competition against one another in such activities as tug-of-war. (b) The considerable hostility that developed between the two groups was expressed in drawings like this one. (c) Hostility was also expressed in fights and in raids on "enemy" cabins. (d) The hostility was eliminated by having the boys perform tasks that needed cooperation, such as pushing a truck that supplied food to the camp.

Although the games began in a spirit of good sportsmanship, tension mounted as the tournament continued. Friendly competition gave way to name calling, fistfights, and raids on enemy cabins. The psychologists had demonstrated the ease with which they could produce unity within the two boys' groups and hatred between them. The experimenters then tried to see what might end the conflict and create harmony between the two groups. They tried to bring the groups together for enjoyable activities, such as a movie and a good meal. This approach failed. The campers shoved and pushed each other, threw food and insults, and generally used the opportunity to continue their attacks.

Next, the psychologists deliberately invented a series of "emergencies" so that the boys would either have to help one another or lose the chance to do or get something they all wanted. For instance, one morning someone reported that the water line to the camp had broken. The boys were told that unless they worked together to find the break and fix it, they would all have to leave camp. By afternoon, they had jointly found and fixed the damage. Gradually, through such cooperative activities, intergroup hostility and tensions lessened. Friendships began to develop between individuals of the opposing groups, and eventually the groups began to seek out occasions to mingle. At the end of the camp period, members of both groups requested that they ride home together on the same bus.

The results of this experiment were striking. A group of boys from identical backgrounds had developed considerable hostility toward each other, simply because they were placed in competition. The crucial factor in eliminating group hostility was cooperation (Sherif *et al.*, 1961).

Social Traps

The question of conflict is not confined just to small groups. It applies to large communities too, but then the possibility of a social trap is greater. A social trap occurs when individuals in a group decide not to cooperate. Instead, they act selfishly and create a bad situation for all.

An illustration of the social trap can be seen in the way Americans have responded to the problems of pollution. We know that automobile exhaust pollutes the air. We know that one way to reduce air pollution is to carpool or use public transportation. Yet the driver who commutes 30 miles a day, alone, and who knows that he or she is polluting the air, thinks: "Yes, I know my car exhaust is bad. But I am only one person. If I stop driving, it won't make any difference." As long as we fall into that social trap, we shall continue to destroy our environment.

Psychologists have been exploring ways to overcome social traps such as this one. One approach is to use laws to bring about behavior changes, such as the law requiring special exhaust systems in cars. Another way to change people's behavior is to educate them concerning the issues and also to communicate the idea that "Yes, you do make a difference." By publicizing the problems and solutions, and organizing groups to act, individuals begin to feel that what they do does have an impact. And their actions are reinforced by the group. In this way, people find it more beneficial to cooperate than to act in a purely selfish manner.

Use the following outline as a tool for reviewing this chapter. Copy the outline onto your own paper, leaving spaces between headings to make notes about key concepts.

I. Needing Other People

   A. Anxiety and Companionship

   B. Comparing Experiences and Reducing Uncertainty

II. Choosing Friends

   A. Proximity

   B. Reward Values

III. Presenting Ourselves

   A. Parent-Child Relationships

   B. Love Relationships

   C. Nonverbal Communication

IV. How People Perceive One Another

   A. Implicit Personality Theory

   B. Personality Versus Circumstance: Attribution Theory

V. What Are Groups?

   A. Interdependence

   B. Common Goals

VI. How Groups Are Held Together

   A. Norms

   B. Ideology

   C. Commitment

VII. Interactions Within Groups

   A. Communication Patterns

   B. Leadership

   C. Diffusion of Responsibility

VIII. Group Conflict Versus Cooperation

1. In what situations do we want to be with other people?

2. Is the saying "Misery loves company" accurate?

3. What is the most important factor in determining the start of a friendship? Why is this an important factor?

4. What are the three kinds of rewards in a friendship?

5. At what stage of a relationship is physical attractiveness of a partner an important concern? Are you likely to ask a very attractive person for a date?

6. Which person is likely to make a better impression on you—one who praises you first and then criticizes you or someone who points out your faults and then discusses your good points?

7. In general, are you likely to choose as a friend a person who is similar to you or a person who complements your strengths and weaknesses?

8. How do passionate love and companionate love differ?

9. How far would you stand from someone to indicate that you would like to talk to that person?

10. What theory do you use when you form an impression of a stranger? If that judgment is based on the stranger's similarity to other people in a given category, what set of assumptions are you using?

11. If you want people to think that you are smart, should you try to do your best on the first, second, or last test in a class? What theory does this illustrate?

12. What features distinguish a group from a non-group? What are the purposes of a group?

13. What factors work to hold a group together? What factors increase the commitment of a person to the group?

14. What technique do psychologists use to study group structure? In what types of group structures will a leader be easily recognized?

15. What are the two kinds of group leaders? Which type will command the loyalty of the group? What are three ways to become a group leader?

16. What are two factors that inhibit group action?

17. If you wanted to reduce conflict between two opposing groups of students, what kinds of activities would you ask them to participate in?

CRITICAL THINKING

1. **Synthesize.** Write down the first ten or fifteen words or phrases that come to mind when you ask yourself "Who am I?" Now, categorize these items as either physical traits, psychological characteristics, or group affiliations. How much of your self-concept is built on your identification with groups?

2. **Apply.** Describe several situations in which you "put on an act" for your family or peer group. Is putting on an act more likely to occur around peers or family? Why do people behave differently around different groups?

3. **Analyze.** Have you ever been jealous of a boyfriend, girlfriend, sibling, friend, or parent? Recall a time when you were jealous of another person. What was the nature of your relationship with this person? How did you feel about yourself? What made you feel jealous? What effect did your responses to the jealousy have on your relationship with the person? Ask several of your friends (both male and female) to respond to these questions. Compare your experience of jeal-ousy with your friends' reactions. Do you notice any similarities? Are there differences between your male and female friends' jealous reactions? If you had it to do over again within the relationship, would you respond the same way?

4. **Analyze.** Friendship and love are often combined in personal relationships, yet loved ones and friends are often selected for different reasons and we often act differently toward each one. Think of people whom you consider your friends. What type of behavior do you expect from them? What do you do with them that you can't do with people you do not call friends? Be as specific as you can. Do different friends fulfill different roles in your life? Think of someone you love now or loved at one time. How would you describe this person? What are or were your expectations of him or her? In what ways do you act similarly toward your loved one and friends? Share your ideas and insights with a classmate, friend, or loved one and get reactions.

APPLYING KNOWLEDGE

1. We may think that stereotyping does not influence us. Watch a television program about (a) a detective, (b) a black family, (c) a white family, (d) an independent woman. What character traits does each have? Do we laugh at some of these characterizations when they do not fit the stereotypes? Which stereotypes do we not laugh at?

2. Examine the interactions between members of your family, your friends, or even strangers, paying as little attention as possible to verbal interaction and noting instead proximity, posture, gesture, facial expression, eye contact, relative position, and nonlinguistic verbal cues. Are you able to interpret the body language? Does this nonverbal communication conflict with what people communicate verbally? What happens if you reply verbally to nonverbal messages?

3. People tend to see other people's behavior as determined by personality traits, while they see their own behavior as a function of the situation they are in. To demonstrate this phenomenon, you will need the help of a friend. Give your friend a sheet of paper and ask him or her to list the following traits across the top of the sheet: sincere, conscientious, aggressive, friendly, independent, and mature. Then have your friend list the following names of people down the left side of the paper: the president, a public figure he or she dislikes, himself or herself, the name of a neighbor he or she hardly knows, and his or her best friend. Then ask your friend to fill in the chart by rating each person on each trait, giving a plus if the person has the trait listed across the top, a minus if the person does not have the trait, and a zero if it depends on the situation. When your friend is finished, sum up the number of pluses, minuses, and zeros for each person, including himself or herself. If your friend is like most people, you will notice that more traits, both positive and negative, were assigned to other people. Share your observations with your friend.

4. Get on an elevator and stand facing the back wall. Have a friend watch the other riders to see how they react to the violation of this simple social norm.

5. Conduct an experiment on personal space by going to the library and sitting at a table with another person. After a few minutes, begin to "invade" his or her space by placing your books and papers across the imaginary line that divides the space between the two of you. Describe his or her reactions to your encroachments.

6. List in detail the main things you look for when you choose close friends. What are your reasons for rejecting certain people as either close friends or acquaintances? Ask two of your friends to make similar lists. After they have made their lists, share your list with them. Discuss the similarities and differences.

7. In the groups to which you belong (clubs, your school, and so on) you have undoubtedly had leaders or people with influence over you. Pick a few such leaders and answer these questions about them. Are they experts? Do they have charisma? Are they socially attractive? How much power do they have? How have they obtained it?

ANALYZING VIEWPOINTS

1. Some people claim that nonverbal communication is a more accurate indicator of an individual's true thoughts and feelings than verbal communication. Others disagree, arguing that verbal communication is most accurate—people are rational beings and they generally say what they mean. Which viewpoint do you agree with? Write an essay that argues both sides of the issue. Before you begin writing, go to the library and locate additional information on nonverbal communication. Look for books or magazine articles. You should also include personal examples in your essay.

BEYOND THE CLASSROOM

1. Choose a person in your community whom you consider to be a leader. This could be a politician, a member of the clergy, the coach of a sports team, or any other individual you consider to be a leader. What qualities does this person have that makes him or her a leader? How does the person demonstrate the characteristics of leadership? Arrange an interview with the individual. Tell the person that you are doing a project for a high school psychology class. Ask him or her the following questions: What is your personal definition of leadership? What do you consider to be the qualities of a good leader? Find out if the person would be willing to come and talk to your class about leadership. If you are unable to arrange a class visit, prepare a report based on your interview and present it to the class.

CHAPTER 18

Attitudes and Social Influence

Key Terms:

attitudes
audience
authoritarian personality
boomerang effect
brainwashing
channel
cognitive dissonance
compliance
discrimination
identification
inoculation effect
internalization
message
obedience
persuasion
prejudice
scapegoat
self-fulfilling prophecy
self-justification
sleeper effect
source

Are you convinced that vitamin C is the best cure for the common cold? Did the oil companies cause the energy crisis? How do you feel about atheism, patriotism, and the Los Angeles Rams? Each of us has a wide variety of opinions, attitudes, and beliefs. Some of them are worth dying for, and others aren't worth the time it takes to explain them.

This chapter is about our attitudes, opinions, and beliefs—where they come from and how they change. It is also about the subtle and complex relationships between what we think, what we say, and what we do.

WHERE ATTITUDES COME FROM

An **attitude** is a predisposition to respond in particular ways toward specific things. It has three main elements: (1) a belief or opinion about something; (2) feelings about that thing; and (3) a tendency to act toward that thing in certain ways. For example, what is your attitude toward the senators from your state? Do you *believe* they are doing a good job? Do you *feel* you trust or distrust them? Would you *act* to vote for them?

We have very definite beliefs, feelings, and responses to things about which we have no firsthand knowledge. Where do these attitudes come from? The culture in which you grew up, the people who raised you, and those with whom you associate—your peers—all shape your attitudes.

Culture. Culture influences everything from our taste in food to our attitudes toward human relationships and our political opinions. For example,

Objectives:

After studying this chapter, you should be able to

- trace the origin of attitudes.
- describe prejudice and its relationship to oppression, discrimination, and authoritarianism.
- cite the sources of attitude change.
- explain the different types of persuasion processes.

Figure 18.1 Our attitudes, opinions, and beliefs can be strongly reinforced and supported by being with others who share them.

most (if not all) Americans would consider eating grubs, curdled milk spiced with cattle blood, or monkey meat disgusting. Yet in some parts of the world these are considered delicacies. Some Americans believe eating meat is essential for good health. Hindus consider our relish for thick, juicy steaks and hamburgers disgusting.

Almost all Americans would agree that in polygamous societies, where a man is allowed to have more than one wife, women are oppressed. But women in polygamous societies feel nothing but pity for a woman whose husband hasn't acquired other wives to help with the work and to keep her company.

Most of us would also agree that parents who interfere in their children's choice of a marriage partner are behaving outrageously and that a person should be able to marry the person he or she loves. However, in some parts of India, parents choose husbands for their daughters, and the girls are relieved not to have to make such an important choice:

> "We girls don't have to worry at all. We know we'll get married. When we are old enough our parents will find a suitable boy and everything will be arranged. We don't have to go into competition with each other.... Besides how would we be able to judge the character of a boy? ... Our parents are older and wiser, and they aren't deceived as easily as we would be. I'd far rather have my parents choose for me" (Mace and Mace, 1960: 131).

The list of culturally derived attitudes is endless. Indeed, it is only by traveling and reading about other ways of life that we discover how many of the things we take for granted are *attitudes*, not facts.

Parents.   There is abundant evidence that all of us acquire many basic attitudes from our parents. How else would you account for the finding that 80 percent of a national sample of elementary school children favored the same political party as their fathers (Hess and Torney, 1967), and 76 percent of high school seniors in a nationwide sample also preferred the same party as both their parents (Jennings and Niemi, 1968)? Parental influence wanes as children get older, of course. A sample of college students selected the same party as their father only 50 to 60 percent of the time (Goldsen *et al.*, 1960). Despite the decline, this study still suggests significant parental influence even after a person has become an adult.

Peers.   It is not surprising that parental influence declines as children get older and are exposed to many other sources of influence. In a now classic study, Newcomb (1943) questioned and requestioned students at Bennington College about their political attitudes over a period of four years. Most of the young women came from wealthy, staunchly conservative families. In contrast, most Bennington faculty members were outspoken liberals. Newcomb found that many of the students were "converted" to the liberal point of view. In 1936, 54 percent of the juniors and seniors supported Franklin D. Roosevelt and the New Deal—although praising Roosevelt to their families would have produced about the same reactions as praising

Karl Marx to Ronald Reagan. Indeed, nearly 30 percent of the students favored Socialist or Communist candidates. Newcomb contacted the subjects of his study twenty-five years after they had graduated, and found that most had maintained the attitudes they had acquired in college. One reason was that they had chosen friends, husbands, and careers that supported liberal values (Newcomb *et al.*, 1967). People tend to adopt the likes and dislikes of groups whose approval and acceptance they seek.

Figure 18.2
Scenes from Bennington College at the time Newcomb was there; Newcomb himself is shown on the left. The marked change in reference groups experienced by Bennington students is shown in a remark by one subject: "Family against faculty has been my struggle here."

ATTITUDE FORMATION

Having suggested where attitudes come from, we can now look at how they develop. The three main processes involved in forming or changing attitudes are compliance, identification, and internalization (Kelman, 1961).

If you praise a certain film director because everyone else does, you are complying. If you find yourself agreeing with everything a friend you particularly admire says about the director, you are identifying with the friend's attitudes. If you genuinely like the director's work and, regardless of what other people think, regard it as brilliant, you are expressing an internalized attitude.

Compliance

One of the best measures of attitude is behavior. If a man settles back into "his chair" after dinner, launches into a discussion of his support of the women's movement, then shouts to his wife—who is in the kitchen washing the dishes—to bring more coffee, you probably wouldn't believe what he had been saying. His actions speak louder than his words. Yet the same man might hire women for jobs he has always considered "men's work" because the law requires him to do so. And he might finally accept his wife's going to work because he knows that she, their children, and many of their friends would consider him old-fashioned if he didn't.

People often **comply** with the wishes of others in order to avoid discomfort or rejection and to gain support. As one Bennington student who professed to be a liberal explained,

> "It's very simple, I was so anxious to be accepted that I accepted the liberal complexion of the community here. I just couldn't stand out against the crowd . . ." (Newcomb, 1943: 132).

But under such circumstances, attitudes do not really change. Social pressure often results in only temporary compliance. Later in this chapter, however, we shall see that compliance can sometimes affect one's beliefs. We shall also discuss in detail how group pressure can lead to conformity.

Identification

One way in which attitudes may really be formed or changed is through the process of **identification.** Suppose you have a favorite uncle who is everything you hope to be. He is a successful musician, has many famous friends, and seems to know a great deal about everything. In many ways you identify with him and copy his behavior. One night, during an intense conversation, your uncle announces he is an atheist. At first you are confused by this statement. You have had a religious upbringing and have always considered religious beliefs as essential. However, as you listen to your uncle, you find yourself starting to agree with him. If a person as knowledgeable and respectable as your uncle holds such beliefs, perhaps you should, too. Later you find yourself feeling that atheism is acceptable. You have adopted a new attitude because of your identification with your uncle.

Identification occurs when a person wants to define himself or herself in terms of a person or group, and therefore adopts the person's or group's attitudes and ways of behaving. Identification is different from compliance because the individual actually believes the newly adopted views. But because these attitudes are based on emotional attachment to another person or group rather than the person's own assessment of the issues, they are fragile. If the person's attachment to that person or group fades, the attitudes may also weaken. Thus, one Bennington student ultimately rejected the liberal point of view:

> "Family against faculty has been my struggle here. As soon as I felt really secure I decided not to let the college atmosphere affect me too much. Everytime I've tried to rebel against my family I've found how terribly wrong I am, and I've very naturally kept to my parents' attitudes" (Newcomb, 1943: 124).

For this student, identification with the college community was only temporary.

Internalization

Internalization is the wholehearted acceptance of an attitude: it becomes an integral part of the person. Internalization is most likely to occur when an attitude is consistent with a person's basic beliefs and values and supports his or her self-image. The person adopts a new attitude because he or she believes it to be right—not because he or she wants to be like someone else.

Internalization is the most lasting of the three sources of attitude formation or change. Your internalized attitudes will be more resistant to pressure from other people because your reasons for holding these views have nothing to do with other people: They are based on your own evaluation of the merits of the issue. A Bennington student put it this way:

> "I became liberal at first because of its prestige value; I remain so because the problems around which my liberalism centers are important. What I want now is to be effective in solving the problems" (Newcomb, 1943: 136).

As this example suggests, compliance or identification may lead to the internalization of an attitude. Often the three overlap. You may support a political candidate in part because you know your friends will approve, in part because someone you admire speaks highly of the candidate, and in part because you believe his or her ideals are consistent with your own.

PREJUDICE

Prejudice means, literally, prejudgment. It means deciding beforehand what a person will be like instead of withholding judgment until it can be based on his or her individual qualities. To hold stereotypes about a group of people is to be prejudiced about them. Prejudice is not necessarily negative—whites who are prejudiced against blacks are often equally prejudiced in favor of whites, for example.

Stereotypes and Roles

Prejudice is strengthened and maintained by the existence of stereotypes and roles. A stereotype is an oversimplified, hard-to-change way of seeing people who belong to some group or category. Black people, scientists, women, Mexicans, and the rich, for example, are often seen in certain rigid ways, rather than as individuals. A role is an oversimplified, hard-to-change way of acting. Stereotypes and roles can act together in a way that makes them difficult to break down. For example, many whites have a stereotype of blacks, believing them to be irresponsible, superstitious, and unintelligent. Whites who believe this expect blacks to act out a role that is consistent with a stereotype. Blacks are expected to be submissive, deferential, and respectful toward whites, who act out the role of the superior,

---

PSYCHOLOGY and YOU

Protest Demonstrations. At the start of the Persian Gulf war, thousands of people marched in antiwar demonstrations in American cities. Some carried signs that said "No blood for oil," or "No corpses for crude."

The antiwar demonstrators marched because they believed that the war was morally wrong or that it was not worth the loss of American lives. Others feared that they or their friends or family members would be called upon to fight. By demonstrating, the protesters both publicly declared their own stand on the war and hoped to persuade others to adopt their point of view.

The protests helped stimulate public debate about whether the war was necessary and the causes were just. The demonstrators also reflected the divisions and doubts among the American public over the war. In America's last major conflict, the Vietnam war, the American public largely supported the conflict at first. But years of antiwar demonstrations gradually changed public opinion about the war to widespread opposition to it.

Figure 18.3
These lines from James Baldwin's novel *Nobody Knows My Name* express the impossible dilemma of being black in a white world and the way it feels to try to break free of the roles and stereotypes which are part of that situation.

condescending parent. In the past, both blacks and whites accepted these roles and looked at themselves and each other according to these stereotypes. In recent years, many blacks and whites have tried to step out of these roles and drop these stereotypes, and to some extent they are succeeding.

Stereotypes are also preserved in the communications media, which have traditionally portrayed American Indians as villains, Italians as greasy gangsters, Jews as misers, and teen-agers as car-crazy rock fans. Many of these stereotypes are changing now, but new ones have replaced them. For example, doctors on television are usually heroes, housewives are charming idiots, and so on. A critical look at television programs and movies reveals a lot about what is widely believed in American society.

Oppression

Group conflict often involves the oppression of one group by another. It is not hard to see how such domination gives rise to feelings of hostility on the part of the oppressed group. In addition, the powerful group stereotypes the oppressed group because it wants to justify its unfair actions and because it wants to stop the oppressed group from fighting back.

This is called a master-slave relationship, for obvious reasons. The present relationship between blacks and whites in America is a result of the fact that at one time blacks were literally the slaves and whites were literally the masters. The oppression of blacks by whites has lessened only gradually. Psychologists are learning that the master-slave relationship exists between other groups, too. For example, the freedom of women has been restricted by men.

The Authoritarian Personality

The most extreme forms of racial oppression were practiced by European Fascists in the 1930s and 1940s. One group of researchers (Adorno *et al.*, 1969) tried to analyze this phenomenon by studying the kinds of people who are attracted to the ideas of racial superiority. They found that highly prejudiced people share a number of traits which they called the **authoritarian personality.** These people tend to have inflexible ideas about themselves and others. Highly conventional, they view differences with suspicion and hostility, and like the sense of security that comes from a very structured authority. They tend to glorify their own qualities and upbringing, despite the fact that their fathers were inclined to be punitive and exacted obedience and unquestioning loyalty through harsh discipline.

The researchers who originally uncovered the relationships among prejudice, personality traits, and upbringing believed that punitive parents create insecure and hostile children. As adults, these people fear their own aggressiveness and cannot admit their own fears and shortcomings. It is easier to claim that others are inferior than to recognize one's own shortcomings. The authoritarian person falls back on the use of stereotypes about others to keep from facing his or her own inadequacies.

This is not the only interpretation of highly prejudiced people, however. The link may be simpler: authoritarian parents teach their views to their children. Or perhaps prejudice and authoritarianism may actually be characteristics of lower social standing rather than quirks of personality.

Prejudice and Discrimination

We can see, then, that there are many possible causes for prejudice. Psychologists have found that people tend to be prejudiced against those less well-off than themselves—they seem to justify being on top by assuming that anyone of lower status or income must be inferior. People who have suffered economic setbacks also tend to be prejudiced—they blame others for their misfortune.

Prejudice also arises from "guilt by association." People who dislike cities and urban living, for example, tend to distrust people associated with cities, such as Jews and blacks. Also, people tend to be prejudiced *toward* those they see as similar to themselves and *against* those who seem different.

Whatever the original cause, prejudice seems to persist. One reason is that children who grow up in an atmosphere of prejudice conform to the prejudicial norm—at first because their parents do and later with the personal conviction that it is the right way to be. Children are socialized into the prejudicial culture of their parents; that is, they encounter numerous forces that induce them to conform to the thoughts and practices of their parents and other teachers, formal and informal.

Prejudice, which is an attitude, should be distinguished from **discrimi-**

Figure 18.4
After the assassination of Martin Luther King in 1968, a third-grade teacher gave her students a lesson in discrimination. On the basis of eye color the teacher divided the class into two groups and favored one group (the blue-eyed children the first day) with privileges. The next day she reversed the situation, favoring the brown-eyed children. On the day they were favored, the blue-eyed children reportedly "took savage delight" in keeping "inferiors" in their place and said they felt "good inside," "smarter," and "stronger." On that day, one child drew the picture shown on the right. The next day, the same child, now one of the "inferiors," drew the picture on the left. The children who had felt "smart" and "strong" on their favored day became tense, lacked confidence, and did badly at their work on the day they were discriminated against. They said they felt "like dying" and "like quitting school."

nation, the unequal treatment of members of certain groups. It is possible for a prejudiced person not to discriminate. He or she may recognize his or her prejudice and try not to act on it. Similarly, a person may discriminate, not out of prejudice, but in compliance with social pressures. Personal discrimination may take the form of refusing to rent to black people or allowing only men to frequent a particular club or paying Mexican-Americans substandard wages.

Scapegoating

One of the most popular theories to explain prejudice is the scapegoat theory (Allport, 1954; Hovland and Sears, 1940). According to this view, prejudice and the associated discrimination are the result of displaced aggression. When people are prevented from achieving their goals, they often react by being aggressive. When there is no obvious target for their aggression, they displace their frustration onto other people who are not responsible for the problem but who cannot strike back or cause them social disapproval. The target of displaced aggression is called a **scapegoat.**

Blacks in this country have been the scapegoats for the economic frustrations of lower-income white Americans who felt exploited and powerless themselves. The anger they felt could not be expressed on an appropriate target (say, the government), so instead they directed their hostility toward those whom they viewed as less powerful than themselves, the blacks. Between 1882 and 1930, the number of lynchings per year in southern states varied according to the price of cotton. When prices were low, indicating economic hard times, the number of lynchings increased (Hovland and Sears, 1940).

465

Integration

Centuries of racial prejudice in the United States and throughout the world seem to indicate that racial hatred poses an extremely complicated problem. One barrier to cooperation between the races is segregation. In one research project, a group of psychologists reasoned that if people of different races had the opportunity to meet as equals, they might come to recognize that their prejudices had no basis. Therefore, they interviewed people who had been placed in integrated and segregated buildings of a housing project just after World War II. The results of the interviews showed clearly that the amount and type of contact between black and white neighbors greatly influenced their opinions toward each other.

In the integrated buildings more than 60 percent of the white house-wives reported having "friendly relations" with blacks. In the segregated buildings less than 10 percent reported friendships, and more than 80 percent reported no contact at all. In the integrated buildings, two out of three white women expressed a desire to be friendly with blacks. In the segregated buildings only one in eleven expressed such a desire. Similar effects occurred in the attitudes of black women toward whites.

The integrated housing situation gave the housewives a chance to have contact with one another and to interact informally and casually. The housewives were likely to encounter each other in the elevators, hallways, and laundry room. In this informal climate they did not have to worry that trying to strike up a conversation might be misinterpreted. In con-trast, contact in the segregated buildings would have to be more deliberate and might be considered suspicious (Deutsch and Collins, 1951).

Contact does not always reduce prejudice, however. Studies of schools that were integrated after the 1954 Supreme Court decision show mixed results. While some students became less prejudiced after a semester in an integrated school, others became *more* prejudiced than they had been before integration (Campbell, 1958). One exception was a community that voluntarily integrated its schools before the 1954 ruling. Children in that community were significantly less prejudiced than children in a similar community with all-white schools (Singer, 1964).

Why does contact reduce intergroup hostility in some instances but not in others? Several factors seem to be involved. First, the need to cooperate forces people to abandon negative stereotypes. Second, contact between people who occupy the same status is more likely to break down barriers than contact between people who do not perceive themselves as equals. Frequent contact with a white landlord is not likely to change a black person's stereotype of whites; nor is the relationship between a white executive and a black chauffeur likely to change the white person's ster-eotype of blacks. The housewives in the integrated buildings were social equals: they had about the same incomes, lived under similar conditions, faced the same problems, and so on.

Finally, when social norms support intergroup cooperation, people are likely to turn contacts into friendships. Presumably parents and teachers in the community that voluntarily desegregated its schools wanted to break down racial barriers. In accepting integration, the children were conforming to group norms. So were the young people whose communities integrated their schools only after they were required to do so by law. Those whose families and friends approved of integration were open to interracial friendships; those whose families and friends opposed desegregation kept their distance.

COGNITIVE CONSISTENCY AND CHANGING ATTITUDES

Many social psychologists have theorized that people's attitudes change because they are always trying to get things to fit together logically inside their heads. Holding two opposing attitudes can create great conflict in an individual, throwing him or her off balance. A socialist who inherits ten million dollars, a doctor who smokes, and a parent who is uncomfortable with children all have one thing in common: they are in conflict.

According to Leon Festinger (1957) people in such situations experience cognitive dissonance (Figure 18.5). **Cognitive dissonance** is the uncomfortable feeling that arises when a person experiences contradictory or conflicting thoughts, beliefs, attitudes, or feelings. To reduce dissonance, it is necessary to change one or both of the conflicting attitudes. Our newly rich socialist, for example, believes that wealth should be shared, but he or she may also be opposed to paying thousands in taxes to the government or contributing to traditional charities. (There might also be a strong temptation to buy fine clothes and a vacation home.) One solution is for the person to give all the money to CARE and forget any reservations regarding capitalist charities. Alternatively, the person could decide that a mere ten million dollars can't do much to stamp out poverty anyway, so he or she might as well hire an expensive tax lawyer and enjoy it.

Some people attempt to evade dissonance by avoiding situations or exposure to information that would create conflict. For example, they may make a point of subscribing to newspapers and magazines that uphold their political attitudes, of surrounding themselves with people who share the same ideas, and of attending only those speeches and lectures that support their views. It is not surprising that such people get quite upset when a piece of conflicting information finally does get through.

The process of dissonance reduction does not always take place consciously, but it is a frequent and powerful occurrence. In fact, remarkably long-lasting changes in attitudes were produced in an experiment in which students were made aware that their emphasis on freedom was inconsistent with their indifference to equality and civil rights. In the initial forty-minute session, students ranked a number of values by importance to themselves—including the key variables "freedom" and "equality." They were also asked to express their attitudes toward civil rights. The students then compared their answers with a table of typical answers, which was interpreted for them by the researchers. The researchers said that the typical tendency to rank freedom high and equality low not only showed

Figure 18.5
An example of cognitive dissonance. Mary has a positive attitude toward Bill and a negative attitude toward certain clothing styles. She can maintain both attitudes until a situation arises in which they are brought into conflict. Then she is faced with a state of dissonance that can be reduced only by a change in attitude. Mary may decide she really does not care so much for Bill; she may decide she really likes the clothes; or she may decide that Bill's "poor taste" is a minor fault.

that students in general are "much more interested in their own freedom than in other people's" but also that such rankings are consistent with a lack of concern for civil rights. Finally, students were asked whether their results left them satisfied or dissatisfied. The control group, who did not receive the researchers' explanation, simply filled out their rankings and went home, oblivious to any inconsistencies in attitude they might have expressed.

Three to five months after the initial test, the researchers sent out a solicitation for donations or memberships on NAACP stationery, to test whether students tested would act on the values they expressed. They received many more replies from students in the experimental group than in the control group. They concluded that the test had somehow made the first group of students more receptive to civil-rights issues. On tests fifteen to seventeen months later, changes in attitude were much more likely in subjects who had been dissatisfied with what they had been told about the results of their original test than in subjects who had not been dissatisfied.

This suggests that cognitive dissonance spurred changes in attitudes toward civil rights.

This is a powerful and lasting impact from a simple forty-minute session and a few follow-up tests. One of the researchers was disturbed by the implications, for "If such socially important values as equality and freedom can be altered to become more important to human subjects, they can surely be altered to also become less important. Who shall decide . . ." (Rokeach, 1971: 458).

ATTITUDES AND ACTIONS

Social psychologists have discovered several interesting relationships between attitudes and actions. Obviously, your attitudes affect your actions: if you like Fords, you will buy a Ford. Some of the other relationships are not so obvious.

Doing Is Believing

If you speak and act as if something is true, you yourself may come to believe it.

It turns out, for example, that if you like Fords but buy a Chevrolet for some reason (perhaps you can get a better deal on a Chevy), you will end up liking Fords less. In other words, actions affect attitudes.

In many instances, if you act and speak as though you have certain beliefs and feelings, you may begin to *really* feel and believe this way. For example, people accused of a crime have, under pressure of police interrogation, confessed to crimes they did not commit. They have confessed in order to relieve the pressure; but having said that they did the deed, they begin to believe that they really *are* guilty.

One explanation for this phenomenon comes from the theory of cognitive dissonance. If a person acts one way but thinks another, he or she will experience dissonance. To reduce the dissonance, the person will have to change either the behavior or the attitude. A similar explanation is that people have a need for **self-justification**—a need to justify their behavior.

In an experiment that demonstrated these principles, subjects were paid either one dollar or twenty dollars to tell another person that a boring experiment in which they both had to participate was really a lot of fun. Afterward, the experimenters asked the subjects how they felt about the experiment. They found that the subjects who had been paid twenty dollars to lie about the experiment continued to believe that it had been boring. Those who had been paid one dollar, however, came to believe that the experiment had actually been fairly enjoyable. These people had less reason to tell the lie, so they experienced more dissonance when they did so. To justify their lie, they had to believe that they had actually enjoyed the experiment (Festinger and Carlsmith, 1959).

The phenomenon of self-justification has serious implications. For example, how would you justify to yourself the fact that you had intentionally injured another human being? In another psychological experiment, subjects were led to believe that they had injured or hurt other subjects in some way (Glass, 1964). The aggressors were then asked how they felt about the victims they had just harmed. It was found that the aggressors had convinced themselves that they did not like the victim of their cruelty. In other words, the aggressors talked themselves into believing that their defenseless victims had deserved their injury. The aggressors also considered their victims to be less attractive after the experiment than before— their self-justification for hurting another person was something like, "Oh well, this person doesn't amount to much, anyway."

Self-Fulfilling Prophecy

Another relationship between attitudes and actions is rather subtle—but extremely widespread. It is possible, it seems, for a person to act in such a way as to make his or her attitudes come true. This phenomenon is called **self-fulfilling prophecy.** Suppose, for example, you are convinced that you are a bad cook. Every time you go into the kitchen, you start thinking poorly of yourself. Because you approach the task of baking a cake with great anxiety, you fumble the measurements, pour in too much milk, leave out an ingredient, and so on. As a result, your cake is a flop. You thus confirm that you *are* a bad cook.

Self-fulfilling prophecies can influence all kinds of human activity. Suppose you believe that people are basically friendly and generous. Whenever you approach other people, you are friendly and open. Because of your smile and positive attitude toward yourself and the world, people like you. Thus your attitude that people are friendly produces your friendly behavior, which in turn causes people to respond favorably toward you. But suppose you turn this example around. Imagine that you believe people are selfish and cold. Because of your negative attitude, you tend to avert your eyes from other people, to act gloomy, and to appear rather unfriendly. People think your actions are strange and, consequently, they act coldly toward you. Your attitude has produced the kind of behavior that makes the attitude come true.

Practical Implications

The psychological findings related to self-justification and self-fulfilling prophecy show that there is truth in the saying "Life is what you make it." What you do affects you directly, and it affects the way the world acts toward you. The fact that all people tend to justify their actions by changing their attitudes has several practical consequences. If you give in to pressure and act against your better judgment, you will be undermining your own beliefs. The next time you are in a similar situation, you will find it even harder to stand up for what you believe in because you will have begun to wonder whether you believe it yourself. If you want to strengthen your convictions about something, it is a good idea to speak and act on your beliefs at every opportunity. If you do make a mistake and act against your beliefs, you should admit that you are wrong and not try to justify yourself.

The phenomenon of self-fulfilling prophecy shows that the way the

MORE about . . .

Behavioral Confirmation. The text describes how beliefs can change actions through processes such as self-justification and the self-fulfilling prophecy. Our expectations can also affect other people's actions. This process is called *behavioral confirmation.*

For example, suppose you are led to believe that another person is friendly and outgoing. To find out more about that person, you would most likely ask that person questions an outgoing person would answer. "What kinds of things do you do with your friends?" "What do you do to have fun?"

Most likely you would get answers that describe the person's outgoing activities. Even a shy person who has only a few friends will think of some outgoing things, though probably not as many as an extroverted person would.

Furthermore, by discussing these activities, the person will actually start to *feel* and *act* more outgoing than he or she usually does. In this way the person's behavior will start to confirm your initial impression, even if that impression was not particularly accurate.

world seems to you may be a result of your own actions. Other people, who act differently, will have different experiences and produce different effects. When you find the world unsatisfactory, remember that to some extent, you are creating it. When you find the world a joyful place, remember, too, that it is making you happy partly because you believe that it can.

PERSUASION

Persuasion is a direct attempt to influence attitudes through the medium of communication. At one time or another everyone engages in persuasion. When a smiling student who is working her way through college by selling magazine subscriptions comes to the door, she attempts to persuade you that reading *Newsweek* or *Sports Illustrated* or *Ms.* will make you better informed and give you lots to talk about at parties. Parents often attempt to persuade a son or daughter to conform to their values about life. Similarly, some young people try to persuade their parents that all their friends' parents are buying them home computers. In each case, the persuader's main hope is that by changing the other person's attitudes he or she can change that person's behavior as well.

The Communication Process

Enormous amounts of time, money, and effort go into campaigns to persuade people to change their attitudes and behavior. Some succeed on a grand scale; others seem to have no effect. One of the most difficult questions social psychologists have tried to answer is: What makes a persuasive communication effective?

Figure 18.6
Successful advertising. This advertisement presents a powerfully emotional picture and headline to shock readers into attention and arouse their concern. It then gives some hard facts to further involve them in the subject matter.
Readers might have ignored the ad if it had simply said, "Doctors need to know about current issues relevant to the medical profession. Subscribe to *Medical World News.*"

Sex in Advertising

Pick up any newspaper or magazine and you'll see dozens of scantily-clad beauties and rugged, sensual he-men trying to sell products in the best way they know how. As they drape themselves over automobiles and puff provocatively on their cigarettes, they tell consumers that sex and their product are a package deal.

This may sound like a message few of us could resist, but according to recent findings, our will power is stronger than advertisers think. Research has shown that sexy ads get readers' attention, but the wrong audience actually reads the message. More women than men read the ads in which a sexy woman appears, and more men than women read ads showing attractive men.

Researchers have also found that sex does not increase product recall, and may in fact get in the way of remembering a brand name. In one study, subjects were shown some ads containing sexy pictures and some without. One week after seeing the ads, subjects could remember more about the "nonsexy" products than they could about the "sexy" ones.

Results like these are sure to change at least some advertisers' approaches. But it will take a lot more than this to convince others that sex is not the advertiser's best friend.

For more details, see Duane P. Schultz, *Psychology in Use.* New York: Macmillan, 1979.

The communication process can be broken down into four parts. The **message** itself is only one part. It is also important to consider the **source** of the message, the **channel** through which it is delivered, and the **audience** that receives it.

The Source. How a person sees the source, or originator, of a message may be a critical factor in his or her acceptance or rejection of it. The person receiving the message asks himself or herself two basic questions: Is the person giving the message trustworthy and sincere? Does he or she know anything about the subject? If the source seems reliable and knowledgeable, the message is likely to be accepted.

Suppose, for example, that you have written a paper criticizing a poem for your English class. A friend who reads the paper tells you about an article that praises the poem and asks you to reconsider your view. The article was written by Agnes Stearn, a student at a state teachers college. You might change your opinion—and you might not. But suppose your friend tells you the same positive critique was written by T. S. Eliot. The chances are that you would begin to doubt your own judgment. Three psychologists tried this experiment. Not surprisingly, many more students changed their minds about the poem when they thought the criticism was written by T. S. Eliot (Aronson, Turner, and Carlsmith, 1963).

A person receiving the message also asks: Do I like the source? If the communicator is respected and admired, people will tend to go along with

Figure 18.7
Winston Churchill, in a speech to the British House of Commons in 1940. Churchill's long record as a soldier (in India, South Africa, and in World War I) and as a political leader made him a source whose knowledge and trustworthiness were beyond question by the time he was needed to lead the fight against Hitler.

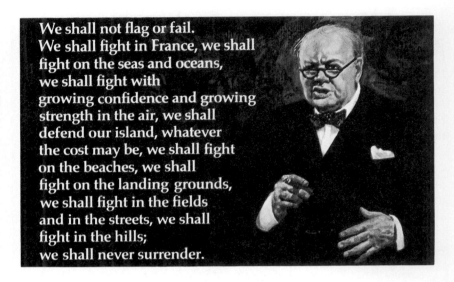

We shall not flag or fail.
We shall fight in France, we shall fight on the seas and oceans, we shall fight with growing confidence and growing strength in the air, we shall defend our island, whatever the cost may be, we shall fight on the beaches, we shall fight on the landing grounds, we shall fight in the fields and in the streets, we shall fight in the hills; we shall never surrender.

the message, either because they believe in his or her judgment or because they want to be like him or her. The identification phenomenon explains the frequent use of athletes in advertisements. Football players and Olympic champions are not (in most cases) experts on deodorants, electric razors, or milk. Indeed, when an athlete endorses a particular brand of deodorant on television, we all know he or she is doing it for the money. Nevertheless, the process of identification makes these sales pitches highly effective.

Similarly, people are much more likely to respond favorably to a physically attractive source than to one who does not make a good appearance. In the 1960 presidential campaign Richard Nixon apparently lost many votes as a result of his poor appearance on a televised debate with John F. Kennedy. During the 1968 campaign Nixon was coached on how to present a likable image to the camera. His campaign managers filmed him in informal settings, hired people to applaud and crowd around him, encouraged him to joke and smile more often, and even used make-up to erase the shadows that gave many people the impression that he had "shifty eyes" (McGinniss, 1970). Nixon, of course, won that campaign.

However, attempts to be friendly and personal can backfire. When a group of college students who opposed the war in Southeast Asia visited homes in the surrounding community in the hope of persuading townspeople to support their cause, they succeeded in further alienating residents. Why? Apparently the townspeople perceived the students as radicals and resented the invasion of their privacy (Nesbitt, 1972). When people dislike the individual or group delivering a message, they are likely to respond by taking the opposite point of view. This is known as the **boomerang effect.**

As the students' failure to persuade townspeople of the wrongfulness of the war suggests, people are more apt to agree with those who are *similar* to them (or who resemble what they would like to be) than with those who are not.

The Message.   Suppose two people with opposing viewpoints are trying to persuade you to agree with them. Suppose further that you like and trust both of them. In this situation the message becomes more important than the source. The persuasiveness of a message depends on the way in which it is composed and organized as well as on the actual content.

Should the message arouse emotion? Are people more likely to change their attitudes if they are afraid or angry or pleased? The answer is yes, but the most effective messages combine emotional appeal with factual information and argument. A communication that overemphasizes the emotional side of an issue may boomerang. If the message is too upsetting, it may force people to mobilize their defenses. For example, showing pictures of accident victims to people who have been arrested for drunken driving may convince them not to drive when they've been drinking. But if the film is so bloody that people are frightened or disgusted, they may also stop listening to the message. On the other hand, a communication that includes only logic and information may miss its mark because the audience does not relate the facts to their personal lives.

When presenting an argument, is it more effective to present both sides of an issue or only one side? For the most part, a two-sided communication is more effective because the audience tends to believe that the speaker is objective and fair-minded. A slight hazard of presenting opposing arguments is that they might undercut the message or suggest that the whole issue is too controversial to make a decision about.

People usually respond positively to a message that is structured and delivered in a dynamic way. But a communication that is forceful to the point of being pushy may produce negative results. People generally resent being pressured. If listeners infer from a message that they are being left with no choice but to agree with the speaker's viewpoint, they may reject an opinion for this reason alone.

The Channel.   Where, when, and how a message is presented also influences the audience's response. In general, personal contact is the most effective approach to an audience. For example, in one study in Ann Arbor, Michigan, 75 percent of voters who had been contacted personally voted in favor of a change in the city charter. Only 45 percent of those who had received the message in the mail and 19 percent of those who had only seen ads in the media voted for the change (Eldersveld and Dodge, 1954).

However, as we saw earlier, personal contact may boomerang: people may dislike the communicator or feel that they are being pressured. Besides, you can reach a great many more people through mailings and radio and television broadcasts than you can in person.

There is some evidence that television and films are more effective media of persuasion than printed matter. People tend to believe what they see and hear with their own senses (even if they know the information has been edited before it is broadcast). In one experiment, 51 percent of people who had watched a film could answer factual questions about the issue in question—compared to 29 percent of those who had only seen printed material. And more of the people who had viewed the film altered their viewpoints than did people who had read about the issue (Hovland,

PSYCHOLOGY and YOU

The Anchoring Effect. Most research on persuasion focuses on large efforts such as political and advertising campaigns. How can you, as an individual, persuade others?

One technique is *anchoring.* When people make judgments under conditions of uncertainty, they are often swayed by suggestions of what is appropriate. One study asked two groups of subjects how many African countries were in the United Nations. One group was asked, "Is it more or less than 65?" The other group was asked, "Is it more or less than 15?" On the average, the first group estimated about 40, the second group about 25. The suggested number serves as an anchor, or starting point, for people's estimates.

Examples of anchors are common. When street performers begin their acts, they often line their hats with dollar bills. People selling cars and houses start with a high price.

We've got over 300 good, steady jobs.

Jobs in construction, transportation, communications, computers.

Jobs for photographers, printers, truck drivers, teachers, typists, TV cameramen and repairmen. Cooks, electricians, medical aides, meteorologists. Motor and missile maintenance men.

Jobs for young men. And young women.

Jobs in Europe, Hawaii, Panama, Alaska. And just about any place in the States.

We'll train you to do the jobs. Train you well, in good schools, under excellent instructors, with the best equipment obtainable.

And you get full pay while you train.

You also get unusually good fringe benefits, including a chance to continue your education. In many cases at our expense. In all cases with at least 75% of your tuition paid.

And if you qualify we'll give you your choice of training. We'll put it in writing, before you sign up.

Today's Army wants to join you.

Figure 18.8
Audiences change from generation to generation, so the means of persuading them must also change. Attitudes toward the armed services, for example, have changed markedly since World War I, thus requiring army recruiters to alter their approach.

Lumsdaine, and Sheffield, 1949). But the most effective channel also depends in part on the audience.

The Audience. The audience includes all those people whose attitudes the communicator is trying to change. Being able to persuade people to alter their views depends on knowing who the audience is and why they hold the attitudes they do (Figure 18.8).

Suppose, for example, you are involved in a program to reduce the birth rate in a population that is outgrowing its food supply. The first step would be to inform people of various methods of birth control as well as how and where to obtain them. However, the fact that people know how to limit their families does not mean that they will do so. To persuade them to use available contraceptives, you need to know why they value large families. In some areas of the world, people have as many children as they can because they do not expect most babies to survive early childhood. In this case you might want to tie the family-planning campaign to programs of infant care. In some areas, children begin working at odd jobs at an early age and bring in needed income. In this case, you might want to promote an incentive system for families who limit themselves to two or three children.

If the people are not taking advantage of available means of birth control, you will want to know who is resisting. Perhaps men believe fathering a child is a sign of virility. Perhaps women consider motherhood an essential element of femininity. Perhaps both sexes see parenthood as a symbol of maturity and adulthood (see Coale, 1973). Knowing who your audience is and what motivates them is crucial.

One way to maximize the chances of persuasion is to capitalize on the audience's emotional needs. For example, one advertising researcher was able to help the Red Cross collect blood donations from men by analyzing their fears. He thought that men associated loss of blood with weakness and loss of manliness. He suggested that the Red Cross publish ads telling prospective donors how manly they were and offer donors pins shaped like drops of blood as medals for bravery. The campaign worked: blood donations from men increased sharply (Dichter, 1964).

The Sleeper Effect

Changes in attitudes are not always permanent. In fact, efforts at persuasion usually have their greatest impact immediately and then fade away. However, sometimes people seem to be persuaded by a message after a period of time has elapsed. This curious **sleeper effect** has been explained in several ways.

One explanation of the delayed-action impact depends on the tendency to retain the message but forget the source. As time goes by, a positive source no longer holds power to persuade nor does a negative source undercut the message. When the source is negative and the memory of the source fades, the message then "speaks for itself" and more people may accept it (Kelman and Hovland, 1953).

Perhaps the original message also sensitizes people to subsequent information and events that reinforce the ideas. Repetition is a valuable tool, and the sleeper effect may simply be the result of hearing or reading similar messages from a number of different sources (Middlebrook, 1974).

It may also be that it simply takes time for people to change their minds. As the message "sinks in," attitudes change more. A dramatic example of this was the experiment mentioned earlier in which students who were made aware of inconsistencies in their values concerning civil rights changed their ideas more after fifteen to seventeen months than after three weeks.

The Inoculation Effect

What can you do to resist persuasion? Research has shown that people can be educated to resist attitude change. This technique can be compared to an inoculation (McGuire, 1970). Inoculation against persuasion works in much the same way as inoculation against certain diseases. When a person is vaccinated he is given a weakened or dead form of the disease-causing agent, which stimulates his body to manufacture defenses. Then, if that person is attacked by a more potent form of the agent, his defenses make him or her immune to infection. Similarly, a person who has resisted a mild attack on her beliefs is ready to defend herself against an onslaught that might otherwise have overwhelmed her.

The **inoculation effect** can be explained in two ways: it motivates the person to defend her beliefs more strongly, and it gives her some practice in defending those beliefs. The most vulnerable attitudes you have, therefore, are the ones that you have never had to defend. For example, you

? FACT OR FICTION

People expect other people to think like they do.

Fact. Common sense tells you that people are unique and hold different values and attitudes. Yet we often expect other people to think and act like we do and are surprised when they do not. This process is called the *false consensus effect.*

The most vulnerable attitudes are those you have never had to defend.

might find yourself hard put to defend your faith in democracy or in the healthfulness of beefsteak if you have never had these beliefs questioned.

USING PSYCHOLOGY

Promoting Energy Conservation

Americans use—and waste—more energy than any other people on earth. The fuel crisis, ad campaigns on the need to conserve energy, and the steadily rising cost of gasoline, oil, and electricity have hardly made a dent in our rate of energy use. How can Americans be persuaded to conserve energy?

Three psychologists attempted to answer this question with an extremely simple experiment (Kohlenberg, Phillips, and Proctor, 1976). The demand for electricity tends to peak in the morning and again in the late afternoon, when people take showers and use vacuum cleaners, washing machines, and other electrical appliances. Unlike other forms of energy, electricity cannot be stored. Power companies therefore have to maintain generators that are in full use for only a few hours each day. One solution to the growing demand for electricity is to build more generators. The other solution is to change people's habits, cutting back the peak demand.

Kohlenberg and his colleagues tried three techniques for convincing volunteer families to reduce their electricity use during peak periods. The first was to provide information. Researchers explained the problem, asked the families to try to cut back, and suggested how they might do so. Monitors installed in each house indicated that this approach had little or no effect. (Considering that all the families were conservation-minded, this was surprising.)

Next, the researchers tried feedback. A bulb that lit up whenever the family approached peak consumption levels was placed in each house. Immediate and direct evidence of electricity overuse was expected to help the families cut back. Although somewhat more effective than information alone, feedback did not break the families' habits of electricity use.

Finally, the researchers gave the experimental households an incentive. Families would earn twice the amount of their electricity bill if they reduced their peak use 100 percent, the full amount if they cut back 50 percent, and so on. This strategy worked. None of the families reduced their peak use 100 percent, but all did cut back. A follow-up revealed that all returned to the convenience of using appliances during peak hours after the incentive was removed.

What this simple experiment demonstrated was that campaigns to reduce the use of electricity during peak periods are largely ineffective. However, if power companies were to provide incentives—say, reduced rates for families that cut back during the peaks—they might save themselves the cost of building and maintaining partially used plants.

SOCIAL INFLUENCE

Brainwashing

The most extreme means of changing attitudes involves a combination of psychological gamesmanship and physical torture, aptly called **brainwashing.** The most extensive studies of brainwashing have been done on Westerners who had been captured by the Chinese during the Korean War and subjected to "thought reform." Psychiatrist Robert Jay Lifton interviewed several dozen prisoners released by the Chinese, and, from their accounts, he outlined the methods used to break down people's convictions and introduce new patterns of belief, feeling, and behavior (1963).

The aim in brainwashing is as much to create a new person as to change attitudes. So the first step is to strip away all identity and subject the person to intense social pressure and physical stress. Prison is a perfect setting for this process. The person is isolated from social support, is a number not a name, is clothed like everyone else, and can be surrounded by people who have had their thoughts "reformed" and are contemptuous of "reactionaries." So long as the prisoner holds out, he is treated with contempt or exhorted to confess by his fellow prisoners. He is interrogated past the point of exhaustion by his captors, and is humiliated and discomfited by being bound hand and foot at all times, even during meals or elimination. Any personal information the prisoner uses to justify himself is turned against him as evidence of his guilt.

At some point, the prisoner realizes that resistance is impossible; the pressures are simply intolerable. Resistance gives way to cooperation, but only as a means of avoiding any more demoralization. The prisoner is rewarded for cooperating. Cooperation involves confessing to crimes against the people in his former way of life.

Throughout the process his cell mates are an integral part of the brainwashing team, berating him at first, then warming to him after his confession. For most of his waking hours, the prisoner is part of a marathon group therapy session built on Marxist ideology. The prisoner is asked not only to interpret his current behavior that way but also to reinterpret his life before capture. Guilt is systematically aroused and defined by Marxist standards. What the prisoner does is to learn a new version of his life, and his confession, provided at first to get some relief from the isolation and pain, becomes more elaborate, coherent, and ideologically based. And with every "improvement" in his attitudes, prison life is made a little more pleasant. Finally, by a combination of threat, peer pressure, systematic rewards, and other psychological means, the prisoner comes to believe his

PSYCHOLOGY and YOU

Psychological Warfare. Psychological warfare refers to any activities and techniques designed to demoralize enemy troops and persuade them to give up the fight. Both sides used psychological warfare extensively in the Persian Gulf war.

As American troops waited in the Saudi Arabian desert for the war to begin, an Iraqi radio announcer nicknamed "Baghdad Betty" tried to persuade them that they would be crushed by Iraqi might. After the war started, Iraq forced captured Allied pilots to denounce the war on TV.

The Allied forces dropped leaflets on Iraqi soldiers and issued false reports of Iraqi defections in an attempt to convince Iraqi soldiers to surrender. In addition, underground radio stations broadcast war news into Iraq. Allied forces also armed resistance fighters in Iraqi-occupied Kuwait so they could wage a secret war against Iraq. No one knows how effective psychological warfare is, but military leaders consider it an essential part of modern warfare.

confession. But as one survivor recalled, "it is a special kind of belief . . . you accept it—in order to avoid trouble—because every time you don't agree, trouble starts again" (Lifton, 1963: 31). These techniques appear to succeed only as long as the person remains a prisoner.

It's hard to say just where persuasion ends and brainwashing begins. (Some researchers believe that brainwashing is just a very intense form of persuasion.) Drawing this line has become particularly important to the courts—from the much publicized case of Patty Hearst in 1977 to lawsuits over deprogramming members of religious cults.

Margaret Thaler Singer (1979) has studied over 300 former members of religious cults. Many had joined during periods of depression and confusion. The cults offered structure and gave life meaning: they provided friends and ready-made decisions about marriage and careers, dating and sex. Being cut off from the outside world and intensive indoctrination into a new ideology often increased the new member's sense of commitment.

When people become dissatisfied and quit, many have trouble readjusting to the world they left behind. Among the problems Singer has observed are depression, loneliness, indecisiveness, passivity, guilt, and

Figure 18.9
Members of the Hare Krishna cult.

blurring of mental activity. The average person takes six to eighteen months to return to normal.

Group Pressure to Conform

Most Americans claim they would never become supporters of Hitler if they had lived in Germany during World War II. Yet a nation of Germans did. Under pressure from others, individuals at least complied with the prevailing attitudes. Everyone conforms to group pressure in many ways. Have you ever come home and surprised your parents by wearing the latest fad in clothing? Possibly the conversation that followed went something like this:

"How can you go around looking like that?"

"But everyone dresses like this."

Psychologist Solomon Asch (1952) designed a famous experiment to test conformity to pressure from one's peers. He found that people may conform to other people's ideas of the truth, even when they disagree. The following is what you would have experienced if you had been a subject in this experiment.

You and seven other students meet in a classroom for an experiment on visual judgment. You are shown a card with one line on it. You are then shown another card containing three lines and are asked to pick the one that is the same length as the first line. One of the three is exactly the same length and is easy to determine. The other two lines are obviously different (Figure 18.10). The experiment begins uneventfully. The subjects announce their answers in the order in which they are seated in the room. You happen to be seventh, and one person follows you. On the first comparison, every person chooses the same matching line. The second set of cards is displayed, and once again the group is unanimous. The discriminations seem easy, and you prepare for what you expect will be a rather boring experiment.

On the third trial, there is an unexpected disturbance. You are quite certain that line 2 is the one that matches the standard. Yet the first person in the group announces confidently that line 1 is the correct match. Then, the second person follows suit and he, too, declares that the answer is line 1. So do the third, fourth, fifth, and sixth subjects. Now it is your turn. You are suddenly faced with two contradictory pieces of information: the evidence of your own senses tells you that one answer is clearly correct, but the unanimous and confident judgments of the six preceding subjects tell you that you are wrong.

The dilemma persists through eighteen trials. On twelve of the trials, the other group members unanimously give an answer that differs from what you clearly perceive to be correct. It is only at the end of the experimental session that you learn the explanation for the confusion. The seven other subjects were all actors, and they had been instructed to give incorrect answers on those twelve trials (Figure 18.11).

How do most subjects react to this situation? Asch found that almost one-third of his fifty subjects conformed at least half the time. These conformers he called the "yielders." Most yielders explained to Asch afterward

Figure 18.10
These two cards were shown to subjects in one trial of Asch's experiment on conformity. The actual discrimination is easy.

Standard Line   Comparison Lines

Figure 18.11
Photographs taken during Asch's experiment on conformity. Subject 6 is the only real subject; the others are confederates of the experimenter (seen at the right in the first photograph). The subject listens to the others express identical judgments that differ from his own. He is in a dilemma: does he express the judgment he knows to be correct and risk being different from the group, or does he conform to the group's judgment?

that they knew which line was correct but that they yielded to group pressure in order not to appear different from the others. Asch called those who did not conform "independents." They gave the correct answer despite group pressure. Why so much conformity? According to one theory, most children are taught the overriding importance of being liked and of being accepted. Conformity is the standard means of gaining this approval.

One of the most important findings of Asch's experiment was that if even one person failed to conform to the group's judgment, the subject was able to stick to his own perceptions. It seems that it is hardest to stand alone. Later researchers have shown that, under some conditions, a minority view can come to win over the larger group (Moscovici, 1976).

Obedience to Authority

The influence other people have on your attitudes and actions is considerable. Sometimes this influence is indirect and subtle; at other times it is quite direct. People may simply tell you what to believe and what to do. Under what conditions do you obey them?

Everyone in this society has had experiences with various authorities, such as parents, teachers, police officers, managers, judges, clergymen, and military officers. **Obedience** to these authorities can be either useful or destructive. For instance, obeying the orders of a doctor or firefighter in an emergency would be constructive. Psychologists are more interested, however, in the negative aspects of obedience. They know from such cases in history as German Nazism and American atrocities in Vietnam that individuals frequently obey irrational commands. In fact, people often obey authority even when obedience goes against their conscience and their whole system of morality.

The most famous investigation of obedience was conducted in 1963 by social psychologist Stanley Milgram. The experiment was set up as follows. Two subjects appeared for each session. They were told that they would be participating in an experiment to test the effects of punishment on memory. One of the subjects was to be the "teacher" and the other, the "learner." (In reality, the learner was not a volunteer subject; he was Milgram's accomplice.) The teacher was to read a list of words into a microphone for the learner, who would be in a nearby room, to memorize. If the learner failed to recite the list back correctly, the teacher was to administer an electric shock. The alleged purpose of the experiment was to test whether the shock would have any effect on learning. In actuality, however, Milgram wanted to discover how far the teacher would follow his instructions; how much shock would he be willing to give a fellow human being?

As the experiment began, the learner continually gave wrong answers, and the teacher began to administer the prescribed shocks from an impressive-looking shock generator. The generator had a dial that ranged from 15 volts, which was labeled "Slight Shock," to 450 volts, which was labeled "Danger: Severe Shock." After each of the learner's mistakes, the teacher was told to increase the voltage by one level, thus increasing the severity of the shock. The teacher believed that the learner was receiving these shocks because he had seen the learner being strapped into a chair in the other room and had watched electrodes being attached to the learner's hands. In reality, however, the accomplice was receiving no shocks at all from the equipment.

As the experiment progressed, the learner made many mistakes and the teacher had to give increasingly severe shocks. At 300 volts the learner

Figure 18.12
Stanley Milgram's experiment on obedience. (a) The fake "shock generator" used by the "teacher." (b) The "learner" is connected to the shock apparatus. (c) Milgram explains the procedure to the "teacher." (d) This subject refuses to shock the "learner" any further and angrily arises in protest. (e) Milgram explains the truth about the experiment. (© 1965 by Stanley Milgram. From the film *Obedience*. Distributed by New York University Film Library.)

pounded on the wall in protest and refused to provide any further answers. At this point the experimenter instructed the subject to treat the absence of an answer as a wrong answer and to continue the procedure. The experiment ended either when the maximum 450 volts was administered or when the teacher refused to administer any more shocks. If at any point the teacher indicated that he wanted to stop, the experimenter calmly told him to continue: "Whether the learner likes it or not," the experimenter asserted, "you must go on until he has learned all the word pairs correctly."

Before Milgram began this study, he had checked with forty psychiatrists in order to get their predictions. These experts thought that most people would not continue beyond the 150-volt level, and that only one in one thousand would actually give the highest shock. Yet in Milgram's experiments more than half of the forty subjects gave the full shock!

These subjects were not sadists. Many of them showed signs of extreme tension and discomfort during the session, and they often told the experimenter that they would like to stop. But in spite of these feelings, they continued to obey the experimenter's commands. They were ordinary men—salesman, engineers, postal workers—placed in an unusual situation.

What accounts for this surprisingly high level of obedience? Part of the answer is that the experimenter represents a legitimate authority. People assume that such an authority knows what he is doing, even when his instructions seem to run counter to their own standards of moral behavior.

Milgram's subjects could have walked out at any time—they had nothing to lose by leaving. Nevertheless, social conditioning for obeying legitimate authorities is so strongly ingrained that people often lack the words or the ways to do otherwise. Simply getting up and leaving would have violated powerful unwritten rules of acceptable social behavior.

Subsequent experiments showed that there were three ways in which subjects could be helped to resist authority in this situation. One was the removal of the physical presence of the experimenter. Even more effective was putting the subject face to face with his victim. The third and most effective variation of the experiment was to provide other "teachers" to support the subject's defiance of the experimenter (Milgram, 1964).

Another experiment that caused ordinary people to act in extraordinary ways was performed by Philip Zimbardo and his colleagues in the early 1970s. Zimbardo randomly divided male volunteers, who were mostly college students, into two groups: "prisoners" and "prison guards." He sent both groups to live in a simulated "prison" set up in the basement of a Stanford University building. He gave the "guards" instructions simply to maintain order. Within two days, most of the "guards" had become intoxicated with power; they acted cruelly toward the prisoners, often without any reason. At the same time, the "prisoners" began showing signs of extreme stress, often acting subdued and depressed. The emotional reactions were so extreme that the two-week experiment was ended after only six days. It seems that the prison environment was much stronger than individual personalities. Although the subjects in this experiment were emotionally mature and stable, the roles these individuals adopted dramatically changed the way they acted. There may be other situations in everyday life that may cause us and those around us to act in ways we do not expect.

Use the following outline as a tool for reviewing this chapter. Copy the outline onto your own paper, leaving spaces between headings to make notes about key concepts.

   I. Where Attitudes Come From

  II. Attitude Formation

     A. Compliance

     B. Identification

     C. Internalization

 III. Prejudice

     A. Stereotypes and Roles

     B. Oppression

     C. The Authoritarian Personality

     D. Prejudice and Discrimination

     E. Scapegoating

     F. Integration

 IV. Cognitive Consistency and Changing Attitudes

  V. Attitudes and Actions

     A. Doing Is Believing

     B. Self-Fulfilling Prophecy

     C. Practical Implications

 VI. Persuasion

     A. The Communication Process

     B. The Sleeper Effect

     C. The Inoculation Effect

VII. Social Influence

     A. Brainwashing

     B. Group Pressure to Conform

     C. Obedience to Authority

1. What is an attitude? What are the three elements of an attitude?

2. What are the three processes involved in changing an attitude? Which process is based on emotional attachment to another person? Which process is the most lasting and has nothing to do with other people?

3. Can prejudice be defined as a negative judgment toward another group of people? What is the name given by researchers to prejudiced persons who share a number of traits in common? According to these researchers, why do these people use stereotypes? Can a person discriminate against another person without being prejudiced?

4. What factors are important in reducing intergroup hostility through integration?

5. What is the name Leon Festinger gave to the uncomfortable feelings that arise when a person experiences conflicting thoughts, beliefs, attitudes, or feelings?

6. Which cognitive act are people engaging in when they convince themselves that they did not like the victim of their aggressive act? Actions can affect attitudes and attitudes can affect actions. What is this latter phenomenon called?

7. What are the four parts of the communication process? What two questions do people ask themselves about the source of a communication? If you listen to the argument of a person whom you dislike and then take the opposite point of view, what effect has just taken place?

8. What will be the effect on listeners if you use a very emotional appeal or if you pressure them to adopt your point of view?

9. How can the sleeper effect be explained? the inoculation effect?

10. What are the steps used to brainwash a person?

11. What percentage of people were "yielders" in Solomon Asch's conformity experiments? Why do people conform? What event will reduce conformity?

12. What are the three ways in which subjects were helped to resist the authoritative experimenter in Stanley Milgram's experiment?

CRITICAL THINKING

1. **Analyze.** One of the primary objectives of advertising is to get the viewers/listeners to remember the product. To what extent do you think familiarity with brand names influences your choices in the market? How many television commercials do you find obnoxious? Do you find that you remember the products advertised in "obnoxious" commercials better than you remember products that appear in less offensive advertisements? Do you think there is a possibility that some commercials are deliberately offensive?

2. **Evaluate.** Parents have an early influence on their children's attitudes and beliefs. Check the degree of similarity between your parents' views and your views on selected issues. First, generate a list of ten statements on issues such as political affiliation, nuclear energy, mandatory retirement, equal pay, and paternity leave. Then develop a questionnaire based on these issues in which a person can respond by agreeing or disagreeing with the statements. Use a five-point scale ranging from 1 (strongly agree) to 5 (strongly disagree). Ask your parents to complete the same questionnaire. Notice the similarity or dissimilarity between your responses and those of your parents.

3. **Apply.** A stereotype is a shorthand, overly simplified description of a group of people, which influences attitudes. People can acquire stereotypes from their social interactions with others, from watching television, or elsewhere. Examine the stereotypes that have emerged about

teenagers by asking a group of adults to describe teenagers. Have them complete the open-ended statement, "Teenagers are . . .," as many times as they can. Ask at least eight to give you responses. Then compile the statements and see whether you can pick out stereotypes of teenagers. How might adults' stereotyped views of teenagers affect the way they act toward them? How can stereotypes be changed?

APPLYING KNOWLEDGE

1. Collect magazine ads of ten different brands of detergent. Using a scale of 0 to 10, have subjects rate the detergent as being weak or strong—0 being the weakest and 10 being the strongest. Have different subjects rate the same brands on the same scale for masculinity or femininity—0 being the most feminine and 10 being the most masculine. Now average your scores. What conclusions can you draw from your results?

2. Collect samples of advertising that depict various techniques of persuasion—identification, social approval, fear of disaster, and so on. Analyze each ad on the basis of effectiveness and what type of person it might appeal to.

3. Choose some issue on which you have a strong opinion. If you were given an unlimited budget, how would you go about persuading people to agree with you? Describe the sources you would employ, the channels you would use, the content of your message, and the audience you would try to reach.

4. To what extent does advertising influence your choice of foods? Find several people who prefer butter to margarine. Ask them why they prefer butter. If they say it tastes better, then ask them to participate in an experiment to test their claims. Get several brands of both butter and margarine and spread them lightly on the same kind of crackers or toast. Blindfold your sub-

jects and provide them with a glass of water to rinse their mouths whenever they wish. Ask them to identify the samples. Run through the series about four times, varying the order of presentation. Try similar experiments with people who prefer certain brands of orange juice, cola, or coffee.

5. Make a list of ten or more nationalities, religions, races, and occupations. Have friends or family members list five things that come to mind when these groups are mentioned. What are your conclusions? How might prejudices be reduced?

6. Choose a controversial topic, such as abortion, drug abuse, war, or women's rights, and devise ten questions to measure people's attitudes toward this issue. Give the questionnaire to a number of different people and see whether your results make sense in terms of what you already know about these people.

7. Write the following list on a separate sheet of paper:
   a blind person
   a child abuser
   a thief
   an elderly person
   a recovering alcoholic
   a wrestler with one leg
   a drug addict
   a homeless man
   a homeless child
   a mentally ill person

   Place a √ by each person on the list you would consider having as a friend. Place a — by each person you would be unlikely to have as a friend. Compare your selections with those of your classmates. Argue against or support the statement: "Everyone has some prejudices." Discuss ways to change prejudices toward others.

ANALYZING VIEWPOINTS

1. Do researchers have the right to fool their subjects, even in the name of science? Consider, for example, the effects on Milgram's subjects of believing they had harmed a fellow subject by obliging the order of a stranger. Do you think this experiment was valuable for allowing the subjects to realize the extent of their conformity? Write an essay that argues both sides of the issue. Be sure to use what you have learned from the chapter.

2. Experiments have shown that enforced integration in housing has resulted in less interracial hostility. What is your opinion of legally enforcing racial integration in housing, employment, and schools? Write a paper that lists the pros and cons of legally enforced racial integration. Before you begin writing, gather additional information on the topic from articles in magazines and newspapers.

3. Research psychologists seek to understand and control human behavior; their overall goal is to promote healthy psychological development of individuals. Through their efforts, however, they have identified a variety of tools that are effective in socially controlling people through persuasion. Write a paper that debates both sides of this question: Is it ethically acceptable for people to use techniques of psychological control to sell merchandise? Look for additional information on the topic in books, magazines, and newspapers.

BEYOND THE CLASSROOM

1. Write down your attitudes about people who receive welfare or unemployment benefits. Put this piece of paper aside. Contact your local department of human/social services and set up an interview. Tell them you are doing a project for a high school psychology class. Ask them to describe the backgrounds and family situations of people who receive social services. Now look at what you wrote earlier. Have any of your attitudes changed? Why or why not?

UNIT 7

Psychological Research

486

CHAPTER 19

How Psychologists Do Research

Key Terms:

case study
control group
correlation
cross-cultural studies
dependent variable
double-blind technique
experimental group
experimental treatment
hypothesis
independent variable
longitudinal studies
naturalistic observation
negative correlation
population
positive correlation
random sample
replication
sample
self-fulfilling prophecy
stratified sample
survey
variable

In this chapter we go behind the scenes to see how psychologists learn about what they don't already know. We poke into laboratories where they are conducting experiments, follow them on surveys, and expose some of the research problems psychologists have.

The surprise is that psychologists do what most people do in everyday life—only more carefully and more systematically. When you turn on the television and the picture is out of focus, you *experiment* with different knobs and dials until you find the one that works. When you ask a number of friends about a movie you are thinking of seeing, you are conducting an informal *survey*. Of course, there is more to doing scientific research than turning dials at random or asking friends what they think. Over the years psychologists, like other scientists, have transformed these everyday techniques for gathering and analyzing information into more precise tools.

As described in Chapter 1, researchers must begin by asking a specific question about a limited topic. The next step is to look for evidence.

GATHERING DATA

How do psychologists collect information about the topic they've chosen to study? The method a researcher uses partly depends on the research topic. For example, a social psychologist who is studying the effects of group pressure is likely to conduct an experiment. A psychologist who is interested in personality theories might begin with intensive case studies of individuals. But whatever approach to gathering data a psychologist selects, he or she must make certain basic decisions in advance.

Objectives:

After studying this chapter, you should be able to

- describe the process of psychological research.
- name the different types of psychological research and some of the methodological hazards of doing research.

Figure 19.1 Psychologists, like students and teachers, use research in a variety of ways.

Samples

Suppose a psychologist wants to know how the desire to get into college affects the attitudes of high-school juniors and seniors. It would be impossible to study every junior and senior in the country. There are just too many. Instead, the researcher would select a **sample,** a relatively small group out of the total **population** under study (in this case, all high-school juniors and seniors).

Choosing a sample can be tricky. A sample must be *representative* of the population a researcher is studying. For example, if you wanted to know how tall American men are, you would want to make certain that your sample did not include a disproportionately large number of professional basketball players. This sample would be *biased;* it would not represent American men in general.

The editors of *Literary Digest* learned about sample bias the hard way. Before the 1936 presidential election, the magazine conducted a massive telephone survey to find out whether voters favored Franklin Roosevelt or Alf Landon. Based on the results of this poll, the *Digest* predicted that Landon would win by a landslide. However, when the votes were counted on election night, it was Roosevelt who won by a landslide. What went wrong? The magazine had only questioned people who appeared on their subscription rolls or who were listed in the telephone book. In those Depression days, conservatives usually subscribed to this magazine, and only the affluent could afford the luxury of a telephone. And these people tended to be Republicans. The *Digest*'s sample did not represent the views of American voters; it was biased toward Landon.

There are two ways to avoid a biased sample. One is to take a purely

Figure 19.2
A survey researcher interviewing a family that is part of the *sample*, the relatively small group selected from the total population under study, for an experiment.

random sample, so that each individual within the scope of the research has an *equal chance* of being represented. For example, a psychologist might choose every twentieth name on school enrollment lists for a study of schoolchildren in a particular town. Random sampling is like drawing names or numbers out of a hat while blindfolded.

The second way to avoid bias is deliberately to pick individuals who represent the various subgroups in the population being studied. For example, the psychologist doing research on schoolchildren might select students of both sexes, of varying ages, of all social classes, and from all neighborhoods. This is called a **stratified sample.**

The size of the sample may also be important. If the sample is too small, the results will be meaningless. For example, a pollster who wants to know what Democrats think about a particular candidate will have to question a relatively large number of people. Why? Because Democrats vary considerably in their political attitudes. Northern and southern, rural and urban, male and female Democrats often disagree. If the pollster interviews only six of the millions of Democrats in the country, the results will not reflect these differences. In most general surveys aimed at large populations, the researcher questions about a thousand people. However, a sample of one hundred may be sufficient *if* those one hundred individuals represent the population as a whole. Indeed, if Democrats were all of one mind, it would only be necessary to interview one!

Sampling techniques apply to the collection of data as well as to the choice of subjects for study. A psychologist who wants to learn how children react to their first years at school might observe them every tenth day (a random sample). Alternatively, he or she might select typical experiences and spend several weeks observing them when they arrive at school, playing alone and in groups, with and without supervision, at different activities inside and outside. This would be a stratified sample of observations.

Correlations and Explanations

A researcher may simply want to observe people or other animals and record these observations in a descriptive study. More often, however, researchers want to examine the *relationship* between two sets of observations—say, between students' grades and the number of hours they sleep.

Scientists use the word **correlation** to describe the degree of relatedness between two sets of data (Figure 19.3). Sometimes the relationship is quite close. For example, there is a **positive correlation** between IQ scores and academic success. High IQ scores tend to go with high grades; low IQ scores tend to go with low grades. On the other hand, there is a **negative correlation** between smoking cigarettes and living a long, healthy life. The more a person smokes, the fewer years he or she may live. In this case, a high rank on one measure tends to go with a low rank on the other.

Establishing a correlation is useful because it enables scientists to make relatively accurate *predictions.* Knowing there is a positive correlation between IQ and academic success, you can predict that a person with a high IQ will do well in school. You won't be right all the time: some people with high IQs do poorly in school. But you will be right most of the time.

Figure 19.3
This series of drawings shows a correlation between the woman's sadness and the man's anger. But is one causing the other? Not necessarily. The woman's sadness may be causing the man's anger; his anger may be causing her sadness; or they may both be responding to a third factor.

Similarly, you might predict that a person with high grades has a high IQ. Here, again, you will be right more often than you will be wrong.

But people often confuse correlations with explanations. Instead of looking at a correlation as a comparison of two things, they think of it as a cause-and-effect relationship. Some years ago, for example, medical researchers discovered a high correlation between cancer and drinking milk. It seemed that the number of cancer cases was increasing in areas where people drink a lot of milk (such as New England) but that cancer was rare in areas where they do not (such as Ceylon). These data suggested to many people that milk causes cancer.

However, when researchers analyzed these data further they found a third factor was involved. Cancer usually strikes people in middle age or later. As a result, cancer is more common in places where people enjoy a high standard of living and live longer than in places where people tend to die at an earlier age. Thus drinking milk is related to cancer, but only because they are both related to a high standard of living. Milk does not cause cancer, but they may be correlated.

As this example illustrates, a correlation between two things may or *may not* indicate a cause-and-effect relationship. Suppose you were told there is a positive correlation between the number of Popsicles sold by ice-cream vendors at swimming pools and the number of people admitted to hospitals for heat stroke. Would you conclude that Popsicles cause heat stroke? To test their hypotheses about cause-and-effect relationships, researchers must turn to experiments.

Experiments

Why would a researcher choose experimentation over other research methods? Because it enables the investigator to *control* the situation and to decrease the possibility that unnoticed, outside factors will influence the results.

This is why, for example, social psychologists Kenneth Gergen, Mary Gergen, and William Barton (1973) put groups of six and seven student volunteers who did not know each other in a dark room for an hour, told them they could do whatever they liked, then photographed their activities with infrared cameras and recorded their conversations (Figure 19.4). What was the purpose of this experiment? To test the hypothesis that a group of

Figure 19.4
The Gergen, Gergen, and Barton experiment. The experimental group was placed in a dark room (darkness is the independent variable), and the amount of talking, moving, and touching was recorded. A control group was placed in an identical room, but with normal light. Again talking, moving, and touching were measured.

strangers left alone in a dark room will do and say things they would not do and say in a lighted room. Darkness provides a cloak of anonymity. The researchers thought that if people can't see each other, they won't worry about being recognized after the experiment and so will be uninhibited. The experiment was designed to prove or disprove this hypothesis. This is the main purpose of psychological studies and experiments—to develop a **hypothesis** or refine and test previous ones.

In designing and reporting experiments, psychologists think in terms of **variables**—that is, conditions and behaviors that are subject to variation or change. In the experiment we are describing, the two significant variables were the amount of light in the room and the amount of conversation, movement, and touching in each of the groups. There are two types of variables: independent and dependent. The **independent variable** is the one experimenters deliberately control so they can observe its effects. Here, the independent variable is the amount of light in the room. The **dependent variable** is the one that researchers believe will be affected by the independent variable. Here, conversation, movement, and touching were the dependent variables. The researchers thought darkness would influence these behaviors.

Of course, there is always a chance that the very fact of participating in an experiment will change the way people act. For this reason, Gergen, Gergen, and Barton put similar groups of students in a lighted room, told them they could do whatever they liked, and photographed and recorded their behavior. Subjects such as these form the **control group.** Subjects who undergo the **experimental treatment**—here, turning off the lights—are called the **experimental group.**

A control group is necessary in all experiments. Without it, a researcher cannot be sure the experimental group is reacting to what he or she thinks it is reacting to—a change in the independent variable. By comparing the way control and experimental groups behaved in this experiment, the researchers could determine whether darkness did in fact influence behavior and how.

What were the results of this experiment? In the lighted room students remained seated (about three feet apart) for most of the hour and kept up a continuous conversation. No one touched anyone else. In the dark room, the students moved around. Although conversation tended to slack off after half an hour or so, there was a great deal of touching—by accident and on purpose. In fact, half of the subjects in the experimental group found themselves hugging another person. Thus the researchers' hypothesis was supported. Anonymity does to some extent remove inhibitions against letting conversation die out and against touching, even hugging a stranger.

Replication. The results of this experiment do not constitute the final word on the subject, however. Psychologists do not fully accept the results of their own or other people's studies until they have been **replicated**—that is, duplicated by at least one other psychologist with different subjects. Why? Because there is always a chance that some unnoticed factor in the original experiment was atypical. For example, perhaps the subjects in the experimental group just happened to be naturally very outgoing.

MORE about . . .

Confounds. When psychologists design experiments, they want the experimental group and the control group to differ *only* in the independent variable. Anything else that differs between the experimental group and the control group is a *confound*.

There are many examples of confounds. In studies of therapeutic effectiveness, for instance, the experimental group (patients who receive the treatment procedure) is usually compared to a wait-list control group (patients who remain on the treatment waiting list for the duration of the study). While these two groups differ in the treatment they receive, they differ in other ways as well. The experimental group receives attention from the research staff, a feeling of belonging to a specified group, and a knowledge of contributing to science. These factors are all confounds, and any of them may affect their behavior. To address these confounds, researchers often run "attention control groups" that receive the same treatment as the experimental group except for the actual therapy.

FACT OR FICTION

Controlled experiments are better than naturalistic observation.

Fiction. Many psychologists prefer the greater degree of control that is possible in experiments. However, this control comes at the price of environmental realism, what psychologists term *ecological validity*. Psychology needs many types of studies, including experiments and natural observations, to prosper as a science.

One example will illustrate why replication is so important. In the mid-1960s, Neal Miller and Leo DiCara (1967) stunned the psychological and medical world by reporting that they had trained rats to control their heart rates. (Before the experiment, researchers believed that animals had no control over the autonomic nervous system.) But all attempts to replicate Miller and DiCara's study failed—including their own. What went wrong? To date, no one has found the answer.

Sometimes, a second researcher purposely changes one or more variables of the original study. For example, he or she may use middle-aged people instead of college students as subjects. The goal is to find out whether the conclusions drawn from the original study apply to people in general, or to just one segment of the population.

Experimentation is sometimes impossible for practical or ethical reasons. Suppose a psychologist suspects that normal visual development in humans depends on visual experience as well as on physical maturation. An ideal way to test this hypothesis would be to raise an experimental group of infants in total darkness, thus depriving them of visual experience, and a control group of infants under similar conditions but with normal lighting. Such an experiment would be impossible, of course. But most ethical problems are not this clear-cut. In the last few years, the American Psychological Association and the United States government have developed a number of guidelines and regulations to ensure that the rights of people who take part in experiments are protected.

Researchers also need to understand the way people and animals behave naturally, when they are not conscious of being the subjects of an experiment. To obtain such information, a psychologist uses **naturalistic observation**.

Naturalistic Observation

One of the most direct ways to learn about psychology is to listen and watch—observing how humans and animals behave, without interfering. For example, a social psychologist might join a commune or participate in a therapy group to study how leadership develops in these settings. A developmental psychologist might position himself or herself behind a two-way mirror to watch youngsters at play (Figure 19.5). Ethologists (scientists who specialize in studying animal behavior) often spend years observing members of a species before even considering an experiment. The cardinal rule of naturalistic observation is to avoid disturbing the people or animals you are studying, by concealing yourself or by acting as unobtrusively as possible. Otherwise, you may observe a performance produced for the researcher's benefit rather than natural behavior.

Case Studies

A **case study** is an intensive investigation of an individual or group. Many case studies focus on a particular disorder, such as schizophrenia, or a particular experience, such as being confined to prison. And most combine long-term observation (by one or more researchers), self-reports (such as

Figure 19.5
Naturalistic observation, sometimes done through a one-way window or mirror, is a useful technique for studying teaching methods and classroom interactions because the observer does not distract the students or the teacher and perhaps cause them to alter their behavior.

diaries, tapes of therapy sessions, or perhaps artwork), and the results of psychological tests.

In the hands of a brilliant psychologist, case studies can be a powerful research tool. Sigmund Freud's theory of personality development, discussed in Chapter 11, was based on case studies of his patients. Jean Piaget's theory of intellectual development, described in Chapter 8, was

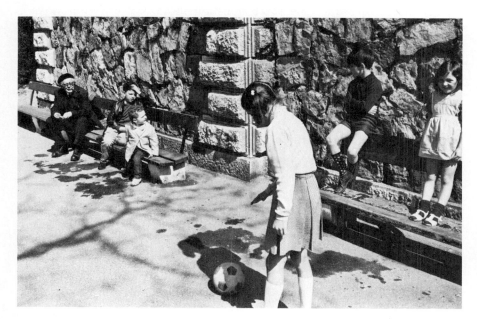

Figure 19.6
Jean Piaget's theories of intellectual development grew partly from case studies of his own children. Here, Piaget observes children playing in a park near his home.

based in part on case studies of his own children. By itself, however, a case study does not prove or disprove anything. The sample is too small, and there is no way of knowing if the researcher's conclusions are correct. For example, a researcher might conduct intensive case studies of families that include an individual diagnosed as schizophrenic. On the basis of these studies she might conclude that a particular kind of interaction produced schizophrenia. However, unless she studies families that do *not* include schizophrenic individuals and finds that they interact differently, she has no way of proving her conclusion. In other words, what is missing from case studies is a control group. The researcher might study a million families that include a schizophrenic person and find similar patterns. But unless she compares these families to others, she cannot be certain that normal families are different.

What, then, is the value of case studies? They provide a wealth of descriptive material that may generate new hypotheses which researchers can then test under controlled conditions with comparison groups.

Surveys

Surveys may be impersonal, but they are the most practical way to gather data on the attitudes, beliefs, and experiences of large numbers of people. A survey can take the form of interviews, questionnaires, or a combination of the two.

Interviews allow a researcher to observe the subject and modify questions if the subject seems confused by them. On the other hand, questionnaires take less time to administer and the results are more uniform. Questionnaires also eliminate the possibility that the researcher will influence the subject by unconsciously frowning at an answer he or she does not like. Of course, there is always a danger that subjects will give misleading answers in order to make themselves "look good." One way to detect this is to phrase the same question in several different ways. A person who says yes, she believes in integration, but no, she would not want her child to marry someone of another race, is not as free of prejudice as the first answer implied.

Perhaps the most famous survey of recent times is the Kinsey report on sexuality. Alfred Kinsey and his staff questioned over 10,000 men and women about their sexual attitudes and behavior—a radical thing to do in the 1940s. The results shocked many people, much as Masters and Johnson's observational studies of human sexual behavior did in the late 1960s.

Longitudinal Studies

Longitudinal studies cover long stretches of time. The psychologist studies and restudies the same group of subjects at regular intervals over a period of years to determine whether their behavior and feelings have changed, and if so, how (Figure 19.7). For example, Lewis Terman followed over a thousand gifted children from an early age to adulthood. He found that they were generally taller, heavier, and stronger than youngsters with average IQs. In addition, they tended to be active socially and to mature

Figure 19.7
The results of a longitudinal study. Kagan and Moss wanted to find out how much continuity there is between individual's behavior in childhood and their behavior as adults. They found the correlations shown here. Traditional sex roles had a strong influence on whether a childhood behavior pattern died out or survived into adulthood. (After Kagan and Moss, 1962)

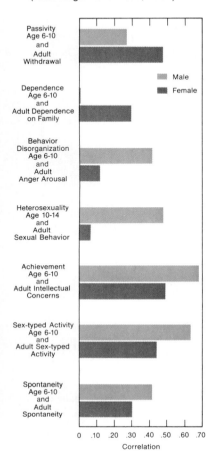

faster than average children. (So much for the stereotype of the skinny, unpopular bookworm.) As adults, they were less likely than people with average intelligence to become involved in crime, to depend on alcohol or drugs, or to develop severe mental illnesses. Some people have said that geniuses are crazy. This study indicates that they are more adaptive, creative, and adjusted than people of normal intelligence (Terman, 1916; Terman and Merrill, 1937).

Longitudinal studies are time-consuming and precarious; subjects may disappear in mid-study. But they are an ideal way to examine consistencies and inconsistencies in behavior over time.

Cross-cultural Studies

Cross-cultural studies are just what the term suggests: comparisons of the way people in different cultures behave, feel, and think. The primary purpose of such research is to determine whether a behavior pattern is universal or reflects the way children are raised and the experiences adults have in a particular culture. For example, Lawrence Kohlberg studied the development of moral reasoning by presenting American, Mexican, and Taiwanese boys age seven and older with a series of dilemmas. (For example, if a man's wife is dying, should he steal a drug that he cannot afford to save her life?) He found that some children in all three societies progress through six stages of moral awareness, from fear of punishment to an inner sense of justice (see Chapter 8). However, the percentage of those in each society who reached stage six varied. Thus although certain values appear to be universal, cultural differences do affect the development of moral reasoning (see Kohlberg and Kramer, 1969).

All the methods for gathering information we've described have advantages and disadvantages; no one technique is better than the others for all purposes. The method a psychologist chooses depends on what he or she wants to learn. It also depends on practical matters such as the amount of money available for research and the kind of training the researcher has had.

TRAPS IN DOING PSYCHOLOGICAL RESEARCH AND HOW TO AVOID THEM

In describing the methods and statistical techniques psychologists use, we have made research appear much simpler and much more straightforward than it actually is. Science is a painstaking, exacting business. Every researcher must be wary of numerous pitfalls that can trap him or her into mistakes. In this section we look at some of the most common problems psychological researchers confront and how they cope with them.

The Self-fulfilling Prophecy

Psychologists are only human, and like all of us they prefer to be right. No matter how objective they try to be in their research, there is always a

PSYCHOLOGY UPDATE

Cross-cultural studies of obedience. Chapter 18 ends with a discussion of Stanley Milgram's experiments on obedience. Recall that in his original study, over half of the subjects (26 of 40, or 65 percent) administered the highest level of shock.

Researchers at Swarthmore College hypothesized that Milgram's findings were due, in part, to the fact that his subjects were mostly middle-aged, working-class men. Most had probably served in the military during World War II and thus had experience taking orders and obeying authority. Young, liberal, highly educated Swarthmore students would obey less. Surprisingly, 88 percent of the Swarthmore undergraduates administered the highest level of shock!

Eventually, Milgram's experiment was conducted in Germany and Japan. To no one's surprise, the German and Japanese subjects showed a high rate of obedience—over 80 percent in both groups.

When Milgram began his study, he doubted that any subject would administer the highest level of shock. Imagine his surprise when he learned that the 65 percent rate he found was the lowest of any group.

Figure 19.8
The Red Queen's fatalistic attitude is likely to be confirmed if she behaves in this way. This common phenomenon is called self-fulfilling prophecy.

chance that they will find what they want to find, unwittingly overlooking contrary evidence. This is what we mean by the **self-fulfilling prophecy.**

Researchers have shown how the self-fulfilling prophecy works in an experiment with experimenters (Rosenthal and Rosnow, 1969). The task was to administer the Wechsler Intelligence Scale for Children to twelve youngsters. Each child was tested by two experimenters, one of whom administered the odd-numbered questions, the other the even-numbered questions. With each child, one of the experimenters was told beforehand that the subject was above average in intelligence. The other was told the subject was below average. The results? The youngsters scored an average of 7.5 points higher on the half of the test administered by the experimenter who had been told they were bright. Thus the experimenters found what they expected to find: the prophecy that a given child would achieve a relatively high score was self-fulfilling.

The Double-Blind Procedure

One way to avoid the self-fulfilling prophecy is to use the double-blind technique. Suppose a psychologist wants to study the effects of a particular tranquilizer. She might give the drug to an experimental group and a placebo (a harmless substitute for the drug) to a control group. The next step would be to compare their performances on a series of tests. This is a *single-blind* experiment. The subjects are "blind" in the sense that they do not know whether they have received the tranquilizer or the placebo.

As a further guarantee of objectivity, the researcher herself doesn't know who takes the drug or the placebo. (She may ask the pharmacist to number rather than label the pills.) *After* she scores the tests, she goes back to the pharmacist to learn which subjects took the tranquilizer and which took the placebo. This is a **double-blind experiment.** Neither the subjects nor the experimenter know which subjects received the tranquilizer. This eliminates the possibility that the researcher will unconsciously find what she expects to find about the effects of the drug.

Observer Effects

Psychologists, like everyone else, are complex people, with attitudes, feelings, and ideas of their own, and their reactions to different subjects may distort the results of a study. Researchers may unknowingly react differently to male and female subjects, short and tall subjects, subjects who speak with an accent or who remind them of someone they particularly dislike. These attitudes, however subtly expressed, may influence the way subjects behave.

In addition, subjects may behave differently than they would otherwise just because they know they are being studied. The presence of an observer may cause them to change their behavior, just as the presence of a photographer can transform a bunch of unruly children into a peaceful, smiling group. Under observation, people are apt to try to please or impress the observer—to act as they think they are expected to act. The use of a control group helps to correct for this, but does not totally eliminate the "observer effect."

Finally, a researcher may not have the equipment to study a subject adequately. For example, psychologists would never have been able to identify the stages of sleep (see Chapter 7) if the electroencephalograph had not been invented. Psychology is a relatively young science, and the tools and techniques psychologists possess may not be equal to the questions they ask.

CONCLUSIONS

What distinguishes psychologists and other scientists from nonscientists is nagging skepticism. Scientists do not believe that they have any final answers, or that they ever will. But they do believe they can learn more about feelings and behavior if they persist in asking questions and studying them systematically. Do people actually behave like that? Does this method work? Does that way of thinking help? When the answer is yes, scientists do not stop asking questions. It is always possible that the next answer will be no, or that it is yes for some people and no for others. Hence it is essential for researchers to *invite* criticism by publishing detailed accounts of their methods as well as their results.

The reason why *students* of psychology need to understand research methods is simple. You wouldn't vote for a political candidate simply because she promised to do something you agreed with. You'd want to know whether she had delivered on past campaign promises, whether she was indebted to special-interest groups, and whether she was an effective bargainer in the legislature. You wouldn't buy a new brand of soap because the company claimed that "tests prove" it is good for your skin. You'd want to know what the tests were, who conducted them, and why other companies make the same claim.

You shouldn't accept what you read about psychology just because a psychologist says so. (The "experts" often disagree.) To evaluate psychological studies for yourself, you need to understand research methods.

It is also important to understand what psychologists do once they have completed their studies. They must organize the information they have obtained in order to draw conclusions. For example, how were the researchers Kagan and Moss able to create the graph presented as Figure 19.7 in this chapter? How did researchers determine that youngsters scored an average of 7.5 points higher on the test administered by experimenters who thought they were bright? What does it mean when reports say that 9 out of 10 dentists recommend that their patients chew a certain type of gum, or, as reported in a recent newspaper article, that 5 to 10 percent of the general population suffers from a dissociative disorder (see Chapter 15)? How do researchers come up with these numbers? In Chapter 20 we will discuss the tools that psychologists use to formulate percentages, create graphs, and derive correlations to prove their hypotheses. We hope that with this information you will become more informed "consumers" of psychology.

Use the following outline as a tool for reviewing this chapter. Copy the outline onto your own paper, leaving spaces between headings to make notes about key concepts.

I. Gathering Data

   A. Samples

   B. Correlations and Explanations

   C. Experiments

   D. Naturalistic Observation

   E. Case Studies

   F. Surveys

   G. Longitudinal Studies

   H. Cross-Cultural Studies

II. Traps in Doing Psychological Research and How to Avoid Them

   A. The Self-Fulfilling Prophecy

   B. The Double-Blind Procedure

   C. Observer Effects

III. Conclusions

CONCEPTS AND VOCABULARY

1. What is the name given to a relatively small group selected from the total population? What is an important quality of this selected group?

2. What are the two ways that a biased sample can be avoided?

3. What word do scientists use to describe the relationship between two sets of data? How is this relationship useful? Does it indicate a cause-and-effect relationship?

4. What is the main purpose of an experiment?

5. What is the name of the variable that experi-

menters can control? Which variable is affected by the other?

6. What is the name given to the group who receive the special treatment?

7. What is an intensive investigation of an individual or group called?

8. What method of experimentation was Freud's theory of personality based on?

9. What is the most practical way to gather data on the attitudes, beliefs, and experiences of large numbers of people? How can this method obtain data?

10. What type of studies obtain data from people at regular intervals over a span of several years?

11. What is the main purpose of a cross-cultural study?

12. What is the name given to the tendency of researchers to find what they want to find despite evidence to the contrary? How can this tendency be avoided in experiments?

CRITICAL THINKING

1. **Synthesize.** Several theories are presented below. How could you attempt to disprove each one? Are there any that could not be disproved?
   a. A person will remember an unfinished task.
   b. Love reduces hate.
   c. You can raise blood pressure by making a subject anxious.
   d. Motivation increases learning.
   e. Making a rat hungry will cause the rat to require less training to find its way through a maze.

2. **Analyze.** Look through a popular magazine such as *Time, Newsweek,* or *Psychology Today.* Read an article about a scientific experiment and try to determine if the results presented cor-

respond to the data given. What approach to obtaining data was used? Did the experiment contain a control group? What were the dependent and independent variables?

APPLYING KNOWLEDGE

1. Measurement is the assignment of numbers to observations. Psychologists face many problems in trying to measure behaviors and feelings. For example, how might the following factors be measured: (1) the number of people in a room; (2) height; (3) the proportion of votes a candidate will receive; (4) hunger; (5) love; (6) liberty. What makes each phenomenon difficult or easy to measure? What can you predict from this exercise regarding the difficulties of measuring such things as personality and intelligence?

2. Select a particular area of psychological investigation that is of interest to you. Go to a main, branch or university library and, by utilizing the card catalog, bibliographical references, and journals or magazines, see how far your research takes you. You may find that, like looking up a word in the dictionary, one thing leads to another, which leads to another, and so on.

3. Design an experiment to study the eating patterns of students in your school. Among questions your experiment should answer are: What do students like to eat? What do they not like to eat? How many students eat lunch in the cafeteria? How many students choose not to eat in the cafeteria? What do students think could be done to improve the food or atmosphere in the cafeteria? Is there any food not currently offered that students would like to see offered? Write a report detailing how you would conduct your study. Be sure you include information about what size sample you would need, how you would select a representative sample, and how you would design your survey. If you want to actually carry out your experiment, write up a research report and present your findings to the class.

ANALYZING VIEWPOINTS

1. One controversy surrounding the use of surveys is the role they can play in influencing future events. For example, political polls have often been criticized because they may cause people to switch their votes or even not vote at all. Television networks survey the viewing habits of select samples of people to determine which shows will be renewed for the following season. This can result in the cancellation of a program that does not fare well in the survey. List the pros and cons of using survey research to predict future events.

BEYOND THE CLASSROOM

1. Choose a traffic intersection near your home or school that has a stop sign. Design an experiment to assess the compliance of motorists with the posted stop sign. Spend several hours at different times of the day observing traffic at the intersection. Some of the research questions you should be considering include: What time of day will I conduct my observations? How will I determine whether motorists comply with the stop sign? How much information do I need to record? For example, do you need to record the number of vehicles, type of vehicles, whether the car stopped, time of day, or gender of the driver? Conduct your experiment and record your observations. Once you have completed your experiment, add up the results. What are your findings? How many vehicles stopped at the stop sign? How many did not? What percentage of the total number of vehicles stopped? What percentage did not? Do these results vary based on the time of day (for example, rush hour versus midday)? Do the results vary based on the make of car? What other factors seemed to differentiate between cars that stopped and cars that did not? What are your conclusions? Prepare a report for the class.

CHAPTER
20
Statistical Evaluation

How many times have you been told that, in order to get good grades, you have to study? A psychology student named Kate has always restricted the amount of TV she watches during the week, particularly before a test. She has a friend, though, who does not watch TV before a test but who still does not get good grades. This fact challenges Kate's belief. Although Kate hypothesizes, or guesses, that among her classmates those who watch less TV get better grades, she decides to conduct a survey to test the validity of her hypothesis. Kate asks fifteen students in her class to write down how many hours of TV they watched the night before their weekly psychology quiz and how many hours they watched on the night after the quiz. To make her study more interesting, Kate collects additional data. She has her subjects check off familiar products on a list of twenty brand-name items that were advertised on TV the night before the quiz. Kate also asks her subjects to give their height.

When the data is turned in, Kate finds herself overwhelmed with the amount of information she has collected. Her data are presented in Figure 20.2. How can she organize it all so that it makes sense? How can she analyze it to see whether it supports or contradicts her hypothesis? The answers to these questions are found in **statistics**, a branch of mathematics that enables researchers to organize and evaluate the data they collect. In this chapter we will explore the statistical procedures that help psychologists make sense out of the masses of data they collect.

DESCRIPTIVE STATISTICS

When a study such as Kate's is completed, the first task is to organize the data in as brief and clear a manner as possible. For Kate, this means that she must put her responses together in a logical format. When she does

Objectives:

After studying this chapter, you should be able to

- define descriptive and inferential statistics.
- name specific research methods used to organize data.
- compare the three measures of central tendency.
- explain statistical significance.

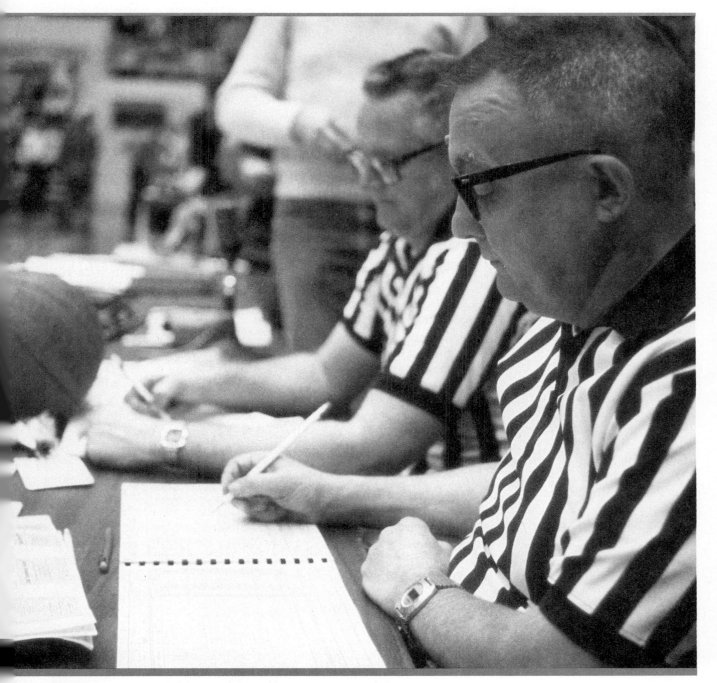

Figure 20.1 Many statisticians analyze and interpret sports statistics.

FIGURE 20.2
Kate's data: number of hours of TV watched before and after the quiz, grade on quiz, number of products recognized, and height in inches.

Before	After	Grade*	Products	Height
0.0	1.5	5	2	71
0.5	2.5	10	4	64
0.5	2.5	9	6	69
1.0	2.0	10	14	60
1.0	2.5	8	10	71
1.0	1.5	7	9	63
1.5	3.0	9	7	70
1.5	2.5	8	12	59
1.5	2.5	8	9	75
1.5	3.0	6	14	60
2.0	3.0	5	13	68
2.5	2.5	3	17	65
2.5	3.5	4	10	72
3.0	3.0	0	18	62
4.0	4.0	4	20	67

* Highest grade possible is 10.

PSYCHOLOGY and YOU

Baseball Statistics. Let us look at how statistics are used in one of our most popular sports, baseball. A batting average is the number of hits per official "at bats" (walks do not count). If a player has a batting average of .250, it means that he gets a hit every fourth time at the plate.

The earned run average represents the number of runs a pitcher allows per 9 innings of play. Consider the pitcher who pitches 180 innings in a season and allows 60 runs. On the average, this pitcher allows one run every 3 innings (180 innings divided by 60 runs). One run every 3 innings equals 3 runs every 9 innings, so the earned run average is 3. The next time you watch your favorite sport, think about the part that statistics plays in it.

this, she is using **descriptive statistics**, the listing and summarizing of data in a practical, efficient way, such as graphs and averages. In this section we will discuss the different forms of descriptive statistics.

Distributions of Data

One of the first steps that researchers take to organize their data is to create frequency tables and graphs. Tables and graphs provide a rough picture of the data. Are the scores bunched up or spread out? What score occurs most often? Frequency distributions and graphs provide researchers with their initial "peek" at the data.

Frequency Distributions. Kate is interested in how many hours of TV her subjects watched the night before and the night after the quiz. She uses the numbers of hours of TV viewing as categories, and then she counts how many subjects reported each category of hours before and after the quiz. She has created a table called a frequency distribution (see Figure 20.3). A **frequency distribution** is a way of arranging data so that we know how often a particular score or observation occurs.

What can Kate do with this information? A commonly used technique is to figure out percentages. This is done simply by dividing the frequency of subjects within a category by the total number of subjects. So, before the quiz, about 13 percent of her subjects (2 divided by 15) watched TV for 2.5 hours. On the night after the quiz, 40 percent of her subjects watched 2.5 hours of TV (6 divided by 15). You are familiar with the use of percentages; test grades are often expressed as percentages (the number of correct points divided by 100). Sometimes frequency distributions include a column giving the percentage of each occurrence.

Graphs. It is often easier to visualize frequency information in the form of a graph. Since Kate is most interested in how much TV her classmates watched the night before their psychology quiz, she decides to graph the results. The graph of the "before the quiz" frequency distribution shown in Figure 20.4 is called a histogram. You are probably familiar with bar graphs. **Histograms** are very similar to bar graphs except that histograms are always vertical, and the bars touch. The X axis, which runs horizontally, lists the number of hours of TV watched, and the Y axis, which runs vertically, is the number of people, or frequency. The height of each bar represents the number of people who reported watching a particular amount of TV. The highest bar shows the number of hours reported most frequently (1.5), and the lowest bar shows the number of hours reported least frequently. In this case, no one reported watching TV for 3.5 hours the night before the quiz. The graph also shows that few people watched more than 2 hours of TV.

Another kind of graph is the frequency polygon or frequency curve. Figure 20.5 is a **frequency polygon**. It shows the same information presented in the histogram. The X axis and Y axis are exactly the same. Instead of drawing boxes, however, a mark is placed on the graph where the midpoint of the top of each histogram bar would be. Then the marks are connected with straight lines.

Frequency polygons are useful because they provide a clear picture of the shape of the data distribution. Another important feature is that more than one set of data can be graphed at the same time. For example, Kate might be interested in comparing how much TV was watched the night before the quiz with the amount watched the evening after the quiz. As shown in Figure 20.6, she can graph the "after quiz" data using a different kind of line. The comparison is obvious; in general, her subjects watched more TV on the night after the quiz than on the night before the quiz.

The Normal Curve. Imagine that Kate could measure how much TV everyone in Chicago watched one night. If she could graph that much information, her graph would probably look something like Figure 20.7. A few people would watch little or no TV, a few would have the TV on all day, while most would watch a moderate amount of TV. Therefore, the graph

Frequency distribution: number of hours of TV viewing on the nights before and after the quiz.

Hours	Frequency Before*	Frequency After*
0.0	1	0
0.5	2	0
1.0	3	0
1.5	4	2
2.0	1	1
2.5	2	6
3.0	1	4
3.5	0	1
4.0	1	1
Total	15	15

* Number of students.

FIGURE 20.5
Frequency polygon: number of hours of TV watched the night before the quiz.

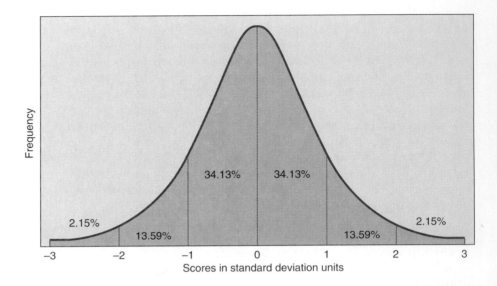

would be highest in the middle and taper off toward the tails, or ends, of the distribution, giving it the shape of a bell. (The standard deviation units shown in Figure 20.6 will be explained later in this chapter.)

This curve is special. It is called the **normal curve** (or bell-shaped curve). Many variables, such as height, weight, and IQ, fall into such a curve if enough people are measured. The normal curve is symmetrical. This means that if a line is drawn down the middle of the curve, one side of the curve is a mirror image of the other side. It is an important distribution because of certain mathematical characteristics. We can divide the curve into sections and can predict how much of the curve, or what percentage of cases, falls within each section. We shall return to this idea later and discuss the importance of the information shown on the curve.

Many curves are not "normal" because scores pile up on one end of the distribution. These are called **skewed distributions** (see Figures 20.7a and 20.7b). Take a look at Figure 20.5 again. Most of the students fell in the lower range of the distribution (they did not watch much TV), and so it is positively skewed (the tail of the distribution points to the right, or positive, end of the X axis). If everyone in your class takes a graduate-school statistics exam, the distribution of grades will also be positively skewed, since most of you will probably get low scores (Figure 20.8a). On the other hand, if everyone in your class takes a sixth-grade math test, most will get high scores, and so the graph will be skewed in the other direction, or negatively skewed (Figure 20.8b).

Measures of Central Tendency

Most of the time, researchers want to do more than organize their data. They want to be able to summarize information about the distribution into statistics. One of the most common ways of summarizing is to use a measure of **central tendency**— a number that describes something about the "average" score. We shall use Kate's quiz grades (refer back to Figure 20.1) in the examples below.

FIGURE 20.6
Frequency polygons: number of hours of TV watched on the nights before and after the quiz.

The Mode. The **mode** is the most frequent score. In a graphed frequency distribution, the mode is the peak of the graph. The most frequently occurring quiz grade is 8; that is, the most students, in this case three, got a score of 8. Distributions can have more than one mode. The data for height presented in Figure 20.1 has two modes: 60 and 71. Distributions with two modes are called "bimodal."

The mode is the simplest statistic to figure out, but it gives the least amount of information. For example, in the distribution 1, 2, 3, 4, 10, 10, the mode is 10. Most of the scores, though, are below 5, so the mode does not provide an accurate portrait of the "average" score. However, if you just want to identify the most frequent score, or observation, the mode is the measure to use.

The Median. When scores are put in order from least to most, the **median** is the middle score. Since the median is the midpoint of a set of values, it divides the frequency distribution into two halves. Therefore, 50 percent of the scores fall below the median, and 50 percent fall above the median. For an odd number of observations, the median would be the exact middle value. Here are the psychology quiz grades, in order: 0, 3, 4, 4, 5, 5, 6, 7, 8, 8, 8, 9, 9, 10, 10. The median is 7. As the middle score it divides the distribution in half: There are seven scores above it and seven scores below it. With an even number of observations, the median would be the midpoint between the two most central scores.

The median does not reflect the value of all the scores in a distribution. If the highest score in a data set were a few points higher, the median would stay the same. Regardless of the numerical value, the highest score represents only a score above the median. If we change the highest quiz grade from 10 to 20, the median remains the same.

The Mean. The **mean** is what most people think of as an "average" and is the most commonly used measure of central tendency. To find the mean, you add up all the scores and then divide by the number of scores you add. Here are some simple symbols that will be helpful in expressing the mean.

X = an individual observation (score)
N = the total number of observations
Σ = "the sum of" (the Greek capital letter sigma)
$\overline{X}$ = the mean

The mean is calculated from the following formula:

$$\overline{X} = \frac{\Sigma X}{N}$$

which reads: The mean equals the sum of the scores on variable X divided by the total number of observations. For the quiz grades, the sum of the scores is 96, and the number of scores is 15. The mean equals 96 divided by 15, to give us a mean quiz grade of 6.4.

$$\overline{X} = \frac{96}{15} = 6.4$$

FIGURE 20.8
Skewed distributions. (a) A positively skewed distribution. (b) A negatively skewed distribution.

a

Positively skewed distribution

Frequency

Scores

b

Negatively skewed distribution

Frequency

Scores

The mean can be considered the balance point of the distribution, like the middle of a seesaw, since it does reflect all the scores in a set of data. If the highest score in a data set is shifted higher, the mean will shift upward also. If we change the highest quiz grade from 10 to 20, the mean changes from 6.4 to 7.1.

This change is not very dramatic because we are working with small numbers. Let us take another example. Five people are randomly chosen at a local shopping mall and are asked their annual incomes. Their answers are: $18,000, $20,000, $25,000, $26,000, and $100,000. The mean income for this group is $41,400! This mean is not very descriptive of most of the incomes. The median, on the other hand, is $25,000—a more accurate portrait of an "average." In skewed distributions, the mean is always pulled toward the most extreme scores. (See Figures 20.7a and 20.7b.) Annual income is positively skewed because a small percentage of the population has extremely high incomes. An "average annual income" that is computed as a mean will be pulled toward these high incomes and will not be as representative of the general population's income as the median.

Measures of Variability

Distributions differ not only in their "average" score but also in terms of how "spread out" or how variable the scores are. Figure 20.9 shows two distributions drawn on the same axis. Each is symmetrical and each has the same mean. However, the distributions differ in terms of their variability. Measures of **variability** provide an index of how spread out the scores of a distribution are.

Two commonly used measures of variability are the range and the standard deviation. To compute the **range**, subtract the lowest score in a data set from the highest score. The highest quiz grade is 10 and the lowest is 0, so the range is 10. Like the mode, the range uses only a small amount of information, and it is used only as a crude measure of variability.

The **standard deviation** (SD) is a better measure of variability because, like the mean, it uses all the data points in its calculation. It is the most widely used measure of variability. The standard deviation is like (but not exactly like) an "average" distance of every score to the mean of the scores. This distance is called a "deviation" and is written: $X - \overline{X}$ (which means a score minus the mean). Scores above the mean will have a positive deviation, and scores below the mean will have a negative deviation. The size of the "average" deviation depends on how variable, or spread out, the distribution is. If the distribution is very spread out, deviations tend to be large. If the distribution is bunched up, deviations tend to be small.

To figure out this "average" distance, deviations cannot simply be added up and then divided by the number of observations. The negative and positive deviations cancel each other out, and the sum of deviation scores is always 0. The traditional way that mathematicians get around this problem is to square each deviation (to make them all positive). These squared deviations are then averaged. To compensate for the fact that the

FIGURE 20.9
Two distributions with the same mean and different standard deviations.

deviations are squared, the square root is taken. The formula for the standard deviation is:

$$\text{Standard deviation} = \sqrt{\frac{\text{sum of (score - mean)}^2}{\text{number of scores}}}$$

or

$$SD = \sqrt{\frac{\Sigma(X - \overline{X})^2}{N}}$$

The mean is subtracted from each score, resulting in a deviation. Each deviation is squared, then all of the squared deviations are added together. This sum is divided by the number of scores. When the square root is taken, the result is the standard deviation. Calculation of the quiz grades' standard deviation is shown in Figure 20.10.

The standard deviation is a measure of distance, describing an "average" distance of every score to the mean. The larger the standard deviation, the more spread out the scores are. Look back at Figure 20.5, where the hours of TV watched before and after the quiz are graphed into two frequency polygons. You can easily see that the observations for the "before" polygon are more spread out than those for the "after" polygon. The standard deviation for "before" is 1.06 and for "after" is 0.67.

The standard deviation does more than summarize information about a data set. When a set of measurements is distributed in the shape of the normal curve, researchers are able to interpret scores by looking at their distance from the mean using the standard deviation as the unit of measurement. In other words, the standard deviation is used to carve up the normal curve into sections. Return to Figure 20.7, where the normal curve is pictured. The numbers on the X axis represent standard deviation units. About 34 percent of the curve lies between the mean and one standard deviation above the mean. Since the curve is symmetrical, the same amount lies between the mean and one standard deviation below the mean. Over 99 percent of the curve lies between –3 and +3 standard deviation units. Only a few standard deviation units are pictured in Figure 20.7.

When a teacher "grades on the curve," it means that there is no absolute standard that equals an A, B, C, etc. The grade a person gets depends on what everyone else gets. If the teacher uses the normal curve to determine the grades, he or she would first compute the mean and standard deviation of the set of test scores. The teacher might then decide that scores above +2 standard deviations receive an A, while those below –2 standard deviations receive an F. Between +1 and +2 standard deviations, the grade will be B; and scores between –1 and –2 standard deviations receive a D. All scores between –1 and +1 standard deviations receive a C. With this system, it is possible for everyone in a class to score between 80 and 100 on an exam, yet most of the students will still get Cs, Ds, and Fs. On the other hand, the entire class can score below 50 on an exam and some students will still get As and Bs.

FIGURE 20.10

Calculations of the standard deviation: grades on quiz

X (Score)	$\overline{X}$	$(X-\overline{X})$	$(X-\overline{X})^2$
0	6.4	–6.4	40.96
3	6.4	–3.4	11.56
4	6.4	–2.4	5.76
4	6.4	–2.4	5.76
5	6.4	–1.4	1.96
5	6.4	–1.4	1.96
6	6.4	–0.4	0.16
7	6.4	+0.6	0.36
8	6.4	+1.6	2.56
8	6.4	+1.6	2.56
8	6.4	+1.6	2.56
9	6.4	+2.6	6.76
9	6.4	+2.6	6.76
10	6.4	+3.6	12.96
10	6.4	+3.6	12.96
		$\Sigma(X-\overline{X})$ $= 0$	$\Sigma(X-\overline{X})^2$ $= 115.6$

$$SD = \sqrt{\frac{115.6}{15}} = \sqrt{7.71} = 2.78$$

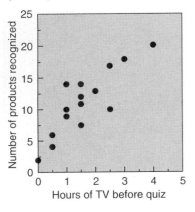

Correlation Coefficients

As discussed in Chapter 19, a **correlation coefficient** describes the direction and strength of the relationship between two sets of observations. While there are many types of correlation coefficients, the most commonly used measure is the Pearson correlation coefficient (*r*). A coefficient with a plus (+) sign indicates a **positive correlation**. This means that as one variable *increases*, the second variable also *increases*. For example, the more you jog, the better your cardiovascular system works. A coefficient with a minus (–) sign indicates a **negative correlation**; as one variable *increases*, the second variable *decreases*. For example, the more hours a person spends at an after-school job, the fewer hours are available for studying. Correlations can take any value between +1 and –1 including 0. An *r* near +1 or –1 indicates a strong relationship (either positive or negative), while an *r* near 0 indicates a weak relationship. Generally, an *r* from 0.60 to 1.0 indicates a strong correlation, from 0.30 to 0.60 a moderate correlation, and from 0 to 0.30 a weak correlation. A correlation of 1.0 indicates a perfect relationship between two variables and is rare in real-life data.

Using correlations, Kate can analyze a number of variables she measured. She uses the data presented in Figure 20.2 to look at the relationship between hours of TV viewing the night before the exam and three variables: number of products recognized, exam grade, and height.

To get an idea of how her data looks, Kate draws some scatterplots. A **scatterplot** is a graph of subjects' scores on the two variables, and it demonstrates the direction of the relationship between them. Figures 20.11, 20.12 and 20.13 illustrate the different kinds of correlations Kate looks at. Note that each point represents one person's score on two variables.

Kate first looks at hours of TV viewing and number of products recognized. She finds that students who watch more TV can identify more products that were advertised on TV. A positive correlation results in a scatterplot in which the points generally tend to cluster on a diagonal from lower left to upper right (Figure 20.11).

She next considers hours of TV and quiz grades. Her original hypothesis was that students who watched more TV would not do as well on the quiz as students who watched less TV. The points on her scatterplot generally tend to cluster on a diagonal from upper left to lower right. This means that, in general, students who watched less TV did better on the next day's quiz than students who watched more TV. This is an example of a negative correlation (Figure 20.12).

Where there is little or no relationship between two variables, the points in the scatterplot do not seem to fall into any pattern. Not surprisingly, Kate finds that TV viewing and height are not related (Figure 20.13)!

Having established that a relationship is either positive or negative, it is also important to note how closely the cluster in the scatterplot approximates a straight line. The stronger the *linear* relationship between two variables, the more closely the points in the scatterplot tend to cluster along a straight line (whether positive or negative) and the higher is the correlation. Data fitting a perfect +1.00 or –1.00 correlation will fall on a straight line. While TV viewing is related strongly to both grades and products identified, Kate finds that the correlation between TV viewing and product identification is higher.

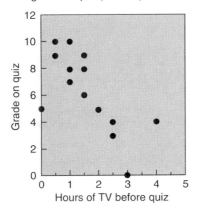

While a correlation tells us something about the relationship or association between two variables, it does not tell us whether one variable *causes* the other. For example, we are all aware that before major holidays, the American Automobile Association predicts, correctly, that more people will be involved in automobile accidents during the holiday period. Does this mean that holidays cause auto accidents? A closer look at the data reveals that holidays and accidents are related to a third variable: the dramatic increase in the number of people who travel during a holiday. Since there are many more people on the roads, the number of accidents increases because the number of people has increased. So, auto accidents and holidays can be correlated, but one does not necessarily cause the other.

To go back to Kate's question, does viewing TV itself cause poorer performance on a quiz? Probably not. Perhaps students who watch more TV have less time to study, and the lack of studying is what affects test grades. Maybe better students are not interested in TV. No matter how high a correlation coefficient is, it tells us nothing about causes.

However, correlations are useful for a different purpose. If two variables are shown to be related, one variable can be predicted from knowledge of the other. Why do you take the SATs before going to college? Because your score tells admissions officers something about how well you will do in your first year of college. The correlation is not perfect. Some students do poorly on standardized tests like the SATs but excel in college. Others have no problems with the SATs but flunk out before the end of the first semester of college. The accuracy of prediction can be increased if other variables are used in combination to predict a single variable (like first-year grades). So, in addition to your SATs, your high school grades, extracurricular activities, and letters of recommendation are considered.

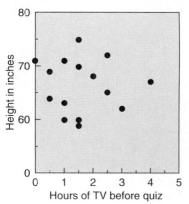

FIGURE 20.13
Scatterplot of hours of TV before quiz and height in inches ($r = -0.06$)

INFERENTIAL STATISTICS

The purpose of descriptive statistics is to describe the characteristics of a sample. But psychologists are not interested only in the information they collect from their subjects. They want to make generalizations about the population from which the subjects come. To make such generalizations, we need the tools of inferential statistics. Using **inferential statistics**, researchers can determine whether the data they collect support their hypotheses, or whether their results are merely due to chance outcomes.

Probability and Chance

If you toss a coin in the air, what is the probability that it will land with heads facing up? Since there are only two possible outcomes, heads or tails, the probability of heads is 0.50. If you toss a coin ten times, you would expect five heads and five tails. What if in nine flips you toss nine heads and no tails? What is the probability that your next toss will be heads? It will

Meta-Analysis. The results of one study cannot provide definite answers to a research question. Studies must be replicated, or repeated. Many studies have looked at the relationship between psychological factors and coronary heart disease (CHD). Some studies have linked heart disease with "Type A" personality (a hurried, impatient workaholic); others have not found this relationship, or have linked CHD with different personality variables. How can conclusions be drawn if numerous studies result in contradictory findings? A statistical technique, *meta-analysis*, can be used to integrate and organize the results of studies. The number of subjects and the size of the effects reported in each study are combined into an "average" effect. A meta-analysis of personality factors and CHD concluded that the stereotyped "Type A" individual is not necessarily the most likely to suffer from heart disease. People at most risk may be those who experience negative emotions such as depression, anger, or anxiety. Other researchers have criticized this meta-analysis, some using meta-analyses of their own. Even a technique like meta-analysis may not provide final answers.

still be 50–50. Each toss has the same probability, if the coin is fair, no matter how many times you toss it. Each toss is independent of the other.

Let's go back to the normal curve pictured in Figure 20.7. The Stanford-Binet, a widely used IQ test described in Chapter 12, has a mean of 100 and a standard deviation of 15. If you choose one person at random walking through your local mall, what is the probability that the person's IQ is between 100 and 115 (between the mean and one standard deviation above the mean)? We know that, with a normally distributed variable, about 34 percent of the population lies between the mean and one standard deviation above the mean. We could say, then, that the probability of randomly choosing a person (or of choosing a person by chance) with such an IQ is about 0.34 (or 34 chances out of 100). What is the probability of choosing a person who has an IQ above 130 (two standard deviations above the mean)? Now the probability goes down to about 0.02 (2 chances out of 100). This would certainly be a rare event!

Let us say that a new diet has been developed and a researcher wants to test its effectiveness. She takes twenty equally overweight people, puts ten of them on the new diet and a program of exercise for three months, and has the other group follow the program of exercise without the diet. At the end of the three months, she finds that, on the average, the diet group lost 10 pounds more than the nondiet group. Is her diet a success? Is her 10-pound difference a real difference (due to the diet), or is it the result of chance? Researchers face this problem whenever they do research: Are the results strong enough to have confidence in them? This is where probability comes in.

Statistical Significance

The normal curve is one of many distributions used by psychologists to evaluate the results of their studies. For example, Kate wants to know if her classmates watch more TV than the "average American." Since daily TV viewing is probably normally distributed, she can compare her results to the normal distribution, if she knows the population's mean number of TV viewing hours. There is a distribution to use when two groups are compared (as in the diet example), a distribution when three or more groups are studied, and a distribution for correlations. All inferential statistics are associated with a distribution. Therefore, all possible outcomes or results are associated with a probability, just as with the normal curve. When psychologists evaluate the results of their studies, they ask: Could the results be due to chance? What researchers really want to know is whether the results are extreme enough so that they are more likely to be due to the variables being studied.

The problem is that this question cannot be answered with a yes or no. This is why researchers use some guidelines to evaluate probabilities. Many researchers say that if the probability that their results were due to chance is less than 0.05 (5 chances out of 100), then they are confident that the results are not due to chance. Some researchers want to be even more sure, and so they use 0.01 as their level of confidence. When the probability of a result is 0.05 or 0.01 (or whatever level the researcher sets), we say that the result is **statistically significant**. It is important to remember that probability tells us how *likely* it is that an event or outcome is due to chance, but not whether the event is *actually* due to chance.

STATISTICS AND YOU

You may never conduct psychological experiments, but statistics can still be useful to you. A basic knowledge of statistics and research principles can help you to become a better consumer and critical thinker.

Look at the backs of some major fashion magazines. There will be advertisements for products that "guarantee" thicker hair, freedom from wrinkles, and huge weight losses in "just two weeks!" Or check the psychology section of a large bookstore. Shelves of books are devoted to self-help—how to achieve the perfect relationship, how to get out of bad relationships, how to find inner talents, how to raise your children. On TV, a trusted actor, who has become famous playing a doctor, makes commercials praising a particular product and is perceived as an "expert." Are any of the claims made for these products, diets, and methods valid?

An advice columnist asks her readers to write in stating whether they would remarry their current spouse if they had the chance. Over 75 percent of the women who respond say that they would not remarry the same person. Before we conclude that most women are trapped in unhappy marriages, let us ask what other information we need. We do not know how many people read this column, and we do not know what proportion of the readers actually responded to the columnist's request. It is very possible that people who are unhappy in their marriages are more motivated to respond than are those who are happily married, so our distribution of responses is skewed.

Whenever you see the results of a "survey" in the media, always ask yourself: "How many people were surveyed? Who was surveyed?" If the survey reports that 40 percent of respondents agree with a statement, ask yourself: "Does that mean that 60 percent disagreed? Did 60 percent have no opinion?" A product is advertised as being 34 percent more effective. Ask yourself: "More effective than what? Another product? No product?"

Finally, just because an "expert" makes a statement or claim, it does not necessarily mean that the claim is true. If you ask a group of psychologists which method of psychotherapy is most effective, many answers will be given. Each psychologist may strongly defend a particular method while claiming that the others do not work as well. You should always ask yourself: "Were studies done to test the effectiveness of these methods? What data support these claims?"

Statistics are used by researchers to organize, summarize, and evaluate data. Advertisers use statistics to sell products, "experts" use statistics to support their conclusions. You can use your knowledge of statistics to become a better-informed citizen.

? FACT OR FICTION

A statistically significant result always represents an important finding.

Fiction. Many statistical tests are affected by sample size. A small difference between groups may be magnified by a large sample and may result in a statistically significant finding. However, the difference may be so small that it is not a meaningful difference.

Use the following outline as a tool for reviewing this chapter. Copy the outline onto your own paper, leaving spaces between headings to make notes about key concepts.

I. Descriptive Statistics

    A. Distributions of Data

    B. Measures of Central Tendency

    C. Measures of Variability

    D. Correlation Coefficients

II. Inferential Statistics

    A. Probability and Chance

    B. Statistical Significance

III. Statistics and You

CONCEPTS AND VOCABULARY

1. What statistics are used to organize and summarize data? Give two examples of the methods researchers use to make sense of their data.

2. What are histograms and frequency polygons?

3. What is the normal curve? What properties make it important in statistics?

4. What is a skewed distribution? Give an example of when a skewed distribution of scores would be likely to occur.

5. What are the three measures of central tendency? What does each measure?

6. What is the preferred measure of central tendency? What is the best measure of central tendency for a skewed distribution? For the normal distribution?

7. What do measures of variability tell researchers? What are two common measures of variability? Which one is more useful?

8. What does a correlation coefficient measure? What does the size of the correlation tell us? What does the sign (+ or −) indicate?

9. What is the purpose of inferential statistics?

10. What does it mean when the results of a study are labeled "statistically significant?"

CRITICAL THINKING

1. **Analyze.** Explain the following statement: "Correlation does not imply causation." Give an example that supports this statement. Then give another example where a correlation *might* imply causation.

2. **Apply.** How are statistics used within your classroom? Within your school? Give specific examples of the different types of statistics discussed in this chapter.

3. **Analyze.** What kinds of statistics are used in sports? Explain your answer with examples from different sports.

APPLYING KNOWLEDGE

1. Look through newspapers and magazines and cut out or photocopy several graphs. Write a short paper that includes each graph. For each example, state what type of graph it is, what the X axis and Y axis represent, and what information or conclusions you draw from the graphic presentation. Compare your evaluation of the graph to the results presented in the text of the article from which the graph came. Do you think the graph is misleading? Do you have suggestions to improve the presentation of information?

2. Collect weights from twenty women and twenty men. Create a frequency distribution for each group. Since there are likely to be many different weights, group them in 5-pound intervals before counting. For example: 110–114, 115–119, 120–124, 125–129, etc. Graph your data for men and women separately as frequency polygons on the same axis. Compute means, medians, modes, ranges, and standard deviations for women and men separately. How are the two distributions alike? How are they different? What would a frequency polygon look

like if you combined the data for women and men into one sample? Write an essay summarizing your results.

3. Is head size related to intelligence? It was once thought that a large head housed a large brain, and that a large brain meant a person was more intelligent. You can look at the correlation between these two variables by getting head measurements and measures of intelligence from ten to twenty of your acquaintances from school. Head size is easily measured with a tape measure. You will also need a measure of intelligence. Since your subjects are unlikely to know their IQ scores, you might ask them what their Verbal SAT score is. (You might consider the question of whether the SAT measures intelligence!) Some of your subjects might be embarrassed to tell you their score. This is easily solved. Have them measure their own heads. They can then write their measurement on a piece of paper along with their SAT score, fold it up, and place it in a large envelope with all the other observations. This way, you won't know which scores go with each subject. When you have collected your data, draw a scatterplot with head size on one axis and SAT score on the other. What does the plot look like? Is the correlation weak, moderate, or strong? If you are ambitious, find a statistics book that tells you how to calculate a correlation coefficient. You will need a calculator. Does your result confirm the conclusion you drew from the scatterplot?

4. Coin tossing can demonstrate some of the concepts illustrated in this chapter. If you toss four coins at once, there are five possible outcomes: (1) four heads; (2) three heads and one tail; (3) two heads and two tails; (4) one head and three tails; and (5) four tails. Create a table with these possible outcomes. Give coins to four friends. Have them toss the coins once. Note the outcome by drawing a slash next to it on your table. Your friends will need to toss their coins 99 more times. Each time you should note the outcome on your table. Draw a bar graph of the results after 25 tosses, 50 tosses, 75 tosses, and 100 tosses. What you should find in each graph

is that your friends will make few tosses resulting in four heads or four tails, and many tosses of two heads and two tails. You have created what is known as the binomial distribution. You should notice that as the number of tosses increases, your graph begins to look more like a normal curve! What do you think would happen if you could toss coins 1,000 times? 10,000 times? What might you suspect if your results do not come out as expected?

ANALYZING VIEWPOINTS

1. Does smoking cause lung cancer? Some scientists cite animal studies as proving that substances in cigarettes cause cell changes, which, in turn, lead to the development of cancer. Representatives of the tobacco industry state that animal studies cannot be generalized to humans. For humans, then, only correlational data is available, and correlations do not necessarily indicate causes. While there seems to be a correlation between smoking and lung cancer, not everyone who smokes get cancer, and non-smokers can develop lung cancer. Write an essay supporting both viewpoints. Be sure to include what you have learned from the chapter about correlations and inferential statistics. Read recent magazine and newspaper articles for more information about this controversy.

BEYOND THE CLASSROOM

1. For the next two weeks, observe how statistics are used in the media. At times they are used to support a point of view. Sometimes they report the results of surveys or studies, or military operations. Television commercials, newspaper and magazine articles and advertisements, and advice columnists will provide you with data. Write a short paper describing your examples. For each one, indicate whether you feel that enough information has been provided for you to evaluate the validity of any reported claims or conclusions. What other information should have been provided? How might additional information change the reported conclusions?

Glossary

absolute threshold: The lowest level of physical energy that will produce a sensation in half the trials.

accommodation: In Piaget's theory of cognitive development, the adjustment of one's scheme for understanding the world to fit newly observed events and experiences.

achievement test: An instrument used to measure how much an individual has learned in a given subject or area.

adaptation: In sensation, an adjustment of the sensitivity of sensory receptors of the brain in response to prolonged stimulation.

addiction: An altered psychological state in the body that causes physical dependence on a drug.

adjustment: The process of adapting to, as well as actively shaping, one's environment.

affective reaction: A type of psychosis in which an individual is subject to excessive and inappropriate mood states of elation or depression.

ageism: Prejudice against the old.

anal stage: According to Freud, the stage at which children associate erotic pleasure with the elimination process.

androgynous: Combining or confusing traditionally male and female characteristics.

anger: The irate reaction likely to result from frustration.

antisocial personality: A personality disorder characterized by irresponsibility, shallow emotions, and lack of conscience.

anxiety: A vague, generalized apprehension or feeling that one is in danger.

applied science: Discovering ways to use scientific findings to accomplish practical goals.

approach-approach conflict: The situation in which the individual must choose between two attractive alternatives.

approach-avoidance conflict: The situation in which the individual wants to do something but fears it at the same time.

aptitude test: An instrument used to estimate the probability that a person will be successful in learning a specific new skill or skills.

archetype: According to Jung, an inherited idea, based on the experiences of one's ancestors, that shapes one's perception of the world.

assimilation: In Piaget's theory of cognitive development, the process of fitting objects and experiences into one's scheme for understanding the environment.

asynchrony: The condition during the period of adolescence in which the growth or maturation of bodily parts is uneven.

attitudes: Predispositions to act, think, and feel in particular ways toward particular things.

attribution theory: A theory that tries to understand how we interpret people's behavior.

audience: In the communication process, the person or persons receiving a message.

auditory nerve: The nerve that carries impulses from

the inner ear to the brain, resulting in the sensation of sound.

authoritarian families: Families in which parents are the "bosses."

authoritarian personality: A personality type characterized by rigid thinking; denial and projection of sexual and aggressive drives onto others; respect for and submission to authority; prejudice regarding people unlike himself or herself.

autism: A childhood psychosis characterized by an inability to relate to others and lack of response to attempts at communication.

autonomic nervous system: Part of the peripheral nervous system that controls internal biological functions such as heart rate and digestion.

aversive control: The process of influencing behavior by means of aversive, or unpleasant, stimuli.

avoidance-avoidance conflict: The situation in which the individual must choose between two unattractive alternatives.

avoidance conditioning: The training of an organism to remove or withdraw from an unpleasant stimulus before it starts.

basic science: The pursuit of knowledge about natural phenomena for its own sake.

behavior modification: The systematic application of learning principles to change people's actions and feelings.

behavior therapy: A form of therapy aimed at changing undesirable behavior through conditioning techniques.

behaviorism: The school of psychology that holds that the proper subject matter of psychology is objectively observable behavior—and nothing else.

binocular fusion: The process of combining the images received from the two eyes into a single, fused image.

biofeedback: The process of learning to control bodily states with the help of machines that provide information about physiological processes.

body language: Nonverbal communication through gestures, positions, and movements of the body.

boomerang effect: A change in attitude or behavior opposite to the one desired by the persuader.

brainwashing: The most extreme form of attitude change, accomplished through peer pressure, physical suffering, threats, rewards for compliance, manipulation of guilt, intensive indoctrination, and other psychological means.

Cannon-Bard theory: A theory introduced by psychologists Cannon and Bard that attributed emotion to the simultaneous activity of the brain and "gut" reactions.

career: A vocation in which a person works at least a few years.

case study: An intensive investigation of an individual or group, usually focusing on a single psychological phenomenon.

central nervous system (CNS):   The brain and spinal cord.

central processing: The second stage of information processing—storing (in memory) and sorting (by thought) information in the brain.

central tendency: A number that describes something about the "average" score of a distribution.

cerebellum: A lower portion of the brain which controls posture and balance and regulates the details of motor commands from the cerebral cortex.

cerebral cortex: The gray mass surrounding the subcortex, which controls most of the higher brain functions, such as reading and problem solving.

cerebrum: The inner part of the brain, in front of and above the cerebellum.

channel: In the communication process, the means by which a message is transmitted from the source to the audience.

charisma: A leader's strong emotional appeal that arouses enthusiasm and loyalty.

chunking: The process of grouping pieces of information for easier handling.

classical conditioning: A learning procedure in which a stimulus that normally elicits a given response is repeatedly preceded by a neutral stimulus (one that usually does not elicit the response). Eventually, the neutral stimulus will evoke a similar response when presented by itself.

client-centered therapy: A form of therapy aimed at helping clients recognize their own strengths and gain confidence so that they can be true to their own standards and ideas about how to live effectively.

closed awareness: The situation in which the medical staff and the family are aware of the patient's terminal condition but the patient is not.

cognitive appraisal: The interpretation of an event that helps to determine its stress impact.

cognitive dissonance: The uncomfortable feeling that arises when a person experiences contradictory or conflicting thoughts, attitudes, beliefs, or feelings.

cognitive preparation: The coping strategy in which the person mentally rehearses possible outcomes.

collective unconscious: According to Jung, that part of the mind that contains inherited instincts, urges, and memories common to all people.

color blindness: Complete or partial inability to distinguish colors, resulting from malfunction in the cones.

complementarity: The attraction that often develops between opposite types of people because of the ability of one to supply what the other lacks.

compliance: A change of behavior in order to avoid discomfort or rejection and gain approval; a superficial form of attitude change.

compulsion: The impulsive and uncontrollable repetition of an irrational action.

concept: A label for a class of objects or events that share common attributes.

conditioned reinforcer: A stimulus that increases the frequency of a response because it has become a signal for a stimulus which is reinforcing.

conditioned response (CR):   In classical conditioning, the learned response to a conditioned stimulus.

conditioned stimulus (CS):   In classical conditioning, a once-neutral stimulus that has come to elicit a given response after a period of training in which it has been paired with an unconditioned stimulus (UCS).

conditions of worth: Rogers's term for the conditions a person must meet in order to regard himself or herself positively.

cones: Receptor cells in the retina sensitive to color. Because they require more light than rods to function, they are most useful in daytime vision.

confabulation: The act of filling in memory with statements that make sense but that are, in fact, untrue.

conflict-habituated marriage: A marriage in which the partners spend most of their time fighting.

conflict situations: The situation in which a person must choose between two or more options that tend to result from conflicting motives.

conformity: Compliance to group standards.

consciousness: A state of awareness, including a person's feelings, sensations, ideas, and perceptions.

conservation: The principle that a given quantity does not change when its appearance is changed. The discovery of this principle between the ages of five and seven is important to the intellectual development of the child.

constancy: The tendency to perceive certain objects in the same way, regardless of changing angle, distance, or lighting.

contingencies of reinforcement: Skinner's term for the occurrence of a reward or punishment following a particular behavior.

contingency management: A form of behavior therapy in which undesirable behavior is not rewarded, while desirable behavior is reinforced.

control group: In an experiment, a group of subjects that is treated in the same way as the experimental group, except that the experimental treatment is not applied.

conversion reaction: A form of hysteria characterized by the conversion of emotional difficulties into a loss of a specific body function.

corpus callosum: A band of nerves that connects the two hemispheres of the cortex and carries messages back and forth between them.

correlation: The degree of relatedness between two sets of data.

correlation coefficient: A statistic that describes the direction and strength of the relationship between two sets of observations.

creativity: The capacity to use information and/or abilities in such a way that the results are new, original, and meaningful.

critical period: A specific time in development when certain skills or abilities are most easily learned.

cross-cultural studies: Acquiring comparable data from two or more cultures for the purpose of studying cultural similarities and differences.

decibel: A measure of the physical intensity of sound, which is lawfully related to the sensation of loudness.

decremental model of aging: This holds that progressive physical and mental decline is inevitable with age.

defense mechanisms: According to Freud, certain specific means by which the ego unconsciously protects itself against unpleasant impulses or circumstances.

delusion: A false belief that a person maintains in the face of contrary evidence.

democratic families: Families in which adolescents participate in decisions affecting their lives.

denial: A coping mechanism in which a person decides that the event is not really a stressor.

dependent variable: In an experiment, the factor that is not controlled by the experimenters but changes as a result of changes in the independent variable.

depressant: A drug that reduces the activity of the central nervous system.

depression: A pattern of sadness, anxiety, fatigue, insomnia, underactivity, and reduced ability to function and to work with others.

depressive reaction: A psychotic reaction in which a person is overcome by feelings of failure, sinfulness, worthlessness, and despair.

descriptive statistics: The listing and summarizing of data in a practical, efficient way, such as graphs and averages.

developmental friendship: The type of friendship in which the partners force one another to re-examine their basic assumptions and perhaps adopt new ideas and beliefs.

developmental psychology: The study of changes that occur as individuals mature.

devitalized marriage: A marriage, originally based on love, in which the partners no longer attempt or expect passion or bliss, but get along well enough to remain together.

difference threshold: The smallest change in a physical stimulus that produces a change in sensation in half the trials.

diffusion of responsibility: The tendency of the presence of others to lessen an individual's feelings of responsibility for his or her actions or failure to act.

directed thinking: Systematic, logical, goal-directed thought.

discrimination: (1) The ability to respond differently to similar but distinct stimuli. (2) The unequal treatment of individuals on the basis of their race, ethnic group, class, sex, or membership in another category, rather than on the basis of individual characteristics.

displacement: The redirection of desires, feelings, or impulses from their proper object to a substitute.

dissociative reaction: A form of hysteria in which a person experiences a loss of memory or identity, or exhibits two or more identities.

distress: The type of stress that stems from acute anxiety or pressure.

double approach-avoidance conflict: The situation in which the individual must choose between two or more alternatives, each of which has attractive and unattractive aspects.

double bind: A situation in which a person receives conflicting demands, so that no matter what he or she does, it is wrong.

double-blind technique: A research technique in which neither the subjects nor the experimenter know which subjects have been exposed to the experimental treatment.

drive reduction theory: A theory formulated by psychologist Clark Hull that states that physiological needs drive an organism to act in random or habitual ways until its needs are satisfied.

DSM-II: The second version of the American Psychiatric Association's *Diagnostic and Statistical Manual of Mental Disorders*. Published in 1968, its classification scheme serves as the basis of organization for this chapter.

DSM-III: The third version of the American Psychiatric Association's *Diagnostic and Statistical Manual of Mental Disorders*. This new classification scheme for mental illness is far more specific than its predecessor.

effectors: The cells that work the muscles, internal glands, and organs.

ego: According to Freud, the part of the personality that is in touch with reality. The ego strives to meet the demands of the id and the superego in socially acceptable ways.

ego-support value: The ability of a person to provide another person with sympathy, encouragement, and approval.

eidetic memory: The ability to remember with great accuracy visual information on the basis of short-term exposure; also called "photographic memory."

electrode: A type of wire used by scientists to detect the minute electrical changes that occur when neurons fire.

electroencephalograph (EEG):   A machine used to record the electrical activity of large portions of the brain.

encounter groups: A type of therapy for people who function adequately in everyday life but who feel unhappy, dissatisfied, or stagnant; aimed at providing experiences that will help people increase their sensitivity, openness, and honesty.

endocrine system: A chemical communication system, using hormones, by which messages are sent through the bloodstream to particular organs of the body.

escape conditioning: The training of an organism to remove or terminate an unpleasant stimulus.

ethology: The study of animal behavior in its natural environment.

eustress: Positive stress, which results from the strivings and challenges that are the spice of life.

experimental group: The group of subjects to which an experimental treatment is applied.

experimental treatment: The manipulation of an independent variable in an experiment designed to observe its effects.

extinction: The gradual disappearance of a conditioned response because the reinforcement is withheld or because the conditioned stimulus is repeatedly presented without the unconditioned stimulus.

extrasensory perception (ESP):   An ability to gain information by some means other than the ordinary senses (such as taste, hearing, vision, and so on).

extrovert: An outgoing, active person who directs his or her energies and interests toward other people and things.

factor analysis: A complex statistical technique used to identify the underlying reasons variables are correlated.

family therapy: A form of therapy aimed at understanding and improving relationships that have led one or more members in a family to experience emotional suffering.

fear: The usual reaction when a stressor involves real danger.

feature extraction: The identification and analysis of specific features of a sensory input.

feedback: Information received after an action as to its effectiveness or correctness.

figure-ground: The division of the visual field into two distinct parts, one being the object or objects, the other the background or space between objects.

fixed action patterns: Patterns of behavior that are inflexible. Such responses are common to many animal species, but not to humans.

fixed-interval schedule: A schedule of reinforcement in which a specific amount of time must elapse before a response will elicit reinforcement.

fixed-ratio schedule: A schedule of reinforcement in which a specific number of correct responses is required before reinforcement can be obtained.

free association: A method used by psychoanalysts to examine the unconscious. The patient is instructed to say whatever comes into his or her mind.

frequency distribution: An arrangement of data that indicates how often a particular score or observation occurs.

frequency polygon: A line graph that indicates how often a particular score or observation occurs.

frontal lobes: The lobes located in the front of the brain, which control intellect and personality.

frustration: The feeling of bafflement or disappointment that results when a person's progress toward a goal is blocked.

fugue: A rare dissociative reaction in which complete or partial amnesia is combined with a move to a new environment.

fully functioning person: Rogers's term for an individual whose organism and self coincide, allowing him or her to be open to experience, to possess unconditional positive regard, and to have harmonious relations with others.

fundamental needs: In Maslow's hierarchy-of-needs theory, these are the biological drives that must be satisfied in order to maintain life.

generalization: Responding similarly to a range of similar stimuli.

generativity: According to Erikson, the desire, in middle age, to use one's accumulated wisdom to guide future generations.

genital stage: According to Freud, the stage during which an individual's sexual satisfaction depends as much on giving pleasure as on receiving it.

Gestalt: In perception, the experience that comes from organizing bits and pieces of information into meaningful wholes.

gestalt therapy: A form of therapy that emphasizes the relationship between the patient and therapist in the here and now. The aim is to encourage the person to recognize all sides of his or her personality.

grasping reflex: An infant's clinging response to a touch on the palm of his or her hand.

group: An aggregate of people characterized by shared goals and a degree of interdependence.

group therapy: A form of therapy in which patients work together with the aid of a group leader to resolve interpersonal problems.

hallucination: A sensation or perception that has no direct external cause.

hallucinogens: Drugs that often produce hallucinations.

histogram: A graph similar to a bar graph that indicates how often a particular score or observation occurs.

homeostasis: The tendency of all organisms to correct imbalances and deviations from their normal state.

hormones: Chemical substances that carry messages through the body in the blood.

human potential movement: An approach to psychotherapy that stresses the actualization of one's unique potentials through personal responsibility, freedom of choice, and authentic relationships.

humanistic psychology: An approach to psychology that stresses the uniqueness of the individual; focuses on the value, dignity, and worth of each person; and holds that healthy living is the result of realizing one's full potential.

hypertension: Unhealthy levels of high blood pressure.

hypnosis: An altered state of consciousness resulting from a narrowed focus of attention and characterized by heightened suggestibility.

hypochondriasis: A preoccupation with imaginary ailments, on which a person blames other problems.

hypothalamus: A small area deep inside the brain that regulates the autonomic nervous system and other body functions.

hypothesis: An educated guess about the relationship between two variables.

id: According to Freud, that part of the unconscious personality that contains our needs, drives, and instincts as well as repressed material. The material in the id strives for immediate satisfaction.

identification: (1) The process by which a child adopts the values and principles of the same-sex parent. (2) The process of seeing oneself as similar to another person or group, and accepting the attitudes of another person or group as one's own.

identity crisis: According to Erikson, a time of storm and stress during which adolescents worry intensely about who they are.

ideology: The set of principles, attitudes, and defined objectives for which a group stands.

illusions: Perceptions that misrepresent physical stimuli.

image: A rough representation of specific events or objects (the most primitive unit of thought).

implicit personality theory: A set of assumptions each person has about how people behave and what personality traits or characteristics go together.

imprinting: A social learning capacity in some species by which attachments are formed to other organisms or to objects very early in life.

independent variable: In an experiment, the factor that is deliberately manipulated by the experimenters to test its effect on another factor.

inferential statistics: Statistical methods used to determine whether research data support a hypothesis or whether results were due to chance.

inferiority complex: According to Adler, a pattern of avoiding feelings of inadequacy and insignificance rather than trying to overcome their source.

innate behavior: Behavior that is part of one's biological inheritance.

inoculation effect: A method of developing resistance to persuasion by exposing a person to arguments that challenge his or her beliefs so that he or she can practice defending them.

input: The first stage of information processing—receiving information through the senses.

insight: The sudden realization of the solution to a problem.

instinct: A behavior pattern that is inborn rather than learned.

intellectualization: A coping mechanism in which the person watches the situation from an emotionally detached standpoint.

intelligence quotient (IQ):   Originally, a measure of a person's mental development obtained by dividing his or her mental age (the score achieved on a standardized intelligence test) by his or her chronological age and multiplying by 100; now, any standardized measure of intelligence based on a scale in which 100 is defined to be average.

interest test: An instrument designed to measure a person's preferences, attitudes, and interests in certain activities.

internalization: The process of incorporating the values, ideas, and standards of others as a part of oneself.

introspection: A method of self-observation in which subjects report on their thoughts and feelings.

introvert: A reserved, unsociable person who is preoccupied with his or her inner thoughts and feelings.

James-Lange theory: A theory formulated by psychologists James and Lange that suggests that emotions are the perception of bodily changes.

kinesthesis: The sense of movement and body position, acquired through receptors located in and near the muscles, tendons, and joints.

laissez-faire families: Families in which children have the final say; permissive families.

latency stage: According to Freud, the stage at which sexual desires are pushed into the background and the child becomes involved in exploring the world and learning new skills.

lateral hypothalamus (LH):   The part of the hypothalamus that produces hunger signals.

learned helplessness: The condition in which the person suffers from a situation so severely or so often that he or she comes to believe that it is uncontrollable and that any effort to cope will fail.

learning: A lasting change in behavior that results from experience.

lens: A flexible, transparent structure in the eye that, by changing its shape, focuses light on the retina.

lobes: The different regions into which the cerebral cortex is divided.

long-term memory: Information storage that has unlimited capacity and lasts indefinitely.

longitudinal studies: Repeatedly gathering data on the same group of subjects over a period of time for the purpose of studying consistencies and change.

LSD: An extremely potent psychedelic drug that produces hallucinations and distortions of perception and thought.

manic reaction: A psychotic reaction characterized by extreme elation, agitation, confusion, disorientation, and incoherence.

marijuana: The dried leaves and flowers of Indian hemp *(Cannabis sativa)* that produces an altered state of consciousness when smoked or ingested.

maturation: The internally programmed growth of a child.

mean: The arithmetic average.

median: The score that divides a distribution of observations in half; the middle score.

meditation: Focusing of attention on an image, thought, bodily process, or external object with the goal of clearing one's mind and producing an "inner peace."

memory: The complex mental function of storage and retrieval of what has been learned or experienced.

menarche: The first menstrual period.

menopause: The biological event by which a woman's production of sex hormones is sharply reduced.

message: In the communication process, the actual content transmitted from the source to the audience.

mnemonic devices: Methods for remembering items by relating them to information already held in the brain.

mode: The most frequent score in a distribution of observations.

motion parallax: The apparent movement of stationary objects relative to one another that occurs when the observer changes position. Near objects seem to move greater distances than far objects.

motivation: Inducement to direct one's energies toward achieving a goal that has acquired meaning.

motor cortex: The portion of the brain located in the front of the somatosensory cortex, which controls body movement.

multiple personality: A rare condition in which one person shows two or more separate consciousnesses with distinct personalities.

mutual pretense awareness: The situation in which both the medical staff and the patient pretend they do not know that the disease is terminal.

naturalistic observation: Studying phenomena as they occur in natural surroundings, without interfering.

negative correlation: A correlation indicating that a high value for one variable corresponds to a low value for the other variable, and vice versa.

negative reinforcement: Increasing the strength of a given response by removing or preventing a painful stimulus when the response occurs.

nerve fibers: The slender threadlike pieces of nerve cells through which messages are sent to and from the brain.

neurons: The long, thin cells that constitute the structural and functional unit of nerve tissue, along which messages travel to and from the brain.

neurosis: A psychological disturbance characterized by prolonged high levels of anxiety. Neurotics often suffer from unrealistic self-images and have difficulty forming satisfying, stable relationships.

neurotransmitters: The chemicals released by neurons which determine the rate at which other neurons fire.

neutral stimulus: A stimulus that does not initially elicit a response.

nondirected thinking: The free flow of images and ideas, occurring with no particular goal.

nonverbal communication: The process of communicating through the use of space, body language, and facial expression.

normal curve: A symmetrical, bell-shaped curve with known mathematical properties.

norms: (1) Shared standards of behavior accepted by and expected from group members. (2) Standards of comparison for test results developed by giving the test to large, well-defined groups of people.

obedience: A change in attitude or behavior brought about by social pressure to comply with people perceived to be authorities.

object permanence: A child's realization, developed between the ages of one and two, that an object exists even when he or she cannot see or touch it.

objective personality tests: Forced-choice tests (in which a person must select one of several answers) designed to study personal characteristics.

obsession: An uncontrollable pattern of thoughts.

Oedipal conflict: According to Freud, a boy's wish to possess his mother sexually, coupled with hostility toward his father. Correspondingly, girls desire their fathers sexually and feel hostile toward their mothers. In order to reduce his or her fear of punishment from the same-sex parent, the child begins to identify with the parent of the same sex.

olfactory nerve: The nerve that carries smell impulses from the nose to the brain.

open awareness: The situation in which the medical staff and patient openly admit to the knowledge of the patient's terminal disease.

operant conditioning: A form of conditioning in which a certain action is reinforced or punished, resulting in corresponding increases or decreases in the likelihood that similar actions will occur again.

optic nerve: The nerve that carries impulses from the retina to the brain.

oral stage: According to Freud, the stage at which infants associate erotic pleasure with the mouth.

organism: Rogers's term for the whole person, including all of his or her feelings, thoughts, and urges as well as body.

output: The final stage of information processing— acting on the basis of information.

parapsychology: The systematic study of ESP and other unusual phenomena.

parasympathetic nervous system: The system that works to conserve energy and enhance the body's ability to recuperate after strenuous activity.

passive-congenial marriage: A marriage based on convenience, in which the partners live together and share responsibilities in order to make it easier to pursue individual interests.

percentile system: A system for ranking test scores that indicates the percentage of scores lower and higher than a given score.

perception: The organization of sensory information into meaningful experiences.

perceptual inference: The process of assuming, from past experience, that certain objects remain the same and will behave as they have in the past.

peripheral nervous system (PNS): A network of nerves branching out from the spinal cord that conducts information from the bodily organs to the central nervous system and takes information back to the organs.

permissive families: Families in which children have the final say; laissez-faire families.

personal space: The space between two people that communicates their feelings about one another and defines the relationship.

personality: The sum total of physical, mental, emotional, and social characteristics that distinguish one person from another.

personality disorder: A psychological disturbance characterized by lifelong maladaptive patterns that are relatively free of anxiety and other emotional symptoms.

persuasion: The direct attempt to influence attitudes through the communication process.

phallic stage: According to Freud, the stage at which children associate sexual pleasure with their genitals.

phobia: A form of severe anxiety in which a person focuses on a particular object or situation.

physical proximity: The physical nearness of one person to another person.

pitch: The sensation associated with a sound's frequency; the "highness" or "lowness" of a sound.

pituitary gland: The center of control of the endocrine system which secretes a large number of hormones.

placebo effect: The influence that a patient's hopes and expectations have on his or her improvement during therapy.

polygraph: A machine used to measure physiological changes, particularly in lie detection.

population: The total group of subjects from which a sample is drawn.

positive correlation: A correlation indicating that a high value for one variable corresponds to a high value for the other variable.

positive regard: Rogers's term for viewing oneself in a positive light, because of positive feedback received from interaction with others.

posthypnotic suggestion: A suggestion made during a hypnotic trance that influences the subject's behavior after the trance is ended.

prejudice: Preconceived attitudes toward a person or group that have been formed without sufficient evidence and are not easily changed.

primary reinforcers: Natural rewards.

proactive interference: The hampering of recall of newly learned material by the recall of previously learned material.

progressive relaxation: Lying down comfortably and tensing and relaxing each major muscle group in turn.

projection: Ascribing one's own undesirable attitudes, feelings, or thoughts to others.

projective personality tests: Unstructured tests of personality in which a person is asked to respond freely, giving his or her own interpretation of various ambiguous stimuli.

psychiatry: A medical specialty that involves the study, diagnosis, and treatment of mental disorders.

psychoanalysis: A form of therapy aimed at making patients aware of their unconscious motives so that they can gain control over their behavior and free themselves of self-defeating patterns.

psychological dependence: Use of a drug to such an extent that a person feels nervous and anxious without it.

psychological needs: In Maslow's hierarchy-of-needs theory, these include the need to belong and to give and receive love, and the need to acquire esteem through competence and achievement. If these needs are frustrated, it will be difficult for the person to strive for fulfillment of the next level in the hierarchy—*self-actualization needs.*

psychology: The study of mental processes and the behavior of organisms.

psychophysics: The study of the relationships between sensory experiences and the physical stimuli that cause them.

psychosis: A psychological disturbance characterized by a breakdown in the ability to accurately perceive reality. Psychotics are unable to relate to other people and to function in everyday life.

psychosurgery: Brain surgery aimed at changing a person's thoughts or actions.

psychotherapy: A general term for treatment used by social workers, psychologists, and psychiatrists to help troubled individuals overcome their problems. The goal of psychotherapy is to break the behavior patterns that lead to unhappiness.

puberty: Sexual maturation; it is the biological event that marks the end of childhood.

punishers: Negative consequences that decrease the likelihood of a behavior occurring again.

pupil: The opening in the iris that regulates the amount of light entering the eye.

random sample: A sample that gives an equal chance of being represented to every piece of data within the scope of the research.

range: A measure of variability; the lowest score in a distribution subtracted from the highest score.

rational-emotive therapy: A form of therapy aimed at changing unrealistic assumptions about oneself and other people. It is believed that once a person understands that he or she has been acting on false beliefs, self-defeating thoughts and behaviors will be avoided.

rationalization: A process whereby an individual seeks to explain an often unpleasant emotion or behavior in a way that will preserve his or her self-esteem.

reaction formation: Replacing an unacceptable feeling or urge with its opposite.

recall: The type of memory retrieval in which a person reconstructs previously learned material.

receptors: Cells whose function it is to gather information and send messages to the brain.

recognition: The type of memory retrieval in which a person is required to identify an object, idea, or situation as one he or she has or has not experienced before.

recombination: Mentally rearranging the elements of a problem in order to arrive at a novel solution.

referred pain: The sensation of pain in an area away from the actual source; most commonly experienced with internal pain.

regression: A return to an earlier stage of development or pattern of behavior in a threatening or stressful situation.

reinforcement: Immediately following a particular response with a reward in order to strengthen that response.

reliability: The ability of a test to give the same results under a variety of different circumstances.

REM sleep: The period of sleep during which the eyes dart back and forth (rapid eye movement) and dreaming usually occurs.

replication: Repetition of an experiment and achievement of the same results.

representational thought: The intellectual ability of a child to picture something in his or her mind.

repression: The exclusion from conscious awareness of a painful, unpleasant, or undesirable memory.

resistance: The reluctance of a patient to reveal painful feelings and to examine long-standing behavior patterns.

response chains: Learned responses that follow one another in sequence, each response producing the signal for the next.

resynthesis: The process of combining old ideas with new ones and reorganizing feelings in order to renew one's identity.

reticular activating system: The system in the brain that screens incoming messages, blocking out some signals and letting others pass.

retina: The innermost coating of the back of the eye, containing the light-sensitive receptor cells.

retinal disparity: The differences between the images on the two retinas.

retrieval: The process of obtaining information that has been stored in memory.

retroactive interference: The hampering of recall of learned material by the recall of other material learned more recently.

rods: Receptor cells in the retina that are sensitive to light, but not to color. Rods are particularly useful in night vision.

role taking: An important aspect of children's play that involves assuming adult roles, thus enabling the child to experience different points of view firsthand.

rooting reflex: An infant's response toward the source of touching that occurs anywhere around his or her mouth.

rule: A statement of the relationship between two or more concepts (the most complex unit of thought).

sample: The small portion of data, out of the total amount available, that a researcher collects.

scapegoat: A person (or group of people) who becomes the target of another person's displaced anger or aggression.

schizophrenia: A group of psychoses characterized by confused and disconnected thoughts, emotions, and perceptions.

selective attention: Focusing one's awareness on a limited segment of the total amount of sensory input one is receiving.

self: Rogers's term for one's experience or image of oneself, developed through interaction with others.

self-actualization: The humanist term for realizing one's unique potential.

self-actualization needs: The top of Maslow's hierarchy-of-needs. These include the pursuit of knowledge and beauty, or whatever else is required for the realization of one's unique potential. Before these needs can be satisfied, people must first meet their *fundamental* and *psychological needs*.

self-fulfilling prophecy: A belief, prediction, or expectation that operates to bring about its own fulfillment.

self-justification: The need to rationalize one's attitude and behavior.

sensation: The result of converting physical stimulation of the sense organs into sensory experience.

sensory storage: The momentary storage of sensory information at the level of the sensory receptors.

separation anxiety: A phase many children experience after twelve months, characterized by fear and anxiety at any prolonged absence of the mother.

set: A habitual strategy or pattern of problem solving.

sex identity: One's biological inheritance; it includes genetic traits and may include some sex-linked behaviors.

sex role: Defined partly by genetic makeup, but mainly by the society and culture in which the individual lives, it is a description of how a person with a given sex identity is supposed to behave.

shaping: A technique of operant conditioning in which the desired behavior is "molded" by first rewarding any act similar to that behavior and then requiring closer and closer approximations to the desired behavior before giving the reward.

short-term memory: Memory that is limited in capacity to about seven items and in duration to about twenty seconds.

signal-detection theory: The study of mathematical relationships between motivation, sensitivity, and sensation.

signals: In operant conditioning, behavioral cues (or stimuli) that are associated with reward or punishment.

situational test: A simulation of a real situation designed to measure a person's performance under such circumstances.

skewed distribution: A distribution of scores where most observations pile up at one end rather than in the middle.

sleeper effect: The delayed impact on attitude change of a persuasive communication.

social functions: In groups, those functions directed toward satisfying the emotional needs of members.

social leader: The leader within a group who promotes group cohesion and commands group loyalty.

social learning theory: Bandura's view of human development, emphasizing interaction.

social rule: Any agreement among members of society about how people should act in particular situations; also called a *norm*.

social support: Information that leads someone to believe that he or she is cared for, loved, respected, and part of a network of communication and mutual obligation.

socialization: The process of learning the rules of behavior of the culture within which an individual is born and will live.

sociobiology: The study of the biological basis of social behavior.

sociogram: A diagram representing relationships within a group.

somatic nervous system: The half of the peripheral nervous system that controls voluntary movement of skeletal muscles.

somatoform disorder: A mental disorder marked by physical symptoms for which there is no apparent physical cause.

somatosensory cortex: An area of the brain, within the cerebral cortex, that receives information from the skin and muscles.

source: In the communication process, the person or group from which a message originates.

species-specific behavior: Behavior that is characteristic of a particular animal species.

spinal cord: The bundle of nerves that run down the length of the back and transmit most messages back and forth between the body and the brain.

stagnation: According to Erikson, a discontinuation of development and a desire to recapture the past, characteristic of some middle-aged people.

standard deviation: A measure of variability that describes an average distance of every score from the mean of the scores.

statistical significance: The degree to which a research study's result will not occur by chance, and, therefore, can be assumed to be due to another factor.

statistics: The branch of mathematics concerned with summarizing and making meaningful inferences from collections of data.

stereopsis: The use by the visual system of retinal disparity to give depth information—providing a three-dimensional appearance to the world.

stereotype: A set of assumptions about people in a given category based on half-truths and nontruths.

stimulation value: The ability of a person or subject to interest or to expose you to new ideas and experiences.

stratified sample: A sample that includes representatives of subgroups or variations of the population being studied.

stress: A person's perception of his or her inability to cope with a certain tense event or situation.

stress reaction: The body's response to a stressor.

stressor: A stress-producing event or situation.

subcortex: The part of the brain where all messages are first received and that, together with the spinal cord, controls and coordinates vital functions and reflex actions. It is sometimes called the "old brain."

sublimation: The process of redirecting sexual impulses into learning tasks that begins at about the age of five.

subliminal advertising: The unsuccessful attempt to influence people with messages that are below normal thresholds of detection.

superego: According to Freud, the process of the personality that inhibits the socially undesirable impulses of the id. The superego may cause excessive guilt if it is overly harsh.

survey: A relatively large sampling of data, obtained through interviews and questionnaires.

suspected awareness: The situation in which some patients begin to suspect that their illness is terminal and endeavor to find out from the medical staff or from their families whether their suspicions are true.

symbol: An abstract unit of thought that represents an object, event, or quality.

sympathetic nervous system: The system that prepares the body for dealing with emergencies or strenuous activities.

synapses: The gaps that occur between individual nerve cells.

systematic desensitization: A technique used by behavior therapists to help a patient overcome irrational fears and anxieties. The goal is to teach the person to relax so that he or she will not feel anxious in the presence of feared objects.

task functions: In groups, those functions directed toward getting a job done.

task leader: The leader within a group who takes over when the group must accomplish something.

telegraphic speech: The kind of speech used by young children. Words are left out, but the meaning is still clear.

thalamus: The portion of the brain that sorts incoming impulses and directs them to various parts of the brain. It also relays messages from one part of the brain to another.

thanatology: The study of death and dying.

thyroid gland: The gland in the endocrine system that produces several hormones, including thyroxin.

token economy: A form of conditioning in which desirable behavior is reinforced with tokens, which can be accumulated and exchanged for various rewards.

tolerance: Physical adaptation to a drug, so that a person needs an increased dosage in order to produce the original effect.

total marriage: A marriage in which both partners are deeply involved in each other's careers and hobbies, spend most of their time together, and seem to live for each other.

trait: A tendency to react to a situation in a way that remains stable over time.

transactional analysis: A form of therapy aimed at helping clients become more flexible by discovering the scripts they play and replay in their lives.

transfer: The effects of past learning on the ability to learn new tasks.

transference: The process, experienced by the patient, of feeling toward an analyst or therapist the way he or she feels toward some other important figure in his or her life.

unconditional positive regard: In client-centered therapy, the atmosphere of emotional support provided by the therapist. The therapist shows the client he or she accepts anything said and does not become embarrassed or angry.

unconditioned response (UCR):   In classical conditioning, an organism's automatic (or natural) reaction to a stimulus.

unconditioned stimulus (UCS):   A stimulus that elicits a certain response without previous training.

unconscious: According to Freud, the part of the mind that contains material we are unaware of, but that strongly influences conscious processes and behaviors.

utility value: The ability of a person or subject to help another achieve his or her goals.

validity: The ability of a test to measure what it is intended to measure.

variable: In an experimental situation, any factor that is capable of change.

variable-interval schedule: A schedule of reinforcement in which varying amounts of time must elapse before a response will obtain reinforcement.

variable-ratio schedule: A schedule of reinforcement in which a variable number of responses are required before reinforcement can be obtained.

ventromedial hypothalamus (VMH):   The part of the hypothalamus that produces feelings of fullness as opposed to hunger, and causes one to stop eating.

vestibular system: Three semicircular canals located in the inner ear and connected to the brain by the vestibular nerve. They regulate the sense of balance.

vital marriage: A marriage in which both partners have a strong sense of individual identity and participate in separate activities.

Weber's law: The principle that the larger or stronger a stimulus, the larger the change required for an observer to notice a difference.

withdrawal: The symptoms that occur after a person discontinues the use of a drug to which he or she had become addicted.

Bibliography

AARONSON, BERNARD, AND OSMOND, H. *Psychedelics: The Uses and Implications of Hallucinogenic Drugs.* Garden City, N.Y.: Doubleday, 1970.

ABRAMSON, LYN Y., SELIGMAN, MARTIN E. P., AND TEASDALE, JOHN D. "Learned Helplessness in Humans: Critique and Reformulation." *Journal of Abnormal Psychology,* 87 (1978): 49–74.

ABSE, D. W. *Hysteria and Related Mental Disorders.* Baltimore: Williams & Wilkins, 1966.

ADAMS, JACK A. *Human Memory.* New York: McGraw-Hill, 1967.

ADLER, ALFRED. *What Life Should Mean to You.* New York: Putnam, 1959 (paper).

ADORNO, T. W., ET AL. *The Authoritarian Personality.* New York: Norton, 1969 (paper).

AHLSKOG, J. ERIC, AND HOEBEL, BARTLEY G. "Overeating and Obesity from Damage to a Noradrenergic System in the Brain." *Science,* 182 (1973): 166–169.

AHRENS, R. "Beitrag zur Entwicklung des Physiognomie- und Mimikerkennens." *Z. exp. angew. Psychol.,* 2 (1954): 412–454.

ALLPORT, GORDON. *The Nature of Prejudice.* Garden City, N.Y.: Doubleday, 1954 (paper).

———. *Pattern and Growth in Personality.* New York: Holt, Rinehart and Winston, 1961.

———(ED). *Letters from Jenny.* New York: Harcourt, Brace & World, 1965.

ALVAREZ, A. *The Savage God: A Study of Suicide.* New York: Random House, 1970.

AMERICAN LAW INSTITUTE. *Model Penal Code: Proposed Official Draft.* Philadelphia: American Law Institute, 1962.

AMERICAN PSYCHIATRIC ASSOCIATION. *Diagnostic and Statistical Manual of Mental Disorders.* 2nd ed. Washington, D.C.: American Psychiatric Association, 1968.

AMES, R. "Physical Maturing Among Boys as Related to Adult Social Behavior: A Longitudinal Study." *California Journal of Educational Research,* 8 (1957): 69–75.

ANASTASI, ANNE. *Psychological Testing.* 3rd ed. New York: Macmillan, 1968.

ANDERSON, A. "How the Mind Heals." *Psychology Today,* 16 (December 1982): 51–56.

ANGOFF, W. H., AND DYER, H.S. "The Admissions Testing Program." In *The College Boards Admissions Testing Program,* ed. by W. H. Angoff. New York: College Entrance Examination Board, 1971, pp. 1–13.

ANTHONY, J. "The Reactions of Adults to Adolescents and Their Behavior." In *Adolescence: Psychological Perspectives,* ed. by G. Caplan and S. Lebovici. New York: Basic Books, 1969.

ARIETI, SILVANO (ED.) *American Handbook of Psychology.* 3 vols. New York: Basic Books, 1959.

ARKOFF, ABE. *Adjustment and Mental Health.* New York: McGraw-Hill, 1968.

ARNHEIM, RUDOLPH. *Art and Visual Perception: A Psychology of the Creative Eye.* Berkeley: University of California Press, 1974.

ARNOLD, MAGDA B. *Emotion and Personality*. New York: Columbia University Press, 1960.

———(ED.) *Feelings and Emotions: The Loyola Symposium*. New York: Academic Press, 1970.

ARONSON, E., AND LINDER, D. "Gain and Loss of Esteem as Determinants of Interpersonal Attractiveness." *Journal of Experimental Social Psychology*, 1 (1965): 156–171.

———, TURNER, J., AND CARLSMITH, M. "Communicator Credibility and Communicator Discrepancy as Determinants of Opinion Change." *Journal of Abnormal and Social Psychology*, 67 (1963): 31–36.

———, ET AL. "Busing and Racial Tension: The Jigsaw Route to Learning and Liking." *Psychology Today*, 9 (February 1975): 43–50.

ASCH, S. *Social Psychology*. New York: Prentice-Hall, 1952.

———. "Effects of Group Pressure upon the Modification and Distortion of Judgments." In *Basic Studies in Social Psychology*, ed. by J. Proshansky and B. Seidenberg. New York: Holt, Rinehart and Winston, 1965, pp. 393–401.

ASH, P., AND KROEKER, L. P. "Personnel Selection, Classification, and Placement." In *Annual Review of Psychology*. Palo Alto, Calif.: Annual Reivews, 1975, pp. 481–507.

ATKINSON, JOHN W. (ED.). *Motives in Fantasy, Action, and Society*. New York: Van Nostrand Reinhold, 1958.

———, AND FEATHER, NORMAN T. *A Theory of Achievement Motivation*. New York: Wiley, 1966.

AVERILL, J. "Studies on Anger and Aggression: Implications for Theories of Emotion." *American Psychologist*, 38 (1983): 1145–1160.

BACHRACH, A. J. *Psychological Research: An Introduction*. 2nd ed. New York: Random House, 1965.

BACK, KURT W. *Beyond Words: The Story of Sensitivity Training and the Encounter Movement*. New York: Basic Books, 1972.

BAKAL, D. A. *Psychology and Medicine: Psychological Dimensions of Health and Medicine*. New York: Springer, 1979.

BALDWIN, ALFRED A. *Theories of Child Development*. New York: Wiley, 1967.

BALES, R. F. "Task Roles and Social Roles in Problem-solving Groups." In *Readings in Social Psychology*, ed. by E. Maccoby, T. M. Newcomb, and E. L. Hartley, 3rd ed. New York: Holt, Rinehart and Winston, 1958, pp. 347–447.

BALTES, P. B., AND SHAIE, K. W. "Aging and IQ—The Myth of the Twilight Years." In *Readings in Aging and Death: Contemporary Perspectives*, ed. by S. H. Zarit, New York: Harper & Row, 1977.

BANDURA, ALBERT. "The Stormy Decade: Fact or Fiction?" *Psychology in the Schools*, 1 (1964): 224–231.

———. "Influence of Models' Reinforcement Contingencies on the Acquisition of Imitative Responses." *Journal of Personality and Social Psychology*, 1 (1965): 589–595.

———. "Analysis of Modeling Processes." In *Psychological Modeling: Conflicting Theories*, ed. by A. Bandura, Chicago: Aldine-Atherton, 1971, pp. 1–62.

———, AND WALTERS, R. H. *Social Learning and Personality Development*. New York: Holt, Rinehart and Winston, New York 1963.

BARBER, T. X. "Measuring 'Hypnotic-like' Suggestibility with and Without 'Hypnotic Induction': Psychometric Properties, Norms, and Variables Influencing Response to the Barber Suggestibility Scale (BSS)." *Psychological Reports*, 16 (1965): 809–844.

BARD, PHILIP. "On Emotional Expression After Decortication with Some Remarks of Certain Theoretical Views: Part I." *Psychological Review*, 41 (1934), 309–329, "Part II," 41 (1934), 424–449.

BARROW, G. M., AND SMITH, P. A. *Aging, Ageism and Society*. St. Paul, Minn.: West Publishing Co., 1979.

BATESON, GREGORY. *Steps to an Ecology of Mind*. San Francisco: Chandler, 1972.

BAUM, ANDREW, AND VALINS, STUART. *Architecture and Social Behavior*. Hillsdale, N.J.: Lawrence Erlbaum Associates, 1977.

BECK, AARON T. *Depression: Causes and Treatment*. Philadelphia: University of Pennsylvania Press, 1967.

BEEBE-CENTER, J. G. "Standards for the Use of Gust Scale." *Journal of Psychology*, 28 (1949): 411–419.

BELLUGI, U., AND BROWN, R. (EDS.). *The Acquisition of Language*. Chicago: University of Chicago Press, 1970.

BELSKY, J. "The Determinants of Parenting: A Process Model." *Child Development*, 55 (1984): 83–96.

BEM, DARYL J. *Beliefs, Attitudes and Human Affairs*. Belmont, Calif.: Brooks/Cole, 1970.

BEM, SANDRA. "Androgyny vs. the Little Lives of Fluffy Women and Chesty Men." *Psychology Today*, 8 (September 1975): 59–62.

BENSON, HERBERT. *The Relaxation Response*. New York: Avon, 1975.

————, AND WALLACE, ROBERT KEITH. "Decreased Drug Abuse with Transcendental Meditation: A Study of 1862 Subjects." In *Drug Abuse: Proceedings of the International Conference*, ed. by C. J. D. Arafonetis. Philadelphia: Lea & Febiger, 1972.

BERGIN, ALLEN E. "The Evaluation of Therapeutic Outcomes." In *Handbook of Psychotherapy and Behavior Change: An Empirical Analysis*, ed. by Allen E. Bergin and Sol L. Garfield. New York: Wiley, 1971.

BERNARD, H. W., AND HUCKINS, W. C. *Dynamics of Personal Adjustment*. 3rd ed. Boston: Holbrook Press, 1978.

BERNARD, JESSIE. *The Future of Marriage*. New York: Bantam, 1973.

BERNE, ERIC. *Games People Play*. New York: Grove Press, 1964.

————, AND WALSTER, A. "A Little Bit of Love." In *Foundations of Interpersonal Attraction*, ed. by T.L. Huston. New York: Academic Press, 1974.

BERSHEID, E. "Emotion." In *Close Relationships*, ed. by H. H. Kelley. New York: Freeman, 1983.

————, ————. Physical Attractiveness." In *Advances in Experimental Social Psychology*, ed. by Leonard Berkowitz. New York: Academic Press, 1974.

————, ————. *Interpersonal Attraction*. 2nd ed. Reading, Mass.: Addison-Wesley, 1978.

BISCHOF, L. *Adult Psychology*. New York: Harper & Row, 1969.

BOTWINICK, J. *Aging and Behavior*. 2nd ed. New York: Springer, 1978.

BOWER, G. "Mood and Memory." *American Psychologist*, 36 (1981): 129–148.

BOWERS, K. *Hypnosis for the Seriously Curious*. Monterey, Calif.: Brooks/Cole, 1976.

BOWLBY, J. "Separation Anxiety: A Critical Review of the Literature." *Journal of Child Psychology and Psychiatry*, 1 (1960–1961): 251–269.

————. *Child Care and Growth of Love*. 2nd ed. Baltimore: Penguin, 1965.

BOYD, J., AND WEISSMAN, M. "The Epidemiology of Psychiatric Disorders of Middle Age: Depression, Alcoholism, and Suicide." In *Modern Perspectives in the Psychiatry of Middle Age*, ed. by J. G. Howels. New York: Brunner/Mazel, 1981.

BRACKBILL, YVONNE, ET AL. "Arousel Level in Neonates and Preschool Children Under Continuous Auditory Stimulation." *Journal of Experimental Child Psychology*, 4 (1966): 177–188.

BRADY, JOSEPH V. "Ulcers in 'Executive' Monkeys." *Scientific American*, 199 (October 1958): 95–100.

BREAN, HERBERT. "Hidden Sell Technique Almost Here." *Life* (March 31, 1958): 102–114.

BRECHER, E. M. *The Sex Researchers*. New York: American Library, 1971.

————, AND THE EDITORS OF *Consumer Reports*. *Licit and Illicit Drugs*. Boston: Little, Brown, 1972.

BRITTAIN, C. V. "Adolescent Choices and Parent-Peer Cross Pressures." *American Sociological Review*, 28 (1963): 385–391.

————. "A Comparison of Urban and Rural Adolescence with Respect to Peer Versus Parent Compliance." *Adolescence*, 4 (1969): 59–68.

BROWN, J. A. C. *Techniques of Persuasion*. Baltimore: Penguin, 1963.

BROWN, ROGER. *A First Language: The Early Stages*. Cambridge, Mass.: Harvard University Press, 1973.

BRUNER, JEROME S., GOODNOW, JACQUELINE J., AND AUSTIN, GEORGE A. *A Study of Thinking*. New York: Wiley, 1956 (paper).

BUCKHOUT, ROBERT. "Eyewitness Testimony." *Scientific American*, 231, no. 6 (1974): 23–31.

BUDZYNSKI, T. H., ET AL. "EMG Biofeedback and Tension Headache: A Controlled Outcome Study." *Psychosomatic Medicine*, 35 (1973): 484–496.

BUEHLER, R. E., PATTERSON, G. R., AND FURNESS, R. M. "The Reinforcement of Behavior in Institutional Settings." *Behavior Research and Therapy*, 4 (1966): 157–167.

BURKE, R. J., AND WEIR, T. "Marital Helping Relationships: The Moderators Between Stress and Well-Being." *The Journal of Psychology*, 95 (1977): 121–130.

BUTLER, R. N. "Psychiatric Evaluation of the Aged." *Geriatrics*, 18 (1963): 220–232.

———. "Successful Aging and the Role of the Life Review." *Journal of the American Geriatrics Society*, 1974.

———, AND LEWIS, M. I. *Aging and Mental Health: Positive Psychosocial Approaches.* St. Louis: Mosby, 1973.

BUTTERFIELD-PICARD, H., AND MAGNO, J. "Hospice, The Adjective Not the Noun: The Future of National Priority." *American Psychologist*, 37 (1982): 1254–1259.

CAHALAN, D. "Subcultural Differences in Drinking Behavior in U.S. National Surveys and Selected European Studies." In *Alcoholism: New Directions in Behaviorial Research and Treatment*, ed. by P. E. Nathan, G. A. Marlatt, and T. Loberg. New York, Plenum, 1978.

CAMPBELL, E. "Some Social Psychological Correlates of Direction in Attitude Change." *Social Forces*, 36 (1958): 335–340.

CANNON, WALTER B. *Bodily Changes in Pain, Hunger, Fear and Rage.* New York: Appleton-Century-Crofts, 1929.

CAPLAN, GERALD. *Principles of Preventive Psychiatry.* New York: Basic Books, 1965.

CAPLAN, R. D., COBB, S., FRENCH, J. R. P., VANHARRISON, R., AND PINNEAU, R. *Job Demands and Worker Health: Main Effects and Occupational Differences.* Washington, D.C.: National Institute for Occupational Safety and Health, 1975.

CARRINGTON, P. *Releasing: The New Behavioral Science Method for Dealing With Pressure Situations.* New York: William Morrow and Company, Inc., 1984.

CATTELL, R. B. *The Scientific Analysis of Personality.* Baltimore: Penguin, 1965.

CHANCE, PAUL. "Telepathy Could Be Real." *Psychology Today*, 9 (February 1976): 40–44, 65.

CHAND, I. P., CRIDER, D. M., AND WILLETS, F. K. "Parent-Youth Disagreement as Perceived by Youth: A Longitudinal Study." *Youth and Society*, 6 (1975): 365–375.

CHOROVER, S. L. "Big Brother and Psychotechnology II: The Pacification of the Brain." *Psychology Today*, 7 (May 1974): 59–69.

CHUKOVSKY, K. *From Two To Five.* Berkeley: University of California Press, 1963.

COALE, A. J. "The Demographic Transition Reconsidered." In *International Population Conference*, Leige, 1973.

COBB, SYDNEY "Social Support as a Moderator of Life Stress." *Psychosomatic Medicine*, 38 (September-October 1976): 300–314.

———, AND ROSE, ROBERT. "Hypertension, Peptic Ulcers, and Diabetes in Air Traffic Controllers." *Journal of the American Medical Association*, 224 (1973): 489–492.

COCH, L., AND FRENCH, J. R. P., JR. "Overcoming Resistance to Change." *Human Relations*, 1 (1948): 512–532.

COFER, C. N. *Motivation and Emotions.* Glenview, Ill.: Scott, Foresman, 1972.

COHEN, A. R. *Attitude Change and Social Influence.* New York: Basic Books, 1964.

COHEN, H., AND FILIPCZAK, J. *A New Learning Environment.* San Francisco: Jossey-Bass, 1971.

COHEN, S., GLASS, D., AND SINGER, J. "Apartment Noises, Auditory Discrimination and Reading Ability in Children." *Journal of Experimental Social Psychology*, 9 (1973): 407–422.

COLE, J. O. "Phenothiazine Treatment in Acute Schizophrenia: Effectiveness." *Archives of General Psychiatry*, 10 (1964): 246–261.

COLEMAN, JAMES. C. *Abnormal Psychology and Modern Life.* 5th ed. Glenview, Ill.: Scott, Foresman, 1976.

———. *Contemporary Psychology and Effective Behavior.* 4th ed. Glenview, Ill.: Scott, Foresman, 1979.

————, AND HAMMEN, CONSTANCE L. *Contemporary Psychology and Effective Behavior*. Glenview, Ill.: Scott, Foresman, 1974.

COLEMAN, J. S. *The Adolescent Society*. New York: Free Press, 1961.

COLES, R. "Life in Appalachia: The Case of Hugh McCaslin." *Life at the Bottom*, ed. by G. Armstrong. New York: Bantam, 1971, pp. 26–42.

CONGER, J. J. *Adolescence and Youth: Psychological Development in a Changing World*. New York: Harper & Row, 1973.

Congressional Quarterly Weekly Report, June 13, 1981, p. 1049.

COOPER, CARY L., AND MARSHALL, JUDI. "Occupational Sources of Stress: A Review of the Literature Relating to Coronary Heart Disease and Mental Ill Health." *Journal of Occupational Psychology*, 49 (March 1976): 11–28.

————, AND PAYNE, R. (EDS.). *Stress at Work*. New York: Wiley, 1979.

CORSINI, RAYMOND J. (ED.). *Current Psychotherapies*. Itasca, Ill.: Peacock, 1973.

COX, T. *Stress*. Baltimore: University Park, 1978.

CRONBACH, LEE J. *Essentials of Psychological Testing*. 3rd ed. New York: Harper & Row, 1970.

CUBER, J. F., AND HARROFF, P. *Sex and the Significant American*. Baltimore: Penguin, 1965.

CULLITON, B. J. "Psychosurgery: National Commission Issues Surprisingly Favorable Report." *Science*, 194 (1976): 299–301.

DACEY, J. S. *Adolescents Today*. Santa Monica, Calif.: Goodyear, 1979.

DAHLSTROM, WILLIAM GRANT, AND WELSH, GEORGE, S. *An MMPI Handbook: A Guide to Use in Clinical Practice and Research*. Minneapolis: University of Minnesota Press, 1960.

DAMON, W. *Social and Personality Development*. New York: Norton, 1983.

DARLEY J. M., AND LATANE, B. "Bystander Intervention in Emergencies: Diffusion of Responsibility." *Journal of Personality and Social Psychology*, 8 (1968): 377–383.

DARWIN, CHARLES. *The Expression of Emotions in Man and Animals*. Chicago: University of Chicago Press, 1967; originally published in 1872.

DAVIS, A. "Socio-Economic Influences upon Children's Learning." *Understanding the Child*, 20 (1951): 10–16.

DAVIS, K. "Near and Dear. Friendship and Love Compared." *Psychology Today*, 19 (February 1985): 22–30.

DAVISON, GERALD C., AND NEALE, JOHN M. *Abnormal Psychology: An Experimental Clinical Approach*. 2nd ed. New York: Wiley, 1978.

DE BONO, EDWARD. *New Think: The Use of Lateral Thinking in the Generation of New Ideas*. New York: Basic Books, 1968.

DEIKMAN, ARTHUR J. "Experimental Meditation." *Journal of Nervous and Mental Disease*, 136 (1963): 329–373.

DELGADO, J. M. R. *Physical Control of the Mind*. New York: Harper & Row, 1969.

DEMENT, W. *Some Must Watch While Some Must Sleep*. New York: Norton, 1976.

————, AND WOLPERT, E. "Relation of Eye Movements, Bodily Mobility, and External Stimuli to Dream Content." *Journal of Experimental Psychology*, 55 (1958): 543–553.

DENNIS, W. "Creative Productivity Between the Ages of Twenty and Eighty Years." *Journal of Gerontology*, 21 (1966): 1–8.

DENNIS, WAYNE. "Causes of Retardation Among Institutional Children: Iran." *Journal of Genetic Psychology*, 96 (1960): 47–59.

DEUTSCH, M., AND COLLINS, M. *Interracial Housing: A Psychological Evaluation of a Social Experiment*. Minneapolis: University of Minnesota Press, 1951.

DICHTER, ERNEST. *Handbook of Consumer Motivations*. New York: McGraw-Hill, 1964.

DION, K. L., BERSCHEID, E., AND WALSTER, E. "What Is Beautiful Is Good." *Journal of Personality and Social Psychology*, 24 (1972): 285–290.

DIXON, N. F. *Subliminal Perception: The Nature of a Controversy*. London: McGraw-Hill, 1971.

DODGE, K. "Behavioral Antecedents of Peer Social Status." *Child Development*, 54 (1983): 1386–1379.

DWYER, JOHANNA, AND MAYER, JEAN. "Psychological Effects of Variations in Physical Appearance During Adolescence." *Adolescence* (1968–1969): 353–368.

DU BOIS, PHILIP H. "Review of Scholastic Aptitude Test." In *The Seventh Mental Measurements Yearbook*, ed. by O. K. Buros. Highland Park, N.J.: Gryphon Press, 1972, pp. 646–648.

DUNCKER, KARL. "On Problem Solving." Trans. by L. S. Lees. *Psychological Monographs*, 58, no. 270 (1945).

———. *The Mechanism of the Mind*. New York: Simon & Schuster, 1969.

DUNPHY, D. "The Social Structure of Urban Adolescent Peer Groups." *Sociometry*, 26 (1963): 230–246.

EDITORS OF THE *Literary Digest*. "Landon, 1,293,669; Roosevelt, 972,897." *Literary Digest*, 122 (October 31, 1936): 5–6.

EDWARDS, J. N., AND BRAUBURGER, M. B. "Exchange and Parent-Youth Conflict." *Journal of Marriage and the Family*, 35 (1973): 101–107.

EKMAN, PAUL, FRIESEN, WALLACE V., AND ELLSWORTH, PHOEBE. *Emotion in the Human Face: Guidelines for Research and an Integration of Findings*. Elmsford, N.Y.: Pergamon, 1972.

ELDERSVELD, S., AND DODGE, R. "Personal Contact or Mail Propaganda? An Experiment in Voting Turnout and Attitude Change." In *Public Opinion and Propaganda*, ed. by D. Katz, *et. al.* New York: Dryden Press, 1954, pp. 532–542.

ELKIND, D., AND WEINER, I. B. *Development of the Child*. New York: Wiley, 1978.

ELLIS, ALBERT. "Rational-Emotive Therapy." In *Current Psychotherapies*, ed. by R. Corsini. Itasca, Ill.: Peacock, 1973, pp. 167–206.

———. "What People Can Do for Themselves to Cope with Stress." In *Stress at Work*, ed. by C. L. Cooper and R. Payne. New York: Wiley, 1978.

ERIKSON, ERIK. *Childhood and Society*. New York: Norton, 1950.

———. *Identity: Youth and Crisis*. New York: Norton, 1968.

ERON, L., HUESMANN, L. R., BRICE, P., FISCHER, P., AND MERMELSTEIN, R. "Age Trends in the Development of Aggression, Sex Typing, and Related Television Habits." *Developmental Psychology*, 19 (1983): 71–77.

ESTABROOKS, G. (ED.). *Hypnosis: Current Problems*. New York: Harper & Row, 1962.

EYSENCK, HANS J. "The Effects of Psychotherapy: An Evaluation." *Journal of Consulting Psychology*, 16 (1952): 319–324.

———. *The Dynamics of Anxiety and Hysteria*. London: Routledge & Kegan Paul, 1957.

———. *The Effects of Psychotherapy*. New York: International Science Press, 1966.

———. *The Structure of Human Personality*, London: Metheun, 1970.

FARADAY, ANN. *The Dream Game*. New York: Harper & Row, 1974.

FESTINGER, L. *A Theory of Cognitive Dissonance*. Stanford, Calif.: Stanford University Press, 1957.

———, AND CARLSMITH, J. M. "Cognitive Consequences of Forced Compliance." *Journal of Abnormal and Social Psychology*, 58 (1959): 203–210.

FIEDLER, F. E. "Style or Circumstance: The Leadership Enigma." *Psychology Today*, 2 (1969): 38–43.

FISCHER, KURT W. *Piaget's Theory of Learning and Cognitive Development*. Chicago: Markham, 1973.

———. *The Organization of Simple Learning*. Chicago: Markham, 1973.

FISHER, S., AND GREENBERG, R. P. *The Scientific Credibility of Freud's Theories and Therapy*. New York: Basic Books, 1977.

"Five Antidotes for Job Tension." *Supervisory Management*, 14 (1969): 32–34.

FITTS, P. M., AND POSNER, M. I. *Human Performance*. Belmont, Calif.: Brooks/Cole, 1967.

FITTS, WILLIAM H. *The Experience of Psychotherapy*. New York: Van Nostrand, 1965.

FIXX, JAMES. *The Complete Book of Running*. New York: Random House, 1977.

FLACK, R. "The Liberated Generation: An Exploration of the Roots of Student Protest." *Journal of Social Issues*, 23 (1967): 52–57.

FLAVELL, JOHN H. *The Developmental Theory of Jean Piaget*. New York: Van Nostrand, 1963.

FLEXNER, L. "Dissection of Memory in Mice with Antibiotics." *Proceedings of the American Philosophical Society*, 111 (1967): 343–346.

FLOOD, J. F., BENNETT, E. L., AND ORME, A. E. "Relation of Memory Formation for Controlled Amounts of Brain Protein Synthesis." *Physiology and Behavior*, 15 (1975): 97–102.

FOULKES, DAVID. *The Psychology of Sleep*. New York: Scribner's, 1966.

FOX, L. JUNGBERG. "Effecting the Use of Efficient Study Habits." In *Control of Human Behavior*, ed. by R. Ulrich, T. Stachnik, and J. Mabry. Vol. 1. Glenview, Ill.: Scott, Foresman, 1966.

FRANCIS, G. J., AND MILBOURN, G. *Human Behavior in the Work Environment: A Managerial Perspective*. Santa Monica, Calif.: Goodyear, 1980.

FRANKL, VIKTOR. *Man's Search for Meaning: An Introduction to Logotherapy*. New York: Clarion 1970.

FREEDMAN, JONATHAN L. *Crowding and Behavior*. San Francisco: Freeman, 1975.

FREUD, SIGMUND. *An Outline of Psychoanalysis*. Ed. and trans. by James Strachey. New york: Norton, 1949; originally published 1940.

————. *A General Introduction to Psychoanalysis*. Trans. by Joan Riviere. Garden City, N.Y.: Garden City Publishing, 1943.

FRIEDMAN, MEYER, AND ROSENMAN, RAY. *Type A Behavior and Your Heart*. New York: Knopf, 1974.

FROMM, ERICH. *Man for Himself: An Inquiry into the Psychology of Ethics*. New York: Holt, Rinehart and Winston, 1947.

————. *The Art of Loving*. New York: Harper & Row, 1956.

FURTH, HANS. *Piaget and Knowledge*. Englewood Cliffs, N.J: Prentice-Hall, 1969.

GALTON, SIR FRANCIS. *Hereditary Genius: An Inquiry into Its Laws and Consequences*. London: Macmillan, 1869.

GARCIÀ, JOHN, AND KOELLING, R. A. "The Relation of Cue to Consequence in Avoidance Learning." *Psychonomic Science*, 4 (1966): 123–124.

GARDNER, R. A., AND GARDNER, B. T. "Teaching Sign Language to a Chimpanzee." *Science*, 1965 (1969): 644–672.

GAZZANIGA, MICHAEL S. "The Split Brain in Man." *Scientific American*, 217 (August 1967): 24–29.

GELDARD, FRANK A. *The Human Senses*. 2nd ed. New York: Wiley, 1972.

GERARD, H. B., AND RABBIE, J. M. "Fear and Social Comparison." *Journal of Abnormal and Social Psychology*, 62 (1961): 586–592.

GERGEN, KENNETH J., GERGEN, MARY M., AND BARTON, WILLIAM H. "Deviance in the Dark." *Psychology Today*, 7 (October 1973): 129, 130.

GERST, M. S. "Symbolic Coding Processes in Observational Learning." *Journal of Personality and Social Psychology*, 19 (1971): 9–17.

GESELL, A., AND THOMPSON, HELEN. "Learning and Growth in Identical Twin Infants." *Genetic Psychological Monograph*, 6 (1929): 1–124.

GHISELIN, B. (ED.). *The Creative Process*. New York: New American Library, 1952 (paper).

GIBB, C. "Leadership." In *The Handbook of Social Psychology*, ed. by G. Lindsey and E. Aronson, Vol. 4, 2nd ed. Reading, Mass.: Addison-Wesley, 1969.

GIBSON, E. J., AND WALK, R. D. "The Visual Cliff." *Scientific American*, 202 (1960): 64–71.

GINSBURG, HERBERT, AND OPPER, SYLVIA. *Piaget's Theory of Intellectual Development: An Introduction*. Englewood Cliffs, N. J.: Prentice-Hall, 1969.

GLASS, D. C. "Changes in Liking as a Means of Reducing Cognitive Discrepancies Between Self-Esteem and Aggression." *Journal of Personality*, 32 (1964): 531–549.

GOFFMAN, ERVING. *Asylums*. Garden City, N.Y.: Doubleday, 1961 (paper).

GOLANN, S. E., AND EISENDORFER, C. (EDS.) *Handbook of Community Mental Health*. New York: Appleton-Century-Crofts, 1972.

GOLDSEN, R., ET AL. *What College Students Think.* New York: Van Nostrand, 1960.

GOLEMAN, DANIEL. "Who's Mentally Ill?" *Psychology Today*, 11 (January 1978): 34–41.

GOODENOUGH, FLORENCE L. "Expression of the Emotions in a Blind-Deaf Child." *Journal of Abnormal and Social Psychology*, 27 (1932): 328–333.

GREEN, DAVID M., AND SWETS, JOHN A. *Signal Detection Theory and Psychophysics.* New York: Wiley, 1966.

GREENBLATT, MILTON, ET AL. (EDS.) *Drugs and Social Therapy in Chronic Schizophrenia.* Springfield, Ill.: Charles C Thomas, 1965.

GREGORY, R. L. *The Intelligent Eye.* New York: McGraw-Hill, 1970 (paper).

———. *Eye and Brain.* 3rd ed. New York: McGraw-Hill, 1978.

GRINSPOON, LESTER. *Marijuana Reconsidered.* Cambridge, Mass.: Harvard University Press, 1970.

GUILFORD, J. P. *Personality.* New York: McGraw-Hill, 1959.

GUSTAVSON, C. R., ET AL. "Coyote Predation Control by Aversive Conditioning." *Science*, 184 (1974): 581–583.

HAAN, N., AND DAY, D. "A Longitudinal Study of Change and Sameness in Personality Development: Adolescence to Later Adulthood." *International Journal of Aging and Human Development*, 5 (1974): 11–39.

HABER, R. N. "How We Remember What We See." *Scientific American*, 222 (1970): 104–112.

HALACY, D. R., JR. *Man and Memory.* New York: Harper & Row, 1970.

HALL, CALVIN S. *A Primer of Freudian Psychology.* Cleveland: World, 1954 (paper).

———, AND LINDZEY, GARDNER. *Theories of Personality.* 3rd ed. New York: Wiley, 1978.

———, AND VAN DE CASTLE, R. L. *The Content Analysis of Dreams.* New York: Appleton-Century-Crofts, 1966.

HALL, EDWARD T. *The Silent Language.* Garden City, N.Y.: Doubleday, 1959.

———. *The Hidden Dimension.* Garden City, N.Y.: Doubleday, 1966.

HALL, G. STANLEY. "The Moral and Religious Training of Children." *Princeton Review* (January 1882): 26–48.

———. *Adolescence.* New York: Appleton, 1904.

HARKINS, E. B. "Effect of Empty Nest Transition on Self-Report of Psychological and Physical Well-Being." *Journal of Marriage and the Family*, 40 (1978): 549–556.

HARLOW, HARRY F. "The Formation of Learning Sets." *Psychological Review*, 56 (1949): 51–65.

———. "The Development of Affectional Patterns in Infant Monkeys." In *Determinants of Infant Behavior*, ed. by B. M. Foss. New York: Wiley, 1961, pp. 75–100.

———, AND ZIMMERMAN, R.R. "Affectional Responses in the Infant Monkey." *Science*, 140 (1959): 421–432.

HARRIS, B. "Whatever Happened to Little Albert?" *American Psychologist*, 34 (1979): 151–160.

HARRIS, C. S. *Fact Book on Aging: A Profile of America's Older Population.* Washington, D.C.: National Council on the Aging, 1978.

HARRISON, R. V. "Job Demands and Worker Health: Person-Environment Misfit." Doctoral dissertation, University of Michigan, 1976. *Dissertation Abstracts International*, 37, 1035B (University Microfilms no. 76–19, 150).

HARTUP, W. W. "Peer Interaction and Social Organization." In *Carmichael's Manual of Child Psychology*, ed. by P. H. Mussen. Vol. 3. New York: Wiley, 1970.

HASSETT, JAMES. *A Primer of Psychophysiology.* San Francisco: Freeman, 1978a.

———. "Teaching Yourself to Relax." *Psychology Today*, 12 (August 1978b): 28–40.

———. "Caution: Meditation Can Hurt." *Psychology Today*, 12 (November 1978c): 125–126.

HASSETT, JOHN. "Checking the Accuracy of Pupil Scores in Standardized Tests." *English Journal*, 67 (October 1978): 30–31.

HASTORF, ALBERT H., SCHNEIDER, DAVID J., AND POLEFKA, JUDITH. *Person Perception.* 2nd ed. Reading, Mass.: Addison-Wesley, 1979.

HATFIELD, E., AND WALSTER, G. *A New Look at Love*, Reading, Mass.: Addison-Wesley, 1981.

HATHAWAY, STARKE R., AND MC KINLEY, JOHN CHARNLEY. "A Multiphasic Personality Schedule (Minnesota): I. Construction of the Schedule." *Journal of Psychology*, 10 (1940): 249–254.

HAVIGHURST, R. J. *Developmental Tasks and Education*. 3rd ed. New York: McKay, 1972.

HAYS, WILLIAM L. *Statistics for Psychologists*. New York: Holt, Rinehart and Winston, 1963.

HEBB, D. O. "What Psychology Is About." *American Psychologist*, 29 (1974): 71–79.

HELD, R., AND HEIN, A. "A Movement-produced Stimulation in the Development of Visually Guided Behavior." *Journal of Comparative Physiology and Psychology*, 56 (1963): 606–613.

HENNING, HANS. "Die Qualitätenreihe des Geschmacks." *Zeitschrift für Psychologie*, 74 (1916): 203–219.

HERNÁNDEZ-PEÓN, R. "Reticular Mechanisms of Sensory Control." In *Sensory Communication*, ed. by W. A. Rosenblith. New York: Wiley, 1961, pp. 497–520.

HERON, W. "The Pathology of Boredom." *Scientific American*, 196 (January 1957): 57–62.

HERRNSTEIN, RICHARD. "I.Q." Atlantic, 228 (1971): 43–64.

HERRON, JEANNINE. "Southpaws: How Different Are They?" *Psychology Today* (March 1976): 50–56.

HESS, R., AND TORNEY, J. *The Development of Political Attitudes in Children*. Chicago: Aldine, 1967.

HIGGINS-TRENK, A., AND GAITE, A. J. H. "Elusiveness of Formal Operational Thought in Adolescents." *Proceedings of the Seventy-ninth Annual Convention of the American Psychological Association*, 1971.

HILGARD, E. R. *Hypnotic Susceptibility*. New York: Harcourt Brace Jovanovich, 1965.

———. *Divided Consciousness*. New York: Wiley, 1977.

HIROTO, D. S. "Locus of Control and Learned Helplessness." *Journal of Experimental Psychology*, 102 (1974): 187–193.

HOCHBERG, JULIAN. *Perception*. Englewood Cliffs, N.J.: Prentice-Hall, 1964 (paper).

HOFFMAN, BANESH. *The Tyranny of Testing*. New York: Collier, 1962 (paper).

HOKANSON, J. E., DEGOOD, D. E., FORREST, M. S., AND BRITTAIN, T. M. "Availability of Avoidance Behaviors for Modulating Vascular-Stress Responses." *Journal of Personality and Social Psychology*, 67 (1963): 60–68.

HOLBORN, HAJO. *A History of Modern Germany 1850–1945*. New York: Knopf, 1969.

HOLDEN, C. "Identical Twins Reared Apart." *Science*, 207 (1980): 1323–1328.

HOLLAND, GLEN A. "Transactional Analysis." In *Current Psychotherapies*, ed. by R. Corsini. Itasca, Ill.: Peacock, 1973, pp. 353–400.

HOLMES, D. L. AND MORRISON, F. J. *The Child: An Introduction to Developmental Psychology*. Monterey, Calif.: Brooks/Cole, 1979.

HOLMES, T. H., AND RAHE, R. H. "The Social Readjustment Scale." *Journal of Psychosomatic Research*, 11 (1967): 213.

HONIG, W. H. (ED.). *Operant Behavior: Areas of Research and Application*. New York: Appleton-Century-Crofts, 1966.

HORN, J. L. "The Aging of Human Abilities." In *Handbook of Developmental Psychology*, Englewood Cliffs, N.J.: Prentice Hall, 1982, pp. 847–870.

HORNER, MATINA S. "Femininity and Successful Achievement: A Basic Inconsistency." In *Feminine Personality and Conflict*, ed. by J. Bardwick, E. M. Douvan, M. S. Horner, and D. Gutman. Belmont, Calif.: Brooks/Cole, 1970.

———. "Towards an Understanding of Achievement-related Conflicts in Women." *Journal of Social Issues*, 28 (1972): 157–175.

HORROCKS, J. E., AND BENIMOFF, M. "Isolation from the Peer Group During Adolescence." *Adolescence*, 2 (1967): 41–52.

HOUGH, R. L., FAIRBANKS, D. T., AND GARCIA, A. M. "Problems in the Ratio Measurement of Life Stress." *Journal of Health and Social Behavior*, 17 (1976): 70–82.

HOUSE, J. S. "The Relationship of Intrinsic and Extrinsic Work Motivation to Occupational Stress and Coronary Heart Disease Risk." Doctoral dissertation, University of Michigan, 1972. *Dissertation Abstracts International*, 33, 2514-A (University Microfilms no. 72–29094).

HOVLAND, C., LUMSDAINE, A., AND SHEFFIELD, F. *Experiments on Mass Communication.* Princeton, N.J.: Princeton University Press, 1949.

————, AND SEARS, R. "Minor Studies of Aggression: Correlation of Lynching with Economic Indices." *Journal of Psychology*, 9 (1940): 301–310.

HRABA, J., AND GRANT, G. "Black Is Beautiful: A Reexamination of Racial Preference and Identification." *Journal of Personality and Social Psychology*, 16 (1970): 398–402.

HUBEL, DAVID H., AND WIESEL, TORSLEN N. "Receptive Fields, Binocular Interaction, and Functional Architecture in the Cat's Visual Cortex." *Journal of Physiology*, 160(1962): 106–154.

HULL, CLARK. *Principles of Behavior: An Introduction to Behavior Theory.* New York: Appleton-Century-Crofts, 1943.

HURLOCK, E. B. *Developmental Psychology: A Life-Span Approach.* 5th ed. New York: McGraw-Hill, 1980.

HUSTON, A., ET AL. "Communicating More Than Content: Formal Features of Children's Television Programs." *Journal of Communication.* 31 (1981): 32–48.

INHELDER, BAERBEL. "Memory and Intelligence in the Child." In *Studies in Cognitive Development*, ed. by D. Elkind and J. F. Flavell. New York: Oxford University Press, 1969, pp. 337–364.

————, AND PIAGET, J. *The Early Growth of Logic in the Child.* New York: Harper & Row, 1964.

IZARD, CARROLL, E. *The Face of Emotion.* New York: Appleton-Century-Crofts, 1971.

————. *Patterns of Emotions: A New Analysis of Anxiety and Depression.* New York: Academic Press, 1972.

JAMES, WILLIAM. *The Principles of Psychology.* Vol. 2. New York: Holt, 1890.

JANIS, IRVING. Psychological Stress. New York: Academic Press, 1958.

JELLINEK, ELVIN M. *The Disease Concept of Alcoholism.* New Brunswick, N.J.: Hillhouse Press, 1960.

JENNINGS, M., AND NIEMI, R. "The Transmission of Political Values from Parent to Child." *American Political Science Review*, 62 (1968): 169–184.

JOHNSON, E. S., AND WILLIAMSON, J. B. *Growing Old: The Social Problems of Aging.* New York: Holt, Rinehart and Winston, 1980.

JOHNSTON, L. D., BACHMAN, J. B., AND O'MALLEY, P. M. *Monitoring the Future: Questionnaire Responses from the Nation's High School Seniors* (1978 Vol.). Ann Arbor, Mich.: Institute for Social Research, 1980.

JONES, EDWARD E., AND DAVIS, KEITH E. "From Acts to Dispositions: The Attribution Process in Person Perception." In *Advances in Experimental Social Psychology*, ed. by Leonard Berkowitz, Vol. 2. New York: Academic Press, 1965, pp. 219–266.

————, ET AL. "Internal States or Emotional Stimuli: Observers' Attitude Judgments and the Dissonance of Theory-Self-Presentation Controversy." *Journal of Experimental Social Psychology*, 4 (1968): 247–269.

JONES, F. H. "A Four-Year Follow-Up of Vulnerable Adolescents." *Journal of Nervous and Mental Disease*, 159 (1974): 20–39.

JONES, M. C. "The Elimination of Children's Fears." *Journal of Experimental Psychology.* 29 (1924): 383–390.

————. "Psychological Correlates of Somatic Development." *Child Development*, 36 (1965): 899–911.

————. "Albert, Peter, and John B. Watson." *American Psychologist*, (August 1974): 581–583.

JOURARD, SIDNEY, M. *The Transparent Self.* 2nd. ed. New York: Van Nostrand, 1971 (paper).

JOUVET, MICHEL. "The Stages of Sleep." *Scientific American*, 216 (1967): 62–72.

JUNG, CARL G. *Memories, Dreams, Reflections.* Ed. by Anna Jaffe, trans. by Richard and Clara Winston, New York: Pantheon, 1963.

KALINOWSKY, L. B. "The Convulsive Therapies." In *Comprehensive Textbook of Psychiatry*, ed. by A. M. Freedman, H. I. Kaplan, and B. J. Saddocks. Baltimore: Williams & Wilkins, 1975.

KALISY, RICHARD A. "Attitudes and Aging: Myths and Realities." In *The Later Years: Social Applications of Gerontology*, ed. by R. A. Kalish. Monterey, Calif.: Brooks/Cole, 1977.

KALMIS, ILZE V., AND BRUNER, J. S. "The Coordination of Visual Observation and Instrumental Behavior in Early Infancy." *Perception*, 2 (1973): 304–314.

KANDEL, D. B., AND LESSER, G. S. "Parental and Peer Influences on Educational Plans of Adolescents." *American Sociological Review*, 34 (1969): 213–223.

————. "The Role of Parents and Peers in Adolescent Marijuana Use." *Science*, 181 (1973): 1067–1070.

KAPLAN, B. (ED.). *The Inner World of Mental Illness*. New York: Harper & Row, 1964 (paper).

KARNASH, L. J. *Handbook of Psychiatry*. St Louis: Mosby, 1945.

KELLEY, H. H. "The Warm-Cold Variable in First Impressions of Persons." *Journal of Personality*, 18 (1950): 431–439.

KELMAN, H. C. "Processes of Opinion Change." *Public Opinion Quarterly*, 21 (1961): 57–78.

————AND HOVLAND, C. I. " 'Reinstatement' of the Communicator in Delayed Measurement of Opinion Change." *Journal of Abnormal and Social Psychology*, 48 (1953): 327–335.

KEMPLER, WALTER. "Gestalt Therapy." In *Current Psychotherapies*, ed. by R. Corsini. Itasca, Ill.: Peacock, 1973, pp 251–286.

KETY, S. S., ET AL. "Mental Illness in the Biological and Adoptive Families of Adopted Schizophrenics." *American Journal of Psychiatry*, 128, no. 3 (1971): 302–306.

KIMMEL, D. C. *Adulthood and Aging*. 2nd ed. New York: Wiley, 1980.

KINSEY, ALFRED C., POMEROY, WARDELL, B., AND MARTIN, CLYDE E. *Sexual Behavior in the Human Male*. Philadelphia: Saunders, 1948.

————, ET AL. *Sexual Behavior in the Human Female*. Philadelphia: Saunders, 1953.

KISKER, GEORGE. *The Disorganized Personality*. New York: McGraw-Hill, 1964.

KLAPPER, J. T. *The Effects of Mass Communications*. New York: Free Press, 1960.

KLEITMAN, NATHANIEL. "Patterns of Dreaming." *Scientific American*, 203 (November 1960): 82–88.

————. *Sleep and Wakefulness*. Rev. ed. Chicago: University of Chicago Press, 1963.

KLINEBERG, OTTO. "Emotional Expression in Chinese Literature." *Journal of Abnormal and Social Psychology*, 33 (1938): 517–520.

KLÜVER, H., AND BUCY, P. C. "Psychic Blindness and Other Symptoms Following Bilateral Temporal Lobectomy in Rhesus Monkeys." *American Journal of Physiology*, 119 (1937): 532–535.

KOENIG, PETER. "Field Report on Psychological Testing of Job Applicants: They Just Changed the Rules on How to Get Ahead." *Psychology Today*, 8 (June 1974): 87–96.

KOESTLER, ARTHUR. *The Act of Creation*. New York: Macmillan, 1964.

KOFFKA, K. *Principles of Gestalt Psychology*. New York: Harcourt Brace Jovanovich, 1963.

KOHLBERG, LAWRENCE. "The Child as Moral Philosopher." *Psychology Today*, 2 (September 1968): 25–30.

————, AND KRAMER, R. "Continuities and Discontinuities in Child and Adult Moral Development." *Human Development*, 12 (1969): 93–120.

————, AND TUNEL, E. *Research in Moral Development: The Cognitive-Developmental Approach*. New York: Holt, Rinehart and Winston, 1971.

KOHLENBERG, ROBERT, PHILLIPS, THOMAS, AND PROCTOR, WILLIAM. "A Behavioral Analysis of Peaking in Residential Electrical Energy Consumers." *Journal of Applied Behavioral Analysis*, 9 (1976): 13–18.

KOHLER, WOLFGANG. *The Mentality of Apes*. New York: Harcourt, 1925.

KOLB, D. A. "Changing Achievement Motivation." In *Behavior Change*, ed. by R. Schwitzgabel and D. A. Kolb. New York: McGraw-Hill, 1973.

KOMAROVSKY, M. *Blue-Collar Marriage*. New York: Random House, 1964.

KRAMER, M. "Statistics of Mental Disorders in the United States: Some Urgent Needs and Suggested Solutions." *Journal of the Royal Statistical Society*, Series A, 132 (1969): 353–407.

KRANTZLER, MEL. *Creative Divorce*. New York: Evans, 1973.

KREPS, J. *Six in the Marketplace. American Women at Work.* Baltimore: Johns Hopkins University, 1971.

KUBLER-ROSS, ELISABETH. *On Death and Dying.* New York: Macmillan, 1969.

LA FRANCE, MARIANNE, AND MAYO, CLARA. "Racial Differences in Gaze Behavior During Conversations: Two Systematic Observation Studies." *Journal of Personality and Social Psychology,* 33 (1976): 547–552.

LAHEY, B. B., AND CIMINERO, A. R. *Maladaptive Behavior: An Introduction to Abnormal Psychology.* Glenview, Ill.: Scott, Foresman, 1980.

LAING, R. D. *The Politics of Experience.* New York: Pantheon, 1967.

———, AND ESTERSON, AARON. *Sanity, Madness, and the Family.* 2nd ed. New York: Basic Books, 1971.

LANGE, CARL G., AND JAMES, WILLIAM. *The Emotions.* Ed. by Knight Dunlap, trans. by I. A. Haupt. Baltimore: Williams & Wilkins, 1922.

LASHLEY, KARL S. *Brain Mechanisms and Intelligence.* Chicago: University of Chicago Press, 1929.

LAZARUS, R. S., ET AL. "The Principle of Short-Circuiting of Threat: Further Evidence." *Journal of Personality,* 3 (1965): 622–635.

LEAVITT, H. J. "Some Effects of Certain Communication Patterns on Group Performance." *Journal of Abnormal Social Psychology,* 46 (1951): 38–50.

LEE, ALFRED M., AND LEE, ELIZABETH. *The Fine Art of Propaganda.* New York: Farrar, Straus, Giroux, 1939.

LERNER, R. M., AND KNAPP, J. R. "Actual and Perceived Intrafamilial Attitudes of Late Adolescents and Their Parents." *Journal of Youth and Adolescence,* 4 (1975): 17–36.

———, AND SPANIER, G. B. *Adolescent Development: A Life-Span Perspective.* New York: McGraw-Hill, 1980.

LEVANT, OSCAR. *The Memoirs of an Amnesiac.* New York: Bantam, 1966 (paper).

LEVINGER, GEORGE. "Sources of Dissatisfaction Among Applicants for Divorce." *American Journal of Orthopsychiatry,* 36 (1966): 803–807.

———, AND SNOEK, J. DIDRICK. *Attraction in Relationship: A New Look at Interpersonal Attraction.* Morristown, N.J.: General Learning Press, 1972.

LEVINSON, DANIEL J., "Living with Dying." *Newsweek* (May 1, 1978): 52–61.

———, ET AL. *The Seasons of a Man's Life.* New York: Knopf, 1978.

LIEBERT, R., SPRAFKIN, J., AND DAVIDSON, E. *The Early Window: Effects of Television on Children and Youth.* 2nd ed. New York: Pergamon, 1982.

LIEM, J. H., AND LIEM, R. "Life Events, Social Supports, and Physical and Psychological Well-Being." Paper presented at the annual meeting of the American Psychological Association, Washington, D.C., 1976.

LIFTON, ROBERT JAY. *Thought Reform and the Psychology of Totalism: A Study of "Brainwashing" in China.* New York: Norton, 1963 (paper).

———. *Home from the War.* New York: Simon & Schuster, 1973.

LINDNER, ROBERT. *The Fifty-Minute Hour.* New York: Bantam, 1954.

LINGEMAN, RICHARD R. *Drugs from A to Z.* New York: McGraw-Hill, 1974.

LITTENBERG, R., TULKIN, S., AND KAGAN, J. "Cognitive Components of Separation Anxiety." *Developmental Psychology,* 4 (1971): 387–388.

LOEHLIN, JOHN C., LINDZEY, GARDNER, AND SPUHLER, J. N. *Race Differences in Intelligence.* San Francisco: Freeman, 1975.

LOFTUS, ELIZABETH. "Reconstructing Memory: The Incredible Eyewitness." *Psychology Today,* 8, no. 7 (1974): 116–119.

———. *Eyewitness Testimony,* Cambridge, Mass.: Harvard University Press, 1979.

———. "Trial by Data: Psychological Research as Legal Evidence." *American Psychologist,* 35 (1980): 270–283.

LOGUE, ALEXANDRA. "Waiter, There's a Phobia in My Soup." *Psychology Today,* 12 (1978): 36.

LORAYNE, HARRY, AND LUCAS, JERRY. *The Memory Book.* New York: Ballantine, 1974 (paper).

LORENZ, KONRAD, Z. *Studies in Animal and Human Behavior*, trans. by Robert Martin, 2 vols. Cambridge, Mass.: Harvard University Press, 1972.

LORENZ, SARAH. *Our Son, Ken*. New York: Dell, 1969 (paper).

LOVAAS, O. I., ET AL. "Establishment of Imitation and Its Use for the Development of Complex Behavior in Schizophrenic Children." *Behavior Research and Therapy*, 5 (August 1967): 171–181.

LUCE, GAY GAER, AND SEGAL, JULIUS. *Sleep*. New York: Coward, McCann & Geoghegan, 1966.

LURIA, A. R. *The Mind of a Mnemonist*. New York: Basic Books, 1968.

LYKKEN, DAVID T. "Psychology and the Lie Detector Industry." *American Psychologist*, 29 (1974): 725–739.

MACCOBY, ELEANOR, AND MASTERS, JOHN C. "Attachment and Dependency." In *Manual of Child Psychology*, ed. by Paul H. Mussen. Vol. 2. New York: Wiley, 1970, pp. 159–260.

MACE, D., AND MACE, V. *Marriage: East and West*. New York: Doubleday, 1960.

MACKAY, CHARLES. *Extraordinary Popular Delusions and the Madness of Crowds*. New York: Farrar, Straus & Giroux, 1932.

MADISON, PETER. *Personality Development in College*. Reading, Mass.: Addison-Wesley, 1969.

MAHER, BRENDAN. "The Shattered Language of Schizophrenia." In *Readings in Psychology Today*. 2nd ed. Del Mar, Calif.: CRM Books, 1972, pp. 549–553.

MAJERES, R. L. "Semantic Connotations of the Words Adolescent,' 'Teenager,' and 'Youth.' " *Journal of Genetic Psychology*, 129 (1976): 57–62.

MARANON, GREGORIO. "Contribution à l étude de l'action émotive de l'adrenaline." *Revue Français d'Endocrinologie*, 2 (1952): 141–147.

MARCIA, J. E. "Development and Validation of Ego Identity Status." *Journal of Personality and Social Psychology*, 3 (1966): 551–558.

MARGOLIS, B. L., KROES, W. H., AND QUINN, R. P. "Job Stress: An Unlisted Occupational Hazard." *Journal of Occupational Medicine*, 16 (1974): 654–661.

MARLATT, G., AND ROHSENOW, D. "The Think-Drink Effect." *Psychology Today*, 15 (December 1981): 60–70.

MARLER, PETER. "On Animal Aggression: The Roles of Strangeness and Familiarity." *American Psychologist*, 31, no. 3 (March 1976): 239–246.

MASLOW, ABRAHAM. *Motivation and Personality*. 2nd ed. New York: Harper & Row, 1970 (paper).

MASTERS, WILLIAM H., AND JOHNSON, VIRGINIA, E. *Human Sexual Inadequacy*. Boston: Little, Brown, 1970.

MASTERSON, J. F. *The Psychiatric Dilemma of Adolescence*. Boston: Little, Brown, 1967.

————, "The Symptomatic Adolescent Five Years Later: He Didn't Grow Out of It." *American Journal of Psychiatry*, 123 (1967): 1338–1345.

MAY, P. R. A. *Treatment of Schizophrenia: A Comparative Study of Five Treatment Methods*. New York: Science House, 1968.

MAY, ROLLO. *Existential Psychology*. 2nd ed. New York: Random House, 1969.

MC CARLEY, ROBERT W. "Where Dreams Come from: A New Theory." *Psychology Today*, 12 (December 1978): 54–65.

MC CLELLAND, D. C. *The Achieving Society*. Princeton: Van Nostrand, 1961.

————. "Need Achievement and Entrepreneurship: A Longitudinal Study." *Journal of Personality and Social Psychology*, 1 (1965): 389–392.

————, AND HARRIS, T. G. "To Know Why Men Do What They Do: A Conversation with David C. McClelland." *Psychology Today*, 4 (January 1971): 35–39.

————, AND WINTER, D. G. *Motivating Economic Achievement*. New York: Free Press, 1969.

————, ET AL. *The Achievement Motive*. New York: Appleton-Century-Crofts, 1953.

MC CONNELL, J. V. "Cannibalism and Memory in Flatworms." *New Scientist*, 21 (1964): 465–468.

MC COY, K. *Coping with Teenage Depression*, New York: Mosby, 1982.

MC GHIE, A., AND CHAPMAN, J. "Disorders of Attention and Perception in Early Schizophrenia." *British Journal of Medical Psychiatry*, 34 (1961): 103–116.

MC GINLEY, HUGH, LE FEVRE, RICHARD, AND MC GINLEY, PAT. "The Influence of a Communicator's Body Position on Opinion Change in Others." *Journal of Personality and Social Psychology*, 31 (1975): 686–690.

MC GINNISS, JOE. *The Selling of the President, 1968*. New York: Pocket Books, 1970 (paper).

MC GUIRE, W. J. "A Vaccine for Brainwash." *Psychology Today*, 3 (February 1970): 36–39, 62–64.

MCKENZIE, S. C. *Aging and Old Age*. Glenview, Ill.: Scott, Foresman, 1980.

MEAD, MARGARET. *Coming of Age in Samoa*. New York: Morrow, 1961.

MECHANIC, D. "Discussion of Research Programs on Relations Between Stressful Life Events and Episodes of Physical Illness." In *Stressful Life Events: Their Nature and Effects*, ed. by B. S. Dohrenwend and B. P. Dohrenwend. New York: Wiley, 1974.

MEEHL, PAUL M. "Schizotaxia, Schizotype, Schizophrenia." *American Psychologist*, 17 (1962): 827–832.

MEYER, W. J., AND DUSEK, J. B. *Child Psychology: A Developmental Perspective*. Lexington, Mass: Heath, 1979.

MIDDLEBROOK, P. N. *Social Psychology and Modern Life*. 2nd ed. New York: Knopf, 1980.

MIKULAS, WILLIAM L. *Behavior Modification*. New York: Harper & Row, 1978.

MILGRIM, STANLEY. *Obedience to Authority*. New York: Harper & Row, 1964.

————. "The Experience of Living in Cities." *Science*, 167 (1970): 1461–1468.

MILLER, GEORGE A. "The Magical Number Seven, Plus or Minus Two: Some Limits on Our Capacity for Processing Information." *Psychological Review*, 63 (1956): 81–97.

————, GALANTER, EUGENE, AND PRIBRAM, KARL, H. *Plans and the Structure of Behavior*. New York: Holt, Rinehart and Winston, 1960.

MILLER, GERALD R., AND FONTES, NORMAN E. "Trial by Videotape." *Psychology Today*, 12 (May 1979): 92–101.

MILLER, L. K. "Behavioral Principles and Experimental Communities." In *Behavior Modification: Principles,*

Issues, and Applications, ed. by W. E. Craighead, A. E. Kazdin, and M. J. Mahoney. Boston: Houghton Miffin, 1976.

————, AND SCHNEIDER, R. "The Use of a Token System in Project Headstart." *Journal of Applied Behavior Analysis*, 3 (1970): 213–220.

MILLER, NEAL E., AND DI CARA, LEO. "Instrumental Learning of Heart Rate Changes in Curarized Rats: Shaping and Specificity to Discriminative Stimulus." *Journal of Comparative and Physiological Psychology*, 63 (1967): 12–19.

————, AND DWORKIN, B. R. "Visceral Learning: Recent Difficulties with Curarized Rats and Significant Problems for Human Research." In *Cardiovas Psychophysiology*, ed. by Paul A. Obrist, *et al.* Chicago: Aldine-Atherton, 1974.

MILLER, S., AND SELIGMAN, M. "The Reformulated Model of Helplessness and Depression: Evidence and Theory." In *Psychological Stress and Psychopathology*, ed. by N. W. Newfield. New York: McGraw-Hill, 1982.

MINER, J. B. "Psychological Testing and Fair Employment Practices." *Personnel Psychology*, 27 (1974): 49–62.

MINTZ, R. S. "Psychotherapy of the Suicidal Patient." In *Suicidal Behaviors*, ed. by H. L. P. Resnik. Boston: Little, Brown, 1968.

MOSCOVICI, SERGE. *Social Influence and Social Change*. New York: Academic Press, 1976.

MOWRER, O. H., AND MOWRER, M. "Enuresis: A Method for Its Study and Treatment." *American Journal of Orthopsychiatry*, 8 (1938): 436–459.

MUNNS, M. "The Values of Adolescents Compared with Parents and Peers." *Adolescence*, 7 (1972): 519–524.

MURRAY, HENRY A., ET AL. *Exploration in Personality*. New York: Oxford University Press, 1934.

MUSSEN, PAUL H., CONGER, JOHN J., AND KAGAN, JEROME. *Child Development and Personality*, 4th ed. New York: Harper & Row, 1974.

————, ————, AND ————. *Essentials of Child Development and Personality*. Philadelphia: Harper & Row, 1980.

NARAJANO, C., AND ORNSTEIN, R. *On the Psychology of Meditation*. New York: Viking, 1971.

NATHAN, P. E., AND HARRIS, S. L. *Psychopathology and Society*. New York: McGraw-Hill, 1975.

————, AND O'BRIEN, J. S. "An Experimental Analysis of the Behavior of Alcoholics and Nonalcoholics During Prolonged Experimental Drinking: A Necessary Precursor of Behavior Therapy?" *Behavior Therapy*, 2 (1971): 455–476.

NEISSER, ULRIC. *Cognitive Psychology*. New York: Appleton-Century-Crofts, 1967.

NESBITT, P. "The Effectiveness of Student Canvassers," *Journal of Applied Psychology*, 2 (1972): 252–258.

NEUGARTEN, BERNICE, ET AL. "Women's Attitudes Toward the Menopause." *Vita Humana*, 6 (1963): 140–151.

New York Times, "Parents on the Brink of Child Abuse Get Crisis Aid," April 17, 1983, pp. 1, 29.

NEWCOMB, T. *Personality and Social Change*. New York: Dryden Press, 1943.

————, ET AL. *Persistence and Change: Bennington College and Its Students After 25 Years*. New York: Wiley, 1967.

NEWMAN, G., AND NICHOLS, C. R. "Sexual Activities and Attitudes in Older Persons." *Journal of the American Medical Association*, 173 (1960): 33–35.

NEWMAN, OSCAR. *Defensible Space*. New York: Macmillan, 1972.

NEWMAN, P. "The Peer Group." In *Handbook of Developmental Psychology*, ed. by B. B. Wolman. Englewood Cliffs, N.J.: Prentice Hall, 1982.

NUCKOLLS, K., CASSEL, J., AND KAPLAN, B. H. "Psychological Assets, Life Crisis, and the Prognosis of Pregnancy." *American Journal of Epidemiology*, 95 (1972): 431–444.

OFFICE OF STRATEGIC SERVICES ASSESSMENT STAFF. *Assessment of Men*. New York: Holt, Rinehart and Winston, 1948.

OLDS, J., AND OLDS, M. E. "Drives, Rewards and the Brain." In *New Directions in Psychology II*, ed. by F. Barron, *et al*. New York: Holt, Rinehart and Winston, 1965.

ORLANSKY, J. "An Assessment of Lie Detection Capability." In *Use of Polygraphs and "Lie Detectors" by the Federal Government*. House Report No. 198, Eighty-ninth Congress, First Session. Washington, D.C.: U.S. Government Printing Office, 1965.

ORNE, MARTIN T. "The Nature of Hypnosis: Artifact and Essence." *Journal of Abnormal and Social Psychology*, 58 (1959): 277–299.

ORNSTEIN, ROBERT. *The Psychology of Consciousness*. 2nd ed. New York: Harcourt Brace Jovanovich, 1977.

PAFFENBARGER, RALPH S., JR., AND HALE, WAYNE, E. "Work Activity and Coronary Heart Mortality." *The New England Journal of Medicine*, 292 (March 1975): 545–550.

PALMORE, ERDMAN. "What Can the USA Learn from Japan about Aging?" In *Readings in Aging and Death: Contemporary Perspectives*, ed. by S. H. Zarit. New York: Harper & Row, 1977.

PARKE, R., AND SLABY, R. "Aggression: A Multilevel Analysis." In *Handbook of Child Psychology. Vol. 14. Socialization, Personality and Social Development*. 4th ed., ed. by P. H. Mussen and M. E. Hetherington, New York: Wiley, 1983.

————, AND LEWIS, N. "The Family in Context: A Multilevel Interactional Analysis of Child Abuse." In *Parent-Child Interaction: Theory, Research and Prospect*. ed. by R. W. Henderson. New York: Academic Press, 1980.

PATCH, VERNON D. "Methadone." *New England Journal of Medicine*, 286 (1972): 43–45.

PAVLOV, IVAN P. *Conditioned Reflexes*. Trans. by G. V. Anrep. London: Oxford University Press, 1927.

PAYKEL, E. S. "Life Stress and Psychiatric Disorder: Applications of the Clinical Approach." In *Stressful Life Events: Their Nature and Effects*, ed. by B. S. Dohrenwend and B. P. Dohrenwend. New York: Wiley, 1974.

PEARL, D., BOUTHILET, L., AND LAZAR, J. (EDS.). *Television and Behavior: Ten Years of Scientific Progress and Implications for the Eighties*. Vols. 1 and 2. Washington, D.C.: U.S. Government Printing Office, 1982.

PENFIELD, WILDER. "Consciousness, Memory, and Man's Conditioned Reflexes." In *On the Biology of Learning*, ed. by Karl H. Pribram. New York: Harcourt Brace Jovanovich, 1969.

————, AND RASMUSSEN, THEODORE. *The Cerebral Cortex of Man*. New York: Macmillan, 1950.

PERLICK, D. "The Withdrawal Syndrome: Nicotine Addiction and the Effects of Stopping Smoking in Heavy and Light Smokers." Unpublished doctoral dissertation. Columbia University, 1977.

PERLS, FRITZ, HEFFERLINE, R. F., AND GOODMAN, P. *Gestalt Therapy*. New York: Dell, 1965.

PETERSON, LLOYD R., AND PETERSON, MARGARET. "Short-Term Retention of Individual Verbal Items." *Journal of Experimental Psychology*, 58 (1959): 193–198.

PIAGET, JEAN. *The Language and Thought of the Child*. London: Routledge & Kegan Paul, 1926.

PILBEAM, DAVID. "An Idea We Could Live Without—The Naked Ape." *Discovery*, 7, no. 2 (Spring 1972): 63–70.

PINES, MAYA. "Infants Are Smarter Than Anybody Thinks." *The New York Times Magazine* (November 29, 1970).

PLUMB, M. M., AND HOLLAND, J. "Comparative Studies of Psychological Function in Patients with Advanced Cancer. I. Self-Reported Depressive Symptoms." *Psychosomatic Medicine*, 39 (1977): 264–276.

POCS, OLLIE, ET AL. "Is There Sex After 40?" *Psychology Today*, 10 (June 1977): 54–57.

PROSHANSKY, H., AND NEWTON, P. "The Nature and Meaning of Negro Self-Identity." In *Social Class, Race, and Psychological Development*, ed. by M. Deutsch, J. Kate, and A. R. Jensen. New York: Holt, Rinehart and Winston, 1968.

QUINN, R., SEASHORE, S., KAHN, R., MANGIONE, T., CAMPBELL, D., STAINES, G., AND MCCULLOUGH, M. *Survey of Working Conditions*. Washington, D.C.: U.S. Government Printing Office, 1971.

RABKIN, LESLIE (ED.). *Psychopathology and Literature*. San Francisco: Chandler, 1966.

RAHE, R. H. "Life Changes and Near-Future Illness Reports." In *Emotions: Their Parameters and Measurement*, ed. by L. Levi. New York: Raven Press, 1975.

————, H., AND ARTHUR, R.J. "Life Change Patterns Surrounding Illness Experience." *Journal of Psychosomatic Research*, 11 (1968): 341–345.

RAUSH, HAROLD L., AND RAUSH, CHARLOTTE. *The Halfway House Movement: A Search for Sanity*. New York: Appleton-Century-Crofts, 1968.

RAY, OAKLEY. *Drugs, Society, and Human Behavior*. 2nd ed. St. Louis: Mosby, 1978.

REID, D. W., HAAS, G., AND HAWKINGS, D. "Locus of Desired Control and Positive Self-Concept of the Elderly." *Journal of Gerontology*, 32 (1977): 441–450.

REISMAN, D., GLAZER, N., AND DENNEY, R. *The Lonely Crowd*. New Haven, Conn.: Yale University Press, 1953 (paper).

REISMAN, J., AND SHORR, S. "Friendship Claims and Expectations Among Children and Adults." *Child Development*, 49 (1978): 913–916.

REPPUCCI, N. D., AND SAUNDERS, J. T. "Social Psychology of Behavior Modification." *American Psychologist*, 29 (1974): 649–660.

REYNOLDS, G. S. *A Primer of Operant Conditioning*. Glenview, Ill.: Scott, Foresman, 1968.

RHINE, JOSEPH B. *Extra-Sensory Perception*. Boston: Branden, 1964.

RHINE, LOUISA E. *Hidden Channels of the Mind*. New York: Apollo, 1961 (paper).

RICE, F. P. *The Adolescent: Development, Relationships, and Culture*. Boston: Allyn & Bacon, 1978.

RICE, M. "The Role of Television in Language Acquisition." *Developmental Review*, 3 (1983): 221–224.

RIGTER, H., VAN RIEZE, H., AND WIED, D. D. "The Effects of ACTH and Vasopressin Analogues on CO_2-induced Retrograde Amnesia in Rats." *Physiology and Behavior*, 13 (1974): 381–388.

RILEY, V. "Psychoneuroendocrine Influences on Immunocompetence and Neoplasia." *Science*, 212 (1981): 1100–1109.

ROGERS, CARL. *Client-centered Therapy*. Boston: Houghton Mifflin, 1951.

————. *On Becoming a Person*. Boston: Houghton Mifflin, 1961.

ROGERS, D. *The Psychology of Adolescence*. 3rd ed. Englewood Cliffs, N.J.: Prentice-Hall, 1977.

————. *The Adult Years: An Introduction to Aging*. Englewood Cliffs, N.J.: Prentice-Hall, 1979.

ROKEACH, M. "Long-Range Experimental Modification of Values, Attitudes, and Behavior." *American Psychologist*, 26 (1971): 453–459.

ROLLINS, B. C., AND FELDMAN, H. "Marital Satisfaction over the Family Life Cycle." *Journal of Marriage and the Family*, 32 (1970): 20–28.

ROSENMAN, R. H. In *Coronary-Prone Behavior*, ed. by T. M. Dembrowski, S. M. Weiss, J. L. Shields, S. G. Haynes, and M. Feinleib. New York: Springer, 1978.

ROSENTHAL, D. *Genetic Theory and Abnormal Behavior*. New York: McGraw-Hill, 1970.

————, ET AL. "The Adopted-Away Offspring of Schizophrenics." *American Journal of Psychiatry*, 128, no. 3 (1971): 307–311.

ROSENTHAL, ROBERT. *Environmental Effects in Behavioral Research*. New York: Appleton-Century-Crofts, 1966.

————, AND ROSNOW, R. L. (EDS.). *Artifact in Behavioral Research*. New York: Academic Press, 1969.

RUBIN, I. "Sex over 65." In *Advances in Sex Research*, ed. by H. G. Beigel. New York: Harper & Row, 1963.

RUBIN, ZICK. "Measurement of Romantic Love." *Journal of Personality and Social Psychology*, 16 (1970): 265–273.

————. *Liking and Loving*. New York: Holt, Rinehart and·Winston, 1973.

RUMBAUGH, DUANE M., GILL, TIMOTHY V., AND VON GLASERSFELD, E. C. "Reading and Sentence Completion by a Chimpanzee." *Science*, 182 (1973): 731–733.

SAHAKIAN, WILLIAM S. *Psychology of Learning*. Chicago: Markam, 1970.

SALK, LEE. "Mother's Heartbeat as an Imprinting Stimulus." *Transactions of the New York Academy of Sciences*, 24 (1962): 753–763.

SARASON, I. G., AND SARASON, B. R. *Abnormal Psychology*. 3rd ed. Englewood Cliffs, N.J.: Prentice-Hall, 1980.

SARBIN, I., AND COE, W. *Hypnosis: A Social Psychological Analysis of Influence Communication*. New York: Holt, Rinehart and Winston, 1972.

————. "Hypnosis and Psychopathology: Replacing Old Myths with Fresh Metaphors." *Journal of Abnormal Psychology*, 88 (1979): 506–526.

SATIR, VIRGINIA. *Peoplemaking*. Palo Alto, Calif.: Science and Behavior, 1972.

SAUL, S. *Aging: An Album of People Growing Old*. New York: Wiley, 1974.

SCARF, M. *Unfinished Business: Pressure Points in the Lives of Women*. New York: Ballentine Books, 1980.

SCHACTER, STANLEY. *The Psychology of Affiliation*. Stanford, Calif.: University Press, 1959.

————. *Emotion, Obesity, and Crime*. New York:-Academic Press, 1971.

————. "Second Thoughts on Biological and Psychological Explanations of Behavior." In *Cognitive Theories in Social Psychology*, ed. by L. Berkowitz. New York: Academic Press, 1978.

————, AND LATANÉ, B. "Crime, Cognition, and the Autonomic Nervous System." In *Nebraska Symposium on Motivation*, ed. by M. Jones. Lincoln: University of Nebraska Press, 1964.

————, AND SINGER, JEROME. "Cognitive, Social, and Physiological Determinants of Emotional State." *Psychological Review*, 69 (1962): 379–399.

SCHEIN, E. H. "The First Job Dilemma." *Psychology Today*, 1 (1968): 26–37.

SCHMALE, A. "Giving Up as a Final Common Pathway to Changes in Health." *Advances in Psychosomatic Medicine*, 8 (1972): 20–40.

SCHREIBER, FLORA RHETA. *Sybil*. New York: Warner, 1973.

SCHULMAN, JAY, ET AL. "Recipe for a Jury," *Psychology Today*, 6 (May 1973): 37–44.

SCHULTES, R. E. *Hallucinogenic Plants*. New York: Golden Press, 1976.

SCHWARTZ, A. N., AND PETERSON, J. A. *Introduction to Gerontology*. San Francisco: Holt, Rinehart and Winston, 1979.

————, AND PROPPE, H. G. "Toward Person/Environment Transactional Research in Aging." *Gerontologist*, 10 (1970): 228–232.

SCHWARTZ, G. E., DAVIDSON, R., AND MAER, F. "Right Hemisphere Lateralization for Emotion in the Human Brain: Interactions with Cognition." *Science*, 190 (1975): 286–288.

SCIENTIFIC AMERICAN. "Psychokinetic Fraud." *Scientific American*, 238 (September 1974): 68, 72.

SCOTT, WILLIAM, AND WERTHEIMER, MICHAEL. *Introduction to Psychological Research*. New York: Wiley, 1962.

SEARS, ROBERT, MACCOBY, ELEANOR, AND LEVIN, HARRY. *Patterns of Child Rearing*. New York: Harper & Row, 1957.

SEIGEL, RONALD K. "Hallucinations." *Scientific American*, 237 (October 1977): 132–140.

SELIGMAN, MARTIN E. P. *Helplessness*. San Francisco: Freeman, 1975.

SELYE, HANS. *The Stress of Life*. New York: McGraw-Hill, 1956.

————. *Stress Without Distress*. Philadelphia: Lippincott, 1974.

————, AND CHERRY, L. "On the Real Benefits of Eustress." *Psychology Today*, 11 (March 1978): 60–70.

SHAPIRO, DAVID. "Preface." In *Biofeedback and Self-Control 1972*, ed. by D. Shapiro, *et al*. Chicago: Aldine-Atherton, 1973.

SHAPIRO, EVELYN (ED.). *PsychoSources: A Psychology Resource Catalog*. New York: Bantam, 1973 (paper).

SHAVER, KELLY G. *An Introduction to Attribution Processes*. Cambridge, Mass.: Winthrop, 1975.

SHAVER, PHILLIP. "Questions Concerning Fear of Success and Its Conceptual Relatives." *Sex Roles*, 2 (1976): 305–320.

SHEEHY, GAIL. *Passages*. New York: Dutton, 1976.

SHERIF, MUZAFER, ET AL. *Intergroup Conflict and Cooperation: The Robber's Cave Experiment*. Norman, Okla.: Institute of Group Relations, 1961.

SHOR, R. E., AND ORNE, M. T. (EDS.). *The Nature of Hypnosis*. New York: Holt, Rinehart and Winston, 1965.

SIFFRE, MICHEL. "Six Months Alone in a Cave." *National Geographic*, 147 (March 1975): 426–435.

SILVERMAN, J. "When Schizophrenia Helps." *Psychology Today*, 4 (September 1970): 62–65.

SILVERSTEIN, B. "An Addiction Explanatin of Cigarette-Induced Relaxation." Unpublished doctoral dissertation, Columbia Unversity, 1976.

SIMON, W., AND GAGNON, J. H. (EDS.). *The Sexual Scene*. Chicago: Transaction Books, 1970.

SINGER, D. "The Impact of Interracial Classroom Exposure on the Social Attitudes of Fifth Grade Children." Unpublished study, 1964.

SINGER, J., AND SINGER, D. "Psychologists Look at Television: Cognitive, Developmental, Personality and Social Policy Implications." *American Psychologist*, 38 (1983): 826–834.

SINGER, J. N. "Job Strain as a Function of Job and Life Stress." Unpublished doctoral dissertation, Colorado State University, 1975.

SINGER, MARGARET T. "Coming Out of the Cults." *Psychology Today*, 12 (January 1979): 72–82.

SKINNER, B. F. *The Behavior of Organisms*. New York: Appleton-Century-Crofts, 1961.

————. *Walden Two*. New York: Macmillan, 1962; originally published 1948.

————. *Beyond Freedom and Dignity*. New York: Knopf, 1971.

————. *About Behaviorism*. New York: Knopf, 1974.

————. "Intellectual Self-Management in Old Age." *American Psychologist*, 38 (1983): 239–244.

————, AND VAUGHN, M. E. *Enjoy Old Age*. New York: Norton, 1983.

SKOLNICK, ARLENE. *The Intimate Environment*. Boston: Little, Brown, 1973.

SLOTKIN, J. J. "Culture and Psychopathology." *Journal of Abnormal and Social Psychology*, 51 (1955): 269–275.

SMITH, MARY LEE, AND GLASS, GENE V. "Meta-Analysis of Psychotherapy Outcome Studies." *American Psychologist*, 32 (1977): 752–760.

SNELLGROVE, L. *Psychological Experiments and Demonstrations*. New York: McGraw-Hill, 1967.

SNYDER, SOLOMON H. *Madness and the Brain*. New York: McGraw-Hill, 1973.

SPERLING, G. "The Information Available in Brief Visual Presentations." *Psychological Monographs*, 74, no. 11 (1960).

SPERRY, ROGER W. "Changing Concepts of Consciousness and Free Will." *Perspectives in Biology and Medicine*, 20, no. 1 (Autumn 1976): 9–19.

SPITZ, RENE, AND WOLFF, K. M. "Anaclitic Depression: An Inquiry into the Genesis of Psychiatric Conditions in Early Childhood, II." In *The Psychoanalytic Study of the Child*, ed. by A. Freud, *et al.* Vol. II. New York: International Universities Press, 1946, pp. 313–342.

SPITZER, R. L., ENDICOTT, J., AND ROBINS, E. "Research-Diagnostic Criteria: Rationale and Reliability." *Archives of General Psychiatry*, 35 (1978): 773–782.

STANLEY, JULIAN C. "Test Better Finder of Great Math Talent Than Teachers Are." *American Psychologist*, 31 (1976): 313–314.

STERNBACH, R. A., GUSTAFSON, L. A., AND COLIER, R. L. "Don't Trust the Lie Detector." *Harvard Business Review*, 40 (1962): 127–134.

STEVENS, S. S. "The Surprising Simplicity of Sensory Metrics." *American Psychologist*, 17 (1962): 29–39.

STEVENS-LONG, J. *Adult Life Developmental Processes*. Palo Alto, Calif.: Mayfield, 1979.

STOKOLS, D. "On the Distinction between Density and Crowding: Some Implications for Future Research." *Psychological Review*, 79 (1972): 275–278.

STONE, ALAN, AND STONE, SUE. *The Abnormal Personality Through Literature*. Englewood Cliffs, N.J.: Prentice-Hall, 1966.

STROMEYER, C. F. "Eidetikers." *Psychology Today*, 4 (1970): 76–80.

SUE, S., SMITH, R. E., AND CALDWELL, C. "Effects of Inadmissible Evidence on the Decisions of Simulated Jurors." *Journal of Applied Social Psychology*, 3 (1973): 345–353.

SURWIT, R. S., SHAPIRO, D., AND GOOD, M. I. "Comparison of Cardiovascular Feedback, Neuromuscular Feedback, and Meditation in the Treatment of Borderline Essential Hypertension." *Journal of Consulting and Clinical Psychology*, 46 (1978): 252–263.

SWEETLAND, J. *Occupational Stress and Productivity* (Work in America Institute Studies in Productivity). Scarsdale, N.Y.: Work in America Institute, 1979.

SZASZ, THOMAS. *The Myth of Mental Illness*. New York: Dell, 1967.

_____. *The Age of Madness*. Garden City, N.Y.: Doubleday Anchor, 1973 (paper).

TART, C. T. (ED.). *Altered States of Consciousness*. 2nd ed. New York: Wiley, 1972.

TAUBE, C. A., AND REDNICK, R. *Utilization of Mental Health Resources by Persons Diagnosed with Schizophrenia*. DHEW Publication No. (HSM) 72–9110. Rockville, Md.: National Institute of Mental Health, 1973.

TAYLOR, S. "Adjustment to Threatening Events." *American Psychologist*, 38 (1983): 1161–1173.

TERMAN, LEWIS M. *The Measurement of Intelligence*. Boston: Houghton Mifflin, 1916.

_____, AND MERRILL, MAUD A. *Measuring Intelligence*. Boston: Houghton Mifflin, 1937.

_____, AND _____. *Stanford-Binet Intelligence Scale: Manual for the Third Revision. Form L-M*. Boston: Houghton Mifflin, 1973.

THOITS, P. "Life Events, Social Isolation and Psychological Distress." Unpublished doctoral dissertation, Stanford University, 1978.

THOMPSON, RICHARD F. (ED.). *Physiological Psychology*. San Francisco: Freeman, 1971.

_____. "The Search for the Engram." *American Psychologist*, 31 (1976): 209–227.

THOMPSON, WILLIAM R., AND GRUSEC, JOAN. "Studies of Early Experience." In *Manual of Child Psychology*, ed. by Paul H. Mussen. Vol. 2. New York: Wiley, 1970, pp. 565–656.

TIMIO, M., AND GENTILI, S. "Andreosympathetic Over-activity under Conditions of Work Stress." *British Journal of Preventive and Social Medicine*, 30 (1976): 262–265.

TOFFLER, ALVIN. *Future Shock*. New York: Bantam, 1970.

TRESEMER, DAVID. "The Cumulative Record of Research on 'Fear of Success.'" *Sex Roles*, 2 (1976a): 217–236.

———. "Current Trends in Research on 'Fear of Success.'" *Sex Roles*, 2 (1976b): 211–216.

TROTTER, R. "Baby Face." *Psychology Today*, 17 (August 1983): 15–20.

TURNER, J. S., AND HELMS, D. B. *Contemporary Adulthood*, Philadelphia: Saunders, 1979.

TYLER, LEONA E. *The Psychology of Human Differences*. 3rd ed. New York: Appleton-Century-Crofts, 1965.

———. "Human Abilities." In *Annual Review of Psychology*. Palo Alto, Calif.: Annual Reviews, 1975, pp. 177–206.

U.S. DEPARTMENT OF HEALTH, EDUCATION, AND WELFARE. "Leading Causes of Death in Middle Age, as Percentage of Total Deaths Between Ages 45 and 64." In *Vital Statistics of the United States, 1968*. Vol. 2, Part B: Mortality. Rockville, Md.: U.S. Department of Health, Education, and Welfare, 1971.

ULLMAN, P. "Parental Participation in Child Rearing as Evaluated by Male Social Deviates." *Pacific Sociological Review*, 3 (1960): 89–95.

VAILLANT, G. E. *Adaption to Life*. Boston: Little, Brown, 1977.

VALENSTEIN, ELLIOT. *Brain Control: A Critical Examination of Brain Stimulation and Psychosurgery*. New York: Wiley, 1973.

VALVO, ALBERTO. *Sight Restoration After Long-Term Blindness: The Problems and Behavior Patterns of Visual Rehabilitation*. New York: American Foundation for the Blind, 1971.

VAN HARRISON, R. "Person-Environment Fit and Job Stress." In *Stress at Work*, ed. by C. L. Cooper and R. Payne. New York: Wiley, 1978.

VICTOR, MAURICE, AND ADAMS, RAYMOND D. "Opiates and Other Synthetic Analgesic Drugs." In *Harrison's Principles of Internal Medicine*, ed. by M. M. Wintrobe, *et al.* New York: McGraw-Hill, 1970, pp. 677–681.

WADE, NICHOLAS. "Sociobiology: Troubled Birth for a New Discipline." *Science*, 191 (March 19, 1976): 1151–1155.

WALD, G. "The Receptors of Color Vision." *Science*, 145 (1964): 1007–1016.

WALLACE, ROBERT KEITH. "Physiological Effects of Transcendental Meditation." *Science*, 167 (1970): 1751–1754.

WALLERSTEIN, J., AND KELLY, J. "The Effects of Parental Divorce: The Adolescent Experience." In *The Child in His Family: Children at Psychiatric Risk*, ed. by J. Anthony and C. Koupernik. New York: Wiley, 1974, pp. 479–505.

WASHBURN, S. L. "Human Behavior and the Behavior of Other Animals." *American Psychologist*, 33 (May 1978): 405–418.

WATSON, DAVID L., AND THARP, RONALD G. *Self-directed Behavior: Self-modification for Personal Adjustment*. Monterey, Calif.: Brooks/Cole, 1972.

WATSON, JOHN B. *Behaviorism*. New York: Norton, 1970; originally published 1924.

———, AND RAYNER, ROSALIE. "Conditioned Emotional Reactions." *Journal of Experimental Psychology*, 3 (1920): 1–14.

WEBB, S. D., AND COLLETTE, J. "Urban Ecological and Household Correlates of Stress-Alleviative Drug Use." *American Behavioral Scientist*, 18 (1975): 750–769.

WEBB, WILSE B. *Sleep: The Gentle Tyrant*. Englewood Cliffs, N.J.: Prentice-Hall, 1975.

WEBER, ERNST H. *De Pulse, Resorptione, Audito et Tactu*. Leipzig: Kohler, 1834.

WECHSLER, DAVID. *The Measurement and Appraisal of Adult Intelligence*. 14th ed. Baltimore: Williams & Wilkins, 1958.

WEIL, ANDREW. *The Natural Mind*. Boston: Houghton Mifflin, 1972.

_____, ZINBERG, N., AND NELSEN, J. M. "Clinical and Psychological Effects of Marijuana in Man." *Science*, 162 (1968): 1234–1242.

WEISS, J. M. "Influence of Psychological Variables on Stress-Induced Pathology." In *Physiology, Emotion and Psychosomatic Illness* (Ciba Foundation Symposium 8). New York: American Elsevier, 1972.

WEISS, JAY M. "Effects of Coping Behavior in Different Warning-Signal Conditions on Stress Pathology in Rats." *Journal of Comparative and Physiological Psychology*, 77 (1971): 1–13.

WELLS, J. A. "Differences in Sources of Social Support in Conditioning the Effect of Perceived Stress on Health." Paper presented at the annual meeting of the Southern Sociological Association, Atlanta, Ga., 1977.

WHEELIS, ALLEN. *The Desert*. New York: Basic Books, 1970.

WHITE, BURTON L. "Child Development Research: An Edifice Without a Foundation." *Merrill-Palmer Quarterly of Behavior and Development*, 15 (1969): 49–79.

WHITE, ROBERT. "Motivation Reconsidered: The Concept of Competence." *Psychological Review*, 66 (1959): 297–333.

_____. *The Abnormal Personality*. New York: Ronald, 1964.

_____. *Lives in Progress: A Study of the Natural Growth of Personality*. 2nd ed. New York: Holt, Rinehart and Winston, 1966.

_____, RIGGS, MARGARET M., AND GILBERT, DORIS C. *Case Workbook in Personality*. New York: Holt Rinehart and Winston, 1976.

WILD, B. S., AND HAYNES, C. A. "A Dynamic Conceptual Framework of Generalized Adaptation to Stressful Stimuli." *Psychological Reports*, 38 (1976): 319–334.

WILL, GEORGE F. "A Good Death." *Newsweek* (January 9, 1978): 72.

WILLIAMSON, J. B., EVANS, L., AND MUNLEY, A. *Aging and Society*. New York: Holt, Rinehart and Winston, 1980.

WILSON, EDWARD O. *Sociobiology: A New Synthesis*. Cambridge, Mass.: Harvard University Press, 1975a.

_____. "Human Decency Is Animal." *The New York Times Magazine* (October 12, 1975b): 38–49.

WOLFE, JOHN B. "Effectiveness of Token-Rewards for Chimpanzees." *Comparative Psychological Monographs*, 12 (1936): whole no. 5.

WOLMAN, BENJAMIN B. (ED.). *Handbook of General Psychology*. Englewood Cliffs, N.J.: Prentice-Hall, 1973.

_____ (ED.). *Handbook of Clinical Psychology*. New York: McGraw-Hill, 1965.

WOOLFOLK, ROBERT L. "Psychophysiological Correlates of Meditation." *Archives of General Psychiatry*, 32 (1975): 1326–1333.

WRIGHT, J., AND HUSTON, A. "A Matter of Form: Potentials of Television for Young Viewers." *American Psychologist*, 38 (1983): 835–843.

WRIGHTSMAN, L. S. "Effects of Waiting with Others on Changes in Level of Felt Anxiety." *Journal of Abnormal and Social Psychology*, 61 (1960): 216–222.

_____, SIGELMAN, C. K., AND SANFORD, F. H. *Psychology: A Scientific Study of Human Behavior*. 5th ed. Monterey, Calif.: Brooks/Cole, 1979.

WYNNE, L., CROMWELL, R., AND MATTHYSSE, S. (EDS.). *Nature of Schizophrenia: New Approaches to Research and Treatment*. New York: Wiley, 1978.

ZARIT, S. H. (ED.). *Readings in Aging and Death: Contemporary Perspectives*. New York: Harper & Row, 1977.

ZIMBARDO, P. G. *Psychology and Life*. 10th ed. Glenview, Ill.: Scott, Foresman, 1979.

_____, EBBESEN, E. B., AND MASLACH, C. *Influencing Attitudes and Changing Behavior*. 2nd ed. Reading, Mass.: Addison-Wesley, 1977.

ZUBECK, J. P. *Sensory Deprivation: Fifteen Years of Research*. New York: Appleton-Century-Crofts, 1969.

ZUBIN, J., AND MONEY, J. (EDS.) *Contemporary Sexual Behavior: Critical Issues in the 1970s*. Baltimore: Johns Hopkins University Press, 1973.

_____, AND SPRING, BONNIE. "Vulnerability: A New View of Schizophrenia." *Journal of Abnormal Psychology*, 86 (1977): 103–126.

Photo Credits

Index